Received 2011 Apl 27

DR. O'BRIEN,

~~~~ 2011

A GROUP OF THE 1969-1 ████████ TOGETHER
FOR A WONDERFUL RE-UN ████████ AUSTIN, TEXAS APRIL 15-17.
WE WANTED TO GIVE YOU THIS BOOK ON BURCKHARDT AS
A COMMEMORATION OF YOUR OUTSTANDING TEACHING
AND LEADERSHIP DURING OUR STUDY YEAR.

D1200637

Robert Jenkins

Thanks, Fred Gillespie, President of
the Swiss American Historical Society

Your intellectual leadership and the opportunity to be exposed
to many differing ideas have changed most of us. Thank you.
Carl H. Cotton

A wonderful, life-changing event in a marvelous
environment with interesting fellow students and
enlightened leadership that allowed us to explore
and examine. Merci viel mal!
Carol Smith Sledge

My independent study project on the geography of Basel —
was one of the highlights of my year with you. Thank you —
Craig Towers

My year in Basel was an incredible
experience. I've been in intercultural
communications and teaching ESL ever
since as a result of my love of other
cultures inspired by that year with you
our great professors, wonderful classmates,
and welcoming swiss families.
Thank you,
Susan Firestone

BASEL
IN THE AGE OF
BURCKHARDT

Johannes Grützke, *Arnold Böcklin, Johann Jacob Bachofen, Jacob Burckhardt, and Friedrich Nietzsche auf der Mittleren Rheinbrücke in Basel,* 1970. Photo: Felix Hoffmann. Courtesy Progressives Museum, Basel (Galerie Miklos von Bartha).

BASEL

IN THE AGE OF

BURCKHARDT

A Study in Unseasonable Ideas

Lionel Gossman

THE UNIVERSITY OF CHICAGO PRESS

CHICAGO AND LONDON

LIONEL GOSSMAN is professor emeritus of Romance languages and literatures at Princeton University. Among his books are *Between History and Literature* (1990) and, with Nicolas Bouvier and Gordon Craig, *Geneva, Zurich, Basel: History, Culture, and National Identity* (1994).

The University of Chicago Press, Chicago 60637
The University of Chicago Press, Ltd., London
© 2000 by The University of Chicago
All rights reserved. Published 2000
Printed in the United States of America
09 08 07 06 05 04 03 02 01 00   1 2 3 4 5

ISBN: 0-226-30498-1 (cloth)

Library of Congress Cataloging-in-Publication Data

Gossman, Lionel.
    Basel in the age of Burckhardt: a study in unseasonable ideas / Lionel Gossman.
        p.   cm.
    Includes bibliographical references and index.
    ISBN 0-226-30498-1
    1. Burckhardt, Jacob, 1818–1897. 2. Bachofen, Johann Jacob, 1815–
1887. 3. Basel (Switzerland)—Intellectual life—19th century. 4. Historians—
Switzerland—Basel Biography. 5. Intellectuals—Switzerland—Basel Biography. 6. Culture—Philosophy—History—19th century. I. Title.
DQ389.6.G67 2000
949.4′32063—dc21   99-43285
                                                                          CIP

This book is printed on acid-free paper.

In memory of my sister
Janice Brason
(26 January 1933–9 March 1961)

Contents

Acknowledgments

In the time it has taken me to write this book on nineteenth-century Basel, Gibbon produced his *History of the Decline and Fall of the Roman Empire*. If one needed a lesson in humility, none could be more effective. So it is with mixed feelings of relief, melancholy, and apprehension that I take my leave of a work that—to borrow Gibbon's words—has amused and exercised near twenty years of my life, and that, however inadequate to my own wishes, I finally deliver to the curiosity and candor of the public. Fortunately, those feelings are mitigated by satisfaction at being able, at long last, to express my gratitude to those who placed their learning and experience unstintingly at my disposal and whose interest and encouragement made the activity of research, reflection, and writing a rewarding and often exhilarating experience.

My greatest debt is to my colleague and friend Carl Schorske. When I met Schorske shortly after I moved to Princeton from Johns Hopkins in 1976, I was already keenly interested in Johann Jacob Bachofen. I had come upon him indirectly, by way of the nineteenth-century French romantic historian Jules Michelet, whose work I had taught in a number of graduate seminars at Hopkins in the early 1970s. The categories of masculine and feminine play a critical role in Michelet's writing and in trying to understand how these categories were used in the nineteenth century, I was led, around 1973 or 1974, to Bachofen's *Mutterrecht,* which appeared in the very same year as Michelet's *La Mer.* I was deeply impressed by Bachofen, especially the *Gräbersymbolik* and the *Griechische Reise.* But I knew little at that time of Jacob Burckhardt, and I had not thought at all of the local political and cultural context of Bachofen's work. It was Schorske who brought Basel to my attention when he suggested that we co-teach an undergraduate seminar in the European Cultural Studies Program at Princeton, which he had originally set up. I undertook to prepare the classes on the social and cultural context of Basel history as well as those on Bachofen. He was to be responsible for Burckhardt and Nietzsche. A graduate student in art history agreed to contribute a class on the painter Arnold Böcklin. I threw myself into the work with enthusiasm and quickly became the local expert on Basel history—not a particularly remarkable achievement given the total lack of competition. The seminar was and remains the high point of my teaching career.

Subsequently, Schorske and I spoke seriously of writing a book together on Basel. In the meantime, however, he retired from the University and took on many other projects. Gradually, it became apparent that if the Basel book were ever to be done, I would probably do it alone. And that is what has happened, though it has not been easy for me either. Over almost twenty years that I have been working on it, I have mostly had to do other things professionally. There have been no opportunities to teach anything connected with it and many obligations to teach and write on other topics for which, as a professor of Romance languages, I bear responsibility. I did what I could during whatever time I could find, but that usually was not much. Moreover, no sooner had I gotten back "into" the topic, during summer vacations, for instance, than it was already time to return to my regular duties. In order to finish, I have had to curtail the original plan, which gave as much place to Böcklin, Nietzsche, and Franz Overbeck as to Bachofen and Burckhardt. But it is done as well as I could do it and it has been a labor of love. Schorske bears none of the responsibility for its many shortcomings, but to the degree that it has any merit, it is his book too.

For both of us Basel has been an important place in our intellectual itineraries. I have visited the thriving, extraordinarily beautiful city on the Rhine many times now since we gave that first seminar; I know and love its narrow, winding streets and steep alleys, its handsome townhouses, its churches and museums, its quiet gardens and riverside promenades, and its attractive outlying villages, as one knows an old friend. It has become part of my inner landscape, along with two other, very different cities that have been important in my life: Glasgow, where I was born and formed, and Baltimore, where as a young teacher I experienced more intellectual stimulation than I ever dreamed of or had any right or reason to expect. Writing about Basel has been an immensely enriching journey of discovery.

Though I am not a professional historian, I have enjoyed the confidence and been able to draw on the knowledge and experience of many distinguished scholars in the Princeton community of historians. I would like to mention in particular the late Laurence Stone, who, with his wife and collaborator, Jeanne Fawtier Stone, befriended my wife and me from the day we arrived in Princeton; the late Felix Gilbert, whose personal copy of the 1927 edition of Bachofen's *Griechische Reise,* given me just after I published my first essay on Bachofen, is now one of the treasures of my own book collection; Peter Paret, who has become a personal friend and precious intellectual interlocutor; and Fritz Stern, whom I first met when his daughter was a graduate student in French at Johns Hopkins but to whom I am now bound, since embarking on the Basel project, by ties of friendship and shared interests.

I owe a special debt to Martin Rühl, presently completing a doctoral dissertation in the history department at Princeton on "Renaissancismus" in late-nineteenth- and early-twentieth-century Germany. I have derived great pleasure and intellectual stimulation from frequent, animated exchanges of ideas and information with this young German scholar over the last couple of years.

Without the support and encouragement of many Baselers and Swiss I could not have gone very far in this work. I would like to thank in particular Charles Gilliéron, the Swiss cultural attaché in New York, who encouraged me at the very beginning; his energetic young successor, the art historian Lukas Gloor, who read most of the manuscript through and offered comments on it; the administrators of the Pro Helvetia Foundation who awarded me a summer grant in the early eighties; the staff at the University Library in Basel; Dr. Andreas Staehelin, director of the Basel State Archives in the eighties; and the Berta Hess-Cohn Foundation in Basel for generously subsidizing the color illustrations that made it possible to retain Arnold Böcklin as a mute but, I hope, meaningful presence in the book. Special thanks are due to two young scholars whose friendship and confidence supported me when I was most doubtful of ever bringing this enterprise to a conclusion: Dr. Andreas Cesana, formerly of the Philosophy Seminar at the University of Basel, now professor at the University of Mainz in Germany, and himself the author of several invaluable studies of Bachofen; and Dr. Niklaus (Niggi) Peter of the Theological Seminar at Basel, who encouraged me to read and even to write about Overbeck, and who is one of the editors of the handsome new edition of Overbeck's complete works and the author of several outstanding studies of the theologian and his thought. I hope both will recognize how much friendship for them is contained in the pages of this book. In the last year, while preparing the manuscript for publication, I have benefited from the advice and practical assistance of two more young Swiss scholars: Dr. Philipp Sarasin, the author of an outstanding study of the Basel bourgeoisie, and Dr. Andreas Urs Sommer, whose book on Nietzsche and Overbeck appeared in 1997.

I would also like to acknowledge the tolerance and broadmindedness of my colleagues at Princeton University. No one at Princeton ever questioned my right to dedicate much of my time and energy to a topic that a professor of Romance languages would not normally be expected to pursue. For similar tolerance and openmindedness I thank the unknown colleagues on the selection committee of the National Endowment for the Humanities who made it possible for me to spend one complete year on the project in the early eighties. Finally, I wish to express my appreciation of the enthusiastic support I have received, from the moment I first contacted him, from my editor at the University of Chicago Press, John Tryneski. With his assistant, Randolph Petilos, he has consistently done everything that lay within his power to make the book as good as it could be. No copy editor could have brought more care and understanding to the final preparation of the manuscript than David Bemelmans.

It goes without saying that in matters of substance I am deeply indebted to Werner Kaegi, Burckhardt's biographer. Kaegi, professor of history at Basel, died before I began serious work on this project and I never met him. But he has been my companion for nearly two decades, informing me constantly of what I needed to know or, occasionally, confirming what I had figured out independently. His magisterial seven-volume study of his predecessor is far more than a biography; it is a rich and stimulating history of Basel and, unexpectedly perhaps, despite its obvious hagiographical aspect (Burckhardt retains to this day the character of the *"Stadtheiliger Basels"* that Heinrich Wölfflin attributed to him a century ago), one of the most comprehensive intellectual histories of the entire nineteenth century. Because of its subject, it embraces both the close-up viewpoint of the local historian and the broad, cosmopolitan viewpoint of the European historian. To make this monumental work, with its vast learning, available in some form to English-speaking readers would be an undertaking of which any publisher and any translator could be proud. I shall be happy to have repaid a small portion of my debt if I succeed in making it a little better known among my academic colleagues than I think it currently is.

In conclusion, I have an apology to make. Burckhardt warned against "monographs on the merest minutiae" in the introduction to his *Weltgeschichtliche Betrachtungen*. "Even the most well-meaning of men will sometimes lose all sense of proportion," he wrote, "forgetting how minute a fraction of his life on earth a reader (unless he has a definite and personal interest in the subject) can devote to work of that kind. Anyone setting out to write a monograph should have the *Agricola* of Tacitus always at hand, and say to himself: the more long-winded, the more short-lived." This book on a small city has turned out to be considerably longer than the *Agricola*. For that I apologize to the reader. I can only hope to have shown that, small as it was, Basel does not belong in the category of minutiae and that it preserved, in the heart of nineteenth-century Europe, a distinct and valuable *geistige Lebensform,* or way of thought and life—to borrow the expression Thomas Mann used of his native Lübeck—in light of which we may still today take the measure of our own.

Lionel Gossman
Princeton, April 1999

BASEL
IN THE AGE OF
BURCKHARDT

Plan of Basel (detail). Courtesy Basel Tourist Bureau.

INTRODUCTION

Rome's overwhelming power was not able to create as much as a single one of those small Greek communities.
> —Johann Jacob Bachofen, *Griechische Reise*

Small states exist, so that there may be some spot on earth where the largest possible proportion of the members of the state are citizens in the fullest sense of the word. In their better times, despite the presence of slavery, the Greek poleis still came closer to that goal than all present-day republics.
> —Jacob Burckhardt, *Weltgeschichtliche Betrachtungen*, II, 1, "Der Staat"

A string of ancient flourishing cities borders the Rhine from where the river turns northward at Basel to the great delta where it finally empties into the North Sea. Many of them were Roman settlements: Basel (*Augusta Raurica,* the present Augst, a few miles up river), Strasbourg (*Argentoratum*), Worms (*Borgetomagus*), Mainz (*Moguntiacum*), Coblenz (*Confluentes*), Bonn (*Bonna*), Cologne (*Colonia Agrippinensis*), Nijmegen (*Noviomagus*), Utrecht (*Trajectum*).[1] Great cathedrals were built later on these same sites: at Basel, Strasbourg, Speyer, Worms, Mainz, Cologne, Utrecht; and there, in the shadow of the minster, merchants and artisans settled and plied their trade under the protection of lord and bishop. For at a time when roads were few and land transportation rudimentary, the river was a natural avenue of communication and exchange.

Around the year 1230 a bridge was thrown across the gorge of the Reuss—the famous Devil's Bridge—and the Rhine–St. Gotthard route between northern and southern Europe was opened. The St. Gotthard quickly became the chief trading route between the two main centers of European economic activity at the time, Flanders and northern Italy, displacing the old route via the fairs of Champagne, the valley of the Saône, and the St. Bernard. As the cities of Champagne went into decline, those along the banks of the Rhine prospered. Basel profited from its position at the point where goods arriving from the south were loaded onto barges for the journey downriver to Strasbourg, then on to Cologne. Other cities imposed *droits d'étape* or staging dues. Cologne, the great entrepôt where goods left the river to be transported by land toward Flanders soon became the largest city in medieval Germany.[2] Basel itself, according to some reports, was one of the chief cities of Germany when the Church Council was held there in the middle of the fifteenth century—larger than Frankfurt or Strasbourg, and, with some twenty thousand inhabitants, twice as populous as it was two centuries later.[3]

By the dawn of the Renaissance, the Rhineland had become—like Flanders and northern Italy—a focus of intense economic, artistic, and intellectual activity. Along the valley there was a lively traffic in men, merchandise, ideas, and skills from Italy and France, Flanders and England, Germany and Scandinavia. Universities were founded at Heidelberg (1386), Cologne (1388), Mainz (1471), Freiburg (1457), and Basel (1460). Out of the ferment came great individual artists and schools of artists—Memling, Urs Graf, Grünewald, Holbein, Konrad Witz—as well as outstanding thinkers and scholars: Reuchlin, Sebastian Brandt, and above all Erasmus, truly a man of the Rhineland cities and as much a citizen of Basel, where he lived for many years and where he is buried, as of Rotterdam, where he was born. The wind of the Reformation—Lutheran and Calvinist—blew powerfully down the valley. Strongholds were established at the northern and southern ends, in Holland and in Switzerland, and in many of the cities. But the traditional Catholic culture survived. To this day, parts of Alsace are a mosaic of Protestant and Catholic villages; the State or *Land* of Baden is 60 percent Catholic; there are also many Catholics in the territories constituting the present half-canton of Basel-Country.[4]

Almost simultaneously in the mid-fifteenth century, at Cologne, Mainz, and Strasbourg, the earliest printing presses went to work, revolutionizing the world of ideas and initiating an original new culture that combined scholarship, religion, and art with trade and technology. The business of culture was born. The Frankfurt book fair was the center and showplace of the new commerce, and the Rhineland printer-publishers held on to a substantial share of it long after printing had spread to other parts of Europe. At the beginning of the seventeenth century, on the eve of the Thirty Years' War, though Leipzig had overtaken Frankfurt as the publishing capital of Europe, the printers of Basel, Strasbourg, Frankfurt, and Cologne still accounted for 40 percent of the total number of titles exhibited at the book fairs.[5] The humanism of the Rhineland cities was not an affair of clerics and theologians. It was mercantile, a culture of merchants and bourgeois, intricately interwoven with the fabric of their everyday lives, their economic activity, as well as their religious practices and beliefs. Book and printing trades thrived on religious and scholarly debate and discussion, on controversy and exchange. The hardening of disagreement into silent antagonism, the closing off of discussion, affected the Rhenish cities economically as well as culturally.

The greatest of them were free cities, enjoying a considerable degree of independence. Having wrested their right to self-government from ecclesiastical or secular overlords and placed themselves, in many instances, under the direct tutelage of the Emperor (Basel, Strasbourg, Speyer, Worms, Frankfurt, and

Cologne were all at one time or another Imperial Cities or *Freie Reichsstädte*), they defended their privileges jealously against all encroachments, including those that might come from the Emperor himself. They were part of no larger state, and no capital or court drained off the skills, talents, or financial resources of their citizenries.[6] "These Rhenish cities are not in states," Lucien Febvre wrote.

> They are states unto themselves. The Baseler is a citizen of Basel, the man of Cologne a citizen of Cologne. If we could ask them, retrospectively, about their origins and, as we say, their "nationality," we would be astonished by their answers. . . . If the Rhenish cities recognized or served any higher political formation, it was the Empire, the Holy Roman Empire of Germany, the cosmopolitan Empire that embraced Italy and Burgundy as well as the Rhineland and the German territories proper. . . . Its tutelage was mild, its orientation to Italy and Burgundy favorable to communities of merchants. Indifferent to all frontiers, other than those that marked them off from their own surroundings, and harboring within their walls representatives of many "foreign" countries, the cities were cosmopolitan by profession, no doubt, but also by taste and temperament.[7]

As the Empire weakened, the cities banded together for protection in leagues or confederations. These, however, remained loosely organized and did not usually last long. The most powerful cities became virtually independent republics, "mistresses and guardians of their own destinies, standing alone and erect in face of the old powers."[8] Yet they shared a common culture. Merchants and scholars moved freely and frequently among them, and members of the same families—often refugees from Italy, France, and the Spanish Netherlands—settled in different cities. Coming from Antwerp, the Bernoullis first established themselves in Frankfurt and then moved to Basel. There are Passavants and De Barys among the merchant elites of both Frankfurt and Basel.[9]

Even today, as Febvre noted, though Basel is Swiss, Strasbourg French, Cologne and Frankfurt German, and Nijmegen Dutch, the Rhine cities have something in common, something that brings them closer to each other than to other cities within their own "national" frontiers.[10] In a fine passage reminiscent of Michelet,[11] Febvre reads Holbein's great portrait of Bonifacius Amerbach, the son of a leading Basel printer and humanist, as an emblem of that common culture.

> Look at him, this young friend of the aging Erasmus—who manages to find a tone of unwonted tenderness when he speaks of him—look at him in his tolerant humanity. He is one of the luminaries of the Reformation at Basel, yet Cardinal Sadolet never misses an opportunity of sending him long and affectionate epistles; a sincere evangelical, fully cognizant of the value of a Farel or a Bèze, yet not hesitating to chide them harshly for speaking one day with partisan narrowness against the memory of Erasmus. A man. There he is as he

prepares, at the age of twenty-four, to journey to Avignon to study with the great Alciatus: handsome in his youthful strength, with a virile grace that springs from modesty and integrity. A living retort to those who keep saying that partiality and blind fanaticism were the unavoidable destiny of the men of the sixteenth century. But who, gazing on this effigy, could articulate the name of a city? He is a Baseler, to be sure, and a great Baseler. But we know that he is a Baseler. No one, seeing him, would say that he is a Swiss or a German. Bonifacius Amerbach, the representative of a rather rare physical and moral human type—no doubt of that. But even more, the product of a culture. Of the authentically humane culture of the cities of the Rhine.[12]

As a Frenchman writing in the interwar years, when it was French policy to neutralize the Rhine, Febvre may have had special reasons for downplaying the role of national politics in the Rhineland and for presenting it instead as an enduring *cultural* entity. Curiously enough, however, a contemporary German historian—a passionate nationalist and ardent Nazi, for whom the Rhine can only have been the "German Rhine" of Niklaus Becker's fiercely anti-French song of 1840—had a similar vision of the Rhineland, from Basel to Amsterdam, as a traditional focus of resistance to the goal of a strong German national state.[13]

Politically, the fierce particularism of the cities left them weak, in the end, in face of powerful territorial lords and incipient centralized monarchies. New methods of warfare also sharply reduced their military significance and effectiveness.[14] Even the stoutest and wealthiest, having survived threats and assaults from ambitious local lords, from Burgundians, and from Habsburgs throughout the fifteenth and sixteenth centuries, finally succumbed. Strasbourg was absorbed into France in 1681, Mulhouse in 1798; Cologne was reduced to a French subprefecture under Napoleon and in 1815 became part of Prussia. Of about fifty free cities in Germany, large and small, only four survived the post-Napoleonic settlement of 1815, and they too, like the other German states, were eventually absorbed into the Prussian-dominated German Empire.[15] In addition, the "independence" of the cities came to be associated in the minds of their less fortunate citizens with the plutocracies that had come to dominate nearly all of them. There was consequently a good deal of support within the cities themselves for the larger political formations that promised to deliver them from these plutocracies—in the Rhineland for the French administration, and subsequently for Prussia; at Basel for a more powerfully centralized Swiss Confederation. Particularism was the policy, above all, of the patriciates.

Economically, the cities along the Rhine began to lose ground in relation to other urban centers around the time of the great voyages of discovery. Just as the opening of the St. Gotthard route had made their fortune, the great discoveries of the fifteenth and sixteenth centuries heralded their relative decline. The center of European trade shifted westward to the Atlantic seaports from where a vast new overseas commerce was conducted with the Indies, Africa, and the newly discovered and colonized territories of the American continent. For the Dutch, turned outward to the oversea trade, the Rhine was now a back door.[16] In the early seventeenth century, moreover, the area suffered devastation and depopulation as a result of the Thirty Years' War.

Yet relative decline does not mean torpor. Though the seventeenth and eighteenth centuries were not comparable in economic terms or in cultural terms to the earlier, more brilliant period, trade continued and men made a living; some became very rich. Certain cities developed thriving new industries—the manufacture of silk ribbon in Basel is a notable instance. And, of course, many of the old trades continued to prosper. Eighteenth century Frankfurt, for instance, supplied printers' materials to clients as far afield as Boston and Pennsylvania.[17] Cultural life, supported by well-established traditions, also went on. The great mathematicians of Basel—the Bernoullis and the Eulers—taught and were taught at the university there in the seventeenth and eighteenth centuries. The handsomely restrained baroque and rococo town houses of Basel and Strasbourg bear silent witness to the taste of a wealthy and educated urban elite. An adjutant of George Washington's, who was in Frankfurt in 1786, reported that about ten thousand visitors had arrived in the city for the fair, and contrasted the liveliness of the "temple of trade" on the Main with the stagnation of formerly wealthy cities like Augsburg and Ulm.[18]

The Basel merchants and ribbon manufacturers did particularly well in the eighteenth century. Their art collections and grand town and country houses testify to the legendary fortunes of the time. Until the middle of the nineteenth century, Basel was by far the wealthiest city in German Switzerland and the chief source of capital for Alsace, Zurich, eastern Switzerland, and southwest Germany.[19] A good deal survived even of the old common life and culture of the region. The eighteenth-century Rhinelander, as Goethe—himself a Frankfurter—depicted him, has a character of his own. He is learned, cultured, and cosmopolitan. "Born in Baden, educated in Basel and Strasbourg," Goethe wrote affectionately and admiringly of Johann Daniel Schoepflin—scholar, antiquarian, author of the celebrated *Alsatia Illustrata,* and enlightened adviser to Maria Theresa's reforming minister in the Austrian Netherlands, Count von Cobenzl—"he belonged in a quite peculiar way to the paradisiac valley of the Rhine, as to an expansive and well situated fatherland."[20]

In the nineteenth century, the industrial revolution and the prodigious development of Germany, especially after mid-century, transformed the Rhine once again into an area of intense economic activity. The region was now divided, however, by the politics of nationalism. Politically and culturally, the pull was east and west toward the centers and great capitals of the new nation-states, which the river separated, rather than north and south along the valley itself. By this time, moreover, only two of the old free cities in the Rhineland survived: Frankfurt (until 1866, when the patriciate paid for their support of Austria by seeing their city absorbed into Prussia) and Basel (which gave up much of its sovereignty by accepting the Swiss federal Constitution of 1848).

In the age of the nation-state, the free city-republics were, of course, vulnerable anachronisms. The pre-1848 Swiss Confederation had been little more than a series of defensive alliances among essentially independent and heterogeneous polities. "Il y a des cantons, il n'y a pas de Suisse," Tocqueville observed in 1836.[21] Basel had joined this loose confederation fairly late, in 1501, after hesitating for half a century between alliance with the neighboring Alsatian cities of Strasbourg and Colmar, which were also under the protection of the Empire, and association with the militarily more effective Confederation. As relations between the Empire and the Confederation deteriorated at the end of the fifteenth century, Basel found itself caught between the two, trying uncomfortably to maintain neutrality. After first rejecting an invitation to join the Confederation, it soon changed its mind, for it had quickly become obvious that the Confederation alone was in a position to defend it against invading and pillaging armies. Even so, the Reformation strengthened Basel's already strong economic ties to the cities to the north, and it was only the French annexation of Alsace in the seventeenth century that finally thrust the city fully into the arms of the Confederation.[22]

Among the Swiss cantons Basel remained distinctive, however, because of its peripheral location at the crossroads of France, Germany, and the rest of Switzerland, its connections to Alsace and Baden, its longstanding international trading relations, its wealth and culture, its predominantly urban character, and even its linguistic separation from the other German-speaking cantons.[23] Not so long ago, old Baselers still spoke of "going to Switzerland" just as they might speak of going to France or Germany.[24] Today, at the end of the twentieth century, as the influence of the old nation-states wanes in the context of European union, Basel has again turned outward beyond the frontiers of Switzerland and is engaged in an ambitious project to strengthen connections with communities in neighboring Alsace and Baden and to provide the *regio basiliensis,* as the Basel agglomeration is called, with a powerful economic, cultural, and communications infrastructure.

Basel's consciousness of its distinction in relation to the rest of the Confederation was consolidated in the early nineteenth century when the Federal Diet intervened to put an end to the so-called *Basler Wirren* (1830–1833)—a revolt against the dominance of the town on the part of the contiguous country districts over which Basel, like other free cities, had gradually acquired overlordship.[25] Under the ancien régime only citizens of the town had been represented in the Senate. As "subjects," the inhabitants of the rural areas had enjoyed no representation at all. With the establishment of the short-lived Helvetic Republic in 1798, the privileges of citizenship and representation had been extended to all, and the town had seen itself outnumbered by its erstwhile rural subjects. The Restoration constitution restored the dominance of the town while guaranteeing a minority representation to the inhabitants of the so-called *Baselbiet:* ninety senators were to represent the town, sixty the countryside (roughly the reverse of the population ratio). In the end, however, this compromise proved unacceptable to the inhabitants of the countryside and the 1830 Revolution in Paris precipitated a revolt of the rural population against the city. In the course of the hostilities, the city suffered a humiliating defeat at the village of Pratteln (August 3, 1833), with the loss of fifty-four men (a huge number of casualties for such a lilliputian conflict) against five killed on the other side. The federal mediating authorities—strongly influenced by the liberal cantons and widely regarded in Basel as prejudiced in favor of the rebels— imposed a resolution of the conflict that divided the canton into two autonomous half-cantons: *Basel-Stadt* (Basel-City) and *Basel-Landschaft* (Basel-Countryside). Though some radicals were convinced that this solution in fact suited the *Herren* or ruling merchant families, since it ensured their continued influence in city politics by eliminating their chief opponents, the entire unhappy episode deepened the Baselers' sense of their distinctiveness with respect to the rest of the Confederation. To the Baseler of the early nineteenth century, in short, the "state" was still essentially the city-republic, and it was to that republic, in the first instance, that he owed allegiance.

By the mid-nineteenth century, however, it was clear that the old Confederation or *Eidgenossenschaft* would have to be reorganized as a more unified state if it was to continue to fulfil its role as a bulwark against the powerful centralized states already existing (France) or rapidly forming (Germany, Italy) on its doorstep.[26] After a brief civil war—the *Sonderbundkrieg*—in which the minority, primarily rural, conservative, and Catholic cantons fought unsuccessfully to preserve maximum cantonal independence against the centralizing and liberal policies of the majority Protestant cantons, a new federal constitution was adopted in 1848, creating for the first time in Switzerland a true central government. The 1874 revision of this federal constitution drastically reduced the remaining autonomy of the cantons and effectively marked the end, for Basel, of six centuries of existence as a more or less independent polity. With the passing of that legislation, a *Ratsherr* of the time is said to have remarked that Basel had finally ceased to be a republic and had become a mere municipality.[27]

By the time of Burckhardt and Nietzsche, therefore, Basel was no longer one of many flourishing and independent city-states, as it had been in the Middle Ages and the Renaissance. Along with a handful of other surviving free cities in a world of nation-states, it was approaching the end of its career. Among the survivors, moreover, there was no longer much communication. Certainly, Basel had something in common with the Hanseatic trading cities—Hamburg, Bremen, Lübeck, themselves also former *Reichsstädte*—which had emerged still independent from the tumult of the Revolution and the Napoleonic occupation and whose patriciates had also proved remarkably resilient. It shared even more with nearby Frankfurt, whose annexation by Prussia in 1866 had been observed by the ruling class at Basel with dismay and apprehension. A century earlier the free merchant cities had collaborated to defend their traditional international trading rights and privileges against the restrictive economic policies of the new nation-states.[28] Now the few survivors stood alone, and each had to come to terms with the reality of the nineteenth century in its own way. Thus in the great struggle for the leadership of Germany, Bremen and Lübeck tended to support the compact *Kleindeutsch* policy of Prussia, whereas Frankfurt, to its cost, sided with Austria and the old idea of a loose federation of heterogeneous communities. Basel, for its part, accepted its place in the modern Swiss Confederation.

Nevertheless, though its political hegemony was finally undermined by the Constitution of 1874, the nineteenth-century Basel patriciate had succeeded in preserving the city's independence and identity and in hanging on to its own power and cultural traditions for seven decades. And that was long enough to provide an original and perhaps unique perspective on the modern world that was the old city-state's nemesis. For a good part of the nineteenth century, the "anachronistic" city-republic of Basel was a place where those whose ideas were *"unzeitgemäss"*—untimely or unseasonable—could feel, to some degree, at home and could even count on a measure of official approval and support. In particular, it became a sanctuary for intellectual practices that ran counter to the reigning orthodoxies of German scholarship: for Johann Jacob Bachofen's antiphilology and Franz Overbeck's antitheology, for Jacob Burckhardt's cultural history and Friedrich Nietzsche's unorthodox philosophy. In Basel, Bachofen, Burckhardt, Nietzsche, and Overbeck found the peace and security they needed to develop or pursue unseasonable thoughts. Though they came from different backgrounds and were by no means uniform in their style of thinking or of writing, they shared in some respects a common outlook. Their work, taken *en bloc,* constitutes a formidable critique not only of *Wissenschaft* as it was understood in the late nineteenth century, especially in Germany, but of the optimistic, self-confident modernism of their time.

This book is chiefly about two of those "untimely" thinkers and writers, the two native Baselers, Johann Jacob Bachofen and Jacob Burckhardt. In Germany, Bachofen was carefully studied by Karl Marx and Friedrich Engels on the left and by Ludwig Klages and Manfred Schröter on the right. He was a major and controversial influence throughout the late-nineteenth and early-twentieth centuries on the scholarly, philosophical, and literary world, from the Stefan George circle to Karl Kerényi, Sigmund Freud, Erich Fromm, Ernst Bloch, Walter Benjamin, and Alfred Bäumler, the Nazi ideologue who headed the science and scholarship division of Rosenberg's Ideology Department. Outside the German-speaking world, however, he remains a rather unfamiliar figure, especially since the discrediting of the theory of primitive matriarchy, with which his name is most often associated.[29] Burckhardt, in contrast, is well known to English readers, but largely as the author of one book, *The Civilization of the Renaissance in Italy,* which has achieved virtually classic status in English as well as German historiography. As writers, the two men are quite unlike each other, the differences of style reflecting differences of personality and thought. At its best, Bachofen's writing has a quality of sustained, elevated poetry, reminiscent of inspired religious oratory, but with a powerful undercurrent of intense personal involvement. Only in his correspondence do we obtain glimpses of a considerable gift for polemic and satire and of a dry, scathing wit. Burckhardt's writing is marked by sobriety, brusque transitions, rapid changes of tone and color, and sly irony. At times, it has an almost telegraphic laconism. Any one familiar with the French Enlightenment would immediately think of Montesquieu.

Stylistically, Bachofen seems quite far removed from our restless, postmodern, fin-de-siècle mentality, whereas Burckhardt may now strike us as wonderfully lively and actual. My endeavor has been to show how both writers are deeply rooted in the culture of a small, somewhat idiosyncratic, but at times illustrious city-state in the heart of Europe in the last decades of its history as an autonomous polity. For that reason I have devoted considerable space not only to Burckhardt and Bachofen, but to the unusual community in which they were born and raised and lived most of their lives, and whose history and character are inevitably little known to generations accustomed to think in terms of the great nation-states of nineteenth-century Europe.

While emphasizing that the ideas and attitudes of Burckhardt and Bachofen are intricately interwoven with the traditions, culture, and destiny of their native city, I do not wish to claim that they are without counterparts beyond the boundaries of Basel. Burckhardt's ideas about politics, culture, and society are often similar to those of Alexis de Tocqueville or Fustel de Coulanges or even John Stuart Mill. Bachofen has much in common not only with Jules Michelet (through Georg Friedrich Creuzer, Jacob Grimm, and Friedrich Karl von Savigny, all of whom Michelet had read attentively) and Fustel (notably regarding the importance of religion and myth), but, as Walter Muschg has shown, substantively and stylistically with the Bernese writer Jeremias Gotthelf (1797–1854) and the Zurich novelist and poet Conrad Ferdinand Meyer (1825–1898).[30] In some respects he is closer to them than to his fellow citizen Burckhardt. The already-noted divergent literary styles of the two Baselers as well as the coolness and guardedness of their personal relations reflect deep differences of temperament and outlook. Though the richness and interest of their work is enhanced, in my view, when it is considered in the context of the polity in which their families enjoyed great prominence and in which they themselves chose, in the end, to settle down for life, it would be diminished if we were to consider them simply as representatives or products of a particular nineteenth-century city culture.

Beyond their historical connection to Basel, Bachofen and Burckhardt—no less than their colleague Nietzsche, if more cautiously and less stridently—raise questions that may be even more challenging today than when they first raised them a century or a century and a half ago. What is or what ought to be, for instance, the relation between the state and culture? Can the influence of the state be limited to providing conditions of security in which individuals may pursue culture or *Bildung,* or must the state inevitably subordinate culture to its own goals? What is the effect on culture when it is mobilized to consolidate or promote the power of the state? Are the interests of power and those of culture essentially incompatible? To Burckhardt and Bachofen, both of whom had been strongly influenced by Herder, the various cultures—especially of the European peoples—still constituted a unity grounded in Christianity and classical antiquity. In our contemporary world, that situation no longer holds. A utopian image of a multicultural state that recognizes and benevolently encourages many different cultures within its borders now confronts a reality in which culture is often deeply involved in the competitive struggles of rival ethnic, linguistic, and economic groups to achieve power in and through the state. The basic question that engaged Bachofen and Burckhardt—the relation between culture and power—has, however, lost none of its pertinence. Another set of questions concerns the relation between culture and various forces in civil society itself. What will be the effect of the rationalization and industrialization of politics and culture, along with so much else in modern societies, which Burckhardt, anticipating Max Weber, was already deploring in the 1840s? Must the market be the Providence that determines virtually every aspect of our lives? And if not, how can that be prevented except through the power of the state and the imposition of restrictions on individual freedom and initiative? Most fundamentally, perhaps, is there a solution, in modern conditions, to the ancient problem of reconciling liberty and democracy? Can democracy be prevented from devolving into demagogy?

As we read Burckhardt and Bachofen, we find ourselves having to review some of our most tenaciously held beliefs. Our belief in progress, for instance— seemingly inextinguishable, until quite recently at least, despite the terrible experiences of the twentieth century. Challenging that belief, Bachofen and Burckhardt urge us to take a more detached view of the past and to evaluate calmly the characteristics of different ages, cultures, and political systems. Or our belief in work and our (growing) tendency to judge everything by how much it contributes to the *bonum utile.* Neither Bachofen nor Burckhardt despises work—and both worked extraordinarily hard. But neither was willing to accept that work is the highest value or that it can be considered independently of the quality of fulfillment or delight it ought to bring to the worker himself no less than to those who use the products of his labor. Moreover, both held that there were other values, equally important and essentially human—values usually related to art and religion, such as a utopian striving toward harmony or the joy that accompanies privileged moments of religious or esthetic experience. Writing shortly after the end of the Second World War, a German philosopher observed that "the 'total work' State needs the spiritually impoverished, one-track mind of the 'functionary.'"[31] In such a state, art ceases to be an occasion of what Burckhardt called *Genuss* and becomes instead the empty article of immediate consumption or the exchange commodity that he feared it would be for the coming "American man of feeling" (to use his own unflattering expression). Such a state also, Burckhardt or Bachofen might well have added, does not need and probably cannot tolerate free, independent-minded citizens.

It does not require great brilliance of insight to see that such ideas are well adapted to the ideology of an elite or leisure class, or of a privileged citizenry, such as both Bachofen and Burckhardt belonged to in their native Basel. Yet one may also feel that such ideas ought not to be dismissed out of hand simply because they offer no obvious solutions to the problems raised, lend themselves easily to political positions one finds objectionable, or are associated with religious positions one does not share. Much of the excitement and benefit of reading Bachofen and Burckhardt derives, I believe, from their ability to get us to think or rethink thoughts we often deem unthinkable. Among our own contemporaries or near-contemporaries, perhaps Sir Isaiah Berlin, with his acute sense of the impossibility of realizing all goods at the same time, comes closest to Burckhardt. As Noel Annan put it, Berlin "believes that you cannot always pursue one good end without setting another on one side. You cannot always exercise mercy without cheating justice. Equality and freedom are both good ends, but you can rarely have more of one without surrendering some part of the other. This is dispiriting for progressives who like to believe that the particular goal which at present they are pursuing is not incompatible with all the other goals which they like to think they value as much."[32]

PART ONE

Nineteenth-Century Basel

Le *genius loci,* c'est Erasme
                    —Jules Michelet, *Journal,* 24 August 1843
O Krähwinkel, mein Vaterland!
              —Jacob Burckhardt, letter to Gottfried Kinkel, 21 April 1844
Un des lieux saints de notre civilisation.
                 —Lucien Febvre, letter to Werner Kaegi, 8 July 1946

1

From "A Community of Citizens" to "A Conglomeration of Individuals"

Passing through Basel on his way to Italy in 1841, Friedrich Engels did not have a good impression. "Such a barren town, full of frock-coats, cocked hats, philistines and patricians and Methodists, where nothing is fresh and vigorous but the trees around the . . . Cathedral. . . . A hole-in-the-corner town, with all the ugliness of the Middle Ages and none of their beauty." Everything about the city was dark, stuffy, misshapen; even the Rhine, Engels claimed, is narrow and mean as it turns northward through Basel. Only after he had climbed up beyond the last spur of the Jura Mountains did Engels feel he had truly entered Switzerland. "The countenance becomes freer, more open, more vivacious, the cocked hat gives way to the round hat," and "the long trailing coat-tails to the short velvet jacket." Zurich lifted the young traveler's spirits completely. "I saw the lake lying before me, glistening in the morning sun, steaming with early mist, enclosed by densely wooded mountains, and for the first moment I was quite overcome by . . . astonishment at the existence of such a strikingly beautiful landscape."[1]

Still confined within its fourteenth-century walls, Basel in 1841 did indeed retain its medieval outline. The baroque palaces of the wealthy merchants had been fitted into the existing town plan. Many humbler dwellings had also acquired new windows or doors in rococo or Biedermeier style—signs of the owners' prosperity, like the fresh façades of Verrières in Stendhal's *The Red and the Black*—but there had been no alteration of the ancient shape of the city. Even the two principal open spaces—the Münsterplatz in front of the Cathedral and the Petersplatz in front of St. Peter's Church to the northwest—dated from the Middle Ages. In this city-state, ruled since 1529 by Protestant merchants and artisans, there had been no ambitious or enlightened prince or prelate to initiate urban projects of the kind that graced cities like Strasbourg, Nancy, or Würzburg. Since the Middle Ages, Basel had been a city of guilds, and like other similar cities—Nuremberg, Augsburg, Frankfurt—it retained that character. It had none of the grandeur of a *Residenzstadt,* even of a small one such as Karlsruhe.[2]

Nevertheless, travelers often commented on the beauty of the setting and on the noble breadth of the river as it flowed through the two formerly autonomous parts of the city, Great Basel on the left bank and Little Basel on the right. Most visitors found much to admire in the numerous churches, public buildings, and private and public art collections.[3] Engels's gloomy account of the city was almost certainly due to something other than its physical appearance, and Basel and its merchants were not being contrasted with the free, fearless Swiss of yore. On the contrary, only a few years later Engels poured ridicule on the popular myths about ancient Swiss freedom and independence then being invoked by the conservative cantons on the eve of the *Sonderbundkrieg,* or Swiss civil war, of 1847. Since the heroic days of Sempach, Grandson, Murten, and Nancy, nothing much had been heard of the legendary but rather stupid *Ur*-Swiss, he would write, for they had withdrawn out of history and "busied themselves in all piety and propriety with milking cows, cheese-making, chastity and yodeling."[4] The contrast Engels drew between Basel and the rest of Switzerland, especially Zurich, had far less to do with the virtues of a simple mountain people and the vices of urban commercial society, with pristine lakes glistening in the morning sun and grimy city streets, than with contemporary politics.

Even though a populist revolt had overturned the liberal regime that had come to power there in 1830, Zurich remained the heart of progressive politics in German-speaking Switzerland, and in fact the liberals staged a comeback within a few years of Engels's visit. It must have seemed an open place—confident, dynamic, and turned toward the future. Characteristically, the city walls—widely viewed everywhere as symbols of the old regime and of the subjection of the peasants to the townsfolk[5]—had been torn down in the 1830s. Basel, on the other hand, then still the largest and wealthiest town in German Switzerland, had become a byword for political conservatism. Like nearly all liberals and radicals at the time, Engels saw it as the stronghold of a mean-spirited, purse-proud, and bigoted bourgeois oligarchy, which in 1833 had accepted the loss of the city's dependent rural territories rather than relinquish its political control by conceding appropriate representation to them on the city-state's Senate. Alone among the major Protestant cantons, Basel had thus withstood the Revolution of 1830 and resisted liberalization of the old *Ratsherrenregiment,* or rule of the merchant elite. On the contrary, the oligarchy had become entrenched as a result of the civil war between the city and its rural subjects—the *"Basler Wirren"*—and the federally mediated *Kantonstrennung,* or division of the canton into the two separate (and still existing) half-cantons of Basel-City and Basel-Countryside, which ensued.[6] In contrast to liberal and progressive Zurich, Basel could only have been perceived by Engels as an obstacle to modernity and to the democratic national state of the future.

Basel's anomalous situation, its relative isolation within the Swiss Confederation, was felt within the city itself. None of its leading citizens was likely to forget the sympathy shown to the rebels in the countryside by almost all the other Protestant cantons or the lack of evenhandedness—so at least it seemed in Basel—of the federal mediators who intervened to resolve the conflict. The city's wealth and independence, together with its orientation to the outside world, had long made it an object of envy and resentment among the other cantons. As a result, there were many in Basel who did not endorse the liberal goal of transforming Switzerland from a *Staatenbund,* a confederation of states, into a *Bundesstaat,* or federal state, and who had little taste for the centralization that to Engels was the indispensable first stage in the movement toward a modern, democratic society. In an article in the *Basler Zeitung* in 1845, Jacob Burckhardt, then a young journalist employed by the conservative publisher of the paper, *Ratsherr* (Senator) Andreas Heusler-Ryhiner, gave expression to the majority *juste-milieu* position. "Switzerland," he wrote, "is no federal state, it is not even a nation, only a federation of states enjoying equal rights."[7] Basel remained loyal to the Confederation during the civil war of 1847, but there were many who sympathized with the conservative cause of maximum cantonal independence. The new federal Constitution of 1848 was passed in Basel in a similar grudging spirit, with many *Ratsherren* simply not voting.[8]

As late as the 1860s, the Basel elite's suspicion of modern political developments and in particular of the liberal-leaning federal Switzerland that emerged after 1848 can be detected in the coolness of its response to a proposal, put forward in 1864, to build a major monument commemorating the victory of a Swiss Confederation force over a far larger Armagnac army at the Battle of St. Jakob (1444). The victory was generally held to have saved Basel—not yet at the time a member of the Confederation—from one of the worst dangers in its history and was traditionally viewed as a symbol of the city-state's indebtedness to and association with the Confederation. In the 1860s, however, the elite appears to have felt that the monument had been proposed in order to signify Basel's full acceptance of the modern federal Swiss state and of the latter's essentially liberal political orientation. Still in the hands of the elite at this time, the government dragged its feet and did nothing to help with the financing of the project. Even when the monument was finally unveiled in 1872 (three years after the 425th anniversary of the battle), the government's role in the celebrations was kept to the strictest minimum.[9]

Not a few members of the Basel elite who were at the opposite end of the political spectrum from Engels concurred not only with the latter's understanding of the social movements of the time but with his description of the city as narrow and suffocatingly provincial. Franz Dorotheus Gerlach, professor of Latin at the University, together with his students Bachofen and Burckhardt, also saw the path of liberal concessions as leading ultimately to communism, and all three complained of the philistinism and meanness of life in Basel. There was no question for them, however, of working to overthrow the existing social order. Belonging to a polity that from Engels's point of view was hopelessly anachronistic and to a class that he considered doomed to be displaced, Bachofen and Burckhardt understandably did not share Engels's historical optimism. On the contrary, they believed it was their duty, in a time of trial, to "stay at their post," as Burckhardt would put it, in order to salvage what they could of "the culture of old Europe." Their situation as Baselers in the age of warring nation-states became for them an emblem of the condition of culture in the age of industrialism and popular democracy.

The city that Bachofen and Burckhardt were born into in the early nineteenth century was still quite small. Estimates of the population vary. Around 1814–1815, it appears to have been about sixteen thousand—a modest figure compared even with Strasbourg (about 50,000) or Frankfurt (40,000), and much smaller than Hamburg (110,000) or Lyons (100,000). Apart from Geneva, however, it was the biggest city in Switzerland, overshadowing Zurich by a considerable margin, and it was certainly the wealthiest.[10] "Das alte würdige Basel, der Sitz des Reichtums" ("Worthy old Basel, the seat of wealth"), the radical *National-Zeitung* called it in 1842, and that is how most people in France, Germany, and Switzerland thought of it.[11]

The modest size of Basel is not an insignificant fact and it was not an accident. Restricting immigration into the city had been the deliberate policy of the *Rat*, or Senate, for centuries. During certain periods of the fourteenth, fifteenth, and early sixteenth centuries, acquisition of citizenship was made easier in order to make up for the catastrophic loss of life caused by outbreaks of the plague (an estimated 14,000 in 1348, for instance, another 8,000 in 1439, another 7,000 in 1564),[12] as well as for the Catholic and conservative citizens who left the city after it embraced the Reformation. Residents who fought bravely for the city in wars were also rewarded with citizenship. But as of 1541, strict limits were again imposed. Prospective immigrants had to demonstrate not only that they had sufficient capital to establish themselves in business but exactly how they proposed to earn their living.[13] Even during times of severe religious persecution of Protestants in France and persecution by the Inquisition in Italy, Basel did not welcome all and sundry—only *"kunstreiche und wohlhabende Welsche,"*[14] those refugees (French and Italian, for the most part, or *"Welsche"*) who might enrich the city with their skills and capital. Few refugees in fact came directly to Basel. Many who finally settled in the city spent some time first in other places—Locarno if they came from Italy, Geneva if they came from France, and Frankfurt if they came from the Spanish Netherlands. Only when it was clear that they could not return to their homes did they move to Basel, arriving in two waves—the first in the mid-fifteenth century, the second in the early seventeenth, at the time of the Thirty Years War. It is an indication of the wealth and talent of these people that they came rapidly to form the ruling elite of the city, the so-called patriciate.

At the beginning of the sixteenth century the population of Basel may have stood at about twenty thousand.[15] In 1726 it was seventeen thousand.[16] In 1779, Isaac Iselin estimated it at slightly more than fifteen thousand. Travelers were struck by the large expanse of land within the town walls. Upward of one hundred thousand people might have been accommodated there, according to one English visitor in 1778, whereas in fact, he claimed, there were not more than about fourteen thousand.[17] Until the mid-nineteenth century, much of the land between the old thirteenth-century inner wall and the newer outer wall dating from the turn of the fourteenth and fifteenth centuries was covered with fields and gardens.[18] Contemporaries were aware that the population of the city had declined. As a good Enlightener, Isaac Iselin inquired into the causes and concluded that, since in all European cities at that time mortality rates were higher than birth rates and population increased only through immigration, the strict control of immigration and citizenship by the city-state's government was the chief reason for the decline.[19]

In fact—despite a brief relaxation of controls on immigration in the early years of the seventeenth century, no doubt to make up for the devastating effect of two further severe outbreaks of plague in 1634 and 1640—the acquisition of Basel citizenship was made extraordinarily difficult by a series of measures passed between 1653 and 1676. Far from easing these restrictions, a citizens' "revolution" in 1691 resulted in a new Constitution that added another turn to the screw.[20] In addition to the existing fees, prospective citizens were now required to turn over 10 percent of their total assets. The native artisans, the citizen-guildsmen of Basel, were clearly not about to make life uncomfortable for themselves by expanding their ranks and increasing competition. For it was they who were concerned to restrict immigration and access to citizenship rather than the wealthy merchants and ribbon manufacturers; to the merchants an increase in the labor pool might conceivably not have been unwelcome. At the beginning of the eighteenth century the door was closed absolutely against all new *Einbürgerungen*. A law of 1706 stipulated that no person was to be admitted to the privileges of citizenship with the exception of unusually "qualified subjects"—that is, those disposing of a fortune of ten thousand Reichsthaler or more. Twelve years later access to citizenship was closed without exception, the few who had claimed sufficient wealth having been found to have deliberately misrepresented their assets. This radical measure was confirmed in 1732 and again in 1749.[21] Thus in the one hundred years from 1691 to 1798, only sixty-four individuals were admitted to citizenship. The significance of that figure is better grasped if it is compared with the corresponding figures for Hamburg or Frankfurt.[22]

To be a citizen of Basel meant to be a member of one of the eighteen officially recognized guilds of the city (fifteen in Great Basel, three in Little Basel). Even merchants and wholesalers who did not practice one of the traditional crafts were required to be members of a guild. "Guildsman" and "citizen" were thus overlapping designations. To become a citizen, a man had at the same time to be accepted into one of the guilds. The officers of the guilds elected the members of the *Grosser Rat,* or Senate, and were themselves eligible for election; it was thus through the guilds that the individual citizen exercised his political rights. Giving an account of the political organization of the city in 1778, an English visitor no doubt had the institutions of early Rome in mind when he described the *Zünfte* or guilds as "tribes" and their leaders as "tribunes." "The citizens are divided into eighteen tribes, called in German *Zuenfte.* . . . Upon a vacancy in the Great Council, for instance, the six candidates [one of whom will be chosen by lot] must be taken from the citizens of that tribe to which the person who occasioned the vacancy belonged, and be nominated by such of the members of the Great and Little Councils [Senate and Cabinet] as are of the same tribe. The candidates for the Senate, and for the tribunes or chiefs of each tribe, called in German *Meister,* are appointed by the Great Council."[23] The electoral system was extremely complicated, and the changes introduced by new constitutions or constitutional revisions[24] did not simplify it or do away with the power of the guilds. What the choice of terms in the visitor's description makes clear is that the *"Zuenfte"* were not simply professional organizations, as the term *guilds,* by which the German word is usually rendered into English, would suggest. They were the basic political organs of the state.[25]

At the same time, however, the guilds were *also* professional organizations, keeping a close watch on the practices of their members and jealously defending their interests and privileges. No one who was not a citizen was entitled to set up for himself in any of the trades organized into guilds. In addition, newly admitted citizens were bound to continue in the trade that they undertook to practice at the time of their admission, no one could change trades, and no one could practice more than one. An ordinance of 1526 had set a limit on the total number of persons authorized to practice any single trade or craft, prohibited sons from setting up with their fathers, and specified the number of journeymen and apprentices permitted to any one workshop.[26] Just as rural society in the ancient régime was characterized by perpetual lawsuits challenging or seeking the application of complex rights, privileges, and property laws, the life of the city was characterized by interminable lawsuits concerning alleged infractions of guild regulations.

The principle behind the elaborate system of regulations governing trade and industry was an old-fashioned precapitalist one. The gist of it is set out in the brief of the plaintiffs in a lawsuit brought in 1686 by a group of nineteen Basel tradesmen against a company of entrepreneurs—Heussler, Sarasin, and

Leissler—who, it was charged, had used unfair and illegal practices in order to drive others out of business and steal their markets and clients: "In all places and at all times it has been the concern of well ordered governments to organize their rule and authority in such a way that their subjects earn an honest and decent living and that none can unduly interfere with his neighbor or be unduly subject to him; and that is also the reason why our forefathers, who have gone to their eternal rest, established certain limits and numbers for all trade, industry, and other forms of business, which each individual was to observe as he made his living from the exercise of his profession."[27]

The principle enunciated here is the satisfaction of legitimate needs and the subordination of individual advantage to the welfare of the community as a whole. Alongside this principle, which supposedly governed the internal affairs of the guild city, there was a second well-established principle that governed external or international commerce and that was, in some respects, the opposite of the first: the principle of *liberum commercium,* of freedom to trade across territorial boundaries. From the seventeenth century on, many members of the Basel elite were engaged in this kind of trade; they bought and sold in different markets, they transshipped merchandise from one place to another, and they participated in international banking operations. The interests of these men were not identical with those of their simpler fellow citizens. At times they were quite opposed. As the governing class responsible for the entire community, the senators or *Ratsherren* had to consider the welfare of the community as a whole and not only what was advantageous to one part of it. If the idea of permitting economic activity within the city to be ruled simply by market forces had entered their minds at all, they would probably have rejected it. The harsh competition unleashed by such a free-for-all would have been incompatible with the religious and moral vision of the community which had been inherited from the Middle Ages, and according to which every citizen should treat his neighbor as his brother. It would have been completely at odds with the inner order of the medieval *Stadtgemeinde* or urban community, and would have destroyed not only the social bonds holding the community together but its unity and identity in face of the outsider. Though they were increasingly inclined to embrace more liberal economic ideas, the wealthy merchants and manufacturers of Basel had an interest in preserving the internal social order of the city and its foundation in the guild regulations, as well as an obligation to do so. When they themselves came into conflict with the artisans and local tradesmen—over the introduction of new machines, for instance—they looked for a solution that would not undermine the economic security of the artisans. Most often, of course, it was the artisans who made the chief concessions, by agreeing for example to allow the merchants to put out to the countryside the manufacture of articles that supposedly required little skill or training.[28]

The immigration policy discussed earlier was itself an expression of the combined will of the wealthy elite and the ordinary citizens. For the latter it was a way of fending off unwelcome competition and avoiding the creation of a population directly dependent on the merchants within the city walls. The merchants, on their side, were content to purchase internal peace in the city at this price and to transfer their work to the villages in the countryside around Basel, where guild regulations did not apply. As citizens, the merchants had a monopoly on the labor of the city's rural "subjects" and could arbitrarily set the rates for it. The "putting-out system" was thus economically attractive as well as politically expedient. The result of this policy of compromise and peaceful coexistence within the city was that the increase in population created by the labor needs of the rapidly expanding silk ribbon industry occurred largely in the countryside around the city. In 1815, for instance, the population of the so-called *Baselbiet* was about double that of the city.[29] Moreover, it was the country dwellers or "subjects" of the city who became directly dependent on the merchant elite.[30] This situation explains why it was unrest in the countryside rather than in the city that was exploited by the revolutionaries of 1830, why the Revolution of that year took the form, at Basel, of a rebellion of the country districts aimed at the privileges of the city as a whole, and why in that conflict the conservative ruling elite had the full support and loyalty of the city's artisans and professional class in resisting demands that representation on the *Rat* or Senate be proportionate to population.

A crucial moment in this policy of compromise and accommodation occurred in 1666, when the *Rat* was petitioned to prohibit the use of a new type of mechanical loom that one of the ribbon manufacturers, Emmanuel Hoffmann-Müller, had succeeded in smuggling out of Holland. While it would vastly increase productivity, the new loom threatened the livelihood of many local weavers working for the passementerie trade. Above all, it bypassed the passementerie worker as a skilled artisan by making it possible for untrained and unskilled operators to execute tasks hitherto entrusted to specialized workers. The *Kleiner Rat,* or Cabinet, deliberated at length on this issue. The decision could not have been an easy one. The passementerie workers were vehemently opposed to the new loom, and it was easy to see that they had reason to fear for their jobs. There was a real danger that a disaffected and impoverished group would be created in the community. On social grounds, the *Rat* would no doubt have liked to prohibit the new machine. On the other hand, the merchants were equally eager to put it to use. In the end, the new loom was approved on the grounds that, if the *Rat* failed to permit its adoption, ribbon manufacturing would simply leave Basel, with far more serious economic consequences for the city than the threatened effects on the passementerie workers. In return, the merchants agreed to pay a supplementary tax on their production into the city treasury.[31] The decision may have been complicated by the fact that the passementerie weavers, like many of the merchants and manufacturers, were relative newcomers to the city, having been admitted as refugees precisely because they brought with them a skill that did not exist among the established artisans of Basel and therefore did not threaten them in any way. Their guild dated only from 1612, and from the beginning it had had to adopt more liberal regulations than the other guilds. In other words, no long-established trade or guild was threatened by the government's decision. So the social damage resulting from what was seen as a necessary concession to the requirements of the market economy could be viewed as less serious than it might otherwise have been.

The Council's approval of the mechanical loom ushered in a brilliant age of expansion and commercial success for the Basel ribbon industry. The city had stolen a march on its chief competitors in Germany (at Krefeld) and in France (at Lyons and Saint-Etienne), as well as in other Swiss and German cities, such as Zurich, Geneva, Frankfurt, Nuremberg, and Augsburg, where the machines had been prohibited. In addition, Louis XIV's wars drastically reduced the French presence in the German market. By the end of the seventeenth century, Basel merchants had captured a dominant share of that market.[32] The French later reversed their decision and with the help of a subsidy from Louis XVI's government smuggled one of the new looms out of Basel to Saint-Etienne in the 1770s.[33] But even by 1811 there were still only one hundred mechanical looms at Saint-Etienne.[34] By the end of the eighteenth century, in contrast, almost twenty-five hundred modern mechanical looms were working for the Basel manufacturers, some in the city, most in the countryside.[35] The *Konsortium* of Basel *Bandfabrikanten,* or ribbon manufacturers, established in the years between 1744 and 1764, comprised twenty-three firms[36] and employed over nine thousand people in the countryside alone.[37]

Throughout this period, however, the city-state's government constantly strove to maintain a balance between two competing forces: on the one hand the economic liberalism called for by the increasingly prosperous and successful merchants and manufacturers, represented by the twelve-man *Direktorium der Kaufmannschaft*—a semiofficial agency given official recognition in 1682;[38] on the other, the traditional guildsmen's ideal of a protected and strictly regulated market guaranteeing a decent livelihood to all honest and hardworking citizens. The artisans pursued that ideal through innumerable petitions, protesting new and unfair trading practices or demanding strict application of the established, officially sanctioned guild regulations and restrictions.[39]

On the whole, the governent succeeded in striking a balance. Though the guilds were abolished during the short period of revolutionary government led by the extreme enlightened and progressive wing of the elite under Peter Ochs in 1798–1803, they were revived under the moderate governments of the Restoration and, despite persistent criticism from committed liberals in the elite like Christoph Bernoulli, survived well into the second half of the nineteenth century, outlasting those at Zurich by several decades.[40] Their members did moderately well economically. While the *Herren,* or great merchants, amassed legendary fortunes, the more modest burghers, the master craftsmen, and the small tradesmen were fairly comfortably off since they operated in a prosperous and protected market. From the time of the Reformation until the brief interregnum of the Helvetic Republic, one historian observes, Basel enjoyed a period of relatively uninterrupted social peace. "The reason for this lies in the effect on the condition of the citizenry of the administration's careful balancing of social and economic objectives. There were no numerically significant groups of poor or disadvantaged citizens within the city walls of Basel during this time, and the cautious policy of the Government with respect to immigration and the granting of citizenship had not fostered the development of a mass of uncontrollable inhabitants."[41]

The population figures from which we started out would nevertheless have been different had there not been quite a bit of immigration into the city. If citizenship was virtually unobtainable except by the very rich, so that the number of citizens hardly increased at all, the number of residents and children of residents (*Hintersassen* in German, *habitants* and *natifs* in French) continued to increase throughout the eighteenth century. Most of those people came from the *Baselbiet* (the villages and the countryside surrounding the city and subject to its rule), from other Swiss cantons, and from neighboring Baden. They were forbidden to exercise any of the traditional trades, which were the privilege of the guilds,[42] or to set up in business and compete with the *Herren;* they could not buy or hold landed property without special permission; and while they paid varying annual dues for the right to reside in the city—depending on whether they enjoyed *Hochschutz* or *Mittelschutz* ("high" or "medium" protection)—they enjoyed no political rights whatsoever. They could not vote and they were, of course, not eligible for office.[43] By the last third of the eighteenth century, the number of these *Hintersassen* was nearly equal to that of the citizenry. The census of 1779 gives a figure of close to seventy-five hundred citizens as against seventy-three hundred noncitizens,[44] but that latter figure would almost certainly have been larger had illegal (*"heimliche"*) as well as legal (*"konzessionierte"*) residents been counted. Many *Hintersassen* were in service. About half of the male and female noncitizens within the *Ringmauer,* or exterior city wall, are listed in the census of 1779 as *"Bediente"* or *"Hausgenossen"* (servants or house staff).[45] On the other hand, the guildsmen often claimed that the increase in the noncitizen population was due to the expansion of the ribbon industry and the employment opportunities created by the large number of warehouses and factories in the city. By the mid-nineteenth century, at least, that was the case. An astonishingly large number of noncitizens were still in service as maids, butlers, coachmen, gardeners, and so on (four thousand out of a population of twenty-seven thousand!), but to their ranks it was now necessary to add about twenty-five hundred journeymen, apprentices, clerks, and other employees, and an equal number of male and female factory hands.[46] The continuous increase in the noncitizen population was a constant source of concern especially to the humbler citizens, and the Senate was frequently petitioned to look into the causes.[47]

In relation to the *Hintersassen,* the ordinary citizen, no matter how humble, belonged to a privileged social class. His livelihood was protected, he enjoyed certain political rights (even if he could rarely afford to exercise them),[48] and he was eligible for community care if he fell sick or upon hard times. The better-off artisan could even aspire to become a kind of grandee in the countryside, the positions of *Vogt,* or bailiff, in the country districts being normally reserved for *Handwerker.* Between the merchants and the more prosperous artisans—masters employing several journeymen and apprentices in a workshop—there was no hard and fast boundary, according to the author of a series of retrospective articles on "Basel in the years after the 1830 Revolution" that appeared in the radical *Schweizerische National-Zeitung* in 1844.[49] One group shaded into the other. That was not surprising, the newspaper contended, since in Basel "money is the surrogate of talent, industry, knowledge, integrity, and virtue."[50] There were, in short, no distinctions among the citizens of Basel other than those established by wealth. The poorer, less successful artisans, correspondingly, were quite sharply distinguished from the rich merchants. According to the *National-Zeitung,* they were narrow-minded and, like the medieval guildsmen, ignorant and suspicious of everything strange, foreign, or not of their guild.

In general, however, poverty among the citizens of Basel was rarely extreme. As a group they were privileged economically as well as politically in comparison with noncitizens.[51] By agreeing to place strict limits on the acquisition of citizenship, the merchants had placed a protective shield around the artisans. If their aim had been to ensure that there would be no large class of disaffected penurious citizens to constitute a political opposition, it seems that they succeeded. An English traveler noted that though there were immense fortunes in Basel, the sumptuary laws were still effective enough to prohibit excessive and provocative display of wealth. Thus "a happy simplicity of manners is still predominant," the community is not visibly divided into extravagantly rich and wretchedly poor, and as a result "the lower ranks of citizens are so strongly prejudiced in favor of their own country as to seem convinced that true felicity is only to be found at Basel; and indeed that class of people are in no part of the world more happy. Every person boasts that he is free, and is so in reality; and as the citizens not only possess very considerable privileges but each individual may also indulge the hope of being one day chosen into the sovereign council, he enjoys a certain degree of respect and consideration extremely flattering to his self-importance."[52]

The preservation of social harmony and a sense of community among all citizens was still one of the stated aims of the school reform introduced in 1817, after the Restoration ended two decades of social and political unrest. The reform, which was intended to create a unified system of education from elementary school to university and which placed education in the hands of the state rather than the church, resulted in the closure of some private schools, notably Christoph Bernoulli's progressive *Philotechnisches Institut.* The advantage of the public school over private schools, according to the principal of the *Gymnasium,* the neohumanist scholar Rudolf Hanhart, lay in its "drawing all citizens together under one roof." Hanhart's vision seems to have been inspired by the examples of classical antiquity and the ancient republic. "In the public school a noble spirit of emulation develops among children from all the different classes of the people and leads them to strive to surpass each other in knowledge and useful skills. In this way, that community spirit, that sense of common citizenship which presides over the founding of free states and ensures their conservation, and above all the sense of fairness which always considers the substance, not the person, and the love of justice, which can be called the source of all republican virtues, are fostered at a very early age, in the schoolboy. The public school may thus rightly be viewed as a 'seed bed of citizens.'"[53]

In fact, merchants made up a not inconsiderable part of the population of Basel. From the sixteenth to the end of the eighteenth centuries, membership of the tradesmen's guilds—the so-called *werbende Hand*—increased by half, while that of the artisan guilds—the *wirkende Hand*—declined.[54] In the sixteenth century only 16 percent of the members of the fifteen guilds of Great Basel had belonged to the *werbende Hand;* by the beginning of the nineteenth century, of fourteen hundred active citizens (those with both voting and office-holding privileges) in the fifteen guilds, 40 percent belonged to the *werbende Hand.*[55] Nineteenth-century Basel was truly a city of merchants and tradesmen, great and small.

In the aftermath of the *Kantonstrennung* of 1833, it looked for a brief time as though the merchants might have to give up a good deal of power in the government of the city-state to the *Handwerker,* or artisans. The latter were rewarded for their loyalty during the *Wirren* with a new, quite liberal constitution that provided for eighty-three members of the Senate to be elected directly by the citizens, in addition to the thirty-six who continued to be elected by the guilds.[56] In fact, however, though more *Handwerker* were indeed elected, they quickly found themselves faced with the reality of the elite's economic power. Either they voted as the merchants wanted or their affairs suffered, the radical *National-Zeitung* reported in 1842 in a retrospective account of the political situation since 1830: "There is evidence for the allegation that as soon as a session of the Senate has come to an end, any recalcitrant artisan is asked to submit his bills, these are paid, and his services are never sought again."[57] The Basel artisan, the paper went on, has qualities—*"den gesetzten Sinn, das Bürger-*

liche" (a steady spirit, an orderly way of life), an aversion to charlatanry and pretension—but he cannot have a free mind and in fact he is obliged to sell his vote to the rich on whose patronage he is dependent. The so-called *freie Bürger* (free citizens) of Basel are often no more than *"verkaufte Plebejer"* (plebeians who have allowed themselves to be bought).[58]

The artisans were the more likely to toe the line as their situation was increasingly precarious. There were frequent complaints that the upper classes were purchasing their clothes and household articles outside the city, especially in France. Occasionally tailors and shoemakers would demand to inspect packages arriving by post from France. Yet the artisans themselves broke their own regulations. Achilles Bischoff reported to the *Grosser Rat* on one occasion that by far the greatest quantity of clothes, shoes, and furniture that entered the city by the post was ordered not by private individuals but by artisans who then resold the goods as their own products.[59] A writer in the *National-Zeitung* appears to have been reporting accurately when he asserted in 1844 that "[t]he young merchant orders his clothes from Paris, the cabinetmaker buys his shoes from the countryside, the stove-fitter gets his porcelain stoves from Strasbourg."[60] As locally produced merchandise is more expensive and of poorer quality, everybody gets round the guild restrictions, "everybody cheats on everybody else." In these conditions, the dependence of the artisans—those "children of a bygone age," as the newspaper patronizingly described them—on the merchants was virtually complete. They needed the merchants as clients and they needed their political support in order to maintain the guild and citizens' privileges, which alone kept them from slipping over into the socially and economically inferior condition of the *Hintersassen, Niedergelassenen,* or non-citizens.

The influx of these poorer immigrants had been a constant cause of alarm and complaints in the eighteenth and early nineteenth centuries. By the middle of the nineteenth century it had become a flood, thanks in part to the growth of factories in the city in the 1840s and the introduction of steam-driven looms in the 1850s.[61] In 1837 Basel had 21.5 new immigrants for every one hundred residents compared with 1.3 for Bern and 2.7 for Zurich. By the end of the century, that figure had risen still further to 37.6, while at Bern it was only 5.5 and even in rapidly industrializing Zurich it did not go beyond 20.3.[62] At mid-century, only 35 percent of the population of Basel were citizens; the rest were immigrants and the children of immigrants from other Swiss cantons and from neighboring Baden. In the humbler ranks of society three thousand artisans and small tradesmen enjoying the protection of the guilds and the privileges of citizenship found themselves outnumbered by four thousand house servants and five thousand journeymen, apprentices, clerks, and male and female factory workers.[63] In the following decades the situation grew even worse. In the 1860s, 1870s, and 1880s, citizens made up only 27 percent of the population of the

L'ILLUSTRATION,
JOURNAL UNIVERSEL.

Ab. pour Paris. 3 mois, 9 fr. — 6 mois, 18 fr. — Un an, 36 fr.
Prix de chaque N°, 75 c. — La collection mensuelle, br., 3 fr.

N° 149. — Vol. VI. — SAMEDI 3 JANVIER 1846.
Bureaux : rue Richelieu, 66.

Ab. pour les dép. — 3 mois, 9 fr. — 6 mois, 18 fr. — Un an, 36 fr.
Ab. pour l'étranger, — 10 fr. — 20 fr. — 40 fr.

Inauguration de la station du chemin de fer à Bâle.

La ville de Bâle a célébré avec pompe, le 11 du mois dernier, la mise en exploitation de la partie du chemin de fer qui pénètre dans l'enceinte de ses murs. Cette inauguration solennelle, celle arrivée d'un premier convoi, on l'a été saluée par les vives acclamations des habitants auxquels elles sem-

(Inauguration de la station du chemin de fer à Bâle, le 11 décembre 1845.)

blaient permettre de regarder comme prochaine la réalisation de leurs espérances d'avenir. Ce n'était pas seulement l'ouverture de la première station sur le territoire suisse et l'achèvement des chemins de fer de l'Alsace que Bâle fêtait, mais le premier pas fait vers l'exécution d'un chemin de fer suisse central, qui doit lier le midi et nord et à l'ouest, les che-

mins de fer de l'Italie à ceux de l'Allemagne et de la France. Depuis un certain temps déjà, les premiers banquiers et les principaux capitalistes de la ville de Bâle se sont réunis pour préparer l'exécution d'un chemin de fer suisse central qui étendra son réseau sur tout ce beau pays, vierge encore de ra l ways et appelé cependant à être le point commun où

viendront se relier les communications de tant d'États puissant d'Europe. Tous les avant-projets avaient été faits, et les études préparatoires des ingénieurs les plus capables avaient mis à même de reconnaître que le seul travail d'art important serait la percée du Hauenstein, par un tunnel de 3,500 mètres de longueur. Cet ouvrage ne présentera même d'autres diffi-

Arrival of the first train from Strasbourg at the new railway station in Basel, the first in Switzerland. From *L'illustration*, January 3, 1846.

city. Professor Kinkelin, the director of the 1870 census, warned that unless measures were taken to facilitate the acquisition of citizenship, Basel would soon reach the point where it was no longer *"eine Bürgerschaft, sondern nur noch ein Conglomerat von Einwohnern"* ("a community of citizens, but only a conglomeration of inhabitants").[64]

In the end, the special relation of merchants and artisans, which had been characteristic of the old Basel and on which its relative internal harmony had rested, was swept away by this tide of newcomers and by the rapidly evolving economic conditions that had attracted them. The artisans put up what resistance they could. They opposed granting any new citizens' rights; they opposed freedom of settlement in the city; they fought bitterly against all attempts to have the guild restrictions lifted, claiming that opening up their protected trades to all comers would put their wives and children on the street. They consistently resisted proposals to permit Jews to settle in the city or to improve the lot of the few who had established themselves.[65] They also tried to halt or at least to slow down the development of factory production in the city, and in 1842–1843 they joined forces with the conservative wing of the elite in the Senate in an unsuccessful effort to block the extension of the Strasbourg–St. Louis railway line into Basel.[66] The construction of the line, they predicted, would be followed by an irresistible influx of French goods, French workers, French ideas, French priests, and French morals. Their tone was alarmist but their perception was correct. The arrival of the railway did indeed mean the opening up of their protected market and of their protected society to the world outside, and the piercing of the city wall to admit the iron horse did announce the end of the old Basel and of their place in it.

2

"A Kind of Family Government"
The Ribbon Lords and Their World

Though political power at Basel until the second half of the nineteenth century was theoretically vested in the guilds, it was in fact in the hands of a wealthy merchant elite. The elite families supplied the majority of the members of the Great Council or Senate and they completely dominated the Little Council or Cabinet, which was the effective organ of government. Their names—and persons—were known to everybody in the town.[1] The *Herren,* as they were called, were treated with great deference by the humbler citizens on account of their wealth and position and because most people were in one way or another dependent on them or beholden to them. They controlled many of the guilds. In addition, the Constitution not only set strict limits both on those who enjoyed citizen's rights and on those among the latter who were eligible for office, it also ensured, by a complex electoral system, that those already in power determined their successors.[2] Finally, the *Honoratiorenregiment*—an ostensibly democratic system of government in which, since it is a citizen's duty and privilege to serve the state in public office, he receives only token remuneration for his pains and may even be expected to subsidize the administration from his own resources—effectively restricted active participation in government to citizens of means.

The typical *Ratsherr,* or senator, was rarely a young man. Most often he had already put in a number of years with the family firm and amassed or added to a considerable fortune by the time he was elected to office.[3] Politics and government, in short, were not a career at Basel. Only business was. In sum, the *Honoratiorenregiment* accomplished two objectives: it kept power in the hands of the moneyed elite and it kept talent and energy in business and did not permit them to be dissipated in politics. Government was what a man did *after* he made money. It would not be farfetched to argue that the state at Basel, in contrast with the France of Louis XIV or the Prussia of Frederick the Great or the nation-states of the postrevolutionary era, was not an end but only a means of securing adequate conditions for the real business of life, which was not after all politics, as it had been in the ancient republics that Basel liked to compare itself with, but the private sphere of trade, work, and family life. The state should therefore be as invisible as possible; it should interfere as little as possible in the lives of its citizens; to serve it, as an end in itself, might even have seemed to these Reformed businessmen a form of idolatry. Most Baselers referred to their city more readily in fact as a community, by which they meant an extended version of smaller "natural" social groups such as the family or a circle of friends. In a popular lecture course given in 1822–1823, the new professor of theology at the University, Wilhelm Martin Liebrecht De Wette, a refugee from the Prussia of the Carlsbad Decrees, presented social life as a series of ever-widening circles extending outward from the family, by way of professional associations, corporations, or guilds, to the larger "national" community, and beyond that to humanity. The basis of social organization was a natural sociability, nothing less than love.[4] In De Wette's lectures, the national life in which all individuals participate was described not as the state, but—in feminine terms—as the common culture, "the maternal lap of all culture and education, the universal mother." And a clear warning was sounded against the "selfishness," albeit "of a higher kind," that marked the patriotism of the Greeks and Romans, "whom national hate and passion for conquest polluted."[5]

In the nineteenth century, the elite of Basel appear to have understood that the increasing complexity of government as well as the accelerating pace of competition and the rationalization of business practices would no longer permit the leisure necessary to sustain the old *Honoratiorenregiment*. They did not abandon it, however. Instead, they tried to breathe new life into it by preparing particular family members for public service. In the years immediately following the *Kantonstrennung* in particular, the study of law appears to have been undertaken by some younger members of the merchant families with a view to public service.[6] The elite's efforts to continue to provide the city's political leadership and administrative cadres out of their own ranks, their unwillingness to yield authority to a professional bureaucracy, reflected both their desire to hold on to their political power and the ideology by which that power was justified. Every Basel *Ratsherr* would have agreed with Montesquieu that in a proper citizens' republic power and authority are not alienated, as they are in monarchical states, to paid public officials. *Senatus populusque basiliensis*, or *S.P.Q.B.*, the inscription placed on most public buildings in Basel down to the present time, was not to be simply an elegant decoration: it was to designate the source of political authority in the city-state. At the same time, there was never any question of giving the political undue significance. In the Switzerland created by the federal Constitution of 1848, moreover, Basel's political influence was mediocre. As a half-canton, with corresponding representation in the Federal Assembly, Basel-City, despite its immense wealth, could only be a fairly minor player.[7]

Though some of the elite families were long established in Basel, many had immigrated to the city in the sixteenth and seventeenth centuries. A large number, with recognizably non-German names (Battier, Bernoulli, De Bary, Legrand, Paravicini or Paravicin, Sarasin, Socini or Socin), had come as refugees from religious persecution in France, Italy, or the Spanish Netherlands at the time of the Counter Reformation; others had sought asylum from the disruption and devastation of the Thirty Years' War;[8] others still had come because of the opportunities offered to enterprising and ambitious individuals by a busy commercial center. As citizens then, most of the so-called patricians were of relatively recent vintage. The Bernoullis acquired citizenship in 1622, the De Barys in 1624, the Vischers in 1649, and the Von der Mühlls, originally from Delft, in 1680. All these people brought with them both capital and technical and commercial skills that the residents of the city believed would enrich the entire community.[9] As we saw earlier, the possession of such resources was virtually the price of admission to Basel. From the very outset, then, these families constituted an elite: more enterprising, more resourceful, more talented, and better off than many in their native countries and the majority of those among whom they came to live.

Even though the Basel elite is often described as a "patriciate"—Nietzsche, for instance, referred to the *"Basler Patrizier"*—this term can be applied to it only in a loose sense. These merchants, shippers, traders in silk and spices, and manufacturers of ribbon and fine cottons were rich. They came to dominate the city politically, socially, economically, and culturally. Some, moreover, achieved distinction not only in business but in the arts and sciences. Nevertheless, they were commercial, bourgeois families. If the model of a patriciate is that of Venice—where the "serrata" of 1297 closed off the ranks of the nobility to all newcomers and the names of the families entitled to exercise political authority were inscribed in a gold book—then there was a patriciate in Fribourg, Bern, Solothurn, Lucerne, but there was none in either Basel or Zurich, both of which, as already observed, were dominated politically by their guilds. Basel developed a ruling elite but this, as the historians of Basel always emphasize, was not a patriciate in any strict sense.[10] No officially recognised division of the citizenry into categories, such as were established in seventeenth-century Frankfurt (patricians, nonpatrician magistrates and merchants, distinguished retailers and professionals, common retailers and craftsmen, unskilled workers),[11] existed in Basel. While it is common and acceptable usage to refer to the stately townhouses of the eighteenth century as *Patrizierhäuser,* that term may create a false impression, according to the authors of a monumental history of the Swiss burgher house.[12] "Though the elite had the upper hand in the running of the state and succeeded at times in turning itself into a formidable oligarchy, it was far from constituting a closed order with political privileges. After the Reformation there was no longer a patriciate at Basel in the sense of a privileged caste, membership in which was either transmitted by birth or specially bestowed. A *Herr* or member of the upper class was simply anyone who appeared to be and to act like one in virtue of his wealth, his occupying one of the higher offices of state, or his having the kind of culture and more refined way of life that usually go with such positions." Another recent scholar sums up the findings of nearly all the local historians: "The government of Basel," according to Alfred Bürgin, "was a kind of family government which was grounded less, however, in membership of particular families than in belonging to the circle of well-to-do merchants and manufacturers."[13]

The Basel *"Patrizier"* resembled more the so-called Brahmins of Boston than the patricians of Venice or—closer to home—of Bern. Money was the condition of entry into the ranks of the "patriciate"; fine manners quickly followed and newcomers were promptly stitched into the elite by marriage, the groom adding the name of the bride's family to his own. Thus the Bachofens' entry into the elite was consecrated by the marriage of an earlier Johann Jacob—the grandfather of the scholar—to the daughter of a wealthy Burckhardt in 1780. In the 1840s, the youthful Jacob Burckhardt's sweetheart, Margaretha (Gritli) Stehlin, the daughter of a former carpenter who had become wealthy as the director of a large building firm, married a young banker from the established and conservative Riggenbach family, and the young couple played a prominent role in Basel society and cultural life. No doubt Jacob Burckhardt, as a member of a modest branch of the Burckhardts that had produced more ministers than ribbon magnates, was not considered a suitable match.[14]

The condition, the culture, and the outlook of the elite was of course constantly evolving over the two and one-half centuries during which it exercised political dominion over the city. From the election of Johann Friedrich Ryhiner as *Bürgermeister* in 1630 until the government of the city was drastically altered in 1875, there was scarcely a single *Bürgermeister,* out of a total of thirty-seven, who was not a Ryhiner, a Battier, a Burckhardt, a De Bary, a Faesch, a Merian, a Socin, or a Sarasin.[15] Not all the prominent or wealthy families sought public office. Some just got on with the most important business of their lives, which was business itself. The Bachofens are an outstanding example of a family that appears to have had no interest in playing a political role. Johann Jacob Bachofen (or Bachofen-Burckhardt) was the first Bachofen to be elected to the *Rat.* Perhaps it was not an accident that by the nineteenth century the Bachofens were probably the wealthiest family in Basel.

Making money and getting ahead in business had been the chief preoccupation of the burghers of Basel at all times. Aeneas Silvius Piccolomini, the humanist scholar and future pope who attended the Council of Basel in the mid-fifteenth century, did not think highly of them even then: "They have no time for the sciences or the fine arts. They have never heard the name of Cicero or any other master of eloquence. . . . They have no inclination to read the works of the poets; they are satisfied at best with some grammar and dialectics."[16] Matters had surely improved since, especially among the elite of the burghers;

moreover, travelers' reports were inevitably marked by the attitudes of their authors: envy, on many sides, of the legendary wealth of mere merchants; contempt for a tiny republic of tradesmen among those accustomed to the feudal-
aristocratic courts of Germany or the great courts of Western Europe; hostility
among sympathizers with the goals of the French Revolution toward a patently
oligarchic political regime and a culture dominated by religion and commerce.
Nevertheless, there seems to have been a remarkable consensus among visitors
to Basel in the second half of the eighteenth century. "The Basel merchants,
constituting the most important segment of the citizenry, are incomparably less
learned, less engaged in politics, less devoted to the arts and sciences than those
of Zurich," a German traveler in Switzerland observed in 1773.[17] A decade
later the same judgment was passed by another traveler from Germany. Though
there are a few citizens of taste and wit, he reported, "for most of the merchants,
the measure of anybody's worth is the louis d'or." Cultural and intellectual interests were not much pursued. "There seems to be a general dearth of ideas
in Basel. People apparently know of no other way to pass the time than by
playing cards."[18]

The University, which had been a center of learning at the time of the Renaissance, was allowed to sink into insignificance. Student enrollment—well
over a thousand in the first decades of the seventeenth century—was so *"mi-
serabel,"* according to one observer in 1720, that it had reached the lowest point
in the entire history of the institution. "Not a single foreign medical student
has matriculated and so few law students have actually completed their course
of study that it has been impossible to hold examinations or graduation ceremo-
nies."[19] A traveler from Saxony explained in 1785 that he had said nothing
about the University in his account of Basel "because, in contrast to the universities in Germany, it is hardly visible. I think a foreigner who did not know
there is a university here could spend a year in Basel without ever finding out
that there is. . . . I barely remember ever seeing a student. In fact, the total
number of students is reportedly between sixty and seventy, and there would be
fewer still, were it not for a special scholarship fund for Hungarian students that
attracts a certain number from that country. There are eighteen professors—an
insignificant figure compared with Leipzig; yet given the student enrollment,
the ratio of professors to students is nowhere more favorable than at Basel."[20]

As Basel citizens enjoyed official preference in professorial appointments and
as salaries were pitifully low,[21] academic offices, like other public offices, were
in fact restricted to Baselers of means. In effect, they became sinecures for the
sons—not always the most gifted or energetic sons—of the elite.[22] A visitor
from Hamburg expressed surprise at the intellectual backwardness of the University. The question up for debate at a scholarly *disputatio* he attended at the
University, he reported in 1785, was whether it is appropriate to apply reason
to matters of faith. The outcome of the debate was that it is, "but the very

fact that this question could be considered worth debating . . . shows that the Enlightenment can hardly have made much headway in such matters here."[23]

At a time when Bodmer, Breitinger, and Haller were bringing luster to Zurich, literary and intellectual life at Basel, in short, was less than brilliant. Passing through the city in 1798, the radical English poet and novelist, Helen Williams—"a clever, badly educated woman," according to her biographer in the *Dictionary of National Biography*—had not much good to say of a society she obviously considered hopelessly philistine and commercial: "At Basil . . . the toils of trade find no relaxation: they begin with the day, but do not finish at its close; since even the hours of recreation are made subservient to the views of interest; and the only species of amusement in which the burghers of that city indulge themselves, is one at which they can arrange their commercial deal-ings, strike bargains, and vigorously pursue that main chance which appears to be their 'being's end and aim.'" At the exclusively male *tabagies* or smoking clubs to which the citizens of Basel repair toward the end of every afternoon, "they drink tea amid the exhilarating fumes of tobacco, discuss the political situation, but far more indefatigably the commercial affairs of the town, calcu-late the gains and losses of the day, form new schemes of acquiring wealth, and separate at the hour of supper, before they have said one word on any subject of taste, or literature." In the judgment of the Swiss themselves, she concludes, "Basil is the Boeotia of their country."[24] Modern historians are hardly more generous. "Apart from some occasional verse," one historian writes, ". . . the old Baselers can point to no poetic achievements. Not a single Baseler ever wrote a tragedy or an epic."[25] It is true that the mercantile outlook is in virtually every respect the opposite of both tragic and epic.

Yet the Baselers were not unfamiliar with the wider world beyond their city. Many traveled to distant shores as agents of their families' companies or to set up businesses for themselves. Burckhardts (or Bourcards) had settled in Nantes and London, Merians in Le Havre, Iselins in London, Norwich, Hamburg, Copenhagen, and New York, and these expatriates worked closely with their relatives and friends in Basel. Even in the nineteenth century, Zurich silk mer-chants depended on agents from Basel and St. Gallen to help them open mar-kets in the Unites States and the West Indies.[26] It became increasingly custom-ary—as in Hamburg or Lübeck or Barmen—for merchants' sons to serve an apprenticeship abroad with a company with which their father's firm had com-mercial connections.[27] Everybody in the merchant class had a good command of French, acquired in most cases by a period of residence in French Switzer-land. Many had learned Italian. More and more also knew English. Both Burck-hardt and Bachofen, for instance, wrote and spoke French and Italian fluently, and many decades after his stay in London and Cambridge, Bachofen was still able to carry on a correspondence in English with the American anthropologist Lewis Morgan. Among women, knowledge of French was *de rigueur* and was usually acquired in the same way, by a couple of years residence in French Switzerland. "An educated girl who cannot speak French would look completely ridiculous," one Basel matron reminded her daughter in the mid-nineteenth century.[28]

But the Baselers' interest in foreign parts seems to have been on the whole, with some remarkable exceptions, strictly economic, or at best religious. Though the city was open to the world of commerce, the cultural atmosphere was stuffy and provincial. There were, of course, citizens who took an interest in literature and the arts and who received visiting literary celebrities: Jacob Sarasin-Battier at the Weisses Haus, Johann Rudolph Burckhardt at the equally elegant Haus zum Kirschgarten or his handsome country estate of Erndthalten, near Sissach. A Basel printer, Johann Jacob Thurneysen played a prominent role in the dissemination of English and, above all, Scottish Enlightenment ideas and letters on the continent.[29] But there was little or no indigenous literary activity. Since joining the Swiss Confederation, as a Swiss historian observed, Basel "had withdrawn from the arena of world politics and even within the Confederation it did not play a leading role but preferred the neutral role of mediator or even outsider."[30] In this respect, it was to Switzerland what Switzerland itself had become to the world at large since the defeat of its armies at Marignano in 1515. "The senators no longer had any fundamental political decisions to make, in contrast to those of Bern or Zurich, and the interests of the ribbon manufacturers and merchants were focused exclusively on the enhancement and display of their fortunes."[31] One of the more unusual Basel personalities of the period, Johann Ludwig Burckhardt (better known as John Lewis Burckhardt, the name under which his accounts of his voyages up the Nile for the British Africa Society were published, or as Sheikh Ibrahim, the name by which he was known to the Arabs and Egyptians he lived among and which is inscribed on his grave in the Bab el Nasr cemetery outside Cairo), once observed that Basel "is one of the richest cities in Europe and yet one of the poorest in happy citizens, for in Basel people know very well how to fill the till, but not many have found real happiness."[32]

The elite's concentration on business paid off in the form of a flourishing economy that procured spectacular rewards for a few and some rewards for almost all. The key sectors of the Basel economy were the manufacture of silk ribbons, introduced in the early 1600s by two Huguenot refugee families, the Battiers and the Passavants,[33] and, to a lesser extent, of fine printed cottons,[34] and—later, from the mid 1830s on—the production of spun silk from silk waste ("schapping") by a process invented at Basel by J. S. Alioth in 1824 and perfected by Braun and Ryhiner in 1833.[35] General shipping or merchandising and finance were also important. The chemical industry, which dominates the city today, developed in the mid-nineteenth century out of the dyeworks associated with the production of ribbons and calico, but did not overtake the ribbon industry as the mainstay of the Basel economy until the second or third decade of the twentieth century. In the production of ribbons, *schappe*, and subsequently chemicals, Basel's lead over all the other Swiss cities and cantons was overwhelming.

The heyday of the *Bändelherren*, or ribbon lords, was perhaps the eighteenth century. Ribbons were in use at that time everywhere—in hair, in hats, in men's clothing as well as women's, and in accessories of every kind. As the clientele was well-to-do, there was relatively little fluctuation in demand. In addition, the availability of cheap labor in the countryside surrounding Basel and timely adoption of the most up-to-date and efficient Dutch ribbon loom[36] had given the merchants of Basel a clear edge over their competitors. Immense fortunes were amassed by all the families engaged in silk ribbon production and export: the Bachofens, the Sarasins, the Wildts, various branches of the Burckhardt, Bischoff, and Thurneysen families, the Forcarts, the Weisses, the Hoffmanns, the La Roches, the Legrands, and the De Barys. "Every Saturday," a German visitor reported, "a large number of wagons trundle into the city bringing the ribbon from the various surrounding villages. It then goes through a number of operations and passes through different hands in the houses of the *Fabrikherren* before being stored in the warehouses or shipped out to customers. Every manufacturer is naturally also a merchant. . . . The ribbon is sent out to every country in Europe. . . . A good deal is even shipped to other parts of the world."[37]

The manufacture of calico, introduced to Basel by Samuel Ryhiner in 1717, also brought substantial profits in the eighteenth century. As tastes began to move toward the end of the century, in conformity with changing political and artistic values, from the heavy satins and brocades of the baroque and early rococo periods to lighter, simpler, printed cottons, the future seemed bright for this branch of Basel industry. But it went through periods of great difficulty, notably at the time of the Continental Blockade when cotton was scarce and expensive and the French market was closed, and again after the peace, when relations with England were restored and the European market was flooded with the cheaper products of mills in Manchester and Glasgow.[38] Some fortunes were built on cotton, that of the Ryhiners in particular; but in the end, silk ribbon remained the chief glory of Basel.

A portrait of Margarethe Bachofen-Heitz, commissioned from the fashionable society painter Alexander Roslin in 1766, conveys some sense of the triumphant confidence of the *Bändelherren* and their families in the golden age of their prosperity (plate 1).[39] Margarethe was the wife of Martin Bachofen, who in 1748 became head of the firm his father had joined as a partner after marrying the owner's daughter. It was Martin who built up the firm and under whose direction its fine properties on the Münsterplatz were acquired. Since Margarethe accompanied her husband to the fairs in Strasbourg and Frankfurt, where she helped him sell his wares, she is said to have been well known to the young men in both cities and to have had many admirers among them. According to one anecdote, when the crowd of admirers got to be too numerous, Martin would tell her in Basel dialect *"gang inne"* ("go inside"), so that she came to be known to the young French officers at Strasbourg as *"la belle Canina."*[40] Whether the story is true or apocryphal, *"la belle Canina"* does indeed appear in Roslin's portrait as an attractive, elegant, rather reserved woman. The impression of aloofness and steely determination conveyed by her pose and features is somewhat softened by the rich texture of her beribboned dress and the pretty length of Basel ribbon that she holds in her hand, like an emblem. The portrait is a celebration of woman and of the worldly culture she stood for in the Age of Enlightenment. But it is also a celebration of—and an advertisement for—the product of industry and ingenuity to which the sitter appears to acknowledge that she and hers owe their social and material well-being, and which is here associated metaphorically and metonymically, as symbol and as cause, with the beauty and refinement both of the sitter and of the successful and prosperous bourgeoisie she represents.

Through their agents in the countryside, the *Bändelherren* of Basel were engaged in the actual production of the materials they traded in. Nevertheless, the "original law of this Polis," as the historian Werner Kaegi put it, was not so much manufacture as "commerce and transit, the buying, reselling, and shipping of goods over long distances linking Italy with the Netherlands, the markets of Champagne with Spain and Germany, Nuremberg with Paris."[41] Even after the *Kantonstrennung* in 1833, most of the actual manufacture of ribbon was still carried out on a putting-out basis by cottage workers in the countryside. The *Bändelherren* were thus also, in a sense, middle-men and merchants, importers of raw materials that they contracted out to be manufactured at piece-work rates in the villages of the *Baselbiet*, and exporters of finished goods.[42] In addition, some wealthy "patrician" families were exclusively engaged in general merchandising—buying a wide variety of goods in one market and selling them to agents in another, or overseeing the transshipment of goods from one market to another, or arranging for the purchase and sale of merchandise between third parties in different parts of the world. The author of an article in the *National-Zeitung* (11 December 1842) supporting the extension of the Strasbourg railway line to Basel in the 1840s underscored Basel's role as a place of exchange: "Basel has grown wealthy not from its manufactures, for they amounted to very little earlier, and even today they are not overwhelmingly important, but from shipping, brokerage, and the commission business."[43]

At a time when communications within Switzerland were poor and impeded by countless tolls and cantonal duties, it was often advantageous to ship goods from one part of the Confederation to another through Basel and by way of France and Baden. In this way, its very peripheral position gave Basel a central role in trade among the cantons. It may be that some of the resistance at Basel to the transformation of Switzerland into a modern unified state was due to the perception that Basel—like Geneva, which played a similar role—stood to lose by such a move, while inner Swiss centers such as Zurich stood to gain by it. But much of Basel's trade was genuinely international. By the late eighteenth century, the city's commercial connections extended to England, the Levant, the United States and the West Indies, Scandinavia, Eastern Europe, and Russia. A diaspora of members of the chief merchant families, who had settled in foreign places or been sent out expressly, acted as agents of the home firms.[44]

A commercial directory for the year 1806—the *Basler Handlungs-Schema*—using the quaint mixture of German and French characteristic of Basel at that time, listed most of the larger general trading companies as "Commissionairs et Speditoren." They were also listed as specialists in one or more particular branches of trade, such as "Droguerie und Material-Handlungen" (apothecaries' goods) or the more general "Specerey und Farbwaren" (grocers and drysalters, literally "spices and dyestuffs") or "Seidenzeughandlungen" (silks) or "Speculations-Handlungen" (brokerage and finance). And, of course, as was common in the age before joint-stock banks, many of the general merchants ("Commissionnairs et Speditoren"), as well as some who were more specialized, also served as suppliers of credit. In general, the trade directories of the end of the eighteenth and the beginning of the nineteenth centuries give the impression that while there was some specialization at this time, there was still a great deal of flexibility in the Basel merchant class. Christoph Mathias Ehinger, for instance, ran a shipping, brokerage, and commission business from his premises in the Aeschenvorstadt, but he also dealt in colonial goods like tea, coffee, spices, and dyestuffs; he speculated on the market and accepted clients' money for such speculations; and he served as a moneylender-banker. Other firms, like Vischer et Sohn, near the Münsterplatz, or Andreas Werthemann et Sohn, also in the Aeschenvorstadt, engaged in a similar range of activities. Firms that specialized in dry goods usually dealt in a variety of textiles. Christoph Burckhardt-Iselin traded in muslin, silks, and stockings; the Bachofen firm dealt mostly in silk ribbons, which they themselves had manufactured in the countryside, but they also imported and sold woolen cloth.

Almost everybody lent money. The ribbon manufacturers could all be properly described as *"fabricants-marchands-banquiers."*[45] Baselers were among the forty-four Swiss bankers represented in Paris in 1714, and by the end of the eighteenth century the city had become a significant source of credit and banking operations.[46] In the early nineteenth century the Burckhardts, the Ehingers, the Forcarts, the Heuslers, the Iselins, the La Roches, the Merians, the Staehelins, and the Passavants were all heavily involved in private banking, and Basel was known as a "city of usurers."[47] Passing through the town in August 1843, the historian Jules Michelet relates with the pious irony of a radical French

"Zum Raben," Aeschenvorstadt 15 (1763–1768), headquarters of
Ehinger et Cie. Photo: Willi Eidenbenz.

ex-Catholic confronted by the "hypocritical" Protestant worship of God and
Mammon that a "Staehelin, professeur de théologie, fort occupé des Hébreux
et de la dixième dynastie des Pharaons," was not above lending money.[48]
Around the time of Michelet's visit, in fact, nearly half of some two hundred
wholesale houses at Basel were also engaged in banking,[49] and capital accumulated by the Basel merchants was financing the industrial development of
Alsace, Baden, and Zurich.[50] Basel banking remained a private, family affair,
however, until the second half of the nineteenth century,[51] and the power of
the elite was due in no small measure to the vital role played locally by their

personal credit at a time when there were no public sources of credit or joint-stock banks.[52]

A relatively small number of families, in various combinations and partnerships, dominated the scene throughout the eighteenth and nineteenth centuries. Some of them had several branches, and all were, in addition, interconnected by a complex web of marriages. At the end of the eighteenth century, there were Burckhardts in banking, the manufacture of calico and muslin, stockings, and tobacco, as well, of course, as silk ribbons; Merians in banking, general merchandising and brokerage, innkeeping, leather-tanning, muslin goods, and tobacco; Sarasins in general merchandising, leather goods, colonial goods and dyestuffs, tobacco, and ribbons; Bischoffs in the book trade, in tobacco, and in colonial goods; and so on. A few families seem to have been more highly specialized. The Geigys, together with five different members of the Bernoulli family, were all in apothecary drugs, which was still slowly emerging as a business from the more general drysalters and in which the Bernoullis had been expert in Amsterdam and Frankfurt before they arrived in Basel.

Strikingly, alongside the long list of firms in the commission business or general trading, a very large number (twenty-three, as compared with seven silk merchants or four hatters or fourteen linen merchants) are listed as "*Speculations-Handlungen*," that is to say, something equivalent to investment brokers. Basel, it would seem, was essentially a city of merchants and middlemen whose chief business, as the *National-Zeitung* claimed, was less to produce and consume—Basel itself was too small a market to sustain much economic activity on that basis—than to facilitate the movement of goods, money, and services among third parties. The typical Basel businessman engaged in a variety of commercial practices, and his success depended on his ability to respond quickly to market opportunities and to keep as many options open as possible.

The eighteenth century was a time of economic prosperity in many parts of Europe, notably in France and England. The wealth of the Basel merchants appears to have increased spectacularly during this period. As early as 1758 Isaac Iselin, deploring the diminishing number of "*mittelmässige Bürger*" (citizens of middling means) in the city[53]—a consequence, as we saw earlier and as Iselin was the first to point out, of the authorities' restrictive policies on immigration and citizenship—remarked at the same time on the enormous enrichment of the elite. "We now have so many more splendid houses than before. Everything is dazzling and brilliant with these people. Their businesses are prospering beautifully."[54]

An analysis of households in the St. Johann section of the city at the end of the eighteenth century (1798–1799) shows that while the *average* wealth of residents who were citizens of Basel-City was hundreds of times greater than that of those who were not, among the citizens themselves the wealth was very unevenly distributed. Of 215 citizens, each worth on average 25,772 pounds,

42 in this single section of the city were worth over 100,000 pounds each.[55] A small number of Baselers were millionaires several times over. Samuel Burckhardt, for instance, who had made his fortune in salt and iron foundries, was worth over 2 million gulden. In 1736, he had his portrait painted by Hyacinthe Rigaud, the painter of the kings of France, and at his magnificent houses in the city and in the countryside he outdid his friend the Margrave of Baden—who also maintained a large and handsome baroque residence in Basel (part of the present Cantonal Hospital)—in luxury and splendor.[56]

Though Basel's wealth, as a traveler from Saxony noted in 1785, was not generally in the form of "houses and land, but in commercial ventures and manufactures,"[57] opportunities for investment were still limited in the preindustrial age. Much of the wealth acquired by the merchants still went inevitably into real estate. During the course of the eighteenth century, numerous town houses were remodeled or rebuilt to fit the prevailing baroque style: for instance, the Schulthof and the Rollerhof on the Münsterplatz, purchased by Martin Bachofen in 1758, which were joined together and provided with a new façade; the house known as Zum Delphin on the Rittergasse, rebuilt by the architect Samuel Werenfels in the 1760s; or Zum goldenen Löwen, in the Aeschenvorstadt, renovated in 1775. Likewise, many imposing new residences were built: the pretty Wildtsches Haus which dominates the north side of the Petersplatz, like a small French château; the palatial Reichensteinerhof (or Blaues Haus) and Wendelstörferhof (or Weisses Haus) on the Rheinsprung, overlooking the river; the more austere neoclassical Zum Kirschgarten on the Elisabethenstrasse. Outside the city, too, the *Bändelherren* and other rich merchants constructed handsome country seats for themselves. At a time when it was not unusual for moderately well-to-do artisans to have a little vineyard in the Basel countryside to which they could repair in the warm summer days, the wealthy merchants built themselves miniature châteaux: Sandgrube, Kleinriehen, the Wenkenhof, the De Barysches Landhaus in Riehen.

Though fairly restrained in internal and external decoration,[58] all these residences were sumptuous by the standards of an earlier age, and they bear witness not only to the immense wealth of the merchants but to the cosmopolitan and refined taste of at least a fair number of them. Widely traveled as they were and familiar with the manners and fashions not only of Strasbourg and Frankfurt, but of Paris and Nantes, of London and Hamburg and Amsterdam, the wealthiest of the Basel merchants demanded and enjoyed the same standards of comfort and elegance that they observed among their well-to-do clients and associates in other cities.[59] Conservative—or less opulent—citizens claimed that these new tastes were dangerous and had led to spectacular bankruptcies, such as that of *Ratsherr* Staehelin in 1713. Saddled with debts of over one hundred thousand gulden, Staehelin fled the city in haste, breaking his ankle as he jumped from the city wall, and sought sanctuary in the Capuchin monastery at

"Wildtsches Haus" (1761–1763) on Petersplatz.

Zur Sandgrube (1745–1751), a Basel country house in Kleinriehen.

"Wendelstörferhof" or "Weisses Haus," "Reichensteinerhof" or "Blaues Haus" (both 1762–1769), and Old University Building from the Rhine. Photo: Peter Armbruster.

neighboring Dornach in Canton Solothurn. The cause of the bankruptcy, a contemporary witness insists, "was not ill luck but excessive spending, show, and luxury."[60]

In general, however, the building projects of the *Bändelherren* did not lead them to behave like princes or end as bankrupts. They still worked within the framework of local practices, and they did not spend money extravagantly. The architects they employed were at first scarcely distinguishable from master builders; they adapted the models they found in French architecture books to local needs, materials, and traditions, and to the requirements of their clients.[61] In some cases the owner himself directly supervised the work of construction. This was the case with Lucas Sarasin, who built the Blaues Haus and the Weisses Haus. Sarasin took over himself from his builder Samuel Werenfels in 1765 and thereafter employed Werenfels only to oversee specific jobs. The first notable Basel architect in the fully professional sense, Burckhardt's brother-in-law Melchior Berri, was a student of Friedrich Weinbrenner in Karlsruhe and of Huyot and Hittorff in Paris. He designed the Stadtcasino, or concert hall, on the Steinenberg (1826, now demolished) and the magnificent Museum in the Augustinergasse (1844–1849), as well as a number of private houses in the city. He was not active, however, until the nineteenth century.

At the same time, along with a characteristic bourgeois concern for economy and comfort, the new homes of the wealthy show a decided interest in stylishness and public show. The principal floors were almost exclusively given over to *Repräsentation*—elegant and imposing public rooms—while the family quarters and bedrooms might be crowded into the top floor, even into attic rooms.[62] These buildings required the outlay of vast sums. The cost of Sarasin's Weisses Haus and Blaues Haus has been estimated at 217,215 gulden (about 3 million Swiss francs in 1930), and that is considered a conservative figure. Samuel Burckhardt spent the equivalent of about 154,000 Swiss francs of 1930 on the design of the garden at Kleinriehen alone. One of his townhouses, the Ramsteinerhof, is said to have cost about half a million pounds (nearly 7 million 1930 Swiss francs), not including the land. If one considers that in addition to these properties, Samuel Burckhardt—who in this respect was no different from many of his wealthy fellow citizens[63]—had built or acquired several other houses in the city and in the *Baselbiet*, it is hard to resist conjecturing that the Basel building mania of the eighteenth century was not only an expression of bourgeois self-satisfaction and pride, or even a means by which the merchants sought to inspire confidence in their liquidity, but a form of capital investment.[64] This may explain why these stately homes passed so frequently from hand to hand. In many cases, of course, they constituted a significant inheritance and the histories of most of them are eloquent testimony to the way marriage was used in the patriciate to form and consolidate business and family alliances.[65] But outright sale was frequent too, often within a few years of construction or purchase.[66]

Great houses in the new style required art collections to adorn and enhance them. Along with the new building style, the Basel merchants adopted the French custom of collecting paintings.[67] Samuel Burckhardt's collection included works of the Flemish, German, French, and Italian schools. *Ratsherr* Samuel Heussler-Burckhardt (1730–1770) owned canvases by Veronese, Palma Vecchio, Luca Giordano, Pietro da Cortona, and Annibale Caracci. Other notable collections were those of Johann Jacob Faesch and Martin Bachofen. The latter, begun by J. J. Bachofen-Strub, Martin's father, contained forty-eight works at the time of the elder Bachofen's death. Martin added substantially to it until it filled two houses, the Rollerhof on the Münsterplatz and Ebenrain, the country house near Sissach in the *Baselbiet,* where Bachofen liked to go hunting with his neighbors Samuel Ryhiner-Werthemann and Peter Burckhardt. The Bachofen collection included not only works by Dutch and Flemish masters (Teniers, Ter Borch, Jordaens, Adrian and Isak Van Ostade, Jacob Ruysdael, Van Dyck, and four Rembrandts) but a fair number of French paintings (a Poussin, a Coypel, four Loutherbourgs).[68] In general, the Basel collections far surpassed those of Strasbourg, Frankfurt, and Zurich.

Like their houses, however, the art collections of the great merchants of Basel in the eighteenth century may well have served not only as an almost obligatory form of representation, but also as a form of investment and speculation.[69] Often a collection was broken up and sold on the owner's death by his heirs, and in economically difficult times, such as the period of the Revolution and the Empire, as some fortunes shrank and others swelled, the pace of buying and selling accelerated noticeably. In the early nineteenth century in particular, we are told, "the content of the various collections was caught up in a perpetual whirl of movement."[70] Significantly, those who conducted their business affairs with special prudence and came through the crises of the revolutionary decades in good shape also built up their art investments prudently and succeeded in holding their collections together. The Bachofens, for instance, had always concentrated on their business and had not sought the prestige of public office. During the hectic period between 1788 and 1806, Johann Jacob Bachofen-Burckhardt, having consecrated his entry into the top echelon of wealthy Basel families in 1780 by marrying the daughter of the ribbon manufacturer Peter Burckhardt-Forcart, made only the most cautious additions to the family collection, seeking always the very best advice before purchasing. His local adviser, Peter Schrocker, was extremely well connected: Le Brun, Napoleon's Directeur des Musées and the husband of the painter Mme Vigée Le Brun, was among his friends. As the Le Bruns stayed several times with the Bachofens at their house on the Münsterplatz, it is reasonable to assume that they gave their hosts the benefit of their advice about acquisitions.[71]

At first paintings were bought and sold at the Frankfurt fair, which was regularly attended by the Basel merchants. Gradually a number of dealers established themselves in Basel or made the city a regular stopping point on their tours of business. By the end of the century, as one might well expect of a place where so many merchants were engaged in "Speculations-Handlungen," Basel itself had become a center of the art trade.

The career of one of the leading Basel artists of the late eighteenth century is revealing. Christian von Mechel, born in modest circumstances in Basel in 1737, was originally destined for the ministry and studied theology at the University of Basel. Though his taste for art proved to be greater than his taste for theology, he would probably not have been permitted by his parents to change careers had it not begun to seem, by the 1750s, when the building boom was in full swing, that art might be quite a lucrative business. Von Mechel was permitted to study in Nuremberg and Augsburg, and then with the famous German-born engraver J. G. Wille in Paris. Though his own manner was quite different from Wille's, being closer to that of Boucher or Hubert Robert, he learned much at Wille's studio, above all urbanity, the ability to deal with rich clients, and a feeling for the art market. Within a short time the businessman and art dealer in him were at least the equal of the artist. While still in Paris he had begun signing his name to many works produced by talented apprentices in his studio and selling them as his own. In 1765 he returned to Basel and in the following year opened a large art dealer's business and engraving workshop in the Erlacherhof on the St. Johannsvorstadt. Here he no longer produced himself, but supervised the work of between twelve and fifteen artists in his employ.[72] In his account of Basel in 1778, the Englishman William Coxe warmly advised his fellow countrymen to visit "M. de Mechel, a celebrated artist of this place," on account of his urbanity, his excellent connections, and his "magazine of prints (in which article he carries on a very considerable trade)" and which is "one of the largest and most complete in Europe."[73]

Von Mechel prospered. He soon became a *Ratsherr* and he was a member of Isaac Iselin's Helvetic Society, where the most enlightened and liberal members of the elite foregathered to consider philosophical and scientific questions. He was a friend and regular correspondent of Winckelmann in Rome. The outbreak of the French Revolution was a blow to his business, but he tried to recoup his losses by speculating on the purchase of large collections from hard-pressed French noble families. These ventures were unsuccessful and Von Mechel was forced into bankruptcy. In the early 1800s he left Basel for Berlin, where he was able to build up his career again.

Von Mechel is not an isolated case. Peter Birmann (1758–1844) is another example of a Basel artist who was also, perhaps in Birmann's case predominantly, a businessman. Birmann studied in Rome, returned to Basel in 1790 and became active not only as the director of an artists' workshop but as an art dealer who bought works of art in Paris during the revolutionary years at knockdown prices and sold them at great profit to Basel collectors.[74]

The market for works of art was considerable in Basel. Public interest in art seems to be confirmed, moreover, by the founding of the *Basler Kunstverein* in

1839, by the strong attendance at the first Exhibition of Swiss Art, held in the Markgräflerhof in 1840,[75] and by the substantial enrollments in Burckhardt's public lecture courses on the history of painting in the mid-1840s. Even so, the city was not a significant art center in the nineteenth century. The wealthy in the elite continued to add to their collections. But as long as business remained the preoccupation of the patrician the latter was more likely to acquire works of established and unquestioned value, at most to speculate on a period or school that was out of favor, than to promote living art and artists. The great nineteenth-century collections of Daniel Bachofen-Wildt, Peter Vischer-Sarasin, Niklaus Reber-Passavant, Johann Jacob Vischer-Staehelin, and above all Johann Jacob Bachofen-Burckhardt and Johann Jacob Bachofen-Merian were the result of careful, informed, and methodical acquisition policies.[76] They do not testify to a lively interest in contemporary art. In an admittedly polemical article under the rubric *"Lokales."* the *National-Zeitung* of June 8, 1843, attacked the lack of real interest in the arts at Basel. What the Baselers are mostly interested in, the newspaper asserted, is money and property; and for all its millionaires and rich collections Basel compares poorly with Geneva, and even with far smaller and less wealthy cities like Neuchatel and Olten, in its support of living artists.

The greatest Basel artist of the nineteenth century, Arnold Böcklin, received encouragement from his teachers at the *Gymnasium* and later from Jacob Burckhardt, but he spent most of his life away from Basel, in Germany (Munich and Weimar) and above all in Italy (Rome and Florence). When he did return to his native city in 1867–1871, having been commissioned—not without misgivings on the part of some members of the Buildings Committee, who were concerned about the expense—to execute three major wall paintings in the staircases of the Museum, the experience was by no means an unqualified success. The city fathers were not pleased with one of the paintings and insisted on changes that Böcklin did not want. They also objected strongly to a couple of satirical medallions they claimed Böcklin had executed without authorization. The artist left in a huff, having quarreled with his old friend Burckhardt, who was a member of the Buildings Committee.[77] It was left to Zurich to honor Böcklin with the freedom of the city and an honorary doctorate at the Federal Polytechnic. Characteristically, while he was in Basel, Böcklin received commissions for several portraits of leading *Ratsherren* and their families.

Local views and portraits were still what many Baselers liked best. Portraits in particular were seen not only as likenesses, in the way photographs are now, but as signs of social distinction. A family of Basel burghers that boasted a gallery of portraits and lived in a fine baroque *hôtel particulier* was hardly to be deemed inferior to the aristocracy of neighboring lands. In the contemplation of their fine houses and fine family portraits, it seems, the *Bändelherren* enjoyed an idealized image of their worldly success.

3

"City of Miracles"
Culture, Religion, and Money

The Basel commercial elite responded positively, on the whole, to the rationalism and practical orientation of the Enlightenment. A number of judicious and respectable citizens even proved favorably disposed at first to the French Revolution.[1] Peter Ochs urged his fellow citizens to carry out a voluntary revolution by granting full equality to the inhabitants of the country districts and his brother-in-law *Ratsherr* Peter Vischer brought a proposal to that effect before the Senate. Though it was turned down at first, the more reform-minded among the citizens, led by Johann-Lukas Legrand, prevailed in the end (some burnings of the castles of the *Landvögte* in the countryside having no doubt helped to convince the waverers). On January 20, 1798, the Senate and Cabinet proclaimed the equality of all the citizens of the canton, making Basel the first of the thirteen old cantons of the Swiss Confederation to break with the ancien régime. This was followed two days later by a "Festival of Brotherly Unity" in the city and the planting of a liberty tree in the Münsterplatz.[2]

Opposition to Enlightenment ideas came chiefly from that part of Basel society that had earned for the city the sobriquet of *"das fromme Basel"* ("pious Basel"). It included some conservative merchants, artisans who had been won over to the Pietist movement and were anxious for their citizen's privileges, and the most orthodox ministers of the established state church. The last named— together with the widows, retired persons, and teachers associated with them— often belonged to the same large families as the merchants, but they were usually considerably less well off. They constituted a distinct section of the elite. Relations between them and their well-to-do cousins were usually not close and it has even been said that the members of each section tended to marry among themselves.[3] Nevertheless, as we shall see, they exercised considerable influence on the life of the city.

The wealthy, worldly merchants of Basel—such as the Sarasin brothers in their palatial residences on the Rheinsprung—were by no means hostile to religion; they simply did not feel that an interest in philosophy, the sciences, and the arts was in any way incompatible with it. In general they did not demand rigorous consistency in their ideas. Jacob Sarasin, for instance, combined an interest in experimental science and a strongly practical bent with considerable piety, traditional moralism, and a fascination with the occult.[4] Despite Maria Williams's charge that "the number of enlightened men in Basil is very inconsiderable" since "they read nothing but their ledgers,"[5] Baselers had in fact been among the leading figures of the Enlightenment in Switzerland. In 1761 Isaac Iselin-Forcart had been one of the founders of the Helvetic Society, the aim of which was to promote education, religious harmony, closer ties among the members of the Swiss Confederation, and more open public discussion of political and social issues. Iselin was also the moving spirit behind the *Gesellschaft zur Aufmunterung und Beförderung des Guten und Gemeinnützigen in Basel* (Society for the Encouragement and Promotion of Works of Public Benefit and Utility in Basel), commonly referred to as the *Gemeinnützige Gesellschaft*, which was established in 1777 at a meeting in Iselin's house on the Münsterplatz and which is active and influential in Basel to this day. The founding members were all "patricians"—businessmen mostly, but at the same time *Ratsherren* or senators, public officials, past or future *Bürgermeisters*. Among them were Friedrich Munch, who was in the grain importing business; Andreas Buxtorf, a member of both the Senate and the Cabinet and *Bürgermeister* in the years immediately preceding the Helvetic Republic; Jacob Sarasin of the Weisses Haus, a prominent ribbon manufacturer or *Bändelherr* and an active member of the Helvetic Society; Andreas Merian; Peter Burckhardt, Iselin's brother-in-law and an influential local freemason; and Johann Rudolf Forcart, another brother-in-law, a wealthy silk merchant, a member of the Helvetic Society since 1773, a founding member in 1795 of the Basel Economic Society, a leading figure among the city's freemasons (he was Grand Master of the Basel lodge *"Zur vollkommenen Freiheit"* from 1778 to 1783), and a member of the Senate at the Restoration (1816–1824).[6]

One of the moving spirits of the Enlightenment at Basel was Christoph Bernoulli, who championed a modern higher education curriculum based on mathematics, the sciences, and practical subjects like political economy and applied mechanics, rather than on the ancient languages. In 1806 Bernoulli founded an innovative high school, known as the *Philotechnisches Institut*, where he offered to provide the kind of education he advocated. The sons of the wealthiest and most distinguished families in the city were enrolled in this school. In 1807 the student body included representatives of the Bernoulli, Bischoff, Burckhardt, Faesch, Heussler, Iselin, La Roche, Ochs, Paravicini, Ryhiner, Wieland, and Wettstein families.[7] Indeed, as the new *Institut* was a private institution and the fees were quite high, it must have been aimed primarily at the children of the elite—in spite of Bernoulli's commitment to education for all citizens (*"Erziehung aller Bürger"*). According to one contemporary account, its object was "de procurer à de futurs commerçans et manufacturiers une institution convenable"—to provide future businessmen and manufacturers with an appropriate education. The author of this account recommends the school to his readers but suggests they enroll their sons early, since at the time of writing all the places are taken by *"de jeunes Bâlois."*[8] As we shall see, the nineteenth-century "patricians" of Basel, despite their growing pride in the humanist tradition of the city and their espousal of German neohumanist ideals, never abandoned their interest in practical subjects and in an education appropriate to the modern world of science, commerce, and industry.

It was the Basel elite, moreover, that produced the man most responsible for inaugurating the Helvetic Republic (1798–1803)—the political embodiment of Enlightenment ideals in Switzerland—which did away with the autonomy of the individual cantons and introduced a democratic constitution designed to subvert the power of the local elites. Born in the prosperous French port city of Nantes, where his family had business interests, Peter Ochs was a member of a distinguished Basel merchant family. Though his championing of the *Helvetik* soon provoked the ire of his fellow citizens, he represented in an extreme political form a tendency that was revived later in a more moderate economic guise by the outstanding Baselers who—despite their city's lukewarm endorsement of the federal Constitution of 1848[9]—contributed signally to the construction of the new federal Switzerland of the second half of the nineteenth century. Achilles Bischoff, the architect of the Swiss customs union, Benedikt La Roche, the founder of the federal postal service, and Johann Jacob Speiser, one of the pioneers of the Swiss railways and a moving force behind the establishment of a national currency, were all products of Bernoulli's *Philotechnisches Institut.*

The new political order ushered in by the Enlightenment and the Revolution did not in fact make life especially comfortable for the Basel merchants. Even after Napoleon put an end to the Helvetic Republic and restored cantonal autonomy (by the Act of Mediation of 1803), the economic policies of the Empire, in particular the Continental Blockade, created difficulties not only for the calico manufacturers of Basel, who found the French market closed to them and the raw materials they needed extremely hard to obtain, even at inflated prices and through illegal channels, but for the whole of the Basel economy, dependent as it was on the free movement and transit of goods and services. The subordination of economic interests to political objectives was not something for which the merchant class of Basel had much sympathy or understanding, nor was the hegemony of a single power over all the other powers of Europe something they looked on with equanimity. From the time of its struggle against the Habsburgs in the late Middle Ages, Basel's policy had always been to prevent the establishment of any such hegemony. What was normal to the Baselers—getting and selling what there was a market for—was often illegal during the Continental Blockade. On one occasion, nine of the most distinguished citizens of the city, including Andreas Merian, were sentenced to prison for "smuggling."[10] Several were ruined. Despite the best efforts of his son Johann to sustain it, the firm of Rudolf Burckhardt—the builder of Zum Kirschgarten, the most elegant town house in eighteenth-century Basel, the friend of Goethe and Lavater, and a patron of music and literature—went under. The town house had to be sold, along with the family's country estate at Erndthalten; and Rudolf's family was scattered to the four corners of the earth.

The elite was therefore glad of the allied victory over Napoleon. Nonetheless, as we have seen, Basel did not return to the *status quo ante* in 1815. On the contrary—though the Ochs family felt their name was such a liability that in 1819 they replaced it with that of an ancestor called His—the men who took over the Basel administration under *Bürgermeister* Johann Heinrich Wieland during the Restoration period accepted the need for change. Wieland himself had served in various administrative capacities under the Helvetic Republic, had worked for the abolition of the subject status of the inhabitants of the country districts dependent on Basel, was a champion of free trade (one of his brothers was a merchant in Nantes, another in Brussels), and advocated educational reforms. In their government of the city-state, the new leaders tried to steer a cautious, pragmatic course, introducing moderate changes and avoiding counterrevolutionary extremism.

Even in the decades following the *Kantonstrennung,* when the name of Basel had become synonymous throughout Switzerland with conservative politics, the elite continued to pursue modest measures of reform. The first progressive income tax in Europe was proposed in 1840 by the conservative *Ratsherr* Bernhard Socin and passed by the *Rat.*[11] Conservative Basel thus accepted the principle of a more equitable distribution of the tax burden before any of its liberal rivals.

In its relations with the great powers, notably Prussia and Austria, Basel also steered an independent middle-of-the-road course. Intellectuals and "liberals" (as they were taken at the time to be)[12] who had to flee Prussia in the wake of the repressive policies that followed the assassination of Kotzebue by the student Carl Sand in 1819 readily found asylum in the city and several were even offered teaching positions at the reorganized University. That is how the distinguished theologian Wilhelm Martin Liebrecht De Wette came to the chair of theology. After the assassination of Kotzebue, De Wette had been suspended from his teaching position at the University of Berlin, the Prussian authorities having laid hands on a letter of condolence he had written to Carl Sand's mother. In the letter De Wette expressed understanding of the young man's motives, even though he condemned the act of assassination itself. Because of this letter and his subsequent dismissal, as well as his friendship with the popular "liberal" philosopher Fries, the darling of the students, De Wette had acquired the reputation of being himself liberally inclined. Moreover, in public statements and lectures in the 1820s he continued to express "liberal" opinions—his opposition to all "selfish" social privileges, for instance, though not to distinctions and hierarchies as such—and these opinions, which his American translator considered "bold and radical even for an American," caused no undue stir among his Basel auditors.[13] The University of Basel made other, similar appointments: Wilhelm Snell in law, Ludwig Snell in classical philosophy, Friedrich Kortum in history, Wilhelm Wesselhoft in anatomy, Carl Follen in law and his friend Carl Gustav Jung in medicine, Carl Seebold in philosophy. All these men had had to leave Germany for political reasons; most enjoyed successful careers at Basel. Several (Jung in 1828, Wilhelm Snell in 1830, De Wette four times—in 1823, 1829, 1834–1835, and 1849) were elected to the rectorship of the University.[14]

Tiny as it was, the revived University of Basel came to be seen by the reactionary governments of Prussia and Austria as a veritable nest of liberals and demagogues, a miniature of the whole of Switzerland, which because of its traditional policy of granting asylum had the reputation at the time of being a dangerous focus of revolution. In May 1824 the king of Prussia formally prohibited his subjects from studying at the University of Basel. This punitive gesture gave the struggling institution rather more importance than it deserved, since no Prussian students—and very few foreign students in general—had been tempted to matriculate at the University. With an enrollment that rarely topped sixty until the mid-1840s—compared with 311 in 1817 at neighboring Freiburg, itself one of the smaller of the German universities—Basel was hardly in the front rank of German-speaking universities of the time.[15]

A special note was sent by the Prussian government to *Bürgermeister* Wieland urging him to cut all ties with Follen in particular. As Basel made no move to comply with this request, the Prussian and Austrian ambassadors warned the Swiss federal authorities that plots were being hatched in Basel to overthrow the entire moral order of Europe. The federal authorities forwarded an official request from Prussia for the extradition of the alleged ringleaders—Follen, Snell, and Wesselhoft—and brought what pressure they could on Basel to comply. By this time Wesselhoft had already left for America, but the Cabinet decided to instruct Follen and Snell, with whose services to the University it declared itself fully satisfied, to remain at their posts until the matter was settled. The attitude the Basel government maintained throughout was that it was a free and sovereign state. It agreed to a proper legal investigation of Follen and Snell, and advised the federal authorities that this had turned up no evidence that either man was maintaining links to any dangerous secret societies in Germany. On the contrary, the investigation had confirmed that both men were honorable and law-abiding citizens. Basel's obstinacy caused the Swiss federal authorities "much anguish."[16] They did not dare to transmit the city's reply to Prussia and Austria, but instead brought further pressure on Basel to yield. A sparring match ensued between Basel, on the one hand, and the three leading cantons of the Confederation—Bern, Zurich, and Lucerne—on the other. Basel insisted that if charges were to be brought against Snell and Follen, this had to be done according to proper legal procedure. The crimes of which they were accused had to be specified, as well as the times and places at which they were alleged to have occurred. Prussia and Austria declined to provide any details, protesting only that they had "sufficient evidence."

Basel's defense of Snell and Follen indicated the city-republic's appreciation of the contribution foreign scholars were making and might still make to the revival of the University, and its determination to protect them. This in itself signaled a new intellectual openness, since in the eighteenth century both the University and the *Gymnasium* had been staffed almost exclusively by native Baselers. The defense of Follen and Snell also indicated the value Basel attached to due process of law in face of the arbitrariness of the reactionary powers. It was by no means an unpopular cause for the Basel government to take up in the heady time following the assassination of Kotzebue. According to Treitschke, the student Carl Sand, who carried out the act of assassination, together with those associated with him, was widely regarded in cultured and "liberal" circles throughout Germany as a hero and as the real victim in the Kotzebue affair. Basel's attitude aligned it not only with the youthful rebels in the *Burschenschaft* movement but with all those, beginning with the executioner himself, who looked on Sand as a martyr in the cause of German freedom.[17] In view of its reputation for extreme conservatism, it is worth noting that in the early 1820s the government of the merchant city appeared more liberal than that of many other Swiss cantons and that, in general, conservatism in the context of a commercial city-republic was not equivalent to the repression practiced in the old monarchical states.[18] "Compared to these gentlemen, we are nothing less than Jacobins," Peter Merian is said to have remarked to his colleague Andreas Heusler, as the two conservative Basel *Ratsherren* drove home in their carriage from a meeting with a couple of visiting Prussian dignitaries, both dyed-in-the-wool Junker reactionaries.[19]

The Basel administration also followed a cautious middle-of-the-road policy in religion. As in similar milieux in other European countries, a fair number of Basel's active and industrious citizens, and even some of its teachers and clergymen, had been attracted to deism or to various simplified and rationalized forms of Christianity, as well as to freemasonry. Isaac Iselin's mixture of moral uprightness, benevolence, scientific curiosity, and moderate piety was probably not atypical. Until about 1816, according to the mid-nineteenth century Basel theologian Karl Rudolf Hagenbach, whose testimony is the more precious for being based on direct acquaintance with the people he described, "the good burghers of Basel were accustomed to going to Church on Sundays, taking Holy Communion on occasion, sending their children to Sunday School, and otherwise not bothering too much about matters of religion."[20] It was thought distinguished to attend the *Eglise française,* which at the time was under the influence of the liberal, predominantly ethical Protestantism common in the French-speaking areas of Switzerland in the eighteenth century.[21] Though the orthodox considered attendance at this *"Modekirche, wo man sieht und gesehen wird"* (in the words of a German visitor) no better than not going to church at all, many of the elite families were members of it. Among the elders between the beginning of the eighteenth and the middle of the nineteenth centuries there were Bachofens, Bernoullis, "Bourcards," Heuslers, Iselins, La Roches, Merians, Passavants, Paravicinis, Ryhiners, Socins, Sarasins, and Vischers.[22]

On the other hand, as we noted, an important part of established Basel society remained deeply religious and traditionally Christian. Many of the city's pastors were from branches of the same families that had produced the well-to-do merchants.[23] Though the two groups in the elite remained fairly distinct, the religious group enjoyed a great deal of influence in a society that was officially Christian and recognized no separation of church and state, the Senate being the effective head of the State Church. Within the religious party, there were two distinct and quarrelsome factions: the Orthodox and the Pietists. The former were pillars of the church and demanded strict obedience on the part of the faithful, the latter stressed the inner life and the experience of conversion. Since the visits of Count Zinzendorf, the founder of the *Herrnhuter,* to Basel in 1740 and 1758, the Pietist movement had grown considerably in strength not only among the artisans but even among the ministers. A *Geographical and Statistical Account of Switzerland* reported in 1786 that in Basel "the *Herrnhuter* are very numerous. Probably their restrained, simple way of life has had an influence on the appearance and behavior of a considerable part of the population."[24] It was not only Basel's central location but the support of a significant part of the population that led the founders of the German *Christentumsgesellschaft*—an evangelical and missionary society established in 1782—to select the city as the center of its activities. One of those most instrumental in attracting the society to Basel was a Burckhardt, the pastor of St. Peter's.[25]

Whatever the influence of Enlightenment ideas on religious thought and feeling, there seems to have been little scope for public dissent. In 1790, for instance, a popular and successful teacher at the *Gymnasium* made the mistake of trying to promote the cause of rationalist theology in his classes and of making his ideas public in a volume entitled *Auswahl der Lehren und Thaten Jesu* (*Selected Teachings and Deeds of Jesus*), which he had somehow succeeded in getting through the censor's net. After long hearings before the *Kirchenrat* (the Department of State for Church Affairs) and the *Censurcommission,* the work was condemned and all copies of it confiscated. The author, Johannes Frey, was forbidden to teach any religion classes. When it was discovered that he had subsequently used a history class to challenge both the authority of the Bible and that of the pastors, he was suspended altogether. He appealed, but it was only some time after his death, which occurred in 1800, in the completely different climate of revolutionary Switzerland when Enlightenment ideas were officially in the ascendancy, that that judgment was overturned on grounds of procedural irregularities. The head of the Department of State for Education was obliged to resign as a result, but he may have been expressing the views of a majority of the parents and of the citizens of Basel when he declared that he had acted out of his conviction that "the Religion of the citizens, no less than their honor and their lives, must be considered a sacred property which it is the obligation of the State to defend and to protect against injury and depreciation."[26]

The social and ideological basis of the influence of the religious party was clearly spelled out by Hagenbach when he described the religious instruction of children in the schools in the early nineteenth century. They were drilled in catechism, he wrote, and in a few simple moral lessons that they learned to repeat parrotwise: "For instance, 'Who are our superiors in a secular sense?' 'The government and its officials.' 'Who are our superiors in a spiritual sense?' 'The pastors and teachers.'" It is clear, Hagenbach commented, that the catechism as taught to the children of Basel reinforced the "patriarchal relation between the authorities and their subjects."[27] The success of Pietism among the *Handwerker*—and among women—may well be understood as a more or less conscious challenge to a religious order that was closely associated, even through its personnel, with the power of the political oligarchy. If that is so, the form the challenge took determined its outcome. It never became a direct political challenge, and in the end, as elements in the elite itself came to support it, became simply an additional instrument of control.

Whatever the experiences and thoughts of individuals, the links between church and state were far too important in Basel—as almost everywhere else at the time—for any government seriously to wish to reduce the influence of religion. Though the Pietists were at times the target of some good-natured jokes among the more worldly citizens, Hagenbach related, and though they were seen as a potential danger to the established church, it was also said that if there had not been any in Basel, it would have been necessary to import a few in order to combat the rising tide of godlessness.[28]

In Basel, as elsewhere,[29] the Revolution provoked a return to religious seriousness and observance in the upper classes. Mme de Krudener made several visits to the city during which her seances in the houses of the well-to-do drew large audiences. Another sign of religious revival was the founding, in 1815, in close association with the *Christentumsgesellschaft,* of the Basel *Mission* as a focus for the missionary action of Protestants from all parts of South Germany, Alsace, and Switzerland. The *Missionsschule,* opened a year later, drew students from missionary societies throughout Europe. The Basel *Mission* sent its graduates to the farthest corners of the globe—to Transcaucasian Russia in 1822, to the Gold Coast in 1828, to southwest India in 1834, to Hong Kong and South China in 1846. According to Hagenbach, the Basel *Mission* rested on a foundation far broader than Zinzendorf's *Herrnhuter:* it was the expression of the religious fervor of wide pietistic circles throughout Germany and Switzerland and it enjoyed broad support among all classes in Basel.[30] The *Allgemeine Encyclopädie* of Ersch and Gruber, published in 1819, refers to "ein sehr ausgebreiteter Hang zu religiöser Schwärmerei, eignen Secten, mystischen Vereinen" ("a widespread tendency to religious enthusiasm, small sects, and mystical associations") in Basel. "Daher die zahlreichen Herrnhuther, die Theilnahme an den Bussübungen der Frau von Krudener und an dem Missionswesen" ("Whence the large numbers of Herrnhuter, the participation in Mme de Krudeners's penance exercises and in the evangelical movement").[31] Basel was a stronghold of the postrevolutionary religious revival movement known in the United States as the "Great Awakening" and in Switzerland as the *"réveil"* or *"Erweckung."* Even at the *Eglise française* the elegant sermons of ministers in the late-eighteenth-century liberal Protestant manner gave way to the passionate evangelism of the great preacher Grandpierre, who achieved a religious awakening, according to Hagenbach, in those strata of society that had hitherto been most distant from Pietism.[32]

Characteristically, however, even in the period of religious revivalism, the generation that came to power at the Restoration seems to have wanted to avoid coming down too strongly on one side or the other in the ongoing conflict between the orthodox and the Pietists. From the time of the Reformation itself there had been a current of resistance in the ruling elites of the Reformed commercial cities to the hegemonic designs of preachers and ministers. As the citizens of Strasbourg reportedly put it, "Man muss dennoch die Welt ein wenig die Welt sin lassen" ("One must let the world be the world at least a little").[33] By stimulating discussion and debate, the chief magistrates of Basel appear to have sought deliberately to relax the hold of both religious parties.

Throughout most of the nineteenth century, the Basel church was notable for its conservatism and for its isolation from current theological discussion in the German universities.[34] Rational and liberal theology made fewer inroads than in Germany or other parts of Switzerland. The liberal or *freisinnig* current in contemporary theology was almost entirely unrepresented. Even the few pastors who had some sympathy with it would not have acknowledged the fact.[35] The alternative was between orthodoxy and Pietism. Inevitably, therefore, the recommendation of the governing board of the newly reorganized University that De Wette be invited to fill the chair of theology in 1821 met with resistance. De Wette was known as a friend and admirer of Friedrich Schleiermacher. In addition, as we saw, he was reputed to have expressed sympathy for the assassin of Kotzebue, the student Carl Sand. In attracting a man who had been a professor at the most prestigious institution of higher education in Germany, the Basel administration almost certainly saw an opportunity of enhancing the reputation of its own much-diminished University. But it is also quite likely that it had in mind to maintain a balance among the religious parties by introducing a prominent figure who could not be characterized as strictly orthodox or Pietist or rationalist, but who attempted to do justice to all three positions. De Wette's inclusiveness endeared him to neither the orthodox clergy nor the Pietists in Basel. Both regarded him primarily as a dangerous rationalist. Inviting him to Basel thus had the effect of keeping religious discussion open and preventing the dominance of one party or another.[36] *Bürgermeister* Wieland made it clear that he favored speculation in theological matters and did not like the narrow self-righteousness and dogmatism of Basel's orthodox guardians of the faith ("unsere dermaligen Zionswächter, [. . .] diese allein rechtgläubigen Baselischen Religionslehrer," as he put it), whose chief concern—in his view—was to oppose anything that might diminish their influence.[37]

There can be no question of anyone's having been ignorant of De Wette's orientation. If anything, it was perceived as more radical than it was. Jacob Burckhardt's father, for instance, the pastor and future *Antistes* or chief minister of the state church, had heard De Wette lecture in Heidelberg in 1807. In the older Burckhardt's eyes, De Wette was a kind of Niebuhr of Scripture, subjecting the biblical texts to philological and historical criticism, questioning their authorship, yet maintaining that their authenticity and truth were independent of the assumed authorship of Moses, David, or Solomon.[38] Nevertheless, the government's policies in no way undermined the dominant position of religion in the life of nineteenth-century Basel. *Bürgermeister* Wieland's position in the Frey affair—when he had been head of the education department—had not altered substantially. Though there was a slow erosion of their relation, church and state remained closely connected in the city-republic throughout most of the nineteenth century.[39] De Wette simply introduced an opening to the kind of thinking that was going on in the world beyond Basel. He in no way sought scandal. On the contrary, in a spirit of conciliation similar to that of his friend Schleiermacher, he sought to combine the various strands in contemporary Christian theology—the liberalism and rationalism of the German universities, the orthodox tradition still strong in church circles in Basel, and the Pietist evangelical current that inspired much of the Basel citizenry. If anything, De Wette became less radical after settling in Basel. His program of reconciliation was carried forward in the so-called *Vermittlungstheologie* (theology of mediation or conciliation) of his student at the University of Basel, Karl-Rudolf Hagenbach.

Thus it was 1870 before religious instruction in Basel's schools was made optional, and it was not till two years later, with the acceptance of an intercantonal concordat establishing a common examination for all candidates for the ministry, that pastors from other cantons and, above all, liberally inclined theologians gained free access to the well-guarded parishes of Basel-City. As late as 1843, just two years after Engels passed through the town, the *National-Zeitung* could still claim that Basel remained, on the whole, deeply conservative in matters of religion, so conservative that what passed for orthodoxy in Germany would be considered heresy there. "And that doctrine is the religion of the State, it dominates public life and private relations. The spirit of our entire community has to breathe that air, and anything that is opposed to it meets with the most stubborn resistance."[40]

Among the elite there was less unanimity than this account would indicate. When the vociferous sermons of Samuel Hebich, a popular Swabian evangelist who drew large and enthusiastic audiences to the Leonhardskirche in 1860, were followed by scenes of public disorder, the authorities were forced to intervene. The episode elicited a mocking account, shot through with patrician disdain, from the pious Bachofen and much merry humor from Burckhardt. The latter had in any case lost his faith and abandoned his early theological studies for history and the history of art. One of the teachers of both men at the Basel *Pädagogium*, Alexandre Vinet, the professor of French, became a passionate advocate, in the interests of religion itself, of the separation of church and state. De Wette himself, as we saw, represented a liberal and modern orientation in Christian theology. Nevertheless, the general atmosphere appears to have been one of fairly strict observance.

The combination of the worldly activity of the elite, their energetic pursuit of trade, commerce, and manufacturing, their hard-nosed devotion to profit, and the religious piety that dominated the city and that they themselves supported, and often shared, gave observers the impression of an oppressively pious, hypocritical society in which God and Mammon were worshipped with equal fervor. "Money," the *National-Zeitung* reported in 1844, "is the surrogate in Basel for talent, diligence, knowledge, honor, virtue; with money one can pay off all one's debts to humanity." The city was not only very rich; it was also reputed for its piety, which came second only to wealth in the Baselers' eyes. "Basel is the city of miracles, where the rich can enter the Kingdom of Heaven more easily than a camel can pass through the eye of a needle. There is a high price on piety. It can almost substitute for wealth."[41] The satirical tone here recalls Engels. But the image presented by the radical newspaper was one that was widely shared. The citizens of Basel have a great reputation for piety, the prospective traveler was told by the author of Murray's *Handbook for Travellers in Switzerland* in 1856.[42] But "the spirit of trade goes hand in hand with that of religion." A few years later the author of this guidebook might have illustrated his point with the example of the Basel Trading Company Limited, founded in 1859 to finance the work of the Missionary Society. The latter was especially active in West Africa, India, and China, and it was to the converts or prospective converts of the missionaries that the Trading Company sold the cotton goods and other products that it exported from Switzerland. After meeting a minimum guaranteed return of 6 percent on all the privately subscribed shares, the company divided the remaining profits equally between the shareholders and the Missionary Society. Bibles and business made happy bedfellows at Basel.[43]

The culture of nineteenth-century Basel was deeply marked by the dominant role of religion in the city's life. There was little theater, for instance, because of the opposition of the Pietists, especially to Sunday performances, without which—since Sunday was the only day of leisure for most people—no theatrical company could hope to survive economically. The city itself provided no subsidy. As late as 1842 a request by a number of citizens for permission to give Sunday performances was turned down in the Cabinet, or *Kleiner Rat*, by six votes to four. Among those who apparently favored a positive response to the petition were Senators Burckhardt-Ryhiner and Abraham Iselin-Iselin, but a majority of the elite either shared the views of the Pietists or were unwilling to cross them on this point.[44] It took several more years before the more liberal elements in the elite were able to overcome the resistance of the Pietists and the orthodox and put through legislation permitting Sunday performances; and it was not really until the very end of the century that theatrical life amounted to anything much in Basel.[45]

As in other communities where religion, and especially Pietism, exercised a strong influence, music fared better than theater or literature, partly perhaps because it appeared to correspond more closely to the Pietists' ideal of inwardness and their distrust of reasoning and rhetoric. In the late eighteenth century there was a music room in almost all the well-to-do houses in Basel and many people took part in private music-making.[46] Lucas Sarasin, who played the fiddle himself, employed a resident concertmaster and held regular musical evenings in a specially designed concert room, equipped with an organ, in the Blaues Haus.[47] Music lovers like Peter Ochs and Daniel Legrand organized concerts in a hall in the Augustinergasse.[48]

Louis Spohr, it is true, had no very high opinion of the musical culture of the Baselers. "The best people here still like music that was already intolerable in Germany in Pleyel's time. They know Mozart, Haydn, and Beethoven mostly as names." Spohr had attracted a large audience to his concert in the spring of 1816 and was pleased with the evening's takings—"but the best thing is that they are easy to please." As the orchestra was composed chiefly of amateurs, with very few professionals, the playing apparently left a good deal to be desired. "The accompaniment of my solo pieces was frightful especially among the wind instruments." Yet bad as it all was, "the audience was very pleased and

Emanuel Burchhardt-Sarasin, *Konzert des Collegium Musikum,* ca. 1790. Private collection, Langenbrück bei Basel.

Sebastian Gutzwiller, *Basler Familienkonzert, 1849.* Öffentliche Kunstsammlung Basel, Kunstmuseum. Photo: Öffentliche Kunstsammlung Basel, Martin Bühler.

found that the orchestra had truly distinguished itself on this occasion."[49] Five years earlier Weber had met with a similar warm welcome in Basel musical circles, especially from *Bürgermeister* Peter Burckhardt, Christoph Bernoulli (the founder and director of the *Philotechnisches Institut*), and the Faesch, Forcart, Merian, and Passavant families.[50]

The elite granted music all the support it withheld from the theater. In 1811 the *Gemeinnützige Gesellschaft* sponsored a mixed male and female choir, which sang major works like Haydn's *Creation* and *The Seasons*. (So much for Spohr's comment about the backwardness of the Basel musical public!) A regular concert series was established in 1813. In 1820 the first Swiss national musical festival was held at Basel. The year 1826 saw the opening of the new *Stadtcasino* or concert hall, designed by the leading architect in Basel and one of the best in Switzerland, Jacob Burckhardt's brother-in-law Melchior Berri-Burckhardt. In 1829 the *Concertgesellschaft* was founded, with the liberal and progressive Christoph Bernoulli as first president, and in the same year a pupil of Spohr's was brought in from Geneva to be music director and to put the orchestra on a more professional footing.[51] Many members of the elite families participated in the activities of the *Gesangverein* (founded in 1824), the *Basler Singverein,* and the *Liedertafel* (founded in 1852). Leading families like the Thurneysens also contributed financially to the support of the orchestra. By the 1880s Burckhardt could write to an old German friend in Crefeld that "Basel has the reputation, even on the outside, of being quite musical," and in one of his regular letters to von Preen he reported that "Basel schwirrt von Musik" and that both Sarasate and Rubinstein had recently given recitals.[52]

The contrast between the relative richness of the city's musical life and the poverty of its theatrical life was underlined in the liberal and radical press, which frequently complained of the exclusive and visibly "social" character of musical activities in Basel. The concerts were occasions for the elite to see and be seen, the *Basler Mitteilungen* noted in 1826, and they were not much frequented by ordinary citizens. The high price of tickets effectively restricted the audience to people of means.[53] Criticism of the "exclusive" character of culture in Basel came to a head in the 1840s, around the same time—as we shall see—that the elite was also coming under attack for its administration of the University and the higher education system. The radical press objected that since concerts were permitted on Sundays while theater performances were forbidden, a double standard was being applied that favored the entertainment preferred by the well-to-do over that desired by the common people. The administration, it was held, was manipulating the cultural institutions and resources of the community for its own ends. In any case, there was no question in a merchant city like Basel of the rich, court-supported musical and theatrical offerings enjoyed by even the smaller German capitals. "In a court theater like yours," Burckhardt wrote to von Preen, who lived in Karlsruhe, "so much can be simply taken for granted and proceed automatically, without a hitch. The same thing can be achieved here only as a result of enormous efforts."[54]

In addition to religion, philanthropy, and music, the recreational activities of the elite often included participation in one of the learned societies that had been founded after the Restoration. Almost all the members of these societies were recruited among the leading families. Between 1800 and 1832 alone, over twenty-five different *Vereine,* or societies, are said to have been established.[55] The *Naturforschende Gesellschaft* (Society for the Advancement of Science) was founded in 1817 and began sponsoring public lectures on popular scientific subjects to "mixed" (that is, male and female) audiences around 1840. The *Freie Akademische Gesellschaft* (Society of Friends of the University), set up in 1834 to muster support for the University and raise money for it, also sponsored a public lecture series. The *Historische Gesellschaft* was founded in 1836, perhaps in response to the trauma of the civil war and the *Kantonstrennung.* Three years later the *Kunstverein* came into being with the aim of promoting "Kunst-Sinn," or an appreciation of art among the citizens, and making the work of local artists better known. The *Antiquarische Gesellschaft* was formed as an offshoot of the *Historische Gesellschaft* in 1842.

The founders of these societies tended to be the so-called *juste-milieu* liberal-conservatives in the elite, that is to say, men who had come to maturity and power at the Restoration and who looked to the historical and legal tradition to provide the ground for a moderate political liberalism and individualism, equally distant from the democratic ideas of the radicals and from the inflexible authoritarianism of extreme conservatives. An outstanding yet typical figure from this group was Felix Sarasin. Head of a successful textile firm (he had traveled in England to study the cotton industry there), Sarasin was one of the leading spirits behind the *Freie Akademische Gesellschaft.* He was also president of the *Lesegesellschaft,* or reading society, and of the *Gemeinnützige Gesellschaft,* was the principal organizer of the *Kunstverein,* and subsequently served as an enlightened *Bürgermeister.*

Prominent among the founders of the Historical Society was the group of liberally inclined university professors (in the sense in which the term *liberal* was understood in Germany in the early 1820s) who had been brought to Basel from Germany in the decade following the Carlsbad Decrees. They had become enthusiastic and loyal supporters of a state and a regime they believed to be more receptive to the ideals of neohumanism than any in Germany. Basel seemed to them closer in character and spirit to the ancient Greek polis than any of the German monarchies or principalities—even constitutional, but still predominantly rural, Baden and Württemberg. These men—Friedrich Brommel, who taught history and had taken part in the War of Liberation against Napoleon (supposedly he had fought at Waterloo); Franz Dorotheus Gerlach, professor of Latin, who had studied with Dissen and Heeren at Göttingen in

1813–1816, and had established a friendship with the great Welcker in his final year there;[56] Wilhelm Wackernagel, professor of German, an enthusiastic
follower of Jahn and his patriotic gymnasts, and one of the founders of *Ger-
manistik*—wished to promote the study of both classical and German history
and literature. Other founding members included Johann Georg Müller-
Burckhardt, who taught theology at the University and the *Pädagogium,* and
was an early student of comparative religion and the author of a book on the
primitive religions of the Americas;[57] Karl-Rudolf Hagenbach-Geigy, the
friend and disciple of De Wette; and above all Andreas Heusler-Ryhiner
(1802–1868). Appointed to a chair of law at the University at the age of
twenty-eight and elected a *Ratsherr,* or senator, a year later in 1831, Ryhiner
was an enormously influential elite intellectual, a conservative who was convinced that it was necessary to make a pact with the devil and enlist the new
forces of the modern world, notably public opinion and specialized expertise, if
conservative policies were to have any chance of success. In 1831 he launched
the *Basler Zeitung* to serve as the political organ of the liberal-conservatives
and counteract the propaganda of the radicals in favor of the rebellious country
districts. He also seems to have encouraged various young men from the elite
to acquire an appropriate training for government service. (It appears to have
been Heusler who planned Bachofen's education, and he later recruited Burckhardt to serve as editor of his newspaper.)[58]

The subjects discussed at the Historical and Antiquarian Societies ranged
from local history and archaeology to wider historiographical speculations such
as those presented by Bachofen. But Bachofen himself did not set much store
by the meetings and did not take them very seriously, especially after a change
in the statutes opened up both societies to a broad membership in the mid-
1860s. "We are short of nothing so much as of archaeologists in our archaeological society," he wrote to a Zurich friend. "In general everything is pretty weak;
about all that is left is a bit of lightweight dilettantism."[59] History and antiquities were simply, for many of the members of these societies, a respectable and
dignified occupation for the increasingly limited leisure time of solid citizens
and businessmen. To show an interest in them was a way of confirming the
value of tradition and culture without taking too much time out from other
more pressing and lucrative activities.

Besides the learned societies, the well-to-do at Basel could, and did, attend
the public lecture series referred to earlier. Given in the evenings by professors
at the University, these lectures had been established as part of a general effort
of regeneration after 1833 and as an outreach to the citizenry, whose efforts had
made it possible for the new half-canton of Basel-City to retain control of the
University by buying back the two-thirds share of the institution attributed to
Basel-Country by the terms of the *Kantonstrennung.* Though the integrity of
the University had been preserved in this way, it had proved necessary to curtail

its offerings drastically and hopes for an eventual restoration of its fortunes rested on the goodwill and the financial support of the community. The *Freie Akademische Gesellschaft* underwrote the public lecture series. Burckhardt had been a popular lecturer in the 1840s with about one hundred subscribers to a course on the history of painting; and when the University authorities invited him to return to Basel from Zurich in 1858, they expressly mentioned their interest in his resuming his evening lecture courses *"vor einem gemischten Publikum."*[60] Burckhardt's own records of the attendance at his course in 1844–1845 give an indication of the social composition of the audience. Many notables attended, beginning with *Bürgermeister* Karl Burckhardt-Paravicini, as did a considerable contingent of colleagues from the University.[61] About one-third of the subscribers consisted of ladies of the town.[62]

Over a decade later, when Burckhardt returned to Basel, nothing much seems to have changed. Bachofen described the lectures in a letter of December 1859: "I don't attend Burckhardt's lectures. I find it simply impossible to subject myself to esthetic outpourings about the beauty of buildings and landscapes. To each his own [*Ein jedes Tierle hat sein Manierle*]. His public here consists largely of noble-minded and sensitive persons [*schöne Seelen*] whose prejudices prevent them from going to the theater. But he won't create much havoc here. The unaesthetic disposition of the Basel public—which is not easily jolted out of its Imperial City composure and which pursues the so-called 'higher' pleasures only out of boredom—will make sure of that."[63]

It seems, in sum, that there was no lively public culture in Basel, no large and varied leisure class, and only a limited artistic and literary life. The city's cultural activities, parceled out according to social classes, and affording few occasions for the entire citizenry to come together, had a narrow, small-town character and could not cast off the constraints imposed by a conservative religious leadership. Even the rigid segregation of the sexes in social activities reported by a traveling Englishwoman at the end of the eighteenth century seems to have been only slightly relaxed by initiatives like the public lecture series for "mixed audiences." The Baselers of the old regime repaired to their *tabagies* or *Kämmerli* to talk of affairs and conduct business over tea and cigars, leaving their ladies to entertain themselves. On the "gala occasions" provided by occasional mixed parties, when the men "sacrificed one evening of smoke and stock-jobbing to the women," "the card-party concludes," Helen Williams wrote acidly, "with a supper, sufficiently luxurious, but which might be more amusing; and as the law forbids any carriages to roll through the streets after eleven, the company usually separate at that hour."[64]

The account Bachofen gave of life in Basel to a Zurich friend in 1861 seems only slightly distorted by the writer's irony. Bachofen had been asked what he would recommend to a young man from Frankfurt who had much enjoyed the dancing parties in Zurich and now planned to visit Basel. He was not encouraging. Mr. Mylius, he wrote, "will have to forgo all that sort of thing here. I do not recall ever hearing of any one dancing in Basel, except at the vile popular balls at Carnival time. With the best will in the world, I have nothing to offer the young man but the advice that he not stay long here. The natives go to bed early and discipline themselves from early youth to have as few needs as possible. A lecture, an interminable symphony concert, and a sermon by Pater Hebich, *voilà tout!*"[65]

Over twenty years later, it was the same story. "Nothing new is to be found either on the Gerbergasse or on the Barfüsserplatz," Bachofen wrote in 1886 to his niece Anita, who was in the south of France and had asked for news of home. "One day here is very much like another. We get up in the morning, consume four meals, then go to bed again. If the sun shines, we go out, if it rains, we take our umbrellas along like every one else. One day I begin my walk with the Sankt Albanvorstadt, the next day with the Aeschenvorstadt, the day after with the great Gerberstrasse. Every morning I drink cocoa, every evening tea.

> Wie intressant, wie intressant
> O du, mein herrlich Schweizerland!"[66]

4

"To Reconcile the Progressive Tendencies of the Time with Resistance to Them"
Neohumanist Ideals and Modern Reality

In the nineteenth century the Basel elite put its greatest cultural effort into the renovation of the University and the establishment of what was to be one of the first important publicly supported (as opposed to princely) museums in any German-speaking land, that is to say, into two institutions whose function, in part, was to celebrate the past and promote respect for tradition. As we saw, the Basel merchants of the previous century had shown no great enthusiasm for academic learning and had allowed the University to stagnate. That was not unusual in the Age of Enlightenment, which set greater store by less traditional institutions of learning such as academies and scientific societies, but it was not to be the policy of the city fathers in the nineteenth century. On the contrary, the University was reconstituted and placed under the direct supervision of the city government. The old habit of filling chairs locally was abandoned and a concerted effort made to attract talented scholars to the city from beyond its gates. Many professors were recruited from Germany at the time of the Carlsbad Decrees, as already noted. In addition, recognizing that their small and financially strapped institution lacked the resources to attract established celebrities (especially after the *Kantonstrennung* depleted the city treasury in 1833), the members of the *Curatel,* or governing board, adopted a deliberate policy of seeking out promising younger scholars, from whom the University and the city might benefit for at least a few years until they were lured away to larger and wealthier institutions in Germany. In this way, the city fathers succeeded in staffing the University with an extraordinary group of gifted men, some of whom stayed only a year, others a lifetime. Among them were Alexandre Vinet and Wilhelm Wackernagel in French and German literature, respectively, Agathon Wunderlich and Rudolf von Jhering in law, Wilhelm Dilthey in philosophy, Adolf Kiessling and Friedrich Nietzsche in classical philology, and Wilhelm Martin Leberecht De Wette and Franz Overbeck in theology.[1]

The revival of interest in education and in the University that coincided with the overthrow of the revolutionary and Napoleonic order and with the Restoration was almost certainly politically and ideologically motivated, but those motivations were complex. A number of influential figures in the Restoration generation recognized that the Revolution had wrought a permanent change in the social and political order of Europe and in people's expectations, and that the effects of the Enlightenment in general would rapidly make themselves felt in economic life and in the conduct of government and administration. If further social unrest was to be avoided, it was felt, the elite would have to concern itself somewhat more directly with the material and spiritual well-being of the population, with education, culture, public health, and finance. And if these expanded and more specialized tasks were to be performed competently, without any weakening of the *Honoratiorenregiment* or of the elite's direct participation in the government of the city—that is, without resort to a bureaucracy—then new cadres of well-trained and technically competent administrators would have to be formed from the younger members of the elite itself. It is not surprising that this group of politically moderate members of the elite included several former students at Christoph Bernoulli's *Philotechnisches Institut* or that Bernoulli himself, the champion of technical and modern education in Basel, was closely associated with it.[2] Already in the 1820s and increasingly in the 1830s, after the *Kantonstrennung,* there was a significant tendency among the elite to provide professional training that would equip at least some of its sons for posts in the government and administration. In addition, a number of activities that had formerly been performed by artisans at Basel were increasingly taken over by the elite as they became professionalized and required more expensive and specialized academic training. The replacement of master builders by architects, for instance, was marked by the arrival on the scene of Melchior Berri-Burckhardt, Christoph Riggenbach, and Amadeus Merian, all members of elite families.

A new seriousness characterized the men who held these reformist views— Karl Burckhardt, Felix Sarasin, Peter and Rudolf Merian, Andreas Heusler (all of whom played significant roles in public life in Basel in the nineteenth century). In some respects they can be considered "modernizers," but they were also respectful of traditional values and religion, and they placed renewed emphasis on philanthropy and public service. It was private funds, for instance, that subsidized the building of new primary schools in the late teens and early twenties, and the function of the *Freie Akademische Gesellschaft,* of which Andreas Heusler, Peter Merian, and Felix Sarasin were the leading lights, was, as already noted, to raise funds for the University. In the appeals of the *Freie Akademische Gesellschaft* it was repeatedly emphasized, first, that a community favored by "Providence" with material success is obliged to take care of the life of the spirit and to complement material well-being with the cultivation of the things of the mind,[3] and, second, that it is vitally important to tend and preserve the traditional culture and the traditional values of the community. Of these the elite presented itself as the guardian and—partly no doubt because of its continued financial disbursements—the legitimate heir.[4] In that role no doubt it found added justification of its political power.

From the outset, however, and for decades to come, there was tension between the two orientations of the program of modernization. On the one hand, there was the need to meet what came to be commonly referred to as "the ever increasing demands of the age"—essentially the practical demands of the new world of commerce and industry—through an overhaul of the educational system that would assign a significant place to "modern" scientific and technical subjects. On the other hand, there was the need to meet the political challenge of the age—that is to say, from the elite's point of view, ensuring that modernization would occur without revolution. The means of achieving this goal was the transformation of the traditional study of the ancient languages from a rhetorical and grammatical exercise into an immersion in the entire life of antiquity in the spirit of the new humanism or study of antiquity that had developed in Germany in the second half of the eighteenth century.

The pedagogical literature, consisting of innumerable tracts, proposals, and public addresses, bears obvious marks of this tension and of the desire to resolve it. Christoph Bernoulli, the founder of the *Philotechnisches Institut,* who, on the whole, represented the first or "technical" tendency, and Rudolf Hanhart, the rector of the *Gymnasium,* who represented the second or "classical" tendency, were both active in the same politically moderate groups of the elite in the 1820s and 1830s.[5] Each of them wrote pamphlets and gave speeches emphasizing the aspect of education he deemed most essential. Yet both were on the whole conciliatory and took care not to appear to be discrediting the views of the other side.[6] In the end, Basel's reformed educational system represented a compromise. In an address to the graduating class of the *Pädagogium* in 1841, Wilhelm Vischer-Bilfinger—who was to be one of the guiding spirits of the University in the middle decades of the century—emphasized this spirit of compromise by evoking the memory of one of his own forebears, Isaac Iselin, and recalling that while Iselin had been an ardent champion of educational reform and modernization, he had also expressed the desire that the study of the classical languages and literatures not be abandoned. Iselin, Vischer declared, "wanted to reconcile the progressive tendencies of his time with resistance to them."[7]

Unlike the neohumanist schools in Prussia, the Basel *Gymnasium* provided an option for those who preferred to concentrate on mathematics and science rather than take the intensive Latin and Greek courses offered in the upper forms. Likewise, at the *Pädagogium,* there were two tracks: a "realist" or modern track and a "humanist" or classical track.[8] The *Pädagogium* itself was a distinctive Basel institution. In Germany the classical *Gymnasium,* or high school, educated students primarily with a view to advanced professional training at one of the University faculties of law, medicine, theology, and philosophy. Most

Gymnasium and *Pädagogium,* Münsterplatz.

graduates then became state civil servants or entered the state-supported church. In the commercial city-republic of Basel, in contrast, the most gifted children of the elite were destined not for a professional career but for a career in business. Government service, as we saw, was not usually a career but rather the unremunerated privilege and responsibility of older, better-off citizens after they had handed the running of their commercial affairs over to their sons. Many young Baselers, in short, required not a professional or preprofessional training but a general liberal education appropriate to their future roles as both cosmopolitan businessmen and members of a governing class.

As part of its general reform of education in 1817, the Basel government undertook to provide its younger citizens with such an education by establishing, in contrast to the nine-year classical *Gymnasium* that was standard in Germany, a six-year *Gymnasium* offering both a classical and a modern track, as we saw, together with a unique two- or three-year post-*Gymnasium* institution known as the *Pädagogium.* Besides being a preparatory college for the University, the *Pädagogium* was designed to offer an appropriate general and classical education to a distinguished class of pupils who *did not* plan to go on to professional studies at the University. These were the so-called *Nichtstudierende,* that is to say, those sons of the Basel businessmen who had been marked out as capable of following in their fathers' footsteps, first in the running of the business and then in the running of the state. For them, the *Pädagogium* served as the capstone of the *Gymnasium* and was the culmination of their educational experience, not a stage on the way to the study of medicine, law, or theology. The teachers at the *Pädagogium* were therefore to be the best available in the city, which is to say they were to be identical with the faculty of the University. Thus Nietzsche taught six hours a week at the *Pädagogium* in addition to seven at the University.

At the same time, it made sense to a governing elite rooted in business that the high spiritual ideals of neohumanism not be separated from the practical goals of modern scientific and technical education and that the state's advanced educational insitutions should offer the opportunity to pursue both. The sons of the elite were in fact enrolled in about equal numbers in the modern and the classical tracks at the *Pädagogium*. The closing down of Bernoulli's *Philotechnisches Institut*, which had been attended chiefly by the children of the elite— the high fees effectively putting it beyond the reach of any one else—coincided with the inauguration of the reformed educational system in 1817; it seems not unlikely that there had been a previous agreement to incorporate the essentials of Bernoulli's educational program into the new state system.

The characteristic Basel reluctance to separate the practical and the theoretical, the modern and the traditional, was reflected as late as the 1860s in the Education Department's refusal to divide the wide-ranging faculty of philosophy at the University into two separate faculties of science and mathematics and of philology and history, as had been done at many institutions. At neighboring Zurich, though the faculty remained formally undivided, it was in practice separated into two sections, each with its own dean; at nearby Tübingen, in Württemberg, two completely separate faculties had been created. At Basel, in contrast, the state Education Department considered it essential that philosophy not be removed from a faculty that also included the sciences, on the grounds that "young people who devote themselves to the study of mathematics and science ought to be no less familiar with philosophy than philologists and historians." Philosophy, it was contended, "is as close to one group of studies as to the other."[9]

At various points in the course of the century the elite was nonetheless accused of favoring classical and traditional disciplines at the expense of newer ones that would be more useful to the community as a whole.[10] The University and the *Pädagogium* were both seen as serving the interests of the elite. In 1844 the *National-Zeitung* denounced the university professors as mere lackeys of the *Herren*,[11] and in 1849 the radicals attempted to shut down the University. In advocating the study of foreign languages, accounting, political economy, and the sciences, the elite's critics were indeed defending a more immediately practical and useful kind of education than any of the spokesmen of the elite would have found acceptable. For both Bernoulli and Hanhart were in agreement that genuine education, whether the emphasis is placed on mathematics and the sciences or on the classical languages, raises the student above what is immediately useful and practical and enhances his humanity as a whole. The two von Humboldt brothers—Wilhelm the philologist, historian, political thinker, and classical scholar, and Alexander the natural scientist—had likewise seen the study of the natural world as offering no less an enrichment and elevation of the student's personality than the study of the human or historical world. Mathematics, Bernoulli insisted, is a way of looking at the world, and the natural sciences should develop the student's understanding and intellect, not merely his powers of observation and his practical intelligence.[12] In the ability to transcend immediate practical concerns and to take a longer view, both Bernoulli and Hanhart saw, in particular, the condition of participation in government. They thus acknowledged the close connection between the city's higher education institutions and the elite and at the same time provided a credible justification for the latter's rule. Whereas the mere artisan or shopkeeper was judged incapable of seeing beyond the narrow interests of his own guild or craft, the sons of the elite, having gone through the *Pädagogium,* could be said to have realized their human potential more fully and to have acquired the ability to embrace the wider and longer-term interests of the community as a whole.[13]

All the same, there was some support for the criticism of overemphasis on classical education among the most enterprising members of the elite—those most convinced, as Consul Thomas Buddenbrooks put it in Mann's novel, that "we musn't let the grass grow under our feet" and therefore most willing to seize the opportunities offered by new technologies, as Johann Rudolf Geigy-Merian was to do around mid-century when he ventured into the production of synthetic chemicals. Bernoulli himself had been prepared to speak out forcefully when he thought the Enlightenment approach to education was threatened. In a tract of 1825 with the provocative title *Über die Entbehrlichkeit des Latein-lernens* ("On the Possiblity of Dispensing with Instruction in Latin"), he denounced what he saw as the political and ideological authoritarianism underlying attempts to enhance the place of Greek and Latin in the school curriculum. These were aimed, he said, at "restoring the domination of the Old even in the lowest strata of the population, and at resurrecting the old obscurantism and the old blind obedience" and they would "make the more advanced schools so inaccessible to the people that, as among the Hindoos, higher understanding will remain the privilege of Brahmins and Rajahs." Some of the champions of Latin and Greek, he charged, were "less concerned to raise the level of classical studies than to suppress new ideas and new views of the world."[14] Bernoulli's was not a lone voice. The elderly pastor of St. Theodor's, J. J. Faesch, who had given energetic support to *Bürgermeister* Wieland's efforts to bring De Wette to Basel, wrote a pamphlet in which he deplored the 2,340 hours spent on Latin at the

Gymnasium and argued that *"Nichtstudierende"* would be far better off learning modern subjects than spending their time on study of the "dead languages."[15]

In the 1840s the proponents of traditional studies such as law, classical philology, and theology could well have felt increasingly under siege as the radical press fired salvo after salvo at the school system, while the moderates in the elite seemed less than fully committed to defending it. The study of Latin and Greek in particular was increasingly identified by the radicals with political conservatism; correspondingly, criticism of classical studies was now interpreted by the most conservative members of the elite as high treason.[16] But the neohumanism that had informed Latin and Greek studies in Basel since the reorganization of the schools at the Restoration was itself a complex phenomenon. As already noted, it was by no means a simple conservatism.

The neohumanist movement in Germany, which the Basel authorities tried to import wholesale into the city at the Restoration, can be viewed as a peculiarly German version of Enlightenment and, by the time it was being promoted by Humboldt, as a rejection of the French road to individual emancipation and social transformation by way of political revolution, in favor of an indigenous German road. The rediscovery of Greece and the elaboration of the neohumanist ideal were seen by Protestant Germans as the peculiar achievement of the freedom-loving Germanic or northern peoples, in opposition to the predominantly Roman or Latin statist culture inherited and developed by the the French—a kind of second Reformation. The Germans, in particular, were believed to have a special affinity with the ancient Greeks: they too were an original, unspoiled, poetic, and creative people, still in close contact with nature, not yet deformed by modern sophistication or by the utilitarian tendencies of the English and French Enlightenment.[17] The alleged similarity of the Greek and German languages appeared to confirm this spiritual affinity. The recovery of the authentic Greek spirit would thus be nothing less than the rebirth of the authentic German spirit.

The primary objective of neohumanist education, at the origins of which stood the great philologist Friedrich August Wolf and the pioneer art historian Johann Joachim Winckelmann, was the free, full, and harmonious development of the human personality. This spiritual rebirth (in the first instance of the individual, but ultimately of the entire nation or people) was to be achieved not through slavish academic imitation but through an internal appropriation of the creative spirit of antiquity as manifested above all in the very language of the ancient Greeks.

The neohumanist ideal of education as a full development of the entire human personality was clearly equally incompatible with the ancien régime division of human beings into ranks and orders, each of which has its function in the state, and with the abstract individualism of bourgeois society, which posits the formal equality of all but may actually require a high degree of specialization

of each particular individual. To that need various Enlightenment and Napoleonic programs of technical education had attempted to respond. Neohumanist
education was thus a complex project, hostile both to the ancien régime and to
the new bourgeois order announced by the French Revolution. As such, it was
well suited to the needs of Prussia in the years after Jena. It promised the renewal that everyone acknowledged was required in order to reverse the disastrous defeat of 1806 and to restore the fortunes of the state, but it did not make
social revolution on the French model either a condition or—except in a very
idealizing way—a consequence of reform. It is not surprising that the new humanist program was adopted as the official educational policy of Prussia as it
set out to mobilize all the resources of the German people in the struggle
against Napoleon.[18]

If neohumanism was appropriate to Prussia in the years of the War of Liberation, it must have seemed in some respects even more appropriate to a city-
republic such as Basel.[19] Both the neohumanist idealization of the ancient polis
and the liberal neohumanist view of the members of a political community as
fully developed individuals and free citizens must have made the doctrines of
Humboldt and his associates seem particularly congenial to the Basel elite. The
neohumanists' enthusiasm for the ancient polis won support for their educational innovations in Basel, in as much as the city leadership was glad to impart
to its own authority something of the aura and prestige of antiquity. The effects
of neohumanist teaching at the *Pädagogium* and the University of Basel were
quickly felt moreover. It is certainly not accidental that *Ratsherr* and Professor
Vischer-Bilfinger, Jacob Burckhardt's teacher, chose to address the topic of
Staaten und Bünden, oder Centralisation und Föderation im alten Griechenland in
a speech given at the *Pädagogium* a year after the passing of the new Swiss
federal Constitution. Nor that he argued, sixteen years after the *Kantonstrennung*, that in Athens "there was no question of one part of the territory's being
subordinate to another, there were no subject inhabitants of the surrounding
countryside [*unterthänige Umwohner (periooichoi)*], but the inhabitants of all
Attica were citizens of Athens."[20]

Nevertheless, the Baselers were aware of an obvious difference between a
purely commercial city of burghers engrossed in their private economic activity
and the early polis, in which public life is everything and the individual is above
all a citizen—a difference well appreciated by Vischer-Bilfinger himself[21] and
developed by his student Jacob Burckhardt in his *Griechische Kulturgeschichte*.
What made neohumanism especially welcome at Basel was a strain in it that
might seem to run counter in a way to its political aspirations: the emphasis on
culture rather than *power*, on the nation or *Volk* rather than the *state*. The association of the German and the Greek carried an implied rejection of the statist
regimes of Louis XIV, the Jacobins, and Napoleon. It was possible to see these
as modern versions of a repressive Roman tradition, contrasting with the Ger-

man (and Greek) preference for loose federations of autonomous communities. In short, the elevation of Greek signified the elevation of culture over power. Few political thinkers of the time were as concerned to limit the powers of the state as Wilhelm von Humboldt, one of the leading figures in the neohumanist movement.

It seems inevitable that this aspect of neohumanism should have exercised a strong appeal at Basel. From the time that it was taken over by the guildsmen, the city-state had effectively given up all territorial ambition and defined its political existence in conservative rather than expansionist terms. Its policy was to avoid becoming embroiled in the struggles of the great princes and powers and to protect itself from the designs of expansionist neighbors—Habsburgs, Bourbons, or Bonapartes. It even kept its distance from the more powerful Swiss cantons, such as Bern and Zurich, and from the reconstituted Swiss state that emerged after 1848 and in which, as a truncated half-canton, it had only a small voice. The Baselers tended to view their own German-ness and German-ness in general as a cultural rather than political phenomenon, and throughout the nineteenth century many were obsessed by the development of the new centralized nation-states. Vischer-Bilfinger, the powerful head of the University *Curatel,* or Board of Regents, and the man most responsible for bringing Nietzsche to Basel to succeed him in the chair of Greek, wrote and gave public addresses, as we just saw, on confederations in the ancient world; his son Vischer-Heussler specialized in the *Bünde* or city-leagues of the Middle Ages; Jacob Burckhardt himself—Vischer-Bilfinger's student and Vischer-Heussler's teacher—continued to defend the "German" position, the vision of Germany as a culture, long after it had been repudiated by "Prussian" nationalist historians like Sybel and Treitschke ("Reichs-Treitschke," as Burckhardt called him)[22] in the 1860s and 1870s. Burckhardt's practice of *cultural* history can be and was interpreted—and was, in part at least, intended—as a challenge on behalf of the smaller and weaker German-speaking communities to the political ambitions of Prussia, and as a reaffirmation of the idea of Germany as a culture against the idea of Germany as a state.

The Baselers of the middle years of the nineteenth century might well have believed that they were in some ways closer and more faithful to the neohumanist ideal than the Germans themselves. Humboldt had no doubt envisaged that those who had been withdrawn from society to be placed in direct contact with antiquity would return to the social world and help to regenerate it. It was expected that the students of the neohumanist *Gymnasium* would go on to the University where the work of rehumanizing them through the study of the Ancients would be completed and that they would then constitute a cadre of leaders and administrators capable of realizing a true renaissance of humanist culture in modern Germany.[23] In fact, however, as is well known, the classical *Gymnasium* quickly became a training ground for the public servants of the new

Prussia, a *"Beamtendrillmaschine,"* as the novelist Theodor Fontane later called it.[24] In addition, classical scholarship in Germany became increasingly professional, technical, and specialized. At Basel, on the other hand, where both the classical and the scientific programs had been designed from the start not for future professionals or specialists but for the so-called *Nichtstudierende,* neohumanist education continued to be conceived as an education for citizens, not bureaucrats or professional scholars.

It is easy to understand that the authorities at Basel embraced and promoted with enthusiasm an educational and cultural ideal that was so well adapted to the ideas and interests of the post-Restoration liberal-conservative elite and to their vision of themselves as free citizens of a small polis, rather than subjects of a monarch or cogs in a vast political or economic machine. Professors were imported from the German universities to staff the reorganized *Gymnasium, Pädagogium,* and University, and the ideals of neohumanism were quickly communicated to the students, among them both Bachofen, who was a student at the *Gymnasium* from 1825 to 1831, at the *Pädagogium* from 1831 to 1834, and at the University of Basel in 1834–1835,[25] and Burckhardt who followed him at a distance of a few years. While most of the students in the "realist" or "modernist" track turned out—like those at Bernoulli's earlier *Philotechnisches Institut*—to be practical men, men of affairs and men of action, the brightest and most imaginative students in the humanist track were filled by their teachers with noble visions of a regenerated humanity and a regenerated community. Though by its emphasis on the inner transformation of the individual it was, in some respects, a conservative doctrine—like the Pietism it both opposed and resembled—neohumanism carried a definite revolutionary charge. In Germany many conservatives quickly came to suspect neohumanist education of fomenting the political discontent among the young that resulted in the activities of the secret student societies of the teens and twenties of the nineteeenth century. Criticism of the world as it is was virtually unavoidable in a doctrine that aimed to regenerate both the individual and society through reappropriation of an inner creative power rather than traditional imitation of external models.[26]

Something of the alienation from the practical world of everyday reality that the new study of the Ancients tended to promote is communicated by Franz Dorotheus Gerlach, one of the Basel Education Department's star imports from Germany, in a speech he gave to the parents of students at the *Pädagogium* in 1822. Gerlach criticized the local champions of practical education for their meanness and lack of vision. They aim, he said, "to form useful, industrious, peaceable burghers, who, once they have grasped the usual course of things in life, will not want to hear of anything except what they already know" and will "consider anything that turns the mind toward the past or the distant future irrelevant and alien."[27] The note of utopian enthusiasm, of contempt for bourgeois "philistinism" and utilitarian specialization found in the writings and speeches of the leaders of the German student movement in the years following the War of Liberation, is still audible here, and it will be heard again among the young men—such as Bachofen, Burckhardt, and Streuber—who studied with Gerlach at the Basel *Pädagogium*. It marks both the critical distance from the contemporary world and the absence of any concrete program of practical reform that were characteristic of neohumanism. Neohumanism aimed, after all, to provide the conditions for the emergence of free creative personalities, to develop the thinking and imaginative faculties, not to prescribe the shape of a new social order.

Lacking experience of the real world, many of the young people who were filled with the ideals of neohumanism found themselves both repelled by the prosaic reality of the nineteenth century and incapable of responding to it in a positive or practical way.[28] The real world, it turned out, did not favor the full, harmonious development of all human capacities in each individual but demanded more and more specialization and division of labor. In the writings of the Baselers—both those who were born in Basel and those who were drawn to the city and settled in it—dismay at the incompatibility of neohumanist ideals and modern reality often led to criticism of modern industrial society, the growing power of the modern state, the narrowness and "philistinism" of bourgeois life, and the smug bourgeois belief in progress. And frequently, especially after mid-century, those objects of contempt were associated with the new Germany of blood and iron that was emerging under the leadership of Bismarck's Prussia.

Many of the features of modern life denounced by the Baselers were equally characteristic, however, of Basel. There were, it is true, some significant differences. Though the growing power of the people, for instance, was as noticeable at Basel as in Germany, it was hard to view the little city-state as a new Leviathan. On the contrary, the very pettiness of conditions at Basel made it possible to suffer the modern world there with irony. In Germany, on the other hand, the might of the new industrial state was so overwhelming that ironical disdain of the *Philister* ceased to be a viable option for the man of "culture" after the mid-century, and especially after Prussia's triumph in 1870–1871. Nonetheless, much of what the neohumanist-educated Baselers reviled in Prussia was to be observed in Basel itself and brought the products of Basel neohumanist education into conflict with their own increasingly industrialized society.

The city, which had hardly changed at all in size or population in the eighteenth century, grew rapidly in the nineteenth, and the pace accelerated after mid-century. The population had stood at 16,420 in 1815. In 1847 it reached 25,787. By 1860 it had climbed to 37,915, having grown more in thirteen years than in the previous thirty-two. In the last four decades of the century, it tripled to pass the one hundred thousand mark.[29] Throughout this period the number of citizens steadily declined in relation to the numbers of noncitizens—

immigrants from other parts of Switzerland and from abroad, overwhelmingly from neighboring Baden.[30] By 1860 only 27.6 percent of the population were still citizens of Basel, 42.8 percent were citizens of other Swiss cantons, and the remaining 29.6 percent were foreigners. Citizenship itself lost a good deal of its significance when the revised Constitution of 1874 extended the right to vote in any Swiss community to all Swiss citizens. The old Baselers became a minority, not only in numbers but in terms of political influence, in the city that they had dominated for over two and one-half centuries. In particular, the refugees of old who had seen their status change to that of *Herren* now felt themselves increasingly pressed by new waves of immigrants and foreigners (so-called *Neu-Schweizer*) to whom they were obliged to concede more and more political power. Finally in the wake of the new federal and cantonal Constitutions of 1874–1875, the old *Ratsherrenregiment*—the system of government that the elite had managed to control for centuries—finally came to an end.

The rise in the population corresponded to increased employment opportunities in the city. Despite severe periods of crisis, especially in the 1860s, at the time of the American Civil War, Basel's industrial development advanced rapidly in the nineteenth century, thanks principally to the entrepreneurial energy of the elite itself. Karl Bücher's statistical survey of the city in 1888 reveals that by 1870 over 50 percent of the population was dependent on industry, as against about 17 percent who were engaged in various forms of commerce. Around ten thousand persons were employed in ribbon and sarcenet weaving alone, and that figure does not include either those still working for the *Bändelherren* in the countryside or the crowds of workers who streamed into the city daily from outlying districts in Basel-Country or in Germany to work in the mills.[31] The fledgling Swiss chemical industry promoted by Johann Rudolf Geigy-Merian was concentrated almost exclusively in Basel and was expanding rapidly. By 1888, it employed nearly two thousand people and toward the end of the century its ouptut, by value, was fully one-fifth that of the entire German industry, then the undisputed leader in the field.[32] The arrival of the Strasbourg railway in 1845, of the Baden line linking Basel with the German network a few years later, and the completion of the Central Railway to Lucerne, Bern, Zurich, and then, in the 1880s, via the great St. Gotthard tunnel, to Italy and the Mediterranean ports, reinforced Basel's position as a major transit center, by far the busiest in Switzerland. By the 1870s the communications sector was one of the fastest growing in the canton.

Living and social conditions were also changing rapidly. In 1818–1819 the *Allgemeine Encyclopädie der Wissenschaften und Künste* of Ersch and Gruber described Basel as a city of *"beinahe holländische Reinlichkeit"* ("almost Dutch cleanliness"),[33] but in 1855 there was a major outbreak of cholera; in 1858 and again in 1865–1866, it was typhus. Massive immigration into the city had not been accompanied by any additional provision for sanitation. While there was much polishing and whitewashing of surfaces, the city relied on the same twenty-four drains or culverts that had been in operation since the Middle Ages to remove waste into the Rhine and Birsig rivers. The Rhine carried the waste away, but the little Birsig, into which sixteen of the drains emptied, did not. A considerable population of hens, ducks, and geese that continued to live within the city walls contributed to the filth and the stench. The drains were in poor condition. No one knew who was responsible for keeping them in repair, and there was no provision for regular cleaning. In addition, most of the houses that had a privy (by no means all) were not connected to the drains. The waste simply seeped through poorly maintained cesspools until finally it poisoned the city wells.[34] The new dyeworks and chemical works were also held responsible for polluting the drinking water, notably in Kleinbasel, and in 1864, after seven people living in the vicinity of one of those chemical works fell ill from arsenic poisoning, the city brought suit against the owner, J. J. Müller-Pack, an associate of Geigy-Merian.[35]

Conditions of work were not good for most of the inhabitants of Basel. Many people apparently had no regular job but picked up work as they found it. In 1841, it was said in the Senate that about six thousand people lived from hand to mouth within the jurisdiction of the city and thus had to be kept under constant police surveillance.[36] Those who had regular employment worked long hours. The Factory Law of 1869 finally set a ceiling of twelve hours per day with two meal breaks of half an hour each.[37] Wages were so low that they had to be supplemented by Sunday work and by whatever extra could be brought in by wife and children. The living quarters of the workers may not have been as horrendous as those depicted by Engels in Manchester, but they were crowded and unhealthy enough, and nothing was done to improve them until the cholera epidemic of 1855. In the factories, large numbers of females worked under the supervision of a male foreman or overseer and were often subject to abuse from him or from other male employees. Sixty percent of the paternity suits brought in the years around 1870 were initiated by female factory workers.[38]

The overcrowding, the factories, and the pollution were at the same time signs of the prosperity of the elite and of the new industrialists who were moving up into it. Basel fortunes in the nineteenth century were immense. According to the calculations of Paul Burckhardt, the Stadtkanton of 1840 with its 24,000 inhabitants was in relative terms wealthier than the canton of Basel-Stadt with 170,000 inhabitants in 1957.[39] Baedeker's *Guide to Switzerland* for 1857 (the seventh edition) declared that the "wealth [of the city] has become proverbial." The celebrated legal scholar Rudolf von Jhering, who taught at Basel from 1845 to 1846, once wrote that the names of the most outstanding citizens are those—"Merian, Bachofen, Vischer, Passavant, and so on"—that can be written with six or seven zeros after them.[40]

The ample fortunes of the elite left plenty over for the charitable works to which its patriarchal, paternalist style of government attributed a vitally important role. In general, the elite was opposed to state intervention and preferred to leave both the enhancement of the city's cultural well-being and the alleviation of social problems to private funds and private initiatives.[41]

The city museum in the Augustinergasse, the noblest structure in nineteenth-century Basel and the principal expression, along with the reorganized University, of the civic humanism of the liberal-conservative elite, was built entirely with funds subscribed by members of the public and foundations. The idea of a city museum that would serve as a cultural center, housing valuable collections and at the same time providing meeting rooms for the learned societies and halls for public lectures, was first mooted in the years immediately after the traumatic division of the old canton. At that time the most imaginative and enlightened members of the old elite—men like Andreas Heusler and Karl Burckhardt—were trying to rebuild the fortunes and the prestige of the diminished, but at the same time more decidedly urban and bourgeois state. The proposed museum had an obvious role to play in those attempts to restore and indeed enhance Basel's self-confidence as a model of urban culture in the new world of the nineteenth century. By 1841 a museum committee—the *Kommission des städtischen Museums*—had been formed of members of other learned and philanthropic societies such as the *Naturforschende Gesellschaft* and the *Kunstverein* to raise some sixty thousand to eighty thousand francs for the construction of the building. The following year, when the subscribers were invited to the founding of the *Museumsverein,* the estimate of the costs had risen to 250,000 francs. Nevertheless, support was forthcoming and the plans went ahead. The project was thrown open to public competition and the winner was Melchior Berri, who had studied with Weinbrenner in Karlsruhe and Hittorff in Paris and was then probably the finest architect in Switzerland. The building was completed in 1849, the famous Böcklin frescoes being added much later, in 1870.

From the beginning, therefore, the museum was the creation of the elite, whose members were largely responsible for its financing. It reflected the elite's ideas and way of life, being turned both to the past and to the present, to historical and scientific research as well as to the fine arts. One of the first museums in any German-speaking land to be founded and funded by citizens rather than a prince, it was planned from the outset essentially as a civic educational and cultural institution. Berri's austere and noble classical design, breaking with the entire tradition of baroque neoclassicism, perfectly captured the intentions of the founders. No doubt the need to convince potential donors in the Basel commercial community of the usefulness of the proposed museum partly determined its character.[42] At the same time, it does seem that the combination of an art collection with a natural history and scientific collection, a library, lecture rooms, and a public auditorium corresponded to the highest aspirations of the

The Museum, Augustinergasse.

Basel elite and to its effort to reconcile the requirements of a modern mercantile and industrial economy with an ideal of civic life borrowed from antiquity.

Even education, which was supported by the state, was also partly dependent on donations from private sources. The extensive building program that followed the reform of the school system in 1817 and led to the construction of some forty new parish schools was largely financed by gifts from individuals and philanthropic foundations.[43] Though the University had been placed under the supervision of the State Department of Education in 1817, as part of the same program of modernization, it still relied to a surprising degree on income from its own endowment and from private foundations. When Burckhardt was called back to Basel to a university chair in history in 1858, for instance, Bachofen explained to him in the letter of invitation, on behalf of the University's

Governing Board, that the ailing professor Floto, whom Burckhardt was to replace, was still drawing his salary. Burckhardt's salary of 3,700 francs, Bachofen wrote, would be contributed largely by the *Freie Akademische Gesellschaft,* an institution that, as he put it, "already stands on an equal footing, as you know, with the State, and has taken the initiative in many instances."[44]

The noninterventionist policy of the Basel government—a policy that often goes hand in hand with Protestant and especially Calvinist religious influence—doubtless reflected the values of a mercantile community whose leaders were active in business, even if they were not "self-made men." At times, however, there was tension between two of the values the policy was supposed to promote: the individual's freedom and responsibility for himself, his obligation to "help himself," and the Christian responsibility to help one's neighbor, to assist the needy, and in general to contribute to the building of a Christian commonwealth.

In the famine years of 1846 and 1847, the government was able to draw on funds subscribed by private individuals to purchase grain and sell it to the public at below cost. Eight years later, in another year of high prices, a single wealthy businessman, Christoph Merian, made cheap subsidized bread available to twenty thousand of his fellow citizens at his own expense.[45] Longer-term projects were also envisaged by private individuals and foundations. In 1846 Frau Elisabeth Burckhardt-Vischer, one of three Vischer sisters who were married young, widowed young, and childless, turned one of her properties, a handsome rococo house at 23 St. Johannesvorstadt, into a hospital for the children of the working class and hired a doctor to run it. A few years later, one of the other sisters died, leaving four hundred thousand francs to secure the future of the *Spitäli,* as it was called. A further legacy of 250,000 francs from Frau Burckhardt-Vischer herself increased the endowment to the point where the state was willing to take over the establishment. A new building was constructed on the Rhine embankment on the Kleinbasel side of the river, where the modern *Kinderspital* still stands.[46] Other well-meaning and charitable ladies opened schools for the children of the poor. The *Gemeinnützige Gesellschaft* set up various committees to study ways of improving the living conditions of the workers, the provision of salubrious and inexpensive housing, and the establishment of sickness insurance and pension funds. The "spiritual" welfare of the workers was promoted by the establishment of public lecture series, a workers' library, nursery schools, and the like.[47]

Despite these private initiatives, there was considerable support in the elite for some kind of state interference to secure minimum living conditions for the working population. Often this support appears to have come from quite conservative, well-established, actively Christian members of the elite rather than from the more aggressive and competitive industrialists.[48] One of the chief spokesmen in favor of a Factory Law and of obligatory sickness insurance for the workers was Adolf Christ, a member of an old Basel family, chairman of the Mission Society for thirty-five years, and one of the most passionate opponents of any separation of church and state. On the other hand, the chief spokesman for "Manchesterism" or complete and unrestrained freedom of trade and industry was Wilhelm Schmidlin, the son of an immigrant from Basel-Countryside, who had worked his way up to be a director of the Central Railway.[49] The lack of concern among some of his fellow citizens for the education of the children of the working classes testified, according to Karl Sarasin, himself a factory owner and subsequent *Bürgermeister*, to "the most conscienceless disregard of their obligations and to a heartless indifference that makes no distinction between men and machines."[50] In a spirit of paternalism characteristic of important sections of the commercial community, Sarasin later proclaimed that "[e]xperience has shown that limits must sometimes be placed on industrialism, that protective measures must be imposed in favor of those classes that serve industry, even against the wishes of the workers themselves. Such measures should include a minimum age for child labor, as well as compulsory school attendance, limitation of continuous and uninterrupted nightshift work, which is contrary to human nature, stipulation of a maximum number of working hours per day, enforcing Sunday as a day of rest for the workers, institution of sickness and accident insurance, regulation of unhealthy and dangerous occupations, and protection of the workers from machine-related accidents and poor working conditions."[51]

The policy of nonintervention was of course chiefly advantageous to the merchants and industrialists, and economic freedom was defined principally in their terms. Strikes were seen as an intolerable interference with economic freedom, equivalent to revolt,[52] but lockouts were an exercise of freedom. In 1837, in keeping with the principle of nonintervention, the state refused to respond to a petition for help from a large contingent of passementerie workers who had been let go in that year, and once again in 1848 the state did not intervene when the employers anticipated a workers' strike by imposing a lockout. Twenty years later, shortly after the founding of the First Workers' International, when workers at the De Bary mills demanded an additional half-day off and many of them quit work in a show of strength, the management again responded by exercising its freedom and firing more than a hundred of them. This time, however, the authorities were called on to provide police protection for those who continued to work. Though the De Bary strike was broken, the leadership of the Basel section of the International Workingmen's Association succeeded in getting all the city workers to draw up a common set of demands. When these were rejected by the employers, the workers laid down their tools in factory after factory. Workers in the mechanical workshops and in the dye works struck in support of the ribbon and silk workers. The situation became tense and threatening. *Bürgermeister* Felix Burckhardt and the Senate voted a proclamation warning the workers not to allow themselves to be led into dangerous adventures and calling on the "friends of order" to be ready to respond to the situation by foregathering at specified rallying points should an alarm be sounded. Rumors spread throughout Switzerland of an impending massacre of the workers by the burghers of Basel. A letter from Bachofen to a friend in Zurich gives an idea of the mood among conservatives at the time. It expresses disenchantment not only with modern developments but with the old *juste-milieu* "liberals" in the elite who had tried to meet modernity halfway. One catches an echo, in this report, of the old tension between the classicists and the modernists, the students of Gerlach and Hanhart and those of Bernoulli.

> I cannot claim to have been stunned with surprise at those heaven-sent events. One should never forget that every present is determined by its past. And what do we find since 1830 but revolution after revolution and a succession of regimes each of which represents a lower stage of morality than the preceding one. The worst of it is that we are not yet at the bottom, but must sink deeper still before the desire for an absolutely new foundation for society can receive any satisfaction. It is amusing to see how many so-called "liberals" are howling pathetically now that they are reaping the whirlwind that they themselves have sown. . . . There are people who only open their eyes when their moneybags are endangered. These same people take what is at best a temporary palliative for a definitive cure, whereas one thing is quite clear: that without *chassepots* there is now no sure foundation for peace and security of persons and property. Long live the freedom of the press, which is permitted to question every foundation of human existence, long live the right to free association of the international thieves who have now claimed the marvelous palladium of progress for themselves as well. It will not be long before we are going at each other with cudgels and pistols.[53]

In the end, the authorities were forced to intervene to mediate a dispute that threatened the economy of the entire city. The industrialists who at first resisted the mediation efforts finally had to accept them. The principle of state intervention and state control was thus conceded and was consecrated by the passing of the first Factory Act in 1869. The preamble to the 1869 act articulates the new situation clearly: "Since, among us also, the more patriarchal kind of relation in which workers previously stood to their employers has unfortunately been increasingly replaced by a modern conception of that relation, and workers and employers are becoming more and more indifferent to each other as individuals, among us also the state can no longer leave the condition of the industrial workers to itself but must intervene to regulate it by law."[54]

The state was visibly no longer simply one aspect of the community's life among others, such as the church or the economy. As its role was to mediate disputes between increasingly powerful opposing parties in a much more closely interwoven web of interests and interdependencies, its power was bound to grow beyond anything that the old Basel elite had imagined. In fact, by the mid-1870s the need to enhance and concentrate the power of the state was such that Basel itself, as an autonomous polity, was obliged to surrender most of its power to the centralized authority of the federal state in Bern.

The changes that had come over the appearance of the city, the living and working conditions of its inhabitants, the composition of the population, the relations among the various classes of the population—all these affected the elite too. New men were coming up, men like Wilhelm Schmidlin, the immigrant's son from Basel-Countryside who became director of a major railway company, and Johann Jacob Stehlin, also originally from Basel-Countryside, who became a highly successful architect, builder, and local political figure and was elected *Nationalrat* (or representative to the Federal Assembly) in 1860. Stehlin, who grew rich from the building boom that followed the demolition of the old city walls in 1859, was referred to disdainfully by Bachofen as *"der Bauer Stehlin, ein grober Zimmermann"* (the builder—or peasant—Stehlin, a crude carpenter).[55] By 1888, when Karl Bücher conducted the first scientific statistical survey of Basel, only slightly over half the factory owners and industrialists had been born in the city. The others were immigrants from Germany (more than a quarter of them) or from other parts of Switzerland. It is true that the influx of "foreigners" was far greater in the working population and—after the relaxing of guild restrictions in 1854 and their complete abolition in 1874—in the lesser trades, among artisans and small shopkeepers. It is quite likely, therefore, that the native merchant and industrial class remained sufficiently powerful and cohesive to impose its values and its codes of behavior on the newcomers.[56]

Within the old elite itself, however, a new economic era was undermining not only the traditional patriarchal relation to the workers (as the preamble to the 1869 Factory Act had openly conceded) but the old, more leisurely way of doing business, the old lifestyle, and the old values. To earlier generations—certainly the generation of Jacob Sarasin in the eighteenth century, but even that of Karl Sarasin in the nineteenth—business had assuredly required application and effort, but in the end the goals of business activity had been seen as partly determined by social and ethical norms. Economic life had not yet come to be thought of as an autonomous sphere with a rationale of its own. Success and failure were not accounted for solely in rational terms: in the minds of the older generation of Basel merchants, divine providence played a part in the destiny of each individual. The merchants of the early nineteenth century, having witnessed the collapse of many brilliant fortunes in the decades of the Revolution and the Empire, were if anything less inclined to speculation and risk, more canny and attentive to sound management, more restrained in their way of life, and more piously Christian than their eighteenth century predecessors.[57] Moreover, a fair number of the old-style patricians had moved toward a *rentier* existence; others still had entered the professions and had become the official representatives and guardians of "culture." In other words, no single power or value—neither politics nor religion nor economics—absolutely dominated the behavior of the old elite. Each was subject to at least some correction or limitation by the others. Similarly, the value of a life, even among those to whom, by all accounts, money mattered greatly, was not measured simply in terms of profit or productivity.[58]

The younger generation of businessmen and industrialists, on the other hand, was affected by the rapidly evolving economic circumstances of the nineteenth century. To these men, adoption of the most modern manufacturing techniques, maximization of profits, and thorough rationalization of production methods and all aspects of business practice were imperatives. They already belonged to the harshly competitive world of modern industrial and financial capitalism, whereas their elders remained to a considerable degree bound ideologically and culturally to an older style of doing business.[59] Specialization was the order of the day for this new generation, the fully rounded personality of the neohumanists an almost unattainable, increasingly irrelevant ideal. Leisure was becoming simply a short respite from work and culture a decorative ornament rather than the substance of life.

As early as 1842, the statutes of the *Gesellschaft für vaterländische Alterthümer* opened up membership to those who were interested in historical research "but who do not have the time to undertake it themselves" and who could not therefore be expected to be active participants in the society's work. In the mid-1860s the Historical Society altered its statutes in an effort to accommodate the same clientele.[60] A decade later Jacob Burckhardt, who himself did not come from the commercial branch of his family, noted in a letter to a friend the profound changes that were taking place in the way of life of the Basel businessman. "We have here a merchant class that is a noble exception in its participation in nonbusiness affairs. Yet among them I find so many individuals who have formally abjured all reading. They say 'with regret' that they have no time, but the truth is that they have no inclination, and the way business is conducted nowadays one cannot hold it against them. From time to time I catch a glimpse into the lives of those who run our big businesses, into that unending race, that continuously being at the ready to telegraph an order or a decision, that impossibility of ever shutting the shop, even when one goes home in the evening."[61] In another letter to the same correspondent—a government official in neighboring Baden—written two years later, Burckhardt evokes the profound changes in the organization of society and of work that he has observed in his lifetime, the growing rationalization of every aspect of social existence.

> We are just at the beginning of it. Doesn't everything we do now appear arbitrary, amateurish, whimsical, and increasingly ridiculous in comparison with the consummate and minutely worked out systematic organization and planning of the military? The military is bound from now on to become the model of all existence. For you . . . the interesting thing will be to observe how the

workings of the state and the administration are transformed according to the military model; for me, how school and education are subjected to the cure. . . . The most remarkable effect will be on the workers. . . . The new military type of state will have to follow the lead of the modern industrialist. Those heaps of humanity in the great human workshops cannot be abandoned eternally to their deprivation and their desire; a carefully measured and supervised proportion of misery to advancement, begun and ended each day in uniform and to the beating of drums—that is what logically must come.[62]

The most vivid emblems of the changes that had overtaken Basel were the development of the railways, which turned the city into a hub of the European network, and the demolition of the fifteenth-century town wall, which began in 1859.

There had been heated debate about permitting an extension of the Strasbourg line into Basel, as we already saw. Most of the guildsmen and even some of the elite looked with suspicion on the opening up of their city to the world that the advent of the railways was bound to bring about. But the majority of the merchants took a longer view of the benefit of the railways to the city's economy as a whole[63] and approved the project, according to the radical *National-Zeitung,* which also favored it. Indeed, Basel soon had to counteract various plans to have the railways bypass the city and displace traffic toward neighboring Saint-Louis (France) and Lörrach (Baden). The completion of the Central Railway line to Zurich and Lucerne (and later, via the St. Gotthard tunnel, to Italy) and the decision to build a large station for both the Central line and the Strasbourg line on the site of the present main railway station spelled, in turn, the last days of the city walls.

There had been talk of pulling down the walls in 1805 and again in the 1820s. City walls were widely seen as symbols of the old regime dependence of the peasants on the towns, and under liberal influence the walls of Zurich and Bern had been torn down in the early 1830s. But during the "Troubles" of 1830–1833, Basel's old walls unexpectedly proved to be a valuable defense against the rural rebels from the *Baselbiet* (who, of course, did not possess heavy artillery). In the years following the "Troubles," the argument was often put forward that the walls still afforded some protection and that, as Basel was a border city, a decision about the fate of its defenses ought not to be taken by the city alone, but required prior consultation with the federal military authorities. Similar considerations were doubtless evoked in Geneva—akin to Basel in so many ways—by those who succeeded in delaying a decision to demolish the walls there until 1849. Against all the efforts of the conservatives, however, land speculators and developers in Basel were successful in obtaining a reduction in the area of the *glacis*—the vacant area beyond the wall, on which no building was permitted. The military authorities also finally acknowledged that the walls were useless as a defense in time of war and had at best a minor role to play in policing the city. Meanwhile, the increase in traffic had required the piercing of new gates into the city. No doubt the shocking awareness of the danger to the entire population of the crowded and unhealthy conditions that had caused the cholera epidemic of 1855 influenced the *Rat* in its decision to demolish the wall. But landowners and land speculators were happy too, as the local wits were quick to note.

> Ein jeder denkt an das Staatswohl nur,
> Ist nicht für sich selber parteiisch.
> Der Güterbesitzer sähe gern,
> Dass bei ihm sich ein Bahnhof erhübe,
> Zwar nicht aus Interesse—des Pudels Kern
> Ist reine Vaterlandsliebe.
> Der kleine Kaufmann, der Handwerker ficht
> Mit einer wahren Rage
> Für das Herz der Stadt, aus Bürgerpflicht,
> Nicht wegen der Cammionage.
> Der Aktionair, der Spekulant,
> Sind frei von Egoismus;
> Sie denken an sich, aber auch auf das Land
> Aus lauter Patriotismus.[64]

The demolition of the walls altered the physiognomy of Basel. The city expanded on all sides. New residential quarters were laid out and a new sanitation system was made possible. Among the consequences of the city's expansion beyond the walls was a growing separation of classes by place of residence, though this never became as pronounced as in cities like London and Paris. While many of the workers continued to live near their workplaces, fewer of the wealthy merchants continued to live "over the shop," as their ancestors had done for generations. There was a tendency to move out to luxurious villas set in large gardens in the outlying districts beyond the old walls. One such district, the Gellert, was developed as a middle- to high-class residential quarter on land to the east of the old St. Alban Gate, previously occupied by the little vineyards and orchards of the citizenry. Many of the sumptuous villas in the Gellert were built in a variety of historical styles by the two architects, J. J. Stehlin and Son, who were quickest to respond to the changed way of life of the well-to-do and to design and build houses that would satisfy their desire for comfort, show, and a wide variety of historical and cultural reference—the sign both of their deference to the past and of their sense of being beyond it and superior to it. "The Gellertstrasse became a *via triumphalis*," writes the art historian who has studied this period most closely, of "English cottages, miniature Versailles, and Böcklin-inspired 'villas by the sea,' all set in extensive grounds."[65]

It was not only speculators who benefited from the demolition of the walls. As any profits accruing to the city from the sale of land around the old fortifications would have had to be shared with the canton of Basel-Countryside, in accordance with the stipulations of the *Kantonstrennung* of 1833, there was considerable incentive for the government to retain some of the newly freed land and develop it as public parks and gardens. Basel thus acquired many of the handsome gardens that aerate the present city in the area of the old city walls.

To many old-timers, however, the demolition of the walls probably signaled the end of Basel as it had been for centuries. A remark by Jean Cuenod, chief of police in Geneva thirty years after the walls of Calvin's city had been belatedly—less than a decade before those of Basel—torn down, would have struck a chord in the ear of many an *Alt-Basler*. "Fifty years ago," Cuenod wrote in 1879, "when our city was still closed, the population of Geneva consisted of one large family. . . . Since that time, much has changed: our city no longer has its walls, new districts have arisen where the fortifications once stood, the air circulates more freely through our streets. Geneva has been emancipated. With the expansion of the city and of our economy foreigners have streamed in, settled within the former walled area, taken over a good deal of our trade and industry and brought us progress, to be sure, but also much trouble."[66]

5

"An Archimedean Point Outside Events"
Anachronism and Modernity—
Parochialism and Cosmopolitanism

In the early nineteenth century Basel had been a small city of narrow ways: "eine Stadt ohne Geselligkeit und fast ohne wissenschaftliche Anregung" ("an unsociable city offering almost no intellectual stimulation"), in Burckhardt's words.[1] Its inhabitants lived out their lives in self-enclosed groups, shut off from each other yet observing each other suspiciously and critically. The composer and musician Louis Spohr was warned by friends in Alsace that the Baselers were "cold and ungracious, given to receiving strangers on their doorstep and terminating the visit before they could cross the threshold."[2] There were few public spaces, and there was little public life, despite the neohumanists' dream of refashioning the city on the model of the ancient polis. Each social group lived in its own sphere.

The annual celebration of *Fasnacht,* or Carnival—a unique popular survival in Protestant Switzerland, with its extravagant disguises, processions, and riotous liberties in which the entire city was supposed to participate—was viewed by the radicals of the 1840s as a token of a future egalitarian order that would replace the deep social divisions of everyday life in the city. But to the elite it seems to have served mainly as a confirmation of general solidarity and a momentary, controlled release of tension that in no way affected "normal" social differences and hierarchies.[3] In that "normal" order of things, the elite governed and went to lectures, to concerts, and to church; the artisans jealously defended their diminishing privileges and sought consolation in religious fervor and sectarianism; the noncitizen population was cowed and respectful. The poet Johann Peter Hebel, who was born in Basel in 1760 to a Swabian couple in service with *Ratsherr* Major Johann Jacob Iselin-Ryhiner, recounts that, as a child, whenever he walked in the street with his mother and they came within twenty paces of a "gentleman," his mother would remind him to stop and tip his cap: "Peter, blib doch sto, zieh gschwind di Chäppli ab, 's chunnt e Her" ("Peter, stop and take your cap off quickly, here's a gentleman coming).[4] Within the social groups, families constituted smaller, tightly knit subunits. Relations were

Tanz der Drei Ehrenzeichen Kleinbasels auf dem Fischmarkt an der Fasnacht, 1857 (*Dance of Mummers from Kleinbasel in the Fishmarket at Carnival, 1857*). Staatsarchiv Basel-Stadt PA 208,37. Photo: Staatsarchiv Basel-Stadt.

at once familiar and formal, and the pressure to conform was considerable. As late as 1866, Burckhardt—who liked to consider himself a free spirit, an exception to the rule in Basel—boasted of the unusual freedom he enjoyed. "I can go about with whomsoever I want," he wrote to a radical friend from Zurich whom he was urging to come and visit him. "'They' have long ago given up on me, and I am none the worse for it."[5] Yet even Burckhardt dutifully attended the family gatherings that were a feature of upper class life in Basel right into his old age.[6]

Two brief anecdotes, involving the two notable citizens whose scholarly work is the focus of this study, will help to convey an idea of the narrowness and pettiness that often characterized life in mid-nineteenth-century Basel. In 1846 Jacob Burckhardt described in a letter to his friend Eduard Schauenberg the elaborate intrigues that were resorted to by the religious conservatives in

order to prevent him from repeating his successful public lecture series of the
previous year on the history of painting.

> As to our more pious citizens, I have already had all kinds of experiences. I
> must tell you one of the more entertaining of these. There is a rich, highly
> respected, and very sagacious man here whom I shall refer to only as the *Rats-*
> *herr* [Andreas Heusler, publisher of the *Basler Zeitung*]. He himself is no fanat-
> ical Pietist, but he is one of the instruments the powerful Pietist clique here
> uses to pull its chestnuts out of the fire. My own relation to him was a sort of
> filial piety. He wrote the lead articles for our newspaper and the perfectly
> worked out system of political law that he expounded in these (in contrast to
> the radicals' system of pure acts of will) won me over to him. I was not too
> bothered by the fact that behind his humanity one sometimes caught glimpses
> of more of the serpent's shrewdness than one normally cares for in ordinary
> intercourse with people. I don't withdraw my trust the very first time I am
> shocked or surprised by something. Well, last winter I gave a lecture series on
> the history of painting to more than a hundred subscribers, which, in terms of
> conditions here, is quite a success. This winter I wanted to give the second part
> of the series, on art outside Italy. Others before me had given four, even up to
> six such lecture series in successive winters. . . . I wanted only one additional
> series, which could surely have been easily accorded me in view of the success
> of the previous year. However, I had offended our most pious citizens, and they
> have a long arm. Not by making indecent or frivolous comments in the course,
> but simply by altogether omitting all the theological and edifying content with
> which Hagenbach (in his quite naturally honorable way) or Gelzer (full of pious
> crap) [Johann Heinrich Gelzer, lecturer in history] had seasoned their lectures.
> As no improvement was to be expected from me, I simply had to be prevented
> from giving the second series. But anybody who is willing to rent a hall can
> lecture here, and it was not advisable to give the real reasons for preventing me
> from repeating my previous performance. I would simply have laughed in the
> faces of these gentlemen. Nor was it possible to dig up a competitor who could
> be said to have got in before me by reserving the room and the hour. So a more
> cunning approach was devised. The *Ratsherr* drew my attention to a scholar
> of the first rank here, one of the great notabilities of his discipline [Wilhelm
> Wackernagel, professor of German literature]; as he was in somewhat straight-
> ened financial circumstances, I was advised, it would be appropriate to ensure,
> as far as possible, that he should have an opportunity to give some lucrative
> lectures without my creating competition for him; since I was a friend of that
> scholar, it behooved me especially so to arrange the matter.
>
> In view of my infinite obligation to the supposedly hard-pressed scholar, I
> shelved my plans and went to see him to encourage him to give one of the
> lecture series "for a mixed public." He immediately guessed who had sent me
> and drew my attention to the fact that he was already engaged on important
> and profitable work, because of which it was both impossible for him to give
> such a series of lectures and entirely possible for him to dispense with giving it.
> Whereupon I returned home, still not ready to recognize what was actually
> going on. In the meantime an effort had also been made to get Hagenbach into
> the act, but in vain. He absolutely did not want to lecture. At this point it was

necessary to bring up the last remaining guns. The *Ratsherr* drew me aside and tried to get me to understand that it was immodest and indelicate for a young whippersnapper like me to want to give two lecture courses one after another. In order not to damage all kinds of connections, I was about to yield, even though I had been sickened by the whole business.

Finally, however, I asked a good old *ordinarius philosophiae* [Friedrich Fischer, professor of philosophy] whether it mightn't be the Pietists who were behind all this. "So it has finally dawned on you!" was the answer. Now I was fired up. I rented the hall, and posted a list for subscribers, on which ninety names soon appeared. We are still not at the end of the story. There is an academic society here [the *Freie Akademische Gesellschaft*] the function of which is to improve the standing of the University and enhance its value to the community through private donations. For years the society has awarded a grant of 300 francs as an incentive to those who plan to give public lectures to reduce the cost of attendance from two French Taler to one Krontaler. The *Ratsherr,* however, is the president of this society. He arranged things in such a way, without the society's knowledge, that, as a matter of honor, I could not accept the 300 francs. However, when I persisted in my plans to give the lectures, he himself subscribed the funds, so that no one would notice anything. Such are our Basel Tartuffes. I am now lecturing in a thoroughly unedifying manner and making the most worldly cracks that I can think up.[7]

In the second episode, Johann Jacob Bachofen explains in a letter to Peter Merian-Thurneysen, head of the Basel Department of Education and president of the three-man *Curatel* or Governing Board of the University, that he must tender his resignation from the Board because of an insult to his family from another member of the Board, Johann Jacob Vischer-Iselin, president of the Criminal Court.

Honored Sir:
  Because of an event that occurred quite recently I am obliged to resign my place on the distinguished University *Curatel.* In justification of this action I feel it incumbent on me to report the circumstances that made it necessary.
  As a result of a complaint filed by widow Iselin-Roulet against my father, three members of the Buildings Court recently carried out an inspection and measurement of a wall in our courtyard. On this occasion President Vischer, acting as the plaintiff's bailiff, made the following remark: There are two kinds of people—honorable people and those who do not deserve that name; the late Herr Iselin belonged in the first category; other people, however, belong in the second. Herr Bachofen-Merian [Bachofen's father] has spoken of friendly relations that he entertained with his neighbor; but he [Vischer] declares in the name of the Iselin family that the deceased would have been ashamed to entertain even the slightest relation with Herr Bachofen. These words were spoken by a young man to the face of a gentleman of seventy, without any reprimand from the president of the Buildings Court [the architect Christoph Riggenbach]—and by a president of the Criminal Court who must know that they constitute a punishable offence. I am sure you will understand that for me . . . any further collegial relations with an individual who flouts every rule of decent behavior in such a manner belong in the realm of the impossible.[8]

Almost a decade later, in the late 1860s, the philosopher Wilhelm Dilthey still found the air of Basel unbreathable. The suspiciousness, the defensiveness, the reserve with which people dealt with each other—"as if one had to reckon with hidden steel traps in all encounters with others"[9]—inhibited both social intercourse and public life, he complained, and were in striking contrast to the expansive, confident openness of Berlin on the eve of the Second Empire. In Basel, it would seem, religious tradition and history had combined to make the world appear full of snares.

The relations between Bachofen and Burckhardt were themselves distant and reserved. There were certainly temperamental differences between the two scholars—and one was also far wealthier than the other, a matter of no small importance in Basel. But intellectually they had a great deal in common; they had also known each other fairly well as young men, were familiar with each other's work, belonged to the same learned societies, and lived within a stone's throw of each other—the millionaire hermit in the opulent obscurity of his grand house on the Münsterplatz and the modest college teacher in his unpretentious rooms on the Sankt Albanvorstadt. Yet their contacts appear to have become more and more rare and guarded.[10] "Whenever I address [Burckhardt]," Bachofen told their common Zurich friend, Heinrich Meyer-Ochsner, in the mid-1860s, "he always seems embarrassed, almost unpleasantly disturbed. Perhaps he resents it that it was I who wrote to invite him back to Basel."[11] (As secretary of the *Curatel* at the time, Bachofen had signed the letter offering Burckhardt a permanent position at the University of Basel a few years after he had been virtually compelled to resign a previous position there and move to Zurich.) The cantankerous and extremely thin-skinned classical scholar was apparently unaware of any irony in his attributing Burckhardt's behavior to his "well known extreme sensitiveness, which with the passing years has developed into ever greater isolation and eccentricity."[12] Bachofen's few comments about Burckhardt's scholarly work hardly indicate much warmth or sympathy on his side. He did not set much store by Burckhardt's enthusing over works of art—*"molto fumo e poco arrosto"* ("a lot of smoke and not much meat"), he told Heinrich Meyer-Ochsner.[13] Above all, he appears to have suspected the slightly younger man of being too liberal. Like Socrates, he noted, Burckhardt prefers the company of "cobblers and carpenters" to that of his colleagues.[14]

Burckhardt's unconcealed distance from the Christian belief of his youth was doubtless another reason for the pious Bachofen to look on him with distrust. Only in face of the common foe—the Prussian *viri eruditissimi,* as Burckhardt called them—do we find Bachofen making common cause with his fellow citizen. When a German scholar and associate from his Berlin University days (Eduard Gerhard, the founder and director of the German Archaeological Institute in Rome) suggested to Bachofen that "Jakob Burckhardt would do better

to leave antiquity out of the sphere of his esthetic endeavors," Bachofen immediately asserted the latter's right to study antiquity from his own point of view.
"Antiquity has room enough for every one to find his place in it," he protested.[15]
Whatever else might be said about him, Burckhardt was "an original and unusual spirit."[16] On that basis Bachofen was no doubt ready to defend him
against the highly organized Prussians.

The pride of the city's elite, the University of Basel itself—with which the
writers and thinkers who will occupy us in the rest of this study were closely
associated—was by current German standards poor and cramped in spite of all
the city's efforts to upgrade it. In 1845, when Rudolf von Jhering was called to
a chair of law there, there were no more than sixty-two students enrolled in all
four faculties. In 1869, the year Nietzsche was appointed professor of Greek,
the total number had just passed the hundred mark.[17] By 1880, Burckhardt
boasted to a German friend that the number of enrolled students had reached
the unheard of figure of 250. "There have been times when Freiburg did not
have so many," Burckhardt noted with humor.[18] Compared with the major
Prussian universities—in 1834 Berlin had 1,777 students, Bonn 828, Breslau
951, Halle 844, Konigsberg 431[19]—these numbers are derisory. Even diminu-
tive Greifswald, with 217 students in 1836, was more considerable than Basel,
which had sixty students that year.

The unusually close ties between the University and the city no doubt imparted to the former a good deal of the spirit of the latter. To those on the
political left, the University seemed part of the apparatus of elite domination.
With only two exceptions, the entire professorate, "liberals" and conservatives
alike, had sided with the city in the "Troubles" of 1830–1833, and for decades
thereafter the radical press derided the professors as lackeys of the merchants,
and the University itself as a backward establishment that had no standing anywhere outside Basel.[20] "One can measure how beneficial and significant its influence is within our walls," the *National-Zeitung* wrote sarcastically, "by the
incredible rush of students to come here from all corners of the globe and by the
great satisfaction the majority of our citizens derive from an institution which is
so useful and so appropriate to our needs."[21] But even the *National-Zeitung*
acknowledged that while there was much to find fault with in the University—
above all the narrowness and conservatism of its curriculum, its slowness to
embrace newer and more modern disciplines, its subservience to the interests
of the elite—the guildsmen and merchants who criticised it were usually motivated only by anti-intellectualism, "hostility to all intellectual and spiritual life,
to whatever does not bring immediate and tangible material advantage."[22]

No wonder the high-spirited Jhering preferred Rostock, one of the less prestigious of German universities, to Basel. As a north German, he wrote in a
letter to Bachofen, he could never get used to Basel ways, especially to the dominance of the moneyed class, which made it necessary for professors to possess

"eine grosse Gewandheit im Bücken und Schmiegen" ("great talents in bowing and scraping").[23] Jhering's letter underscores the drawbacks of the close connection at Basel between the elite and the University. It was a disadvantage as well as an advantage that professors were not regarded as an autonomous, professional class distinct from the rest of the citizenry but were expected to play their part in the limited social life of the city. Purely professional qualifications were for that reason not always sufficient to ensure appointment to the faculty. As late as the beginning of the twentieth century, Wilamowitz answered an inquiry about candidates for a chair in classics at Basel by observing that one of the most qualified (he was referring to Giorgio Pasquale, then his student) was totally unsuitable socially: "In einem alten Hochsitz wirklich vornehmer gesell-schaftlicher Cultur wie Basel ist er einfach unmöglich." ("In an ancient seat of truly refined social culture such as Basel he is simply unthinkable.")[24]

As industry expanded, as communications became increasingly easy and frequent, and as the population itself was swollen by immigrants from all parts of Switzerland and southwest Germany, the narrow world of old Basel gradually changed, giving place to a somewhat more open, impersonal, and unfamiliar one in which the city was destined inevitably to lose some of its distinctiveness along with some of its narrowness.[25] In this transformation from a small medieval-looking city-republic into a moderate-sized, nineteenth-century industrial town, Basel was gradually overtaken by Zurich. As the center of a large and populous canton, Zurich had far more political clout in the new federal Switzerland and emerged more and more after 1850 as the largest and most dynamic city in the country, the center of the modern machine tool industry and, increasingly, of the modern banking industry.[26] The new University of Zurich and the Federal Polytechnic, which the Baselers had tried unsuccessfully to have located in their own city, had likewise grown faster than the ancient but rather conservative institution to which Burckhardt had returned in 1858.[27] It seems likely that the old Basel families looked on Zurich, which owed most of its success to "new men," with something like the envious disdain they expressed more openly for Berlin, especially during the *Gründerzeit,* the period of rapid expansion following the founding of the German Empire in 1871. But Berlin and Zurich were only *relatively* more brash and vulgar, in the eyes of old Baselers, than the new Basel. And the outbursts against Prussia and Berlin by Bachofen and, on occasion, Burckhardt too may well have had targets closer to home.

Bachofen and Burckhardt observed the transformation of Basel with growing unease. To both, as to many others in the elite, the developments they deplored in Europe as a whole and saw as a threat to the culture and political independence of their native city—the rise of popular democracy and the formation of mighty nation-states capable of mobilizing vast populations—were of a piece with the transformations they observed with dismay in Basel itself:

the growing power of the "masses" (in which they lumped together not only the ever increasing numbers of factory hands and state employees, but new self-made men; the influx of foreign workers and the arrival of foreign entrepreneurs; the development of the railway network, factories, and banks; the heightened communications with the world outside and the slow disappearance of the old Basel ways; the altered conditions of business; even the new buildings, the construction of entire new districts, the planting of public gardens where once the old walls stood. In 1872 Burckhardt wrote that Basel was being "ringed round with railway constructions: it gives you a feeling of emptiness and sadness. Embankments, cuttings, and a ceaseless whistling and wailing, that is what our future holds."[28] Bachofen saw his fellow citizens putting all their energy into "credit banks and other swindles that go by the name of Progress."[29] When his friend Meyer-Ochsner of Zurich asked him to find out about investing in one such "swindle"—the *Basler Handelsbank*—he provided quite detailed information and had his father subscribe fifty shares (at a cost of about five thousand francs) on Meyer-Ochsner's behalf. "I myself have not participated in the affair," he wrote, however, "because I have a particular dislike of these institutions" (*"Ich habe auf alle diese Institute einen speziellen Stich"*).[30]

The social and industrial crisis of 1868 only confirmed Bachofen's skepticism about "this much touted civilization" and the "demi-culture that is being propagated by newspapers and popular lectures."[31] By the beginning of the eighties, he was grumbling bitterly that a rootless, alien population had taken control of the old city-republic and transformed it into a hideous modern metropolis. "Bâle officielle," he wrote in French to a Genevan correspondent,

> ne mérite pas les éloges, dont vous comblez notre ville, car ce que vous en dites ne peut avoir trait qu'aux vieux éléments indigènes de la population, éléments devenus l'objet de haine et de poursuite à une majorité qui a son origine dans tous les pays de l'Europe centrale et cherche avant tout de vivre et de s'amuser aux frais d'autrui. Quel beau ideal qu'une petite république gouvernée non par les gens de bien mais par la populace animée par les passions les plus hideuses. Quelle presse, quel usage de la liberté d'écrire et de publier tout ce que le bon sens et la moralité condamnent et rejettent! Que les héros de Saint-Jacques sont à plaindre d'être devenus après quatre siècles le beau prétexte de mauvais principes! Hélas, un Winkelried serait-il mort pour une liberté pareille à celle qui nous accable? Ah, si ces grands hommes revenaient, ils se couvriraient le visage pour ne pas voir ce que nous sommes devenus. . . . S(entina) P(opuli) Q(uondam) B(asiliensis): voilà l'explication des quatre initiales qui brillent sur plus d'un de nos bâtiments publiques.[32]

The older Basel of the early years of the nineteenth century with its frock coats and cocked hats, its orthodox Calvinists and Pietists, had seemed at times a cramped and depressing place to many besides Friedrich Engels. The generation of Bachofen and Burckhardt in particular had been encouraged by an enthusiastic cohort of neohumanist teachers at the *Gymnasium* and the *Pädagogium* to imagine that Hellas might be resurrected in the free city-republic of Basel and that their state might thereby recover some of the glory it had enjoyed during an earlier Renaissance. De Wette, for instance, had repeatedly compared Basel to the ancient Greek cities, encouraged the development of public spirit and public life, and advocated the institution of festivals and games to promote civic unity and "kindle noble zeal and emulation." In addition, De Wette had argued that, since "patriotism cannot prosper without publicity," the administration of law and the administration of government should be public. "[P]ublic judgment upon national affairs should be free, and each one should be able to state his mind regarding them, either with pen or voice, in order that a free public opinion may be formed."[33] The young men who had been raised on these ideas and who were sent abroad—to France, to England, to Berlin—to complete their education were often impressed by the public character of life and culture they found in the first two countries, just as they were intoxicated by the idealism and intellectualism of Berlin. To many of them the return to Basel was a devastating experience.

The young Bachofen, for example, wrote home to his friend von Speyr in Basel of his enthusiasm for the public character of life in Paris where he was spending the year 1838–1839 learning about French law. The contrast between the openness of French public life and the narrow provincialism and secretiveness of Switzerland, and of Basel in particular, left him discouraged.

> The public character of things is what dominates the entire scene here, in every possible way. You don't pay a single sou to visit the greatest art collections and the most important cultural institutions, to see all the great buildings, to attend sessions of the High Court, to go to all the courses in the various educational institutions, to listen to the speeches in the Chamber. The French are far superior to the Germans in this respect; and this public character of things is truly made use of by the population. Everywhere there is active participation in public affairs and events. No one tries to do what we still did a few years ago in Basel, when any one who was not formally enrolled as a student at the university was absolutely prevented from attending any classes. . . . I find all this beautiful, quite beautiful, and the sign of an enlightened government. Everything that facilitates public and general education is a step forward, a service to the state. . . . Next to the public character of life, what is especially striking here is the enormous degree of centralization and the resulting immensity of all the public institutions. The Faculty of Law alone has as many students as the entire University of Berlin. Naturally, the more energy and effort are combined in a single whole, the greater the result. If we in Switzerland could only be convinced of that simple principle, we would have a single really significant central university, at least for the German-speaking cantons, instead of three small, insignificant universities that no one pays any attention to. I have always held this view and I was reminded of it when I heard that at a salary of 800 francs it had proved impossible to discover any professor willing to replace the late Adolf Burckhardt. It is a disgrace to expect to get a professor for 800 francs. But

rivalry, envy, and suspicion among the cantons are so deep-seated that each of them would rather go it alone with 800 francs or even less than try to achieve something worthwhile with three times 800. What is to be done? Nothing. But it is certain that nothing worthwhile will ever emerge from our present conditions.[34]

Bachofen's resigned perception of Swiss conditions as irremediably parochial and petty coincides with that of other observers coming from different backgrounds and holding different political views, such as Engels and Gobineau, who was First Secretary at the French Legation in Bern from 1849–1854.[35] His eulogy of his friend Wilhelm Streuber, who had been a fellow student at the University of Berlin and who on his return to Basel became an untenured professor of Latin at the University and one of the editors of Heusler's *Basler Zeitung* (from 1847 to 1856), contains one of the most moving testimonies to the cramped and stifling cultural climate at Basel. Bachofen quoted from a letter Streuber wrote to his father in which he conveyed his apprehension at leaving Berlin—which he clearly experienced, like many young Baselers at the time, including Bachofen himself, as a center of intellectual vitality, a new Athens— in order to return to the old commercial city on the Rhine. "I see that I shall soon be leaving this place, to which I owe so much, that I shall no longer enjoy the intense intellectual exchanges that are the rule here, and that I must return to my native city where, for all my respect for it, an iron commercial spirit and a crude materialism dominate everything to an excessive degree. Do not think that I lack respect for Basel: it has great qualities of many different kinds, and in recent times, thanks to the influence of the cultivated men who are now at the helm, it has made considerable progress." But, Streuber continued, culture and education were still not highly regarded at Basel. "Unfortunately, there are people among us who consider themselves cultivated; indeed, they do know what philology is. But when they consider the vocation that I have taken up— the noblest that there is, that is to say: the study of the immortal spirit and soul of Man—they are at best moved to observe, with a shrug of the shoulders: 'Poor fellow! He won't go very far.'"[36]

Only a few years later, Burckhardt, who had also returned from Berlin to Basel, wrote to his friend Gottfried Kinkel that "Basel strikes me as so tedious and mean-spirited that I am grateful to the good Lord for granting me even a winter in Berlin. No decent person can stand it for long here among those purse-proud merchants."[37] And in 1851, even Gerlach, once so confident that the vision of antiquity he worked so hard to promote among the young people of his adopted city would win out over orthodoxy and Pietism, confessed in a letter to Bachofen, who had been his student and had become his friend and collaborator, that he was relieved to be getting away for a few days "from the nest," even if it was only to attend a Philological Congress in Erlangen. "With all its qualities," he conceded, "our good town of Basel has an overwhelming tendency to tedium and narrow-mindedness. One breathes them in, God knows, with the very air."[38]

If the old Basel had been depressing and mean, however, the city that was emerging in the second half of the nineteenth century—the Basel of factories and banks, railways and chemicals, opulent modern villas and new avenues and public gardens—was not exactly what the students of Gerlach and Hanhart had dreamed of, and it did not inspire them with much confidence or enthusiasm. Nothing essential had changed for them, except the pace of commercial activity and the ever-growing influence of the new industrialists and the working people—who together made up the "masses."

The new Basel, with its easier links to the outside world and its huge foreign-born population, seemed only more dominated by narrow commercial motives and more exposed to the dangers of demagoguery and international revolution than the old, cramped, but socially and politically stable city-republic of the 1820s, 1830s, and 1840s, which had survived the *Kantonstrennung* with surprisingly little damage. The conservatives themselves had become opportunistic, according to Bachofen. "Convictions are put up for sale, egoism emerges completely naked; . . . the good of the state is not a goal but a pretext."[39] In such circumstances it was impossible to retain the respect of the people. "Das junge Basel taugt nicht viel" ("The new Basel isn't worth much"), he wrote sourly in 1868.[40]

Still, compared to those states, such as France and Prussia, that were even further advanced on the road of modernization, Basel's marginal position in great power politics could be seen as an advantage; its very parochialism and provincialism were qualities by which the city-state might be held back for a while from the abyss to provide an excellent observation post for the historian. There was no turning back, to be sure, and regeneration would be possible only after the road had been traveled to the bitter end.[41] But in the meantime one could "stay at one's post," as Burckhardt wrote, and salvage whatever one could of the old culture.[42]

Neither Burckhardt nor Bachofen believed it was possible to turn back the tide. But if open battle was pointless, quiet resistance was not. To the citizens of a city-republic visibly under great pressure from History, the fact of historical success was not in itself a justification of anything. On the contrary, standing up for one's principles against the steamroller of "modern" ideas and facing down the smug doctrine of "Progress" was a moral imperative, as Burckhardt made clear when he defended Demosthenes' resistance to Philip of Macedon, in his lectures on Greek culture in the 1860s, against Droysen's contemptuous dismissal of it as historical blindness. In Bachofen's case taking an independent position meant arguing—in an age of ruthless industrial and political competition, ever-expanding state and military power, and European colonial conquest—that the complex "feminine" web of tradition was no less important in the construction of culture than the "masculine" drive for innovation, that hierarchy and community were equally indispensable in any society, that authority was not the same as domination, and that the exercise of it was in fact incompatible with violence. It meant adopting the standpoint of the cultural historian or anthropologist rather than that of the political historian, and eschewing the forward-striving narrative form in which the latter's historical optimism was enshrined. In Burckhardt's case, resistance to "modernism" was a significant factor in the decision to pursue cultural history and the history of art rather than political history, and here too that decision affected the scholar's writing: the relentless forward surge of historical narrative was replaced in all Burckhardt's work, from *The Age of Constantine the Great* (1851) on, by paintings made of many short brushstrokes and accumulations of synchronic tableaux.

Certain features of Basel's situation in the modern world seem to have made the old city-republic congenial to those who were out of step with the prevailing optimism and progressivism of nineteenth-century thought. But if the city was well placed to serve as a *refugium* or place of refuge for these men, it was at the same time an *exilium*, a place of exile—and not only for Nietzsche and Overbeck, who came to Basel from Germany, but for the native sons Bachofen and Burckhardt also. The connection between Basel as a society and the critics of modernism who came to be associated with it should probably not be thought of as causal (a certain society "producing" a certain ideology) but rather as coincidental, a matter of converging interests. A conservative elite had succeeded in holding on to power and influence in Basel for far longer than anywhere else in Switzerland—not least, ironically, as a result of the *Kantonstrennung,* through which the disastrous struggle with the rebellious inhabitants of the countryside had finally been brought to a close and which older Baselers continued to resent for many years. The elite's defense of its peculiar polity made it keenly conscious of the tradition of learning and intellectual independence it had inherited from the Renaissance and the Reformation, and sympathetic to dissidents and heretics critical of the new world of popular democracy, the nation-state, and the mass literary market. At the same time, the hiring policy adopted by the city for its relatively impecunious University led it to seek out young and promising scholars, of whom those eager to be part of mainstream academic culture moved on in due course to more lucrative and prestigious positions in Germany, while the quirkier ones, those that were alienated from the reigning opinions and scholarly currents of their time, remained behind, finding Basel, because of its eccentricity, more tolerable and tolerant than the institutions of the new German Reich. Burckhardt pointed out on several occasions that even Imperial Rome, in contrast with modern states like Germany and France, did not much interfere in cultural matters and made little attempt to control them.[43] Culture was not yet seen, then, as an instrument of state power or a territory to be appropriated by the state. In comparison with Germany or France, the very weakness of the state in a small city-republic like Basel was an advantage from the point of view of the artist or intellectual. Petty interferences were to be expected, but there was no danger of a massive takeover. Above all, professors and artists were not regarded as employees or officers of the state and therefore subservient to its ends. They were seen as pursuing long-established cultural objectives that are independent of any state.

The historian Emil Dürr explained the peculiar "fit" between Burckhardt and his native city in the second half of the nineteenth century as an unexpected result of the *Kantonsstrennung*.

> In the year 1833, in consequence of a revolution, Basel experienced the great political misfortune, as is often said, of separation from its surrounding countryside. But if one considers the higher, cultural fate of the city, this separation was its true good fortune. For it was only because of that separation that Basel and its urbane culture were spared from falling under the influence of the country districts, the peasants, and the populations of the small country towns; it was only because of that separation that it was saved from the cultural and moral centralization that was the fate of all other Swiss cities and urban cultures—with the exception of Basel and Geneva. Basel did not have to go through the process of complete democratization and rationalization until 1875 . . . but in the meantime, it had consolidated, expanded and saved its urban culture. That urban and urbane culture always remained the climate that best suited Burckhardt. And so it came about that this city-state, created forcibly out of a revolution, allowed Burckhardt to live as what he truly was: a cosmopolitan in that high spiritual sense and in that ideal world imagined and lived by a Schiller or a Goethe, or by the ancient Greeks themselves.[44]

Portrait of a City from
Romain Rolland's *Jean-Christophe*

He was living in an old town, full of intelligence and vitality, but also full of
patrician pride, self-satisfied, and closed in on itself. A bourgeois aristocracy
with a taste for work and the higher culture, but narrow and pietistic, was quietly convinced of its own superiority and of the superiority of its city and was
quite content to live shut off in family isolation. It was composed of ancient
families with vast ramifications. Each family had a day for a general gathering
of the clan. They were hardly at all open to the outside world. These influential
houses, possessing fortunes generations old, felt no need to show off their
wealth. They all knew each other, and that was enough. The opinion of outsiders counted not at all. Millionaires dressed like humble shopkeepers, they spoke
in their own raucous dialect, with its pungent expressions, and went conscien-
tiously to their offices every day of their lives. . . . Their wives prided themselves
on their domestic skills. Their daughters received no dowry. Rich men had their
sons go through the same hard apprenticeship in their turn that they themselves
had served. In their daily lives they practiced strict economy. But they made
noble use of their huge fortunes in collecting works of art, in picture galleries,
and in social work: they were forever giving enormous sums, nearly always
anonymously, to charitable foundations, to enrich the museums. . . . This small
world, for which the rest of the world seemed not to exist—(although its members knew it thoroughly through their businesses, their far-flung family and
commercial connections, and the long trips to far-off places that were a required
part of the education of their sons)—this small world, in which fame and reputation acquired in another land only carried weight after they had been acknowledged and accepted at home, subjected itself to the severest self-
discipline. Every member of it kept watch upon himself and upon all the others.
The result was a collective conscience that covered over all individual differences (though among these robust personalities differences were more marked
than in other places) with a veil of religious and moral uniformity. Everybody
was a practicing and believing Christian. Not a single soul had any doubts, or
none would admit to any. It would have been impossible to know what went
on in the depths of those souls, which had sealed themselves off from prying
eyes all the more hermetically as they knew that they were the focus of the most

intense scrutiny and that every one claimed the right to examine the conscience of others. It was said that even those who had left the country and imagined themselves liberated were caught up again in the traditions, habits, and atmosphere of the town the moment they set foot in it again. Even the most skeptical had to practice and believe. . . . It was never admitted that a man of their world could be absolved of his religious obligations. If a man did not practice their religion, he was at once unclassed, and all doors were closed to him.

Even the weight of all this discipline was apparently not enough for them. They did not find the bonds of caste sufficient. Within the great *Verein* they had formed a multitude of small *Vereine* in order to tie themselves up completely. There were several hundreds of those. . . . There were *Vereine* for everything: for philanthropy, for good works that were charitable and commercial at the same time, for the arts, for the sciences, for singing, music, spiritual exercise, physical exercise, and simply to provide an opportunity for meeting and enjoying themselves together. There were *Vereine* for different city neighborhoods and for each guild or corporation. There were *Vereine* for men of the same social position, the same degree of wealth, the same weight, or who had the same forename. . . .

Beneath this triple corset formed by town, caste, and association, the soul was cramped and bound. Character was repressed by a hidden force of constraint. The majority had been brought up to it from childhood—had been for centuries. . . . Moreover, they found it wholesome. They would have considered it improper and unhealthy to go without such a corset. Their satisfied smiles gave no indication of any discomfort they might be feeling. But Nature took her revenge. Every now and then some individual personality in revolt would emerge, some vigorous artist or unbridled thinker who would brutally break his bonds and give the city fathers something to worry about. They were so clever that, when they did not succeed in nipping the revolt in the bud, when the rebel proved to be the stronger, they never got involved in a long, obstinate struggle. . . . They bought him up. If he was a painter, they found a place for him in the museum; if he was a thinker, in the libraries. It was useless for him to shout himself hoarse with outrageous observations; they pretended not to hear. His protestations of independence were made in vain; they incorporated him as one of themselves. . . . But such cases were rare, most of the rebellions never emerged from obscurity to the light of day. Unsuspected tragedies were played out in those quiet houses. . . .

These solid burgesses, who were hard upon themselves because they knew their own worth, were much less hard on others because they esteemed them less. They were even quite liberal in their treatment of foreigners who, like Christophe, had taken up residence in the town—German professors and political refugees—because ultimately they felt indifference toward them. Besides, they loved intelligence. Advanced ideas held no terrors for them: they knew that they would have no effect on their sons. So they behaved toward their guests with a cold cordiality which kept them at arm's length.[1]

PART TWO

Johann Jacob Bachofen

As no Time stretches before it, I imagine that the Divinity surveys all historical humanity in its entirety and finds value everywhere. The idea of the progressive education of mankind contains indeed an element of truth, but in the
eyes of God all the generations of Man appear equally justified, and that is
how the historian too should see things.
— Leopold von Ranke, *Über die Epochen der neueren Geschichte*

Johann Jacob Bachofen. Universitätsbibliothek Basel, Porträtsammlung.

6

"An Exile in My Own Homeland"
Withdrawal and Renunciation

Like many other families in the elite, the Bachofens had immigrated to Basel. Heinrich Bachofen, a tailor from eastern Switzerland, became a citizen in 1546. Two centuries later the Bachofens' star began to rise when Johann Jacob Bachofen (1701–1784) married the daughter of the ribbon merchant Martin Strub and at the age of twenty-three became a partner in his father-in-law's well-established firm. On Strub's death the business passed entirely into the hands of the Bachofen family, where it remained for the next 180 years. During the eighteenth century, fortunes were made by the Basel *Bändelherren*. The Bachofen business seems to have been particularly well run.[1] It survived the economic crises of the Revolutionary period, of the continental blockade, and of the nineteenth century, and was dissolved only in 1906, when the family itself died out.

The success achieved by Bachofen-Strub's son, Martin Bachofen-Heiz, enabled the Bachofens to become integrated into the elite through the usual web of marriages. One of Martin's daughters married a Merian, another a Burckhardt, while his only son Johann Jacob married Helena Burckhardt, the daughter of the head of another ribbon firm and later *Bürgermeister*, Peter Burckhardt-Forcart. But the family tradition was one of piety and austerity. The Bachofens tended literally to mind their business, did not seek political office, and eschewed high living. Bachofen-Strub is said to have been something of a recluse who did his best to restrain what he saw as a propensity for luxury and ostentation—characteristic of a time of growing fortunes and increasing worldliness—in his son Martin Bachofen-Heitz (whose wife's portrait by Roslin was evoked in an earlier chapter). When Bachofen-Heitz went to Frankfurt or Strasbourg on business trips, the elder Bachofen apparently insisted that he use the same riding breeches and boots and the same raincoat that had already served him on such occasions.[2] To Bachofen-Heitz's son, Johann Jacob Bachofen-Burckhardt the Elder—the scholar's grandfather—the specter of financial ruin facing his father-in-law, *Bürgermeister* Peter Burckhardt-Forcart, could well have been a warning not to neglect business for politics or to speculate too adventurously in real estate. The scholar's father,

Johann Jacob Bachofen-Merian, continued the conservative tradition of the family. In a *Short History of Ribbon-Weaving in Basel,* written at a time of increasing worker militancy in the mid-nineteenth century, he deplored the relaxing of discipline and deference, the "unrestrained character of the modern age, the war of each against all," and the "disdain, especially in our day, that is the sole reward granted to our ancestors and to the past."[3] A relative of his wife, Valeria Merian, remarked of him that he was "not a sociable man" and that he looked with suspicion on everything outside his immediate family.[4]

The immense wealth acquired by the Bachofens can be surmised from their impressive real estate holdings. The original Bachofen *Fabrik,* or factory—a combination of family dwelling, business office, warehouse for the silk yarn distributed to the weavers in the countryside, and stockroom for the finished products delivered by the weavers and shipped to markets throughout Europe and the world[5]—had been in the old Friedhof in the Petersgasse. Under Bachofen-Heitz it was moved to the Rollerhof (bought from the wealthy Joseph Ochs) and the adjacent Zum Mägerlin, directly on the Münsterplatz, which were rebuilt and embellished in up-to-date rococo style. At the same time, following the example of other *Bändelherren,* Bachofen-Heitz acquired a fine country house—built after plans by Samuel Werenfels, the leading local architect—in the Basel countryside near the village of Sissach, where he could indulge his passion for hunting. Though the Sissach property was sold by Martin's widow in 1816, the family acquired other country houses in Weil, Lauwylberg, and Frenkendorf. Subsequently, at the time of the troubles in the countryside, the Frenkendorf house was sold and another property (presently the Institute for the Deaf and Dumb) was purchased in the more conveniently located nearby village of Riehen, which was included in the new half-canton of Basel-City. After the accidental death of his daughter there, Bachofen-Merian sold this property as well. In its place he bought a house in the Klybeckstrasse, beyond the old Bläsitor in Kleinbasel, where for sixteen years his family spent the warm summer months.

In 1811 Bachofen-Burckhardt the Elder again moved the headquarters of the firm, this time to one of the most desirable properties in Basel, the imposing baroque Weisses Haus on a rise overlooking the Rhine. This remained the chief office of the Bachofen company until it was dissolved in the early twentieth century. A little over a decade later, Bachofen-Burckhardt's son, Bachofen-Merian, commissioned the leading neoclassical architect of early-nineteenth-century Basel, Melchior Berri-Burckhardt, the brother-in-law of Jacob Burckhardt, to design a house for him on the Sankt-Alban-Graben (presently the city's Museum of Ancient Art, opposite the modern *Kunstmuseum*). After his marriage to Louise Burckhardt in 1865 Bachofen-Merian's son, Johann Jacob Bachofen-Burckhardt, the scholar, had a new house built on the

Münsterplatz—until then he had lived in his father's house—to plans by the well-regarded architect Christoph Riggenbach.[6]

All these fine properties had to be furnished and decorated and that is no doubt the origin of the Bachofens' rich art collection. Begun by Bachofen-Strub and abundantly enhanced by Bachofen-Heitz and his son Bachofen-Burckhardt the Elder—both of whom spent carefully, sought expert advice, and became themselves increasingly knowledgeable as collectors—it now belongs, by a bequest of the scholar's widow, Louise Burckhardt, to the Basel *Kunstmuseum.*

On his mother's side, Bachofen belonged to one of the largest and most distinguished families in the city. Unlike the Bachofens, the Merians—who were in many lines of business, from fine printing and engraving to general merchandising and banking—also served the city frequently as *Bürgermeister* and *Ratsherren.* In addition, they produced a large number of university professors and scholars of European reputation, such as the philosopher and translator of Hume, Johann Bernhard Merian (1723–1807), who became Perpetual Secretary of the Berlin Academy under Frederick the Great. Two of Valeria Bachofen's uncles were partners in the notoriously successful firm of Merian Brothers that amassed a fortune by skillfully exploiting every loophole, legal or otherwise, in Napoleon's Continental Blockade and thereby won for the family name the Emperor's undying hatred. Burckhardt once observed merrily that the income of one of these brothers, Christoph Merian-Hoffmann, was considerably greater than that of the Crown Prince of Prussia.[7] Christoph Merian-Burckhardt, Merian-Hoffmann's son and Valeria Bachofen-Merian's cousin, used his immense wealth to set up a foundation that financed important community projects in the city, such as the rebuilding of the Middle Rhine Bridge, the Women's Hospital, a large new wing of the City Hospital (since demolished), part of the Insane Asylum, and the Trade School, and that continues to be a significant force in the life of Basel to this day. It was in the elegant eighteenth-century garden house of the Ritterhof, the home of his maternal grandfather, Samuel Merian-Hoffmann—which his father and mother occupied in the years immediately following their marriage—that Bachofen himself was born, as the young couple's first child, on December 22, 1815.

The future scholar and writer thus belonged to the cream of Basel society, was heir to one of its greatest fortunes—even if, in typical Basel fashion, the full extent of the family's wealth was never displayed—and might well have expected to play a considerable role in the city's government if he chose to do so. As a child and then as a young man attending the various educational institutions of his native city, Bachofen could look around him and find everywhere confirmation of his family's prominence: at Sunday Church services, which were, of course, attended regularly; on the customary visits to other members

Birthplace of Johann Jacob Bachofen, Ritterhof, Garden house.

of the family and at "family day" receptions; in the many handsome *hôtels parti-culiers,* all in close proximity to his own house and all Basel landmarks, where members of his family lived—his pious great-aunt Margreth in the Rollerhof, his paternal grandparents and his Burckhardt cousins in the Weisses Haus, his maternal grandparents in the Ritterhof. In the summers, like other elite fami-lies, the Bachofens would move to one of their properties in the countryside immediately adjacent to Basel.

At the age of four, Bachofen was enrolled in Herr Munzinger's private infants' school, which his father had attended as a child and where the three-and-a-half-year-old Jacob Burckhardt was to follow him a year afterward. At six, in

1822, he transferred to the best-run public elementary school in the city, the *Münstergemeindeschule,* which was a stone's throw from his home. At the *Gymnasium,* then presided over by a student of the great neohumanist classical scholar Friedrich August Wolf, the young Bachofen gradually distinguished himself, and in 1831 was selected to read the German oration (three orations were read by the best students, one in Latin, one in French, and one in German) at the graduation ceremony in the Cathedral, before the two *Bürgermeisters* and the assembled members of the state Cabinet. The topic chosen by Bachofen was "On Patriotism" (*Über die Liebe zum Vaterlande*): the fifteen and a half year old undertook solemnly, as a citizen of the republic of Basel, to promote the public good, following the example of the heroes of antiquity and of Swiss history, and to combat evil through dedication to religion and the pursuit of knowledge.[8]

Bachofen's religious faith, which was to inform all his writing and which appears never to have been disturbed, was instilled in him by his pious, churchgoing family and reinforced by Jacob Burckhardt's father, the *Antistes* or chief minister of the state church at Basel (who had less success with his own son).[9] It was the elder Burckhardt who prepared Bachofen for confirmation in the Cathedral in 1833, two years before young "Köbi." An officially approved *Lehrbuch des christlichen Religionsunterrichts für die Kirchen des Kantons Basel,* compiled by the elder Burckhardt and published anonymously in that same year, gives an idea of the religious teaching Bachofen received at the minister's hands. The harshness of orthodox Calvinism was moderated, in Burckhardt's catechism, by Enlightenment, Pietist, and humanist influences. In particular, the doctrine of predestination was distinctly underplayed. Instead, emphasis was placed on the preeminence of man as the noblest part of creation and on God's desire that his creature share in eternal life.[10] That was a theme to which Bachofen frequently returned as a scholar in later years. It justified his conviction that the study of history was more important than natural science. "The human is always the highest, not nature, from which, despite their close relation, the human is separated by an infinite gulf. Besides, since all understanding presupposes kinship, we are capable, in some measure, of understanding only the human spirit."[11] Likewise, *Antistes* Burckhardt taught that all the good in man was not eradicated as a result of the Fall. "Traces of the image of God are still present in man." For that reason "the heathen who do not know the Law, nevertheless act naturally according to the Law, and as they do not have the Law, they are for themselves a Law. They demonstrate that the work of the Law is inscribed in their heart." The lesson was evidently not lost on the scholar who later wrote in defense of the most ancient cultures and peoples that with the introduction of new laws, "what is virtue comes to be called sin, and following the path of duty is branded error." But in fact "there is no sin in polyandry, none in promiscuity," and as a consequence "generations of human beings, who

saw in one or the other of these social arrangements the rule of conduct of their
lives and in the religious observance of traditional ways the fulfillment of their
highest duty, carry no burden of guilt."[12] Above all, the entirety of Bachofen's
historical and anthropological work on "Mother Right"—the law of an early
matrilinear and matriarchal phase that Bachofen believed occurred in all societies—can plausibly be read as an expansion of the answer given in Burckhardt's
catechism to the question "What is the nature of the body?" That answer ran:
"The body is indeed of the earth, but it is so fashioned that it may become the
instrument of the soul and the temple of God."

When he entered the *Pädagogium* in the fall of 1831, Bachofen was enrolled
in the two-year modern track (*Realisten-Abteil*), where the subjects studied
were mathematics, physics, chemistry, natural history, mechanics, and technology, together with modern languages and some history, rather than in the
three-year classical or humanist track with its heavy emphasis on Latin and
Greek.[13] No doubt, as he was the eldest of Bachofen-Merian's three sons, he
was expected to take over the running of the firm, and a broad general education, with an emphasis on modern subjects, was considered appropriate. By the
middle of the first year, however, his passionate interest in philology and history
had declared itself and his parents allowed him to switch to the classical track.
Soon he was impressing all his teachers with his dedication, enthusiasm, and
imaginativeness. Their influence on him is likewise unmistakable. Though he
turned out to be more conservative politically than his French teacher, Alexandre Vinet, a confirmed liberal, he responded eagerly to Vinet's historical and
cultural approach to the study of literature and to his Jansenist sympathies in
religion. (Until Sainte-Beuve, with whom he later developed a close friendship,
Vinet was the leading Pascal scholar and interpreter of the nineteenth century.)
The same general approach to literature was promoted by the German teacher,
Wilhelm Wackernagel, whose *Deutsches Lesebuch* Bachofen took with him on
his first journey to Rome.[14]

The young Bachofen's greatest debt, however, was to his Latin teacher, Franz
Dorotheus Gerlach, an ardent champion of neohumanism but also a loyal defender, during the *Wirren* of 1830–1833, of the city government that had appointed him to his position at the *Pädagogium* and the University and entrusted
him with the education of its sons. As Gerlach became increasingly conservative in his outlook after the *Kantonstrennung* (the final Latin theme he set for
Bachofen's graduating class at the *Pädagogium* in 1834 was "De bello civile" and
it is apparent that the students were expected to treat it with Sallustian severity), it was easy for his favorite pupil to collaborate with him later on an unsuccessful *History of the Romans,* of which the first and only volume appeared in
1851.[15] After Gerlach's death in 1876, Bachofen continued to look after the
interests of his widow.[16]

It was during those student years also that the future scholar struck up a friendship with several students who had been brought from Greece to study at the *Pädagogium* in a program devised by De Wette and others to serve as a nonrevolutionary alternative to the Philhellenic movement. The plan was apparently to educate an elite of young Greeks in Basel and send them back to work for reform in their homeland. Bachofen appears to have kept in touch with these men, for years later, at the time of his own journey to Greece in 1851, he renewed his early relationship with them. When he graduated from the *Pädagogium* in 1834 Bachofen had the reputation of being "undoubtedly one of the best students formed by the institution since its founding."[17]

In 1834–1835 Bachofen went on to the University of Basel to pursue his studies of history and philology. His teachers were essentially the same as at the *Pädagogium,* notably Gerlach in Latin and Wilhelm Vischer-Bilfinger in Greek. In addition, he probably took some courses with the theologian De Wette, who was so highly regarded in the city where he had found refuge from persecution in Germany that Burckhardt's mother thought of sitting in on his classes.[18] There certainly seem to be echoes of De Wette's teaching in Bachofen's later work. De Wette had interpreted the entire Old Testament canon, together with a good part of the New Testament, as myth rather than factual history but had sought at the same time to rebuild what he might seem to have destroyed by rehabilitating myth and symbol, in the spirit of his friend Georg Friedrich Creuzer, the widely read Heidelberg philologist and mythologist, as valid sources of historical understanding. As a consequence of his endeavors, as he himself understood them, dogma might appear shaken, but not the authority or validity of the biblical narratives. Bachofen and Gerlach were to adopt a similar approach to the sources of early Roman history. De Wette also laid great store, as Bachofen was to do (and as Humboldt had already done), by *Ahnung,* or "divination," as an instrument of historical understanding by means of which the scholar may sometimes arrive at privileged instants of insight transcending anything he might hope to achieve by rational and analytical processes alone.

One of Bachofen's professors at the University of Basel—he referred to him in later years as "my teacher of blessed memory"[19]—was Johannes Georg Müller, the author of a work on the religion of the American Indians. The influence on the young Bachofen of Müller's course on "The History of Polytheistic Religions" is probably to be seen not only in the mature scholar's keen and growing interest in nonEuropean cultures and religions, but in the unshakable faith, underlying all his work, in the universality of religious experience among all the peoples of the earth. Likewise Müller's attitude to "natural" or polytheistic religions and their relation to monotheism anticipates that of his student. With all his genuine respect for "natural" religions, Müller always insisted that they end in pantheism ("among the German philosophers as among the Hindoos") and that there is a radical difference between them and monotheism. The latter may well instruct man through nature, but it always leads the human spirit beyond nature to the point where it becomes aware of itself as "different from the world, even though not separate from it."[20]

For a small institution, the University of Basel offered a range of interesting courses taught by men of some intellectual distinction. At the time Bachofen began his studies, however, it was going through a crisis. Impoverished by the settlement with the country districts in 1833 (the city had had to buy back the share of the University attributed to Basel-Country by the terms of the *Kantonstrennung*), it had had to curtail its offerings drastically and was virtually reduced for a time to serving as a feeder to the German universities, where most students had to go to complete their professional preparation.

In the spring of 1835, therefore, Bachofen matriculated at the University of Berlin, where he spent five semesters, until August 1837. Although no longer, in the last years of the reign of Frederick William III, quite the New Athens it had seemed to be in the first two decades of the nineteenth century, Berlin was still an exciting, stimulating place in the mid 1830s. To Bachofen, it offered an exhilarating contrast with Basel. Its recently founded university, one of the glories of the neohumanist movement, seemed to be a token of the cultural regeneration neohumanism promised. In contrast to the University of Basel which was old, poor, and provincial, and was frequented almost exclusively by students from Basel and vicinity (and by not many of them: the total enrollment in 1835 was forty students)[21], Berlin had two thousand students[22] drawn not just from Prussia but from all the countries of central Europe, as befitted a capital that many thought better suited than Vienna to serve as the center of a revived German nation. Its professors made up probably the most distinguished academic body in the world. Hegel, Friedrich Schlegel, and Schleiermacher had died, but Bachofen studied history with Ranke, philology with Böckh and Lachmann (characteristically, the only one of his teachers to whose instruction—a critical, closely textual philology—he failed to respond), geography with Karl Ritter, and law with Savigny. Above all, Berlin was not dominated, as Basel was, by business and money. Over twenty years later, in a eulogy of a fellow student from those days—the modest, rather unsuccessful Wilhelm Streuber, who took over the editorship of the *Basler Zeitung* after Burckhardt gave it up, but in the field that commanded his deepest interest never got to be more than an untenured lecturer or tutor at the University—Bachofen recalled "the magic which the Friedrich Wilhelm University exercises on sensitive and eager young minds." In contrast to Basel, where, as he was to put it in a long autobiographical letter written later to Savigny, "study for study's sake is something that is not understood by a people whose character is distinguished by practical concerns,"[23] in Berlin "the combined presence of so many respected scholars, the high position they occupy, the importance attributed to scholarship in life and in the state, the coming together of so many hundreds of young men, filled with the desire to learn, from all the German speaking lands, all this highlights the beauty and dignity of the scholarly life." No doubt Bachofen was not aware that among those hundreds of young men in his own last year at Berlin was Karl Marx, who also followed Savigny's course.[24] Bachofen was considered an unusually devoted and committed student at Berlin, and he never forgot what he learned there. References to the writings of his teachers are frequent in his later work.[25]

By 1837 Bachofen appears to have decided to take his degree in law rather than philology. In all probability, he chose to spend the winter semester of 1837–1838 at the University of Göttingen in order to take courses in Roman law with Gustav Hugo, the founder of the historical school and an older friend of Savigny's. The switch to law did not mean that the interest in philology and classical antiquity that had led him to abandon the modern track for the classical one at the *Pädagogium* years before had abated. On the contrary, Bachofen also attended the lectures of Hugo's colleague at Göttingen, the great classicist Carl Otfried Müller, to whom he had been provided with a letter of introduction by his old Latin teacher Gerlach,[26] and he always insisted that "it was philology, from which I started out and to which I returned, that led me to the study of law." In this respect, he wrote in his autobiographical letter to Savigny, "my attitude to my scholarly work has always been the same. I saw Roman law as an integral part of classical and in particular of Latin philology, that is to say, as a piece of the great whole embraced by classical studies [*die klassische Altertumswissenschaft*] in general."[27] In addition, he pointed out, as judges in Switzerland are unremunerated and are usually laymen rather than trained professionals, the study of Roman law for a Swiss has little practical value. "Nowhere has jurisprudence been less debased into a career-related object of study [*'zum Brodstudium herabgewürdigt'*] than among us," and for that reason "the historical study of law has been raised to a level of disinterestedness that is one of its greatest virtues."[28] The preeminence of classical philology and the disinterestedness or nonutilitarian character of scholarly study were, as we saw in chapter 4, the two fundamental principles of neohumanism. Clearly, there was no break between the student at the Basel *Pädagogium* and the future Dr. Iuris. In fact, Bachofen's extreme emphasis on the nonutilitarian and nonpractical aspect of legal studies, his distrust of all attempts at legal codification, and his determination to treat the study of Roman law exclusively as a branch of historical study were to lead two decades later to a disagreement with his teacher Savigny, whose position in this regard was more flexible than Bachofen's.

The long autobiographical letter Bachofen wrote to Savigny on that occasion, explaining and justifying his position, indicates that it had been Savigny who turned Bachofen toward the study of law. Savigny's teaching, however, was of a piece with that of Ranke and Böckh. All three belonged to the "historical school," and it was their combined influence—the general outlook of all three rather than any specific theory—that won Bachofen's allegiance and is discernible in all his work. More than a theory or method, it was a common outlook or worldview, notably opposition to Enlightenment rationalism, that held the school together and defined it. The components of the historical school's worldview have been described as "reverence for the old, the ancestral, the product of organic evolution; sympathy for the truly popular, for tradition and national culture; recognition of the privilege of everything that has developed organically or has come to be historically over what has been artificially constructed; preference for the authentic and the original; love of the individual and particular; delight in diversity and plurality."[29]

The historical school of law, in particular, of which Savigny was the outstanding representative, opposed the natural law theories of the Enlightenment and denied both the need for and the possibility of a codification of German civil law, such as had been proposed at the highpoint of the Prussian reform movement in 1814. To Savigny a rationally grounded code of law was an impossibility, since law is an organic historical development and, like language, custom, and political constitution, an integral part of the culture of a people: "Law grows and develops with a people, and dies off when a people loses its specific historical character."[30] It is separated from those other manifestations of a people's energies and activities only in thought, not in "nature" or reality. The legitimacy and authority of law is thus grounded in its relation to the historical evolution of the people among whom it lays claim to legitimacy and authority. The key to the formulation of new law is correspondingly a deep understanding of the legal tradition, both in Roman law and in the older German law. And just as the imitation of classical antiquity for the neohumanists was not a mechanical imitation of the products of classical culture but rather fresh creation in the spirit of classical culture, it was not blind admiration for Roman law that was expected of the legal scholar, since "it would be fruitless and foolhardy to recommend a return to that past condition."[31] Rather the legal scholar was expected to investigate the very roots of the law in Germany in order to unearth the organic principle that would allow the legislator to distinguish what is still living from what is already dead and lost to the past. The historical legal school could fairly claim that its aim was not mere conservatism, resistance to change, but the grounding of legislation in the historical legal tradition. History thus took the place, for Savigny and his followers, that reason held for the natural law theorists, and historical study usurped the place occupied by rational philosophical reflection in the field of jurisprudence. For reason was now seen as itself subject to history, not independent of it; consequently, any attempt to put law on a purely rational basis, without consideration of the historical situation, was bound to fail.[32]

Bachofen never wavered in his commitment to the essential doctrines of the historical school or in his opposition to the natural law theorists, whom he probably viewed as apologists of Jacobinism and revolution. There is no record of his having taken any courses with the leading light of the philosophical or rationalist school at Berlin, Eduard Gans, whose polemical exchanges with his colleague Savigny reached their height in the late 1830s. The war between the two schools, a French jurist wrote, is "spectacular. In the historical school they are afraid of philosophy. . . . In the philosophical camp, they look down with pity on the purely historical jurists."[33] Bachofen, as we shall see, always claimed—as Burckhardt was to do—that he distrusted philosophy and that his method was "empirical" and historical. In 1839, just after he had returned to Basel from Göttingen and on the eve of a journey to France and England, one of his student friends wrote him enthusiastically of the instruction he would derive from observing the practice of English and Scots law, since they are not founded "on abstractions and metaphysical speculations" but on "a thousand years of history." They cannot be considered in abstraction from the life, manners, and history of the English and Scottish peoples, the correspondent declared.[34] Many years later, Bachofen reiterated his opposition to all efforts to rationalize the law. In 1866 a committee was appointed to draw up a new civil code for Basel, but when *Bürgermeister* Carl Felix Burckhardt wrote to Bachofen inviting his opinion, as an appeals judge, of the committee's work, Bachofen declined to respond on the grounds that he could not approve of "this entire legislative enterprise." He was thoroughly opposed, he explained, to "extending the search for novelty into the area of civil law" and he also "could not share the expectation that a comprehensive code will improve the administration of justice and raise the level of our jurisprudence here. Experience . . . teaches us that the regimentation of juridical thinking by legislative prescription benefits neither the study nor the practical application of the law."[35]

In 1838, after first returning to Basel to write his doctoral dissertation and take his degree, Bachofen left to spend a year in Paris. The following year he was in England. The proficiency he acquired in both French and English later allowed him to correspond freely with French- and English-speaking scholars. In Paris he took courses at the Ecole de Droit and followed the lectures on political economy given at the Collège de France by Pellegrino Rossi, an Italian expatriate and citizen of Geneva, who had helped to make the work of Savigny known in France and Switzerland.[36] He also worked briefly in the office of a French law firm. In England, he studied law and English legal practice in London and at Cambridge, read Bacon, Blackstone, and Burke, spent some time in Edinburgh, where he had introductions to a number of Scottish lawyers,[37] and traveled as far north as the Hebrides, one of the great romantic travel destinations. "No year in my life has been so rich in work, instruction, and enjoyment as the one spent in England," he later declared.[38]

While it was normal for sons of the leading Basel merchant houses to spend time learning the business and improving their foreign language skills with one of the home firm's foreign associates—in Italy, in France, in England, or, as in the case of Bachofen's brother Carl, in the United States[39]—Bachofen's two-year sojourn in France and England seems to have had other objectives. Most probably, since he showed considerable scholarly and intellectual talent and no inclination to enter the family firm, it had been decided that he should be groomed for public service as part of the elite's plan to introduce a degree of professionalization into its government of the city without resorting to a professional bureaucracy. The influential Andreas Heusler may even have had a hand in designing Bachofen's program of foreign study, since it closely resembles that followed by Heusler himself several years before. The idea appears to have been that the young scholar would return to Basel after acquainting himself with the laws, institutions, and customs of the two chief European powers and combine a professorial appointment in law at the University with public office. That, at any rate, is what seemed about to happen. Six months or so after his return to Basel, barely turned twenty-six, Bachofen was appointed Professor of Roman Law at the University of Basel; in the following year (1842), he was called to fill the first vacancy on the bench as a criminal court judge; and in 1844 he was elected to the Senate.

Almost immediately, however, Bachofen's public career began to unravel. Questions were raised about his University appointment. The *Neue Basler Zeitung,* which as suggested by its subsequent title *Schweizerische National-Zeitung* was the liberal radical counterpart of Andreas Heusler's *juste-milieu* conservative *Basler Zeitung,* demanded to know what such a young man had achieved to merit appointment to a chair at a large salary in a field with virtually no students, while other professors and lecturers at the University, who did not have his vast private fortune, were miserably remunerated and vital modern subjects were not taught at all, because the University claimed to lack the resources to hire qualified staff.[40] In a way Bachofen himself was incidental to the polemic, which was directed not at him personally but at the elite's alleged high-handed governance of the University as though it were a private fief and, implicitly, at Heusler's pervasive influence in all affairs of state. Nevertheless, to a young man, who probably did not question that he deserved to occupy a high position in his community because of his fortune, social position, and brilliant education, it was probably extremely distasteful to see his name dragged through the mire of public polemic in the newspapers. Sensitive and haughty, Bachofen did not respond but preferred to withdraw in contempt, as he would do again and again. "Scholarship is generally held in low esteem in our country," he wrote to Savigny. "Whoever is not in tune with the spirit of the times in trade and industry gets put down."[41]

In 1844 Bachofen resigned his university position, and a year later he gave up his seat in the Senate. As a man of learning and a contributor to the academic treasury, he continued to be consulted on appointments to the University

Residence of Bachofen after his marriage to Louise Burckhardt, Zur St. Johanneskapelle, Münsterplatz 2.

and he served briefly on the *Curatel,* or Governing Board, from 1855 to 1858, when he once again resigned on account of an alleged insult. (The episode in question was described in chapter 5.) To all intents and purposes, however, Bachofen's public career in Basel was over before it had even begun. He was to spend the rest of his life as a private scholar, living almost like an exile in the heart of his native city—first in his father's house on the Sankt Alban Graben, then, after his marriage, in the handsome house he had built in the very center of the city, on the Münsterplatz—yet never thinking of leaving. In 1850, for instance, he declined an invitation to fill the chair of Roman law at the University of Freiburg.[42] Unlike his near-contemporary Burckhardt, who was also to feel himself alienated from Basel, Bachofen never found a satisfactory way of restoring his connections with the city's community life. He served for many years as an appeals judge and kept up with the more interesting appointments at the University—Nietzsche, for instance, was a regular guest at his home— but his most intense and sustained exchanges were with people outside Basel, above all with his Zurich friend Heinrich Meyer-Ochsner, a wealthy private scholar like himself. He also kept up an active correspondence with a number of individuals in Geneva, France, Belgium, and the United States who had similar interests to his own. He never contributed to the public lecture series that were a tradition of Basel cultural life and that made Burckhardt a familiar and popular local personality. He read several papers at the city's learned societies, but desisted even from that degree of participation when the societies tried to open up to a larger public. "My life revolves around my family, my studies and some close friends," he wrote to Meyer-Ochsner in 1867. "Nothing else has any value anyway."[43] By the time of his death in 1887 Bachofen was virtually unknown to his fellow citizens, except for a few older men, such as Burckhardt, who knew of his scholarly interests.[44]

His disappointment and bitterness were expressed in veiled personal remarks, in the increasing conservatism of his political views, and in his frequently proclaimed disenchantment with the evolution of affairs in Basel and in the world generally. He appears to have found some relief from his sense of rejection and alienation only in frequent scholarly trips abroad to Germany, France, Italy, Spain, England, and Greece; in the maliciousness, typical of the so-called Basel spirit, with which he described the events and personalities of his native city to his many correspondents;[45] and above all in his scholarly work, the character of which is unlikely to have been unaffected by the role it played in his life, as a refuge from the present. *"Monotonie sans égale,"* was how he described his day-to-day life in what he called *"dem langweiligen Musen- und Fabriksitze Basel"* ("the boring seat of the muses and of factories, that is Basel").[46] Without new ideas and projects for scholarly work, "existence, at least in dreary Basel, would be an impossibility for me."[47] Whenever he did get away, especially to Italy, "the idea of having to return to our Basel philistines [*zu unsern Basler Kümmertürken*]" filled him with "real dread."[48] His little niece Anita was smart to spend the winter in the south of France, he told her. The first storks had been spotted in Basel, heralding the return of spring. But they sounded "hoarse from the cold Basel air" they had to breathe. "If I were a stork, I would not come to Basel, but would follow your example and sit in the sun instead of a heated room."[49]

The study of other times and other places was an escape not only from Basel but, above all, from the depressing political reality of a world fast sinking into the abyss of democracy, nationalism, militarism, and materialism. "If I am not depressed," Bachofen wrote, "it is only because I am little occupied with the present and live instead in the tranquilizing world of my studies." In the aftermath of the Franco-Prussian War he returned to this theme: "I have never felt as intensely as I do today the value of an activity that distracts our minds from contemporary events and silences the dismal thoughts provoked by the lugubrious spectacle presented at this moment by the history of civilized Europe."[50]

Before the scandal that led to his resignation from both the University and the Senate, Bachofen appears to have been moderately liberal—the way young Germans and Swiss raised on neohumanism were at the time. By joining the

Zofingerverein—a national association of well-meaning, moderately reform-minded Swiss students from well-to-do families established in 1819—he declared his opposition to the narrow and restrictive *Kantönligeist* (exclusively local patriotism and parish pump politics) prevalent among his countrymen and his sympathy with the goal of a more unified Switzerland than had survived the Restoration. In an address to the Basel *Zofingia* in 1834, on the anniversary of the Rütli oath, the legendary founding act of the Swiss Confederation—Bachofen was then nineteen years of age—he praised his native country as one of the few states that owed its origin to an act of popular will rather than the dynastic ambitions of a prince.[51] This was not a strikingly original or radical position to take, but not an extreme conservative position either.

Three years later, in a letter to Gerlach from Göttingen, he expressed his disgust at the summary dismissal of seven university professors (the so-called Göttingen Seven—among them the Grimms, Dahlmann, and Gervinus) who had protested at the suspension of the Hanoverian Constitution.[52] In 1839, as we saw in chapter 5, the man who later deplored every extension of state power wrote enthusiastically from Paris to his friends in Basel about the advantages of a centralized state, the intellectual and artistic vitality it promotes in the capital, and the open public character of all state institutions in France, in contrast to the secretiveness of public administration at Basel and the jealously guarded local autonomies of Switzerland.[53] One thinks of Burckhardt's youthful determination, when he took on the editorship of the *Basler Zeitung*, not only to oppose the "raucous Swiss radicals" but "to exterminate . . . the odious sympathy . . . among the ruling clique [in Basel] for absolutism of every kind."[54]

The circle of devotees of Savigny in which Bachofen moved in his mid-twenties—it embraced French, Italian, German, and even Greek scholars[55]—was not composed of diehard conservatives either. As Donald Kelley has pointed out, Savigny at this time "loomed as large on the European scene as did Guizot and Goethe, and his teaching was . . . adaptable to politics right or left."[56] Pellegrino Rossi, for instance—whose kindness to him during his stay in Paris Bachofen later recalled in his so-called autobiography (written in the form of a letter to Savigny), and to whom he had been recommended by his Göttingen teacher Gustav Hugo—had been an Italian patriot with Joachim Murat, the self-styled King of Italy, and then a professor of law and a liberal parliamentarian in Geneva, before being called by Guizot to fill the chair of political economy at the Collège de France after the July Revolution. Rossi had the reputation in Switzerland of being a moderate liberal: he advocated limited reinforcement of the authority of the Diet with respect to the individual cantons, some extension of the suffrage, and public reporting of debates in cantonal senates. A strong champion of Savigny against the "dogmatic" natural law schools, Rossi believed that Europe had entered upon "the third reformation of the new social era, the legislative reformation" which, though "less dangerous in its effects and more immediately useful than the political revolution," nevertheless "follows the same path and is the product of the same causes." For him, the partnership instituted by Savigny between Clio and Themis, history and law, was a condition of the "social revolution."[57] That Bachofen carried a letter of introduction to him and that he expressed his admiration for Rossi's course, which he called the best at the Collège de France,[58] seems to confirm his own *juste-milieu* political position at this time.

Edmond Laboulaye was another French Savigny follower with whom Bachofen established relations in these years. On the eve of a projected trip to Paris in 1844 he had asked a German disciple of Savigny, Leopold August Warnkönig of Tübingen—one of the moving spirits behind the organ of Savigny legal doctrine in France, *La Thémis*—for a letter of introduction to Laboulaye because of the "similar orientation of our studies."[59] Laboulaye himself had studied in Germany, had written a sympathetic *Essai sur la vie et les doctrines de Frédéric-Charles de Savigny* in 1842 (subsequently he succeeded still another of the French Savigny scholars, Eugène Lerminier, as professor of comparative law at the Collège de France), and his interest in the history of the social role of women parallels Bachofen's, for in 1843 he published his *Recherches sur la condition civile et politique des femmes depuis les Romains jusqu'à nos jours*. A staunch defender of private property against what he saw as the utopian fantasies of the socialists of his time, Laboulaye remained all his life an outspoken champion of liberalism in France and later devoted himself to the study of American culture and the advocacy of American democracy.[60] Some of Bachofen's Paris friends from the late 1830s and early 1840s—with whom he kept in touch throughout his life—would later tease him on account of his extreme conservatism. Congratulating him on his marriage in 1865, Henri Michelant, an editor of French medieval literary and historical texts and the keeper of French manuscripts at the *Bibliothèque Impériale* in Paris, warned him, with a playful reference to his work on Mother Right, that "tout votre échaffaudage de despotisme, . . . comme tous les despotismes, même les plus intelligents, est moins solide qu'on ne pense. . . . Vous serez obligé de partager le pouvoir sur une foule de questions et si Mme Bachofen est habile, et elle le sera, soyez-en sûr, elle rétablira l'équilibre par un système de pondération quelconque. Vous supprimez les journaux, fort bien, pas de liberté de la presse, mais vous ne pouvez supprimer la liberté de penser, et c'est la plus dangereuse de toutes. Enfin n'oubliez pas que sous les gouvernments despotiques les mieux établis, ce sont toujours les influences féminines qui règnent."[61]

In Rome, as in Paris, Bachofen moved in moderately liberal circles. During his fist visit there in 1842–1843, he was an habitué of the *Società storica romana*, a gathering of patriotic and idealistic young intellectuals, who met at the home of the U.S. Consul in Rome, George Washington Greene, on the Via del Quirinale, near the Quattro Fontane—"*il centro di quanto di generoso e di liberale viveva allora in Roma."*[62] An entry in his travel notebook entitled "dispute with Pantaleone [*sic*] at Greene's" is an early sign that he did not share all the views that were expressed at the group's meetings. (Diomede Pantaleoni, a doctor, patriot and politician, worked on behalf of Cavour, played a role in the Revolution of 1848 in Rome, and served as a senator in the new kingdom of Italy.) But he remained in touch with the men he met at Consul Greene's house for years. Pantaleoni's many references to Bachofen's *Mutterrecht* in his own *Storia civile e costituzionale di Roma* (Turin, 1881) suggest that the two men maintained personal and scholarly contacts long after their first meeting at Consul Greene's in the early 1840s.

Bachofen's inaugural lecture at Basel, "On Natural Law and Historical Law," which he gave on May 7, 1841, is true to the ideas of the historical school of Ranke, Savigny, and Grimm. Referring frequently to Bacon and Burke, Bachofen first aligned himself with the empiricist, who submits to the existent and grounds his understanding on objective realities independent of the ideas of particular individuals or particular generations, and against the rationalist, who is accused of constructing his theories arbitrarily out of his own mind and with complete disregard for the existent. That is recognizably an antirevolutionary, Restoration stance, as is the rejection of the radical Hobbesian pessimism on which some modern theories of law are founded. Law, according to Bachofen, is not the result of the Fall, nor a means of preventing further degeneration. It is not a *Kunstwerk,* as Burckhardt might have said, not something artificially contrived. As far back as we can see, there never was a condition in which man lived without laws or an organized community. On the contrary, "in ancient times, the state contained everything; religion itself did not exist separately or independently of the state." Far from being an arbitrary convention, the state—according to the student of Ranke—is "the embodiment of our better nature—not a dam to prevent an even greater fall, but a 'brothering' ['*Verbrüderung*'] for the purpose of attaining the highest ends, a combining of our best energies in every field of science, art, virtue and perfection." Correspondingly, law, to the student of Savigny, is like language, "the unconscious expression of the popular spirit [*Volksgeist*]."[63] As such, it is not rigid and unmoving but evolving; in fact its function is to facilitate the progress of man and society toward ever higher moral and spiritual achievement. That is the law of the cosmos itself, to which man and his institutions are no less subject than the rest of Creation.[64]

To those who accused the historical school of honoring only the past and knowing no higher law than positive law, Bachofen replied that it is the historical school that recognizes "in the finite a revelation of the infinite and in the earthly a gradual development toward perfection." For the aim of the historical school is to "free the historical from the reproach of arbitrariness and lawlessness." On the contrary, the historical school attributes to every historical entity and to every age its place and meaning—a meaning that lies not in the destruction of what preceded, but in its fulfillment, in the progressive realization of a perfect law that is, however, at the end, not the beginning of history.[65] In this process, every age, every people has its part to play, and the ultimate goal is not national perfection but the perfection of all humanity. Nationality, if it were the highest law, would isolate peoples from each other and inhibit progress. Thus it is a mistake to regret the displacement of the old Germanic law by Roman law. The former knows only the group, it does not recognize the individual as an autonomous legal person or the corporation as an autonomous legal entity within the state. In Rome, in contrast, private law was developed to a high degree. For that reason Roman jurisprudence is an invaluable gift that should be hailed and revered, even though it came from the hands of another people.[66]

Thus Bachofen's (and Savigny's) evolutionary conception of law is presented as truly compatible with the historical progress of man and society (albeit this progress has a markedly spiritual and nonmaterial character) whereas the eternalist and universalist notions of rational or natural law are presented as opposed to historical evolution. Bachofen's position, which owes much, as is obvious, not only to Savigny but to Ranke and—beyond Ranke—to Herder, seems not substantially different from that of Rossi with his idea of a "legislative reformation . . . less dangerous in its effects and more immediately useful than the political revolution." It was opposed to radical reform but not incompatible with moderate reformism.

It was probably a combination of the personal humiliation and failure he suffered in the early 1840s and his shocked reaction to political developments in Switzerland and in Europe in the mid and late 1840s that led Bachofen to take up a much less optimistic and more rigidly conservative position than he had occupied in his youth. Before the outbreak of the 1848 revolutions all over Europe seemed to put an end to what Burckhardt later described as the "illusions" of the "spirit of 1830" (that is, of *juste-milieu* conservative liberalism),[67] the optimism of many in Switzerland had already been shaken by events peculiar to that country. The Basel elite, in particular, had been alarmed by the so-called *Züriputsch* of 1839, in which the liberal government of the canton of Zurich, in itself not very sympathetically regarded at Basel, was toppled as a result of a violent popular protest, beginning in the country districts and spreading to the city, against the appointment of the controversial liberal theologian David Strauss to a chair at the new University of Zurich. Two years later, in a climate of increasing polarization of religious and anticlerical groups, the radical regime in canton Aargau reacted to pressure from religious conservatives by forcing the closure of eight convents. The Catholic government of canton Lucerne responded by abrogating the laws against the Jesuits and inviting them to return to take over their schools again. This move outraged the Protestant liberal cantons. In December 1844 and again in April 1845, brigades of volunteers from all over Switzerland—the so-called *Freischaren*—were organized for a march on Lucerne to bring pressure on the cantonal government. The upshot of the growing unrest was the Swiss civil war or *Sonderbundkrieg* of 1847.

Though Basel remained loyal to the Confederation when it finally came to armed conflict, there was a good deal of sympathy among the elite of the staunchly Protestant city with the conservative Catholic cantons.[68] Liberty, for the elite, meant above all the rule of law, which they saw as their chief protection against the arbitrariness of "tyrants" and "demagogues" alike. As a result, they had a scrupulous, almost superstitious respect for legal procedure. In 1837 Bachofen had reacted to the dismissal of the "Göttingen Seven" by expressing indignation at the "tyrannical decrees of the Hanoverian Prince."[69] In the internal Swiss context, however, the law represented first and foremost a barrier to popular pressure and tyrants were often associated, as in antiquity, with democratic and popular parties rather than patriciates or aristocracies.[70] The popular uprising that had overthrown the liberal regime at Zurich and the demagogic character of the popular Catholic parties in Lucerne and Schwyz were viewed with almost as much consternation at Basel as the efforts of the radical *Freischaren* to overturn by force the lawful acts of the legitimate government of an autonomous canton. In every case, the Basel regime took the side of law against popular pressure. While expressing the hope that Lucerne would reconsider the recall of the Jesuits, it firmly denounced as illegal every attempt to oblige it to do so. On a different occasion, Adolf Christ—though a descendant of Huguenot refugees—insisted that a new Constitution in the canton of Valais, according to which Protestant church services were prohibited, ought not to be resisted since each canton had full authority to make its own decisions in such matters.[71] Perhaps because the elite remembered that similar volunteer bands of radical antiurban peasants had been organized against Basel itself at the time of the *"Wirren,"* or "Troubles," a decade or so earlier, Basel was the only canton that prosecuted and punished those of its citizens (a small number, as it happened) who had participated in the *Freischaren*. Burckhardt's emphasis, as editor of the *Basler Zeitung* in 1844–1845, on "the simple truth that freedom and respect for law are indissolubly linked" and that "the former is an illusion without the latter" seems to have reflected the view of most people in the Basel elite.[72]

Bachofen was horrified by the lawlessness of the *Freischaren,* the release of popular political passions, and the seeming triumph of radical democratic principles. Then, in 1848, he returned to Basel from a journey to Italy to find that a new Constitution for Switzerland, in which the principle of popular sovereignty was virtually acknowledged, was about to be laid before the people. "Quanta nunc rerum mutatio," he wrote to an Italian fellow-scholar in a lan-

guage reassuringly remote from the contemporary world. "Civilibus armis pa-
tria absumpta, coelum horridum, terra aspera, sine amicis quos longinquos ha-
beo omnes domi ut ita dicam exul" ("What a change in affairs now! My native
land destroyed by civil war, the oppressive gray sky, the rude landscape, and I
myself, deprived of my friends, all of whom are in far-off places, so to speak an
exile in my own home").[73] A few years later he elaborated, in his autobiographical letter to Savigny, on his dismay at the turn taken by politics in Switzerland:

> Since . . . Lucerne, the doctrine of popular sovereignty and of the omnipotence
> of democracy has in practice become the basis of our public affairs. . . . But
> complete democracy is the ruin of everything good. Republics have most to
> fear from it. I tremble at its gathering strength not for the sake of my material
> well-being, but because it is thrusting us back into barbarism. The doctrine of
> popular sovereignty runs counter to my deepest historical and religious convic-
> tions. Not that I ever despised the people or shrank in disgust from contact
> with it—all the misery it endures would rather win my heart—but because I
> recognize a higher world order to which alone sovereignty and majesty belong.
> The authority of governments derives from that higher world order. It is an
> agency of God—that is the doctrine of both Roman paganism and of Chris-
> tianity. The magistrate's office also stems from God, and whoever exercises it,
> exercises a right that has a higher source. My office comes to me from God,
> only my appointment to it comes from the people.[74]

Bachofen's sentiments were probably quite widely shared among the Basel elite.
The spectacle of revolution throughout Europe in 1848 prompted *Ratsherr*
Bernhard Socin (1777–1854), who designed the enlightened progressive income tax that Basel was one of the first governments to adopt, to remark that
"[e]very one must accept the authority of government, for there is no government except as willed by God. The government that does not fulfill its obligations will not escape the judgment of God, but it is not for the people to exercise judgment."[75] A lapidary phrase of Bachofen's—"It is because I love
freedom that I hate democracy"—sums up the position of a significant segment
of his social class.[76]

With the fall of the Orleans monarchy in France, the civil war in Switzerland, and revolution in all the major European states, the *juste-milieu* position
had become untenable. Like Burckhardt and so many others, Bachofen turned
his back on the liberal-conservative views of his youth. Pellegrino Rossi's lectures at the Collège de France, so warmly commended in 1839, were now
judged to have been worthless and trivial. Rossi's support of trial by jury, consti-
tutionalism, freedom of the press, Polish independence, and other liberal causes
was seen retrospectively as a hypocritical concession to the revolutionary catch-
words of the day, which in the end failed to stave off the moment of honest
decision. Rossi himself was recast as a slippery opportunist, with no depth of
conviction—too much of an actor and an orator to be a genuine statesman or
scholar.[77] His assassination, in 1848, at the opening of the Parliament in Rome,

where he had been called by the reforming Pius IX in a last attempt to reassert the authority of his government in the Papal States, must have seemed emblematic to Bachofen, who was in Rome himself when the event occurred. Many years later, on the death of his erstwhile mentor Andreas Heusler in 1868, Bachofen again repudiated the *juste-milieu* politics of the thirties and expressed the view that the attempt to strike a compromise with the new popular spirit had been misguided and ultimately self-defeating. Heusler, he wrote, belonged to the old Switzerland of the time before the 1848 Constitution. But "he tried in vain to ingratiate himself with the new world by making ill-fated moves in the direction of liberalism, which only resulted in his ruining his credit with the champions of the old ways."[78]

The outlook for the future now seemed anything but reassuring. "None of the peaceable burghers of Basel knows how things really stand with Switzerland," Bachofen wrote in 1850 to a friend in Rome. "But my inner voice tells me grave events are on the way. They are coming because they must come. . . . We have reached the final stage of demagogy and nothing now remains but to plunge into the abyss."[79] In France the democratic excesses of 1848 were certain to be followed by despotism.[80] The Second Empire confirmed Bachofen's worst fears: a repressive regime that ensured order by naked force ("without chassepots the order and security of persons and property rests on shaky foundations")[81], while pandering to the most vulgar materialism. "Not a soul is interested in political freedoms. . . . Spiritual decline, blatant adoration of material pleasures, vulgar display, conspicuous consumption, and immorality in most social milieux. . . . That is Paris today. Who will think of freedom there? Such people need despotism and are happy under it." But Bachofen insisted that it was the *juste-milieu* liberalism of the 1830s that had led directly to the current situation. "Under Louis Philippe, a parliamentary France, with people making all kinds of speeches about freedom; today the consequences of that: an emperor who holds down dangerous elements with a firm hand and is therefore praised by the majority of the people as the savior of the country." Bachofen's old friends among the moderate liberals of the late 1830s and 1840s themselves "say openly that the present situation is a golden age compared with what preceded it [that is, the Second Republic]. May God preserve us, they say, from a return to freedom."[82]

The expansionist policies of Bismarck's Prussia and the transformation of the compact Biedermeier and classical Berlin Bachofen had loved in the late 1830s into the raucous commercial capital of a growing military and economic power provided no consolation for the turn events had taken in France and Switzerland. On the contrary, Bachofen, along with many in the merchant elites of both Basel and Frankfurt, now supported Austria's efforts, at the Congress of German sovereigns in Frankfurt in 1863, to recover the leadership of Germany.[83] The Austro-Prussian War so incensed him that in the fall of 1866 he refused to attend a scholarly meeting in Prussia. "I have a deep inner revulsion against Prussia," he wrote, "which makes the society and even the sight of that robber-nation extremely unpleasant."[84] After the Franco-Prussian War he refused to read the German newspapers any more.[85] Like Burckhardt, he believed that Europe was "devouring itself" and that the civilization he had known was approaching its end. "Victors and vanquished alike are about to experience a hangover from this war, the like of which no one has seen before." The age of revolutions was about to culminate in repressive military regimes of hitherto unknown cruelty. "The principles of 1789 are too deeply ingrained now in men's minds for any power to root them out. . . . In Germany the people will demand free democratic institutions in return for the blood it has given; as in 1815, Prussia will not grant them; and so, disappointed and frustrated, the people will become dissatisfied and will turn to revolution." Meanwhile chauvinism and national hatreds among the peoples will spawn new wars.[86] The Germans in particular will thirst for more wars and more conquests. So much, Bachofen noted bitterly, for the years of peace the Second German Empire was supposed to bring. "For years to come honest Fritz will have nothing to do but Boom! Boom! Boom! . . . Any other sound coming from him will be pursued as high treason."[87] In the aftermath of the Franco-Prussian War, the beginnings of civilization seemed to Bachofen in many respects preferable to the current age of decline: "The age of Mother Right now seems less barbarous to me, a golden age, compared with the century of the chassepot."[88]

To the "much touted civilization" of the new commercial and industrial order and the democratic-militarist despotisms accompanying it corresponds, according to Bachofen (who on this point is even more severe than Burckhardt), the mass "demi-culture that is being fostered by newspapers and popular lectures."[89] Ideas and works of art will inevitably become market commodities like everything else, and will be valued accordingly.

Bachofen did not advocate struggle against the forces of destruction he saw all around him. First, resistance was futile. The plunge into the abyss was inevitable, he believed, and had to be accepted as the necessary prelude to any regeneration. "There is a time when the public life of states and peoples falls victim to fate. We are in such a time. Every one has the feeling that we can only let things run their course as God wills."[90] Second, struggle would necessarily implicate anyone who engaged in it in the very "demi-culture"—propaganda, demagogy, "market" literature—that it was hoped to eradicate. Third, the forces of conservatism had themselves been corrupted by the opportunism of the times.

In face of the collapse of traditional societies and traditional values, the only reasonable policy was to withdraw, cultivate those things that would enrich one's own inner being and that might be shared with a few other individuals similarly inclined, and thus wait out the coming crisis, as it were, in order that beyond it, when humanity had come to its senses again, the torch of true learning and wisdom might be handed on. For though Bachofen described himself as a "pessimist," he did not believe—any more than Burckhardt did—that the present age was the last word of human history. "The old world of Europe lies on a sickbed from which it can expect no lasting recovery," he wrote to Meyer-Ochsner,[91] but this did not signify the end of history, only the destruction of that which had to be sacrificed so that the history of mankind could take a new turn.[92] Sickness and death were the prelude to regeneration. Whatever the fate of the established states, therefore, "at the individual level, much that is good can be salvaged, much that is worthwhile can be newly created." So too, at the local level: "The best seek a sphere of activity in the concerns of their municipality. From there they hope to win back later a part of the ground that has been lost. My past experience and my studies indicate that my province should be that of the magistrate and judge."[93] All the effort and energy expended on politics and the state is now best directed toward the improvement of individual lives, for it is individuals who will transmit what can be salvaged of the old culture, not states.

It is at this point that Bachofen's personal career and the course of world history, as it appeared to him, converge. Both the shipwreck of his hopes for a career in public life and the coming collapse of "the old world of Europe" threw him back upon himself and on the duty of self-cultivation. His writing expresses two responses to this situation, which would be echoed in his larger historical and anthropological studies: elegiac regret at what had been lost, sometimes accompanied by passionate evocations of long-gone conditions of life, and stoical resignation, submission to what was assumed to be a providential plan, even a kind of austere joy at the destruction of the old, since it is the necessary prelude to the coming of the new. The description of the pain suffered by his friend Wilhelm Streuber, when he had to leave Berlin to return to Basel, is almost certainly also a confession of his own feelings of disappointment and loss—at leaving Berlin and subsequently observing it progressively transformed from the city of poets and professors he had known and loved into the capital of an aggressive modern power; at the collapse of his own career plans in the early 1840s; at the failure of the moderately optimistic politics of his youth. "Like one newborn Streuber enjoyed in Berlin what no later time of life ever brings back—the doubly blissful experience of a present full of contentment and satisfaction and of a proud and confident anticipation of the fruits of the future. . . . Leaving Berlin he felt like a man who had been flying in a dream and now found himself, as he awoke, sinking back down to the harsh ground. . . . Now he suffered the double pain of memories full of melancholy and a future without help. He had girded himself up for life as for a joyful feast, but he had hardly begun to drink from the cup when the last lamps were extinguished and the last note fell silent."[94]

The melancholy, elegiac tone of this passage is complemented by the determined acceptance of what fate has ordained in the opening pages of what is arguably Bachofen's finest literary achievement, the so-called *Griechische Reise,* an account of a journey to Greece in 1851 that he wrote, not long before the eulogy of Streuber, for private circulation among a small circle of friends. The allusion to his withdrawal from the University and the Senate in the early 1840s is unmistakable here: "Can someone who feels himself called to a particular office be affected by anything more shattering than when he finds that it is impossible for him to exercise this One Thing. That very thing is what is taken from him, and thereby life loses for him all its external value. But it must be taken from him, in order that nothing may remain that might distract him from the One Great Thing that alone has value. Even our best qualities can become the very obstacle that hinders us on the path to perfection. When external action, effective activity in the world in the way we best understand it becomes impossible, we have to assume that the life's task being pointed out to us is that of bringing ourselves to greater perfection. As Tertullian says so beautifully: Nemo alii nascitur, sibi moriturus. [No one is born for another, since we shall all die for ourselves alone.]"[95]

Bachofen's insistence on personal cultivation and personal salvation in face of what to him was a collapsing public and political order resembles Burckhardt's evocation of the hermits and monks of the declining Roman Empire in *The Age of Constantine the Great.* For Bachofen, moroever, self-cultivation was not a simple personal solution, a matter of individual free choice. It was an obligation, because it was part of the same Providential design and of the same history of humanity in which the disintegration of the European political order had been decreed. "In the life of the soul, egoism is justified; indeed, it is an obligation," Bachofen wrote in 1855.[96] In the end, the choice is not really ours. We are the willing or unwilling instruments of a higher plan. "In the decisive moments of our lives," we read in the eulogy of Streuber, "we seldom freely determine our own actions. What appears to be our work has its origin in a higher design. We believe we choose our vocation, but in fact we are chosen by it."[97]

The experiences of the 1840s had shaken Bachofen to the core and caused him to reconsider completely the career he had been pursuing. "There must come a time when the scholar seriously asks himself about the relation of his studies to the highest things," he wrote.[98] Looking back on his work as a student of Roman law, he questioned what he had been doing up until that time and developed a view of the study of Law that was sufficiently at variance with that of his master Savigny to prompt him to write the latter a letter explaining and justifying his position. Like the eulogy of Streuber and the *Griechische Reise,* which date from the same years, this long letter took a decidedly autobiographical form and is usually referred to in the Bachofen literature as the *Selbstbiographie,* or autobiography.

The aim of Savigny, like that of his older Göttingen colleague Hugo, had been to reconcile the "empirical" or historical and the "dogmatic" or systematic currents of legal scholarship, the idiographic and the nomothetic, in a new legal systematization informed by history (Savigny's last work was a monumental six-volume *System of Modern Roman Law*).[99] As a student of Savigny's, Bachofen subscribed to this goal. In 1845, for instance, when he was asked for his opinion of Rudolf von Jhering, who was being considered for a chair of law at the University of Basel, he responded positively to Andreas Heusler that Jhering's articles on Roman law had impressed him as following truly scholarly methods. "A comprehensive investigation of sources allows him to gather together and elucidate all the judgments of the Roman jurists about the matter in hand that are scattered throughout the *corpus juris*. In this way he establishes a positive basis for the inquiry. From that basis the principle underlying the doctrine is derived, and this, finally, is applied with a sure touch to reach a resolution of cases that had not been expressly considered. Thus the exegetical, the historical, and the dogmatic treatments of the case are combined."[100]

The empirical method Bachofen attributed to Jhering is visibly similar to the method he himself claimed to have adopted in his own scholarly works. Six years later, however, in 1854, the letter to Savigny highlighted a difference in emphasis between Bachofen's approach to the study of Roman law and that of his teachers. "If it had been up to me," the young scholar declared, "I should have given the interpretation of Pandect titles precedence over all systematic lectures with their dogmatic principles and the so-called proofs so painstakingly collected in support of these."[101] He had always regarded Roman law, he explained, "as a branch of classical . . . philology, hence as part of a vast field encompassing the whole of classical antiquity." What interested him was "the ancient world itself and not the applicability of its lessons to present-day needs; it was ancient and not modern Roman law that I really wanted to study." He now claimed that this outlook, "taken over from philology," had often brought him, as a student, into "painful opposition to the instructors and books I had chosen as my guides." As he succeeded in freeing himself from the modern point of view and "subordinating it in every particular to the ancient one," he developed an increasing ill will toward "all modern systems." Whereas he "would have liked to see the cloth in its original folds," the efforts of the systematizers to "adjust the material to modern ideas" produced only "distortions that made the understanding of ancient conditions even more difficult."[102]

Around the same time, a difference between his own approach and that of Jhering, who had become a good friend during his stay in Basel, also became more apparent. In the letters the two men exchanged in the late 1840s and early 1850s, after Jhering had left Basel to take up posts at Rostock, Kiel, and Giessen successively, there are several references to Bachofen's dislike of dogmatics and his insistence on regarding Roman law historically, as part of ancient culture, rather than systematically. Thus Jhering wrote in a tone of friendly independence that he intended to continue "thinking dogmatically, as much as I can, in Roman law too, even if it means coming under a sentence of banishment and exclusion from you,"[103] and reminded Bachofen pointedly that his radically historical view of Roman law was only possible because of the favorable material circumstances that allowed him to abstract himself from practical affairs and pursue purely scholarly concerns.[104] When Jhering sent Bachofen a copy of his *Geist des römischen Rechts* (1852) he was pleasantly surprised by the courteous comments it elicited, but Bachofen's underlying opposition emerged a decade later in *Das Mutterrecht* in a testy attack on Jhering's rationalizing and systematizing method of interpretation.[105]

In his letter to his old teacher and, somewhat less directly in the exchange with Jhering, Bachofen was highlighting a tension between the historical and the legal outlook that the historical school of law obviously preferred not to emphasize. Having as a practical objective the reform and systematization of modern law in Germany (on an historical basis, to be sure), the legal scholars were interested in discovering principles relevant to their own time. From a rigorously historical point of view, however, Roman law was part of the culture of the ancient world and had to be studied in its relation to that culture, not for what could be adapted from it to benefit the present. Increasingly, it seems, Bachofen was coming to consider ancient and modern, the Roman and the Germanic world, as two distinct cultures, and to emphasize the discontinuities in the overall but often inscrutable Providential design of history, which he continued to believe in. He was thus moving away not only from Savigny but from Ranke and the moderate optimism—the search for a reconciliation of ancient and modern, Romanic and Germanic—that was characteristic of the entire historical school. The spectacle of continued social unrest in Switzerland and in Europe had not only solidified his political conservatism; it had made his historicism, his insistence on particularity, and his rejection of everything that smacked of generalizing categories even more extreme than that of his teachers. Roman law, he now declared, was "a part of ancient, and not of modern life, an aspect of classical philology, an integral part of conditions long past, a product of fundamental ideas that have only the most tenuous relation to those of the Christian Germanic peoples."[106] From that perspective, the only correct relation the modern could have with the ancient in a time of accelerating change was one of reverential contemplation. "Let us give to Antiquity its law and to Modernity its law," he declared, "to each its own."[107]

To underline his difference with his teacher on this point, he even came to the defence of the French, whose ignorance and lack of professionalism had often been criticized by Savigny.[108] Jurisprudence can be rejuvenated either by direct contact with traditional legal wisdom or by involvement in the practical affairs of everyday life, Bachofen claimed. If Paris had little to offer in the first regard, it at least prepared the student more effectively than German legal education did in the second.[109] As it happens, the practical jurisprudence that was associated with the *Cour de Cassation* at the time Bachofen was in Paris and that emerged out of legal commentary on and interpretation of the Napoleonic Code had created a practice of law more in keeping with Bachofen's notions of judicial discretion and authority, as opposed to mechanical application of statutes, than the rationalist spirit of the Code itself. For it was judicial authority and creativity, informed and disciplined by understanding of legal principles and tradition, that were the heart of the law in Bachofen's view.[110] The life of the law was in the culture of which it was part; if that was healthy, so would be the theory and practice of law; if it was not, no amount of formal manipulation would save the day.

7

"Far from One's Father's House"
A Prepatriarchal Order

After resigning from the University and the Senate, that is to say for most of his seventy-two years, Bachofen led the life of a wealthy private scholar. It was a life marked by little participation in public affairs and by few events. The death of his mother, Valeria Merian, in 1856, marriage to Louise Burckhardt in 1865, when he was already fifty years old, the birth of a son a year later, and the death of his father in 1876 were the most important of these. There was a good deal of travel: to philological congresses in Frankfurt, Stuttgart, and other cities; to London, especially to see the Near Eastern and classical antiquities at the British Museum, in 1847 and again in 1852; to Paris in 1852, 1860, 1864, and 1865; to Spain and the south of France, to inspect the antiquities there, in 1861; to Greece in 1851; and most frequently and gladly to Italy, above all to Rome (1842–1843, 1848–1849, 1851–1852, 1863, 1865, 1868)—though with increasing contempt (as in Burckhardt's case) for the new Italian state created by the *Risorgimento*. Otherwise nothing interrupted the *"monotonie sans égale,"* as he himself put it,[1] of his existence, except the internal passions and the occasional exchanges with others provoked by his research, reflection, and writing on the remote past of humanity. Even the publication of his works caused few ripples and passed virtually unnoticed by the scholarly world, as he often complained. It is hardly surprising, in light of his negative view of the events of his time and the uneventfulness of his own existence, that Bachofen was little interested in what we now refer to as *"histoire événémentielle."*

The real events of a life that had been removed from politics and public affairs were his thinking and writing, and these have the same character of permanence or repetition that Bachofen found in history. Throughout his writings we find the same concerns and the same themes, sometimes even the same phrases, just as in history, according to him, "an imperishable truth emerges from the husk of ever-changing phenomena."[2] And in Bachofen's case everything was informed by his profoundly Christian spirituality.

The unpublished "Politische Betrachtungen über das Staatsleben des römischen Volkes" (1850), the *Geschichte der Römer* (1851), an uncompleted study of "Das alte Italien" (1855), and "Die Grundgesetze der Völkerentwicklung und der Historiographie," an important paper read to the Basel Historical Society in 1864, reflect Bachofen's lifelong preoccupation with the history of Rome, which he saw as the central act of the history of humanity,[3] and outline his ideas about the interconnectedness of law, religion, and the state; the evolution of humanity; the meaning of history; the relation of history to myth and to the natural world; and the value, purpose, and proper method of historical scholarship. Two remarkable essays on the funerary symbolism of the Ancients ("Die drei Mysterieneier" and "Öknos der Seilflechter"), published as *Versuch über die Gräbersymbolik der Alten* (1851), turn on the fundamental theme of all his work, whatever its specific subject: death and resurrection, the life of nature and the life of the spirit, and the universality of basic religious notions and of the symbols in which they are expressed.

In the best known of all his works, *Das Mutterrecht* (1861), he presented once again his ideas about myth and history, the evolution of humanity, and the place of religion in social life and the life of the state. Here these ideas were placed in the context of an overarching theory of the evolution of human society from primitive "hetaerism" or the law of material nature, the body, the eternal cycle of birth and death, to patriarchy or the rule of human law, the redemption of nature by spirit, and the conquest of death. This law of development, he declared, was part of the law of the cosmos, an assertion buttressed by countless references to the myths and customs of both ancient and modern "primitive" peoples, as recorded not only in classical texts and on ancient monuments but in the writings of modern ethnographers, missionaries, and travelers. Within this evolutionary process, Bachofen claimed to distinguish an intermediate stage of "regulated naturalism"[4]—"an archaic humanity," in the words of the only scholar who ever referred to himself as Bachofen's disciple, the Geneva sociologist Alexis Giraud-Teulon—"in which the Mother ruled alone in the family, gave her name to the children, transmitted the property of the kin group, and played, within the tribe, the role that later fell to the Father and Husband. In the religions corresponding to this period of civilization," Giraud-Teulon went on, "the goddess is higher than the god and the Mother is worshipped as the representative of the divinity on earth."[5]

All these texts proposed the view that the culture of classical antiquity contained within itself an even more ancient—and primitive—form of culture, the culture associated with the rule of the Mother or "Matriarchy," which the classical world had both overcome and preserved in a transformed state. Classical culture was thus to be thought of not as serenely self-sufficient, but as the outcome of a never quite completed struggle with the "antiquity of antiquity," as Bachofen called it.[6] Well before Nietzsche, who knew his work, Bachofen had both elaborated the theme of ancient Greek culture as a battleground of the Dionysian and the Apollonian, and contrasted that earlier antiquity with the Socratic and rationalistic culture of democratic Athens in the fifth century B.C.

In 1862, *Das lykische Volk und seine Bedeutung für die Entwicklung des Al-*

tertums focussed on one of the early societies in which "matriarchal" elements were particularly visible, and in which Bachofen believed he had found something akin to the early traditions of the mountain communities of his native Switzerland. *Die Unsterblichkeitslehre der orphischen Theologie auf den Grabdenkmälern des Altertums* (1867), printed in a private edition of fifty copies, took up again the themes of funerary symbolism and the perennial human hope in redemption from the cycle of material birth and death, as did a long essay in Italian on *"La lupa Romana su monumenti sepolchrali,"* published in the *Annali dell'Istituto di Archeologia* (1867, 1868, and 1869).

In the first of the two masterworks of his maturity, *Die Sage von Tanaquil* (1870), Bachofen returned to the theme of the central significance of Roman history and of Rome as the juncture of Orient and Occident, the ancient and the modern worlds, matriarchy and patriarchy, nature and law. Rome was the nodal point from which all history can be surveyed and the key to its understanding, since "as modernity, it looks down on antiquity, and as antiquity on modernity, transmitting to us everything that it did not create itself."[7] In the second, *Antiquarische Briefe* (vol. 1, 1880, vol. 2, 1886), inspired partly by the support and interest of the American anthropologist Lewis Morgan, with whom he had begun exchanging letters in 1874, Bachofen took off from a vast reading of modern ethnographic and anthropological writings and travel reports to develop in detail one aspect of early kinship relations associated with "matriarchal" societies and first broached in *Mutterrecht,* namely the so-called avunculate, or "relation of the mother's brother to his sister's children."[8] While the basic concerns of this work remained rooted in those of *Das Mutterrecht,* the horizon was now much wider, and thanks to the development of anthropology as a discipline and to Bachofen's keen interest in that development—by the late 1860s he was following the writings of MacLennan, Lubbock, and Tylor, and shortly afterwards began corresponding with Bastian and Morgan[9]—the questions began to assume a more visibly anthropological and "scientific" character. This was still "imaginary anthropology," as a modern scholar has called it[10]—"je voyage en Afrique, en pantoufle seulement," Bachofen admitted himself[11]—but the range of reference had widened remarkably from that of the classical world and of classical texts.

Bachofen's final work—a series of commentaries on ten illustrations of funerary lamps in his own collection, entitled *Römische Grablampen nebst einigen anderen Grabdenkmälern vorzugsweise eigener Sammlung ... mit Ausführungen zu einzelnen Theilen der Römischen Gräbersymbolik*—was published posthumously, in 1912, by his widow and his son, with a fine introduction by Giraud-Teulon. In it, in the last weeks of his life, the elderly scholar returned, appropriately enough, to the themes of funerary symbolism and ancient religious ideas.

Besides these formal scholarly writings—even the *Antiquarische Briefe,* despite the deliberate selection of a more informal structure, remains a recognizably scholarly production—Bachofen produced two major texts of a different kind. The first is his correspondence, especially the letters to his Zurich friend Heinrich Meyer-Ochsner, a wealthy private scholar like himself, and the long autobiographical letter to Savigny, dating from 1854 and usually referred to as the *Selbstbiographie*, or autobiography. The second, entitled *Griechische Reise*, was written for private circulation on his return from a journey to Greece in 1851 and published only in 1927[12]—a combination of travel journal, with comments on contemporary Greece, and powerful poetic evocations of the ancient sites of the eastern Peloponnese, interspersed with reflections on the vanished cultures to which the material remains bear mute witness.

From a literary point of view, these may well be Bachofen's most successful works. In the correspondence he expresses many of his views more succinctly and vividly than in his scholarly works, burdened as the latter often are by the excessive quotation and textual references that he believed gave his ideas an empirical foundation. There is also much wit, humor, and malicious satire in this writing. The *Griechische Reise* achieves a similar liveliness by artfully combining, in a characteristically romantic mixture, a down-to-earth, often humorous narrative of a journey to what was then still an exotic and quite primitive land, with sustained lyrical descriptions of the unchanging Greek landscape and elevated, elegiac, intensely personal meditations on man's relation to nature and to the divine, the meaning of human history, and the religious foundations of political authority.

It is not surprising that Bachofen is at his best, as a writer, in those two bodies of work (neither of which has been translated into English). He did not like to write for *"das grosse Publikum."* It was cold, disinterested, and anonymous, he declared, striking a Platonic as well as a modern note, and the writer could never be sure how his words would be received by it, whether a completely different image might not arise in the reader's mind from the image the writer had had in his. As this image cannot respond to questioning or tell anything about its source,

> I prefer not to let it loose in the world. True joy and genuine satisfaction are to be had only from an immediate relation of minds, in which one spark ignites another, and each one gives and receives. Since the invention of printing this joy has fallen out of sight, become exceptional. . . . For the book has communicated its character to oral communication also. Wherever the modern scholar is heard, in universities, academies, or learned societies, he never seems to me to be anything but a book reading itself. A book that I have delivered to the public is like money I have spent. I come out poorer, not just for having lost some of my wealth—it would be possible to get over that—but for having lost a part of my Self.[13]

As Bachofen, like Burckhardt, virtually withdrew from what both referred to contemptuously as the "demi-culture" of the time, the writings they addressed to the select public they deemed worth communicating with assume particular importance. In addition, Bachofen's entire view of scholarly study ran against the grain of mid-nineteenth-century institutionalized scholarship and academic discourse. Since the scholarly career for him was truly a vocation, the scholar's engagement with the object of his study had to be total and personal. All cognition being, in the end—as he had learned from his Platonizing neo-humanist teachers at the Basel *Pädagogium*—recognition, the investigation of the object was at the same time a process of self-discovery and of personal education. Writing about the object, the scholar was also writing about himself and, conversely, in discovering what was deepest in himself, he was also discovering the object of his study. It was inevitable that Bachofen's finest work would be essentially confessional in nature.[14]

Even his seemingly most scholarly productions have a significant confessional element. *Das Mutterrecht,* for instance, in which Bachofen first systematically presented his theory of ancient society and which he himself considered his first major scholarly achievement, is deeply rooted in personal experience. He offered this work as a monument to the memory of his mother, who had died in 1856, five years before its publication. It bears a moving dedication in Greek, "To the lovely image of the Mother," and another, in German, "To the memory of my mother, Frau Valeria Bachofen, née Merian" with an addition in Greek: "We shall not cease from speaking of your goodness and sweetness for as long as we live." Valeria Merian appears to have been a deeply pious, sensitive woman who never recovered from the accidental death of her two-year-old daughter at the family country house in Riehen in the late 1830s and who spent the rest of her life in mourning. (The property was sold when it became clear that Frau Bachofen would never return to it.) No doubt, we shall never know the role she played in the life of her eldest and most gifted son. Bachofen's direct comments about her are as sparing as the prose of his dedications. Only once, in his correspondence, does he evoke her memory. Expressing his regret that Meyer-Ochsner's wife has fallen sick just when their daughter is expecting a child, he alludes to the recent pregnancy of his own wife and notes: "The presence of a mother is a precious thing and one feels it bitterly when, as in our family, none is with us any longer."[15]

The absence of Valeria Merian from Bachofen's private correspondence is amply compensated for, however, by the inscription of the grieving, sorrowing mother and the mother-daughter pair of Demeter and Kore on almost every page of her son's scholarly writing.[16] Nor can there be much doubt that it is once again Valeria Merian who is being honored and adored in the massive figure of the matronly Roman goddess Tanaquil to whom Bachofen devoted his second large-scale scholarly work (plate 2). *Die Sage von Tanaquil* appeared in the same year as an article rejecting the Coriolanus story as a poetic fabrication by the Basel scholar's nemesis, the Berlin professor Theodor Mommsen, the leader of the modern critical school of philologists. The Coriolanus story plays a significant role in Bachofen's text and he reacted to the article with even greater vehemence than usual.[17] Apparently he felt that the man who had come to represent for him the entire orientation of modern scholarship, the man whose critical method he constantly denounced as destructive and sacrilegious because of its rejection of myth as a genuine source of knowledge of the past, had taken aim at the most sacred of all targets. Among the protagonists of the Coriolanus story was P. Valerius Publicola, who advised the matrons of Rome to approach Coriolanus in his camp and try to persuade him to mitigate his resentment. Publicola belonged to the Valeria *gens,* one of the most distinguished patrician houses of Rome; his sister, the first priestess of Fortuna Muliebris, another mother-goddess to whom the Latins, according to Bachofen, transferred significant features of the Tanaquil figure, bore the name of Bachofen's mother, Valeria.

One can speculate that, however much affection she continued to give her remaining children, Valeria Merian's inconsolable grief at the death of her daughter, added to her piety, may have made her appear distant and inaccessible to those in need of her maternal warmth. Renunciation and hope in a future restoration of what has been lost may well have been a lesson that Bachofen had had to learn early in life—and not only from his religious teachers. He certainly learned it well, for it became central to all his thinking. "I have always hoped and hope always springs anew in me," he would note in his mid-thirties. "And through the hoping I have become a man, and suffer now in proud consciousness of my strength. Not to be crowned with success is not the same as failure. Conscious renunciation awakens a remarkable confidence in oneself, a pride, such as even the consciousness of successfully applied powers can scarcely bring."[18] Renunciation is one of the great themes of Bachofen's work. It is through renunciation that woman creates culture by raising the law of material nature to the highest point it can attain in the world of Mother Right. It is through renunciation again that this highest point of natural existence is transcended and the order of paternal law instituted. By renouncing material satisfaction the greatest spiritual rewards are obtained, ultimate reality is reached, and it becomes possible to "embrace the goddess herself," in Bachofen's own words, instead of her passing earthly forms.[19] Correspondingly, it is through renunciation that the infernal cycle of birth and death, the law of material nature, which Mother Right alone could not go beyond, is finally overcome in the promise of eternal life. Likewise, it is the austerity of the mother and "the chastity and restraint she exacted of young men," as opposed to the destructive facility of the chthonic hetaera figure, that makes men into heroes and founds all chivalry.[20]

Bachofen himself always acknowledged the deeply personal character of his interest in and reflection on antiquity. "How various were the points of connection between an impoverished present and the long vanished heroic age of Hellas," he noted at an inn in Megara where he and his guide spent the night, "and how pleasingly memories of antiquity, interwoven in a golden image of the past with memories of my own youth, played in the mirror of my thoughts! But now both were gone and lost beyond repair."[21] Later on, at Mycenae, he reflected on the power of the ancient site to "transport the curious modern traveler for a few hours from his own time and his entire intellectual universe" to a world still largely under the sway of the natural law of the mothers. How does that come about, he wonders.

> To be so far from one's father's house, to be roaming in every thought through a time that is so far removed from the present or from any exact measurement, and yet to be so at home, and from the very first step so well acquainted and so familiar with what is revealed only gradually to the eye. How does that come about? Is it not as though, instead of treading for the first time the soil of a strange land, one was in fact rediscovering sites long known to us, where once, in our youth, we played with innocent pleasure?[22]

The suggestion made here—that there is a correspondence between the history of humanity and the history of each individual—is repeated over and over again, most memorably in a passage of the autobiographical letter to Savigny, in which Bachofen compares the way "the walls of Rome arouse what is deepest in man" with striking a bronze disk, so that "it keeps resounding until you set a finger on it to stop the vibrations."[23] In light of this correspondence, a new and poignant significance is assumed by the scholar's often-confessed longing for Italy; his predilection for archaic, matriarchal societies; the glowing colors in which he painted cultures that he believed *had* to be transcended by a higher paternalist law; his acknowledged tendency to set off impulsively on journeys to the always dangerously alluring South, to *"vagari,"* as he put it himself, even if the price to be paid for such ill-considered voyages was often sickness and fever curable only by returning to gray, old Basel, his "rainy protective fatherland."[24]

But we may read our modern psychological truths into Bachofen's prose only with caution. Like many romantics, Bachofen believed firmly in the spiritual unity and meaningfulness of the universe. As everything was connected, everything was also a key to or a symbol of something beyond itself. Of the symbols he found everywhere Bachofen was an eager and imaginative interpreter. In his own life he scrutinized the most seemingly banal events or coincidences for the providential message they might contain. Thus he read the attacks on his appointment to the University faculty in 1841 as a sign that Providence had other plans for him than those he had had for himself, and he carefully noted in the opening paragraph of the *Griechische Reise* that the eleventh of the month—the day on which he set out on this journey—was "always a fateful day for me."[25] There was virtually nothing in the universe that did not point to something beyond itself. It was because the events of individual history were figures of universal history, in fact, that it was not only empirically but theoretically impossible for the scholar to separate his personal experience from his scholarly work.

It is true that Bachofen was keenly sensitive to the erotic significance of many ancient symbols and myths, and few modern readers will not be struck by a resemblance between the movement from hetaerism, through ever-increasing discipline, to paternal law, and the Freudian evolution from polymorphous infantile eroticism to the genital sexuality of the adult. But for Bachofen, as for Georg Friedrich Creuzer, whose *Symbolik* (1819–1823) the Basel scholar had studied closely, the erotic itself concealed spiritual truths, which it was the task of the initiator or mystagogue to interpret. Thus the massive stone walls rising out of the earth at Tiryns or Mycenae, he believed, symbolize the phallus, but the phallus itself symbolized fixedness, unity, identity, and authority—the security of the civil order, as Creuzer himself remarked[26]—and in general physical love, properly interpreted, was a figure of the longings of the soul, a point particularly well developed in Bachofen's reading of the myth of Amor and Psyche in *Die Gräbersymbolik*. In Freud's deliberate *Umwertung* of romantic symbolism, everything erect and towering becomes a symbol of the phallus, and the human body is the secret about which men dream in symbols that those initiated into the new mysteries interpret for them. To Bachofen, however, the Freudian reading of the language of symbols would probably have seemed only another sign of the regressive materialism of the modern age.

It is difficult for us today to go back behind Freud to the cosmic spiritualism of the romantics. We cannot help asking ourselves to what extent the preoccupation of scholars like Creuzer and Bachofen with erotic symbolism and the length and detail of their descriptions—whatever the interpretations they come up with—were not in fact a way of indulging their erotic imagination in the only form permissible at the time, that is to say, in the guise of learned discourse, even if in so doing they also aimed consciously, as scholars, to challenge the bloodless and idealized view of antiquity held by many of their contemporaries.[27] And we cannot help wondering to what degree the immense popularity of Creuzer in the learned world (and the posthumous popularity of Bachofen) might have been due precisely to the erotic character of the myths and symbols that were their principal topic. Bachofen's version of the story of Amor and Psyche, for instance, is no less powerfully erotic for being made subservient *in the end* to a spiritualizing interpretation. And his work is full of such passages. Even the astonishingly insightful analysis of the difference between "sanctum" and "sacrum" in *Die Gräbersymbolik* has an inescapably erotic character in the repeated veiled depictions of male sexual arousal.[28] The modern reader who does not subscribe to the spiritualism of the romantics cannot view as unproblematical the enormous energy of barely suppressed eroticism in these texts or ignore the strains of narcissism and homoeroticism that emerge from Bacho-fen's remarkable evocations of female adoration of the male and that so often accompany the representation of the phallus as the image of the sacred, the source of authority, and the pillar of moral and civil order.

To Bachofen, however, the spiritual significance of the erotic was not a dis-guise or something added on, as it tends to be for us; it was its truth. Similarly, sublimation did not simply have a pragmatic value for the development of hu-man culture and society; it was the way to the truth and to the divinely ap-pointed end of human existence. The sublimation of all erotic desire, whether desire for the mother or, through identification with the (earthly) mother, long-ing for the (divine) father, is thus an essential aspect both of the personal history of the individual and of the providentially directed history of mankind as a whole. Hence in *Das Mutterrecht* the glowing tribute to Sappho and the un-compromising apology of male and female homosexuality in the ancient world, presented as an effort to transcend the world of matter and the body, to rise "from the morass of hetaeric sensuality to a higher stage of existence." Behind the *arrenes erotes*, Bachofen claims, we do not find "sensuality, as Ovid, the poet of a decadent age supposes, but a sublimation, an ethical transcending of the lower Eros."[29] No less than desire, renunciation and sublimation turn out to be not only strategies of the psyche but providentially ordained dynamic principles of cultural transformation and spiritual progress, moving humanity forward, first out of the chthonic world of undifferentiated nature toward the gentle law of the mothers, and then higher still, from the natural warmth of mother law to the austerity and purity of paternal justice—from the tribe or nation to the state.

Three topics will occupy the remainder of our section on Bachofen: his view of the nature and proper method of historical study, his interpretation of ancient symbolism and myth, and his understanding of history. These three topics are inseparable in his work. Each reflects and repeats the others and all three are also, on Bachofen's own admission, closely connected with his own situation and with what he believed to be the critical questions of his own time. As we shall see, Bachofen accused many of his contemporaries of "modernizing" his-tory, of comfortably reading the present into the past in order to justify the present, and thus of refusing to discern what in the past is radically different and for that reason challenging, but he never held that scholarship was or should be neutral or purely "scientific." Just as he claimed there was an intimate connection between personal history and universal history, he readily acknowl-edged that his own interest in antiquity, in particular his lifelong preoccupation with the history of Rome, arose out of the experience of his own time—which he became more and more convinced was marked by a deepening crisis in the history of humanity—and was part of an effort to understand it and to come to a clearer idea of what his personal obligation as an individual and a citizen, living in such a time, might be.

The enormous and often contradictory resonance of Bachofen's writings in the century since his death—on the political left and the right, among Marxists and anarchists, and among the literary and intellectual apologists of National Socialism—is a complex and tangled story, the working out of which would throw light on the promiscuous relations of modern left-wing and right-wing critiques of liberal democracy in recent times. Strikingly, the legacies of Bachofen's colleagues in Basel, Jacob Burckhardt and Friedrich Nietzsche, are no less complex and contradictory.

8

"At Its Greatest in Its Graves"
The Dark Side of Antiquity

Compared to the Age of Enlightenment, the nineteenth century appears obsessed by death. Jules Michelet, one of its outstanding historians, acknowledged that he was "too much in love with death," and placed the fascination with death at the origin of his historical vocation. Private letters and diaries, as well as the works of romantic poets and artists, testify to an increasing awareness of the historicity of things once taken to be eternal and universal and to intense feelings of isolation in a world become suddenly unfamiliar and impenetrable. No doubt the political and industrial revolutions, the dissolution of old traditions and communities, and the erosion of long-established religious beliefs had a good deal to do with the new preoccupation with death. Death signified not only discontinuity but the healing of discontinuity—in a communal sense as well as a personal one. Soldiers in the murderous American Civil War and in the aptly named "Great War," which marked the true end of the nineteenth century, appear to have found in combat and death a community not only with their compatriots but with the "enemy," the Other, that was unattainable or prohibited in life and the world. The historian may well wonder what obscure "Dionysian" impulses might underlie the infatuation with combat and death, in the latter part of the nineteenth century especially, and to what extent sacrifice and the constantly reiterated expectation of reparation in the world beyond may have served to reinforce various forms of paternal authority, by compensating for the harshness of a present strained by social alienation and economic competition.

In an astounding passage of one of his letters to the poetess Karoline von Günderode, as early as 1805, Georg Friedrich Creuzer offered consolation for the frustrations of their unhappy love affair in the thought of death. (Creuzer apparently believed marriage ought not to stand in the way of passion and was disappointed by what he considered the bourgeois philistinism of friends and colleagues, notably the Savignys, who tried to get him and Karoline to renounce their love for the sake of Creuzer's marriage.) "How beautiful it will all finally be in death, or rather in the great All, in which individuality will be transcended . . . and the difference between the state and the individual citizen, the master and the servant, the teacher and the student, will be no more—in which all that loves, dissolved in love itself, can seek itself without fear or hesitation, and without the apprehension of being separated again, since separation itself will no longer exist."[1] A couple of decades later, Jules Michelet, whose adolescence had been marked by the premature death of his mother and of his best friend Paul Poinsot, told how his imagination was stimulated by frequent visits to the Père Lachaise cemetery in Paris. The historian's journal shows him obsessively preoccupied subsequently by the deaths of his wife, his close friend Madame Dumesnil (whose son was to become Michelet's student and marry his daughter Adèle), his father, and the little son his second wife Athénaïs Mialaret bore him in his later years. In Bachofen's case, the accidental death of his sister, from which his mother never recovered, cast a shadow over the scholar's entire childhood and adolescence. Mourning, for him, was a normal condition.

It is in no way surprising, therefore, that the grave—where the past is laid to rest, revered, remembered, and resurrected to eternal life—is at the center of Bachofen's work, determining both his idea of historical method and the substance of his history of antiquity. It was during a stay in Rome in 1842, he related, that repeated visits to the Villa Pamphili, where a columbarium "distinguished by the great number and unusual diversity of its mural paintings" had recently been unearthed, set him on the course of study he was to pursue for the rest of his life. "The beauty of the gardens, the magnificent view, the ancient works of art which banish, for some moments at least, the centuries that separate us from antiquity, and in addition the novelty and freshness of a young man's first visit to Rome—all these combined to arouse an interest that has been with me ever since. It is to these visits that I owe my first impulsion to study the world of the ancient tombs—a preoccupation that has brought me twice to Italy and has found new nourishment in Greece. In my constant reading of the ancient authors I have paid close attention to everything they say about tombs and tomb cults."[2]

Bachofen's highest goal was the contemplation of a past redeemed from the ephemerality of worldly existence and restored to eternal life by the pious labors of scholarship. He was fully aware of the political, ethical, and philosophical implications of this conception of the task of historical scholarship.

> Either life obeys the law of the divine world, which it accepts in faith and humility, and in that case selfish desire is crushed and sinks to the bottom of the soul; or that faith grows weak and yields ground, allowing desire to occupy the throne it has abandoned. Mankind then falls to the dust before its false brilliance. In this single opposition lies the whole secret of the rise and fall of states. . . . It is the only valid philosophy of all history and it is the same for all peoples and all times. What it comes down to is that the pot should bow before the potter, the creature before the creator. What I discovered in antiquity, so rich in faith and in wonders, was always far more to me than a mere object of antiquarian learning. I gave to it the veneration appropriate to religious feeling.[3]

Arnold Böcklin, *Der heilige Hain* (*Sacred Grove*), 1882. Öffentliche Kunstsammlung Basel, Kunstmuseum. Photo: Öffentliche Kunstsammlung Basel, Martin Bühler.

The study of antiquity removes us, in short, from the pursuit of ephemeral, fragmentary, immediate satisfactions that Bachofen considers characteristic of democratic and revolutionary societies and restores a sense of the whole and the enduring. The history of Rome, in particular, is exemplary, and it is vital, in times of "confusion," that we learn from it "what sustains the state and what precipitates its fall, what is good and what springs from evil."[4] His aim, Bachofen declared in the foreword to *Die Gräbersymbolik,* was to "communicate the sublimely beautiful ideas of the past to an age that is very much in need of regeneration."[5]

The grave and grave symbolism are the essential subject matter of virtually all Bachofen's writing. Antiquity, he stated, is "at its greatest in its graves."[6] From the symbols of funerary art and the myths that, in his view, developed out of them, he would weave a philosophy of history, grounded in the millennial experience of the species, that he believed held the key not only to the past but to the present and the future, permitting men to escape from the limitations of their own time-bound existence and their own historical moment—that is to say, from the short-sighted clichés of nineteenth-century capitalism, socialism, and democracy—toward that *philosophia perennis* and that vision of eternity, which, according to him, was the goal of the great civilizations of antiquity.[7] "The passing centuries and all the innovations they bring have little power over tombs and tomb cults," he wrote. "Their symbolism . . . forms a bond between early and late generations, annulling distinctions of time, space, and nationality." Thus the symbols studied in *Die Gräbersymbolik*—the egg, the motif of the rope plaiter—are found "in Egypt, Asia, Greece, and Italy."[8] One of the finest of Bachofen's many meditations on the meaning of history—in some respects it recalls Gibbon's celebrated account of how he conceived the *Decline and Fall*—is placed, with perfect artistic propriety, in a passage of the *Griechische Reise* where he describes how, from a height above the little city of Nafplion, the first capital of modern Greece, in that timeless hour when the world seems suspended between light and dark, day and night, he watched the sun slowly set over the bay and the plain stretching behind it.

> The setting sun is nature's evening prayer. Its last rays fade, trembling, like the reverberations of the Requiem Aeternam, over the broad plain from which Mycenae and Tiryns, Argos and Palamedes rise like four tombstones. Nature and creature alike bow silently to its song of praise. No sound struck my ear there other than the plashing of water wantonly teasing the jutting rocks at the foot of the wall, now splashing a light foam over them, now quickly withdrawing. Eternal youth is the privilege of the blue sea with its ever new and ever repeated play. And so, at the foot of the Palamedes hill, more vividly than anywhere else, we encounter the difference between the laws that God has prescribed for his own works and those that govern the works of his creatures. The former are changeless like the divine ideas themselves, the latter transitory, as a flower of the field over which the wind has passed. . . . And yet there is something in human things that connects them with eternity. As in all our being, what is highest and what is most base lie close together. There is immortality under dust and decay, and time weaves the living cloth of the divine out of fragile threads. In those very sites where the ruins of prehistory remind us of destinies long ago played out, the transitory aspect of things fades into the background and only their eternal aspect remains for us to contemplate. History then seems to resemble the great creations of ancient art, which display nature's eternal ideas rather than mere copies of her imperfect products, images of calm remembrance rather than figures of the living present.[9]

In this view of history as leading beyond the grave to a transcendent vision in which the past is saved from its transience to become an enduring object of contemplation, Bachofen was far closer than he himself ever acknowledged, or his dismissive references to Burckhardt's "estheticism" would encourage one to believe, to the celebrated fellow citizen with whom he never entertained more than rather reserved and formal relations.[10] Both seem to have shared the view of history expressed by their common teacher at the *Pädagogium*, Franz Gerlach, in an address to the parents of the school's students in 1822: "Nothing is more sacred than history. It is the great mirror of the world spirit, the eternal poem of the divine Intelligence."[11]

Bachofen's view of history focuses, like Burckhardt's, not on the gradual and progressive developments that the liberals and the more optimistic of the liberal-conservatives of the nineteenth century liked to recount in detail, but on the essential and permanent features of cultures and on the dramatic turning points when one culture is overtaken by another, the crises of death and transfiguration. Thus in the history of Greece, it is not Athens but Mycenae that held Bachofen's attention, since to him Mycenae was the crossroads of East and West, the place that buried the culture of the Orient and at the same time preserved its essence in the new culture of the Occident, so that "a reflection of Oriental splendor falls over Agammemnon and his kingdom."[12] "Before the Lion Gate at Mycenae," he wrote, "one feels one is standing in the middle point, as it were, between two worlds, that of the Orient and that of the Occident. To the latter was handed over that which was received from the former."[13]

So too Homer stands between the old "Pelasgian" world of mute, immobile nature symbols and the new Greek world of anthropomorphic gods and mythical narratives.

> Whereas the highest Being had hitherto been considered incomprehensible and unrepresentable, so that it could at best be hinted at through mute signs, now it was given human form, human thoughts, and human passions and made to resemble the creature in everything except the perfection of beauty. . . . The symbol stirred and acquired movement. Hermes, hitherto a heavy stone inseparably bound to earth becomes the winged messenger of the gods, fleeting light-footed over the earth without ever touching the tips of her plants. . . . The meaning of the symbol that spoke directly to the mind and the intuition was transformed and laid out in myths. Hellas is the fatherland of myths and Homer their father. Seen in that light, Homer is the author of the ruin of ancient religion, and that is indeed how he is portrayed by Herodotus, to whom familiarity with the wealth of symbols, the depth of feeling, and the immobility of the Orient made the contrast [between the world of symbol and the world of myth] especially vivid.[14]

Finally, Rome—whose history was the constant focus of Bachofen's writing and reflection—is seen as standing at the limit of the ancient Orient and the modern Occident, the graveyard of the one and the birthplace of the other. Rome struggles against the Orient within—that is, against the principle of its own religion, which is more material and therefore more profoundly rooted than the idea of the state, and which can never be entirely subdued by the latter, but constantly returns to oppose it. It struggles against the Orient without— laying low first Alba, then Carthage, and in the same year "wealthy Corinth, the sumptuous abode of Aphrodite," and above all Etruria, which gave Rome so much, but could not overcome the deep Asiatic "nature principle" in itself.[15] Thus Rome lays the Oriental Tanaquil into the grave but at the same time preserves her transfigured as the matronly goddess of the new state.

Were it not for the historian's work of redemption, the grave would constitute an almost insuperable barrier between the world of the past and the world of the present from which men look out toward it. "An immense abyss separates the new from the old," the thirty-six-year-old traveler wrote on setting foot in the land of Homer. "The thread of tradition was cut long ago."[16] The very names of the ancient fortified places that dot the Greek landscape have sunk into oblivion. The modern Greek uses the same generic term to refer to all of them.[17] Again and again, Bachofen remarked on the contrast between the unchanging landscape, which in his mind's eye was still the scene of ancient heroic life,[18] and the mediocre ambitions of the "progressive" Greeks of the mid-nineteenth century, with their dress coats and top hats, their petty European-style politics, their civil servants in the uniform of the Bavarian monarchy, their dreams of a brilliant future of tourist hotels, and their complete unconsciousness of antiquity.[19] As for modern scholars, the religious basis of all life in ancient times had become so completely foreign to their essentially rationalist and critical spirit that they could barely begin to understand antiquity. "How far our spirit has diverged from that of antiquity! How incapable we are, for that reason, of grasping that ancient world. Hence the monstrous productions of modern history. You cannot fetch water in a sieve. Whoever mocks his own religion cannot respect that of the Ancients."[20]

To understand the other, in sum, one must become the other. Understanding supposes participation.

> Whoever would understand a people must adopt the standpoint which that people itself occupied and whoever would write its history must work out of its spirit and not out of his own. He must not let himself be ruled by the views of the nineteenth century, but must appropriate those of the Romans, and see with their eyes. What profit is there in rediscovering the ideas of the nineteenth century in Roman history? The only value for us is in rediscovering the views of the Romans themselves, knowing what *they* thought of their origins, what *they* knew, what *they* believed. That is my position . . . , and all my efforts are directed toward making me as Roman as possible. I reject so-called scientific criticism, which measures the life and deeds of a noble people, filled with the idea of God, by the decadent and corrupt views of a decadent and corrupt age, and transfers its own giddiness to that earlier time and to that energetic people. What would the Middle Ages of the German nation look like if their faith and their deeds were analyzed to bits by the modern spirit?[21]

The difficulty is felt doubly by the writer who has to convey the spirit of antiquity to a reader remote from the ancient sites. "Everything is so completely different from our accustomed notions that it is hard to remove the comfortable Westerner from the artificiality that accompanies every step in his life from the cradle to the grave and place him in the unspoiled pristine naturalness of conditions in Greece."[22]

To bridge the gulf between the ancient world and our own exceptional means are required. "What a leap from that race of men to ours! What kinship is there between the man who heard the voice of his god in the rustling branches of a tall oak at Dodona and contemporary man, who seems to stand in no relation at all to creation? Therein lies the difficulty of understanding that distant time.

If we wish to return to it, we must first lose ourselves."[23] Only by "losing himself," then, only by rediscovering the other in himself, can the modern scholar hope to find his way back beyond the grave in which "wasted and turned to dust, the corpse" of the past lies buried.[24] "Abundance of information is not everything, it is not even the essential. . . . Without a thorough transformation of our whole being, without a return to ancient simplicity and health of soul, one cannot gain the merest intimation of the greatness of those ancient times . . . when the human race had not yet, as it has today, departed from its harmony with creation and the transcendent creator."[25] Winckelmann's greatness among classical scholars was in his having achieved such a transformation; his "magical" history of art was written "beneath the warmer sun of Italy . . . ; it is no product of our smoky study rooms, with their rancid smell of tallow candles and oil lamps."[26]

Far from facilitating our journey back to an earlier, simpler time of life, the instruments of criticism and analysis developed by the modern intellect bar our way. All they reveal to us, in Bachofen's view, is ourselves. Oppressed by overcast skies, shrouded in hyperborean mists or shut up in his smoky study, reading by the artificial light of a lamp, the northern scholar can never see antiquity as it is in the glorious natural light of Greece. Images of the Platonic cave return again and again as Bachofen mocks modern German scholars— *"Rauchclubbisten"* ("smoking club men"), as he calls them disdainfully[27]—and their puny efforts to reconstitute the life of antiquity from books. The claim of those same scholars to legislate what was to count as the true voice of antiquity and what was to be rejected as false roused him to indignant protest. History is not "a mere appendage of philology," he protested,[28] and the worth of a testimony cannot be measured simply by determining the age or authenticity of a document or by applying criteria of probability that tell more about the scholar's own age than they reveal about the objects to which they are applied.[29]

As time went on, Bachofen's expressions of outrage at the imperialist claims of the critical philological school, which had established itself in all the major universities of the German-speaking world, grew more and more vehement. The "Wolves of the North," who have "hacked Homer to pieces," he once called them, punning on the name of the founder of modern Homeric criticism, Friedrich August Wolf, and referring to the theory that the *Iliad* was not the work of an individual poet but a communal production.[30] And it was as predators that he saw them, lacking all sympathy with the remote past, reaching out to it violently and brutally with instruments of dissection and appropriation, more intent on furthering their careers in the contemporary world by coming up with provocative and attention-getting theories and speculations than on gaining true insight into the past they purported to be studying, and impotent, because of their resentment of everything grand and heroic, to appreciate its greatness. (Characteristically, Bachofen used an economic metaphor to refer to the theory of the collective composition of the *Iliad:* the "gigantic figure" of Homer, he wrote, was "dissolved into a collective idea that could be offered for sale in a quantity of small lots, like a great property after the owner has died, so that it can be put within reach of the feeble resources of the poor.")[31] More caution, piety, and humility are in order. "Our objective should not be to resolve all problems. He who strains his eyes in the dark loses his vision."[32] The true scholar, in contrast, accustoms himself gradually to the dark, and slowly learns to guide his steps on unfamiliar paths.

Almost invariably, Bachofen identified the object on which the philologists exercised their critical skills with the "Oriental" aspect of ancient culture, that "antiquity of antiquity" still connected with the ancient culture of Mother Right that the Ancients themselves tried to repress. Homer, the harbinger of the new age, as we already saw, was also for Bachofen the last representative of the matriarchal cultures of the Orient.[33] The outrageous *"Zerstückelung"* ("dissection") of Homer[34] thus belongs in the same category as Mommsen's critique of the Coriolanus myth. In both cases, it is the mother, the emblem of wholeness or totality, that is being attacked, and Bachofen is the pious son who comes to her defense. "If woman is man's stick and staff," he wrote to a friend on the birth of his own son, ". . . this boy should in turn be her shield and where necessary also her lance."[35] The scholarly approach Bachofen advocated is not aggressive or invasive or analytical; it is—he claimed—"empirical," that is to say, the object will not be violated or penetrated but explored cautiously, with respect for its integrity. In the end, knowing the object is not possession or domination but a form of loving contemplation, in which the barrier between subject and object falls as the subject recognizes himself in the object.

"I repudiate all that pedantry [*Schulmeisterei*] that rejects instead of explaining, and that substitutes constructions based on the critic's own conceptions," Bachofen announced to Meyer-Ochsner in 1851. "I am conservative, not destructive, and I still believe Livy, Cicero, Dionysius knew far more of their people's customs and history than Niebuhr. The historical scholar hearkens and elucidates; he does not master and he does not destroy."[36] The same idea recurred later in a letter to Ludwig Ross, a professor of classics at Halle who had become, like Bachofen, a somewhat eccentric and lonely figure among the classical scholars of his day on account of his impenitent opposition to the school of Niebuhr and his insistence on the Oriental origins of classical culture.[37] "The effort to achieve understanding is the only genuine form of criticism," Bachofen wrote to Ross.[38] That *"die wahre Kritik liegt im Verständnis"* was again, many years later, the motto of the *Antiquarische Briefe.* But it was in a letter to the pioneer American ethnologist Lewis Morgan, in which he denounced the way Mommsen had portrayed Coriolanus "in the attire of a guard of Louis XIV" and the Roman kings and *gentes* as "prototypes of the German Emperor and the penurious aristocracy surrounding his throne," that Bachofen expressed most clearly, in still fluent but by the 1880s no longer idiomatic English, the essence of his critical credo. "The task of the historian consists in showing the difference of what has been and what is now. But historians of this description are a great exception now a days. . . . German historians especially follow another way. They propose to make antiquity intelligible by measuring it according to the popular ideas of our present days. They only see themselves in the creations of the past: hence their stupidity to reject [stupid rejection of] all traditions that will not allow [themselves] to be mistreated in that way. To penetrate the structure of a mind different from our own is a hardy work."[39]

As early as 1841, in his inaugural lecture at the University of Basel, Bachofen had defined the proper method to be followed by the student of antiquity. It was recognizably that of the historical school, as he might have learned it from Ranke's lectures at the University of Berlin. Only a reference to the "ancient mother" added a characteristic personal note: "Let us not be deceived about historical truth by brilliant systems. Let us follow . . . the old oracle, as it was communicated to Aeneas: *Antiquam exquirite matrem*. . . . The observation of that which history has produced, the empirical study of the past is the great principle on which all true knowledge and all progress rest."[40]

This essentially anti-Enlightenment, anti-*philosophe*, anti-Revolutionary position—common enough among the scholars of the Restoration, particularly the members of the German historical school who were Bachofen's teachers, and restated repeatedly throughout Bachofen's career[41]—was intensified by the experience of his first visit to Italy in 1842–1843. By the 1850s he was describing that visit as a revelation, through which antiquity appeared to him with a vividness and immediacy that no book study had been able to achieve. "How oppressive the poverty of our German life is, how inadequate to the true contemplation and enjoyment of antiquity. Whoever has seen Italy but once with his senses will immediately feel how we in these parts, with all our study, can only manage to peer out from our obscure corner at the great spectacle of antiquity; whereas the scholar who lives and meditates in Italy is already placed in the midst of it; life and study unite to form in him a fundamental conception of antiquity that penetrates everything he produces like a living breath."[42]

Human beings, their cultures, and their natural habitats are all intimately related, Bachofen would write—in the *History of the Romans* and in the account of his journey to Greece—and living nature often speaks louder to us than inert signs on a printed page. Books cannot deliver to us the living spirit of antiquity as effectively as the physical remnants of ancient culture and the unchanged landscape in which the Ancients themselves once lived,[43] and where occasionally, even among the inhabitants, the practiced eye can still discern present traces of ancient beauty.[44] Texts, moreover, can be disputed, manipulated, diminished by petty criticism. The demolition work of the German *"Rauchclubbisten"* illustrates abundantly, in Bachofen's view, the helplessness of texts before the arbitrary constructions of critics more taken with their own theories than with recovering the truth and reality of what lies before them. If it were possible to deal as easily with the massive walls of the Ancients as it is with literary documents, he observed, the Germans would already have cleared the hill on which Tiryns stands.[45]

Paradoxically, the physical decay of the material remains of antiquity is not a disadvantage in Bachofen's view. Just as death to him is the gateway to eternal life, so we must pass through absence to rediscover presence. Ruins, he claimed, do not excite the intellectual ingenuity and the analytical, dissecting talents that the study of texts excites in the philologist. Instead, by releasing us from the immediacy of material reality, ruins stimulate the effort of the imagination to reconstitute a vanished humanity in its wholeness and to reach beyond its passing empirical existence to the contemplation of its enduring essence.[46] This view of ruins brings Bachofen again close to his countryman Burckhardt. According to the poet Carl Spitteler, who was his student at the *Pädagogium,* it was not so much antiquity itself that Burckhardt cared about, as the study of antiquity. For Burckhardt, as for Bachofen, the object of desire was not the past itself but what only the study of it can deliver: its enduring beauty and significance, redeemed from time and death.

The special value Bachofen attributed to physical ruins and natural landscapes underlines the most important feature of his hermeneutics. Understanding, for him, is not a purely intellectual process. Along with virtually the entire Restoration and romantic generation in Germany, he believed that reason detached from feeling and other nonrational faculties is a dangerous and corrupting guide, as the French Revolution had, in their judgment, amply demonstrated. "Where the head moves ahead faster than the heart," he noted in the *Griechische Reise,* "man succumbs to the dark drives buried in the lowest depths of his soul."[47] A humanity that represses the qualities characteristic of its earlier stages is preparing trouble for itself. Instinct and habit will always be capable of much that is beyond the power of reason. Picking his way through the rocky pass of Dervenaki south of Corinth, Bachofen admired the skill of his horse and observed that "the glory of man's intelligence and the superiority of his mind are put to shame by the instinct and habit of the beast."[48] It is one of the misfortunes of modern political life that love has been banished from it to the private domestic sphere, he noted in the *Politische Betrachtungen über das römische Staatsrecht,* for in law and right human beings are isolated from each other, whereas love and religion bind them together.[49] The state that rests on law alone is already in decline.[50] The healthy state, in contrast, is one in which law and love or religion work together; the healthy culture, one in which the paternal rule of spirit and the maternal law of nature have been substantially reconciled. Thus the Latins, according to Bachofen, represented "the author of their freedom," King Servius Tullius, as the son and as himself the founder of the cult of Fortuna Muliebris, who "protects faithful wives from male high-handedness."[51]

Correspondingly, the ideal form of understanding is one in which there is continuity between the knowing subject and the object of its quest or desire. Knowledge is founded not on the techniques by which the subject attempts to master the object, but on the object itself—conceived as living, enduring manifestations of spirit, as "the spirit of the times as it is disclosed in tradition," not as inert and ephemeral facts or "empirical events"—and on the subject's respect for it. "What distinguishes our scientific method from the modern method that likes to call itself critical," Bachofen explained, "is chiefly our conception of the object of investigation and attitude toward it."[52] Understanding and "appropriating to ourselves" the history of early times is thus not a purely intellectual process [*keine Verständnisoperation*].[53] The meaning of the mute and dense symbols in which the Ancients expressed their deepest thoughts, for instance, is "more sensed by us in the interior of the soul than comprehended by the mind."[54] We immediately recognize this kind of understanding, because it possesses us entirely and fills us with "a feeling of unspeakable joy similar to that of a man born blind when the scales are removed from his eyes. We feel richer than all the kings of the earth. And it is only gradually that we discover all the articulations of our thought, get a grasp of what we have won, and hope to win yet more." At such moments, everything is intensified, and we are rewarded with a vision of eternity. "What we enjoy, we enjoy more deeply, and so too our inner suffering, the unfulfillable longing of our souls, wells up more powerfully in us. . . . Knowledge becomes indistinguishable from feeling. All our thoughts, all our experiences, all our struggles rise from their slumbers in the depths of the soul, come to the surface, and are there united in a glorious and unfathomable intuition of the eternal, which rises as our highest prayer to the throne of the heavenly father."[55] That this mode of acquiring understanding is not without its dangers Bachofen himself acknowledged when he admitted to Savigny that he might easily "have strayed into metaphysical bypaths" and been "led to phantasms of the Huschke variety." By the reference to Huschke, a professor of law well known for his attachment to the ideas of Schelling, Bachofen clearly intended to distance himself from Schelling and his alleged "pantheism."[56]

The understanding acquired by flashes of insight is not only capable of leading the scholar astray, it is hard to communicate or even to retain. "These are great, rich moments in which the scholar of antiquity feels he is one with his object!" Bachofen wrote. "But they can last only a short time."[57] Not being the result of a pure process of reasoning, they cannot be retained or called up at will. Likewise, their content cannot be communicated by means of concepts or through the discrete signs of ordinary language. Not even visual representation is adequate. Trying to put down on paper the scene that had moved him deeply at Mycenae, Bachofen noted that he could not "find a way to retain it. The best of everything we sense and feel is unsayable. What had been living and moving within us becomes a rigid skeleton on paper. Instead of the vivid and colorful picture, all you will be able to set down and hold is the outline of the shadows."[58] In these conditions, the best the writer can hope for from his writing or the scholar from his interpretation is that it will in turn be the occasion of a moment of insight on the part of the reader. It is consistent with Bachofen's romantic hermeneutics that his prose often rises to poetry, and that his interpretations often take the form of poetic restatements, in different terms, of the materials he is ostensibly analyzing (and, consequently, that they can be invoked in support of quite contradictory discursive arguments and political ideologies).

The modern student of myth, as Bachofen conceived him, thus finds himself in this respect in a position remarkably similar to that of the ancient poets and tellers of myth themselves. For as narrative, myth is already an unfolding, unraveling or opening up—in Bachofen's understanding of it, and in this he follows Creuzer—of the dense, closed oneness of symbol. "Myth is the exegesis of the symbol. It unfolds in a series of outwardly connected actions what the symbol embodies in a unity. It resembles a discursive philosophical treatise in so far as it splits the idea into a number of connected images." At the same time, however, myth respects the mystery embedded in the symbol. "To expound the mystery doctrine in words would be a sacrilege against the supreme law; it can only be represented in terms of myth."[59] Myth is thus situated between the ancient mute materiality of the symbol and the modern world of the concept, participating—unlike either of these—in both the Orient and the Occident, the natural world of the mothers and the spiritual world of the fathers, doing justice to both and excluding neither. Myth therefore enjoys the privileged status in Bachofen's work of other points of juncture that preserve what they have displaced, like Rome and Mycenaean Greece.

The authentic modern interpreter of myth does not abolish the mystery. Interpretation in his hands does not supersede myth; it becomes another version of it. The mythographer participates to some degree in the world of myth. He has not made himself a complete stranger to it. Hence his frequent designation in Bachofen's letters as an "Oedipus."[60] As already noted, Bachofen's explanations of classical monuments and myths are often highly poetical texts that discover unsuspected and strikingly suggestive layers of meaning in the old material. Thus in *Mother Right,* he can recognize the erotic significance of Jocasta's clasp-pin, or of Oedipus's swollen "foot"—the sign of his "shamelessness" and of his roots in "the unregulated tellurian sexuality of the swamp."[61] But the erotic is not a fact for Bachofen; it is itself symbolic. The work of exegesis, as he practiced it, is intended to enrich the meaning or signifying power of the myth or symbol that is being interpreted, not reduce it to a single reference; it develops the myth, it does not try to eliminate it.

The scholar who arbitrarily applies the methods of critical philology to the mythical tradition and fails to respect its integrity, Bachofen maintained, will never truly understand it or reveal anything significant about it. "Pour comprendre une tradition, il faut commencer par l'accepter."⁶² Whoever refuses to en- ter the tradition sympathetically and chooses instead to remain outside cannot hope to understand its richness and coherency or what it meant to those who lived by it and in it. In the end, the goal of such an individual cannot be to interpret but only to destroy. It is unlikely that Bachofen did not consider his reflections on myth in the context of the highly charged nineteenth-century debate around the criticism and interpretation of the Bible. "Without human truth," he conceded in the Introduction to *Tanaquil,* "divine truth cannot satisfy the Western mind. But the opposite extreme, so highly regarded today, is as- suredly far worse, namely the exclusive emphasis on human truth, which with- out divine truth remains sterile and unsanctified."⁶³ These views seem to situate Bachofen close to De Wette, who acknowledged the mythical character of a large part of the Bible but insisted equally that the biblical text is not thereby disqualified as a valid source of genuine understanding and of truth. Certainly Bachofen placed himself squarely in the camp of the antimodernists in that debate by adopting a positive attitude to myth and refusing to view it simply as a "primitive" anticipation of philosophical notions that have finally been brought to such clear conceptual articulation that they can now replace religion.

Bachofen's idea of the scholar's task led him to take a dim view of the armies of career scholars who had turned classical philology in Germany into some- thing quite different from what the neohumanists of the early years of the cen- tury had envisaged. Where the neohumanists had seen the study of antiquity as a vocation, the new philologists saw it as a career; where the neohumanists saw it as a total inner education or formation of the individual (*"Bildung"*), the philologists saw it as an exercise in critical method and an accumulation of reli- able information (*"Wissenschaft"*). On both counts, Bachofen remained faithful to the neohumanist doctrines he had absorbed at the Basel *Gymnasium* and *Pädagogium,* while integrating them into his own more highly colored roman- tic vision.

His almost religious conception of scholarly work seems to have taken deep root in the period of uncertainty and confusion following his resignation from the University and the Senate, when he began to review the study of Roman law as he had been pursuing it until then. The acute sense of providential guid- ance in the affairs of men that he developed in those years, combined perhaps with the Calvinist doctrine of calling, appears to have reinforced his conviction that the study of antiquity was a vocation. "It is not the man who has chosen his studies," he remarked of the Duc de Luynes, "but they that have chosen him."⁶⁴ In addition, there is a close connection between the idea of scholarship as calling and the inner affinity with the subject matter that Bachofen believed essential to the student of the past. If the kind of understanding Bachofen ex- pected was to occur, the scholar—as we have seen—could not stand back from the object; above all, he could not be disdainful of it. Confirmed rationalists hostile to religion, for instance, were simply incapable of understanding ancient societies, since these were founded on religious beliefs. Not anybody, therefore, was fit to study the Ancients. Some, probably a fairly small band, were chosen.

The idea of scholarship as vocation also sat well with Bachofen's frequently professed "empiricism"—by which he meant a kind of Goethean attentiveness to the object world with a view to discovering its internal laws, as opposed to the Kantian and Enlightenment effort to grasp the world by the activity of "comparing, examining, distinguishing, abstracting, deducing, and demonstrating."[65] "The material alone is my preceptor," he declared, and vowed he would never try to "arrive at a picture of the origins by philosophical speculation, to fill in the great gaps in our historical records with the shadowy figures of abstract reasoning." Instead he would steer a "course close to *terra firma,* following the bends and bays of the shoreline, avoiding the dangers and accidents of the high seas."[66]

Consistently with his elevated notion of scholarship as the vocation of a chosen few, Bachofen had only contempt for the busywork of discovering, describing, and classifying the remains of antiquity that, according to him, occupied the legions of German academic philologists—not to mention the *"kleine Winckelmännchen,"* as he called them, of the local Basel antiquarian society.[67] "We have far too many details, and almost no comprehensive views," he complained.[68] "Paraphrasing the scene and identifying the figures represented" on Greek vases or sarcophagi, for instance, is simply not enough.[69] It won't do to say: "This is Alcestes, this is Telephus, this is Niobe, etc." The scholar must interpret, bring home "living thoughts, not just dry notices."[70] But most modern scholars have no feeling for the greatness of antiquity[71] and are not willing to recognize anything that goes beyond their own prosaic understanding. "People want to find in antiquity the ordinariness and the dearth of ideas by which they themselves are afflicted. I am more and more convinced that every one sees in antiquity exactly what he is capable of."[72] Above all, there is a general refusal to acknowledge the religious element in ancient life, to go beyond surface description, classification, and aestheticizing commentary, to recognize the symbolic character of nearly all ancient art. "This is the sort of thing you hear: 'Gentlemen, you see here a girl playing ball; the Ancients often manifest their child-like sensibility in the choice of such naive scenes; probably the deceased had been partial to such innocent pleasures during her lifetime. A few mystical minds have imagined they could discern deeper ideas, but they did not take into consideration that the clarity of the Hellenic spirit rejects everything mystical. Let us stick to the simple and obvious content; the image belongs among Panofka's Scenes of Everyday Life.'"[73]

Partly because of their "narrow political circumstances" (by which Bachofen doubtless was referring to the Germans' exclusion from participation in the affairs of the polis, in contrast to the active involvement in government of the humanists of Basel), partly as a result of a "false admiration for a so-called classicism" inculcated in them in their schools, Bachofen wrote to Morgan, the German philologists suffer from "a pitifully one-sided vision. . . . Everything is isolated from everything else, torn out of its context and then judged, criticized and thoroughly disfigured in accordance with modern tea-table ideas."[74] The term *"schulmeistern"*—as in *"Köchly schulmeistert den Homer"*[75]—conveys Bachofen's contempt for the myopic labors of scholars whose reputations have been built on reducing the grandeur of antiquity to the dimensions of a school textbook fit for general consumption. With these ambitious, career-minded, scholar-workers, comparable to the revolutionaries of 1848 in their deliberate disrespect for everything that is sacred in antiquity (Köchly's Homer is described as "authentic Garibaldi-literature"),[76] Bachofen would have no truck. "Not being a schoolman," he told the French anarchist Elie Reclus, in terms strikingly similar to those often used by his fellow citizen Jacob Burckhardt, "I do not write for scholars like the grand Academicians of the Pont-Neuf [i.e., of the Académie des Inscriptions] but for intelligent individuals who are interested in learning about the origins of our species and in studying a condition of barbarism of which we have no right to be ashamed."[77]

By the late 1850s Bachofen's disagreement with the mainstream philologists of his day had assumed the form of a bitter polemic in which the wealthy patrician citizen of the republic of Basel set himself up as the representative and champion of tradition, hermeneutic, and old-style humanism in opposition to Theodor Mommsen, the highly successful northern professor (Mommsen hailed, like Niebuhr, from Schleswig-Holstein), president of the Royal Prussian Academy, political liberal, and advocate of modernization and of philology as a "science." Mommsen was also the prize-winning author of a popular *Roman History* (1854–1856), the success of which contrasted painfully with the failure of Bachofen's slightly earlier *History of the Romans* (1851). It was an additional source of embitterment and frustration to Bachofen that the polemic remained entirely one-sided and that his work was, in his own words, "studiously ignored" in Germany.[78] No one need fear, he told Meyer-Ochsner many years afterwards, that "I shall be set upon by howling mobs. The only punishment a Swiss is deemed worthy of by the Prussianized Berlin clique, which now enthusiastically supports Bismarck as it previously supported the Augustenburgs, . . . is absolute silence."[79]

It must have been obvious to Bachofen from the start that the odds were strong against him. Even his good Zurich friend Meyer-Ochsner was shocked when he dared to find fault with Niebuhr, the revered father of the new critical historiography of the ancient world. Both Creuzer and Hegel had criticised Niebuhr, but by the 1850s the philological school was so firmly entrenched that any divergence seemed like madness. "How can a reasonable man accuse the

genius who created the early history of Rome of being reckless and imprudent?"
Meyer-Ochsner wrote. Bachofen responded that he had expressed himself with
unusual vehemence because "I am engaged in a genuine struggle. . . . Niebuhr
is a genius, and I honor him. But I am opposed to his orientation and to his
conception of scholarship in general, and the further I advance in my own work,
the more vehemently I shall oppose both."[80] His attention turned to Theodor
Mommsen as the scholar on whom the mantle of Niebuhr had fallen and who
stood out more and more as the leader of an increasingly entrenched, organized,
and monolithic philological profession. Bachofen was convinced that it was the
deliberate policy of the profession to marginalize and effectively silence any
individual who, like himself, refused to "blow the trumpet of the latest scholarly
fashion" or who "permitted himself to diverge from the Royal Prussian point of
view."[81] "It is impossible to fight successfully against an entire insurance company of scientific—or rather—unscientific cliques," he declared.[82] "If I were a
Berliner, I would be taken at my word. As a Baseler, I do not enjoy that privilege."[83] The critique of Mommsen did not, therefore, turn simply on a disputed
point of scholarship. It was directed at the basic principles of the philological
school and at the overwhelming influence it exerted through its control of university teaching posts and learned journals. "My business is not with Mommsen
as an individual," Bachofen explained. "He is for me the very type of the modern way of thinking, and deserves to be dealt with as such."[84]

Mommsen had favorably reviewed an early academic essay of Bachofen's,
dating from before the latter's reassessment of his scholarly aims and career in
the late 1840s, but he responded to the *Geschichte der Römer* (1851), the first
major publication in Bachofen's new manner, with a scathing denunciation in
Zarncke's *Historisches Centralblatt*. The work was a complete failure, he declared, due to the author's disregard of the most elementary principles of Niebuhrian criticism. There is no sifting of early tradition from later accretions, no
serious attempt to distinguish authentic ancient tales from the later "chatter of
schoolmen and poets" ("*Schul- und Poetengeschwätz*"). It is as though Niebuhr
had never written. The style itself, hovering between the pedestrian and the
inspirational, is an "aesthetic and logical disaster." And finally, the basic idea—
that the ancient Roman constitution rested on a theocratic foundation—is an
"illusion," ideologically motivated rather than scientifically founded.[85]

On his side, Bachofen had taken an early dislike to Mommsen, in whom
he saw, from the beginning, an ambitious academic careerist, and whom he
immediately associated with the wheedling commercialism and sycophancy of
the day. "His motto is: 'I smear words on paper, like polish on boots,'" he told
Meyer-Ochsner.[86] He was outraged by the "criminal" portrayal of the Roman
people as "rationalists" in the *Roman History* and began to attack Mommsen in
letters to Savigny, Meyer-Ochsner, and Eduard Gerhard, a leading figure in

classical studies at Berlin and a former fellow student under Böckh.[87] His opposition to Mommsen became public in a review of a work by Gerlach written for the *Augsburger Allgemeine Zeitung.* "What would the world know of Rome," he asked, "if the only source of knowledge left to it were Niebuhr and Mommsen?"[88] In 1861 Mommsen was portrayed disdainfully as an entrepreneur, sending his *commis-voyageurs* or salesmen to Spain and other places in order to corner the market in the popular inscription collecting business.[89] The same year, the publication of a third edition of the *Roman History*—of which Bachofen still received a courtesy copy—and the award of the Bavarian Academy's Gold Medal to the author unleashed a flood of hostile feelings. From the moment of this official consecration of a work that for Bachofen epitomized the modern philological approach to antiquity, the Basel scholar's hatred was unrelenting. Mommsen was now established as the emblem of everything he found repugnant not only in modern classical studies but in the modern world in general.

In a letter to Meyer-Ochsner that is filled with echoes of traditional European republicanism—including that of Rousseau, with whom Bachofen was not otherwise much in sympathy![90]—he wrote that Mommsen's *Roman History* has filled him "with rage and deep revulsion."

> I have read the book several times over, very attentively, and I can say with absolute conviction, *sine ira et studio*, that there are no words to characterize the author's truly villainous infamy. It is a duty to protest publicly against such a book for it is a mark of this century's ignominy that such a miserable production could actually be awarded a prize and acclaimed as a significant accomplishment. I have to overcome a genuine distaste for participating in public discussion; but, as I observed, I regard it as a duty to speak out in protest. I do not hope to convince or convert. But at a later time, when humanity has returned to its senses, it should at least not be possible to say our age had sunk so low that it did not even enter a protest.
>
> So "Mommsen and the History of Rome" is my new project. I want to expose the entire method and procedure of this so-called historian and to depict the shameless insolence of the modern, mindless Berliner in all its repulsive nakedness. . . . At times one wonders if one is dealing with a person who is in his right mind. The reduction of Rome to the most insipid clichés of Prussian salon liberalism is especially nauseating. All the jargon of demaguery crops up as early as the age of kings, so that absolutely everything is hauled in under the most miserable concepts and completely stood on its head. The only moving force of ancient life, it appears, was trade and commerce. You read constantly of imports and exports, the balance of trade, speculation, competition, free ports, navigation acts, factories and emporia, as though these could provide the principal, indeed the only point of view from which to consider and judge the lives of nations. This "practical point of view" is even extended to religion. There is talk of the "clear-minded rationalism" of the Romans, Roman law is considered from the point of view of personal credit and credit based on real estate, economic liberalism, the abolition of tariffs. And those who are not yet

ready for such high ideals are dismissed in expressions such as "There are scholars against whom it is not worth invoking such arguments, who are incapable of thinking," etc. etc. The Romans, we are now to believe, had records enough and to spare, but they could no longer understand them, so they served up as many tall tales as their imagination could concoct. Thus we would do well, "if we would be impartial scholars, to get rid, first and foremost, of all the stuff that goes by the name of tradition," in order to make room for the most arbitrary historical inventions, and thus cause the good Lord to take note of our suggestions, so that he can make history unfold in a more logical manner in the future. . . . History is no more than a dialectical game, it is nothing real, and truth is what can be made credible by sophistry. The entire modern age lies contained in this book, in all its arrogant, narrow, vacuous Prussian demagoguery.[91]

Meyer-Ochsner appears to have urged Bachofen to moderate his criticism, but Bachofen was unmoved. "I cannot let up in the struggle against Mommsen. Registering my protest against this view of history is an absolute necessity for me. Rome shall not be judged in the forum of Berlin. . . . Mommsen may go on copying inscriptions . . . but his hands are not worthy to hold the stylus of the historian."[92] At the end of that same year (1862) he returned to the attack. At a time when the minds of men are filled from morning to night by nothing but "building plans, loans, trade associations and other stuff of that ilk," so that one envies "the inhabitants of the northernmost Hebrides their isolation from it all," what should be the subject matter of a correspondence between two scholars, he asked Meyer-Ochsner, if not literature? The world of scholarship, in other words, should be a refuge from the ephemerality of modern commercial culture. It should be dedicated to enduring values. In Mommsen's *History,* however, precisely the opposite is the case. Far from offering the vision of another, different world, antiquity in Mommsen's account of it is invaded and taken over by modernity. "The twaddle of tradesmen and capitalists . . . runs through the entire work," encouraging "the illusion that the greatness of a people is grounded in the degree of perfection of its theories of political economy." Bachofen's mission was now not only to expose all the errors in Mommsen's account of Rome but to alert the world to the dangers of the path on which it has embarked. "I want to show our entire age what principles it has bred up and raised to power over men. Only now that I have studied this work carefully do I have a clear insight into the latest stage in the development of the spirit in Germany." In fact, we can be grateful to Mommsen "for expressing so nakedly and unreservedly everything that the times carry in them. It is always good when a disease declares itself decisively and unambiguously."

The political and moral basis of Bachofen's opposition to Mommsen was now openly acknowledged. "Don't think for a moment that all that is at issue here is the credibility of the traditional accounts of the early history of Rome. That aspect appears as only a modest consequence of a cultural trend. . . . In general, Rome and the Romans are not Mommsen's real concern. The heart of the book is its application of the latest ideas of the times, its apotheosis of the boundless radicalism of modern Prussia's Friends of Light. Only a Carl Vogt or some other of that species would ever have dreamed of abusing scholarly discussion of historical material from classical antiquity and turning it to partisan ends in such a manner. . . . I leave aside the question of scholarship altogether. The book is without any. . . . I have not come upon a single page that has the least scholarly merit. But the basic doctrines which the author seeks to propose to the youth of our time, by way of Roman history, . . . are of a kind to make Satan rejoice."[93]

The criticism of Mommsen was now made increasingly in the name of the free city-republics of Europe. Those guardians of the old humanism find their independence threatened by an upstart, cynical, increasingly powerful and imperialist state whose rulers, Bachofen charged, aided and abetted by myriads of dependent bureaucrats, flatter the appetites of the masses in order to enroll them in the service of their ambitions. "I intend to show the rabble of court councilors in those petty German capitals that, even in its decline, republicanism still preserves a healthier outlook than the mean resentment of everything that once was great on this earth, which in the present condition of general decay is spreading everywhere."[94] The narrowness and the unimaginativeness of German classical scholarship reflects the narrowness of the Germans' political experience and their lack of a republican tradition of individual freedom and responsibility. The most open and inquiring spirits writing in German all belong to free cities: "Burckhardt [i.e., Johann Ludwig or John Lewis Burckhardt, known as 'Sheikh Ibrahim'—a distant relative of Bachofen's], Münziger, Ruppell, Barth: all citizens of small republics [i.e., of Basel, Solothurn, Frankfurt am Main, and Hamburg] and on that account provided with love and understanding of men and of remarkable small human communities."[95] In Bachofen's mind Mommsen, the dictator of the Prussian scholarly empire, was more and more associated with Bismarck, the manager of Prussian political imperialism, and he saw the German scholars as toadies of power and inveterate enemies not only of traditional authorities but of traditional freedoms. Just as scholars associated with the National Liberals had supported the Augustenburgs' attempt to usurp the Danish throne during the 1848 revolt of Schleswig-Holstein against Danish rule, so twenty-two years later they were massed behind Bismarck and his new German Empire. Of Adolf Kiessling, a German scholar who had occupied a chair at Basel for a number of years, Bachofen remarked that he was "an enthusiastic Bismarckian, a bootlicker of Mommsen's" and "an admirer of Tiberius."[96] Mommsen himself would later describe modern scholarship as *"Grosswissenschaft,"* on the model of the modern *"Grossstaat"* and modern *"Grossindustrie,"* and argue that like these, it must be *"nicht von Einem geleistet, aber von Einem geleitet"* ("carried out by many, but led by one").[97]

Mommsen thus represented everything Bachofen had grown to loathe and feel oppressed by: modern critical philology, with its irreverent scrutiny or outright rejection of traditional sources, its narrow vision, its focus on the accuracy of individual facts, and its contempt for myth; a "modernizing" approach to ancient history in which concepts borrowed from modern economics and *Realpolitik*, but utterly alien—in Bachofen's view—to the Ancients themselves, and inadequate to the task of understanding a culture built on different premises from those of the nineteenth century, became the interpreter's guiding threads; the use of ancient history to lend ideological support to the goals of modern liberalism, nationalism, and imperialism—as "the handmaiden of current interests," in Bachofen's own words;[98] the organization of scholarship itself along business lines, for the production of *"Wissenschaft"* rather than to enhance the culture (*"Bildung"*) of the individual and the community; and finally the rise of modern Prussia and of the new German Empire (in contrast with "Renaissance" Basel), seen as marking the culmination of modernity, capitalist economics, technical progress, industrialism, militarism, the welfare state based on popular suffrage, and the end of the humanist "culture of old Europe" (in Burckhardt's words).

Bachofen turns out to be no less concerned than Burckhardt, who had also reacted with outrage to Mommsen's *Roman History*[99]—or for that matter, Nietzsche—at what they all considered the disappearance of individuality and the banalization of moral and intellectual life under modern democracy and the modern centralized state. As early as 1847, recommending the appointment of Bernhard Windscheid as professor of law at Basel, he had warned that while the candidate had solid virtues, he was "not a creative nature who will open up new paths in scholarship." Such creative persons, rare at all times, were particularly hard to find in the present age. Even lesser geniuses were thin on the ground. "In our time, minds too have been made uniform. Only in a few cases does individuality [*ihr eigentümliches Ich*] survive the school and the lecture room." In 1847, Bachofen had not yet forgotten the favorable impression made on him by the cultural achievements of centralization in France and he was still ready to acknowledge that "in compensation, we have a certain general culture that is spread widely throughout the world of learning."[100] After 1848 this note is no longer heard. Increasingly, the dominant theme is contempt for the demos: Socrates was too fond of it; even Burckhardt is faulted for being, like Socrates, too favorably inclined toward the people![101] The individual, he now insists, is the source of all creativity—"In all ages, everything great has sprung from individuals"—and the individual is nurtured only in small communities. These alone "have the capacity to create. In the midst of an enormous mass, no one can stir; the mass is never favorable to independence of spirit."[102] The rise of modern mass societies is for that reason a fateful development. Even the Italians are losing their originality in the new Italian state. To the man who once wrote that "beneath the warmer sun of Italy . . . one feels everything more deeply, pain and joy and the true meaning of things," a trip to northern Italy in 1868 proved deeply disappointing. "The greatest joy of travel, making contact with different and original people and circumstances, is no longer to be had anywhere. Everything is so stale and degraded and ruled by fashion. Only nature has kept her ancient beauty and all her charm."[103] Where modern society has given us "pygmy natures," "railways and Prussian criticism," the Renaissance city-states produced great individuals and heroic scholars.[104] The benefit France may yet reap from her disastrous defeat in 1870, Bachofen wrote to a Genevan colleague, is the abolition of Caesarism and a return to republican government, for *"la république en s'adressant à l'individu est seule capable d'éveiller les vertus personnelles, qui doivent inaugurer toute régéneration politique."*[105]

For Bachofen, in short, there was a clear social and political dimension to the dispute about method. Neither his hermeneutical method nor the understanding it yields can be taught to crowds of eager, ambitious young professionals or to the mass modern reading public; neither can be expressed in unequivocal, communicable, and universally intelligible terms. Only those individuals who have retained their independence of mind and persisted in pursuing their own demon can be genuine interpreters of antiquity. While such individuals might be found in any social class or country (though old-style republican governments and small states, such as Basel, provided the most favorable conditions) and could hold widely divergent views (and Bachofen did establish contact with an extremely varied group of such independent figures in Germany, France, and America, not to mention his friend and faithful correspondent Heinrich Meyer-Ochsner in Zurich and his disciple Alexis Giraud-Theulon in Geneva), it is not hard to see that a certain degree of financial independence made it very much easier to retain intellectual independence, as Jhering had already pointed out, and as Bachofen appears to have acknowledged himself. The genuine scholar, as Bachofen saw him, is not a salaried professor or a state employee, like the German university philologists and the members of the Royal Prussian Academy, but a man of independent mind and independent means. "I have the greatest respect," he once wrote, "for people, who belong to no clique, and receive no professional salary, yet spend year after year . . . living only for their work."[106]

The Basel elite's horror of paid bureaucracies, its obstinate old-republican belief that government is an obligation of all citizens (which meant, in fact, of a wealthy, educated class intellectually and financially capable of assuming responsibility for it) was carried over by both Bachofen and Burckhardt into the field of intellectual activity. It is not in the least surprising that Burckhardt was as repelled as his fellow citizen by Mommsen's vision of a trained professional bureaucracy as the mainstay of state power and that he vehemently denounced the subordination of education to the goal of producing efficient civil

servants, which such a vision appeared to imply.[107] Bachofen's idea of philological method thus has the stamp of a political and cultural commitment and his
opposition to contemporary critical practice was the continuation of a political
and cultural struggle on behalf of aristocracy—rule by a traditional (though not
necessarily hereditary) elite governing class—against democracy; on behalf of
those endowed by birth with a natural (though not necessarily hereditary) propensity for creating and appreciating culture and for exercising authority
against those who sought to acquire both "artificially"; on behalf of the old-
style humanism still pursued in the few surviving city-states against the modern philological "science" promoted by the *Grossstaat;* on behalf of the old free
city-state against the modern *Grossstaat* (post-1866 Prussia and, *a fortiori,* post-
1871 imperial Germany); and, in general, on behalf of the traditional small
European city and its way of life against the modern national metropolis
(*Gründerzeit* Berlin or Second Empire Paris, the *"Pharaonstadt an der Seine"*)[108].
In this struggle, aristocracy, the free city-state, and old-style humanism were
pitted, in Bachofen's eyes, against regimentation, uniformity, and tyranny. They
constituted a space appropriate to the *human,* a space that Bachofen also
praised, as we shall see, in his account of the development of human society.
Method and matter in Bachofen's work convey the same message.

9

"Spinning and Weaving"
The Forming of Matter

Human history and society—as Bachofen presented them—describe a movement that is also played out in the life of each individual, a movement from primitive chaos and promiscuity, the infinitely fertile "swamp" of unbridled sexuality,[1] to a superior condition in which sexuality and the body are governed by "higher" ends. The movement begins with the pure "law of nature"—the subordination of the individual to the species and the inevitable natural cycle of birth and death. (Bachofen liked to recall that in ancient symbolism "the veil of youth conceals the wrinkled forehead of the primordial mother.")[2] Its goal is the law of spirit, the subordination of the bonds of blood and natural affection to legal and ethical obligations and of the natural community or the tribe to the state, the emergence of the individual from the mass. Here the male or paternal principle at last achieves primacy over the female or maternal principle—not, as in the earliest, most primitive stage of human development, when the male exercised violence on the female while remaining himself a mere instrument of the natural order, but as a spiritual force, freed from the law of the body and the natural economy of procreation. Religious faith in the rebirth of the individual to eternal life has here taken precedence over the natural religion of regeneration through the material cycle of birth and death. The binary oppositions (body–spirit, chaos–order, female–male, East–West, left [sinister]–right, and so on) that mark the terms of this movement are ancient. Aristotle traced them back at least to the Pythagoreans and to Alcmaeon of Croton.[3] The pattern described by the movement from the one to the other informs all the triumphant epic narratives of the West from Homer to Hegel, Droysen, and Michelet.

Into this familiar pattern Bachofen introduced an intermediate stage—itself suggested by the writings of the Ancients, notably Plutarch, an author who anticipated Bachofen's loyalty in an imperial age to the ideal of the small polis—which he portrays in glowing colors and on which he dwells lovingly. This is the stage at which nature begins to be transformed into culture and the pure materiality of the body to be infused with an element of spirit, as the female hetaera is replaced by the mother who imposes the first laws restricting sexuality. Between the swamp and the city there is the world of agriculture; between the hetaera and the father, there is the mother; between the cult of Aphrodite and the cult of Apollo, there is the cult of the mother-goddess, Demeter. The East and the female are thus represented in Bachofen's work not as the radically Other, that which has to be excluded from the city, but as that from which all subsequent culture sprang. Though he does not question the relative inferiority of this early stage of culture, Bachofen emphasizes not only its achievement in preparing the way for the still "higher" culture of the fathers but—in the spirit of Ranke—its unique and irreplaceable qualities. He thereby moderates the triumphalism of the story of the victory of the West over the East, the male over the female, the state over the community, without repudiating it. His work urges more humility, less arrogance. It is hard not to recognize in the words inspired in him by the memory of antiquity and the simplicity of life even in present-day Greece the voice of the bourgeois of Basel cautioning not only against the illusions of Enlightenment optimism but against the hubris of those contemporaries—such as Droysen—who glorify the state beyond all measure and express contempt for whoever has reservations concerning the onward march of modernization, in particular the allegedly providential, historically *necessary* creation of a unified German state under Prussian leadership.

> How foolish it is to praise so loudly the progress of our Western culture and the good fortune of the peoples that participate in it. All that may be more appearance than reality, more illusion than truth. Do we not pay for each new-won benefit with the loss of two earlier ones? Are they not right who hold that the very qualities making for the greatness of man's works are also the source of their weakness? So it is also in the life of the individual. We become the victims not only of our bad deeds and qualities but, even more often, of our good ones. How frequently must we hear it said that the gigantic progress of man's technical skills justifies the hope that he will achieve complete command of nature. But do we not become with each passing day not so much nature's master as her slave? How much more free than our own are the people among whom I am peacefully passing my days? As they end their day's work with the sun, so they rise again with the sun on the morrow, and everything they think and do is informed by complete harmony with the laws of nature. Between them and nature there is not that continuous conflict that makes our lives into a never-ending struggle. Awareness of that fact can help to bring one of the most fundamental characteristics of the Ancients' view of the world far more alive before our understanding than could ever happen in some dim northern study by the flickering light of a stinking tallow-candle. In antiquity man walked hand in hand with the powers and all the phenomena of nature and, being closer to the earliest beginnings of mankind, was far more keenly aware of the common origin of all things. Everything inevitably took on a living form for him, while he himself stood in a relation of friendship and respect to the powers of the Cosmos. Thus there arose that brilliant world, in which heaven came down to earth and earth rose up to heaven. It is all gone now. But as

memories of youth throw a golden glow over old age, the spiritual riches of antiquity can shed a last beneficent glimmer of light on our own harsh and faded spiritual universe.[4]

Bachofen proposed innumerable versions of the basic movement from "tellurian" culture and religion, marked by veneration of the reproductive powers of the earth and the female body, through an intermediate "lunar" stage, "hermaphroditic" and "androgynous,"[5] to "solar," masculine spirituality. He discovered it in the history of law and the history of religion, in the evolution of the individual psyche, in the history of the species and in the histories of individual peoples, in the history of the arts and of literature; and he found it already represented in the ancient myths and legends handed down by poets, early historians, and early philosophers and exploited by the great dramatists of antiquity. (The vivid and ingenious interpretations of the works of Aeschylus and Sophocles as dramas of the overcoming of matriarchy by patriarchy are among the high points in *Das Mutterrecht* and were to be taken up again by George Thomson, the English classicist, in his *Aeschylus and Athens* [1941].) It is described as the passage from East to West; from the cult of the chthonic divinities, Aphrodite and Poseidon, to the cult of Apollo and "motherless Athena";[6] from feeling and intuition to reason and reflection; from nature and custom to law; from image to word, and symbol to myth; from the mortal and material tribe, the mass with its communal property (represented, for Bachofen, by the beehive),[7] to the state as the ideal union of the individuals composing it and the guardian of individual property (where property also has the significance of individual identity, as in the expression "proper name"). This movement is recognized anthropologically in the gradual imposition of the idea of paternal authorship, accompanied by that of paternal authority, first through the ritual of the couvade, by which the male "participates" in the process of childbearing, and then through the institution of adoption—the adopted son being "always motherless"[8]—and in the shift from Mother Right or Law to Father Right or Law, kinship systems based on descent through the female line to kinship systems based on descent through the male line. It informs, Bachofen claimed, the history and historiography of Athens and of Rome, both of which triumph as centers of paternal authority and law, and it informs the history of mankind as a whole.[9] In the conquest of Antiope, Queen of the Amazons (representing "the matriarchal state"), by Theseus (representing "the patriarchal state") and the latter's founding of Athens Bachofen claimed to see "the first act in the struggle between Europe and Asia that is the very essence of Greek history."[10] Roman history, in turn, is "the struggle by which the little community on the Palatine hill, surrounded by swamplands, leads the ethical idea of the state to victory over the materialism of the antique world,"[11] while Scipio's defeat of Carthage and Flavius's conquest of Jerusalem, which "liberated the religion of the future from Mosaic Orientalism," are considered the chief turning points in world history.[12]

The progress from the swamp to the city—the undifferentiated to the highly articulated, the mass to the individual—was for Bachofen the providentially determined and proper path of all history, as it was, *mutatis mutandis,* for Hegel and as it would be for Freud. But it was not an inevitable linear movement. Reversals and regressions might occur at any time, both in the history of mankind or of a people and in the development of the individual. Often—as one might expect the student of Ranke and Savigny to argue—these result from hubris, the attempt to erase the past and construct a revolutionary future owing nothing to anything other than present willing and conceiving. Such revolutionary, Fichtean idealism, Bachofen held, inevitably leads to the opposite of what it aspired to, as Euphorion's attempt to leave the earth in Goethe's *Faust* ends in disaster.

Bachofen's rejection of a political order from which the affective has been completely banished has already been noted in chapter 8, as has his claim for the religious foundation of political authority. The earliest forms of the state, he had argued as early as some youthful anti-Machiavellian "Observations on Livy," rest on religion. The state is seen as a divine, not a worldly institution. For Ranke, the nations are "ideas of God"; similarly, for his student all the "passing manifestations of history" are "expressions of divine creative ideas."[13] Progress consists in the state's becoming more and more worldly [*"Verwelt-lichung"*], more and more purely ethical. At first it inherits the tribe's domination of the individual. Little by little, however, the individual achieves autonomy and the bonds of religion and custom that bind him to the state are eased. In this process, however, it is vital, according to Bachofen, that the rupture never be complete. "It is custom, ancient custom that sustains the state, animates it, and reconciles us with it."[14]

History shows that in the struggle between newer and older forms of social organization, the newer forms often strive to erase every vestige of the older ones. No matter how zealously this task is pursued, Bachofen claimed, it is not only ill advised, it is never successful. The creation of new forms always requires "a long period of arduous apprenticeship."[15] The Romans, for instance, did their best at first to stamp out every vestige of the maternal, Oriental culture on which they were originally dependent and from which they arose. They destroyed Etruria (which Bachofen was convinced was settled by Pelasgi from Asia Minor and is thus "Oriental") "with incredible fury . . . and eradicated every trace of its culture." Nevertheless, "they did not succeed in suppressing every monument of this sort. Even after the people itself and its entire literature, including even its language, had disappeared, a fragment of Etruscan history was preserved in Roman history."[16] In the end, there was a "return of the repressed," as the defeated Oriental cults revived in imperial Rome. To Bachofen, the victors' eagerness to purge the historical record of all trace of the vanquished and thus of every reminder of their own early dependency on a conquered civilization forms in fact the best guarantee of the authenticity of the few surviving testimonies to an earlier, matriarchal stage of culture in the Roman annals.[17]

Bachofen's argument was that transcendence can never mean the annihilation of what has gone before, but only its transformation. Nothing dies, nothing is irretrievably lost, victory subordinates but does not abolish the vanquished or their influence. "Nowhere in history do we find a beginning, but always a continuation."[18] As the seed will always be affected by the terrain in which it is sown, the ideas of men can never grow out of nothing; they must always be partly formed by the context in which they develop. Material and historical dependency is integral to the human condition. "No pedagogue," we are told, "is more strict than nature," which shapes our spirit as well as our body.[19] Every attempt to deny or repress this "nature," the humble and too often humiliated source from which we spring, every move to abolish feeling or tradition, our "material" origin, and establish the rule of reason alone, every effort, in other words to make man into god, results in the opposite of what is intended, that is, in regression to a more primitive stage of existence. The best order we may hope to achieve, it thus turns out, is not homogeneous or uniform, but mixed—a hierarchy, in which every aspect of existence is included in its proper place, and body is not eliminated but transfigured by and subordinated to spirit. In contrast, all attempts to achieve absolute spirit end by collapsing into their opposite: absolute matter. Socialist democracy (Bachofen was convinced) prepares the way for tyranny and tyranny in turn encourages the materialism of the mass (*panis et circenses*).

This fundamental wisdom, Bachofen claimed, was understood by the Ancients who discovered it in their own history and communicated it in their legends. In the *Eumenides* of Aeschylus, though the Erinyes—the "primordial goddesses"—are defeated, "they are not banished, they are not fallen." Countering their angry resolve to "hide in the subterranean depths . . . Athene wins them over and reconciles them with the new law. Henceforth they shall serve piously by her side. . . . Beloved of maidens, they will prepare nuptial joys."[20] The healer-god Asklepeios who "from a mortal man became an immortal god" and who comes as close to a Christ figure, in Bachofen's account, as any god of antiquity, scrupulously respects the great powers of the underworld and enlists them in his work of salvation.[21] In the same way Rome, having first "sought to repress everything that was contrary to its spirit, . . . once the victory was won, . . . knew how to bend to its purposes elements that at first had been fiercely combated."[22] The hetaeric Tanaquil was not excluded from the city; instead, she was made over into a mother-goddess whose function is to represent the legitimate claims of our affective nature and to intercede on behalf of the people with the ruling fathers. As "the advocate and protectress of maternal rights against men's stern insistence on the power conferred on them by the positive civil law, . . . the champion of humanity in a society weighed down by the severity of the positive state order,"[23] she moderates the decrees of the fathers and pleads for those gentle obligations of charity and community care that the conservative patrician leaders of Bachofen's native city believed must accompany the exercise of authority. (See plate 2: Arnold Böcklin, *Das Drama.*)

Bachofen's understanding of the "Oriental" origins of both Greek and Roman civilization[24] was maintained in the face of the concerted opposition of the majority of his contemporaries and ran counter to the prevailing idealized view of Hellenic culture as somehow autonomous, owing nothing to any origin, and thus eternally youthful, perfectly harmonious, blissfully ignorant both of the terrors of death and of the insatiable longing for salvation—a perfect Eden. It was consistent not only with his Christian faith (he could not accept that some men had escaped the common lot that all human beings share with Adam)[25] and with his resolutely historical approach to all periods of the past, his insistence that "there are no autochthons," but also with his attempt to outline a universal pattern of historical evolution common to all men and all societies. The efforts of his contemporaries to discredit myth as a source of knowledge of the past undoubtedly struck him as a continuation of the Romans' own attempt to erase an "Oriental" past of which they did not wish to be reminded, and he denounced them: "A distinction between myth and history may be justified where it refers merely to a difference in mode of expression, but it has neither meaning nor justification when it creates a hiatus in the continuity of human development."[26] The argument for the "Oriental" origins of classical civilization, the theory of an intermediate "matriarchal" culture, and the rehabilitation of myth as a source of historical knowledge, are, in short, of a piece. In each case continuity is affirmed against revolution, the necessity of mediation against creation ex nihilo or radical dualism. And not surprisingly, just as Bachofen lingered lovingly over the myths of antiquity, repeatedly interpreting and commenting upon them, so too he repeatedly painted a glowing portrait of those intermediate, "matriarchal" stages of culture that have been overtaken by time. In the justification of the work of mediation, the faithful son, the pious Christian, and the Basel patrician all had a stake.

In the age of the complete triumph of paternal authority in both private and public life, Bachofen's designation of woman as the founder of culture must have seemed a startling innovation, and he himself evidently understood it in that light. His exposure of what he claimed were the early efforts of patriarchal societies to suppress or distort the truth about the matriarchal societies they had defeated is inseparable from his unrelenting critique of the modern "bootlickers of Mommsen" and admirers of Bismarck who deliberately set out to malign the preclassical age and diminish the role of woman and of religion in the early development of civilization. It took a journey to Greece itself, a radical break with the bookish scholarship and pedantic ratiocination of the smoke-filled study rooms of the foggy north, to open his own eyes, he related. But standing on Mycenae's high hill, he saw through the deceit.

> What a different idea I had previously had of the time of the Trojan War! How primitive and savage I had judged those men who expiated murder with murder, who believed in the wildness of their imagination that at the graveside of their friends they could pacify the furious shades with the blood of captured enemies, and who held it was a mother's greatest joy on her son's return from war to remove the armor of a slain enemy from his shoulders and embrace his blood-bespattered body. Now my inner eye beheld a world of infinite sweetness and gentle ways, a world so vigorously blooming in all the joy and beauty of youthful strength ... that it reminded me of an innocent, curly-headed boy next to a bald, bewigged old man.[27]

Bachofen's rehabilitation of woman is inseparable not only from his rehabilitation of ancient religion and of the civilizations of archaic Greece and Italy. It is also intimately associated, as suggested earlier, with his memories of Valeria Merian, the pious grieving mother of his youth. And it is to her defense that he came when he asserted, against the followers of Niebuhr and Mommsen, the "essential greatness of the pre-Hellenic culture" and the deep religious piety of the matriarchal order. "In the Demetrian mystery and under the religious and civil primacy of womanhood," he wrote, archaic culture

> possessed the seed of noble achievement which was suppressed and often destroyed by later developments. The barbarity of the Pelasgian world, the incompatibility of matriarchy with a noble way of life, the later origin of the mysterious element in religion—such traditional opinions are dethroned once and for all. It has long been a hobby with students of antiquity to impute the noblest manifestations to the basest motives. Could they be expected to spare religion, to acknowledge that what was noblest in it—its concern with the supernatural, the transcendent, the mystical—was rooted in the profoundest needs of the human soul? In the opinion of these scholars only self-seeking false prophets could have darkened the limpid sky of the Hellenic world with such ugly clouds, only an era of decadence could have gone so far astray. But mystery is the true essence of every religion, and wherever woman dominates religion or life, she will cultivate the mysterious. Mystery is rooted in her very nature, with its close alliance between the material and the supersensory; mystery springs from her kinship with material nature, whose eternal death creates a need for comforting thoughts and awakens hope through pain; and mystery is inherent in the law of Demetrian motherhood, manifested to woman in the transformations of the seed grain and in the reciprocal relation between perishing and coming into being, by which death is revealed as the indispensable forerunner of higher rebirth.[28]

Woman was now to be restored by Bachofen to the privileged place in the annals of civilization from which the scholarship of the cigar-smoking bootlickers of Mommsen would have excluded her. In the history of the species, "the initial determined resistance to the bestial state of universal promiscuity is woman's."[29] It was woman who "was the first to feel the need for regulated conditions and a purer ethic," who struggled to impose "the strict discipline which is one of the distinguishing features of matriarchal life," and who thus accomplished the first and most significant advance both in human society and in human religion. The institution of marriage, which she introduced, far from being "a necessary and primordial state," as most people believe, was represented by the ancients "as an infringement on an older principle and . . . as an offense against a religious commandment." At first, therefore, it "demanded propitiation of the godhead whose law it transgressed by its exclusivity," and it was only gradually that "the Demetrian principle" triumphed, allowing the expiatory sacrifices (in the form of "hetaeric practices surrounding marriage") to be steadily restricted until they were reduced to the symbolic sacrifice of the hair, "regarded as equivalent to the body" and "identified with the chaos of hetaeric generation and with swamp vegetation."[30] It is thus woman who succeeded in taking the first "step toward civilization." By beginning the process of "elimination of the natural state" and introducing regulated marriage, she prepared the way for "civil law and a definite order of inheritance"—Bachofen's basic definition of civilization.[31]

Woman also initiated the movement from hunting and food gathering to agricultural societies and to the first permanent and orderly human settlements. "The observation of still living peoples has shown that human societies are impelled toward agriculture chiefly by the efforts of women, while the men tend to resist this change. Countless ancient traditions support this same historical fact: women put an end to the nomadic life by burning the ships; women gave most cities their names, and, as in Rome or in Elis, women inaugurated the first apportionment of the land."[32]

Finally, to the "culture-bringing, benign power of woman" humanity owes also a refinement of religious consciousness and the idea of justice, not in opposition to nature but in harmony with it. Bachofen recalled that Strabo imputes woman's beneficent influence to *deisidaimonia* or the fear of God, "which first dwelled in woman and which she implanted in men." Woman was held to be "closer than man to the godhead and endowed with a superior understanding of the divine will. . . . She manifests justice unconsciously but with full certainty, she is the human conscience; she is naturally *autonoë* (in herself wise), *dikaia* (just) . . . ; she is the prophetess who proclaims the *fatum;* she is Sibyl, Martha, Phaennis, Themis."[33] The matriarchal peoples in general are "distinguished by *eunomia, eusebeia, paideia* (rectitude, piety, and culture)."[34]

In contrast to most of his contemporaries, for whom Greece meant chiefly fifth-century Athens and Italy late republican or imperial Rome, it was an archaic antiquity, still close to the realm of the mothers, that held Bachofen's attention. In Greece, Argos and Mycenae drew him far more than the Athens of the philosophers. In Italy, he was drawn to "the mighty realm of Alba, which is so little regarded nowadays that it is virtually considered only myth and legend."[35]

Against the *"so-genannte Classicität"* of established classical philology, Bachofen sketched innumerable sympathetic portraits of the archaic world of the mothers. Acknowledging that "[t]he close relation between child and father requires a far higher degree of moral development than mother love, that mysterious power that equally permeates all earthly creatures . . . ," he also demanded recognition of the fact that it is the relation between the child and the mother that "stands at the origin of all culture, of every virtue, of every nobler aspect of existence; it operates in a world of violence as the divine principle of love, of union, of peace. Raising her young, the woman learns earlier than the man to extend her loving care beyond the limits of the ego to another creature. . . . Woman at this stage is the repository of all culture, of all benevolence, of all devotion, of all concern for the living and grief for the dead."[36]

Though destined to be overtaken by the father-child relation and the "higher" and more "advanced" religion and social organization that go with it, the social order based on the mother-child relation is not to be regarded as inferior to what came after it. It had qualities that were unique to it; the loss of them has to be accepted, but it need not and should not be without regret.

> The love that arises from motherhood is not only more intense, but also more universal. . . . Whereas the paternal principle is inherently restrictive, the maternal principle, like the life of nature, knows no barriers. The idea of motherhood produces a sense of universal fraternity among all men, which dies with the development of paternity. . . . Every woman's womb, the mortal image of the earth mother Demeter, will give brothers and sisters to the children of every other woman; the homeland will know only brothers and sisters until the day when the development of the paternal system dissolves the undifferentiated unity of the mass and introduces a principle of articulation.
>
> The matriarchal cultures present many expressions and even juridical formulations of this aspect of the maternal principle. It is the basis of the universal freedom and equality so frequent among matriarchal peoples, of their hospitality, and of their aversion to restrictions of all sorts. It accounts for the broad significance of such concepts as the Roman *paricidium* (parricide or murder of a relative), which only later exchanged its natural, universal meaning for an individual, restricted one. And it is rooted in the admirable sense of kinship and *sympatheia* (fellow feeling) which knows no barriers or dividing lines and embraces all members of a nation alike. Matriarchal states were particularly famed for their freedom from intestine strife and conflict. The great festivals where all sections of a nation delighted in a sense of brotherhood and common nationality were first introduced among matriarchal peoples, and there achieved their finest expression. . . . An air of tender humanity, discernible even in the facial expression of Egyptian statuary, permeates the culture of the matriarchal world. And now an aura of Saturnian innocence seems to surround that

older race of men who, subordinating their whole existence to the law of motherhood, provided later generations with the main features of their picture of the silver age. How natural we now find Hesiod's world, with its dominant mother lavishing eternal loving care on an ever dependent son who, growing more physically than spiritually, lives beside his mother to a ripe old age, enjoying the peace and abundance of an agricultural life; how close it is to those pictures of lost happiness that always center around the dominance of motherhood.[37]

There seems little doubt that, in contrast to "the north"—the world of commerce, industry, Prussian imperialism, and Prussian criticism, but also of the more moderate patriarchalism of his own native city—Bachofen believed that in Greece and Italy it was still possibe to reestablish contact with the "world we have lost" and to be regenerated by that contact. In those landscapes of the remote matriarchal past, he wrote, "one feels everything more deeply, pain and joy and the true meaning of things."[38] There, "nature, by the warmth and richness of her sensuous manifestations, invites mortal man to yield to her charms and to enjoy the life of the senses under the guidance of a religion which hopes to elevate him not by repressing, but on the contrary by developing and educating his sensuality, to which the law of struggle is foreign, and in which the distinction between this life and the other life is not an absolute one."[39] Basel, he would complain, is a desert compared with the south. To return from Italy to the gray old city on the Rhine is to go from "All to Nothing," or—as he put it with humor in another letter to Meyer-Ochsner, "from Schnapps to water."[40]

The Greece depicted in the *Griechische Reise* was essentially a land in which significant traces of Mother Right survived—a land in which nature, the animal, and the human (and, to some degree, past and present) were still in harmony with each other, and "all the different sides of our spirit find satisfaction." The ancient sites teach us that in antiquity "no one side is enriched at the expense of others, no one feeling is stimulated to the point of excess, while another is allowed at the same moment to be dulled or deadened."[41] Even in 1851, the division of labor that comes with "the progress of so-called cultivated life" was largely undeveloped in Greece,[42] and it was still possible to observe in some simple people "the glory of the human form when all its powers are developed to the full and in perfect equilibrium."[43] Animals still shared the landscape with humans. Huge herds of goats that might have walked through the pastoral scenes of Theocritus still picked their way among the rocky hills. "Observing the proud gracefulness of these goats as they hurry shyly by among the rocks and scrub," the young traveler noted, "one can understand how antiquity could imagine Amaltheia, the most beautiful of women, transformed into one of these creatures."[44] In the weeks just before his death, the seventy-one-year-old scholar was no doubt reminded of these goats as he wrote down his reflections on the frequent occurrence in funerary art of the she-goat nursing her kid. The pastoral scenes represented on the funerary monuments, he claimed, "cannot be assumed to have been simply taken from everyday life and used for purely decorative purposes. Rather the pastoral idyll becomes the image of a former peaceful and untroubled happiness, and the group of the she-goat nursing her kid a symbol of mother love and of the renewal of the blessedness of childhood that awaits the sleeper on his or her awakening."[45] In the culture of Mother Right, in other words, everyday life was not a mere matter of fact, distinct from the world of meaning. Symbol and reality were one. "Heaven came down to earth and earth rose up to heaven."[46]

Above all, what distinguishes Greece is its inclusiveness. All the features of nature and all the aspects of human existence are acknowledged and represented in Greek life and find their proper place in it.

> The combination of water and land, mountain and sea into a unity in which neither of the elements composing it is subjected to the other lends to every view in Greece a quite peculiar, but always sublime expressiveness. . . . The combination of the highest degree of plenitude with the highest degree of moderation, from which the perfection of form and content arises naturally, lends to antiquity and all its creations a quality of greatness that we can no longer achieve. The prototype for it is found in that clime in inanimate nature itself, from which it is carried over to the spirit of the people. The coastal mountains of Acarnania, rising darkly and abruptly from the depths of the Ionian sea, do not have the oppressiveness of the Alps, which annihilate everything around them and which, far from elevating man by the harsh life they impose on him, rather weigh him down. Nor, however, can the sea claim dominion for itself . . . for wherever it turns, land mingles with the waters.[47]

In the same way nature and culture appear always in harmony with each other, never in conflict. At Mycenae the lay of the land itself combines with the massive, seemingly immovable stonework to give to the defenses the grandeur and simplicity of something eternal.[48] At Epidauros the ruined architecture of the theater and the magnificent landscape are not antagonistic or mutually exclusive; rather the creation of man (and to Bachofen, architecture, being nonmimetic, was the most autonomous of all the arts, the most completely a product of the human spirit) and the creation of nature reach out to include each other. The theater seems hewn from the natural rock, as if the hillside had been given a beautiful functional form. It never has the appearance of an autonomous, foreign product placed among the shapes made by nature herself.[49] At Epidaurus "nature becomes art and art nature," to the point that the viewer is unaware of the labor of production and feels only the contentment of the finished work. The problematic tensions that would be introduced by the awareness of division and discontinuity are thus avoided in an impression of wholeness and harmony. Bachofen contrasted the equilibrium of Greek architecture and the feelings of calm and repose that it brings with the sense of power and of being overpowered that is produced by the gigantic proportions and the accumulation of detail in the Gothic cathedrals of northern Europe.

The Gothic cathedral exhibits the enormous difficulties of its execution. The Greek theater achieves something different and, to my mind, far higher. It makes one forget the difficulties of creation in the impression of the perfect grace of the whole. There is no astonishment, only contentment. The impression we have is one of perfect unity: no whole and no parts; rather every part is itself as good as the whole, and the whole in turn is no more than a part of the natural context in which it is set. . . . Buildings in the Germanic spirit, whatever the end they serve, violently tear the soul from its harmony with itself and with creation and always set themselves in sharp opposition to nature; it is the special quality of those of the ancients, in contrast, that they make the blessed feeling of that harmony flow beneficently over us whenever it has been disturbed or has not yet come to consciousness.[50]

The fullness and harmony of ancient life was epitomized for Bachofen by the proximity of Lerna, with its sacred "swampy marshlands," to the sanctuary of Asklepeios in the hills near Epidaurus barely fifty miles—a day's journey—away, that is, by the proximity of the most archaic chthonic forces, which once exercised exclusive dominion over mankind, to the forces that represent man's highest spiritual aspirations.

The contrast between the beginning and the end of that day of journeying could not have been greater. On our setting out, the stillness and isolation of the wooded vale of the Hieron and all the feelings that the view of a beautiful mountain landscape awakens in our soul; now, at day's end, the sea shore, among marshy lowlands, the air damp and heavy. It is as though the contrasting topographies of Switzerland and Holland had been placed alongside each other and enclosed within the space of a single day's journey. But such rapid transitions are characteristic of the Greek landscape. Because of them the greatest variety and the greatest richness of individual forms are made possible in a small space. And the assortment of thoughts that pass through one's mind is as varied as the nature of the country. Hieron, then Lerna. The powers of Asklepeios, friendly to man and beneficent; the bright friendly halls and the graceful games in the shade of those lovely woods, and then the terror of the underworld at Lerna; the dark all-swallowing waters of the Alkyonic sea; the unfathomable depths Nero could not measure; the entrance to the Underworld, through which Dionysus descended to Hell and Pluto carried off Proserpine; the nocturnal service of the underworld divinities, all the mystery of the dread presentiments evoked by the sight of this stretch of land that is equally alien to the sea and to the mountains and by all those ancient cults; finally the river Amymone, the certain lurking place of the many-headed monster that yielded only to the high, superhuman strength of Heracles: does myth offer greater contrasts or ritual pursue ends more distant from each other? But chance, and the power that rules it, had ordained that the very time of day at which I came to each place appeared to have an inner connection with the range of ideas each draws one into. The rising sun lighted up from the east the mountain peaks in whose vicinity Asklepeios grew up, nourished by a she-goat; the dancing Hours, descending from the golden source of light—as in Guido Reni's magnificent ceiling-fresco—strewed flowers over these valleys; and now darkest night shrouded Lerna's swampy marshland and concealed in her bosom all those dread fears from which the imagination of the earliest generations, so close to the divine and so rich in presentiments, had called forth a world of mysterious terror.[51]

Yet the world of terror has its place in the economy of a universe that is still a unified totality. Though no human settlement has ever succeeded in establishing itself at Lerna, the currents there are suitable for driving the mills needed in irrigation works. It is the Amymone that drives the mills of Nafplion. "Thus the wealth of waters of this stretch of coast was destined to relieve the aridity of the rest of the country. The area of Lerna is a necessary, indispensible complement to Nafplion and the entire great plain of Argos."[52] Characteristically, however, the ancient water control systems of Lerna had been allowed to fall into ruin along with the temples where Demeter and Dionysus were worshipped, so that the neglected marshlands had become far more extensive— and far more dangerous—than in antiquity.

In Italy, a similar fate befell the Roman *campagna*, long considered sacred ground because of its innumerable fresh water springs, which supplied the city abundantly. Here "in the cool well watered groves the leaders of the people would come together to take counsel with each other . . . or benevolent divinities decipher for troubled mortals the secrets of the future. . . . From earliest times a grove and temple were dedicated to Feronia at the spring of that name, three miles north of Terracina. No pilgrim . . . ever passed by this place without washing hands and face in the sacred waters."[53] Though the same conditions that infect the air in modern times and make the *campagna* a breeding ground of mortal fevers were already present in antiquity, they were rendered harmless by diligent cultivation and management of the land.[54] The deterioration of the *campagna* began only "after the Roman sword drove the old established, hardworking inhabitants from the many independent communities in which they had organized themselves; the small *heredia* or freeholdings of two, at most seven acres, were combined to form massive latifundia; and grazing lands for cattle replaced fields sown with corn." The violent destruction of the old ways has proven irremediable. "No legislation can conjure up from the soil the energetic industrious population that was once so thickly settled on this plain, none can reestablish the free cities that once flourished here, none can revive the ancient simplicity, the vigor and activity of the golden ages of Italy."[55] The once flourishing *campagna* had become desolate, dangerous, and virtually deserted. Catching a glimpse of a dark form "lurking in the hollow of a half-ruined mausoleum or in the recess of some grotto formed by nature, its limbs wrapped in rags tied round with shaggy, filthy sheepskins," the traveler might well imagine he was seeing creatures from another time.[56]

Archaic Greece and Italy, Bachofen would have us conclude, possessed a wisdom that more modern times have lost: they knew, acknowledged, and respected the powers of the archaic mother goddesses, and so were able to "win them over," as Athene won over the Erinyes. They did not try to exclude them. "Where the head advances more rapidly than the heart," we have already read, "man falls victim to the dark drives that lurk in the lowest regions of his soul."[57]

Bachofen's vision of antiquity as inclusive—accommodating the marshland and the mountain, night and day, Lerna and the Hieron of Asklepeios, the dark chthonic goddesses of the past and the bright new gods of the future—had an obvious bearing on his political convictions, on his philosophical and religious ideas, and on his own enterprise as a writer and scholar.

There cannot be much doubt that when he wrote glowingly of the beauty of Greece with its "countless self-contained landscapes, each having its own particular character and its peculiar aspect" and claimed that, at a time when man was still close to nature and guided by her example, no other land "manifested so fully every possible side of the human spirit,"[58] he was thinking (in all probability, not without irony) of his native country. The comparison of the Greek city-states with the Swiss cantons and of Hellas with the Swiss Confederation was a fairly familiar topic of historians and essayists, English as well as Swiss, and was taken up again in 1849 in two important lectures by Wilhelm Vischer, Nietzsche's predecessor in the chair of Greek at the University of Basel, as well as in the account of his own journey to Greece in 1853–1854 that Vischer published in 1857 (*"Erinnerungen und Eindrücke aus Griechenland"* ["Memories and Impressions of Greece"]).[59] It is hard to imagine that Bachofen's image of antiquity—differentiation and variety without conflict, unity without uniformity, aspiration toward a future of ever greater human autonomy without sacrificing respect for the powers of the past—was not intended, at least in part, as a justification of the allegedly anachronistic political structure not only of his native country but, even more, of his native city in the age of democracy and increasingly centralized, uniform nation-states. *"La variété, c'est la vie, l'uniformité, c'est la mort,"* another Swiss, Benjamin Constant, had declared around the time that the Napoleonic Empire reached its zenith. Bachofen's sketch of the Roman *campagna* was an exemplification of that argument.

The archaic world of Greece and Italy was also for Bachofen an epitome of all history. Within the limited space stretching between Lerna and the Hieron of Asklepeios and between the *campagna* and the Palatine hill were contained, in his view, the essential elements of all historical development. Enshrined in symbol and myth, the history of "the antiquity of antiquity" transcended particularity, overcame time and death, and was preserved as an enduring object of contemplation and reflection for all time. It thus satisfied Bachofen's demand for knowledge of enduring truth, rather than the trivial knowledge of isolated facts, far better than the detailed histories of modern historians or the positivistic studies of antiquity produced by classical philologists of the Niebuhr and Mommsen schools.

If the history of the ancient world is an epitome of all history, the landscape and art of antiquity are enduring symbols, permitting the modern student and, more particularly, the traveler to leap over the chasm separating the ancient from the modern world and to grasp in a single instantaneous vision a history of many centuries that could only be pieced together imperfectly, and by dint of long and laborious efforts, through historical analysis and argument. So it had been for the author of *Griechische Reise* himself, that night in 1851, by the dark shore of the Gulf of Argos, when he recapitulated the sights and emotions of a journey of less than a day that had taken him back through aeons of time from the wooded hills of Epidaurus, where sunrise over the sanctuary of Asklepeios the healer-god seemed to announce the dawn of a new age, to the low marshlands round the bay from Nafplion, where nightfall cast a veil of mystery over the dwelling places of the archaic mother goddesses. There is no reason to be surprised by Bachofen's partiality for the landscapes and visual monuments of antiquity or by his little-noted tribute to Winckelmann in the autobiographical letter to Savigny: "To my reading of Winckelmann's works I owe an enjoyment of a far higher order [than learned notations could provide]—indeed, one of the greatest pleasures of my whole life. Since then I have dwelt much in the regions that it opened, especially at times when everything else seemed to lose interest for me. Ancient art draws our heart to classical antiquity, and jurisprudence our mind. . . . Philology without concern for the works of art remains a lifeless skeleton."[60]

Ancient Greece and Italy, in sum, were not only, as objects of study, cultures in which the scholar could recognize and admire the vitality of symbolic and mythical thought and the achievement of a unique equilibrium of imagination and reason, heart and mind, community and individuality, the natural law of the mothers and the constructed law of the fathers; they were themselves, as physical landscapes and sites of ancient art, living symbols through which the past was communicated immediately and in a flash to the mind and heart of the modern visitor. "There are two roads to knowledge," Bachofen wrote to Savigny. "The longer, slower, more arduous road of rational combination and the shorter path of the imagination, traversed with the force and swiftness of electricity. Aroused by direct contact with the ancient remains, the imagination grasps the truth at one stroke, without intermediary links. The knowledge acquired in this way is infinitely more living and colorful than the products of the understanding."[61]

In his own writing, Bachofen often tried to lead his reader on this second, superior road, to reproduce in him or her the immediate insights that the landscapes and art objects of antiquity had produced in the writer, and thus to repeat for the reader the experience, comparable almost to an act of grace, that to Bachofen was virtually the condition of genuine understanding of a world separated from us by an immense, almost unbridgeable gulf.[62] This may account in part for the peculiar structure and rhythm of Bachofen's scholarly works, in which the language of scholarly discourse seems to be interrupted from time to time by epiphanic moments of great poetic power, where the voice that speaks is no longer that of the scholar presenting arguments and evidence but that of an inspired prophet. It also helps to explain why *Griechische Reise,* which was not published until almost a half century after his death, is the most successful and consistent of Bachofen's writings from a literary point of view. The *sole* purpose of this work is to recreate a visual symbol—the landscape of Greece—in language, and so to reproduce in the reader the marvelous and immediate effect that the writer claims the visual symbol had had on him. The work does not pretend to offer a scholarly argument and there is none of the tedious, almost desperate piling up of learned evidence, which Bachofen apparently felt would impart credibility to the insights of *Das Mutterrecht* and other scholarly writings.[63] The result is a consistency of design and a degree of correspondence between intention and method that are not to be found in any of the specifically scholarly writings. One could argue that in *Griechische Reise* Bachofen did achieve, as nowhere else, that middle position of oneness with the object and distance from it, unity and differentiation, that he admired in so many different forms, but most strikingly in the world of Mother Right.

At the same time, one has to reflect on the implications of Bachofen's insistence on the leap of imagination that genuine historical understanding of the ancient world is said to require and of his consequent downgrading of the laborious, though admittedly useful processes of philological scholarship. In antiquity there was still continuity, it would appear, between insight and discourse, feeling and reasoning, nature and culture. In the modern world, in contrast, the wholeness of the cosmos and the autonomous human individual are divided by such an abyss that the vast majority live in a condition of alienation, cut off from nature and their own past, not understanding the meaning of their lives or their labors. It thus falls to a privileged few, endowed with special insight, to maintain on behalf of the community as a whole the essential links binding the present to the past and human civilization to the total cosmic order. Bachofen's epistemology thus corresponds to his ideas about the value and necessity of authority and hierarchy in the state.

In his scholarly works, as already noted, Bachofen's most glowing prose is reserved for evocations of those stages in the history of ancient culture—stages of incipient differentiation which has not yet become alienation and conflict, of individuation which is not yet isolation—that appeared peculiarly blessed to him, as they had already appeared a century earlier to the celebrated *citoyen* of another Protestant Swiss city-state, Jean-Jacques Rousseau. Over the years, the tension in Rousseau's work between the poet of immediate experience and the individual moment and the theorist of general laws and permanent political constitutions—between the author of the *Rêveries d'un promeneur solitaire* or the first part of *La Nouvelle Héloïse* and the author of the *Contrat social* or the second part of *La Nouvelle Héloïse*—has been a major focus of Rousseau interpretation. In the same way, readers of Bachofen have usually pointed to the seeming inconsistency with which he sang hymns to the world of the mothers while resolutely espousing the authority of the fathers. Some have considered the former secondary, mere outbursts of lyrical nostalgia in an austere philosophy of history; to others it was the philosophy of history that was secondary, tacked on arbitrarily to privileged texts expressing a unique, but subversive poetic imagination and sensibility.[64] The problematic relation, in the form and method of Bachofen's work, between insight and discursive argument thus seems to be repeated, on the level of the argument itself, in the problematic relation between unstinting praise of the world of Mother Right and determined affirmation of the superiority of Father Right and the order of abstract law. We must now turn our attention directly to the problem of Bachofen's "philosophy of history."

To an age shaken by massive historical upheavals, history had become the prime question of the day. Reason having met its Waterloo and failed to impose itself on the historical world, the latter could no longer be treated with the cool detachment and irony of the eighteenth-century *philosophes*. For those who accepted the settlements of 1815, liberals and conservatives alike, the task was to discover a meaning and direction in the profusion of events that would impart a character of necessity to the world as it had emerged from the revolutionary and Napoleonic crisis, to go beyond the Enlightenment confrontation of reason and history—history as the record of the crimes and follies of mankind (Voltaire and Gibbon)—to a vision of reason *in* history or *as* history. In this way, the sacrifices and sufferings of historical existence, highlighted by recent events, could be justified, the past redeemed from meaninglessness, and the present securely grounded in historical necessity.

Observers of the contemporary scene who, like Bachofen and Burckhardt, quickly came to hold a less optimistic view—namely, that with the end of the old regime mankind had entered on an age of extreme instability and violent change—were no less driven to seek an antidote to despair in the discovery of some enduring spiritual meaning behind the welter of ephemeral particulars and the succession of revolutions. The analytical philosophers of the Enlightenment had fought hard to release the individual—the individual moment as well as the individual person—from oppressive totalities; but victory, as Constant observed in the aftermath of the revolution, brought its own anxieties and discontents. "Man looks on a world depopulated of protective powers, and is astonished at his victory. . . . His imagination, idle now and solitary, turns upon itself. He finds himself alone on an earth which may swallow him up. . . . The generations follow each other, transitory, fortuitous, isolated; they appear, they suffer, they die."[65] The aim of the philosophy of history pursued equally by the liberal Frenchman Jules Michelet and the conservative Baseler Johann Jacob Bachofen was to recover a sense of the wholeness and meaningfulness of history. The difference between historical optimists and historical pessimists was that, whereas for the former the totality pointed unmistakably toward a telos or end, be it the progressive realization of the objectives of the revolution or the progressive identification of the real with the rational, for the latter the modern age promised to be an extended time of cataclysmic upheavals the end of which was unforeseeable and would be reached only after a descent into the depths of the abyss.

Bachofen often wrote of the need to go beyond particulars, beyond proximate causes in history to the larger, meaningful structures underlying them. Hoping to interest the famous publishing house of Cotta in *Mother Right,* he explained that his aim as a historian was to dig out the "characteristic content" of particular events and phenomena, and then determine "its place in the development of a country, an epoch, and of mankind generally."[66] A few years later, in a paper read to the Basel Historical Society on December 15, 1864, he emphasized the need to consider not simply the immediate material causes of events but higher, invisible ones. Every event can be understood both causally, in relation to what preceded and what followed, and symbolically, as the manifestation of the whole in the part.[67] Causal explanation focuses attention on particular time sequences, whereas symbolic understanding supposes a view of the whole; the first is analytical, the second supposes powers of imagination, insight, and sympathetic understanding that far exceed the methods of analysis. The preoccupation of most of his contemporaries "with the facts, personalities, and institutions of particular epochs,"[68] in Bachofen's view, followed from the materialism of the age and its emphasis on the proximate, from the fact that "we men of the nineteenth century . . . are content for the most part if we know what we are going to eat and drink, how we are going to dress and entertain ourselves." The view of history promoted by a culture that has sacrificed the eternal for the ephemeral, the whole for the part, and feeling and imagination for analytical and critical reason is narrow and short. Virgil, in contrast, took the long view, seeing "a close connection between the Punic Wars and the myth of Aeneas," and regarding the former as "the culmination of a development begun thousands of years before." The modern historian who would judge events correctly must likewise "take equally vast periods of time under consideration, because history always operates in long perspectives."[69]

In the introduction to *Tanaquil* (1870) Bachofen again rejected what he called "the prevailing modern view, according to which history is a natural process set in motion by material forces." We do not know events, he argued, we know only the traditions in which events have been reported and already encoded as meaningful. The only genuine history, in other words, is cultural history—the history of traditions, not of the events and personalities that figure in them. The historian's task is not primarily to establish names of persons or dates of events, but to recover the feelings and ideas, the ways in which human beings have understood and represented themselves and their world, and the relations that obtained among them, as these are expressed in mythical and historical traditions, whatever the factual accuracy of the particular events these traditions report. The rest is nothing—"*Schutt*" ("rubble" or "rubbish"), as Burckhardt would say.

> Since all human activity on earth is transient and ephemeral, empirical events in themselves can never be the object of our observations. We can only fixate the ephemeral through the intermediary of tradition. But the tradition too shares the nature of the underlying event. Like the outward action, the inner act by which beliefs and traditions are formed springs from a principle that is not stable and immutable but fluid and transient, and hence, like everything in which there is life, itself subject to history. From this it follows that historical inquiry always deals with a spiritual manifestation that develops and progresses; that the factual and ideal elements of a tradition are not juxtaposed, but are so interwoven as to defy any attempt to sift them apart; and finally, that the truth we can attain in regard to the history of the past is not of a physical but of a purely spiritual character. When pretentious scholars approach a tradition . . . with the question of what "actually happened," and, by a so-called critical sifting of the material at hand, seek to determine the actual course of events, it would be basically unsound and ineffectual for us to respond to their denial of the factuality of a historical tradition (this is the "critical approach" to historical traditions) by affirming its factuality, or to examine the plausibility of any new hypothesis regarding the actual course of events—for such an argument would imply an acceptance of the false notion that the investigation of former times revolves around the discovery of factual rather than spiritual truth, around empirical events rather than the spirit of the times as disclosed in tradition.[70]

The closeness of Bachofen's position to Burckhardt's is striking here. Neither concerned himself with political history, the history of events. Both addressed themselves rather to the history of the ways in which human beings have understood themselves, the universe, and their own history—Burckhardt chiefly through the representation of these understandings in literature and art, Bachofen through their representation in myth, legend, religion, and law. Bachofen's refusal to distinguish between myth and history except "in mode of expression" and his insistence on the continuity of myth and history are entirely consistent with the view that the subject matter of history is essentially culture. It is not surprising that, as Virgil saw a connection between the story of Aeneas and the Punic wars, Bachofen established one between Orestes and the emperor Augustus. "Orestes appears in legend, Augustus in history as the avenger of an offense against the father."[71]

No valid history is possible, to sum up, that is not at the same time philosophy of history or anthropology, in the sense of a philosophy of man. The scholar who so often denounced the modern taste for "systems" (understood as constructions of the human mind) instead of patient attentiveness to "empirical" reality (that is, the material transmitted by tradition) not only acknowledged his confidence that there is an objective order or system of history transcending any order that we might invent—"Everywhere there is system, everywhere cohesion; in every detail the expression of a great fundamental law"[72]—but acknowledged as well the systematic character of his own work insofar as it claimed to have revealed that order. In a letter to a Genevan friend, Bachofen spoke boldly of *"l'édifice de mon système."*[73]

The general outline of this *"système"* has already been noted: it describes human history as a double, simultaneous movement of ever greater differentiation (as "all the parts of large homogeneous masses strive to develop their own selves") and ever greater unification (through the unending encounters, collisions, and mutual determinations of different peoples),[74] as a progressive evolution from the dominance of instinct to that of reason and reflection, from the preeminence of matter to that of spirit, from nature to culture, from matriarchal to patriarchal authority, from religion to law, from the Orient through Rome to the modern Christian and Germanic world.[75] We today are inclined to associate that pattern with Hegel, but it was widely diffused, in one form or another, among nineteenth-century writers.[76] We find it developed quite programatically, for instance, in Michelet's early *Introduction à l'histoire universelle* of 1831 and it is easily discernible as the informing structure of all the French historian's work, including his popular studies of natural history. The association of the female with the origin, matter, religion, and the East, and the distinction between the chthonic female and the maternal female, as well as that between the violent and aggressive male wielding arbitrary power and the legitimate husband who exercises authority justly, gently, and without repression, are likewise not unique to Bachofen but are essential features of all the historical writings of Michelet.

The total system is what provides the separate parts or moments of history with meaning and continued life. Those nations that remain isolated and do not enter into the pattern of world history through migration, conquest, war, or other forms of exchange remain historically sterile, according to Ranke. "Not all nations are equal," he declared in a lecture course given in 1857–1858, "and not all have a history that is worth our trouble. . . . One could well distinguish between nations that deserve to be described in a natural history of humanity and properly historical nations. The latter become historical through their participation in the development of humanity, in culture. Since culture has been developed peoples have come into contact with each other through it. A people that cut itself off would condemn itself to eternal barbarism."[77] At the same time, within the pattern of world history, each age has an intrinsic value of its own. "Every age stands in immediate relation to God," Ranke was to say, "and its value does not depend on what emerged out of it, but in its existence as such." Part of the charm of historical study lies in the fact that "every age must be seen as valid in itself and as worthy of being studied for itself."[78]

As Ranke's student, Bachofen took into account both the intrinsic value and significance of each culture and its effect or impact on the cultural history of humanity. Because of its extraordinary talent for abiding legal and political ideas and institutions, Rome, for example, was more effective historically than Greece, and mankind "owes less to Apollo than to the idea of the imperium."[79]

> Living closer to Asia, the Greeks cast off Asiatic domination more quickly and completely [than the Romans]; but soon local influences deflected them from any great national idea. More given to the glitter of genius than to greatness of character, they disintegrated everything they touched, first and most completely themselves. In their heroic undertakings against the powers of the Orient they remind us of those Olympic champions who, after achieving fame in their youth, soon sank into oblivion. The types of Greek genius are Achilles, Alexander, Pyrrhus, who rise and fall like meteors on the horizon of history. . . . Not Alexander, but Rome completed the millennial struggle against the East which was the leitmotif of Herodotus' history; hence it was Rome, not Greece, which transferred the universal monarchy from the East to the West, and so put an end to the old world. What is Marathon, what are Salamis and Plataea, compared to the war against Hannibal? As infinitesimal as the brief decades of Athenian power compared to Roman eternity. What were Agathocles' battles against Carthage compared to the Roman campaigns? The Greek thought it a simple matter to subjugate the Phoenician city, and what did he accomplish? The destruction of Carthage, that greatest turning point in the destinies of mankind, was the work of the Italic nations under the republican leadership of Rome. In these years the city fulfilled its true historical mission. The West had conquered the inheritance of the East for all time, and the victorious nation had achieved its ethical summit.[80]

Two powers—"the Delphic Apollo and the Roman political ideal of the masculine imperium"—had seemed capable of "fully realizing the paternal principle." But of those, only the latter prevailed and was historically successful. As pure spirituality, religion could not withstand the seductions of the senses. It had to be institutionalized, invested with the consistency of ethics and the staying power of law and the state.

> Though perhaps less spiritual than the Delphic idea, the imperial principle possessed in its juridical form an intimate bond with all public and private life, a support that was utterly lacking in the purely spiritual power of the god. Thus while the idea of the imperium could triumph against all attacks and hold its own against barbarization and the steady relapse into material views, the Apollonian idea was unable to withstand the increasing assaults of baser doctrines. We see paternity falling back from Apollonian purity to Dionysian materiality, so preparing the way for a new victory of the feminine principle, for a new flowering of the mother cults. Although the intimate union that the two luminous powers concluded in Delphi seemed calculated to purify Dionysius's phallic exuberance through Apollo's immutable repose and clarity, and to lift it

above itself, the consequence was the exact opposite: the greater sensuous appeal of the fecundating god outweighed his companion's more spiritual beauty.... Instead of the Apollonian age, it was a Dionysian age that dawned.[81]

Instead of the victory of the West, what occurred, in other words, was a reconciliation of the Greek and the Oriental worlds.[82] The Roman political idea, in contrast, ensured the "enduring victory of paternity" by giving it a strict juridical form that "enabled it to develop in all spheres of existence . . . and safeguarded it against the decadence of religion, the corruption of manners, and a popular return to matriarchal views."[83] A basic, widely acknowledged difference between Greek and Roman culture epitomizes the higher historical destiny of the latter. "The Greek genius never relinquished its bond with the outward manifestations of material life; the Greek ideal of beauty has at all times aroused sensualism and given rise to aesthetic judgment, the badge of ethically enfeebled peoples. Rome's central idea, on the other hand, the idea underlying its historical state and its law, is wholly independent of matter; it is an eminently ethical achievement."[84]

Nevertheless, historical effectiveness was not for Bachofen the only measure of worth. Peoples and cultures that appear to have been left behind by the continual migrations, wars, invasions, and conquests that bring the nations together into a general history of humanity[85] also deserve to be remembered and honored. Every page of *Griechische Reise* is a testimony to the writer's love and admiration of the ancient Greece of independent city-states. Against Droysen's glorification of the power of Philip of Macedon—whom he saw as having done for Greece what he expected Prussia to do for Germany—Bachofen recalled the judgment of his teacher Böckh: "If extent of territory and numbers of population were the only criterion of the greatness and significance of states, Athens would be placed well behind the hordes of the Huns and the Mongols. But massive size arouses only our astonishment."[86] "Rome's overwhelming power," Bachofen asserted in turn, "could not create as much as a single one of these small Greek cities."[87] Likewise, in Italy, it was the "ancient realm of Alba," the world of the Sabines and the Etruscans, on the ruins of which Roman power was built, that engaged, as we saw, his interest and imagination.

The overall design, in short, does not absorb or exhaust any of the individual component parts and does not determine their intrinsic worth. The realization of the state does not cancel the value of the cultures that failed to achieve institutionalization as enduring and powerful states.[88] The entire journey counts, not only the point of arrival. Every moment, every stage, every culture is necessary, is what it had to be, and realizes some aspect of human potential. No historical existence is for another, each has its end in itself ("*Selbstzweck*"), Bachofen wrote in the paper he read to the Basel Historical Society in 1864.[89] Years later, in *Antiquarische Briefe,* he reiterated the "never to be forgotten truth, that each stage of man's development has a charm that is lost to the stage that follows, even as it receives gifts of a higher order."[90] In the eyes of the Divinity, as Ranke put it, there is no time: the whole of historical humanity is thus embraced in a single simultaneous view and all parts of it appear equally worthy.[91]

There is nothing contradictory, therefore, in the glowing accounts Bachofen gave not only of the Demetrian, Mother Right culture, for which he obviously had special fondness, but even of certain stages of the earlier, more primitive "Aphroditian" culture, notably the ecstatic worship of Dionysus. In comparison with the chthonic gods and heroes like Neptune or Peleus, he wrote, Dionysus marks no doubt an important step in the dissociation of the male principle from the female: "Bursting the shell of the egg, he discloses the mystery of phallic masculinity that had hitherto been hidden within it." Nevertheless, Bachofen claimed, the Dionysian cult only appears to be an affirmation of the rights of the male against the female; in fact, it remains in close alliance with the "hetaeric trend." Dionysus still "stands as a son to feminine matter; . . . and the mother herself rejoices in him as in her own demon. The phallic god cannot be thought of separately from feminine materiality."[92] Naturally, the worship of the "phallic lord of exuberant natural life," who remains bound to Aphrodite and "whose combination of sensuous beauty and transcendent radiance made him doubly seductive," appeals particularly to women and to the people. The "magic power," with which that cult "revolutionized the world of women, is manifested in phenomena that surpass the limits of our experience and our imagination," Bachofen noted suggestively. "Yet to relegate them to the realm of poetic invention would betoken little knowledge of the dark depths of human nature and failure to understand the power of a religion that satisfied sensual as well as transcendent needs."[93] Dionysus is also a threat to the good order of society. His cult "loosed all fetters, removed all distinctions. . . . This sensualization of existence coincides everywhere with the dissolution of political organization and the decline of political life. Intricate gradation gives way to democracy, the undifferentiated mass, the freedom and equality that distinguish natural life from ordered social life and pertain to the physical, material side of human nature." Ceres herself had always been "the great protectress of the plebs,"[94] but the Dionysian religion introduced an ecstatic element into the serious brotherhood fostered by the goddess. It represented "the apotheosis both of Aphroditean pleasure and of universal brotherhood; hence it was readily accepted by the servile classes and encouraged by tyrants, . . . since it favored the democratic development on which their tyranny was based."

Having pointed out what he considered the negative and regressive features of the Dionysian cults, however, Bachofen also underlined the attraction of the "virile god." Under his influence "the symbols of Demetrian regulated maternity, the ear of grain and the loaf of bread, give way to the Bacchic grape . . . ;

milk, honey, and water, the chaste sacrifices of the old time, ceded to wine, the inducer of sensual frenzy. . . . The Dionysian cult brought antiquity the highest development of a thoroughly Aphroditean civilization, and lent it that radiance that overshadows all the refinement and all the art of modern life."[95]

Just as the achievements of modern life are overshadowed by the radiance of the cult of Dionysus, "the humanized Tanaquil of the Roman tradition . . . seems an impoverished figure, scarcely comparable to the colossal Oriental conception,"[96] and the arrival of the Romans marks an impoverishment of ancient Greek culture: "The thin brick, baked in the sun out of clay and water, takes the place of natural stone hewn from the rock and fine marble, life becomes hard and is stripped of its incomparable grace."[97] There is loss as well as gain as humanity moves toward a higher, more purely human existence, further and further from the warmth of nature. Bachofen's position was that that loss must be accepted because it is the price of man's fulfillment of his spiritual destiny. Reviewing the transformations of the Tanaquil figure in ancient Italy and Rome, he conceded that "we might be tempted to regard the subordination of the divine to a human idea as the last stage in a process of degeneration from an earlier, more sublime standpoint. And indeed, who will deny that beside the cosmic world-spanning ideas of the Bel-Heracles religion, which gave rise to the notion of a woman commanding over life and throne, the humanized Tanaquil of the Roman tradition, adapted as she is to everyday life, seems an impoverished figure, scarcely comparable to the colossal Oriental conception." But such a view of the evolution of the tradition would be mistaken: "And yet this regression contains the germ of a very important advance. For every step that liberates our spirit from the paralyzing fetters of a cosmic-physical view of life must be so regarded."[98] Similarly, "great knowledge and experience" were lost as a result of the destruction of Carthage. "But," Bachofen noted firmly, "we have no regrets."[99] Nevertheless, the loss ought not to be denied or the defeated erased from memory.

On the contrary, it seems to have been Bachofen's aim to reinstate them and acknowledge them, as—by his own account—it was Michelet's. "Il faut faire parler les silences de l'histoire, ces terribles points d'orgue où elle ne dit plus rien et qui sont justement ses accents les plus tragiques," Michelet had noted in his journal in 1842. But the object of the enterprise was not simply to call up the shades of the past, it was also to quiet the anger of the victims and avoid a potentially dangerous "return of the repressed." Having had their chance to speak, "alors seulement les morts se résignent au sépulcre."[100] The desire for inclusion, the rejection of the *funeste sagesse* of the modern men of reason— namely, that the historian arm himself with the sword of Aeneas to ward off the shades and their bewitching charms—implies no surrender to the dark forces of the underworld that have been overcome. "Sachez . . . que sans épée, sans armes, sans quereller des âmes confiantes qui réclament la résurrection, l'art, en les accueillant, en leur rendant le souffle, l'art pourtant garde en lui sa lucidité entière."[101]

Ultimately, Bachofen's ideal is neither the absolute empire of spirit—always beyond the power of mortals—nor the absolute empire of the senses that no longer befits them, neither dictatorship nor democracy, which he regarded, in any case, as complementing each other rather than as opposed. It is a well-ordered hierarchy in which what has been overcome—the origins, women, the people, with all their pristine mysterious powers—is included, assigned its proper place, respected for its contributions, and at the same time itself in turn freely respectful of the authority of the higher spiritual power that replaced it and now regulates it. *Antistes* Burckhardt's lessons to his catechism class on the proper relation between the body and the spirit had clearly not been lost on his pupil, nor had the student at the Basel *Pädagogium* forgotten the lesson that Franz Gerlach, the Latin professor, who later became his collaborator, had always tried to convey to the young men entrusted to his care:

> We should joyfully honor and admire what is great and noble, wherever it appears, and not ask, amid anxious investigations, whether even here the divine has been clouded over by the human. For nothing perfect is to be found on this earth, as wise men and fools have told us for centuries. . . . Man stands in the middle, between God and the animals, and reveals his dual nature in all his productions. Related in spirit to the heavenly, but to animal nature by his body, he would be destroyed by the unending struggle between the two parts of his being had not understanding set him a worthy goal toward which to strive.[102]

The model, one is tempted to say, is an idealized Basel, where the productive, material energies of civil society, the inextinguishable and indispensable "maternal" energies of trade and industry (the principal activities of the great "Oriental" centers, such as Carthage or Corinth, the description of which in *Griechische Reise* is strongly evocative of Basel) are informed, guided, and elevated by the wisdom and law of the *patres* or governors of the state.

There seems not much doubt that in the Roman patricians Bachofen venerated an idealized image of his own class. In an important exchange of letters with Morgan, he defended his view of the Roman gens as a cultural construct—"an artificial agglomeration of families not related by blood ties"—against Morgan's claim that, as among the Iroquois, it was "to be regarded as a natural growth,"[103] with a tenacity that was not characteristic of his general relations with the American ethnologist and that indicates considerable ideological investment in his theory. According to Bachofen, the Roman patriciate (the plebs being much more closely tied to "nature") made the crucial contribution that differentiated Rome, from its founding, from the other cities of Italy and ensured its world-historical role in leading humanity to a higher level of culture than any known thitherto. That contribution was the displacement of nature by culture, of the natural family by the family as a juridical concept, and of the tribe or nation by the state.[104] "We never ought to forget that the Romans never have been a nation, but a political body," he wrote to Morgan in English, "that they owe their very existence to the negation of what makes and constitutes a nationality founded on common origin, that finally from beginning to end one idea only, the idea of a political state, governed the brain of all citizens."[105]

Morgan demurred: In the Roman gens "I see the same institution I find in the Iroquois gens," with a few changes due to experience and time. "Much of this development is expressed by the change of descent from the female line to the male" but "it is still the same institution known the world over as a kinship and founded on blood ties."[106] Delighted as he was to enlist Morgan on his side in the struggle against the Prussian philologists and to applaud the anthropologist's criticism of their narrow vision, Bachofen's commitment to his vision of the Roman patriciate was such that he resisted the arguments of his new friend. When Morgan reiterated his view that "the Roman gens was a body of consanguines descended from a supposed common male ancestor. . . . An Omaha gens and an Iowa and a Maya gens are the same, nothing more, nothing less—a body of kindred,"[107] Bachofen wrote a conciliatory reply reaffirming his conviction that the anthropology of contemporary native American societies could not be ignored by any serious historian of early European societies, but avoiding the disputed issue of the nature of the Roman gens.[108] Morgan, however, would not let the matter drop: "You European and particularly German scholars will be obliged to recast some portion of your work upon the institutions of the Greeks and Romans and place these societies upon their true basis. In the time of Solon and of Romulus these societies were founded upon kin, and were purely gentile, having little in common with the political society as it came in some years later."[109] Bachofen again struck a conciliatory note, agreeing with many of the points in Morgan's letter but maintaining firmly that, on the question of the Roman gentes, "difficulties remain," and reiterating his basic view that the founding of the eternal city marks a new stage in the history of Italy and of mankind: "From the first day we are able to discern a political idea, that guided the distinguished leader, who recruited the scattered elements of the neighboring principalities fallen into decay." Thus we can accept that "gentilism" (or social groupings based on kin relations) is "a groundwork of Roman history, but not the only one. It fights for an existence already questioned." Though vestiges of it remain in Rome, "its undisputed existence is to be traced to a period anterior to any historical tradition." That is where comparisons with the Iroquois and other New World tribes are in order. The oldest ideas are borne by the Sabines; the Romans, however, are the bearers of a new idea "that has been introduced into the occidental world by the city of convenae and refugees hostile to the states based on elder convictions."[110] Rome thus remains essentially the creation of the patricians: older, native elements persist but they have been subordinated to the "higher" principles and authority introduced by the patricians.

Nevertheless, Bachofen had high respect for the prepolitical culture that the Romans subordinated to the political idea of the state. In the first part of *Griechische Reise,* he painted two city portraits, one of Patras and one of Corinth, that communicate the grandeur of their material culture even as they make its limitations clear. Both portraits seem to have been intended to evoke significant features of Basel that no Baseler could afford to despise, least of all one so closely associated with the city's commercial prosperity. Both cities, for instance, were described as advantageously situated between north and south, east and west, as transshipment centers, and as having flourishing factories.

> Situated where the Corinthian Sea meets the Adriatic, opposite the Ionian islands and at the midpoint between the northern and the southern parts of the kingdom, Patras is an important rung in the ladder joining the East and the West, and it owes to this mediating position the mixed character by which it is distinguished and in which Italian encounters Greek, the Orient the Occident. It is one of those places that never yield to their fate. Here on this gently rising strand, between the sea and the mountains, provided with nourishment from one of the most fertile countrysides in all Hellas, a city inhabited by an industrious, entrepreneurial, and profit-seeking people will stand until the last day dawns on earth. An excellent situation for trade and exchange ensures a longer future than any other advantage can, and Rome is perhaps the only example of a city that owes its eternity and indestructibility to a spiritual principle alone.[111]

The description of Corinth again emphasizes the value of industry and commerce, here explicitly associated with "feminine" and material rather than "masculine" and spiritual culture.

> The aspect of the place is so grand, one can easily understand how the first thought of the Greek people after they rose up to claim their independence was to locate the new capital of the country here, on the site of Corinth, at the midpoint of the new kingdom, equidistant from and equally accessible to north and south, east and west, and in one of the most heavenly spots that this earth has to offer. If in the end Athens was preferred, that represented an homage due to the superiority of greatness of spirit over the advantages of situation and external natural conditions. For in the highest things the world can produce, the works of the mind, Corinth stands far behind the brilliant brow of Athens, and of many a lesser city. In the entire time of its republic, it produced no intellectually distinguished man, writer, orator or statesman that we know of. The direction it took was quite different and remained the same from the moment it first emerged until its disappearance: that of industrious artisanal production, guided and ennobled by artistic development. This is the home of the vase painting that Demarat took over to Etruria when, dissatisfied with Kypselos's leadership, he found a new fatherland in Tarquinii. Even so, two thousand years later, did industrious artisans from the Netherlands, fleeing the rule of Spain, lay the groundwork in England for that country's later greatness. More-

over, Corinth blossomed in every branch of industry. . . . Over a long period of time its factories were as celebrated throughout the entire ancient world as those of England are today. . . . Corinth is also one of the first places in Greece to have become great through trade. Its superb situation made it one of the great emporiums of the trade of the ancient world. For it is not only, like Patras, one of the chief outlets for the inner Peloponnese, it is also the natural link between East and West, through its two harbor cities, Lechaeon on the Corinthian Sea and Kenchrae on the Saronic Gulf. Traders preferred to discharge their goods here and have them transported by land across the narrow isthmus rather than undertake the long and dangerous journey by sea around the southern tip of the Peloponnese. This was the line taken by all the trade from the Italian coastal cities to the Near East, until the founding of Alexandria brought the route to Egypt and Syria into favor. And so, through trade and industrial activity of every kind Corinth came to occupy first place among all the rich and brilliant cities of Greece.[112]

Bachofen added that "Corinth's most famous sanctuary was dedicated to Aphrodite, the divine being that produces all things from the womb of the earth, distributes fullness and fertility to every thing, and clothes it in the magical charm of love."

In the end, no citizen of Basel could deny the enduring value of the productive material labor associated with "maternal" and "popular" cultures, certainly not the heir to one of the most important ribbon weaving businesses in the city. In 1861, the year in which Bachofen published *Mother Right,* there also appeared a modest, but quite well-researched *Kurze Geschichte der Bandweberei in Basel* (*Short History of Ribbon Weaving in Basel*) written by his father, Bachofen-Merian, who had run the Bachofen firm for years. Perhaps it is not surprising that weaving occupies an important place in the work both of the father and of the son and that woman—the founder of culture, according to the son, and the first to give form to raw matter—appears so often in his scholarly writing as spinner and weaver, Arachne the spider-woman.[113]

"The action of the creative, formative energy of nature is represented by the image of spinning and weaving," we read in *Gräbersymbolik.* "The work of the great archaic Mothers is compared with the art of plaiting and braiding that imparts symmetry, form, and refinement to raw, crude material." Both the "erotic significance" that inheres in "the work of weaving and in the criss-crossing in-and-out movement of the threads," and the symbolic representation of man's life "as the great web of fate" point back "to a single basic notion, namely the first, purely physical idea of the spinning and weaving birth mothers." From the beginning, then, spinning and weaving are not neutral industrial activities; they are also religious symbols, symbols of the universal labor of articulation and form-giving, from the elementary natural (and sacred) processes of sexual intercourse and procreation to the designs of Providence itself. Equally, the development of the weaver's art manifests the increasing refinement of these processes as they are more and more informed by spirit. The contrast between the crude products of Ocnus ("not a single fine thread, not the least artistry in the yarn") or of Aphrodite, "the archaic mother of raw tellurian generation," and the fine materials due to the "highly developed skill" of Pallas Athene symbolizes the advance from "tellurian" toward "solar" culture; and the struggle between the "tellurian" and the "solar" principles is represented by the mythical competition between Aphrodite and Athene for the weaver's prize. "Aphrodite weaves the gross web of tellurian patterns from cruder materials, Athene fine raiments of perfect beauty. Aphrodite's work belongs to the earth, . . . it is the image of Aphroditian earth products; Athene's reaches a higher level of perfection, the heavenly level. The former remains unfinished and will be again unraveled; but what comes from Athene's hands is perfect. The basis of the former is material generation, always associated with the pains of birth; on Pallas's side, however, there is pure Olympian being, free of all material desire and exempt from the pains of birth, as befits the goddess who knows only a father, her father Zeus." Both weavers, nevertheless, participate in the sacredness of maternal creation. "Though they spring from different conceptions, they are still manifestations of the same essential quality—namely the power of maternity preserved in the fruitful opening of the womb of the female." Increasing refinement and spiritualization do not abolish the essential link with sacred origins.[114]

Weaving, "creation" as "skilled handiwork," enjoys a privileged place in the writing of the Basel ribbon-weaving magnate's son. It represents the peaceful, productive labor that is woman's—and the people's—crucial, founding contribution to human culture. Bachofen contrasted it with "the work of pure force," the violence, rapine, and destruction that the ancients attributed to "daemonic animal nature" and that he appears to have associated with materialistic and aggressive military regimes, whether ancient or modern, primitive or sophisticated. For a member of the Basel elite, and for a Bachofen in particular, weaving was not simply an industrial process and it was not intelligible solely in terms of technical and market considerations. On the contrary, it had its place in a "hierarchy"—a sacred order—and had been ennobled and purified by accepting the "paternal" spiritual authority that occupied the summit of that order. To tamper with the hierarchy was ruinous and sacrilegious. From that perspective, both the socialism of the increasingly militant workers' movements in Basel and the new impersonal organization of industrial production in factories—which Burckhardt compared to the military—imperiled the highest achievement of culture to date and threatened to bring about a regression similar to that produced in imperial Rome by the revival of Oriental mother cults and the rise of military dictatorships.

In the closing pages of his *History of Ribbon Weaving in Basel,* Bachofen-Merian addressed himself to the younger generation of Basel *Bändelherren.*

They might well judge the strict regulation of production methods, employers' hiring practices, and salaries that he had described in his book, he said, "with the disdain that, in our time particularly, is the only reward granted to our forebears and our past." They ought to consider, however, whether that older regulated order did not have many advantages over the current anarchic (in Bachofen Senior's eyes) market conditions. In these new conditions, export of the technically superior looms built by Basel craftsmen was no longer prohibited; as a result, the Basel ribbon firms were experiencing growing competition in foreign markets. Uncontrolled expansion of the number of looms had likewise made it difficult to keep them all busy despite the efforts of the manufacturers to seek outlets for their products in ever more remote overseas lands. Finally, import duties placed on Basel manufacturers in many foreign markets—notably the countries of the German *Zollverein*—were forcing many manufacturers to transfer production to the states within the customs union in order to remain competitive. Bachofen-Merian's final paragraph might have been written by his son: "These remarks may help to encourage a fair judgment of the point of view and the system prevailing in the past that now lies behind us. The future must teach our descendants whether the quite opposite, totally unrestrained character of modern times, the war of each against all, will have good or bad consequences for Basel and its industry."[115]

PART THREE

Jacob Burckhardt

The saying I heard most often from his lips was: "The world is thoroughly evil." Each time he uttered it, it was with the deepest, innermost conviction; now and then he would say it repeatedly, or for no particular reason, always with a deep, pious sigh. . . . He rejected the concept of a personal God. I once heard him cry out bitterly, with a shrug of his shoulders: "The idea of God?! When one animal devours another?!" However, he said that in no way light-heartedly, but under the compulsion of an earnest and melancholy convic-tion. . . . The son of the chief pastor of the city of Basel was so far removed from Christianity that he could only appreciate it historically and anthropolog-ically. Naturally, from that point of view, the most appealing Christian is the most authentic and uncompromising. . . . At the top of the list of those for whom Burckhardt felt sympathy were monks and ascetics, the only ones he ac-cepted as full-blooded Christians; at the bottom were progressives and reform-ers. . . . One day he gave me a commission, in the form of an authorization: "Spread it about without any hesitation, tell it fearlessly, tell it in your student circles, that I believe in nothing. I don't mind at all if people are informed about it; I am quite happy for the young people to know it." . . . When one thinks of a freethinker, one usually imagines a skeptical and frivolous person. Burckhardt was certainly skeptical, at least in some of his forms of expression; his Voltaire had washed off on him a bit. On the other hand, he was the oppo-site of frivolous. He was the most earnest thinker I have met in my life. Who-ever has heard a single one of his lectures will know what I mean. I have in mind the cosmic seriousness that pulsed through his lectures and raised them to a form of ceremonious devotion. . . . Private conversation with him rein-forced that impression of seriousness, despite all the humor he expressed in word and gesture. One could even detect in Burckhardt's spirit a trait that one normally encounters only in connection with religion: he was *mysterical.* Even if he did not believe in a guiding Providence, he still believed in mysterious shoves from behind toward a goal of some kind. . . . How he might have con-ceived of this mysterious impulse in the absence of a God, no one of course could know but himself, and quite probably he did not know.

—Carl Spitteler, "Jacob Burckhardt und der Student."

Jacob Burckhardt. Universitätsbibliothek Basel, Porträtsammlung.

10

"A Man Who Held Out amid the Collapse of Everything"

Serene Resistance

The Bachofens had made their way into the Basel elite at a relatively late date. The Burckhardts, citizens since the early 1500s, were already, by the year 1600, among the richest and most influential families in the state.[1] They had come to Basel in the second major wave of immigration, at the turn of the fifteenth and sixteenth centuries, just as the city was settling into its new role as an independent, commercial city-state in the Swiss Confederation. More recent arrivals than the oldest families—the Iselins, the Falkeners, the Faesch—they preceded the great influx of religious refugees—the Sarasins, the Socins, the Bernoullis. Having started out in a modest way as haberdashers, the Burckhardts were soon trading in silk cloth in every part of Europe and had become members not only of the *Krämerzunft* or tradesmen's guild but of the powerful merchants' guild *"zum Schlüssel."* Simultaneously, they advanced to political prominence. From 1655 to 1798 there was not a year when one of the two *Bürgermeisters* of Basel was not a Burckhardt or the husband of a Burckhardt. Many established themselves in various foreign capitals and ports and some attained high rank in the service of foreign princes. By the mid-eighteenth century one of the most distinguished of the Iselins confided to his diary the wish that "Heaven would deliver us from these Medicis!"[2]

The large and expanding Burckhardt clan was not only active in business and in government, it also provided the University of Basel with an impressive contingent of professors. Ten times, in the course of the seventeenth and eighteenth centuries, Burckhardts occupied chairs of law, theology, eloquence, rhetoric, logic, ethics, and mathematics. Before 1700, on the other hand, they seem not to have played much of a role in the ministry, perhaps because they were too preoccupied with amassing wealth and influence, or because they shared the coolness of some other city families like the Amerbachs and the Iselins to the Reformed church. By the time of Jacob Burckhardt's birth in 1818 they had made up for this. The historian's grandfather, Johann Rudolf (1738–1820), had been chief minister of St. Peter's Church, one of the principal churches of the city, and had been active in both Christian and Enlightenment philanthropic causes. He had helped to found the *Gemeinnützige Gesellschaft* and the *Christentumsgesellschaft*, from which the celebrated Basel *Mission* was to emerge in 1815. His son Jacob, the historian's father, rose to become the chief minister or *Antistes* of the state church after studying at Heidelberg, where he was close to men as varied in their outlook as Jung-Stilling, the leader of the Pietist movement, Daub, a professor of theology who tried to reconcile Kantian philosophy and orthodox theology, and Creuzer, the great scholar of classical mythology, whose teaching made such an impression on the elder Jacob Burckhardt that he almost abandoned theology for classical history and philology. According to the testimony of one of his nephews, *Antistes* Burckhardt was "neither a Rationalist nor a Pietist, but a simple, solid Bible Christian, knowledgeable in history and in art, and in general broadly cultivated."[3] Around 1780, the author of *Athenae Rauricae*, a history of the University of Basel, could quite properly describe the Burckhardts as *"gens amplissima et virorum de Republica, Ecclesia et Academia nostra praeclare meritorum feracissima."*[4] As Werner Kaegi noted in his rich biography of Jacob Burckhardt, "To write the history of the family in the seventeenth and eighteenth century would be equivalent to writing the history of the city of Basel."[5]

On his mother's side, the historian belonged to a well-to-do and respected family that still had close links with the ordinary guildsmen of Basel. The Schorndorffs had settled in Basel before the Burckhardts. They had been tailors, coopers, furriers, and then innkeepers. In the mid-seventeenth century Hans Schorndorff, innkeeper at the "Stork," was elected a *Ratsherr*, married the daughter of *Bürgermeister* Johann Rudolf Wettstein, who was to play an important role at the Peace of Westphalia, and acquired the inn known as *"zum Wilden Mann"* on the Freie Strasse, in the heart of the city, where he was host to numerous captains and dignitaries during the Thirty Years' War. Between the two of them, *Antistes* Jacob Burckhardt and his wife Susanna Schorndorff were connected with almost all the families in the Basel elite, including even the legendary Amerbachs and Frobeniuses. At the same time, like so many Basel families, they were descended from artisans and small traders in Germany, France, Italy, and the Netherlands. These people, in sum, were at once thoroughgoing Baselers, products of the peculiar social, political, religious, and commercial culture of their native city, and in their way, more cosmopolitan and European than many citizens of much larger nations.

Though his father did not belong to the wealthiest branch of the Burckhardt family and, as a minister, did not himself possess great wealth, there was nothing narrow about the circumstances of Jacob Burckhardt's upbringing. He was familiar with the milieux of business and international trade from his earliest years and there was virtually no time when he was not fully aware of the larger world beyond the frontiers of the city-state and the precincts of the Cathedral and the University. As a child he regularly spent part of the summer at Mayen-fels, in the Basel countryside, where his uncle Johann Lucas Burckhardt had acquired a fine eighteenth-century country house. This older brother of his fa-ther's had developed trade connections with Russia, settled there, and been ap-pointed Swiss consul in Moscow. At the time of Napoleon's continental block-ade, he had amassed a fortune—like other Basel merchants—by smuggling goods to and from England. His wife, the so-called *Moskowiterin,* had adopted two Russian children saved from the burning of Moscow and it was the govern-ess she hired to take care of these children, a young woman from Königsberg in East Prussia, who had herself been orphaned at the time of the Napoleonic occupation of that city, that pastor and *Antistes*-to-be Burckhardt chose as his second wife after the premature death of Susanna Schorndorff in 1830.

Both the Russian and the business connections were kept up, moreover, by Jacob Burckhardt's younger brother Lucas Gottlieb, whom the *Antistes* and his wife had considered the brightest of their children and whom, in the Basel tradition, they had therefore groomed for a business career. Gottlieb's career followed the typical path of the Basel merchant patrician. He learned French in French-speaking Switzerland, was apprenticed to the firm of Vischer and Co. in Basel, and was then attached to companies in northern Italy and En-gland that had business links with Basel in order to round out his training. At the age of twenty-two he left for Moscow to help run his uncle's business there. A few years later he returned to Basel to marry Laura Alioth, whose parents owned a large silk spinning mill (*Florettspinnerei*) in the adjacent village of Arl-esheim. Gottlieb immediately entered his father-in-law's well-established firm as a partner and served as its technical director. At the age of fifty, after twenty-eight years in business, he was elected to the Senate and made a member of the Cabinet, where he specialized in educational matters. In 1874 he became president of the *Gemeinnützige Gesellschaft.* An educated and cultivated man, Gottlieb Burckhardt remained close to his brother Jacob all his life.[6] When Burckhardt later wrote about the humanist education and interests of the Flor-entine merchants, Basel and his own brother were assuredly not far from his mind. His "aestheticism" was always moderated by familiarity with practical affairs and knowledge of the way these affected the lives of his relatives and friends in the small world of the Basel elite. In 1883, for instance, that world was shaken by the *"Riesenbankrott"* ("colossal bankruptcy") of the firm of Leo-nard Paravicini. Burckhardt wrote at length to another member of the elite who was out of town, describing how the calamitous consequences of the event had spread outwards from the three principals involved—"Manni" (Emanuel) Burckhardt-Burckhardt, *Bürgermeister* Carl Felix Burckhardt-Sarasin, and "Manni" Paravicini—to many of their close relatives. *Bürgermeister* Burckhardt-Sarasin was on the point of declaring insolvency; his wife, a Sara-sin, had lost a million; Frau Heusler-Wegner had lost everything except her

house, as had Manni Burckhardt-Burckhardt's mother-in-law, old Frau Burckhardt on the St. Albanvorstadt. The losses of many creditors, both companies
and individuals, were measured in the hundreds of thousands. A member of
the Vischer family whose daughter had just married Burckhardt-Sarasin's son
had felt obliged to resign from his position and had agreed to be reinstated only
at the insistence of the board of his company. Burckhardt himself had had to
go through the sumptuous home of one of the firm's directors in order to put a
value on the works of art in it.[7]

Jacob Burckhardt was born on May 25, 1818. His education was almost identical to Bachofen's: Herr Munzinger's elementary school (1821–1824), the Basel
Gymnasium (1826–1833), and the *Pädagogium* (1833–1836).[8] His teachers were
essentially the same as Bachofen's: Vinet in French, Gerlach in Latin, Vischer
in Greek, Wackernagel in German, Brommel in history, J. R. Merian in mathematics. To these should be added the sometime *carbonaro* Luigi Picchioni, the
teacher of Italian, to whom the historian dedicated the second edition of *The
Civilization of the Renaissance*. Because of his participation in various plots to
free Lombardy from Austrian rule in the years following the Congress of Vienna, Picchioni had found himself under sentence of death and in 1821 had
fled to Switzerland. Five years later he succeeded in obtaining a lectureship
in Italian language and literature at Basel, where he settled down peacefully,
respecting a commitment to steer clear of further subversive activity and taking
no part in the 1830 revolutions, as a report of the University Governing Board
noted with satisfaction in 1834.[9] But in 1848 his old revolutionary enthusiasm
flared up, and while Burckhardt took over his classes, he left to take part in the
liberation movement in Lombardy. On the collapse of the uprising against the
Austrians, he returned to Basel and devoted himself from then on to his teaching and to a series of studies of Dante on which he may have received some
help from his former pupil. Jacob Burckhardt loved Picchioni. Even after he
himself had veered away from the liberal convictions of his student days, he
continued to admire the warmth and nobility of his old teacher's dedication to
liberty. Above all, he loved him for his human qualities, his lack of bitterness,
and his ability to stay "young and full of mischief" after sixty years of exile and
disappointment. "A German, whose youthful illusions have collapsed, easily becomes morose and hard to bear; but it is precisely in such circumstances that the
Latin becomes truly engaging," Burckhardt observed of Picchioni to a friend.[10]

The remark highlights an aspect of Burckhardt's personality that distinguishes him from Bachofen. Both men shared, to a surprising degree, the same
judgment of their own time, both had the legendary wicked tongue of the Baseler, but Burckhardt was determined never to allow himself to become gloomy
or embittered, always to retain the inner freedom and serenity, the sociability
and the capacity for artistic and intellectual enjoyment that he admired in Pic-

chioni. The early death of his mother, he said of himself much later, recalling the exact date (17 March 1830), "caused him his first experience of deep pain and produced in him, very early in life, a keen sense of the fragility and uncertainty of everything earthly, but at the same time his temperament (doubtless inherited from his mother) was naturally disposed to joyousness."[11] Bachofen, in contrast, might have been the model of the German whom Burckhardt contrasted with the Latin. It seems appropriate that of all his teachers it was to the increasingly cranky and disenchanted German idealist Gerlach that Bachofen remained faithfully attached, while Burckhardt was until the end the *"particolare e carissimo amico"* of the lively and amiable Italian ex-*carbonaro* who knew how to turn even the bitterness of exile to sweetness.[12] It was an art for which Burckhardt was to have a special appreciation, since he had to acquire it himself.

After the *Pädagogium,* there followed the stint in French-speaking Switzerland, in Burckhardt's case at Neuchâtel, that was normal for the children of better-off Basel families, who were expected to have a good command of French. Burckhardt appears to have thought that knowledge of French would be all the more necessary for him as he was unlikely to be able to make a career in Basel. "I realize very well that there are not many prospects for me in Basel," he told a Freiburg friend and mentor in 1836[13]—an indication, incidentally, that at that point he may already have had doubts about entering the ministry, since as a theology graduate he would probably have had no trouble finding a pastoral position in Basel.

In Neuchâtel, Burckhardt lodged with Charles-Henri Godet, a distinguished citizen of the town and a man of learning and worldly experience. Godet had started out as a classical scholar and tutor to various foreign dignitaries. He had traveled in Sweden, Poland, Russia, the Crimea, and the Caucasus. In France, just before the July Revolution, he had been tutor to the family of Count Pourtalès, the legal scholar (a relative of the prominent Neuchâtel family that had immigrated from France at the time of the Revocation of the Edict of Nantes), and in this milieu he had met some of the leading lights of Paris at the time: Cousin, de Gérando, Guizot, Villemain, Alexander von Humboldt. An ardent botanist, Godet had collected over twelve thousand specimens (his *Flore du Jura,* published in 1852, remains a classic), as well as an unusual number and variety of insects. He still retained enough Greek to go through Aristophanes' *Clouds* with his young charge. Godet's sister, who had been a governess in England, seems to have taught Burckhardt some English.[14]

During his stay in Neuchâtel, Burckhardt compiled a collection of excerpts from classical texts and commentaries to which he gave the title *"Noctes Novocastrenses"* (no doubt an allusion to the *Noctes Atticae* of Aulus Gellius, a second-century Roman studying in Athens). From this collection it is possible to glean an idea of his interests at the time. These turn out to have been remarkably similar to those of his fellow student at the *Pädagogium*, Bachofen. Many of the excerpts concern the world of ancient myth, ritual, festivals, and sacrifices. For instance, there were transcriptions of many of the eighty or so Hellenistic poems known as the Orphic hymns—hymns to Dionysus, Kronos, Aphrodite, Pan, and so on—which had been made popular by the romantic interpretation of myth and the theories of comparative religion Burckhardt had already encountered or was about to encounter in Basel in the lectures of Gerlach, De Wette, and Johann Georg Müller. Excerpts from and commentaries on the *Phaedo* and on Sophocles' *Oedipus at Colonnus* focus on the theme of death and the immortality of the soul and show Burckhardt struggling with traditional Christian dogma on these topics and rejecting the claim that there is no eternal life except through Christ.[15] Later, in 1851, *The Age of Constantine the Great* was to bear traces of this preoccupation with ancient myth and religious symbolism.

Burckhardt up to this point had shown himself to be a gifted youngster, with a broad range of interests. He knew Latin and Greek well and was soon to add some knowledge of Hebrew, spoke French and Italian fluently, and also had some English. Like many people of his class in Basel, and in the German-speaking countries as a whole, he had a fair musical education and had learned to draw competently. He found it as natural to compose music as to play or sing it, to write poems as to read them, and to sketch scenes and buildings as to look at them. By the age of fifteen he had bound together a number of his musical compositions into a sort of musical sketchbook, on the cover of which he inscribed with naive pride *"Composizioni di Giacomo Burcardo."* They included a choral, *"O Haupt voll Blut und Wunden"* and a *"Dies Irae"* for voices and pianoforte. Right into the 1840s Burckhardt continued to add to this little collection, the compositions becoming gradually more secular in tone and inspiration. A *"Salve Regina"* of 1834 and a *"Stabat Mater"* of 1835 were followed by settings of choruses from Schiller's *Die Braut von Messina* in 1836–1837, of Goethe's *"Trost in Tränen,"* of *"Des Mägdleins Klage"* from Schiller's *Wallenstein*, for voice and pianoforte in 1837–1838, and of the concluding stanza of Goethe's famous poem *"Die Braut von Corinth,"* with its striking final line, *"Eilen wir den alten Göttern zu"* ("Let us hasten back to the old Gods")—the last named having been composed some time between the young Baseler's first foray into Italy in 1837 and his first real journey through the peninsula in 1838.

Along with these musical compositions, Burckhardt had compiled a collection of sketches of antiquities, ranging from the gargoyles of Basel's Cathedral to items in the Cathedral treasure and plans of Greek and Roman theaters and private homes; these were placed in a volume to which he gave the title *"Alterthümer."* In addition, he took his sketchbook with him on his travels through Switzerland and Italy and brought back drawings of landscapes, buildings, and city views—a practice he continued for decades to come in his travels in Germany and Italy and on which he was to rely when he was working on *The*

Cicerone: An Introduction to the Enjoyment of the Art Works of Italy.[16] No doubt he never imagined he might contribute anything original as an artist—as he imagined for a while that he might be a poet—but drawing lessons had taught his eye to see and encouraged his interest in art and art history.

Naturally, Burckhardt had also tried his hand at poetic composition, as his father had done before him[17]—once again gathering the pieces together in a volume on which he wrote the title *"Gedichte."* The themes are romantic: death, the transitoriness of everything earthly, providence and the meaning of life, the immortality of art (poems on Tasso and Dante), occasionally the *"carpe diem"* theme. Some of them have a surprising power, like *"Nach dem Weltgericht"* ("After Judgment Day") of 1835, in which the poet evokes the planets crashing into nothingness: Sirius itself, its light extinguished, rolling through the darkness of space until it strikes and crushes the sun; the earth plunging headlong into the black abyss like a burned out Aetna or a horrifying, deserted field strewn with corpses. It would be hazardous to assume that these juvenile works "express" original thoughts and feelings that were formed independently of Burckhardt's literary reading. In addition, like all such compositions, they were partly exercises through which the writer hoped to appropriate the techniques of admired masters. The young student's poetic productions can be taken as testimony of inner experience only in the sense that that inner experience was itself shaped largely by literature. There seems little doubt, however, that some of the concerns of the young poet remained alive in the mature historian, and not only in his explicit statements. Just as the work of poetry itself was an attempt by the seventeen-year-old to salvage what is essential in a feeling or an experience from what he described as the "dark abyss"—subsequent poems, written at the time of his journey to Italy in 1838, aimed to capture, like sketches, particular experiences of time and place ("To the poet Platen, from the heights above Pisa, 22nd July 1838," "Palazzo Doria," "Fiesole")—so the work of history for the later historian was not simply a scholarly investigation, the object of which is to produce knowledge, or even a means of enhancing the self-awareness of the individual in history, but an instrument for saving the spirit of the past for eternal life. We should not be surprised that Burckhardt took some time to be convinced that poetry was not his true vocation or that he regarded history as "the highest form of poetry."[18] Several experiments with the historical novella form (*"Der schwarze Tod," "Nero"*) point to an early but at the time by no means unusual interest in combining history and literary art.[19]

Shortly before his departure for Neuchâtel, Burckhardt had already become initiated into the world of historical research. An acquaintance of his father's, the Freiburg theologian and historian Heinrich Schreiber—a dissident Catholic very popular in Protestant circles because of his questioning of the authority of the Curia, of eternal vows, and of the celibacy of the priesthood[20]—had engaged him to do some copying and bibliographical and archival research in the

Basel libraries, in connection with a projected biography of Glarean. With some assistance from Gerlach and his father, the young Burckhardt supplied the Freiburg scholar with careful and critical summaries of the material he was interested in, winning both an acknowledgment (the first public mention of Burckhardt's name) in the final published work and his enduring friendship. On his side, in gratitude to Schreiber for his guidance and encouragement, Burckhardt later dedicated to him the first edition of *The Age of Constantine the Great*.

If Bachofen wavered for several years between law and classical philology, unable to decide between two disciplines that were closely related in his mind, Burckhardt hesitated between theology and history. In those early decades of the nineteenth century, when theologians like De Wette and Hagenbach tried to do justice both to the demands of modern historical method and to those of faith, while historians like Ranke believed that the nations of the earth are "ideas of God,"[21] the two disciplines were in practice not so far apart. Out of deference to his father, Burckhardt first committed himself to theology when he matriculated at the University of Basel in 1837. But that did not yet mean giving up history and literature. In addition to the lectures of the theology professors—Hagenbach, De Wette, and Johann Georg Müller—Burckhardt attended those of Wilhelm Vischer, the professor of Greek, and Wilhelm Wackernagel, the professor of German, at whose home he and several of his friends had gathered every week when they were students at the *Pädagogium*, to read poetry and discuss their own compositions.[22]

From his copious notes on these lectures, it is possible to reconstruct what he got out of them. The notes on Wackernagel's course on "Poetics, Rhetoric, Stylistics" (1837–1838) underline the idea of an epic age, prior to the age of prose, novels, and discursive reason, and of an oral culture in which the transmission of heroic legends consolidating group identity fell to the poet, with memory and song playing a far more significant role than in later literate cultures. This romantic notion of a historical development from belief to criticism, from poetry to prose, from myth to history, from epic to romance, was to be an essential ingredient in Burckhardt's later view of history.[23] As for Vischer's course on the *Agamemnon* of Aeschylus (1839), the "basic idea," in Burckhardt's own words, was a religious one: "the insufficiency of human capacity with respect to divine Providence; every attempt of man to break out of his limits meets with rejection. The [representation of] the vain struggle of the free individual against blind fate is moral, not fatalistic. It arouses fear and compassion in the spectator but at the same time points to a reconciliation in a higher order. Only with Euripides does the accident of individual passion take the place of divine Providence."[24] The themes addressed in the lectures Burckhardt attended on German and Greek history and literature were thus by no means unconnected with those he was to encounter in his theology classes.

Plate 1. Alexander Roslin, *Frau Margaretha Bachofen-Heitz*. Private collection, Basel; reproduced by kind permission of the owner.

Plate 2. Arnold Böcklin, *Das Drama* (*Drama*). Private collection.

Plate 3. Arnold Böcklin, *Der Krieg* (*War*). Staatliche Kunstsammlungen, Dresden. Photo: Sächsische Landesbibliothek/Staats- und Universitätsbibliothek Dresden, Deutsche Fotothek.

Plate 4. Arnold Böcklin, *Kentaurenkampf auf beschneiter Bergkuppe* (*Battle of Centaurs on Snow–Capped Mountain Top*). Offentliche Kunstsammlung Basel, Kunstmuseum. Photo: Offentliche Kunstsammlung Basel, Martin Buhler.

Here Hagenbach's carefully prepared and well-honed lectures on church history offered a richly detailed introduction to the Italian Middle Ages, the struggle between the popes and the emperors, and the work of the Italian humanists. In his account of recent church history, the moderate and conciliatory Hagenbach apparently stressed the need to accept the historical and critical orientation of modern theological thought. "Scripture must be interpreted grammatically and historically," Burckhardt noted. At the same time, when Hagenbach lectured later on the early church, it became obvious to Burckhardt—and this lesson coincided with the teaching of Wackernagel and Vischer—that belief itself had paid a high price for the commitment of modern theology to the principles of historical criticism.[25]

That same problem—the impoverishment of religion through modern critical reflection—was raised by the lectures of De Wette, the most complex and original, as well as the best known, of Burckhardt's teachers at the University of Basel. In his youth, *Antistes* Burckhardt had attended some lectures by De Wette at Heidelberg. "He is giving an introduction to the Old Testament," he had written back to Basel. "But he follows a curious path. For example, he claims that the Pentateuch is not by Moses, that the writings of Solomon are not by Solomon, that Moses, David, and Solomon are collective names to which everything that was thought to be written in the spirit of one or the other was retrospectively attributed; that they are, however, authentic. The Book of Jonah, he says, is an instructive tale."[26] The *Antistes'* son did not have his father's ironic reserve. He had no sympathy with strict orthodoxy. "Nothing in the world is better suited to laziness than orthodoxy," he declared. "If you gag your mouth, stop up your ears and put a blinder over your eyes, you can sleep peacefully." But the new theology could not restore what it had undermined. "De Wette's system grows daily more colossal before my very eyes. One *has* to follow him; nothing else is possible. But every day another bit of the familiar teachings of the church comes away in his hands. Today I have finally reached the conclusion that he considers the birth of Christ a myth—and so now do I. A shudder came over me when I thought of a whole series of reasons why this virtually must be so. . . . Prayer is still a possibility for me, but there is no Revelation, I now know that."[27]

The outcome of Burckhardt's theological studies was that he could not envisage ever serving as a minister of the church. "Given my present convictions (if I may call them that), I could never in good conscience accept a position as a minister, not at least as long as the current view of Revelation prevails, and it does not seem about to change any time soon. . . . If I have to assume responsibility, I want at least to be free to assume it for myself alone, and not for others." This did not mean that he would abandon theology, but that he could no longer consider the ministry as a career. Perhaps there was a way of avoiding classes on the doctrines of faith and Revelation and concentrating exclusively on history and language studies, for which he had both talent and inclination, he wrote his friend Johannes Riggenbach, a future professor of theology. A career as a teacher at the *Gymnasium* was something he might aim at. At any rate, he was not inclined to stifle his doubts: "Let us remain honest heretics."[28]

The fact that his father was elected *Antistes* precisely at this point of crisis in his religious faith obviously did not make matters simpler for Burckhardt. He decided to put off a decision concerning his theological studies. But there was no doubt that his relation to theology had become extremely problematical. Characteristically, he remained unresponsive to the efforts of his friend Alois Biedermann—a young Zuricher whose father had sent him to college in Basel in order to protect him from the influence of the Zurich radicals, but who fell despite these precautions under the spell of Hegelian philosophy and evolved in later years into the leader of the liberal and reforming theological party in Switzerland—to restore his faith by philosophical argument. "I would not want to burden anybody with my doubts," Burckhardt noted, "for, as I was evidently not born to be a thinker but have a very unclear head, I would only bore every one. In any case," he added, with characteristic irony, "I see that things are not any better with those who have clear heads."[29]

In his own way, however, Burckhardt now distinguished between two things that he described as "Religion" and "the Bible" and that seemed irreconcilable to him. The former designated a general religiosity or sense of the mystery of life, the latter Protestant orthodoxy.[30] He could no longer subscribe to orthodoxy, but he could not give up religion altogether, despite heroic attempts to achieve a kind of stoic renunciation.[31] A passage from a letter to Riggenbach, in which he recalls his emotions one evening during a journey to Italy a few months earlier, gives some idea of what "Religion" meant to Burckhardt. If one disregards the fervent sentimentality to which romantic young men in the first half of the nineteenth century seem to have been especially prone, this letter affords an insight into thoughts and feelings that may not have vanished with youth but on the contrary may well have defined and continued to define Burckhardt's historical vocation.

> The pain I felt that heavenly evening in Pisa will never vanish from my memory. In the beautiful green meadow in the midst of which stand the Cathedral, the Campanile, the Baptistry, and the Camposanto, I was leaning against the wall of the Seminary, sketching. As I gazed on the Byzantine arches I was led by a natural association of ideas to think of all of you [Burckhardt had made a brief but memorable foray into Italy the previous year with Riggenbach and two other close friends from Basel, his cousin Jacob Oeri and Alois Biedermann], and was soon hardly in a state to draw any more. . . . I followed the old city wall and found my way through gardens and vineyards to the furthest downriver of the bridges over the Arno. The sky was now very dark blue, the Apennines stood out violet-hued in the evening light; the Arno was flowing by

beneath my feet, and I could have wept like a child. All my heroic resolve melted away. . . . And so it happened again three days later as we watched the sunset on the dome of the Cathedral in Florence. At times I felt as if I were Faust, full of overflowing longing. . . . Before me lay all the treasures of nature and art, as though the divinity had passed over this land like a sower.[32]

The idea that the beauty of art and nature is a manifestation of the divine takes the place here, for Burckhardt, of his lost belief in Revelation, at least as it was understood in traditional Protestantism. And so it was to be until the end of his life. Years later, in his *Cultural History of Greece,* he observed that the final great chorus of Aeschylus's *Eumenides,* with the interspersed speeches of Athene, was comparable in the sublimity of its inspiration to Isaiah's vision of the Jerusalem to come.[33] In contrast with the vanity of political events, art in particular offered intimations of eternity. In an account he wrote of his journey to Italy in 1838, Burckhardt described the Cathedral of Milan: "Here the Milanese governed themselves as a commune, then obeyed first the Sforzas, later the Spaniards, the Emperor, the French Republic and Napoleon, and finally mighty Austria; and the Cathedral looked down upon all this and lived through it all, and moss grew on it and was scraped off again, and it had to learn of the constant political turmoil from all the chattering magpies, and it continued to smile down from the blue sky as in days gone by."[34]

In the spring of 1839, after a candid discussion with his father, Burckhardt gave up theology, and in the fall of that year left Basel for the University of Berlin to study history. He spent four years in Berlin, interrupted only by a period at the University of Bonn in the summer of 1841. By the time he returned to Basel in 1843, he had come to terms with his loss of faith and had brought his thinking about history into sharper focus.[35]

At Berlin, Burckhardt enrolled in several of the courses that Bachofen had attended a couple of years before him—Böckh's course on Greek history and philology, Ranke's on German history and on modern European history, Ritter's on geography. In addition, he read Tacitus's *Germania* with Jacob Grimm, newly arrived and covered with glory as one of the suspended "Göttingen Seven" who had stood up against "tyranny" (see chapter 6, p. 125). Among the brilliant younger men at Berlin with whom Burckhardt studied were Johann Gustav Droysen and Franz Kugler. Droysen, who at thirty-one was not much older than Burckhardt, already was celebrated as the author of important works on Alexander the Great and the Hellenistic world. He took an interest in the young student from Basel, but their relationship was entirely academic and impersonal.[36] In contrast, Burckhardt found in Kugler, the art historian and one of the most humane and liberal minds in Prussia at the time, "a dear friend, full of ideas, kindness, and patience";[37] he remained close to him for the rest of Kugler's life, as assistant, collaborator, and friend. At Bonn, Burckhardt took

Friedrich Welcker's course on the history of ancient art and he also appears to have attended for a time a course on the history of the Rhineland by von Sybel, who was only a few years older than he and who was just starting out.

In addition, he made many friends. A bachelor all his life, Burckhardt had a genuine vocation for friendship. In adolescence, his friendships were often intense and romantic, clouded by jealousies and disappointments; in later years the private circle of his friends and regular correspondents, to whom he maintained an unswerving loyalty, seem to have constituted a surrogate community and public for the community he could no longer find in the rapidly changing world of mid-nineteenth-century Europe. The young student in Berlin and Bonn, it appears, was especially drawn to restless or rebellious and idealistic spirits, like the two Schauenburgs, Eduard and Hermann, Willibald Beyschlag, Ernst Ackermann, and above all Gottfried Kinkel, the future socialist revolutionary, then a young *Privat-dozent* in theology at Bonn with strong interests in poetry, music, and art and the center of a merry romantic circle of young poets and radicals known as the *Maikäfer.* The high-spirited Baseler even managed to get himself listed in the Prussian police files as a "revolutionary" for having participated in a serenade honoring the liberal ruler of Baden.[38] Through Kinkel's future wife, Johanna Matthieux, the *"Liebe Directrix"* of Burckhardt's correspondence, he gained entry to the salon of the fabled Bettina von Arnim in Berlin, where he sang lieder, was admired by the hostess for his "fine bass voice," and may have met his fellow student Karl Marx.[39]

Throughout these years, filled with ardent discussions of religion, history, politics, and philosophy, Burckhardt also continued to write poetry, to make music, to visit galleries and buildings, and to make sketches of what he saw. Kinkel—who did not have a low opinion of himself—was fascinated by the many-sided talents and accomplishments of the young man from Basel. "To visit galleries or buildings with Burckhardt was the highest form of delight," he wrote some years later, in the early 1870s, after his somewhat theatrical engagement in revolutionary politics had caused a considerable cooling of the friendship on Burckhardt's side. "He had a perfect understanding both of the subtlest nuances of meaning and of the sensuous appeal of art and could relate every work to the ideas and tendencies of the age in which it had been produced. Regrettably, he himself had too low an opinion of his poetic talent to get the best out of it; for as he was capable of doing and succeeding at anything he wanted, he practiced all the genres of poetic composition with unimaginable facility and taste. . . . I have never known a more gifted person. . . ."[40]

For a while, under the influence of Droysen in particular, Burckhardt accepted the need to choose a field of scholarly specialization. "In view of the enormous expansion of the field of scholarship, one must now concentrate on one area and pursue it thoroughly," he wrote. "Otherwise one's efforts are completely dissipated."[41] But, in the end, the many-sidedness of talents and interests that had struck Kinkel was one of the factors that led Burckhardt to follow an independent path as a historian and that distinguished him from the *viri eruditissimi*—as he was to call the German professional historians—who, in his opinion, had betrayed the freedom of history and sold it into bondage to the Prussian state.

By the time Burckhardt reached Berlin, Hegel had been dead eight years. But his influence at the University that he had helped to launch remained enormous. Above all, the ambition underlying Hegel's philosophical program—the reconciliation of reason and existence, the demands of Enlightenment and the weight of historical reality, Revolution and historical continuity—had presided over the foundation of the University of Berlin (in 1807) and was shared by many who did not accept all of Hegel's solutions, by Ranke as well as by Droysen or Böckh. "I was born in the year the Peace of Basel was signed," Ranke noted later, "that is to say in the year of the first attempt to produce a new line of descent by bringing together a France transformed by the Revolution and a Prussian state that represented the conservative principle of the European world."[42] Ranke's intellectual enterprise, as Werner Kaegi shrewdly observed, was a constantly renewed endeavor "to establish such a Peace of Basel between the revolutionary and the conservative powers of his age."[43]

Such an endeavor could hardly have failed to appeal to Burckhardt. It had not been fortuitous that when the Basel authorities undertook to reform the city's education system they looked to Prussia for ideas and inspiration. They too wanted to reconcile change with respect for the values of tradition. Compromise solutions, moreover, had always been preferred in Basel—for the practical reasons suggested earlier—to dramatic conflicts. Even conservatives like Andreas Heusler—of whose newspaper, the *Basler Zeitung*, Burckhardt was shortly to become editor—recognized the need for concessions and were partisans of the *juste milieu* rather than dyed-in-the-wool reactionaries.

In Ranke's lectures, as Burckhardt reported them in his class notes, the balance between conservatism and acceptance of change, between Herder's prerevolutionary vision of nations as primarily cultural communities and the postrevolutionary awareness of the importance of political and state organization, was finely maintained. On the one hand, history is destiny. "The nations are ideas of God." Each one is an organic growth with its proper telos or end and each has its specific contribution to make to the total divine plan. The state is therefore not evil in itself, but is justified, as the historical embodiment of a national spirit, by its contribution to the realization of the divine plan. Even revolution, provided it is "organic"—provided it "erupts unconsciously and unsummoned from the ground"—can be considered "lawful."[44] Ranke's viewpoint as a historian, Burckhardt noted, was that of historical fate itself: the historian stands above the mêlée, above the individual tragedies and catastrophes, his eyes trained on the grand design.[45] From Ranke's own writings it is clear that he dreamed of a "book of history" that would be a kind of narrative of the divine mind, a new book of revelations.[46] "The book of history lies open before us," he wrote. "[W]e can know how nations achieve greatness and how they fall into ruin. The examples of the more distant past and those of recent history come together before our eyes."[47]

On the other hand, Ranke himself realized the dangers of such a lofty vision of the total grand design. "You look upon the bloody handiwork of war as a competition between moral energies," he has "Karl" object to "Friedrich" in the dialogue *Politisches Gespräch,* dating from the early 1830s. "Beware that you do not become too sublime."[48] And in his lectures to Maximilian II of Bavaria in the mid-1850s he rejected, in the spirit of Herder, the progressivist idea that "each generation surpasses the preceding one, so that the latest is always the most favored and the preceding generations are only the bearers of those that follow."[49] Burckhardt's notes from the lectures on "History of the Middle Ages" (1840–1841) contain a similar admonition: "No generation may take itself to be the goal of universal development."[50] Moreoever, if Ranke's eye was constantly trained on the grand design of universal history, he also emphasized the value of the individual phenomena in and through which we receive intimations of the universal. Ranke's history is in that sense in line with the contemporary romantic emphasis on symbol, as opposed to neoclassical allegory. In allegory, the romantics often argued, the individual phenomenon vanishes in the general truth it signifies; the symbol, in contrast, being both a particular instantiation of an essence or universal and the sign of that essence or universal, is the locus of reconciliation of the particular and the general.

The point of departure of Droysen's lectures was also, as Burckhardt reported it in his class notes, a fairly familiar romantic view of universal history as providential design: "History: humanity's re-membering of itself. The daily task of humanity, to approach fulfillment of its destiny. . . . That destiny is: to work toward freedom and full consciousness of freedom. Spirit wills to dominate the existent and turn it to its own ends. History is the remembering of that work."[51] Droysen presented a much stricter version of the idea of history as providential development than Ranke's. In all historical conflicts, Droysen saw one party as the bearer of fate, the elect of Providence, and this party "subsumes" everything that preceded it. In Droysen's lectures on Greek history, for instance, everything points toward the triumph of the Macedonians. The evils and weaknesses of Greek democracy, the internecine struggles and civil wars, and the corruption of political mores are described in great detail. Philip of Macedon thereby acquires the prestige of a hero whose imperial state constitutes the direly needed salvation of Greece. "Philip maligned by Theopompus and Demosthenes," Burckhardt wrote in his lecture notes. "A man of fine culture, but adapted to Macedonian simplicity. He is deceptive in that he is honorable and nobody believes it. His goal is the highest and his political strategy the most grandiose."[52] The view of history as providential design in Droysen's course thus lent itself easily to a justification of conquest and tyranny, and made it possible to view Machiavellian *Realpolitik* as an instrument for promoting the ends of providence. As G. P. Gooch later observed in a lecture on Machiavelli, the Prussian historical school transformed Machiavelli's *raison d'état* into a moral law.[53]

Burckhardt had already been tempted by the idea that history is nothing less than the handwriting of God and the study of history the interpretation and appreciation of the divine text. The lectures of Ranke and Droysen reinforced that idea in him. In the spring of 1840, he wrote that whereas he had once considered the free play of the imagination the highest goal of poetry, he now placed "the development of spiritual or inner conditions even higher" than that of the imagination, so that he now found the greatest satisfaction in history, "which reveals this development to us in two parallel but constantly intersecting, indeed identical waves—i.e. the development of the individual and of the totality." To the degree that he regarded "the visible brilliance of *external* history as colorful clothing on the real course of the world," he added, he now found himself in agreement with "the old saying, not often understood, that 'our good Lord is the greatest of poets.'"[54] "The highest poetry," in other words, "is in history." A year or two later, in the summer of 1842, he professed his commitment to his teachers' philosophy of history: "When I see the present lying quite clearly in the past, I feel moved by a shudder of profound respect. The highest conception of the history of mankind: the development of the spirit to freedom, has become my leading conviction."[55]

By the end of the same year, Burckhardt's idea of universal history had acquired something of the awesome "sublimity" of Ranke's and Droysen's. Responding to the manuscript of a historical drama by Kinkel, which appears to have borne some resemblance to the contemporary dramatic works of Hebbel, he congratulated his friend on having emancipated himself from old poetic ideas of moral justice and written a play motivated by the "real" and the necessary "in the true historical sense." In that genuine historical perspective, he declared, "ethical conflicts are accidental and determine the external decoration and support of the play rather than its essential core. The real topic is made up of *historical* and therefore *unresolvable* conflicts between rival world forces, where it must first be shown which proved victorious for us to know which was right."[56] History, in other words, is a play of forces whose real ethical value is revealed by historical success. It is beyond ordinary good and evil, a spectacle in which the players are marionnettes of the world spirit, and which appears in ethical guise only to those caught up in it. "For the spectator, or the reader, an immeasurable fascination—which you have exploited with great boldness— ensues from the fact that the oppositions appear to the participants and their time in ethical dress, whereas the spectator, with his modern consciousness, knows very well that that is not their true nature and that the conflict can be resolved only by time and historical development. Only in this way can history, which in general knows no Good or Evil, but only Thus or Otherwise, be made into drama."

The reader of the mature Burckhardt of the *Welthistorische Betrachtungen* (*Reflections on History*)—the Burckhardt who had become an acerbic critic of nineteenth-century progressivism and optimism and had withdrawn to his native city-state in order to stand his ground against them—is likely to be taken aback by such utterances, even though it might be argued that they highlight the disjunction between ethical judgment and the "course of world history" as much as they argue for the identity of rightness and historical success. And the later Burckhardt—the Burckhardt who distinguished scrupulously between the moral quality of individual acts or the aesthetic value of individual works of art and the apparent direction of history—did of course repudiate them, explicitly in a public lecture delivered in Basel in his later years, for instance:

> In saying that Philip of Macedon was the man of the hour and his policy that of the future, I am very far from casting the slightest aspersion on Demosthenes for having opposed him. Demosthenes remained an authentic citizen of the dying polis. But monarchy and the idea of the polis are as irreconcilable as fire and water. Each one must either triumph or die. Demosthenes was an Athenian yoked body and soul to his native community and as a citizen he vigorously stood his ground. In antiquity there were citizens such as no longer exist today. Demosthenes was such a one. That is why Niebuhr and Jacobs steeped themselves in Demosthenes and translated him at the time of the Napoleonic Empire. . . . Droysen says: "History knows few figures more pathetic than the great Athenian orator. He misunderstood his time, his people, his opponents, and himself. With the obstinacy of impotence and habit, even after the complete victory of Macedonia and the beginning of a new era that was to reshape the world, he did not give up his old hopes and plans, which had outlived their time, along with him." But here no one cuts a more pathetic figure than the *vir eruditissimus* Johann Gustav Droysen himself. Whether Demosthenes knew or did not know that his judgment of Philip was false is irrelevant. There are desperate moments in the lives of nations when it is a crime against patriotism to speak the [historical] truth. Had Demosthenes appeared before the people and said, *"Andres Athinaioi* [You men of Athens], behold, you have been judged politically and morally. Your Republic is a *leros* [a trumpery]; today it is the monarchical principle that is being born along by the *Zeitgeist.* Submit to it like reasonable men and bow deeply before the great king," he would stand branded in the eyes of posterity like Aeschines, Philocrates and their entire condemned society. Whether it triumphs or dies, it is always the minority that makes world history. For what fills the hearts of men with enthusiasm and pride is to see a noble personality, a great character stand firm like the Titans against the unalterable decree of historical development and go under rather than give up what it believes in.[57]

Explicit repudiation of teleological fatalism is again found in the *Reflections on History*, where the author seems to be responding to Droysen as well as to

Hegel. To Droysen, "the secret of all movement is in its end. . . . In discerning the forward march of the moral world, . . . in observing end after end fulfilled, historical study divines that the movement will close with the fulfillment of the end of ends." To Burckhardt, in contrast, "we are not privy to the purposes of eternal wisdom: they are beyond our ken. This bold assumption of a world plan leads to fallacies because it starts out from false premises."[58] Burckhardt expressed his position succinctly in a letter to Nietzsche in 1874, a few years after the Franco-Prussian war—not the greatest of times for the World Spirit: "I never taught history for the sake of the thing that goes by the highfalutin name of Universal History."[59]

That that was truly the case is demonstrated by the distress Burckhardt's approach initially provoked in one of his most gifted students, Heinrich Wölff-lin, who came to Basel to study with him in the early 1880s and subsequently succeeded him in the chair of art history at the University of Basel. Wölfflin complained of the general lack of a philosophical orientation at Basel, and in Burckhardt's course in particular: "Is there a man here who represents science ['die Wissenschaft'] in its highest sense? I cannot devote my life to study that is conducted in this way. Take J.B.: a course in universal history, prettily narrated, but with absolutely no metaphysical underpinning. . . . This history is totally aimless. It is a show, a theater, in which everything is colorfully mingled. But the Whole only acquires a soul when one observes according to certain principles. Universal history is unintelligible without the idea of providential guidance ['Die Weltgeschichte ist ohne Weltregierung nicht verständlich']. So says W. von Humboldt. The scientific point of view is: the laws of human development."[60]

Probably Burckhardt never wholeheartedly embraced the optimistic faith of the Restoration and of some of his Berlin teachers in the providential course of historical development. There seem always to have been reservations or reversals. Distaste for the self-confident Hegelianism with which his friend Alois Biedermann had tried to answer his religious uncertainties had no doubt alerted him to the smugness as well as the seductions of "pantheism," as the holistic philosophies of the time were referred to by those unsympathetic to them. Perhaps too the memory of the *Basler Wirren* of 1830–1833, which remained very much alive in Basel until late in the nineteenth century, had made him more cautious and skeptical than some of his German friends.

As a Baseler, he was also more attentive than many German historians to French historiography and had almost certainly read some of the criticisms leveled by the liberal French historians of the Restoration—Barante, Thierry, and Michelet—at the so-called *doctrinaires* of the 1820s and at the popular Hegel-inspired lectures on the philosophy of history that Victor Cousin had delivered at the Sorbonne in 1828. (These had been available in a printed version since 1827.) "It is because God or Providence is in nature that nature is governed by necessary laws, which the vulgar sees as fate," Cousin had asserted. "It is because Providence is in history that humanity has its necessary laws and history its necessary course. History is the demonstration of God's providential design for humanity; history's judgments are God's own judgments. . . . If history is God's government made visible, everything in history has its place and everything is as it should be in it, for everything is leading toward the goal marked out by a benign power. Whence the high optimism that I am proud to proclaim and profess." In Cousin's philosophy of history, "war is only a bloody exchange of ideas, involving the thrusting of swords and the firing of cannon balls; a battle is nothing else than the combat of truth and error. . . . Victory and conquest are nothing else than the victory of today's truth over yesterday's truth, which has become tomorrow's error. There is no injustice in the great battles." This extreme optimism, which vindicated the victors of Hastings and of Waterloo, was too much both for the historian of the Norman conquest (Augustin Thierry) and for the future historian of France and of the Revolution (Jules Michelet), however much they might themselves wish to justify the political results of the Revolution by appealing to history and Providence. After reading Cousin's lectures, Michelet's cousin Célestine Lefèbvre wrote the historian that she could not accept a "fatalistic system . . . from which it follows that circumstances are always right, that one should submit to force because, in the end, it is always on the side of the right, that Brutus was wrong to oppose Caesar, that courage and virtue are an error." Even the moderate Barante was moved to complain in the Preface to his immensely popular *Histoire des Ducs de Bourgogne de la Maison de Valois* (1824) that "[s]ome men hold it to be a matter of unquestionable doctrine that power is not only permitted but determined by Providence. . . . They ask only that success be lasting for it to be recognized as a divine mission. They reject the idea that God put a law of justice in our consciousness so that we might correctly judge human acts. Force, according to them, is the Holy Spirit; since it has triumphed, men have only to obey and adore! It is pride to believe one has rights and rebellion to claim them. Disorder and corruption are always the result of resistance by the weak. . . ."[61]

In addition, there were elements in the teaching of Welcker, Ranke, and even of Böckh that were capable of challenging easy confidence in "universal history." Welcker, for instance, questioned the view that different ages constitute organic totalities. "The periods into which art history falls do not usually coincide with those of literary history or political history," Burckhardt wrote in his notes on Welcker's class at Bonn.[62] Likewise, whereas Droysen subordinated every manifestation of life to the political, Böckh recognized a plurality of spheres—private life, religion, the arts—alongside the sphere of politics and the state. Ranke noted that different activities—such as art, religion, and technology—may flourish at different times and that an age remarkable for the achievements of one of these may see the decline of others.[63]

It is noteworthy that at the very time he was echoing his teachers' philosophy of history in the 1842 letter to Kinkel, Burckhardt was also questioning Germany's special character as a fully "organic," traditional nation—the foundation stone of Ranke's historical optimism. The continuity of European culture, in Ranke's view, was based on the mutually enriching and correcting contributions of the Romance and Germanic peoples. To Burckhardt, however, The *entire* European world had been shaken to the core by the Revolution, and something new had emerged that it would not be possible to reconcile with the old and with tradition. "What we might call the historical ground," he wrote to Kinkel a few months earlier,

> has been dug away from under the feet of nearly all the peoples of Europe, including the Prussians. The spirit of radical negation that entered the state, the church, art, and life toward the end of the last century has filled every moderately animated mind with such a mountainous mass of objective awareness . . . that a reestablishment of the old immaturity seems unthinkable. As art has lost its naivete and it has become possible to observe the styles of all the ages laid out objectively alongside each other, so it is with the state. The special interest people once took in the particularity of their own state has had to yield to a selective, self-conscious idealism. No Restoration, however well intended and however much it may have seemed to be the only solution, can disguise the fact that the nineteenth century began by making tabula rasa of all previously existing relations. I neither praise nor blame. I simply note a fact. Princes would do well to consider clearly wherein their present situation is different from their previous one.[64]

There is still some optimism here, but rather less serenity than with Ranke; and there is a degree of apprehension of the future that could easily wing over into historical pessimism.

Burckhardt returned to Basel in 1843, after a trip to Paris, passed his *Habilitation* (the examination establishing the right to teach at the University), obtained an untenured post at the University, and began to offer classes in both history and art history. The latter were offered not only within the University of Basel but to the broad public of ladies and gentlemen of the town, colleagues, and *Ratsherren* that attended the open lecture series the University had instituted after the *Kantonstrennung* as part of its undertaking to serve as a *"bürgerliche Akademie,"* or citizens' academy. He also took on the editorship of Heusler's *Basler Zeitung,* which defined him in the eyes of the local radicals as a conservative and a lackey of the *Herren.* In his own eyes, however, Burckhardt had been emancipated from Basel parochialism and prejudice by four years of absence and was at this point no champion of the local conservatives. The liberalism of the preceding few years in Switzerland, he assured a Berlin friend in 1844, had been "only the first sour bloom that encloses the fruit" and it would be followed by "a new liberalism and public opinion . . . stronger and . . . purer of every kind of extravagance." That liberalism, he promised, "grounded in the people, will gather strength and be able to put together a new Confederation."[65] His own task at the *Basler Zeitung* would be not only to oppose the "raucous Swiss radicals" but "to exterminate . . . the odious sympathy . . . among the ruling clique here for absolutism of every kind (e.g., the Russian)."[66]

To his teaching, likewise, Burckhardt brought the modern ideas and approaches of Berlin, introducing new courses to the Basel curriculum, notably courses on German history, the history of the Middle Ages, and a completely revamped history of Switzerland.[67] For the first two of these he drew on his lecture notes from Ranke's and Jacob Grimm's classes in Berlin and adopted a point of view virtually identical with Ranke's: the idea of Europe as a community of individual nationalities that gradually emerged out of the fusion of Christianity and classical culture, the Germanic and Romanic, Celtic and Alemannic, Norman and Saxon peoples.

Two features of these lectures are especially noteworthy. First, the evolution of European culture was characterized as a movement toward freedom (in the manner of Droysen). It was in this respect that the Christian West was said to be distinguished from the Islamic and "Mongol" East and assured of the leading role in human history.[68] Second, the chief reason for the privileged historical role of the West was that European history is not a mere succession of conquests, with one culture simply replacing another, but a continuity, a constant integrating and gathering up of the vanquished by the victors: "Settlement of the Germans in the territory of the Roman Empire; fusion with the Romanic peoples to form a third, fresh, energetic whole, the bearer of world-history until the present time and for all time."[69] The Middle Ages offer the perfect example of that process of integration and progress—they are "the highest and most comforting object for our contemplation, since they show new life springing demonstrably out of every destruction. In ancient times, one people simply displaced another. Now we have the co-existence of mixed Germanic-Romanic peoples in a common Christendom. The scene is vaster and more varied, the connections international and unlimited, forming systems that serve as the preparation for the present European system."[70] In an original move, which was to become characteristic of him, Burckhardt constructed the "Middle Ages" as a historical concept, designating periods of cultural differentiation and encounter, and compared different such "Middle Ages" in order to point out the advantages of the European version. Thus, in the Near East, he claimed—perhaps remembering Droysen—the Greek component was so enfeebled by the time of Alexander the Great that it was simply "reabsorbed" by the Oriental element from which it had originally differentiated itself. "In the history of America, on the other hand, the European element overwhelmed the indigenous culture, preventing any genuine interaction between the victors and the vanquished and thus rendering the development of a genuine Middle Ages impossible."[71]

The central idea developed by Burckhardt in these lecture outlines—that the goal of history is freedom and that it will be realized through mediation and integration rather than substitution and elimination or repression—is strikingly close, despite many differences, to the central idea of Bachofen's interpretation of ancient history. No doubt it reflects the influence on both Basel scholars of their common teachers in Berlin. But for both, the moderate optimism with which Ranke regarded his own age—even in the 1850s Ranke believed that the dangerous "destructive tendencies" in the age's striving for popular sovereignty could be held in check by the influence of traditional monarchy and that a healthy balance of democracy and tradition was attainable[72]—became impossible to sustain in face of the revival of revolutionary activity in Switzerland in the mid-1840s and the growing threat to the European "system" presented by aggressive, popularly based nation-states. In place of Ranke's serene confidence in Restoration—from which it seems impossible to separate both his political confidence and his confidence in the possibility of objective historical knowledge based on critical evaluation and interpretation of sources[73]—Bachofen and Burckhardt came to be convinced that a seismic break divided their own modern period from the cumulative "culture of old Europe," as Burckhardt would call it.[74] In both the relative historical optimism they had espoused in their youth gave way to anxiety and pessimism. Yet neither ever renounced the Rankean vision as a *value*. Freedom within a plural system, under a benign and freely accepted leadership, remained their political ideal long after they had ceased to believe it was the inevitable end point of a providential history. In the same way, it was a moral imperative, in Burckhardt's eyes, to do everything one could, against all odds, to maintain a historical continuity that, not for the first time, was under dire threat and that for him was to be found not so much externally in a divine plan as internally in man's continued consciousness of and imaginative participation in the culture of the past.

Burckhardt was not happy in Basel. Like the young hero in the first version of Gottfried Keller's *Der grüne Heinrich,* he had felt at home in Germany, where he had found so many kindred spirits. "I acknowledge the motherly embrace of our great common German fatherland, which I once mocked and rejected like nearly all my Swiss compatriots. . . . I want to devote my life to showing the Swiss that they are Germans," he had written to Kinkel at the end of the year 1841.[75] "I have been spoiled by Germany," he confessed on his return to Basel. "I think of nothing else."[76]

After almost four years of freedom as a student in Berlin and Bonn, he felt constrained in a town where he was known to every one and where business success was rated higher than the things of the mind. "Basel is so narrow and so small. There is nothing of the free and uplifting stimulation that made Bonn a great city as far as I was concerned."[77] The problem was neither his family nor the faculty. It was the narrowness and maliciousness of Basel society. "Not a word is ever forgotten or forgiven; scandal mongering such as exists nowhere else spreads poison over everything. . . . It is not good in our day and age when a little corner of the world like this is so completely turned in on itself."[78] He wanted nothing more than to escape from the stifling climate of his native city. "God, how sour 'home' tastes after four years of living as one pleases," he wrote to a friend in Berlin.[79] "Basel," he complained to Kinkel, "will always be unbearable to me. I hope I will not have to stay more than two years."[80] "Out of here! Out of here! That is and will remain my motto," he told his *"liebe Directrix,"* Johanna Kinkel.[81] In addition, a heavy teaching load, which brought in very little money, left him no time for independent research and writing.[82] Above all, he lacked companionship and saw no prospect of anything approaching the lively social existence he had known in Berlin and Bonn. "In Basel," he explained, "I can expect a life of extreme reserve and politeness; there will be no one I can trust fully, no one I can communicate with without constraint. The two or three university teachers in the same position as myself are young gentlemen from the leading families in the city, to whom I would never make the first advances, for you have no idea how grotesque and all-pervasive the Basel reverence for wealth is. Some of the professors are well disposed towards me, but you know better than any one what an abyss separates a professor from a mere lecturer."[83]

From time to time he tried to adopt a more positive attitude. "Not a single person," he wrote, "is in mourning because I have withdrawn from society. No one was sitting waiting for me and if I remain silent until I turn gray, not a soul will bother. And that is right and as it should be. . . . There are quite a number of people here who are my intellectual superiors. . . . If I don't spoil my chances through excessive haste, I may perhaps gradually succeed in establishing good relations with the educated circles here."[84] But the overall feeling remained bleak. As far as his personal life was concerned, his reserves of optimism and humor seem to have run out: "It is winter in my soul."[85] The first *Freischaren* were the last straw. As in the case of Bachofen, private and public disappointment and disgust converged and provoked a crisis that affected Burckhardt's entire outlook.[86]

"Conditions in Switzerland have spoilt everything for me," he wrote to his old Bonn friends in 1845. "The word *freedom* sounds rich and beautiful, but no one should talk about it who has not seen and experienced slavery under the loudmouthed masses called 'the people.'" The erstwhile moderate who had planned to "exterminate the odious sympathy of the ruling clique" in Basel for "absolutism of every sort" now feared tyranny from another source. He knew "too much history," he announced, "to expect anything from the despotism of the masses but a future tyranny," and warned his romantic, radical friends in the anti-Prussian Rhineland that they were "political innocents." They should "thank God that there are Prussian garrisons in Cologne, Coblenz and other places, so that the first crowd of communized boors cannot fall on you in the middle of the night and carry you off bag and baggage."[87] Two months later he was again complaining of "this constant Swiss agitation." A song in the old Basel hymn book that ran 'Save us, Lord, from the people's rage' had been dropped, he observed sardonically, "Heaven knows why. I have the sovereignty of the people up to here . . . ." (The suspension points at the end of this sentence led to a drawing of a head, reaching it just above the neck.)[88] Above all, the future for culture in the coming democratic, egalitarian world was bleak. The attack on private capital would be used to justify the most deadly philistinism.[89] The historical optimism that might have seemed, on the whole, justified under the Restoration regimes and that Burckhardt's Berlin teachers had all espoused in one degree or another, collapsed. Nothing was to be expected, Burckhardt now declared, from the public sphere, the sphere of history. Instead of being the basis of our aspirations and our value judgments, it was now something that, as free and thoughtful individuals, we must take our distance from and judge. Burckhardt's attitude became one of ironical detachment. "I mean to be a good private individual, an affectionate friend, a good spirit. . . I can do nothing more with society as a whole; my attitude towards it is willy-nilly ironical."[90] Convinced that the arguments in favor of law and respect for cantonal rights that he had been presenting in the *Basler Zeitung* had no chance against the fanaticism and demagoguery on *both* sides in the Lucerne affair, he announced his refusal to "throw away the best years of my working life in this political upheaval" and his determination to "expatriate myself next year and then carry on my work in peace."[91]

Six months later the decision had been taken. Having "quietly but completely fallen out" with "this wretched age," he was "escaping from it to the beautiful lazy south, which has dropped out of history."[92] Burckhardt's journey through Italy in the spring, summer, and fall of 1846 marked him for life. From that time on, Italy and the world of art never ceased to hover in his eyes above the ephemeral world of journalism and everyday events, as an intimation of what is enduring in human life and history. "Italy opened my eyes," he told his Berlin friend Hermann Schauenburg later, "and ever since my whole being has been filled with longing for the Golden Age and the harmony of things."[93] The message was driven home in some verses expressing his disaffection for the cold, crooked north, with its *"trivialen Horden,"* and his longing for the warmth, light, and undying beauty of the south.

> O nimm, du heissgeliebter Süden,
> Den Fremdling auf, den Wandermüden!
> Erfülle seine Seele ganz
> Mit Deinem heitern Sonnenglanz!
>
> . . . .

Lass rings um ihn den Wunderreigen
Der alten Götter leuchtend steigen!
Zeig ihm aus alt und neuer Zeit
Gestalten voll Unsterblichkeit![94]

Later in 1846, when an opportunity arose to leave Basel and go to Berlin to assist his former teacher Franz Kugler on a revision of the latter's *Handbook of the History of Art*, Burckhardt seized it eagerly. Berlin was certainly not *Italia aeterna*, but at least it was not Basel or Switzerland. For a while, Burckhardt even thought he might settle in Berlin and pursue a career there as an art historian. The Prussian government had set aside funds for the promotion of art and artists, and Kugler hoped a suitable post might be found for his former student. On his side, Burckhardt conceived the plan of a "Library of Cultural History— small, readable, inexpensive little volumes by me and others who have an interest in popularizing knowledge" on topics such as the Age of Pericles, the Late Roman Empire, the Age of Raphael.[95] (These were in effect to be the themes of Burckhardt's major works: *The Age of Constantine the Great* [1851], *The Civilization of the Renaissance in Italy* [1860], and the *Cultural History of Greece* [1860–1870; published posthumously]). "I would have lived quietly for myself until old age caught up with me," he later wrote to his former protector and employer Andreas Heusler, "having no close relations except with the people of this house [the Kuglers], where for four years I have been treated like a son."[96]

Even at this point in his life, then, Burckhardt was still far from being the "patron saint" of Basel—the role he later came to fill, in the words of his student, the celebrated art historian Heinrich Wölfflin, after he had returned to Basel for good and turned his back on the culture of the modern. Quite to the contrary, Henning Ritter has emphasized, "the plan of life which Burckhardt seems to have had in the forties was modern. It was more akin to the way people like Heinrich Heine or Karl Marx wanted to live than to his later academic existence in Basel."[97] Hence his willingness to write for the newspapers, not only the *Basler Zeitung* but the liberal *Kölnische Zeitung,* to which he contributed several articles and to which Marx was also a contributor. He even applied—unsuccessfully—for the post of editor of the *Kölnische Zeitung's* feuilleton section.[98] His eagerness to give popular lecture courses on the history of art and his plan for a series of popular, readable books on cultural history—a genre closely associated at the time with the feuilleton and popular taste, and generally frowned upon by serious professionals, indicates a general flexibility and pliancy, an almost bohemian disposition quite at odds with the later image of *"der Stadtheilige Basels"* ("the patron saint of Basel").

As there was no sign that a permanent position was going to materialize in Berlin, however, Burckhardt left the Prussian capital on another journey to Italy in October of 1847. At the beginning of 1848 he was contacted in Rome by Andreas Heusler about returning to Basel to serve as keeper of the new city museum on the Augustinergasse, which was nearing completion. To supplement the extremely modest salary (for the sake of economy, the museum's opening hours were restricted to two hours on Sundays—"after Church," as the regulations stipulated sternly—and a couple of hours during the rest of the week, and the post was remunerated accordingly), it was proposed that he also do some hours of teaching at the *Pädagogium*. Heusler appealed to his patriotism. "You are really made for Basel, and you should also consider how much you owe to the city of your fathers. . . . Remember that with all its faults, Basel is still a city where—as Pius II and Erasmus both said—one lives not too badly. The climate of Berlin is not for you."[99] After a good deal of hesitation, and in the absence of any sign that Berlin was about to move, Burckhardt decided to return to Basel. "Ad vos veniam. Vester ero," he wrote Heusler on February 14, 1848.

It is possible that the uncertain political situation in Rome contributed to the decision to go back to Basel. Burckhardt had been writing reports from Rome to the *Basler Zeitung* about the difficulties facing the new liberally inclined Pope Pius IX, who had just succeeded the rigidly conservative Gregory XVI. As early as November 1847, he had noted that demands for a constitution and for secular representation in the papal government had been intensifying; the outcome of the Swiss civil war had been hailed with joy in liberal, anti-Jesuit, and democratic circles in Rome, he added, and it was going to be difficult for the pope to meet the expectations of the "real progressives."[100] Burckhardt constantly hinted at a connection between the events he had tried to escape by leaving Switzerland and the political turmoil in Rome. In December a great spectacle—*La Presa di Lucerna* —had been organized: "a huge popular crowd, many of them in workingmen's clothes, assembled in the Piazza del Popolo carrying banners and torches, with men from the Ticino and German workmen placed in the lead." The tricolor flag with a Helvetic Cross sown on to it was unfurled as the crowd marched toward the house of the Swiss consul shouting *"Viva la Svizzera, il Console, Dufour* [the commander of the victorious Swiss Federal army], *Pio Nono, la presa di Lucerna."* By the new year the cries had become shriller: *"Evviva l'independenza italiana, Abasso i Gesuiti! Abasso la polizia! Evviva la nazione svizzera!"*[101] On February 11, three days before he wrote to Heusler announcing that he would return to Basel, there was another mass gathering at the Quirinal, again with banners, torches, and red, white, and green tricolor flags. Burckhardt reported the great speech in which Pius IX explained what he could and could not do. "When he stepped back inside from the balcony, the usual Evvivas stuck in people's throats and the huge crowd broke up in silence."[102]

Burckhardt had already sent off his letter to Heusler when for the first time laymen were brought into the cabinet and news of the banquets in Paris reached Rome. In the midst of the Eternal City, Burckhardt found himself overtaken by the political restlessness and the spirit of revolution from which he had sought refuge when he left Switzerland. "How transitory is our entire existence," he wrote to Heusler on March 4. "The bombshell of the Revolution in Paris burst upon us in the middle of the riotous celebration of Carnival. It was as though the old pestiferous Lacus Curtius had suddenly opened up again among the grand processions and merry crowds of the Roman forum."[103] The news from Paris was followed by news of the Revolution in Vienna and men's "spirits were at once filled with wild enthusiasm."[104] Shortly afterwards, Burckhardt was writing of armies of volunteers setting out from Rome to fight the Austrians and of pressures on the pope to participate in the national struggle. The connection with the events in his homeland was now inescapable. "Es ist ein Freischarenzug in kolossalen Verhältnissen," he wrote in the *Basler Zeitung*.[105]

It had thus taken the events of the mid-1840s in Switzerland—the radical *Freischaren* against the canton of Lucerne, followed by the civil war or *Sonderbundskrieg*—and the outbreak of the 1848 Revolutions in the rest of Europe to make Burckhardt break decisively with the optimism of his Berlin teachers and strike out on his own idiosyncratic path as a historian. It was only then that he began to "burn what he had adored and adore what he had once burned" by challenging the view, shared by all his Berlin teachers, that the judgment *of* history is the final judgment, and by laying claim to the unqualified legitimacy of a human judgment *on* history. Curiously, he seems to have returned to a view expressed earlier by Herder. "You seem to believe," Herder had written his imaginary correspondent in *Letters Concerning the Advancement of Humanity* (1797), "that a history of humankind is not complete as long as one does not know the *outcome of things,* or, as it is said, one has not experienced the Last Judgment. I am not of this opinion. Whether the human species improves itself or worsens, whether it will turn at some time into angels or demons . . . we know what we have to do. *We* view the history of our species on the basis of the firm principles of our convictions regarding right and wrong, let the final act end as it may."[106] If there was a locus outside history from which a judgment *on* history could be made, it was clearly not modern Berlin, the centrally situated capital of an increasingly ambitious, expanding Prussian state, but eccentric, anachronistic Basel in its marginal *Dreiländereck* between Germany and France on the one hand and the rest of Switzerland on the other.

As a historian, Burckhardt was to occupy a position similar to that of his native city. Just as he probably never fully subscribed to the historical optimism of his teachers, he did not completely burn what he had adored. By abandoning a good deal of the theological underpinnings of the Rankean vision of history as an ordered and unified whole, he was led to confront the dilemmas and aporias of historicism. At the same time, though he became increasingly persuaded of the *catastrophic* character of history and of the recurrence of discontinuity

and breakdown, he could never completely renounce the idea of unity and continuity or write history off as a *Wirrsal* or chaos. In the Introduction to his
Cultural History of Greece, which dates from shortly after the 1874 letter to
Nietzsche repudiating universal history, he announced that the Greeks must be
studied "not in a narrative manner, but historically all the same, and inasmuch,
above all, as their history is part of universal history."[107] Similarly, though he
could not accept historical success as the absolute criterion of good and bad, his
judgments of men and actions took account of their historical contexts. In the
matter of historical knowledge, he accepted both the relativity of all historical
understanding and the goal of objectivity and impartiality as proper to the historian. Throughout his career, as Wolfgang Hardtwig has demonstrated, he
struggled with contradictory demands and convictions, trying to find a foundation for historical meaning and continuity, for ethical judgments on past actions, and for the validity of our knowledge of the past as itself historical, something existing *within* history, rather than in some extra-historical realm.[108] In
many respects Basel was the living emblem of the innerworldly "Archimedean
point outside events"[109] that Burckhardt was looking for, being situated within
the historical world yet at the same time anachronistic and thus capable of serving as a vantage point from which to survey and judge the historical world.

Burckhardt's renunciation of the historical optimism of his teachers—the "illusions of 1830," as he now called them bitterly—was certainly reinforced as the
revolutionary upheavals of 1848 spread from France to Germany and Austria
and to the classical land he had loved because it had "dropped out of history."
Moreover many of his closest friends from his student days in Berlin and Bonn
were caught up in the maelstrom. Hermann Schauenburg, for instance, by then
a doctor in Westphalia, wrote and harangued against political oppression and
economic exploitation, acquiring the reputation of a communist. Quickly disillusioned, he spoke, like many other German activists, of going to America:
"There are not many democrats in Germany, not many men who are capable of
a little nobility of soul."[110] As for Kinkel, he turned out to be one of the most
colorful actors in a Revolution not lacking in theatricality; his imprisonment by
the Prussians at Spandau, his dramatic escape to England with the help of his
wife Johanna and his devoted disciple Carl Schurz, their journey to America
(where Schurz was to have an outstanding career as a highly respected journalist
and politician), and his final appointment to the chair of art history at Zurich,
where he was such a popular figure that his funeral in 1882 turned into a mass
demonstration, are only the best known moments in an adventurous career that
stands in striking contrast to that of his erstwhile fellow *Maikäfer.*[111]

While sympathizing with his radical friends (he was severely critical only of
Kinkel), Burckhardt stood well back from the tumultuous events by which they
were carried away and kept his eye trained on the unchanging values he had

sought and found in Italy. "I knew from the beginning that you would be swept up in the events," he wrote to Hermann Schauenburg. "You wanted to act, and so you had to mix with everything that was breaking down and in disorder. But I am a man of contemplation and I seek that which is harmonious. . . . I follow a different road. . . . As you now want to cross to the other side of the ocean, I shall some day once again set off on my pilgrimage to the other side of the Alps; maybe I shall live in the south as an old beggar. These years of dark passion will pass after all."[112] His skepticism about the 1848 Revolution, no less than his conviction that revolution was a dangerous fundamental feature of the age, was ineradicable. "Do what you will or must, but do not imagine you are free as long as the darkest spirits of nature are playing pranks with you."[113] He retained some sympathy with the aspirations of the Italians—too much for Bachofen, who later declared his "horror" of "this man [Burckhardt], because of his demoniacal Mazzinism"[114]—though even that faded quickly as he watched *das regno d'Italia*" (the term, tinged with contempt, by which he always referred to the modern Italian state) spread its mediocrity over the spirited independence of the old Italy.[115] But his enthusiasm for Germany— *"heilig grosses Vaterland,"* as he had once called it—was a thing of the past. In 1841 he had "wanted to kneel down before the sacred soil of Germany and thank God that my mother-tongue is German," for he had "Germany to thank for everything." His best teachers had been German and he had been "nourished at the breast of German culture and learning." For the people and above all for German youth he had had unbounded admiration. The land itself was "a paradise."[116] By the mid-1840s, with workers' revolts and even an attempt on the life of the king, his enthusiasm had cooled. "Germany has changed," he wrote. ". . . Things there are no longer the way they were."[117] The messianism, nationalism, and militarism he sensed among the German radicals of 1848 filled him with misgivings and led later to his well-known predictions of despotic and militarist regimes to come once nationalism and democracy had triumphed.[118] Curiously enough, the unholy mixture of radical politics with romantic and rhetorical posturing which repelled Burckhardt and in which he discerned the seeds of a later surrender to unbridled nationalism—in his later years Kinkel proved to be not indifferent to the blandishments of Bismarck[119]—also led Marx to turn with violent sarcasm against some of the leading figures of the 1848 Revolution.[120]

Though Basel itself had not been a scene of revolutionary violence, Burckhardt was aware that changes had occurred there too. Andreas Heusler, for instance, lost his seat in the Senate. A new generation less fixated on the history and independence of Basel, less resentful of the federal mediation in 1833, and more willing to accept the city's new destiny in a reformed confederation was coming into positions of leadership. In some respects, on his return to Basel, Burckhardt found that he belonged to the men of yesterday.[121] In a letter to Heusler, in which he attempted to console the old *Ratsherr* for the loss of his seat, he evoked for the first time the figure of the courageous exile, which was to figure so prominently in his later work. "If you would like to read something consoling, have a look at the Life of St. Severin in Pez. There you will see a man who held out amid the collapse of everything."[122]

In the years between the first radical *Freischaren* in Switzerland and the coming to power of a new Napoleon in France, Burckhardt could claim with some justification that he had become a "stranger to the world and its ways."[123] The detachment and irony to which he referred in his letters of these years remained a permanent part of his character and put their stamp on all his work. Detachment and irony did not imply indifference, however. On the contrary, in freeing himself "from the generally accepted bogus-objective recognition of the value of everything, whatever it may be"—that is from the obligation to show how everything contributes to and is justified by the grand plan of History—Burckhardt assumed a different obligation, that of making independent judgments of the men and events of history, and of becoming, as he put it, "thoroughly intolerant."[124] Nor did it imply that he was no longer interested in politics. Not only did he take every opportunity to exercise his voting rights as a citizen of Basel, his abundant correspondence bears eloquent testimony to his lifelong concern with politics insofar, at least, as it affects culture and the life of the spirit. Likewise, despite his growing sense—which he shared with Bachofen—that a sharp break divided the modern world not only from the ancient world but from "the culture of old Europe," he did not completely give up the idea of historical continuity. In *The Age of Constantine the Great* (1851) he still referred to the "higher decrees," which the "great man, often unconsciously, consummates," even while he believes "he himself is ruling his age and determining its character," and to the "high historical necessity" that brought Christianity to the world "as a period to antiquity, as a break with it, and yet in part in order to preserve it and transmit it to new peoples who, as pagans, might well have utterly barbarized and destroyed a purely pagan Roman Empire."[125]

The larger historical scheme those "higher decrees" might be thought to reflect was now, however, something more hoped for than confidently believed in, something human beings themselves, as the subjects of history, had to assume responsibility for. Burckhardt had become convinced that man's task was not to attempt to read what was beyond his ken, but to understand and judge as freely and honestly as possible according to his own lights—just as it had not been Demosthenes's job to recognize the historical "necessity" of the triumph of Philip of Macedon, but rather to oppose the tyrant who threatened the destruction of everything he believed in and valued. If there was a historical necessity, in other words, the proper way for men to serve it was not by trying to anticipate it and sacrifice everything to it, but by acting according to their own best judgment. It is as though Burckhardt was denouncing Ranke's glossing over of incompatibilities in the two guiding principles he proposed to King Maximilian

II of Bavaria: "die Welt verstehen und dann das Gute wollen; . . . in seiner Zeit stehend, . . . dasjenige tun, was . . . notwendig erscheint, und was sein Gewissen diktiert" ("to understand the world and then to will the Good; . . . standing fully in one's own time, . . . to do that which seems to be historical necessity and which one's conscience commands").[126] Only genuinely free individuals were capable of thinking and acting independently, of course. And it was in that sense that "the minority . . . makes world history." It was also in that sense that Burckhardt himself could hope "to help save things, as far as my humble station allows" and thus "take part in the inevitable restoration" that would follow the social revolution of the age.[127]

The return to Basel in 1848 was still not definitive. Within a few years Burckhardt had again taken his leave after a dispute with the Education Department over his teaching obligations. In an important concession to the liberals and progressives, the Department had decided to create a separate "realist" or scientific *Gymnasium* and a separate *Gewerbeschule*, or trades school, in place of the "realist" or scientific tracks that had hitherto been included, alongside the "classical" tracks, in the city's central *Gymnasium* and in the *Pädagogium*. Burckhardt agreed to teach at the new *Gewerbeschule*—whose rector was Wilhelm Schmidlin, a mathematician and economist of humble origins, a convinced liberal and free-trader, and later a director of the Central Railway—but requested that he not be saddled with the correcting of students' written work, since that would be an intolerable burden on top of his already heavy and poorly remunerated teaching obligations. "I am convinced," he explained, "that students learn nothing from written exercises in history that they cannot acquire through good oral repetitions."[128] Burckhardt obviously wanted to ensure that he would have some time for scholarly research and writing, but his faith in oral repetitions as opposed to written exercises also seems characteristic of his entire understanding of *Bildung* or the transmission of culture. The "objective" and often routinized character of the written exercise, which is essential to mass education, held no advantage, for him, over the immediacy of oral interchange between teacher and student. Burckhardt's request was turned down. He was given a week to think the matter over and, when he stood his ground, was dismissed. This outcome was easily interpreted as a triumph for those at Basel who were hostile to what they saw as the "patrician"-dominated University and its values.[129]

To Burckhardt, it was deeply depressing. Though his public lecture courses on "The Age of the Thirty Years' War" (1848–1849) and "The Heyday of the Middle Ages" (1849–1850) had drawn large, loyal audiences of between 250 and 300 men and women of the Basel bourgeoisie,[130] his life in Basel seemed to him lonely, drab, and without much future. In May 1852 he complained to a woman friend of "the heavy, noxious, mist-laden atmosphere in which we are condemned to live our lonely lives."[131] In November, after being dismissed by the Education Department, he wrote that "few people here live as isolated and as cut off from the life of this place as I do."[132] A month later he told his old mentor, the historian and theologian Heinrich Schreiber, that he was "positively going to pieces here" because of the "all-controlling small-town parochialism" (*"kontrollierende Krähwinckelei"*) of the cultural climate at Basel.[133] In March 1853 he again sought refuge in Italy from the pettiness of his native city.

His friends in Basel, notably Heusler, had already begun a campaign to bring him back in an acceptable position, but all they could come up with was a makeshift arrangement that did not carry enough salary for Burckhardt to live on. The authorities were not prepared to appoint him to a chair of history.[134] Burckhardt nonetheless considered accepting these unsatisfactory terms. "Many people besides myself have had to hold out as tutors, without capital and incurring debts, until better times came around."[135] In the end, with his book on the Age of Constantine already published and *The Cicerone: An Introduction to the Enjoyment of the Art Works of Italy* coming off the presses, he decided to apply for a real job—the post of professor of art history at the newly founded Federal Polytechnic in Zurich.[136]

The significance of that move deserves notice. By applying to the federal authorities, Burckhardt might have seemed to be aligning himself with those in the Basel elite who accepted the challenge of working within the framework of the new federal state instead of the old city-republic. He also seemed to be indicating greater confidence in a new institution supported by the federal state and committed to a modern ideal of technical education than in the established but increasingly precarious humanist University of Basel. (The model of the Polytechnic was, of course, the Paris *Ecole Polytechnique,* which had been established by the revolutionaries during the Terror, and it had been a minister in the government of the Helvetic Republic, Philipp Albert Stapfer, who conceived the original idea of the Swiss Polytechnic.) Moreover, by applying for the post rather than waiting to be "called," as was customary with older institutions, he appeared to be submitting willingly to modern bureaucratic procedures for professional appointments. The *Antistes* worried that his son might be seduced by the "radicalism" of Zurich. "Who is not capable of radicalism," he wrote to his son-in-law. "That is the dark side of Jacob's appointment to the Polytechnicum."[137] While he was still waiting to hear from the federal board of education, Burckhardt received an invitation from the recently founded university in the new federal capital of Bern. These developments appear finally to have convinced the Basel authorities that they had failed to recognize the merits of a native son and that his departure would be a serious loss.[138] They hurriedly put together an offer that approached the terms of the Zurich appointment. But it came too late. Burckhardt had accepted the Zurich offer and he intended to keep his word. His father, in the end, saw the importance of the move. "For Jacob, it is the great turning point in his life. He is coming into a completely new atmosphere, and he is gaining a degree of independence such as he never had before. Most important, he will have time to work, to develop, and to become what his natural bent demands that he be."[139]

Burckhardt moved to Zurich in October 1855. In the mid-nineteenth century Zurich was an open, expanding, confident, and progressive city. Economically and demographically, it had already begun to challenge Basel's centuries' old place as the largest and wealthiest German-speaking city in the Swiss Confederation. Its industrial expansion—based not only on textiles but on the modern machine-tool industry—had been financed in part by Basel capital but had quickly become itself a generator of capital. By setting up modern banks with publicly traded shares, the Zurichers had rapidly turned their city into a financial center capable of rivaling and in the end outstripping Basel, which, with all its wealth, was still dominated by private banks owned and operated by a few leading families. Zurich had also set out to become the railway center of the new federal Switzerland, which it was far better positioned by geography to be than the frontier cities of Basel and Geneva. The city's leaders eagerly promoted plans for the construction of a federal rail network. As the destiny of Zurich was visibly far more bound up with that of the new federal Swiss state than that of either Basel or Geneva, it was not surprising that it became the center of Swiss liberalism and progressivism. Characteristically, the walls of Zurich were knocked down in the 1830s, while those of Basel were still in place when Burckhardt left in 1855. Characteristically, too, it was to Zurich that liberal artists and intellectuals (Richard Wagner, Gottfried Semper, Theodor Mommsen, and Francesco De Sanctis are only the best known) flocked after the collapse of the 1848 Revolutions in Germany and Italy. When Burckhardt arrived there from Basel in the fall of 1855 he found himself in a lively, stimulating, cosmopolitan society of artists, musicians, writers, and scholars, many of whom were his colleagues at the Federal Polytechnic.[140] The years in Zurich, as he himself noted in the text he prepared, according to Basel tradition, to be read at his graveside, provided him with "stimulation and experiences of all kinds."[141]

Burckhardt might have been put off by the overwhelmingly liberal politics of Zurich. But he was not. He made many friends, among them De Sanctis and Gottfried Keller. Even though he had little love for the liberal German refugees of 1848, he maintained more than decent collegial relations with the architect Gottfried Semper, whom he admired for his energy and honesty. "Semper began learning Greek when he was already a fully grown man and studied everything in the original," he remarked with admiration years later to Heinrich Wölfflin. "He often grumbled and complained, like a child, but he was a marvel of energy and industriousness. No affectation whatsoever. . . . In certain matters there was much to learn from him."[142] Moreover, for all its liberalism and internationalism, Zurich remained profoundly Swiss and in some respects not so different from Basel. Just as the contrast between Keller and Burckhardt should not be exaggerated, so the antithesis of Basel and Zurich may have more rhetorical value than historical foundation. Mommsen noted, for instance, that "the university has no foundation here, not because the number of auditors is small, but because the public does not respect it." The creation of the radicals, it was only tolerated by the townspeople and was entirely dependent on the government, with the result that most of the faculty were deferential to the point of servility.[143] In Basel, in contrast, the leading townspeople took great pride in their ancient university, and it was the radicals who constantly challenged it and accused the faculty of being "lackeys of the *Herren.*" But the net result—narrowness and parochialism—was the same. In a strange echo of Burckhardt, Mommsen—for whom, as we saw in chapter 8, Burckhardt like his fellow countryman Bachofen had scant sympathy—feared that he might deteriorate in the close atmosphere of "Athens on the Limmat." "That's the way it is in these cozy little backwaters. One declines without really knowing how."[144]

The Zurich Antiquarian Society, of which Burckhardt was an active member, was one of the more conservative circles in the city and in this familiar climate it was easy for a man from Basel to form good relationships. Burckhardt formed such a relationship with one of the pillars of the society, Heinrich Meyer-Ochsner—a wealthy private scholar, distinguished numismatist, and, as we saw in chapters 7–9, close personal friend of Bachofen. He read a number of papers at the Antiquarian Society, and was also invited to participate in the Town Hall Public Lecture Series, a signal honor, since these were an old and prestigious Zurich tradition. On the whole, then, Burckhardt was happy in Zurich—happier than he had been for years in Basel, he told a friend, though he also claimed he had "only as much to do with Zurich as he wanted."[145] Part of the pleasure of Zurich for him was the freedom it gave him. "One of the decisive reasons for going to Zurich," he had told the poet Paul Heyse, a friend from his Berlin days, "is that I shall be able to live virtually incognito there."[146] With Burckhardt seemingly well established and happy in Zurich and a recently appointed scholar in his early thirties occupying the chair of history at Basel, there was no reason to believe that the *Antistes*'s son would return any time in the near future to his native city.

Yet three years later he resigned from the Federal Polytechnic, to the deep regret of the federal education authorities, and moved back to Basel, definitively this time. The thirty-two-year-old occupant of the chair of history at Basel had suffered a massive stroke,[147] and the authorities were now ready, with financial help from the *Freie Akademische Gesellschaft,* to create a new chair of history and to offer the position to Burckhardt. The invitation came from Bachofen, who was then serving on the *Curatel* or Governing Board of the University. "You are not only the favorite of the general public, . . . you are the person most ardently desired by your future colleagues," Bachofen wrote. "So come joyfully; help us to develop our cultural life and to impart to it the vigor it is undoubtedly destined to attain among us, so long as we do not lose our confidence and determination."[148] Burckhardt did not find it easy to resign from the Polytechnic, but he accepted the invitation. It was an earnestly and carefully considered decision and it expressed Burckhardt's mature understanding of himself, his historical situation, and the role he wished to play. The national recognition implied by his appointment to the Federal Polytechnic, the esteem he was held in at Zurich, and the personal freedom he had enjoyed there had allowed him, as his father had foreseen, to develop a degree of independence and self-assurance that he would probably never have attained had he remained in his *"Krähwinckel"* of a fatherland. The man who returned to Basel in 1858 did so deliberately and in full consciousness of his own merit. He saw the call back to his native city not only as a "complete rehabilitation" after the humiliation of 1855, in his own words,[149] but as an opportunity to realize his true vocation: "It will be the object of my earnest endeavor to justify this confidence and to pursue as my life's goal the employment of all my energies in the service of the office that has been so generously offered to me for as long as it is given me to see the light of day."[150]

After 1858 Burckhardt never again left Basel except to make fairly short visits to Germany, France, England, and above all Italy—always for him, as for his compatriot Bachofen, an indispensable source of personal recreation. He still felt keenly the limitations of life in a small town where everyone knows everyone else. "You don't know these small cities," he wrote to Paul Heyse in 1860. "I have just spent fourteen days in London and eleven in Paris, primarily to take a great bath of neutrality, to torture the English language and chatter in French among utter strangers. . . . But the bit of detachment from things that I brought home with me has almost evaporated, and the locals, who know me well and whom I also know, have me in their power again."[151] But he was satisfied now if he could get away from time to time to clear his mind of the misty air of Basel. In 1872 Burckhardt was sounded out by no less an eminence than Ernst Curtius, the distinguished classicist, about succeeding his old teacher Ranke in the most prestigious chair of history in the world at the time, at the University of Berlin, but he made it plain that he was not interested in leaving Basel.[152] "I could not have gone to Berlin at any price," he explained to Friedrich von Preen, a lawyer from Baden, later a state official there, with whom he corresponded for many years. "A malediction would have fallen on me if I had left Basel."[153] A couple of years later he recalled the episode in a letter to Bernhard Kugler, the son of his old art teacher in Berlin, Franz Kugler. "My business is simple," he wrote. "[I]t is to stay at my post, even though I have had several

Burckhardt's lodgings, St. Albanvorstadt 64.

attractive opportunities to leave."[154] After coming home to Basel, Burckhardt also virtually stopped writing for publication. With the exception of the volume on *The History of the Renaissance* (1867) which he contributed as an act of piety to the *History of Architecture* planned and originally launched by Kugler, *The Civilization of the Renaissance in Italy* (1860) was the last work he published in his lifetime. He refused to assume responsibility for revising the enormously successful *Cicerone: An Introduction to the Enjoyment of the Art Works of Italy* (1854) for later editions, entrusting the task to others instead. "Having completed the writings he had begun in his early years," he declared in the obituary he wrote for himself, following Basel tradition, around 1869, "he devoted himself exclusively to his task as a teacher. . . . He believed he should see the obligations of his university chair, as befits the needs of a fairly small university, less in the communication of specialized knowledge than in a general awakening of his students to an historical way of looking at the world."[155]

The public to which he now chose to address himself was clearly not the new public created by modern, democratic state-run school systems and bourgeois pretension (as he saw it), and vividly represented for him by the armies of earnest German tourists—often armed, ironically enough, with his own *Cicerone*—who now regularly descended on the Italian cities, depriving him of his old pleasures,[156] nor was it the international public of professional scholars, the *viri eruditissimi,* as he called them with hardly veiled contempt.

"He made no claim to the celebrity of the specialized scholar," his student and successor in the chair of art history at Basel, Heinrich Wölfflin, said of him in a speech commemorating the hundredth anniversary of his birth. "He looked on the mere professional as a philistine, a laborer, in the classical Greek sense. The dilettante to whom work always remained pure pleasure (*diletto*) was the truly human person." Consequently, "he was repelled by large collaborative scholarly ventures ['*korporative Arbeit*'] and by servitude to a single task, where the author commits himself to making a complete inventory of the material."[157] No one should stay at the same task for more than three years, he would say to Wölfflin, for it is important always to remain open to new things.[158] To underscore his distance from the industrious professionals being turned out in their thousands by the modern German universities, he liked to claim that his own books had been written "in bright sunlight" ("*bei Sonnenlicht*"), in contrast—as with Bachofen—to works produced by the dim light of oil lamps. From the *viri eruditissimi*—the bureaucrats of scholarship—he did everything possible to distance himself. He avoided writing reviews. He discouraged young foreign scholars from coming to Basel to study with him. He made himself notoriously difficult to approach. "He wanted to pass for dead abroad," observed one young German admirer who came to study with him in Basel but never succeeded in getting into private conversation with him.[159] At the same time he punctiliously fulfilled his obligations as a teacher and public figure in his native city and worked hard at refining his lectures and his lecturing style. "The main thing in life," he told Wölfflin, "is the satisfaction that comes from doing your daily work. To be happy, you need a regular task."[160] Relations with close colleagues, he added, "are not to be recommended. Better to seek out colleagues in the natural sciences and merchants. Or family."[161] In the end, "reserved as he was toward the outside world," Wölfflin noted, "he was a thoroughly public figure in his native city." The elderly Burckhardt, affectionately known as Köbi, even became, in Wölfflin's words, "a kind of patron saint of Basel" ["*Stadttheiliger*"].[162]

The audience Burckhardt aimed to reach was made up of his students at the University of Basel, the local citizens who attended his public lectures, and a number of personal friends and associates with whom he corresponded regularly. Just as he discouraged foreign scholars from coming to study with him, he regularly turned down invitations to speak to foreign audiences. "I have never hawked my lectures beyond the gates of Basel, in spite of more than one invitation to do so," he wrote in 1869 to Eduard Schauenburg, his old friend from student days in Germany, who had pressed him to come and give a lecture at Krefeld, where Schauenburg was principal of the *Realgymnasium,* "and I mean to stick to that rule. . . . I should regard myself as robbing Basel if I were to act differently. Every shred of nervous energy I have belongs solely to this piece of ground." Turning his back on the modern lecture circuit and a professional or scholarly "community" that he appears to have found sterile and self-serving—"Congresses are attended by people who like to sniff at each other," he once told Wölfflin[163]—Burckhardt dedicated himself to the civic culture of the place to which, despite everything, he still felt attached by concrete bonds of birth and long family tradition. "I envy the celebrities of Bonn and Heidelberg their appearances within your and other walls," he added, with ironcial self-deprecatoriness, in his letter to Schauenburg, "but I cannot compete. . . . It is a sort of moral duty for us lecturers born in Basel to preach before large mixed audiences; and any one born abroad who joins us is doing a good deed. We guarantee the public a great series of thirty-eight to forty lectures every winter, and a series of fourteen pitched a bit higher for a more discriminating audience. . . . I am convinced that if there were a lecture every evening in the winter, it would be well attended."[164] A dream recounted by the poet Carl Spitteler, who had been Burckhardt's student at the Basel *Pädagogium* toward the end of the historian's career, reflects a common view of the old man's priorities. In the dream Spitteler visited his old teacher and told him he had been awarded an honorary doctorate, whereupon Burckhardt cried out, "So you are an honorary doctor, are you, an honorary doctor! I'd rather you were an honorary citizen!"

Because of this deliberate repudiation of the world of the press, the literary market, and international professional scholarship, several of the most important works in the present Burckhardt canon had to be put together from lecture notes after the historian's death. The *Erinnerungen aus Rubens* appeared in 1897 (Engl. trans. *Recollections of Rubens,* 1950); the *Griechische Kulturgeschichte* in 1898–1902 (partial Engl. trans. *History of Greek Culture,* 1963); and the celebrated *Weltgeschichtliche Betrachtungen,* assembled by the historian's nephew Jacob Oeri from notes for courses taught in the late 1860s and the 1870s, in 1905 (Engl. trans. *Reflections on History,* 1943).[165] Of these the *Weltgeschichtliche Betrachtungen*—rightly viewed as Burckhardt's most concentrated and original statement on politics and the state and as a work comparable in kind to Plato's *Republic,* Machiavelli's *Prince,* and Montesquieu's *Esprit des Loix*—began to have a major impact only in our own time. As Werner Kaegi put it, writing of the early 1940s, "the nineteenth century saw the Basel historian as the author of *The Civilization of the Renaissance in Italy*, the twentieth century discovered him as the thinker of the *Weltgeschichtliche Betrachtungen.*"[166]

Burckhardt's attitude toward publishing and the press also suggests that his correspondence—now at last available in a superb edition by the late Max Burckhardt—deserves to be treated as a major literary achievement, in some respects perhaps his masterpiece. Nowhere is the writing more lively, the language more racy and concrete, the imagination more rich and inventive, the wit sharper, or the observation more keen than in these texts intended for a privileged and intimate audience. It was certainly not by chance that Burckhardt chose Mme de Sévigné as the topic of one of his public lectures.

He was not oblivious to the changes taking place in Basel nor did he in any way imagine that his native city was the backwater some later Burckhardt scholars have pictured it as. Burckhardt knew very well that by withdrawing to Basel he had not withdrawn out of the world of modernity. He was fully aware that economically, socially, and politically the Basel of 1858, to say nothing of the Basel of 1868 or 1878, was a very different place from the Biedermeier city of his youth. In fact, that Biedermeier Basel, whose narrowness he had once found so stifling, came to seem unexpectedly attractive in retrospect. In 1852 he had expressed the hope that with "the new railway Basel . . . will, along with some disadvantages, have the advantage of blowing the controlling clique here sky-high; their insularity embitters the lives of both natives and foreigners."[167] In 1871, the year a triumphant Prussia founded the new German Empire, the tone was less sure: "As to the way the smaller European cities have changed, I fear it is not only to us, because we were young then, that the thirties and forties of this *seculum* appear far more attractive than the present time, but that they really were incomparably more enjoyable. Remember Renan's comment on the July Monarchy: *ces dix-huit années, les meilleures qu'ait passées la France et peut-être l'humanité.*"[168]

The correspondence is full of allusions to the increasing drabness of the mill town that Basel had become. Only the "ceaseless whistling and wailing" of locomotives in the rail yards breaks the "sadness and emptiness" of the place.[169] Politically, too, the city was more and more in the hands of a new class of people. "No Baseler can expect anything good" from a proposed revision of the federal Constitution.[170] When it came, in 1874, Burckhardt knew that it sounded the death knell of the old Basel. "Conditions here are moving in the direction of an ultra-democratic swing," he wrote.[171] The following year the Basel Constitution was revised to bring it into line with the democratic provisions of the revised federal Constitution. The last remaining privileges of the old guilds were abolished, as was the essential distinction between the city and the canton. Burckhardt was deeply apprehensive. "I long ago predicted the present developments here, which promise to be none too pleasant, and I know that for me there will be no peaceful old age and all that."[172] The outlook, a decade later, was grim. "We here in Basel are now unfortunate, threatened people, and we must face up to the reality that every sign of our way of thinking and our culture will be removed from every city office, court, inspectorate, etc."[173] By 1890, Burckhardt was keenly aware that hardly any of those in the city government who were pursuing the kind of legislation in public education and health insurance that he deplored—he considered such social legislation "calculated to promote the despotism of the State over the private life of individuals"—were what he would call Baselers, "even though one or another of them may have been born here." But he was resigned to the elite's loss of political power to this *nuova gente.* "We old Baselers are quite accustomed to swallowing a good deal of this kind of thing."[174] Above all, there was no question of leaving. "Things will turn out as they will at Basel, but I shall be there."[175] One cannot help recalling the figure of St. Severin—"a man who held out amid the collapse of everything"—which he had proposed to Heusler in 1848.[176]

Notoriously, Burckhardt did predict such a collapse of the old Europe and of the essentially individualist, patrician-style culture he associated with it. After the shock of 1870, it seemed clear to him that a new age of nationalistic wars and intensified class struggles was about to begin and that the so-called educated classes would have to "throw overboard, as a spiritual luxury, much that they held dear." In other words, they might have to steel themselves to accept harsh authoritarian regimes that were not to their liking but were alone capable of protecting them from an ever more demanding demos.[177] For there would soon be no choice except between full democracy and an absolute despotism without the protection of laws.[178] "One day the dreadful capitalism from above and the driving desire from below will run into each other like two express trains on the same track."[179] Only an armed and organized military state will be able to ensure a certain *"beata tranquillitas,"* an *"imperium Romanum."* Traditional politics will seem like a game played by amateurs as the militarized state adopts the rational organization of the modern factory.[180] With schools and cultural institutions completely subordinate to the state, it is to be expected that the humanity we are familiar with will gradually die off. The men and women of the generation to come will be a different breed.[181] With such a catastrophic view of history, the former student of Ranke found himself separated from his teacher by an abyss. (See plate 3: Arnold Böcklin, *Der Krieg.*)

Already the symptoms of cultural degeneration were unmistakable, according to Burckhardt. As early as 1843 he had begun predicting doom. "No tyranny is worse than that of the journalist," he wrote to Johanna Kinkel. Because of it, "nothing enduring is being created any more."[182] A few years later, the graduate of the Basel *Pädagogium,* the student of Gerlach and Wackernagel, had reached the conclusion that there had "never been such a vulgar, unattractive period in the history of the world as that since 1830."[183] What concerned him even then was the erosion of individuality and originality by a pervasive "culture" that the new middle class produced, bought, sold, exchanged, and displayed like other products of the market economy. Reporting from Paris for the *Basler Zeitung* in 1844–1845 he had noted with dismay that, with the progress of the newspaper feuilleton, literature in the French capital was becoming a commodity. Thiers, for instance, had made more from the productions of his pen than any historian before him. "Though generously remunerated, Gibbon, Hume, and Robertson, taken all together, did not obtain as much for their immortal works as Thiers alone receives from the joint-stock company formed to market the *History of the Consulate and the Empire.* . . . Even Chateaubriand . . . has sold his Memoirs, which were originally supposed to appear only after his death, to *La Presse* for a cash advance of 80,000 francs and an annual income of 4,000. The *Mémoires d'Outre-Tombe* will thus appear while the author is still alive, in feuilleton form, sandwiched between fashion news and reviews of the latest shows. It is obvious what must become of literature in these conditions of fragmentation, enslavement to party press organs, and day-to-day existence."[184] The fat contracts French novelists were signing with newspaper magnates, he warned, will lead to the collapse of a host of small belletristic publishing houses and deliver writers into the hands "of a few large speculators who will do with them what they will."[185] The very future of French literature was in question. At best, there would be two literatures: a literature of mass consumption and a literature produced by bohemian artists such as Baudelaire, "a great independent poet." If literature was to retain its moral value, "a literature that is not for hire must appear alongside a literature that is made for renting out, and great independent poets must appear alongside those who are for sale."[186]

This experience of culture in the very center of nineteenth-century modernity gives a certain urgency to some further remarks Burckhardt made on the topic a year or two later. Looking around at his contemporaries, he was struck that so many who had been "volcanoes of originality and poetry" had since become "either servile or liberal philistines." Taking up the theme of the deleterious effects of education on the individual personality already articulated by Diderot and Stendhal, he now expressed pessimism concerning modern democratic culture in general: "It is a long story . . . the spread of culture and the decrease of originality and individuality, of will and of capacity; and the world will suffocate and decay one day in the dung of its own philistinism."[187] Serious historical research was especially vulnerable. The social and cultural forces that had created the modern press and modern literature had also created a public that required constant titillation and that expected to be as entertained and distracted by works of history as by novels. As a result, "genuine history, and especially historical research" will never win the favor of a "lazy, overstimulated populace."[188] Toward the end of his life, Burckhardt reiterated the views he had formed in the 1840s. In the France of the Third Republic, he declared in 1890, "you must be mediocre, or woe betide you!"[189]

It was of the very essence of the new democratic, middle-class culture, in Burckhardt's view, that it blunted originality, discouraged independence, and forced all opinion to conform to the dominant opinion of the moment.[190] Were not strict rationalization of the means of production and technical progress, geared toward uninterrupted, mindless innovation, the dominant features of the new economy? The constant revisions of the Basel Constitution, which so outraged the old Baselers, not least among them Burckhardt and Bachofen, were the political manifestation of a modernizing culture of whose material basis no one in a small trading and manufacturing community like Basel—certainly not any one as close to it, through his family and friends, as Burckhardt—could be ignorant. The historian knew very well what he was saying when he described the spirit of the modern age as *der Geist der ewigen Revision* ("the spirit of eternal revision").[191] Likewise modern methods of industrial production and the huge capital investments they required left little room for the kind of inspired improvisation that had marked the Basel businessman of an earlier era. The alliance of the state and industry and the assumption by the state of many social responsibilities previously entrusted to individuals or to independent institutions (for health and education, for instance) were equally deleterious to individualism and initiative.[192] Absolute uniformity and constant, distracting novelty were the essential features of the modern way of life, as Burckhardt understood it, and in that way of life he saw a mortal threat both to the traditional culture of Europe and to the continuity of a history that had been saved during previous crises (the collapse of the Greek polis, for instance, or the end of the Roman Empire) only by the almost providential intervention of unusually capable individuals—an Alexander or a Constantine. To an important degree, Burckhardt's entire historical enterprise was an act of resistance to that modern way of life and to what, according to him, it entailed: the disappearance of a genuine connection with history and, as a result, ignorance of the values handed down by history that allow us to measure and judge the present.[193]

Time and again Burckhardt excoriated the banality and vulgarity of the new "barbarism." For a long time Italy was the antidote to it—not so much the "pinched, malicious," middle-class Milanese as the Romans, "who have armed themselves against work for centuries, as against their worst enemy," have "not the smallest trace of industry," and "no such thing as a 'Daily Advertiser.'"[194] But Burckhardt lived to endure the spread of the hated middle-class culture, like the spread of republican and socialist ideas, into the land where history was supposed to be dead. For a time he could close his eyes and ears to everything that was not *"Italia aeterna"*[195] but in the end the modern culture of politics, business, and the manipulation of public opinion forced itself upon him. "The sound of the boys shouting *la gazittah! la stellah!* with their shrill voices goes right through one."[196] In 1878, he found "the air thick with revolutionary miasmas" and nationalist passions. "Italy wanting to be a great power and a military state and a centralized state," he lamented in dismay, "is . . . a colossal untruth."[197] The Italy of the end of the nineteenth century bore no relation to anything imagined by the poet-heroes who had dreamed of a new united Italy. "We in Basel live in constant communication with that bit of the south, but I could not say that I hope for anything very good where its future is concerned," he wrote to his friend and fellow Italophile, the writer Paul Heyse, in Munich. "Your heroes, who since the days of Parini and Alfieri have been crowned with laurels, all hoped for an Italy very different from the prostrate country now being exploited in every possible way, and the real Garibaldians [Burckhardt may well have been thinking of his beloved old teacher of Italian, Luigi Picchioni—L.G.] also fought for a different one. . . . Now we know who really wanted to get to the top, and who really got there."[198] The last word, in 1891, is of sadness and defeat. The culture of the modern, which he spent his life resisting, had overwhelmed even Italy. "In Italy, where forty or fifty years ago I had the illusion of a centuries-old way of life, the 'present day' is forcing itself upon one in a horrifying way; careerists on top, and beneath them a nation that is gradually becoming appallingly disillusioned."[199]

In Germany, middle class culture was certainly no better. Revealing that he was by no means immune to the antisemitism endemic in all strata of society, at Basel as elsewhere in Europe, Burckhardt often associated the new middle-class culture with Jews, who served for so many critics of liberalism and democracy at the time as emblems of modernity—the quintessential *nuova gente* in their alleged rootlessness, intellectualism, commercialism, and parasitism, their inability to produce an authentic, original culture. In Frankfurt, he complained, there is "furious building of palaces by Jews and other company promoters, and what is more in *German* Renaissance style, which our friend Lübke has made the fashion. Clumsy ornamentation of every description, naturally, has been smuggled in under that rubric; people who are incapable of producing something beautiful are unable to do so whatever the style, and all the 'motives' and 'themes' in the world won't help a man without imagination. Most of what is built in Italian Renaissance style is hideous, despite its richness. . . . And you should see the classical buildings! 'For the wealthy Jew/Only caryatids will do' ['Denn die reichen Jüden/Bau'n mit Caryatiden']."[200]

Jews were associated with "journalism and the unspeakable, awful business of the press,"[201] with professionalism in scholarship, and above all with the very heart of the alienated culture of uniformity, fashion, and the mass media—the metropolis or *Grossstadt*. The *Grossstadt*, for Burckhardt, was the monstrous product of all the forces that he believed were undermining what he called "the culture of old Europe." When he was young, he wrote at the age of seventy-three—prophetically, as it may appear to us at the beginning of the twenty-first century—"it was taken for granted that the aim of art was ideal beauty, and harmony was still one of the conditions of creation. But since then life has been influenced to an incalculable degree by life in large cities, and the spirit that formerly existed in small centers of influence has departed. In large cities, however, artists, musicians, and poets become nervous. A wild, pressing competition infects everything, and newspaper feuilletons play their part in this. The actual amount and degree of talent at the present time is very great, but it seems to me that with the exception of an occasional, often fanatical, little circle of supporters nobody really enjoys individual works any more."[202]

Basel, of course, was one of those "small centers of influence" whose decline Burckhardt lamented. Even so, the relative calm of these small centers, their distance from the frenetic activity of the great metropolises, was at least not a disadvantage. Burckhardt could have been speaking for Bachofen or Franz Overbeck as well as for himself when he declared that "[w]hoever wants to keep his mind fresh and alert can do so in a small city by fulfilling his obligations and reading good books, and whoever is destined to turn stale will do so also in Berlin and Paris."[203] A small city-state also had the advantage of providing conditions for freedom of thought in an age of increasing state pressure. "It can at least be said in favor of the five wooden planks of my podium [in Basel] that they do not require me to preach either *grossdeutsch* or *kleindeutsch*, either etc. or etc. but let me express my own opinion in any way I like."[204] Nevertheless, he was aware that Basel was by no means immune to the influences on culture that he had observed in Paris and Berlin. There, no less than in Berlin or Paris or Manchester or Philadelphia, "the industrialization of the world has proceeded apace" and "machine production has far overtaken all older techniques of production," with the consequence that "large amounts of capital have to be brought together to set up factories and large masses of men brought together to work them."[205] In such circumstances, in Burckhardt's view, the spirit of individual responsibility, enterprise, and improvisation that had characterized the old merchant class of Europe, and that of Basel in particular, was bound to be displaced by different features: those that Max Weber was to associate with "bureaucracy" or that are now often associated with "corporate culture," such as a high degree of rational organization. Burckhardt could observe the effects of these changes among the many Basel businessmen he knew personally through his family connections. The business class at Basel once was an honorable exception to the rule, he wrote as early as 1870, in that it tried to maintain a generally high level of education and culture. Traditionally, the Basel merchant was a well-developed individual with a genuine love of literature and learning as well as an acute practical sense of economic realities and the energy and initiative to exploit them. (The fine portrait of the Florentine merchant in *The*

Civilization of the Renaissance may well be an idealized vision of the merchant of Basel—and a discreet compliment to him.)[206] Modern business conditions, however, require such undivided attention, that the Basel merchant no longer has the time—and increasingly no longer has the habit or the inclination—to read.[207]

From Burckhardt's point of view the outlook for the old European culture he was committed to—a culture whose essential characteristic was variety and lively competition[208]—was grim. "The final act," he wrote von Preen at the time of the Franco-Prussian war, "could be once more . . . an *imperium Romanum*. . . . Such an empire, as we know, no longer has a dynasty, but a central administration and—with the help of soldiers—a *beata tranquillitas*. Unbeknown to themselves, the men and women of today in their vast social strata have gradually renounced nationality and really hate all forms of diversity. If it comes to that, they will all sacrifice their particular literatures and cultures in exchange for 'through sleeper trains.'"[209]

There was no hope of turning back the historical tide. "No one has any remedy to hand. . . . All power now lies with the forces of dissolution and uniformization. . . . There are no remedies."[210] In such a situation, the model of Severin calmly continuing to carry out his ministry to the Germans from the monasteries he had set up along the valleys of the Inn and the Danube, as the empire collapsed around him, must have acquired a new pertinence for the historian.[211] Burckhardt's monastery was perhaps not so much the city as the University of Basel. It was from there that he hoped to do what Severin had done before him: preserve what could be salvaged of the old culture, to serve as a link between a world that was dying and one not yet born. "For my part," he wrote, "I have long since simplified my outlook by relating every question to the University of Basel and asking whether this or that is good or not good for it."[212] Though he could fairly claim that he had finally made his peace with his native city—"In my youth," he told von Preen, "my imagination was always turned toward distant, even far distant places, and only in recent years do I feel properly at home here"[213]—he had to confess that between himself and the hard-working commercial and industrial city that he had once considered a place of exile and had now withdrawn to as a place of refuge, there was still a considerable and perhaps unbridgeable distance. "At bottom we are all everywhere in a foreign land," he wrote, "and our true homeland is wonderfully composed of things earthly and real and things spiritual and distant."[214] The citizen of Basel was also, as he claimed the great philosophers of antiquity and the great artists of the Renaissance had been, a citizen of the world and, in particular, of the transcendent and enduring world of art and literature. As Athenian democracy careered inevitably downhill, he told the students in his course on the cultural history of Greece, driving all decent and talented citizens to withdraw from participation in politics and public life, "the most important people, for the world and its culture, were no longer statesmen . . . but men of the spirit, in the broadest sense of that word."[215]

From the beginning, Burckhardt had been drawn to music, art, and poetry, and had sought in them a surrogate for the religious faith he was unable to sustain. The mixture of joy and reverence in the contemplation of the eternal, which the religious person finds in the divine or the philosopher in the truth, he appears to have experienced in beauty. "History, to me, is always poetry for the most part, a series of the most beautiful painterly compositions," he wrote Willibald Beyschlag, a fellow student at Berlin and Bonn, in the summer of 1842. A philosophical understanding of the meaning of history—"from an a priori standpoint"—might be the affair of the *"Weltgeist,"* it was not that of the human being living in history. "Everything about my study of history, like my passion for travel, my mania for landscapes and my interest in art, springs from an enormous desire for attentive contemplation."[216] A few days later, in a letter to Karl Fresenius, another fellow student at Bonn, this Goethean position was developed in greater detail. Burckhardt took his distance from speculative philosophy, asserting in particular that it was his intention not to start out from Hegel's philosophy of history but rather to see to what extent it might correspond to his own experience and understanding of history's concrete manifestations. At the same time, he affirmed that what he looked for in the world of the particular and the historical was, in the end, glimmerings of the eternal.

> Dearest friend, you have become a philosopher; but you will have to grant me the following: Some one like myself, who is incapable of speculation and is not for a single moment in the year inclined to abstract thought, does best when he tries to understand the higher questions of his life and his studies in the way that best corresponds to his nature. My surrogate is attentive contemplation, which in my case means turning on the objects of my study a gaze that becomes with each passing day more and more penetrating and more and more oriented toward the essential. My nature impels me to cleave to matter, to visible nature and to history. But through ceaselessly drawing parallels among particular *facta,* I have succeeded in abstracting much that is general. Above this still multiform generality there hovers, I know, a higher generality, and it may be that I shall never attain that level. . . . Permit me to get to know history, to experience it from this lowly vantage point instead of grasping it from its first principles. . . . The infinite treasures that have been showered on me through this lowly form of immediate sensation have already filled my cup to overflowing and will enable me to accomplish a few things that, however unphilosophical in form, might even be of some value to philosophers. . . . I respect speculation as one of the highest expressions of the spirit in every age; only I seek out its historical correlates rather than the spirit itself. . . . History is and remains for me poetry on the grandest scale; naturally, I do not mean this in a romantic-fantastic way, which would serve no useful purpose; I mean that I look on it as an extraordinary process of chrysalis-like transformations [*Verpuppungen*] and ever new revelations of the spirit. I shall remain standing at this outer edge of our world with my arms stretched out toward the ultimate ground of all things. That is

why history for me is pure poetry, and is to be grasped only through attentive contemplation. You philosophers, however, go further. Your system penetrates to the depths of the mysteries of the universe, and history is a . . . science for you because you see or think you see the *primum agens* where I find mystery and poetry.[217]

History, like art and poetry, is thus made up of discrete revelations of spirit, of the eternal, and as such—as the antechamber to the divine, as "the last words before the last," to borrow an expression of Siegfried Kracauer's—can properly be an object of reverential looking. To experience this reverence there is no need to penetrate further, to whatever design or order may underlie the successive *Verpuppungen*. Indeed, to do that one would have to tear aside the last veil of phenomena and submit to the blinding light of the divine itself. For Burckhardt, one suspects, that would provide an insight uncommunicable in any human form—whence his skepticism about the neat patterns the speculative philosophers claim to have found. It might also, to this barely lapsed Christian, have represented a transgressive act, an act of hubris, comparable to Noah's son looking on the nakedness of his father. For Burckhardt, therefore, the phenomenal world itself remained the object of the historian's most intense contemplation. In later years, moreover, the "spirit" of these early letters to Beyschlag and Fresenius was relieved of much of its metaphysical and transcendental baggage, even though it always remained completely in the purview of philosophical idealism. Increasingly, the "spirit" Burckhardt evoked was not the Hegelian "Geist" but "the human spirit," the creative and imaginative power of man "as he is, was, and always will be."

The highest forms of the *Verpuppungen* of the spirit—those that were already themselves the product of an attempt to reach that "essential" aspect of things, to which Burckhardt claimed that his own attentive looking was increasingly directed—were art and literature. In his teaching and writing, he made clear in the *Weltgeschichtliche Betrachtungen,* his object was not only to evoke those *Verpuppungen* and re-present them for the reader but to investigate the relation of art and literature to politics and religion, that is to say, to explore the relation among three modes of activity, three different kinds of revelation of the spirit (as he saw them): that of practice and worldliness, of states and institutions and power struggles (politics); that of men's various attempts to rise above the world to the pure sphere of the divine and the eternal (religion); and that which appears to be located between the other two, between pure worldliness and pure otherworldliness (culture). None, he would claim, exists in a pure form: the state may sometimes be treated as subordinate to religion, this world to the other; religion may become embroiled in the world through its efforts to maintain itself in history by dogmas and institutions; art always fluctuates between the pure ideal and the real, between the world and religion, and it may on occasion be made completely subordinate to either, or it may undermine both.

In the shadow cast by the Franco-Prussian War, Burckhardt expressed his foreboding that the future would be quite unlike the world with which he and his friends were familiar: "Es wird Anders als es gewesen ist." Much of modern literature would simply die off. Novels and plays that had won wide applause would become unreadable and unperformable; authors who had pleased publishers and won the hearts of the public with their eager modernity, their talent for adapting to the tone of the decade, the year, even the month, would be forgotten. "Only what contains a fair portion of eternity will survive. And new works that are to have a chance of enduring will result only from the most arduous efforts of genuine poetic imagination." It is a time, therefore, to "'Put one's house in order. . . .'"

There is no doubt that Burckhardt had had such ideas in mind for many years. The war simply gave them greater urgency. Nor can there be any doubt that he had arranged his life and designed his own work with a view to the coming crisis. "As a history teacher," he noted, the war and the crisis it signals have "made one phenomenon unmistakably clear: the sudden devaluation of all mere 'events' of the past. From now on, my courses will emphasize only cultural history and will retain only what is indispensable of the external scaffolding."[218] Cultural history, in other words, was that "essential" history toward which, as early as 1842, he had told Karl Fresenius he was increasingly turning his attention.

11

"From Now On My Courses Will Emphasize Only Cultural History"

The Age of Constantine the Great and *The Civilization of the Renaissance in Italy*

Though Burckhardt's name is inseparably connected with cultural history, he did not invent it. Following Pierre Bayle, nearly all the writers of the Age of Enlightenment denounced traditional historical narratives. Not only were they said to contain much that was fabulous or legendary, not only were they heavily influenced by rhetorical and narrative models, their effect was to deaden the activity of the critical intellect—the highest value known to the *philosophes*—rather than to stimulate it. What was essential to Enlightenment history was not narrative but the historian's reflection on the materials of history, whether in the form of critical evaluation of the reliability of testimony or in the form of the analysis by which he sought to discern the order underlying the apparent chaos of events, the regularities hidden in the mere positivity of facts: the laws (or "spirit" in Montesquieu's terms) of the laws, of economics, of demography, of politics. The function of many traditional narratives, in contrast, had been to legitimize established authority by tracing an unbroken chain of transmission from remote origins to the present in a text that rigorously excluded any sign of self-reflection.

In addition, as its focus was on the notable deeds of the great princes or churchmen whom the historian served and was expected to celebrate, traditional historical narrative had nothing to say about the uneventful, industrious lives of the artisans, merchants, writers, artists, and philosophers to whom was due—in the eyes of the men of the Enlightenment, themselves members of that category of useful, industrious persons—whatever order and refinement there is in human affairs, the process of "civilization" that, to them, was the enduring part of human history. In his *Essai sur les moeurs,* published in the mid-eighteenth century, Voltaire contrasted the busy, violent, and pointless history of "eagles and vultures tearing each other apart" with the peaceful, purposeful, but invisible history of "ants that silently dig out dwelling places for themselves" beneath the surface of things, a contrast of political history—we might say—with the history of civil society.[1] Similar judgments of political historiography were pronounced throughout the eighteenth century by d'Alembert, Rousseau, Turgot, Adam Ferguson, Adam Smith, Malthus, and many others, and again in the nineteenth by Macaulay, Carlyle, and Emerson. Voltaire intended his *Siècle de Louis XIV*, he said, to be the history of an age, not of an individual, however powerful. His *Essai sur les moeurs* (original titles: *Abrégé d'histoire universelle*, 1753 and *Essai d'histoire universelle*, 1754), opened provocatively on the early history of China instead of the traditional Biblical stories, and maintained throughout its almost two hundred chapters an admirable openness to the variety of human history. It thus constituted a brilliant challenge to the established narratives of universal history, of which the most celebrated in Voltaire's time was still that of Bishop Bossuet.[2] Despite its length, the *Essai* remained an *essay*, held together primarily by the voice of the reflecting and commenting historian and by the repeated pattern of struggle, discerned throughout most of history, between reason and "superstition," or "fanaticism." Cultural history, "histoire des moeurs," *Kulturgeschichte*, was in short, in Thomas Nipperdey's phrase, an *"Oppositionswissenschaft."*[3]

The cosmopolitanism and openness of the English and French Enlightenment, which Voltaire himself represents very well, reflected a firmly held neoclassical belief in the uniformity underlying the most varied peoples and histories. Humanity was everywhere the same. The variations were relatively superficial—different masks and costumes—though some conditions were superior to others in terms of moral, aesthetic, and material refinement. In contrast, the cosmopolitanism of the German eighteenth century, as we find it in Herder, for example, reflected a pluralist view of times, nations, and cultures. Each age, each people, and each culture marked the realization of a different aspect of humanity, a different human potential, which could only be realized in that age, by that people, through that culture. Humanity was not a universal representing itself in a variety of particular, accidental guises, and history was not simply the indifferent, featureless space or theater in which that universal was represented or in which a gradual improvement in "civilization" had been achieved. On the contrary, humanity could be actualized only in and through history; and history was real time, not an abstract, featureless space. As a result, each historical manifestation of humanity had to be thought of as at once related to all the others and yet unique and uniquely valuable (*"unmittelbar zu Gott"* in Ranke's celebrated expression).[4] In the same way, the individual was perceived in this tradition not as the notional end product of a process of abstraction and analysis—as in the main Anglo-French Enlightenment tradition—but as a personality, a part of a larger cultural and historical whole, neither fully separate from that whole nor completely identifiable with it.

An idea of culture was thus developed in late-eighteenth-century Germany that diverged both from the English and French Enlightenment idea of civilization—which had also been embraced by a fair number of German Enlightenment scholars—and from the encyclopedic accounts of different states and peoples ("*Staatskunde*") developed at certain German universities, notably Jena and Halle, by Martin Schmeitzel, Gottfried Achenwall, and Johann Peter Süssmilch. Culture was understood neither as a certain high level of material and intellectual cultivation and refinement, which may be reached from time to time in any country in favorable circumstances (as in Voltaire or Gibbon) or toward which a continuous movement could be observed throughout history (as in Condorcet, Guizot, or Macaulay), nor yet as the sum total of discrete elements—population, political constitution, agriculture, industry, trade, and so on—making up civil society (as with the practitioners of *Staatskunde* or *Statistik*). Culture rather was understood to be an autonomous system, a self-contained and enduring organism, like a Goethean plant, all of whose parts reflect and contribute to the life of the whole.[5]

Romantic, postrevolutionary historiography inherited the outlook of the Age of Herder and Goethe. It was above all a historiography of the various cultures through which humanity had expressed itself. The historian's chief task, Ranke observed, is to discover and convey "how human beings thought and lived in a particular period of time."[6] However, the Revolution and its Napoleonic aftermath—which included the dissolution, in 1806, of the Holy Roman Empire of the German Nation, the somewhat ghostly political entity that had embraced the many small German states—had focused attention in Germany on the state as the political expression of the culture of a human group and its means of defense against other cultures. As the initial successes of Napoleonic imperialism were taken to have made clear, each *Kulturvolk* or nationality needed to be able to defend itself, as a culture, against the aggressive designs of others if it was to fulfil its mission of contributing to human history and development as a whole. To that new awareness is due Ranke's explicit emphasis on the state and on foreign affairs as the core of his practice of history. "We can counter the dominance that another nation threatens to exercise over us only through the development of our own nationality," Ranke wrote at the end of an essay on "The Great Powers," published in 1833. "I do not mean an imagined, chimerical nationality but the fundamental, truly actual nationality that is expressed in the state."[7] With Ranke, as Burckhardt certainly must have realized from his course and seminar work with his teacher, the emphasis on the state as the moral and political fulfillment of the nation did not eliminate the pluralist, cosmopolitan ideals he had inherited from the Age of Goethe. Immediately after the passage from "The Great Powers" just quoted, Ranke raised the question whether the competition among peoples and cultures and among the states that give them moral and political definition might not impede the development of humanity toward ever greater solidarity. "The situation," he responded, referring to the Goethean ideal of *Weltliteratur,* "if I am not mistaken, is like that of literature. There was no talk of world literature when French literature dominated the whole of Europe. The idea of world literature has been conceived, articulated, and disseminated only since the majority of the great peoples of Europe have developed their own literature independently, and often enough in opposition to other literatures."

The special situation of Germany in the first half of the nineteenth century—the "nation" or linguistic and cultural community, as defined primarily by writers and scholars, was still divided among a wide variety of states only loosely linked in a kind of alliance or confederation[8]—may help to explain the popularity enjoyed by cultural history in the German context,[9] as well as the reason why cultural and political history represented for German historians two genuinely different options, the gap between which grew deeper as the power of Prussia and its claim to leadership gathered strength in the course of the century. Whether his emphasis fell on culture or on politics might well reflect a historian's judgment about the character of the nation—whether it was to be defined primarily as a linguistic and cultural community or as a polity based ultimately on an implicit contract among its members—as well as about the proper political form to be taken by the nation. Should Germany, for instance, be a *Staatenbund,* a league or confederation of independent states, or a *Bundes-taat,* a more centrally organized federal state?

A passage from Wilhelm von Humboldt, one of the classical neohumanists most admired by Burckhardt's Berlin mentor, Franz Kugler, conveys an idea of what was involved. While acknowledging that "only a nation which is externally strong can preserve the spirit from which all domestic blessings flow,"[10] Humboldt warned that the true aim of any German confederation must not be forgotten and that the state should never be viewed or pursued as an end in itself, only as an auxiliary to culture. The purpose of the German confederation of states, he declared, must be "peace and security." "The insertion into the European state system of a new collective German state . . . would work directly against this purpose. Nobody could then prevent Germany as Germany from becoming another aggressive state—something that no true German can desire; for we know what significant advantages the German nation, with no external political ambitions, has enjoyed until now in the areas of culture and the pursuit of knowledge, and it is by no means clear what the effect of acquiring such ambitions would be."[11]

Humboldt's view is the view of those Germans of the Age of Goethe to whom culture and the free development of the individual personality were infinitely more important than the creation of a politically powerful nation-state. In fact, they feared the latter and sought to restrict it to the bare minimum necessary for guaranteeing "peace and security." Their highest value was not economic activity or political power but *Bildung,* the fullest possible development of the individual and the continued life of culture. Politics, for them, ought never to be more than the handmaid of culture. Goethe's view of culture as something that elevates above politics and *is* above politics is characteristic of the neohumanist generation.[12]

In England and in France a different situation obtained. As long as the German nation was defined primarily as a *Kulturvolk* rather than in political terms, and as long as it was not embodied in a single state, it was easy to maintain a clear distinction between cultural history and political history. In France, in contrast, the history of the nation and its culture was presented as inseparable from that of the state: by consolidating a variety of territories, the kings of France had united the nation under a single state administration and thereby created the conditions in which the nation could wrest political control for itself and reconstitute the social contract on which the state was based. The history of the nation was thus virtually indistinguishable from the history of the state.[13] Moreover, in a society that had undergone major revolutions and where the history of the people was understood as that of its progressive rise to power, history was almost inconceivable in any form other than narrative. The people simply replaced the prince as the hero of the tale. Cultural history remained recognizably history. Its essentially diachronic, narrative character was not in danger. This is abundantly clear in the work of Jules Michelet, who is both the political and the cultural historian of the French nation. Michelet's close friend and colleague, Edgar Quinet, had translated Herder into French; he himself strongly supported all the European national movements (Ireland, Poland, Italy); and he was acutely sensitive to manners, language, laws, the arts, architecture, and institutions—even eating habits—as expressions of particular cultures. (Thus Michelet's aggressive, rapacious English are great eaters of red meat, whereas the diet of the "sociable" French includes more vegetable and milk products; the witty, satirical *fabliaux* and a celebrated sparkling wine are both produced by the flinty soil of Champagne; the rich soil of Burgundy, in contrast, produces the famous full-bodied reds and the eloquence of Bossuet.) If Michelet is not usually thought of as a cultural historian, it is because in the French context the nation as a culture (*"une âme et une personne,"* in Michelet's own words)[14] and the nation as a polity of free citizens based on consent and law, the history of culture and the history of the state, were inseparable. One could not be told without the other.

In Germany, in contrast, where the bourgeoisie remained excluded from power and the nation was still not embodied in a single state, conditions were favorable to a form of cultural history without events or heroes. In the first part of the nineteenth century, such a history did develop into "a small, but recognized special field of history," as Felix Gilbert observed in the short study of Ranke and Burckhardt that he wrote shortly before his death.[15] This cultural history sometimes retained the encyclopedic sweep of the old universal histories—as in Wilhelm Wachsmuth's *Europäische Sittengeschichte* (1831–1839) and

Allgemeine Kulturgeschichte (1850), or in Gustav Klemm's *Allgemeine Cultur-geschichte der Menschheit* (1843)—or of the *Staatskunde* of the eighteenth century. It could come close to being a compilation of facts about population, agriculture, industry, trade, religion, the arts, folklore, and so on, within the historical framework of a general account of the evolution of civilization. The work of Karl Dietrich Hüllmann, professor of history at Bonn in the 1820s and 1830s, whom Felix Gilbert singled out as a typical practitioner of the genre in the third and fourth decades of the nineteenth century, seems to have been of this kind. (Burckhardt may even have heard him lecture, as Hüllmann gave a course on the cultural history of the Middle Ages when Burckhardt was a student at Bonn.) Hüllmann defined the objectives of cultural history as follows: "So far, history has always been treated in a very one-sided way; it has been exclusively concerned with those who have been influential and have written about their experiences. Scant attention has been paid to the lower classes [*'Niederes Volk'*] or to the age in general. This is the aim of cultural history, which, without regard to social status or to language, encompasses the whole of humanity. It illustrates the outstanding stages of development through which the prominent nations of the whole world have passed till they reached the situation in which they are now."[16]

The task of cultural history, in other words, is twofold: to record the daily life of society and its various constituent groups, and to distinguish among the various historical epochs and describe the stages of development through which the "prominent" nations of the world have passed. Cultural history thus deals both with material and popular culture—in his book on city culture in the Middle Ages,[17] Hüllmann, who had already written on the history of trade and finance in antiquity, Babylonian times, and the Middle Ages, dealt with topics as varied as guild regulations and festivities, drinking habits and gambling, the relation of dress and social rank, family life, and prostitution—and with the "high" culture of the elites: literature and art, education and scholarship. Hüllmann's scholarly reach was broad. It embraced the whole of Europe. Gilbert claimed that in the early years of his scholarly career, Burckhardt's idea of cultural history was similar to Hüllmann's.

To the degree that it had become a rallying cry for national regeneration or national affirmation, however, cultural history easily assumed a less universalist character and became instead a means of defining and reinforcing national identity. One of the earliest journals devoted to the topic of cultural history in Germany was entitled *Zeitschrift für deutsche Kulturgeschichte.*[18] With the disastrous failure of the 1848 Revolution in Germany, many who had expected the German *Kulturvolk* to achieve political form under liberal auspices began to look to the strongest of the German states—Prussia—to impose the political unity that had eluded the men of 1848. Political history—the history of the state power that, even in the eyes of those who claimed to be primarily concerned with culture, enabled a people to fulfill its cultural and historical mission, that is, to make its contribution to Universal History—acquired ever greater prestige. The state itself undertook to protect and promote culture, and the new German Empire saw itself as a *Kulturstaat*. By the time of the First World War an *"Aufruf an die Kulturwelt"* ("Appeal to the World of Culture") (1915), signed by many eminent German men of letters and science, including the writer Gerhart Hauptmann, the painter Max Liebermann, the physicist Max Planck, and the literary scholar Karl Vossler, affirmed the intimate association of culture and military might. "It is not true," the signatories protested, "as our enemies hypocritically contend, that the attack on our alleged militarism is not an attack on our culture, for without German militarism German culture would long ago have been wiped from the face of the earth."[19]

Even where reaction to the failure to create a unified political state in 1848 seems to have been a general denial of the significance of politics, cultural history continued to promote the idea of the nation and to assert its reality as a cultural community. In the work of Wilhelm Riehl, a contemporary of Burckhardt's, cultural history, the history of society, was virtually released from political history and brought close to what we might call ethnography or folklore studies. Cultural history, according to Riehl, should be concerned with the permanent ground or soil on which, in his view, the ephemeral forms of the state are constructed and which outlives them all—that is to say, with the nation or people. Riehl devoted himself entirely to studying the life, manners, and beliefs of peasants and artisans, seen as the most important and enduring elements of the nation. This popular, nonpolitical emphasis led him in effect to take up an extremely conservative political position, in that he accepted the division of society into orders (peasants, townsfolk, gentry) as a permanent or "natural" feature of social life, analogous, in his own terms, to the difference between male and female, and advocated a politics that took that division as its starting point. Thus Riehl's chief works, *The Society of the Town* (*Die bürgerliche Gesellschaft*, 1851), *The People of the Land* (*Land und Leute*, 1853), and *The Family* (*Die Familie*, 1855), were designed as contributions to what he called "The Natural History of the People as the Foundation of a German Social Politics" (*"Naturgeschichte des Volkes als Grundlage einer deutschen Socialpolitik"*). The appropriation of the term *Natural History* here was clearly intended to emphasize the autonomous, organic nature of the *Volk* and its culture.[20]

Perhaps it is not surprising that cultural history came to be viewed in some quarters as a popular, less rigorous form of history, so much so that its practitioners felt obliged to defend themselves against the charge of dilettantism.[21] Political history, in contrast, based on scrupulous analysis of documentary sources and practiced by the majority of university-trained professionals, claimed to be not only the only genuinely scholarly kind of history but the only truly relevant history—the only history that could address the questions of historical action and historical destiny—and for that reason the form of history to which all "specialized" historical practices, such as cultural history, economic history, and the history of art and literature must be subordinate. On the eve of the celebrated *"Methodenstreit"* in the early 1890s between the Leipzig historian Karl Lamprecht and the Berlin historians usually considered as having inherited the mantle of Ranke, this view was forcefully expressed by Dietrich Schäfer in an inaugural lecture provocatively entitled "Das eigentliche Arbeitsgebiet der Geschichte" ("The Proper Field for Historical Study"), which created quite a stir.[22]

As a citizen of a small, politically powerless state within the Swiss Confederation, Burckhardt may have been naturally drawn to cultural history rather than political history.[23] All the city-states were "commercial republics," to borrow the term they used to describe themselves. All were run by their merchant elites and were better known for their wealth and industry than for their roles as actors on the stage of European political history. It is surely not fortuitous that when he tried to describe to a Basel correspondent the perspective from which the modern historian-*philosophe* should write history, Voltaire picked that of a city-state. Working on his *Siècle de Louis XIV,* he told Johann Bernoulli, the Basel mathematician, "je me mets à la place d'un hambourgeois" ("I put myself in the position of a citizen of Hamburg").[24] The interest of both Bachofen and Burckhardt in cultural history is thus hardly surprising. The political history of his "hole-in-the-corner fatherland," as Burckhardt called it, was scarcely of universal significance.[25] As a German-speaking Baseler, moreover, Burckhardt had an idea of Germany as a *Kulturvolk,* a culture-nation, embracing many communities and forms of state, including that of his own native city. It was that larger Germany that had inspired his enthusiasm as a student at Berlin and Bonn. His outlook inclined him, almost of necessity, toward a *grossdeutsch* rather than a *kleindeutsch* vision of a future Germany.[26]

At the same time, because of the geographic position of Switzerland and in particular of Basel's position at the crossroads of France, Germany, and Italy, of northern and southern and of western and central Europe, Burckhardt retained a cosmopolitan, European outlook a good deal closer to that of Herder and his own teacher Ranke than to that of the newer German nationalist historians and poets, the Hoffmann von Fallerslebens, the Max Schneckenburgers, the Max von Schenkendorfs. As the cultural nationalists moved increasingly toward demagogic politics, finally embracing Prussia as their champion—Wilhelm Riehl himself ultimately lined up behind the Iron Chancellor—Burckhardt's orientation toward *European* cultural history became, if anything, even more marked. He turned away from the German Middle Ages to the great moments of classical and general European cultural history: to later Roman antiquity, to the Italian Renaissance, and finally, to ancient Greece. The cultural community his works of cultural history—as well as his studies of art history—were designed to promote, was Europe, not Germany.[27]

In addition, no member of the ruling Basel elite, least of all a Burckhardt, and no student of Ranke, could be indifferent to political power. Power and the state were realities, for Burckhardt, which had to be reckoned with. While he shared to some extent the romantic understanding of culture as a self-contained organic system, therefore, he saw it as something more dynamic and shifting, and less easily isolated from the play of power than Riehl.[28]

The term *cultural history,* for him, meant study of the underlying dynamics of a given time or society—"understanding of the living forces, both constructive and destructive, that were active in Greek life" ("Erkenntnis der lebendigen Kräfte, der aufbauenden und zerstörenden, welche im griechischen Leben tätig waren"), as he put it in the Introduction to his *Cultural History of Greece,*[29] in terms reminiscent of those used by Michelet in his 1869 Preface to the *Histoire de France:* "résurrection de la vie intégrale, non pas dans ses surfaces, mais dans ses organismes intérieurs et profonds."[30] As we know from the *Weltgeschichtliche Betrachtungen,* roughly contemporary with the *Cultural History of Greece,* Burckhardt saw those forces as inseparable from and in constant interaction with the power of the state and of organized religion. Heinrich Wölfflin, who studied cultural history with both Riehl and Burckhardt (he had taken courses with Riehl at Munich before coming to Basel) considered Burckhardt's approach "vastly different" from Riehl's. "Burckhardt is a historian through and through," he noted. "His cultural history is an elaborated form of history [*ausgeschmückte Geschichte'*]. Riehl has no real core. What he provides is a mosaic of pieces taken from art, literary history, social theory, etc. Burckhardt's definition of cultural history is the 'history of the forces that have been operative in history.' Riehl on the other hand: 'Representation of the manners of peoples in their interrelated development.'"[31] Burckhardt himself explained that his manner of writing about culture would indeed be "not narrative, but certainly historical" [*"nicht erzählend, wohl aber geschichtlich"*].[32] In the end, his fundamental position appears to have been far closer to that of his teacher, Ranke, than to that of Riehl.[33]

Burckhardt also retained a narrower humanist view of culture as the supreme contribution of exceptionally talented, imaginative, and cultivated (*"gebildete"*) individuals. Through the outstanding works of literature, art, and music produced by such individuals, the culture of a particular time or nation may achieve universality and become part of the heritage of all humanity. This "high" culture is by no means unconnected with the common culture of a given time, people, or nation. On the contrary, it grows out of it, develops it, and returns to it. In the best conditions, for Burckhardt, popular and "high" culture work together. As sons of distinguished families among the citizens of their small city-state, neither Burckhardt nor Bachofen was likely to forget the leadership role assumed by particular families in all aspects of the city's life. The transformation of the local weaving craft into a far-flung international commerce in fine ribbons, the basis of the city's economy, for instance, had been the achievement of enterprising individuals.[34] It is hard to see how they could not have viewed the more complex and refined products of culture as the work of gifted individuals building on and enhancing traditions shared in by the people as a whole.

Wolfgang Hardtwig's thorough analysis of Burckhardt's own uses of the terms *culture* and *cultural history* shows that they refer sometimes to a totality of social, material, and spiritual conditions and forces informing all particular aspects of history at a given moment, while at other times they refer more specifically to a power or activity that takes its place, in the *Weltgeschichtliche Betrachtungen*, alongside and often in opposition to religion and the state, as one of the three *"Potenzen"* that dominate history and determine, according to the particular relations among them at any given time, the specific character of any age. In that more specific sense, "culture" is an expression of human creativity and freedom, which often turns out in fact to be a destabilizing influence on the two stabilizing and ordering forces of the state and religion. In a still narrower and more specific sense, "culture" may also refer to the highest achievements of art, literature, and music. Culture in this sense aims to create "an imperishable world out of the merely earthly, a second creation that in the end is the only imperishable and universal thing on earth"; it strives to "eternalize that which is momentary or has validity only for particular times, places or parties."[35] But culture in this sense is never immune from the influence of culture in the broader sense or even, to a greater or lesser degree, of state and religion. There is ample material in Burckhardt's writings on art, for instance, to serve as the foundation of a sociology of art—that is, a study of the way social and political conditions affect the production of art.

As most of Burckhardt's published works—including those published posthumously from his lecture notes and papers—have been in the field of cultural history, and as Burckhardt himself made several polemical pronouncements about the superiority of cultural history to political history, that is, of "the recurrent," "the constant," "the typical" (*"das sich Wiederholende," "das Konstante," "das Typische"*), to the momentary and the singular event (*das Einmalige*),[36] it is often overlooked that he continued to give courses on political history (notably a course on the Age of Revolution) until very late in his life. In addition, both in his courses and in his private letters, he followed and commented on the *events* of the day (the Austro-Prussian War, the Franco-Prussian War, the revision of the Swiss Constitution) with anxious attention. Burckhardt never argued either against detailed historical study of particulars or against historical scholarship. He was simply opposed to mindless fact-grubbing for its own sake. "I do not intend to spare historians the task of studying all the rubble," he wrote. "I would only have them refrain from exhibiting it all in their works."[37]

In the introduction to the *Cultural History of Greece,* he articulated his position clearly: "The particular, especially the so-called event, will receive mention here in so far as it bears witness to the general, not for its own sake."[38] Once again, his position was closer to that of his teacher Ranke than the popular "parallel" of Burckhardt and Ranke would lead one to believe. For Ranke too had declared in his old age that the aim of his historical work was "to distinguish between what is accidental and passing and what is enduring";[39] Ranke too, while always retaining a keen interest in politics, had carefully distinguished in his inaugural lecture at the University of Berlin in 1836 between the active engagement of the politician and the historian's goal of understanding;[40] and Ranke too had defined the "chief goal of the historian" as that of reporting "how human beings in a particular period lived and thought" (*"wie die Menschen in einer bestimmten Periode gedacht und gelebt haben"*).[41]

Culture in its more specific and narrow sense, could not, to sum up, be treated as something completely independent of politics and state power. Instead, culture, political power, and religion were constitutive elements of any historical society and stood in any historical society in a dynamic and changing relation to each other, which might be more or less favorable to each. They might be very closely imbricated in each other, as in the early stages of the Greek polis, or the connections could be more tenuous, as in modern society. The state and religion traditionally provide the framework and stable conditions necessary for the work of the artist, but they may be so dominating and oppressive that the space of culture ("the sum total of those mental developments which take place spontaneously and lay no claim to universal or compulsive authority")[42] is drastically reduced and art becomes simply the handmaid of religion or of power; conversely, where it achieves a high degree of autonomy, culture may be capable of undermining the respect for authority, sense of community, and religious belief that are the foundations of a stable political order. The action of culture on state and religion, Burckhardt wrote, is "one of perpetual modification and disintegration and is limited only by the extent to which they have pressed it into their service and included it within their aims."[43]

No citizen of Basel could have failed to be aware that culture in Burckhardt's narrower sense had flourished in the city intermittently—most brilliantly perhaps in the period that corresponded to the one Burckhardt was to celebrate in *The Civilization of the Renaissance in Italy,* the period when Basel had been the preferred residence of Erasmus, Reuchlin, and Holbein, and when a member of a merchant family, such as Bonifacius Amerbach, could become a notable humanist and connoisseur.[44] It is tempting to discern in the magnificent account of the city of Florence in Burckhardt's book the ideal model of humanist Basel and even—in anticipation of the nostalgia with which the mature historian came to look back on the city of his youth—of the paler neohumanist Basel of the early nineteenth century.

Equally, however, no one in Basel could have been unaware that the state, including the city-state, could be repressive and unfavorable to cultural development. If humanist and neohumanist Basel is dimly perceptible behind the brilliant description of Renaissance Florence, as I believe it may be, it is another Basel—the narrowly orthodox and Pietist Basel from which Burckhardt suffered grief enough as a young professor and from which he escaped as often as he could, and above all, the new "democratic" Basel of the second half of the nineteenth century—that is evoked by the rather grim picture of the Greek city-state of the fifth and fourth centuries in the posthumously published *Cultural History of Greece*. Neither Burckhardt's idea of culture nor his practice of cultural history can be conceived apart from political considerations. As many commentators have pointed out, the opening section of *The Civilization of the Renaissance in Italy* is primarily political—an account of the breakdown of the political order of medieval Italy, resulting in the creation of the political and social conditions that permitted the astonishing release of individual energies in the course of the fourteenth, fifteenth, and sixteenth centuries that we refer to by the term *Renaissance*.

Cultural history, for Burckhardt, could not, in other words, be the antiquarian recovery of the past that still informed much of Riehl's work and that flourished in hundreds of local learned societies throughout Europe,[45] nor could it be the basis of a populist, nationalist ideology. To both Burckhardt and Bachofen, as to the humanist scholars to whose legacy they always laid claim, the study of past culture had a moral and social function: it was intended to instruct and fortify the current generation, faced as it was, in the opinion of both scholars, with the prospect of drastic decline and catastrophic revolutions, and it was addressed neither to the mass of the people nor to professional specialists, but to independent-minded (and that usually meant socially and economically independent) laymen of culture throughout Europe. This was preeminently the class of people referred to in Burckhardt's own city as the *Nichtstudierende,* that is to say, well-to-do, educated men destined to pursue a career in business while also participating in government and public life. They were not the *plebs,* not the manual workers, not the unenfranchised, but the *populus* referred to in the official designation *Senatus populusque basiliensis.* It was to this class, together with their spouses, that Burckhardt lectured on the history of art in his public lectures of the early 1840s and that he again addressed the popular lectures on art, literature, and history that he gave regularly after he returned to his native city in 1858 and seemingly turned his back on modern academic scholarship and publishing. Through his family and friends, he knew this class personally and was himself part of it. His own brother, Lucas Gottlieb, can probably be considered typical of the readers he sought and wrote for.

In his relation to the public and in his view of the historian's function as formative rather than purely *"wissenschaftlich,"* if not in the political message he had to transmit, Burckhardt was probably as close to the French historians of the Restoration, with whom he had been familiar since his early youth, as to his German academic masters.[46] Moreover, those French historians were highly self conscious; they practiced the genre of theoretical and methodological essays and prefaces with great energy; and in these, as well as in their historical writings proper, they had laid out an ambitious program of cultural history, as distinct from a history of events. Prosper de Barante tried to reproduce the tone of his chronicle sources in his own narrative, on the grounds that the texts of the chroniclers, their style and language, were as valuable as testimony to the mentality of the age in which they were written as their narratives were valuable as sources for the history of events. "The history of a nation does not consist simply in the chronicle of its wars and revolutions or in lively portraits of its illustrious men," he declared.[47] In his popular *Histoire de la Conquête de l'Angleterre par les Normands*, Augustin Thierry quoted liberally from literary and poetic sources, as did Michelet in the copious *"notes et éclaircissements"* he appended to his concise, highly schematic *Introduction à l'histoire universelle* of 1831. In addition, Michelet made increasing use of visual, artistic, architectural, and archaeological artifacts, and drew upon the evidence of clothing, sexual practices, eating habits, and the like to portray what we would nowadays call the "mentality" of past times. Burckhardt acknowledged his debt to the French historians in a conversation with Kurt Breysig in Basel in 1896, a year before his death.[48]

A course taught in the summer semester of 1851 and entitled "Introduction to the Study of History"—an extremely sketchy and hesitant anticipation of the later course on the study of history, which was published posthumously as *Weltgeschichtliche Betrachtungen*[49]—contains an early attempt by Burckhardt to articulate his ideas about cultural history. The historical view, he explained, has come "to pervade our entire culture." "It is a high, indeed a late stage in culture, which attains to an objective view of the past—and along with it, of a good part of the present; which can recognize relative justification and necessity where earlier centuries passionately took one side or another; and which can discern historical development even in decline and barbarism."[50]

Like Barante, Thierry, and Michelet—as well as Ranke—Burckhardt acknowledged the subjective element in historiography: every one comes to history in his own way, every one follows his own path, every one has more sympathy with some ages than with others.[51] Nevertheless, like his French predecessors no less than his teacher Ranke, Burckhardt insisted that the aim of the modern historian is to achieve a broad, nonpartisan view. In earlier times, the historian was determined by a single point of view—that of the sovereign in "histories of states, with their rulers, conquests, losses of territory, wars, and the like," or that of a principle, usually a religious one, according to which all the facts were organized and judged. In contrast, the new historiography aims at a universal point of view. Though he came increasingly to share Michelet's keen sense that the historian himself is swept along on the powerful waves he tries to describe,[52] Burckhardt never abandoned his conviction that the modern historian's vision can and should be universal, free of narrow interests or polemical purposes, and that such a broad general vision is more easily realized in cultural history than in political history. "Facts," he declared, should be "gathered not according to their external connections"—with the plans of particular rulers or of divine Providence—but for the sake of what they hold in themselves that is "characteristic of the age." "Alongside the history of states stretches an infinitely vast cultural history. . . . Everything that has survived becomes an eloquent witness of the age in question, a monument. Historical investigation gains thereby an immense range."

For the *writer* of history, however, there is a downside to the infinite expansion of the field of inquiry. "Beauty and integrity (*Abrundung*) of form suffer. No one can write an Agricola or a Germania any more."[53] Burckhardt appears to have sensed from very early on that the choice of cultural history would have a significant effect on the *writing* of history. "In my research, it is the background that is central, and that is the affair of cultural history, to which I plan to devote all my energies," he wrote to Gottfried Kinkel in 1842. "Epic form," as he put it, "doesn't come easily to me."[54] The historian had to find new principles of composition to replace the old narrative principles.

In the late 1840s Burckhardt had planned a series of small, inexpensive volumes of cultural history on topics such as "The Age of Pericles," "The Times of the Later Roman Emperors," "The Century of Charlemagne," "The Period of the Hohenstaufen," "German Life in the Fifteenth Century," and "The Age of Raphael." A course he gave at Basel in the winter semester of 1849–1850 on the "Heyday of the Middle Ages" provides some insight into the way he may have expected to carry out these projects. He did not intend to deal with political developments or to proceed "by countries or chronologically," he explained at the outset of this course. Instead he would combine an account of many aspects of medieval life with a discussion of the all-pervasive, unique character of the period.[55] This traditional objective of cultural history remains important in the major works that Burckhardt began producing after mid-century: *The Age of Constantine the Great* (1852), *The Civilization of the Renaissance in Italy* (1860), and *The Cultural History of Greece* (1898; posthumous). All of them deal with religion, ritual, folk festivals, carnivals, and other aspects of popular culture as well as with art, philosophy, literature, and theology. Nevertheless, as Felix Gilbert pointed out, none of the actually completed works corresponds exactly to the idea or the practice of cultural history at the time or to the plan Burckhardt himself laid down in the course on the "Heyday of the Middle Ages."

Burckhardt set out to write *The Age of Constantine* neither as "a history of the life and reign of Constantine," that is, as a political history, "nor yet [as] an encyclopedia of all worthwhile information pertaining to his period," that is, as a cultural history in the manner of Hüllmann. His aim was rather to outline and shape "the significant and essential characteristics of the contemporary world into a perspicuous sketch of the whole," as he put it in the Preface to the first edition (1852).[56] He admitted that he soon ran into difficulties. These are only partly accounted for by the reason he alleged, namely that many areas of the life of the time, notably its economic and financial aspects, were still unexplored, and only partly by the problem, already referred to, of achieving formal unity and balance in *any* cultural history, that is, of finding a way of writing that would result in neither a piling up of fragments nor a pure narrative. The chief reason for what he himself considered "the unevenness of the book" was, in Felix Gilbert's view, the difficulty he encountered in trying to reconcile two distinct historiographical goals: the description and evocation of a period of the past for its own sake, as an autonomous self-contained unit, and the evaluation of that period in relation to universal history and its significance for the present. In other words, Burckhardt had difficulty reconciling the two basic goals of early-nineteenth-century German historicism: the evaluation of each age of the past in its own terms and the evaluation of each age in relation to its place in the whole of history, in universal history as a total design.

The compositional difficulty Burckhardt alluded to in relation to *The Age of Constantine* must have been aggravated by the fact that, by the early 1850s, he no longer subscribed to the view—if he ever truly did—that history follows a progressive evolution, so that the value and meaning of each action or condition is determined by the subsequent unfolding of the plot. Nor was he inclined to accept the pious Rankean view that virtually everything is justified by the very fact that divine Providence had permitted it to exist.[57]

Only months before the publication of *Constantine,* he had begun to distance himself from the Rankean vision of history as well as from the Hegelian one and to reclaim the historian's traditional role as independent judge. His historical outlook had changed radically, he told his friend, the poet Paul Heyse. "I would never have believed that such a rotted-through old cultural historian as myself, who thought he would allow all points of view and all ages their own value, could become as one-sided as I am. But it is as though the scales have fallen from my eyes. I tell myself what St. Remy told Chlodowig: *incende quod adorasti, et adora quod incendisti!* [throw to the flames what you adored in the past and adore what in the past you threw to the flames]. . . . It is high time for me to free myself from the general, bogus-objective recognition of the value of everything and anything and to become thoroughly intolerant again."[58]

If we must acknowledge our ignorance of God's designs in human history and renounce as pure hubris all attempts to decipher them, we cannot evaluate the morality or beauty of human actions in terms of those designs. The historian must no doubt recognize what in his judgment appears to have been inevitable, but the attribution of value to particular acts, particular works of artistic creation (the only truly enduring elements in any historical existence), or even entire ages is the freely exercised responsibility of the historian. Universal history should not be regarded as the universal court. Historical judgments should not be pronounced simply in terms of the supposed contribution of individual acts and events to the advancement of a putative historical destiny; right and wrong, beauty and ugliness, are not a function of historical success or failure. At the same time, the historian must continue to evaluate and to judge. Everything in history is not admirable or even forgivable. On the contrary, history is full of cruelty, violence, waste, and suffering, and these should be denounced for what they are. Having come to this understanding, Burckhardt no longer had the basic optimism about history that had allowed the leading spokesman in Ranke's *Politisches Gespräch* of 1836 to challenge his partner to name a war that had not resulted in the victory of "the authentic moral force."[59] In evaluating the past, the historian is therefore thrown back on his own purely human resources, on his moral judgment and conscience, his political values, his practical sense of what in any given circumstances was possible, honorable, and most likely to promote human well-being. His judgments will be the better and more refined as he himself is more informed about the concrete historical situation, has more experience of the world, and has reflected more about his own standards. There is certainly an ironical, contemplative side to Burckhardt's mature vision of history. It led him to a detached acceptance of what seemed to him inevitable. But it did not allow him to confuse what he deemed unavoidable with what is good, or to renounce judgment altogether.

In fact, he became increasingly convinced that the chief value of historical study lay in its capacity to refine the understanding and make informed and nuanced judgment possible. The ability to reflect on the past was one of the features distinguishing humans from animals and "civilized" humans from "barbarians," as the historian might have read in his favorite philosopher, Arthur Schopenhauer. Awareness of history—again in Schopenhauer's words—is what "restores unity to the consciousness of the human race."[60] In one of the lectures attended by Wölfflin in the early 1880s, Burckhardt declared in terms that reflect not only Ranke but Schopenhauer that "every period of history is there for its own sake; one does not need to seek out the threads in it that lead forward to the present. The mere contemplation of the struggles and the creative acts of mankind in particular ages of the past is useful in itself. The difference between the thinking human being and the ordinary crowd lies in that capacity to contemplate and compare."[61] The same point had been made, in greater detail, in the Introduction to a course on "Modern History, 1450–1598," which probably dates from 1872:

It is not so long ago that people looked on the period from 1450 to 1598 from an essentially optimistic perspective and saw in it the beginnings of that "progress," in the continuation and expansion of which they believed that they themselves were living. That was the general picture anyway. For, when the details were examined, it was granted that the absolute power and tyranny of the great states, the Counter-Reformation, and other such things had demanded significant sacrifices. (It is not hard to hear those who suffered if one is willing to hear.) Still, in general, people stuck to the view that the supposed excellence or, at any rate, the brilliant promise of the situation they had been living in since 1830 was to be directly linked to the great innovations that had been carried through after 1450.

In light of the looming crises of the end of the nineteenth century, these gratifying products of historical reasoning have all collapsed. We have good cause to be more circumspect in pronouncing on the desirability of events and developments since 1450 in relation to us. In fact, we would do well to give up the notion of desirability in the past altogether. But that entails not the slightest diminution of the high interest with respect to the human spirit that that period should have for us. As long as our present Western culture can keep its head above the waves, we shall continue to find inner enrichment in appropriating for ourselves the colors and figures of the past and in treating the spiritual conditions and transformations of earlier historical periods as a primary requirement of our own intellectual awareness. Indeed, the ability to compare different times in the past with each other and with our own time is one of the principal powers that insulate us from the frenzied preoccupations of the day and from barbarism, which is incapable of comparison.[62]

Though these articulations of Burckhardt's ideas about historical study and historical judgment date from his later years, the ideas themselves were not new. They had been germinating for decades.

In the early 1850s, to be sure, it was still not so long since the enthusiastic student of history in Berlin, the friend of Gottfried Kinkel, had pronounced that "the highest conception of the history of mankind: the development of the spirit to freedom" was his "leading conviction."[63] There may be traces of that conviction, with its implication that the historian's judgment must coincide with the supposed judgment of history itself in a course on imperial Rome, which Burckhardt taught at the University of Basel in the winter semester of 1848–1849 and which was the prelude to his *Constantine*. In those lectures, Burckhardt justified the passage from republic to empire as a historical necessity. Rejecting Barthold Niebuhr's elegiac account of the end of the republic together with his judgment that Augustus's effort to retain some republican forms was a "farce" (*"Possenspiel"*), Burckhardt argued that any attempt at a full restoration of the republic would have been a disaster. It would have meant civil war and some one less worthy would probably have seized power.[64] Perhaps that was simply a hard, realistic assessment of the state of affairs, a sober-minded repudiation of Niebuhr's idealism. But when Burckhardt subsequently found some justification in Vespasian's persecution of the "philosophers" and chided the latter for not recognizing, as they ought to have done, "that Vespasian and the empire were necessities,"[65] it is hard not to hear an echo of Droysen—even if, in that instance also, it could be argued that Burckhardt was simply scolding the philosophers for obstinately closing their minds to facts that they did not want to acknowledge. One recalls how he had scolded his liberal friends in Bonn and Coblenz in the mid-1840s for failing to see the true nature of popular revolutionary movements.

The Age of Constantine, at any rate, shows little of Burckhardt's earlier "leading conviction" and the larger context of universal history is not clearly defined. There are certainly suggestions that history may be governed by a higher Providence. "Christianity," we are told, "was brought to the world by high historical necessity, as a period to antiquity, as a break with it, and yet in part to preserve it and transmit it to new peoples who as pagans might well have utterly barbarized and destroyed a purely pagan Roman Empire."[66] The ironical historical structure of *The Age of Constantine*—by persecuting the Christians and trying to eradicate their religion, Diocletian planted the seeds of their triumph, while Constantine, by making Christianity a state religion, ensured the survival of classical culture—also points either to some kind of divine comedy or, more probably, to the supreme irony of a world in which good and evil are so closely intertwined that nothing is either purely the one or purely the other, and in which good intentions may produce undesirable consequences and evil intentions desirable ones.

As has already been noted and will be noted again in relation to the *Cultural History of Greece,* Burckhardt never gave up the unity and continuity of culture as a moral imperative, a goal that mankind must strive to realize in the world, even after he had begun to be impressed by the catastrophic character of history: the permanence of suffering, the ineradicability of evil, and the constantly recurring threat to continuity itself.[67] The continuity of culture—the survival in later generations of the highest human aspirations and the deepest experiences of the past—was the only counterweight to and consolation for the untold miseries of actual historical existence. In contrast to Ranke, however, Burckhardt, who had lost his faith, could no longer ground the unity and continuity of history in God's Providence and benevolence. The references to "high historical necessity" are not only scarce and scattered; they have an ironic quality that points to the problematical character of the assumption that there is a providential plan of universal history and to the purely human basis of the requirement that what is best and most essential in past ages survive for the sake of the future. By the time of *Constantine,* and with even greater intensity thereafter, Burckhardt seems to have been ready to conceive that what actually happened to make cultural continuity possible might *not* have happened and need not have happened, that it was "necessary" only in the sense that the unity and continuity of culture are a kind of categorical imperative both for mankind (in as much as without an awareness of the past, man would not be distinguishable from the animals) and for the historian (in as much as the idea of a continuity of culture is the foundation of his ability to order and narrate).

The Constantine project itself, which Felix Gilbert has traced to Burckhardt's close friend in Bonn, Gottfried Kinkel, was originally envisaged by Kinkel as a study of the first three centuries after the birth of Christ, and an analysis of "political and intellectual developments in the course of which Christianity became"—in Kinkel's own words—"a 'historical necessity.'"[68] In the wake of the French Revolution and new critical approaches to the study of scripture and sacred history, many people had come to believe that history had taken a new turn and that the era of Christianity was over. The Constantine project may originally have been conceived as a reflection on the beginnings of a great age in the development of civilization that was thought to be finally drawing to a close as it yielded to a new and presumably "higher" stage. By the time he came to write *The Age of Constantine,* however, Burckhardt, as we saw, had become less convinced of the progressive character of history and more impressed by the recurrent threats to the continuity of the one part of it that was capable of enduring and that deserved to endure: culture, the accumulated product of the activities of the human spirit. The Age of Constantine probably appealed to him as a time of crisis and perilous transition that corresponded strikingly to his increasingly bleak view of his own time.[69] According to G. P. Gooch, in his classic study of nineteenth-century historians, it was Burckhardt's intention in *Constantine* "to depict the psychology of an age in which the leading characteristic was insecurity and the dominant tendency was a longing for novelty."[70]

Like the new age that appeared to Burckhardt to have been ushered in by the French Revolution and the Napoleonic empire,[71] the fourth century, in his view, was a time of uncertainty and disintegration. It was dominated, however, by a single extraordinarily astute and energetic individual. The memory of Napoleon seems to me to hover over Burckhardt's book, stimulating a persistent underlying question about the role of the "great man" in history, and illuminating the portrait of Constantine himself. It was Napoleon, one could say, who freed Burckhardt equally from the one-sided picture of the "sanctimious devotee" in Eusebius's sanitized *Life of Constantine* and from the Enlightenment vision (notably in Voltaire and Gibbon) of a cruel tyrant who was the true destroyer of the Roman Empire. Eusebius's biography, according to Burckhardt, is "basically insincere": the Bishop of Caeserea was not interested in telling the story of a forceful individual, "the man who with all his faults was always significant and always powerful," but in defending a cause, "the hierarchy so strongly and richly established by Constantine."[72] On the other hand, most of the pagan historians were, for obvious reasons, as Voltaire himself acknowledged, hostile to the emperor: "Ce serait une étude curieuse et instructive que l'histoire politique de ces tems-là. Nous n'avons guère que des satires et des panégyriques."[73] Gibbon's attempt to provide such a history seemed to Burckhardt enmeshed in the typical judgments and opinions of his own age. At this point the example of the Napoleon of the Concordat seems to have come to Burckhardt's rescue. "We can only surmise . . . that virtually throughout his life Constantine never assumed the guise of or gave himself out as a Christian but kept his free personal convictions quite unconcealed to his very last days." An impartial account would thus free Constantine from "the odious hypocrisy which disfigures his character" and reveal "instead a calculating politician who shrewdly employed all available physical resources and spiritual powers to the one end of maintaining himself and his rule without surrendering himself wholly to any party."[74]

> Constantine consistently acted according to the principle which energetic ambition, as long as the world has endured, has called "necessity." It is that remarkable concatenation of deeds and destiny to which ambitious men who are highly gifted are drawn as by some mysterious power. In vain does the sense of righteousness enter its protest, in vain do millions of prayers of the oppressed rise to Nemesis; the great man, frequently unconsciously, consummates higher decrees, and an epoch is expressed in his person, while he believes that he himself is ruling his age and determining its character.[75]

This conception of the role of the "great man" in history resembles that of Hegel (who had also, of course, been much impressed by Napoleon), except in two important particulars. For one, Burckhardt made no attempt to talk away the sufferings imposed on the "oppressed" or the insults to the human "sense of righteousness" by invoking the larger plans of Providence. What *men* see or present as "necessity" is usually, on the contrary, he suggested, a mask for their interest and ambition. As for objective necessity, we can no more know what it is than the great man himself. Those "higher decrees" that he "frequently consummates" are impenetrable and history is full of ironies. The "necessity" people claim to be serving may turn out to be entirely different from what they imagined. "We are not privy to the designs of eternal wisdom and we cannot know them," Burckhardt declared later in a strong statement repudiating Hegel in the lecture course on "The Study of History" that was published posthumously as *Weltgeschichtliche Betrachtungen.* "This presumptuous assumption of a universal plan leads to errors since it derives from erroneous premises."[76] Burckhardt's contemplation of the seemingly inevitable shifts and transformations of cultures and societies remains free of any attempt to justify behavior that promotes those shifts and transformations. Philosophy and history are two distinct disciplines, he maintained in the *Betrachtungen,* as are ethics and metaphysics. If we cannot deduce anything about a divine plan from the observation of apparent historical inevitabilities, equally we cannot deduce norms of behavior from the movements of history. It may be a moral obligation, he observed on another occasion, not to assist, and even to resist, the "inevitable."[77] Contemplation of the spectacle of history, in short, reinforced Burckhardt's leaning toward Stoic *constantia;* it did not make the direction and goal of history a criterion of right action.

In another, equally important respect, Burckhardt's view of the role of great men differed from that of Hegel and, for that matter, of his teacher Ranke. Ranke and Hegel both subordinated the great man, in the end, to the impersonal historical forces he embodies or represents, whereas Burckhardt, anticipating Nietzsche, saw the great individual rather as impressing his will on the world. For Ranke, the great man realizes changes that were, in any case, bound to occur. He is the instrument of historical providence. To Burckhardt, by the 1850s, the continuity that for Ranke was unquestionable no longer appeared inevitable. At various points of crisis, he had come to believe, history might have taken a different turn. "Instead of one wave of history, which we know, another, which we do not know, might have arisen."[78] Only in retrospect does everything appear to have been "inevitable" and "necessary." At such points of crisis, the unity and continuity of culture, which were as desirable and even necessary to Burckhardt as they had appeared unquestionable to Ranke, were truly threatened, and the greatness of the great man consists in his stepping in—consciously or more probably unconsciously, but in any event energetically—in such a way that they were preserved. The great man is not the mere agent of history, but carries a heavy burden of historical responsibility, even if, as usually happens, he does not understand what that responsibility is or the significance of his actions. "The view that spirit is unconquerable and will always emerge victorious is utterly banal. In fact, whether peoples and cultures go under or not can depend entirely on whether a particular man possesses a particular degree of energy at a particular moment. At such times great individuals are needed, and they need to be successful." It is by no means inevitable that such individuals will be available. All one can say is that so far, ultimate catastrophe has been avoided, though there has been infinite suffering and loss. "At important moments Europe has often found great individuals."[79]

Later on, when he turned to the Italian Renaissance, Burckhardt was again guided by the same concern to study the past as a key to the understanding of the present, not in the sense that there is a necessary evolution of human society from its origins to the present time, "a development toward freedom, in which in the Orient one was free, among the peoples of classical antiquity a few were free, while the modern age makes all free,"[80]—not, in other words, for the sake of some alleged historical philosophy—but for the sake of a better understanding of the complexities and ironies of history. History for Burckhardt was always, first and foremost, *Bildung*—part of education and of the formation of a fully human person. It did not provide a God-like view of destiny, "laws" of historical development, or useful answers to particular practical questions; nor, on the other hand, did it simply offer lively and interesting material for the curious mind or spectacles for our amused contemplation. It offered, in the celebrated formula, "to make us not shrewder (for next time) but wiser (for ever)."[81] A scholar writing in the 1950s, whose own experience as a refugee from Nazi Germany may have given him special insight into Burckhardt's practice of history, described cultural history, in the form Burckhardt gave it, as a form of "historical sociology," "a phenomenological description of the human situation in a historical setting."[82] In contrast to other sociologists of the nineteenth century (Marx and Saint-Simon), according to Albert Salomon, Burckhardt did not aim to discover immanent or transcendent laws on which to base a science of social manipulation; he sought instead to derive wisdom from consideration of the various historical situations in which human beings had found themselves, of the ways in which they had responded to these situations, and of the consequences of these responses. We can know nothing of the immanent or transcendent meaning of history. "We can only present observations and reflections on the way human beings act and are acted upon."[83] History in general, as Burckhardt understood it, was *passio humana*—"the study of the greatness and the limitations of men." In times of great historical upheaval, Salomon concluded, reflection on that greatness and those limitations might provide some modest comfort.[84]

Certain passages in Burckhardt might lead one to believe that history for him was an escape, a pure aesthetic contemplation, and a number of interpreters have emphasized his alleged "aestheticism." With Burckhardt, however, it is always dangerous to simplify. He certainly sought to rise above the strains of his own time, but it cannot be an accident that he so often chose to study periods of crisis or transition or that so many of his comments and judgments seem inspired by and relevant to his own experience and his own world. Exile and engagement, detachment and active concern did not rule each other out in Burckhardt's mind or behavior. Dante, in the historian's vision of him, was at once an exile and a man deeply involved in the affairs of his time. Saint Severin, to whom he alluded so frequently, is seen serenely continuing his mission even as he observed the empire crumbling around him. There is most probably at least as much affinity between Burckhardt and late humanism—notably the neostoical doctrines of the end of the sixteenth and beginning of the seventeenth centuries, which had a major impact not only in France and England but in Germany and Switzerland, and not least in humanist Basel, with its close links to Erasmus and the Netherlands—as there is between Burckhardt and *fin de siècle* aestheticism. Many essential aspects of Dutch and Flemish neostoicism seem recognizable in the outlook and attitudes of the nineteenth-century *civis basiliensis:* the overriding concern with peace and order; the aversion to dogmatic dispute; the characteristically humanist view of learning as not an end in itself, not pure *Wissenschaft,* nor merely useful knowledge, but education for a full life;

the deliberate policy of addressing substantial citizens—humanist merchants and men of learning—and of ignoring the uneducated mass, seen as the object, not the subject of good government; the view of the political community as always subject to the natural law of change, growth and decline; above all, the conviction that the chief duty of the citizen is to remain firm or constant and to follow his best judgment *in publicis malis*[85]—or, in Burckhardt's own words, when *"politica erscheinen ziemlich trostlos."*[86] It is not certain that Burckhardt had read Justus Lipsius; but it is more than likely that he knew something of him, if only because he had been a teacher of Burckhardt's beloved Rubens, whose portrait of him the historian could easily have seen in the Palazzo Pitti in Florence.

Some of the most important features that Burckhardt attributed to the Age of Constantine the Great seem to reflect his understanding of the character of his own time, most notably the decadence and vulgarization of religion and culture, the emergence of "strong men" to maintain order, and the importance of ensuring that the essentials of the culture that is dying will be preserved and transmitted, beyond the crisis, to future times.

Finally, Burckhardt's discussion of late paganism introduced a motif that is also found in Bachofen—as well as in a number of romantic scholars such as the Dane, Georg Zoega, and to a certain extent Georg Friedrich Creuzer and Friedrich Gottlieb Welcker—and that was to become widely disseminated thanks to Nietzsche. The image of classical antiquity propagated by Hegel and the Young Hegelians and by the German *Gymnasia* and universities, according to Burckhardt, was a false, idealized one. "Enemies of Christianity make it their constant charge that Christianity is an other-worldly religion that regards life on earth only as a period of preparation, grim and rich in trials, for eternal life in the world to come. Paganism, on the contrary, is praised as a joyous doctrine that taught ancient man to give untrammeled expression . . . to his potentialities, his inclinations, and his individual destiny. It might be objected at once that even at its most powerful the worldview of the Greeks was far from being as joyous as is customarily believed." Contrary to prevailing views, Burckhardt argued—and this argument would later be developed powerfully in his *Cultural History of Greece*—the Ancients were not happy. Late paganism in particular was even more concerned with the afterworld than Christianity. "Christian dogma places its doctrine of death and immortality at the end of its doctrine of man." But with the paganism of the third century "we must begin with death and immortality, because comprehension of late pagan religions depends entirely upon this point." To be sure, "the lamentable condition of the state and society certainly contributed greatly to the development of this other-worldliness, but it cannot explain it fully. New tendencies such as these draw their essential strength from unplumbed depths: they cannot be merely deduced as consequences of antecedent conditions."[87] Religion, in other words, is as fundamental and essential to man "as he is, was, and always will be," as society or artistic creation, and the religious dimension of classical antiquity is far more important than modern classical scholarship has been willing to acknowledge. Like art, religion, it would appear, enjoys a kind of autonomy within the context of humanity's overriding historical existence.

In the eyes of the historian, nevertheless, conditions of life in the late empire did give added prominence to concerns about death and immortality and spread them among ever wider segments of the population, coarsening and debasing religious sentiment. Whereas early paganism (like early Christianity) had been elitist, allowing that only a small number of people to whom the gods were particularly favorable were destined to sojourn in Elysium or in the Isles of the Blessed, late paganism was democratic: "the circle of these favored ones was suddenly enlarged and soon every one made claim to eternal blessedness."[88] Almost all the surviving religious cults of the late Roman world (the mysteries of Bacchus, Hecate, and Venus, the Taurobolia or mysteries connected with the cult of the Great Mother, the cult of Isis, the worship of Mithras), reflect the "gloomy anxiety concerning the beyond" that "overpowered" the late pagans and "drove them to the most extraordinary doctrines and rites."[89] Late Roman religion appears as a vulgarization of earlier religious beliefs and practices. Anxiety about their "troubled earthly destinies" led the third- and fourth-century inhabitants of the empire to astrology, magic, and demonology, which soon gained "the upper hand over earlier sacrifices, oracles and penances." Astrology in turn provided "a strong impulse toward atheism,"[90] in that to the person convinced of the fate made manifest in the stars, no moral consideration or religion could offer either comfort or aid. Philosophy itself declined, and vulgar, sometimes cruel magical practices proliferated. "From the lives of the philosophers themselves, as Eunapius tells them, superstition rises to meet us like a gray fog."[91] Christianity, the attraction of which was largely due to the hope in immortality that it justified, suffered the fate of all the other religions. "Each century has its own view of the hypersensual within and without man,"[92] according to Burckhardt, so that "the Christians in their belief in daimones, partly of Judaizing and partly of popular origin, run parallel with the pagans" and "[p]agans, Jews, and Christians were equally convinced that spirits and the dead could be conjured up."[93] All in all, Burckhardt proposed a bleak picture of the decadent moral and spiritual condition of "a people which even during the bloom of its culture was alien to the idea of a divine world order and an all-embracing system of moral purpose, and which now more than ever was confused by uncertainty and apprehension concerning the great questions of life."[94] Religion had degenerated into a search for quick answers, magic tricks, and easy consolations.

The Age of Constantine anticipated to a surprising degree, in Burckhardt's view, his own. Nineteenth-century religion, to Burckhardt, was as debased by the influence of the masses as the religion of the fourth-century empire. More concerned with comforting beliefs than with truth, incapable of the courage and austerity that had characterized the strong-willed men and women of an earlier age, the nineteenth-century *"Spiessbürger"* practiced a religion appropriate to their insipid confidence in "progress" and their vulgar ideal of happiness and wellbeing.[95] Far from countering the prevailing democratic culture of optimism, religion had, in short, been contaminated by it. "Our present-day Christianity is not strong enough [to challenge that optimism], since for the last hundred years it has itself been strongly penetrated by it and intermingled with it."[96] As "the expression of an eternal metaphysical need" in man,[97] religion was a potent force and deserved respect, but in the nineteenth century it had truly become the "opium" of the people for Burckhardt in his way, no less than for Marx. The collusion of church and state had likewise not been to the religious benefit of the church. One of the themes of *The Age of Constantine,* G. P. Gooch noted with his usual perceptiveness, was that Christianity deteriorated as a religion from the moment that it became the official religion of the empire, and that this led the nobler elements to seek refuge in asceticism and monasticism. In modern times no less than in antiquity, however, association with the state had diminished the church's spiritual authority. There was no doubt, in Burckhardt's mind, that the nineteenth century was an *"Auflösungsperiode"*—a period of dissolution—and that *"das Christentum seine grossartigen Stadien hinter sich hat"* ("the great epochs of Christianity lie behind it").[98] To the concerned citizen of the mid-nineteenth century—and especially, no doubt, to the patrician citizen of an old humanist city-state—the Age of Constantine was more than a curious spectacle; it was a mirror for the present.

There was a similar implicit parallel between the state of the arts in the Age of Constantine and at the end of the nineteenth century. The Romans never had in equal degree the Greek dedication to beauty, according to Burckhardt. Theirs was already a culture of irony, removed from the immediacy of the beautiful. To illustrate his point Burckhardt evoked a scene from Lucian's "masterly" *Dialogues of the Dead,* in which Hermes, the conductor of souls to Hades, shows the cynical and worldly wise Menippus the skeletons of "famous beauties of antiquity, Narcissus, Nereis, and others. 'But I see nothing but skulls and bones; show me Helen.' 'This skull here is Helen.' 'Was it for this that a thousand ships sailed, that countless men died, that cities were destoyed?' 'Ah, Menippus,' Hermes answers, 'you never saw the woman alive!'"[99]

Nevertheless, "a need for the beautiful was inherent" in the Romans. Despite criticism from their moralists, "the demand for artistic surroundings for life continued unbelievably strong. Pompeii alone, in Goethe's words, shows 'an appetite for art and pictures on the part of a whole people of an extent of which the most ardent *amateur* of today can have neither concept nor feeling.'" By about the middle of the second century, however, "the active production of works of art . . . ceases and degenerates to mere repetition, and . . . hencefor-ward internal impoverishment and apparent over-elaboration of forms go hand in hand."[100] An inordinate demand for luxurious materials develops—por-phyry, jasper, agate, and marbles of all colors—and, along with that, a deepen-ing separation of structure and ornamentation. As a result, "art and the artist could only retire." Not only did the hardness of the newly fashionable materials "limit the scope of the chisel" and give the supplier of the stone itself greater importance than the artist, "the taste for simplicity" was corrupted. "Despite mass, the impression is often trivial and confusing, because external architec-tural richness, once it has been conceived of as the guiding principle, soon ex-ceeds all measure and is also applied to structural members whose function makes them incapable of receiving decorative treatment." In an early applica-tion of his principle of writing art history *"nach Aufgaben"*—in terms of what a society commissions and expects its artists to do—Burckhardt explained that Christianity contributed to the decline of classical form by its demand for very large interior spaces. This resulted in new forms of construction and consider-able "mechanical virtuosity" but "contributed no less to the final dissolution of the structural system inherited from the Greeks." Soon columns ceased to be a structural element of Christian basilicas and became purely ornamental. Chris-tianity's overriding concern with preaching further aggravated the separation of structure and ornamentation and led to a "predominance of luxurious embel-lishment and of figured representation, in the interior as on the facades," where mosaics soon "covered every space and every surface with biblical figures and stories," making "genuine architectural articulation impossible."[101]

Sculpture and painting declined for the same reasons: the hardness of the fashionable materials, which were often mixed in a single figure, and the over-riding importance given to symbolism and the communication of specific ideas and messages. In the working of the "incredibly hard and unyielding stone" from which the colossal porphyry sarcophagi of Helena and Constantia (the mother and daughter of Constantine) were constructed, for instance, "there can be no question of any direct touch of artistic genius . . . ; what is involved is slave labor after a given pattern."[102] Called upon to mass produce sarcophagi in an age of revived religious cults of the most varied deities, many of them foreign and unfamiliar, the artist no longer had any inner relation to his subject matter; he had become little more than a supplier of artifacts, following an externally provided set of requirements, to a clientele he in turn knew only externally. "Work was seldom done to special order, but produced for the trade, and hence had to follow the vulgar and florid taste of the average purchaser."[103] The inner relation between form and substance, the harmonization of the ideal and the real—which to Burckhardt was characteristic of the greatest art, be it that of ancient sculpture or that of Renaissance painters like Raphael—was lost. "Sub-ject matter grew dominant in a tendentious sense, to the detriment of art. The relevant myths were represented as symbolic husks of general ideas, and the separation between kernel and shell could in the long run only be injurious to art."

Everywhere, in sculpture and in painting alike, the "message" dominated.[104] Sheer mass and size in themselves became objects of admiration as artistic draftsmanship and modeling declined and people proved less and less able to appreciate artistic refinement. The tension between the ideal and the real, artistic form and empirical observation and representation, which in true art, according to Burckhardt, saves the universality of form from vacuity and gives universality to the representation of particular phenomena, was lost.

> Luxury in material and passion for decoration had largely deprived acute perception of the place of honor which is its due. The few wall paintings of mythological content which have been preserved show crude repetition of older motifs and a stunting and ossification of the system of arabesques which was once so decorative. . . . The new Christian subjects spread a sunset glow over ancient art, but new content did not bring fresh quality. . . . Ecclesiastical merit and completeness of the subject, along with magnificence of execution were the only relevant considerations. For the artist's own joy in his work, there is no room. Art had become serviceable to a symbol which lay outside itself.[105]

There was a development of portraiture, but the portrait celebrated neither the ideal qualities and energies of the human character nor the particular features of an individual. Instead, the "ceremonial picture," to borrow Burckhardt's term, gave an exact representation of "official vestments and solemn posture, frequently with symbolic accessories." The portrait, in other words, represented neither the human nor the individual; it represented rank and power. Costume was so essential in such portraits that the head was replaced by the entire upper body, even on coins and tombstones, in order that an individual's rank and dignity might be clearly designated by dress. Portraits of the emperor, in particular, functioned as symbols of his power and authority. In Burckhardt's view, such portraits "no longer had much to do with true art. . . . Art had largely become the handmaid of propaganda."[106] This process had set in before Christianity became the religion of the empire, but Christianity aggravated it.

Literature was also in decline. "Poetry continued to be composed in most categories, to be sure, in a consciously academic manner; but ever paler reminiscences of a better age, as is displayed for example in the bucolic and didactic poets of the third century . . . cannot suffice to produce a living literature, however much talent may appear in individual cases." Some works of unusual artistic merit were produced, especially in the lyric, which, being a private rather than a public genre, "is always capable of rejuvenation, as is the human heart, and may produce individual lovely blooms even in periods of general wretchedness, though their form be imperfect."[107] For the most part, however, literature breathes "too plainly of the air of the schools," and the officially promoted and admired literature in the Age of Constantine "was the most deplorable of all productions, grammatical tricks with words and verses; . . . figured poems, which when carefully written out, take the form of an altar, a pan-pipe, an organ, or the like; . . . anacylic verses, which could be read backwards or forwards; and other such aberrations."[108] Once again, the spread of Christianity brought no improvement. Ancient myth had been malleable and so "with poetry and through it could serve as a continuous revelation of the beautiful." Biblical history, in contrast, was "delivered to poetry in a fixed and completed form; epic or plastic decoration might be dangerous from the point of view of dogma. Hence the dryness of the versified harmonies of the Gospels." The total impression of the best of the Christian poets, the Spaniard Prudentius, in whose work the portentous shift from quantity to stress can already be felt, is "disproportionately rhetorical."[109]

Significantly, however, Burckhardt did not support the romantic condemnation of rhetoric. On the contrary, he acknowledged the vital role of rhetoric and school exercises in sustaining cultural continuity in times of dissolution—in preserving, for instance, the basic sense of beauty and proportion that in his view was typical of classical culture and was so singularly lacking in his own fragmented age.

> Did not antiquity exaggerate the importance of education in discourse and writing? Would it not have done better to fill the heads of boys and young men with useful realities? The answer is that we have no right to make a decision as long as formlessness in discourse and writing persists among us everywhere, as long as perhaps barely one of a hundred of our educated men possess any notion of the true art of periodic structure. To the Ancients, rhetoric and its collateral sciences were the indispensable complement to their norm of beautiful and free existence, to their arts and their poetry. Modern life has higher principles and aims in some respects, but it is uneven and disharmonious. What is most beautiful and delicate in it is found alongside the crudest barbarism. And our multitudinous preoccupations do not leave us leisure to take offense at the contradictions.[110]

In the fourth century "rhetoric still ruled as queen." But by then it had been developed as a school discipline to a degree unknown in the heyday of antiquity. "Every sort of sentence structure, figure of speech, and artifice of construction" was classified, given a name, and described in circumstantial detail. To a belated age that had lost its inner relation to classical culture and was capable only of exploiting its external forms, codified and teachable techniques were far more necessary than they had ever been previously.[111] Nevertheless, Burckhardt's final judgment is extremely nuanced. Like Helen's skull, academicism preserved at least the memory of what had once been lively and beautiful. It thus became the agent of cultural continuity.

> If almost all the productions of the fourth century betray decline by labored and tortured form, by heaping up of *sententiae*, by the misuse of metaphor for

the simple and the commonplace, by modern turgidity and artificial archaic aridity, still a peculiar reflection of the classical period rests upon many of these writers. They still show the requirement of artistic style, which is normally alien to us; that the style emerges as something calculated and self-conscious is the fault of the sinking age, which felt quite clearly that it and its culture were something secondary and derivative, and imitated the great models painstakingly and unevenly. But it is impossible to dismiss lightly authors like Libanius and Symmachus, for example, whose every little letter was wrought into a minor work of art. Symmachus at least knew that the Ciceronian period of epistolography was over and why it was over.[112]

In the end, it is to the "reverence for the ancient literature" of writers like Symmachus that we owe not only their "dainty affectation" and "conscious artifice" but the preservation of the classics.[113]

The faults that Burckhardt deplored in the arts and the literature of the Age of Constantine—vulgarity and materialism, excess and extravagance of materials, the arbitrary use for purely ornamental purposes of motifs whose inner "organic relation" to a once coherent style and culture had vanished, the subordination of artistic production to the demands of a clientele that was less and less familiar with artistic traditions and more and more lacking in taste and discrimination, the increasing subservience of art to dogma, ideology, even propaganda—were those he believed afflicted his own time. And just as he defended the very rote learning and rhetorical routines to which true art had sunk in that age of decline because these at least preserved some recollection of the great artistic traditions and might therefore, in a happier time, facilitate a revival, he approved every effort to maintain, in his own age, the great traditions of Renaissance painting, sculpture, and architecture. Likewise, just as he occasionally showed, even as early as *The Age of Constantine*, a surprisingly evenhanded recognition of the interest and artistic value of "decadent" art, so later on would he come around to reevaluate the universal sympathy, the capacity to appreciate all styles and all cultures, which come with the very belatedness or "Alexandrianism" that removes a period from spontaneous, "natural" participation in a living and dynamic culture, and which is the positive side of the often denounced commodification of art and literature. Art history, the young discipline of which Burckhardt was a passionate pioneer, was the most striking and brilliant manifestation in the nineteenth century of that expanded sympathy and appreciation.

The Age of Constantine was a study of a period of historical and cultural crisis and transition: it described an end and, at the same time, a beginning, of which the men and women of the period could themselves barely have had glimmerings.[114] It also pointed to the curious process by which the very force that seemed to be destroying the old culture of antiquity and the fabric of the empire—Christianity—provided the means for its preservation, not to be sure as it had once been, but as a respected memory that might one day be reinvigorated.[115]

To Burckhardt, already anticipating the coming mass culture, the Roman Empire of the fourth century carried vital and poignant lessons for the men and women of his own age. He wrote his *Age of Constantine,* as he said in the Preface to the 1852 edition, not for professional historians but for "thoughtful readers of all classes." In Burckhardt's eyes, as we have seen, the "culture of old Europe," the humanist culture that resulted from the combination of Renaissance individualism and Christian religion and in which the life of his native city as he knew it was rooted, seemed to be running out, undermined by the politics of democracy, the rise of mass culture, and the ever greater rationalization of all aspects of economic life and public administration. How could the historian not have expected that the reader of his *Constantine* would be moved by the elegiac reflections at the end of the chapter on "The Senescence of Ancient Life" to reflect on his own time and experience? "Does a formal decline in poetry and representational art always imply a people's national decline also?" the historian asked. With apparent evenhandedness, he suggested the "modern" notion that religious or scientific truth and "useful knowledge" may represent a more advanced stage of human "progress" than the arts and the old-fashioned poetic vision of the world that theology, philosophy, and science have superseded. Though it is quickly evident that Burckhardt did not entertain that notion seriously, a note of uncertainty remains amid the irony. Perhaps the Constantinian solution was as good as could be hoped for in the circumstances: "Are those arts not blossoms which must fall before fruit can mature? Cannot the true take the place of the beautiful, the useful of the agreeable? The question may remain unsolved, and between such alternatives as the last there can be no solution. But anyone who has encountered classical antiquity, if only in its twilight, feels that with beauty and freedom there departed also the genuine antique life, the better part of the national genius, and that the rhetorizing orthodoxy which was left to the Greek world can only be regarded as a lifeless precipitate of a once wonderful totality of being."[116]

Certain passages of *The Age of Constantine* seem even to have a discreet though curiously concrete contemporary reference, which Burckhardt himself may or may not have consciously intended. In the evocation toward the end of the book of "another city in the ancient world empire, a city that was perhaps never named under Constantine, but concerning whose life and survival our sympathetic curiosity may well be aroused," that is to say fourth-century Athens, some of Burckhardt's readers from the Basel elite—former fellow students at the *Pädagogium* raised on neohumanist enthusiasm for the ancient polis and the ardent hope of reviving it on the banks of the Rhine and the Birsig—could conceivably have recognized or thought they recognized an allusion and a gently ironical compliment to their own native city. For like Athens under Constantine, Basel too had become an anachronism, "greatly diminished" and "reduced to a small compass" since its heyday in the Renaissance and, like Athens in relation to Rome and Constantinople, it no longer counted for much in comparison with the powerful empires that had emerged in the postrevolutionary world of mass culture and political democracy. In particular, many Baselers from the city's elite might have been vividly reminded of their dream of Basel in Burckhardt's account of "the aura of glory which surrounded [Athens], its easy and pleasant life, the majestic monuments" that "drew a continual stream of free and educated spirits to the city" and led to the creation of "a sort of university." To the former center of the Western world, which history had turned into a backwater, Burckhardt attributed the characteristics that had formed the basis of the educated Baseler's ideal since Erasmus and that always remained his own: freedom, moderation, and the leisure to devote oneself to learning and self-cultivation.

At the same time the *Antistes*'s son included in his description what might well have been a warning of the threat to that ideal from excessive preoccupation with work and economic success. "All who cherished antiquity in these late ages must needs love the Athenians," we are told. Lucian, for instance, "has his Nigrinus utter beautiful and moving words concerning this people, among whom philosophy and poverty were equally at home, and who were not ashamed of their poverty, but regarded themselves rich and happy in their freedom, the moderation of their life, and in their golden leisure." A phrase quoted directly from Lucian must surely have had a direct, personal significance to the young scholar. Athens is for the philosophically inclined, Lucian wrote: "One who wishes luxury, power, flattery, lies, servitude, must live in Rome." In the 1850s Burckhardt was still hesitating between "Athens" and "Rome." It had been only a few years since he returned to his native city from fast-developing Berlin, soon to be the capital of a second German Empire; and in another four years he would again leave to try his luck at the new Swiss national university in Zurich; in 1858, however, he returned definitively to Basel, having finally made his choice. As he had no illusions about Basel, he did not attempt to conceal the fact that Athens had not been spared the general intellectual and artistic decline that afflicted the entire age. Nevertheless, those "who could not be at ease either in the organized life of Rome or in the Christian Church, adhered to the most sacred site of ancient Greek life with a genuine tenderness. Anyone who could spend his life in that environment counted himself happy."[117]

Cut off from the mainstream of political life, Athens figures in *The Age of Constantine* as a kind of refuge or asylum for values that have become increasingly *"unzeitgemäss,"* or out of season. Unexpectedly, it thus echoes the celebrated account of eremitism in an earlier chapter. The third- and fourth-century Christian anchorites were motivated, according to Burckhardt, by a natural inclination of man "to find his proper self in solitude when he feels lost in the large and busy external world." What they sought was partly to do pen-

ance for the sins of mankind, partly to owe the world as little as possible—
"nothing more than the barest subsistence"—but "partly also to keep the soul
capable of constant intercourse with the sublime." The premise of eremitism is
"a not wholly healthy state of society and the individual" and a period of "crisis,
when many crushed spirits seek quiet, and at the same time many strong hearts
are puzzled by the whole apparatus of life." The phenomenon cannot be
grasped in medical or economic terms; the attempt to do so reveals only an
incapacity "to have any comprehension of the spiritual forces which drove those
towering personalities into the desert." Above all, "there remains an enormous
effect upon history, which the student must evaluate after his own manner." By
that Burckhardt meant the influence of eremitism and monasticism on Christianity and indirectly on the whole of culture. "It was these anchorites who
communicated to the clerical order of succeeding centuries the higher ascetic
attitude toward life, or at least the claim to such an attitude; without their pattern the church, which was the sole pillar of all spiritual interests, would have
become entirely secularized and have necessarily succumbed to crass material
power."[118] It was the anchorites, in other words, who preserved the spiritual
core of Christianity from contamination and corruption by the world and, by
acting as a perpetual reminder of the transcendent aspirations of religion, saved
the church from becoming simply an institution of power. With his usual sympathy and insight, Burckhardt noted that the authentic—that is to say, disinterested—pursuit of art, literature, scholarship, and science in modern secular society is motivated by a similar reserve with respect to the world, and that it still
profits, in the respect accorded it and the freedom it continues to enjoy, "from
the halo of the supermundane which the medieval Church imparted to science."[119] In his darker moments, Burckhardt envisaged a time when this might
no longer be the case and when all art and thought might be subject to the
manipulations of power and the forces of the market. Like so much else in
The Age of Constantine, Burckhardt's Christian anchorites spoke directly to the
readers of the mid-nineteenth century. There is much learning in this early
essay in cultural history, but it is unquestioningly a work of *Bildung* rather
than *Wissenschaft.*

Burckhardt's best known and most widely read work of cultural history, *The
Civilization of the Renaissance in Italy,* appeared in 1860, shortly after his definitive return to Basel. It has become a classic of historiography in English translation as well as in the original German. To this day, despite well over a century
of subsequent scholarship, it retains much of its freshness and pertinence.[120] In
a recent essay on the so-called new historicism in Renaissance studies, which
focuses on the work of Stephen Greenblatt and, indirectly, on the influence of
Michel Foucault, David Norbrook, an Oxford Renaissance scholar, argued that
the political, philosophical, and cultural issues raised in Burckhardt's account

of Renaissance Italy may be more vital to historians and critics today than the historical account itself. According to Norbrook, Burckhardt's portrait of Renaissance man, whatever its historical validity, has provided a model for a contemporary ideal of freedom that seeks refuge in the sphere of art—or self-fashioning—from the disillusionments of politics, perceived as a sphere of "mere expediency."[121]

While pointing to the continued presence of Burckhardt's vision of the Renaissance in the work of contemporary scholars, Norbrook also recognized that that vision was rooted in a particular historical experience. "If we take [Burckhardt's] portrayal of Renaissance Italy as mirroring his own era, what emerges is a potentially satirical anatomy of a society in which a superstructure of culture and courtesy masks a complete lack of any moral legitimacy, a ruthless entrepreneurial competitiveness. But Burckhardt regarded this society of conspicuous consumption as far preferable to any predecessor or likely successor. His cult of the depoliticized individual meant that his writings potentially legitimized the power of capital while expressing contempt for the political process."[122]

Norbrook's reading of Burckhardt, however one may respond to it, has the considerable merit of treating *The Civilization of the Renaissance in Italy* as a work that—far from being "escapist"—is intensely concerned with questions of politics, as Burckhardt lived them, albeit in a negative and deeply pessimistic way. Burckhardt himself never attempted to conceal that concern. On the contrary. Florence, he tells us, "deserves the name of the first modern state in the world." It was "the workshop of the Italian and indeed of the modern European spirit." The Florentines "are the earliest types of Italians and modern Europeans generally." The "record of the collapse of the highest and most original life that the world could then show," as found in the *Istorie Fiorentini* of Machiavelli and in the works of his contemporaries and successors, is therefore no matter of merely local interest, but "will be an object of thought and study to the end of time."[123] The analysis of the exacerbated individualism of the Italian Renaissance is likewise an object lesson for all modern readers, who are its inheritors.[124] Above all, the development of the modern state, which finds its raison d'être in itself and which is "scientifically organized with a view to this object," Burckhardt declared at the beginning of part I, chapter 2, presents "to us a higher interest than that of mere narrative."[125] To Burckhardt, as we saw in chapter 10, the nineteenth century had "begun by making tabula rasa of all previously existing relations," and with the settlement of 1815, "the historical ground [had] been dug away from beneath the feet of nearly all the peoples of Europe, including the Prussians." The emergence of the state as artificial construct or *Kunstwerk* was something the historian had observed in his own time and immediate environment.[126] In Burckhardt's view, in other words, the "Restoration," no less than the revolutionary and imperial regimes it was supposed to bring to a close, had not prevented conditions strikingly similar, in some respects, to those of fourteenth- and fifteenth-century Italy as described in the opening chapters of *The Civilization of the Renaissance*. Even the German monarchies and duchies—Bavaria, Baden, and Württemberg, no less than Prussia—had emerged from the settlement of 1815 as states organized on different lines from those of the ancien régime. They no longer rested on historical tradition but on modern principles of administrative rationality and efficiency. It would have been surprising indeed if Burckhardt's readers had not glimpsed parallels as well as differences between the new world described by the historian at the beginning of *The Civilization of the Renaissance* and their own.[127]

If Burckhardt's history suggests a comparison of the situation of early Renaissance Italy and that of Europe as a whole in the nineteenth century, it may not be entirely fanciful to discern at least the hint of a parallel between the Florentine historians of the sixteenth century and their nineteenth-century counterpart. At the end of part III, chapter 8 of *The Civilization of the Renaissance*, Burckhardt remarked that, unlike their humanist contemporaries Pietro Bembo and Paolo Giovio, the Florentines wrote not in Latin but in Italian, and that they did so

> not only because they could not vie with the Ciceronian elegance of the philologists, but because, like Machiavelli, they could record only in a living tongue the living results of their own immediate observations—and we may add in the case of Machiavelli of his observations of the past—and because, as in the case of Guicciardini, Varchi, and many others, what they most desired was that their view of the course of events should have as wide and deep a practical effect as possible. . . . They were not humanists, but they had passed through the school of humanism, and they have in them more of the spirit of the ancient historians than most of the imitators of Livy. Like the Ancients, they were citizens who wrote for citizens.[128]

It does not take a special lens to perceive in these observations a reflection of Burckhardt's image of his place among the historians of *his* time. As Niccolo Machiavelli and Francesco Vettori, citizens of Florence, were not humanists but had more of the spirit of the ancient historians in them than the philologists, even when, like Vettori, they wrote "only for a few friends" or, like Machiavelli himself, "not . . . for the public, but either for princes and administrators or for personal friends,"[129] Burckhardt, the citizen of Basel, thought of himself as writing a more meaningful and usable history—a history by citizens for citizens—than the ponderous volumes of the German scholar-bureaucrats of his day, even when he presented his work only in the form of lectures to his students or fellow citizens at Basel. His devastating comment on the *viri eruditissimi*, as he liked to call the philologists, is well known. "In front of them a mountain of history; they dig a hole in it, create a pile of rubble and rubbish behind themselves, and die."[130]

Above all, the deeply ironic central theme of *The Civilization of the Renais-*

sance is one that Burckhardt believed to be of great relevance to his own time. According to Burckhardt, the simultaneous development of the modern individual and the modern state in fourteenth- and fifteenth-century Italy, of personal ambition and an enormously heightened subjectivity, and of a completely objective, rational, and desacralized view of the world of nature and politics ultimately turns back upon itself and undermines both the integrity of the individual as a moral being and the foundations (in tradition, religion, community feeling) of the state and of social order. It is possible to overlook this story. The emphasis commonly placed on the synchronic aspect of Burckhardt's cultural history—the evocation of all the interlocking aspects of a culture—has sometimes led to underestimation of the importance of the dynamic aspect. But *The Civilization of the Renaissance* does have an important story to tell as well as a picture to draw. Writing of the later *Cultural History of Greece*, Karl Joachim Weintraub noted Burckhardt's "methodological difficulties . . . : how can one obtain a valid view of the typically Greek and how then can one present this both with structural coherence and in chronological sequence as a changing thing? Burckhardt knew these difficulties. In each of his great books he lamented the need to take apart what ought to be presented as a continuum. Each time he tried to present the historical, the developing dimension, within the generalized panorama of the cultural conditions."[131] If the panorama of cultural conditions might seem to encourage detached aesthetic contemplation, the "developing dimension" of *The Civilization of the Renaissance* brought its problems directly into the reader's present.[132]

The historical argument of Burckhardt's history is fairly well known and can be briefly summarized. Its general outlines are not entirely new. The rise of modern individualism and the modern state, and the concomitant loosening of traditional community bonds, had been a major theme of the reflections that the experience of the French Revolution and the empire inspired in Benjamin Constant, a fellow Swiss, in 1813. It is true that Constant's work is written in the abstract, universal language of political theory, not in the colorful and concrete language of the historian, and that his view of the development he described was on the whole more positive and optimistic than Burckhardt's, though not without a strong elegiac note. Still anchored in the preindustrial era, the modern individual evoked by Constant was recognizably the relatively restrained and well-educated private citizen of the Enlightenment, the sober, often quite pious merchant entrepreneur of Holland or Switzerland. By the time of Burckhardt's *Civilization of the Renaissance,* however, the modern world that had emerged out of the French Revolution was no longer that of Constant's *De l'Esprit de conquête et de l'usurpation.* Already the outlines of a far more dynamic and disturbing world were clearly visible—a world of powerful, rationally organized states emancipated from nearly all ties to tradition and of Promethean captains of industry (the coming Carnegies and Krupps), a world in which all human values would be subordinated to the goals of power and profit by means of an almost military industrial discipline. This is the amoral world announced by the state as *Kunstwerk* and the *Gewaltmenschen* of Burckhardt's Italian Renaissance.

The disintegration in fourteenth-century Italy of the "common veil . . . woven of faith, illusion, and childish prepossession" beneath which, in the Middle Ages, "both sides of human consciousness—that which was turned within as that which was turned without—lay dreaming or half awake"[133] resulted, Burckhardt argued, in a radically realistic view of politics, in which states depended for their existence on themselves alone and were scientifically organized to that end,[134] and in "unbridled egoism" in the individual. The latter felt himself "inwardly emancipated from the control of the state and its police, whose title to respect was illegitimate and itself based on violence."[135] The foundation of the political system "was and remained illegitimate," in Burckhardt's words—that is to say, it lacked any transcendental legitimation—"and nothing could remove the curse which rested upon it."[136]

International politics became as realistic as internal politics. "The purely objective treatment of international affairs, as free from prejudice as from moral scruples, attained a perfection which sometimes is not without a certain beauty and grandeur of its own. But as a whole, it gives us the impression of a bottomless abyss."[137] Just as nominally Christian states might now form "alliances with the Turks . . . with little scruple or disguise," since "they were reckoned no worse than other political expedients,"[138] individuals who no longer found their identities as members of a "race, people, party, family, or corporation"[139] pursued their own personal ends, unencumbered by the restraints of tradition or religion. "The enjoyment of intellectual and artistic pleasures, the comforts and elegancies of life, and the supreme interest of self-development, destroyed or hampered the love of country."[140] In the same way, "each individual in Italy went his own way, and thousands wandered on the sea of life without any religious guidance whatever. . . . It is probable that most of them wavered inwardly between incredulity and a remnant of the faith in which they were brought up."[141]

The balance sheet of this massive transformation, as Burckhardt saw it, is mixed. In the credit column: greater freedom, tolerance, ambition, and energy; the unrestricted development of human capacities; a more cosmopolitan, less narrowly local and prejudiced outlook; the achievement of a detached, scientific point of view and of a new kind of "modern enjoyment";[142] an explosion of artistic and literary talent and creation; the invention of manners and a new sociability; and a more open, meritocratic society, in which the barriers between nobles and burghers ceased to exist, "birth and origin were without influence, unless combined with leisure and inherited wealth," nobility was identified, as in Dante's *Convivio*, with the "capacity for moral and intellectual eminence," and, in the exaggerated but pithy phrase of the humanist Pope Aeneas Silvius, "a servant can easily become a king."[143] In the debit column: unbridled egoism, violence, and cruelty; the beginnings of a portentous separation of elite and popular culture,[144] and of a new, brilliant and corrupting kind of literature, aimed at instant effect and success, an incipient journalism;[145] and, most important, the undermining of the individual and the state by their very success.

In a passage that recalls Montesquieu's view of honor as the substitute for virtue in men after they have ceased to be citizens and patriots, Burckhardt argued that the only remaining "bulwark against evil"[146] was the sense of honor. "All the noble elements that are left in the wreck of a character may gather round it, and from this fountain may draw new strength." Because it is "compatible with much selfishness and great vices," honor "often survives in modern man after he has lost . . . faith, hope and charity." This is no less true in the nineteenth century than it was in the fifteenth, Burckhardt suggested, and in this respect as in so much else the modern age is heir to the Renaissance. The sense of honor "has become, in a far wider sense than is commonly believed, a decisive test of conduct in the minds of the cultivated Europeans of our own day, and many of those who yet hold faithfully by religion and morality are unconsciously guided by this feeling in the gravest decisions of their lives."[147] What saves the individual from dissolving into a mere agent of his desires and protects society from sinking into lawlessness is thus not authentic moral conviction but a concern for public reputation that is itself by no means unselfish.

Burckhardt was here characteristically and uncompromisingly un-idealistic. The admirer of Machiavelli—for centuries anathema to the *bien pensants* on account of his undisguised realism—belongs in the disabused and hard-headed company of his great contemporaries: Feuerbach, Marx, and Nietzsche. "It would indeed be better and nobler," he declared, if conscience rather than honor were the force motivating us; "but, since it must be granted that even our worthier resolutions result from 'a conscience more or less dimmed by selfishness,' it is better to call the mixture by its right name."[148] In the figure of the giant Margutte, in Pulci's parody of romance, the *Morgante Maggiore*, Burckhardt saw the larger-than-life image of modern Renaissance man: "Disregarding each and every religion," Margutte "jovially confesses to every form of vice and sensuality, and reserves to himself only the merit of never having broken faith." He presents "in grotesque proportions the figure of an untamed egoism, insensible to all established rule, and yet with a remnant of honorable feeling left."[149]

If throwing off the "illusory" constraints of tradition or established rule and pursuing the goals of "unbridled egoism" with calculated efficiency—substituting *Zweckrationalität* for traditional or transcendental norms—threatens the modern individual with shipwreck, the scientific pursuit by the state of its equally selfish goals of conquest and aggrandizement sets in motion a process that results in the end in the destruction of the state. *Ragione di stato* is a policy with no long-term winners. "It was understood too late [in Italy] that France and Spain, the two chief invaders, had become great European powers, that they would no longer be satisfied with verbal homage, but would fight to the death for influence and territory in Italy," Burckhardt wrote. In fact, "they had come to resemble the centralized Italian states, and, indeed, to copy them, *only on a gigantic scale.*"[150]

The process of disintegration accompanying the extraordinary development and autonomization of both the individual and the state was thus already clearly visible in Renaissance Italy. Then, however, it was amply compensated by an enormous release of fresh energy and cultural creativity and by the exhilaration of emancipation and discovery. In the nineteenth century, in contrast—and Burckhardt invites the reader to make the comparison—genuine individuality is on the wane, having succumbed to the very rationalization of all aspects of existence that Renaissance individualism itself initiated; and a prudish veil of hypocrisy has been thrown over the blemishes of reality. One of the chief features of the Renaissance in Italy, the candor with which men pursued their desires—"The Italians of the fourteenth century," we are told, "knew little of false modesty or of hypocrisy in any shape; not one of them was afraid of singularity, of being and seeming unlike his neighbors"[151]—has been drastically reduced in the age of Blood and Iron. Several passages containing an explicit critique of his own age in Burckhardt's history suggest strongly that the entire work—as Norbrook proposed—is not simply a scholarly portrayal of a moment in the past but also a not too veiled critique of the civilization of the nineteenth century. The Revolution that inaugurated the nineteenth century was carried out in the name of individual freedom and was supposed to release men from what was left of traditional beliefs and from the restraints of discipline and coercion which the post-Renaissance secular states had imposed in order to restore social order. In fact, it only created the conditions for a further reduction of the scope of individual freedom and self-cultivation. There is an implied contrast in Burckhardt's history between the relative independence of the merchant entrepreneurs and artisans of Renaissance Italy (or of Basel in the seventeenth, eighteenth and early nineteenth centuries), who were still able to use rational methods for their own ends—"Favorable economic conditions. Profitable industry in many places. But no proletariat," Burckhardt had written pointedly of Renaissance Florence in his lecture notes for a course on "Architecture of the Renaissance" at the Federal Polytechnic in Zurich in 1856–1867[152]—and the growing subordination of the leaders of industry and the uprooted, faceless proletariats of the later, industrial stage of capitalism to the iron laws of an ever more competitive market and of mass production in factories. Burckhardt's view coincides with that of Tocqueville, whose work he knew and admired. The growing influence of the "masses" was detrimental to genuine individualism and fostered uniformity, while at the same time—as Burckhardt had had occasion to observe among the merchants even of still relatively idiosyncratic Basel—commercial success now demanded iron discipline, strict and single-minded dedication, and the subordination or sacrifice of all other human interests and activities to the needs of business.

The Renaissance Italian "shrank from no dissimulation in order to attain his ends, but was wholly free from hypocrisy in matters of principle," Burckhardt noted.[153] Unlike the man of the nineteenth century, in other words, he had not lost the independence of mind needed to recognize the truth or permitted his spirit to be invaded and dominated by social convention. A generous portrait of Machiavelli contains the pointed observation that "virtuous indignation at [Machiavelli's] expense is thrown away upon us who have seen in what sense political morality is understood by the statesmen of our own century."[154] In a chapter on Renaissance champions of humanism, the official nineteenth-century reverence for "culture," for classical culture in particular, is contrasted with the "enthusiastic devotion to [antiquity], the recognition that the need of it is the first and greatest of all needs," found among Florentines of the fifteenth and the early sixteenth centuries.[155] Here, as in the passage on the writing of history referred to earlier, Burckhardt might well have also had in mind the difference between the academic study of classical antiquity, which in Germany functioned as a kind of state-sponsored religion of culture, and the lively personal enthusiasm that moved individual *dilettanti*—the word he used of the Florentines—such as his colleague Johann Jacob Bachofen, in Basel. It is a far cry, Burckhardt maintains, from the keen epicurean worldliness, the materialism, the eager grasping after sensation and possession of the Renaissance, to the ingrained, uninspired worldliness of his own time, which never dares to avow itself but drapes itself prudishly in noble seriousness. "The worldliness, through which the Renaissance seems to offer so striking a contrast to the Middle Ages, owed its first origin to the flood of new thoughts, purposes, and views which transformed the medieval conception of nature and man. This spirit is not in itself more hostile to religion than that 'culture' which now holds its place, but which can give us only a feeble notion of the universal ferment which the discovery of a new world of greatness then called forth. This worldliness was not frivolous, but earnest, and was ennobled by art and poetry."[156]

The great portrait of the Florentine "merchant and statesman" (the two functions were combined in Florence, as in Basel) and of his relation to the world of culture in part II, chapter 2 of *The Civilization of the Renaissance* demonstrates how Burckhardt's study of the Renaissance often functions indirectly as a critique of his own time. The historian's fellow citizens could easily have read into this portrait an allusion and a discreet compliment to the Basel patriciate, whose traditions and way of life the historian had known in his youth and compared favorably with the values and way of life of the ruling classes of the great modern European states. At the same time, they might also have reflected that they were themselves pale shadows of those lively predecessors. The politics of the citizen of old Basel come together here with the scholarship of the historian of Renaissance Florence to create an elegiac portrait, the effect of which is to underline how much poorer and more narrow modern man has become under the unavoidable pressures of utilitarianism and specialization.

> The Florentine merchant and statesman was often learned in both the classical languages; the most famous humanists read the ethics and politics of Aristotle to him and his sons; even the daughters of the house were highly educated. It is in these circles that private education was first treated seriously. The humanist, on his side, was compelled to the most varied attainments, since his philological learning was not limited, as it now is, to the theoretical knowledge of classical antiquity, but had to serve the practical needs of daily life. While studying Pliny, he made collections of natural history, the geography of the Ancients was his guide in treating of modern geography, their history was his pattern in writing contemporary chronicles, even when composed in Italian; . . . and besides all this he acted as magistrate, secretary, and diplomatist.[157]

To the somewhat depressing view of historical development presented in *The Civilization of the Renaissance in Italy*, Burckhardt responded with neither optimism nor pessimism but a kind of serene stoicism. There is no going back; this history must run its course. Moreover, if what is looming on the horizon of the nineteenth century—"socialism" and the end of individual culture—cannot be considered desirable, no modern individual could possibly wish to return to the Middle Ages either. And the civilization of the Renaissance itself, with all its brilliance, was marked by unbridled greed and cruelty. No age, in other words, is without its drawbacks. There are no historical utopias. As Gooch noted, Burckhardt always presented a nuanced and complex picture of the past and was careful to point up the darker sides even of the cultures most admired in his own time, such as that of ancient Greece.[158] Since human beings cannot escape from history and few can affect it, the only wise course is to try to achieve serenity and avoid despair by seeking to understand it, while at the same time doing what one can to preserve whatever one believes to be of enduring value.

In the case of the Renaissance, Burckhardt himself declared, it was not so much the historical reality that he admired as the art it produced, for almost no other age had succeeded so well in elevating the real to the ideal and redeeming through artistic representation the inevitably flawed reality of temporal and historical experience. Still, the example of the Renaissance indicated that some historical conditions might be more favorable than others to the production of what Burckhardt considered the greatest art. Much as Raphael is admired in *The Cicerone,* published only a few years earlier, for combining the real and the ideal in his painting, Florence is admired in *The Civilization of the Renaissance* because, as a polis, it reconciled the real and the ideal, economic success and artistic achievement, better than any other of the Italian states. In the same way, Italy is considered fortunate in that the division between popular and elite culture, which Burckhardt argued was one of the consequences of the Renaissance, was less severe there than elsewhere. "The most artistic of her poets, Tasso, is in the hands of even the poorest."[159] The division between townspeople and country folk was also "far from being so marked here as in northern countries." Class differences and hostilities were likewise more muted. "Nowhere do we find a trace of that brutal and contemptuous class-hatred against the *vilains* which inspired the aristocratic poets of Provence, and often too, the French chroniclers. On the contrary, Italian authors of every sort gladly recognize and accentuate what is great or remarkable in the life of the peasant."[160] As he wrote those lines, might not Burckhardt have had somewhere in mind the patriarchal ideal of old Basel before the bitter civil war that culminated in the *Kantonstrennung* of 1833?

In general, Burckhardt's countrymen would have had no difficulty in recognizing many passages where the experience and perspective of the nineteenth-century Baseler had informed his picture of Renaissance Italy. The portrait of the Florentine merchant has already been alluded to. There are other points of resemblance between the Italian cities of the Renaissance and the old humanist city on the Rhine. Most notable, of course, the fact that the leading citizens of Renaissance Italy were mostly not defined by their birth, according to Burckhardt. The Italian ruling class, like the Basel patriciate, was a meritocracy of wealth and culture. It embraced old nobility that had gotten rich in business and new men who had risen in society through their wealth and culture. "In Venice the *nobili*, the ruling caste, were all merchants. Similarly in Genoa the nobles and non-nobles were alike merchants and sailors, and separated only by their birth. . . . In Florence a part of the old noblity had devoted themselves to trade. . . . The decisive fact was that nearly everywhere in Italy even those who might be disposed to pride themselves on their birth could not make good their claims against the power of culture and of wealth." Burckhardt recorded admiringly a "good old Florentine custom, by which fathers left property to their children on the condition that they should have some occupation."[161]

In addition, various minor features of the life of the Renaissance Italian, as Burckhardt depicted it, recall features of the life of Basel. With obvious pleasure Burckhardt evokes the country villas to which the well-to-do Italian citizen repaired to seek peace, happiness, and respite from the activities of the city. In the villas around Florence, "as in those on the Brenta, on the Lombard hills, at Posilippo, and on the Vomero," wrote the historian, who had tasted every summer for many years the pleasures of his uncle's estate in the Basel countryside at Mayenfels, "social life assumed a freer and more rural character than in the palaces within the city. We meet with charming descriptions of the intercourse of the guests, the hunting parties, and all the open-air pursuits and amusements."[162] The position of women in Renaissance Italy, as described in *The Civilization of the Renaissance,* may also contain an oblique reference to Burckhardt's native city. The historian had good reason to appreciate the commitment of the Basel patricians to the education of their wives and daughters: his own mother had been a highly cultivated woman and women had made up a significant part of the audiences for his public art history courses in the 1840s. Bachofen's wife, herself a Burckhardt, had been a good enough Greek scholar to coach her sons in the language. In Renaissance Italy, the historian noted, the citizen "felt no scruple in putting sons and daughters alike under the same course of literary and even philological instruction. Indeed, looking at this ancient culture as the chief treasure of life, he was glad that his girls should have a share in it." As a result, the individuality of women in the upper classes was developed no less than that of men. At the same time—and here we can discern the accents of the conservative nineteenth-century Basel patrician—the development of individuality did not imply that all individuals were equal. "There was no question of 'women's rights' or female emancipation," since the high standing of women made this unnecessary, according to Burckhardt. Likewise, though "the same intellectual and emotional development that perfected the man was demanded for the perfection of the woman," she was not expected to be active in literary production herself. "These women had no thought of the public: their function was to influence distinguished men and to moderate male impulse and caprice."[163] Burckhardt even attributed to the inhabitants of Renaissance Florence something of the malice and denigrating wit widely attributed to the inhabitants of Basel. "'Sharp eyes and bad tongues' is the description given of the [Florentines]. An easy-going contempt of everything and everybody was probably the prevailing tone of society."[164]

Some of the problems that beset the Renaissance cities might also have reminded Burckhardt's Basel readers of problems confronting their own city. "The keynote of the Venetian character," we are told, for instance, "was a spirit of proud and contemptuous isolation, which joined to the hatred felt for the city by the other states of Italy, gave rise to a strong sense of solidarity within."[165] A fair number of readers are quite likely to have heard in those lines an echo of the experience of nineteenth-century Basel in the years following the *Wirren* and the *Kantonstrennung.* And in the report of Dante's comparison of Florence, "which was always mending its Constitution, with the sick man who is continually changing his posture to escape from pain," Burckhardt could hardly have expected that his readers would not find an implicit allusion to that spirit of *"ewige Revision"* that he considered characteristic of postrevolutionary Europe in general and of postrevolutionary Basel in particular. Both he and Bachofen commented acidly, as we saw, on the revisions of the Basel Constitution. Burckhardt's judgment of Florence mirrors perfectly his judgment of his native city: "The great modern fallacy that a constitution can be made, can be manufactured by a combination of existing forces and tendencies, was constantly crop-ping up in stormy times; even Machiavelli is not wholly free from it. Constitu-tional artists were never wanting who by an ingenious distribution and division of political power, by indirect elections of the most complicated kind . . . sought to found a lasting order of things, and to satisfy or to deceive the rich and the poor alike."[166]

Even Burckhardt's notorious remark that "political impotence does not hin-der the different tendencies and manifestations of private life from thriving in the fullest vigor and variety" and that the "cessation" of political life in the des-potisms of the fourteenth century in fact furnished the necessary leisure for the growth of individual thought[167]—a remark that challenged liberal pieties about the intimate and necessary relation between culture and political freedom—has an obvious reference both to his own situation as a member of one of Basel's patrician families in the age of democratic revolution and to the situation of his native city itself in its vulnerable *Dreiländereck.*[168]

If Burckhardt's account of Renaissance Italy reflects many of the concerns of his own time and his own society, there is, equally, an autobiographical element in some of his portraits of individual writers and thinkers of the Italian Renais-sance. In the Florentine historians—Dante, Machiavelli, Vittorino da Feltre, Fra Urbano Valeriano of Belluno, Cardano, Luigi Cornaro—the citizen-historian of nineteenth-century Basel appears to have discerned various *Verpup-pungen* of himself. There can be little doubt that fragments of a self-portrait lie scattered throughout the historian's text or that the scholars of the Italian Renaissance were models after which Burckhardt tried to shape his own life and character.

Burckhardt's own complex relation to his native city is reflected in the close relation that bound Dante, "matured alike by home and by exile," to Florence. Dante's contempt for political trimmers was fully shared by Burckhardt; like-wise, his passionate local patriotism was combined, like Burckhardt's, with a broad cosmopolitan and human vision.[169] The realism and matter-of-factness, the avoidance of pathos and sentimentality, and the passion for truth that the historian admired in Machiavelli are characteristics he tried to impart to his own work. "He seeks to mislead neither himself nor others. No man could be more free from vanity or ostentation; indeed, he does not write for the public, but either for princes and administrators or for personal friends. . . . The objec-tivity of his political judgment is sometimes appalling in its sincerity."[170] The praise of Vittorino da Feltre for his learning, his good humor, his contempt for worldly titles and other "outward distinctions," the friendship he cultivated with "teachers, companions, and pupils," the moderation with which he lived, "so that till his old age he was never ill," and his pedagogical principle of "giving each pupil that sort of learning which he was most fitted to receive"[171] recalls the praise Burckhardt lavished on his old Italian teacher, Luigi Picchioni, and

probably indicates the qualities for which he wanted to be known himself. Fra
Urbano Valeriano is another "type of the happy scholar." A tireless traveler
through many lands, he "never had a penny of his own, rejected all honors and
distinctions, and after a gay old age, died in his eighty-fourth year, without, if
we except a fall from a ladder, having ever known an hour of sickness."[172]
Burckhardt admired Picchioni for never having allowed himself to become embittered by his repeated political disappointments. Likewise he praised Cardano for the simple courage and liberating gaiety with which he looked truth
in the face—he brought to his own self-portrait, we are told, "the same simple
and sincere love of fact which guided him in his scientific researches"—while
never allowing himself to lose his curiosity or his capacity for enjoying life.
"What to us is the most repulsive of all," Burckhardt noted ironically, "the old
man, after the most shocking experiences and with his confidence in his fellow
men gone, finds himself after all tolerably happy and comfortable." He counts
his blessings and "after this, he counts the teeth in his head, and finds that
he has fifteen."[173] From his letters and from the testimony of his friends and
acquaintances, it is certain that such serenity and even gaiety in the face of a
vision of the world devoid of illusion was Burckhardt's own goal, as it was to be
in remarkable degree his achievement.

Burckhardt was only a little over forty when he wrote *The Civilization of the
Renaissance in Italy*. But the portrait of Luigi Cornaro, author of the "famous
treatise *On the Sober Life*," anticipates in an almost uncanny manner the celebrated scholar of twenty-five years later. Burckhardt not only discovered himself in many of the Italian Renaissance figures he portrayed in his book, he
appears to have modeled himself on them in true humanist style. The "philosopher of practical life," we are told, invited those who despise life after the age
of sixty-five (that is, after the exhaustion of illusions) as a living death, to consider how he, at the age of eighty-three, continues to find delight in it. Cornaro
is quoted at unusual length:

> Let them come and see, and wonder at my good health, how I mount on horse-
> back without help, how I run upstairs and up hills, how cheerful, amusing, and
> contented I am, how free from care and disagreeable thoughts. Peace and joy
> never quit me. . . . My friends are wise, learned, and distinguished people of
> good position, and when they are not with me I read and write, and try thereby,
> as by all other means, to be useful to others. Each of these things I do at the
> proper time, and at my ease, in my dwelling, which is beautiful and lies in the
> best part of Padua, and is arranged both for summer and winter with all the
> resources of architecture, and provided with a garden by the running water. . . .
> In the spring and autumn I also visit the neighboring towns, to see and con-
> verse with my friends, through whom I make the acquaintance of other distin-
> guished men, architects, painters, sculptors, musicians, and cultivators of the
> soil. I see what new things they have done, I look again at what I know already,
> and learn much that is of use to me. I see palaces, gardens, antiquities, public

grounds, churches, and fortifications. But what most of all delights me when I travel is the beauty of the country and the cities, lying now on the plain, now on the slopes of the hills, or on the banks of rivers and streams, surrounded by gardens and villas. And these enjoyments are not diminished through weakness of the eyes or the ears; all my senses (thank God) are in the best condition, including the sense of taste; for I enjoy more the simple food which I now take in moderation than all the delicacies which I ate in my years of disorder.[174]

12

"Not Narrative, but Historical"
The Cultural History of Greece

If *The Civilization of the Renaissance in Italy* is the best known of Burckhardt's works in English and is still widely read after almost a century and a half, *The Cultural History of Greece* is virtually unknown and unread in Britain and the United States. This may be partly due to the fact that, until quite recently, the only English translation, published in 1963, was even more incomplete than the abridged German edition on which it was based and also contains many errors.[1] It did not include either the important programmatic Introduction or the founding initial section on myth; the sections on religion and the diachronic account of the different moments of Greek culture, which makes up Section 9, were also dropped.[2] Moreover, Burckhardt shared many ideas about the ancient world with Nietzsche and it was through *The Birth of Tragedy* that these reached the English-speaking public and with Nietzsche that they are now chiefly associated. As a result, Burckhardt's *Cultural History of Greece* is rarely commented on or referred to—or perhaps read—even by English and French classical scholars.[3] For that reason this powerful and provocative work of scholarship will be presented here in rather greater detail than Burckhardt's more familiar writings.

About the time he completed the manuscript of *The Civilization of the Renaissance* Burckhardt paid a visit to London, partly to see the Elgin Marbles at the British Museum. A year later, some time in 1861–1862, he and a colleague in classics at Basel, Otto Ribbeck, talked of working together on a history of Greek culture. But after little more than a year at the University of Basel, Ribbeck left for Kiel and the plan hatched by the two men over a beer or a glass of wine at a pub opposite the Baden Train Station in Basel came to nothing. Burckhardt himself dismissed it humorously—"an idea *inter pocula*," he remarked.[4]

Nevertheless, the thought of a course or even a book on the history of Greek culture did not go away. Burckhardt had had something of the kind in mind for many years. In the outline of a projected series of inexpensive books on cultural history drawn up in the late 1840s, one volume, it will be recalled, was to have been devoted to the Age of Pericles, and in 1847 he wrote to *"herzliebster Ete"* (Eduard Schauenburg) from Berlin that he was going back to the Greeks, Homer, and the tragedians: "Now for the first time the road leads *con amore* to antiquity."[5]

The idea of a course or a book on Greek cultural history seems to have been resurrected after the Austro-Prussian War of 1866, that is to say, around the time that Burckhardt began to develop the reflections on history, and on the history of Europe in particular, that culminated in the celebrated lecture course published posthumously as *Weltgeschichtliche Betrachtungen* (*Reflections on History*, 1943). To get some perspective on the tumultuous course of recent events, he told his nephew Jacob Oeri in 1867, he had plunged into ancient history. "At my age," he explained with his usual humor, "you have to swing into a new saddle from time to time, if you are not to stand stock still."[6] *Reflections on History* and *The Cultural History of Greece,* Burckhardt's learned biographer Werner Kaegi has argued, are equally products of the five years from 1867 to 1872, when the two wars were fought that Burckhardt saw as harbingers of catastrophes to come—the Austro-Prussian War and the Franco-Prussian War. Burckhardt himself declared in a manuscript note that the first plan for *The Cultural History of Greece* was drawn up on the first day of the year 1870.[7] The central themes of the work, as we shall see, are in fact those that deeply concerned the historian at this time: the relative merits of confederations of small states and of larger, centralized states; the relation between individual freedom and state power and, in particular, between liberty and democracy; the effect on culture of unrestrained power struggles among rival states and of democratic resentment of elites within them; and democracy as a breeding-ground of demagogy, chauvinism, and war. At the same time, the Introduction contains Burckhardt's most programmatic statement about the nature and aims of cultural history.

Comparisons of the Swiss cantons with the Greek poleis had for some time been a topos both of the historiography of Switzerland (in the work of Johannes von Müller, for instance)[8] and of the historiography of ancient Greece, which until the mid-nineteenth century was largely a British affair, according to Arnaldo Momigliano.[9] In late 1847, in the immediate aftermath of the Sonderbund War, the latest British historian of ancient Greece, George Grote, published *Seven Letters on the Recent Politics of Switzerland.* As the twenty-two cantons present "a miniature of all Europe," he declared in the Preface, being extremely various with respect to "race, language, religion, civilization, wealth, habits, etc." and "exhibiting the fifteenth century in immediate juxtaposition with the nineteenth," they are "interesting, on every ground, to the general intelligent public of Europe." To him in particular, however, they presented "an additional ground of interest, from a certain political analogy (nowhere else to be found in Europe) with those who preeminently occupy my thoughts, and on the history of whom I am still engaged—the ancient Greeks."[10] Grote thus drew parallels among three situations: the Greek poleis of antiquity, the Swiss cantons or republics, and the modern European states. His *Letters* went through several editions and were known in Basel. It is unlikely that Burckhardt was not aware of them.

Several decades later, and only a few years before Burckhardt got down to thinking seriously about a course or book on the cultural history of Greece, another eminent English historian, Edward Freeman, brought out the first volume of his *History of Federal Government* (1863), which was to have spanned the entire period from the Achaean League to the Civil War in the United States. Though only the first volume, on ancient Greece, was ever published, Freeman's work did not pass unnoticed in Basel. It received a sympathetic and detailed review in the *Schweizerisches Museum* from Wilhelm Vischer-Bilfinger, Burckhardt's colleague in the chair of Greek at the University and former teacher. Vischer noted that Freeman had recently visited Switzerland to study those cantons where direct democracy was still practiced and that his next volume was expected to cover the Swiss Confederation and the various German Leagues of the late Middle Ages. The first volume of Freeman's work, Vischer wrote, "takes a decidedly contradictory stand in relation to a number of recent German publications, in which the unification movement of the German peoples has too often clouded clear and unprejudiced historical vision by making the unique goal of the state appear to be the development of its external power and by overlooking the infinitely rich cultural life that small states, and in the first instance the small city-states of Greece, have been able to promote."[11] Vischer made no secret of the German scholars he had in mind: he named specifically Theodor Mommsen with his "idolatry of pure power" and Gustav Droysen with his excessive partiality for Macedonia—the Prussia of antiquity, according to Droysen himself. Immediately after the publication of his *History of Hellenism* in 1843 Droysen had in fact turned his attention to the history of Prussia, so that by the time Vischer wrote his review he had already established himself as the highest authority on the subject.[12] No one mistook the drift of Droysen's historical argument. It had already been obvious in his enormously successful biography of Alexander the Great (1833), which, we are told, was to be found on every German middle-class bookshelf: "Macedonia was Prussia, Greece Germany, Asia Europe."[13]

The context of Droysen's historical work, of the historical analogy between Prussia and Macedonia, and of the entire discussion of the relative merits of small states and large states was an ongoing reflection among German scholars in particular, in the wake of Napoleon's defeat of Prussia and Austria in the first decade of the nineteenth century, on the relation between the enduring German *Kulturvolk* as defined by the romantics and its shifting political organization. When Francis II was compelled to abdicate as Holy Roman Emperor and assume the title of Emperor Francis I of Austria, even the shadowy form of the old Empire ceased to provide a minimal unifying political form for the German *Kulturvolk*. "I feel as I do, when an old friend is very sick, the doctors have given up on him, we know he is going to die and yet we are shattered when the letter finally comes announcing his death," Goethe's mother wrote to her son on hearing the news in the old imperial city of Frankfurt in August 1806. "Die Deutschen sind kein Volck keine Nation mehr und damit punctum" ("The Germans have ceased to be a people, a nation, and that's the end of it"), she had noted matter-of-factly as early as 1798.[14] Not everybody had taken matters so lightly, however. More and more it was argued, even by those who started out from Herder's vision of the nation as a cultural entity rather than a political one, that in order to protect itself against conquerors like Napoleon and to be free to develop all its potential, the German *Kulturvolk* needed a strong political state—a "center," as Jules Michelet said, when he contrasted France, which had one in his view, with Germany and Italy which did not.[15] The political state was thus the fulfillment, from that perspective, of the cultural nation. It marked the transformation of a natural community into a moral one according to Bachofen who, like Burckhardt, had been a student of Ranke's in Berlin. Burckhardt himself had not been hostile in his youth to the search for a new political form for Germany. But by the 1840s he had become convinced that nationalism was a revolutionary force more likely to destroy the varied yet closely interrelated cultures of "old Europe" than to preserve them. Wilhelm von Humboldt's warnings about state power and in particular about the creation of a new German national state have already been referred to in chapter 11.

Freeman's book thus addressed questions that were of great concern both to German-speaking Swiss as members of the German *Kulturvolk* and to Baselers as citizens of an old city-republic within an increasingly centralized Swiss federal state. It is by no means surprising that it was reviewed attentively by Vischer. The professor of Greek had been meditating on its central topic for years. As early as 1849, when it fell to him to give the public lecture to the students and their parents that was a regular feature of the opening exercises at the *Pädagogium,* he had chosen as his topic the question of centralization and federation in the construction of the ancient polis—a topic that was obviously of more than antiquarian interest to a Swiss audience only two years after the Sonderbund War.[16] Equally, the relation between *Stadt* and *Land* in the state or polis—the core of the lecture concerned the relation of the Greek city-state to the simpler communities or *demoi* out of which it had been forged—must have struck a chord in an audience of Basel parents, many of whom could well have participated in the painful events of 1830–1833.

Vischer distinguished between two models of the ancient polis: on the one hand, a centralized model, characterized in the case of Athens by the complete identification of the polis and the erstwhile inhabitants of the communities or *demoi,* and in the case of Sparta by the dominion of a conquering and invading core group (in Sparta's case, the Dorians) over the erstwhile indigenous communities; and, on the other hand, a confederate model, characterized by a fairly loose association of the communities, as in the Aetolian and Achaean Leagues. As evenhandedly as possible he evaluated the advantages and disadvantages of the various political structures he had described—a centralized city-state in which all citizens were equal and which tended toward democracy; a centralized city state with a hierarchy of full citizens, *perioikoi,* and helots, which tended toward aristocracy; and a confederation constituted by the free banding together of autonomous communities. While acknowledging that the ancient Greeks never succeeded in developing a viable and lasting constitution for a confederate state and that the centralized states had also proved incapable of uniting to form a single national state, Vischer emphasized at the close of his lecture that "if, on the one hand, the particularism of the Greek people presents a sorry picture, we ought not to forget, on the other, that out of that very particularist spirit grew the infinitely varied life which flowered in glorious achievements of art and thought that will be objects of admiration for all ages and that fully make up for the political shortcomings of the state."[17] Burckhardt almost certainly knew of this lecture by his colleague and former teacher, since it had been published immediately in Basel, and in any case he could not have been ignorant of Vischer's ideas about the ancient polis or of their connection in his colleague's mind with the politics of Basel, Switzerland, and Germany.

The Cultural History of Greece is in fact deeply marked by Burckhardt's experience as a citizen of Basel and by the characteristic Basel reflection on the relations of politics, power, and culture, the *Grossstaat* or *Machtstaat* and the *Kleinstaat.* That is not to say, however, that Burckhardt accepted without qualification the analogy between the Greek poleis and the Swiss cantons. On the contrary, his work seems to have been intended in part as an examination and, ultimately, even a rejection of that analogy in any strict sense. In general, Burckhardt's aim seems to have been to provide a more sober and realistic evaluation of the polis than those who had represented it as a model of liberty or culture. He did not dispute its great cultural achievements, as we shall see—though he argued, in a strikingly Hegelian move for a professed anti-Hegelian, that the universalization of those achievements and their integration into the general cultural heritage of mankind could occur only as a consequence of the *political* ruin of the polis and the transformation of its citizens into *Bildungsmenschen* or men of culture—but he persistently emphasized the price in terms of individual happiness that had had to be paid for those achievements. Similarly, like his fellow Swiss Benjamin Constant a generation earlier, he drew a sharp distinction between ancient liberty and modern liberty. He had himself been deeply influenced as a schoolboy in Basel by the idealistic philhellenism of the German neohumanists—Wolf, Winckelmann, Schiller, and Goethe—but some time before he embarked on *The Cultural History of Greece,* he had already questioned both their vision of ancient Greece and the enthusiasm it had inspired in him as a young man. In 1859, for instance, when he delivered the memorial address on the centenary of Schiller's birth in the great hall of the new Basel Museum in the Augustinergasse, he pronounced a surprising judgment on the celebrated *Hymn to Joy* (*An die Freude*). Schiller's poem was "an intoxication . . . unable to stand up to logical examination," he declared, maliciously reminding his listeners that with all his enthusiasm for the Gods of Greece, in the well-known poem of that title, Schiller had remained primly monotheistic. The enthralling neohumanist picture of ancient Greece as a uniquely happy age of mankind, an age of beauty, harmony, and joy, he went on to argue in *The Cultural History of Greece,* was "one of the greatest historical frauds ever perpetrated."[18] In Burckhardt's mature view, there are no perfect ages in history. Since the human condition does not change, all historical situations inevitably mix good and evil, suffering and fulfillment. The historian can only point to the relative advantages and disadvantages of different situations and to the complex ways in which good and evil are interwoven.

In revising the neohumanist image of antiquity, Burckhardt was reaping the harvest of ideas already sown by some of the neohumanists themselves. For instance, in the Introduction to *The Cultural History of Greece* he quoted from a classic work of 1817 by his former teacher at Berlin, August Böckh, on the *Staatshaushaltung der Athener:* "The Ancients were unhappier than most people believe."[19] In fact, in the very first chapter of his work Böckh had articulated a position with which Burckhardt could not but have sympathized. "I took the Truth as my goal," Böckh declared, "and if we must moderate our unconditional admiration of the Ancients because it turns out that where they touched gold, their hands also got dirty, I will not regret that. Or should our accounts of the past be written only to inspire and edify the young? Should the classical scholar conceal that then, as now, everything under the sun was not perfect?"[20] Burckhardt could also have read in F. W. Riemer's *Mitteilungen* a remark of Goethe's dating to the year 1813: "The Greeks were lovers of freedom, to be sure! But each one of them only of his own. For that reason there was within every Greek a tyrant for whose development only the opportunity was wanting." That comment, which may have been inspired, in part at least, by the turn the original enthusiasm for liberty of the French revolutionaries had taken, would echo throughout Burckhardt's work, in one place almost word for word.[21]

Finally, local conditions at the University of Basel also impelled Burckhardt to offer a course on Greek cultural history. The colleagues in Latin and Greek who might have undertaken a major synthetic view of antiquity had for one reason or another failed to do so. The form in which most of them published their work was that of *Kleine Schriften,* or short articles, even though several of them (Gerlach and Vischer, for instance) were critical of the increasingly

professional and scholarly orientation of classical studies and the narrowly philological, rather than broadly humanistic and historical, turn they had taken.
Burckhardt himself later gave as one of his reasons for not publishing *The Cultural History of Greece* the destructive, nitpicking reviews he was certain it would
receive from the *viri eruditissimi*. Böckh, who still sympathized with the goals
of the early generation of neohumanists and was himself of the generation of
Hegel, had been aware of a growing problem. "The study of Greek antiquity
is still at its beginnings," he wrote in the foreword to *Die Staatshaushaltung
der Athener:*

> Large masses of material abound; most people do not know how to make use
> of them. Few topics are adequately treated because whoever wishes to treat a
> particular topic thoroughly must know the whole. An outline of the whole by
> a scholar and connoisseur, not a mere compiler, executed in a scholarly spirit,
> with breadth of vision and conceptual rigor, and not, as heretofore, simply
> thrown together in a welter of raw, unorganized data, is especially necessary in
> the present age; for the mass of classical scholars, the younger ones in particu-
> lar, are more and more inclined to pursue complacently a form of philological
> scholarship which, in itself not unworthy of respect, is nevertheless chiefly ori-
> ented toward the smallest details and is scarcely any longer a study of words,
> but rather of syllables and letters.[22]

Such an "outline of the whole, executed in a scholarly spirit," but "with
breadth of vision," is what Burckhardt believed was direly needed as part of the
curriculum at Basel and what he set out to provide. He certainly discussed it
with Nietzsche, to whom he was extremely close in these years. (Nietzsche had
arrived in Basel as a new, very young professor of Greek in 1870 and Burckhardt
had attended the public lectures on "The Future of our Educational Institutions" in which the newcomer had bravely taken on the entire German philological and scholarly establishment.) In fact, Nietzsche himself had plans for a
comprehensive work on Greek cultural history,[23] and there is a great deal of
overlap between the views expressed on the philosophy, philology, and rhetoric
of the Greeks in Nietzsche's early lectures and courses at Basel and those of
Burckhardt. But Nietzsche's effectiveness had been temporarily undermined—
or so he himself believed—by the accusation, following the publication of *The
Birth of Tragedy,* that he was philologically ignorant and unsuitable for a teaching position in a university.[24] Word of the famous negative review by Ulrich
von Wilamowitz-Moellendorff, himself then a recent doctoral graduate barely
twenty-two years old, had apparently reached Basel—Nietzsche tells of one
student who wrote to his relatives in Basel that he had decided to stay on at
Bonn instead of coming to study philology at Basel, as he had originally intended, and that he thanked God he had not enrolled in a university where
Nietzsche was a teacher[25]—for in the fall of 1872 Nietzsche found that only
two students had signed up for the course he had announced on "Greek and

Roman Rhetoric" and that of those one was a law student, the other a Germanist. "Our Winter term has begun and I have no students!" he told Richard Wagner. "Our classical philologists have stayed away. It is truly a *pudendum* [a matter of deep shame] that must be withheld from every one."[26]

Within a couple of years the affair would blow over, and enrollments in Nietzsche's courses would again be respectable. But in 1872, with Vischer ailing (he died two years later), the damage to Nietzsche's reputation affected the entire program in classical philology. Until 1872, according to Nietzsche, there had been a steady increase in the number of students in classical philology at the University, but all those gains had "been blown away" because of him, and his colleagues, including *Ratsherr* Vischer, to whom he owed his appointment, were having to experience a falling off such as they had never experienced in their entire careers. It was clear in those conditions that the broad review of Greek cultural history, which Burckhardt believed was an essential element in the curriculum, could be taught only by him. Perhaps the University authorities also had the idea that only he, with his great reputation, was capable of reviving the study of classical antiquity at Basel. When he offered his course for the first time in the winter term of 1872, the weekly four hours of class drew almost sixty students—fifty-four matriculated students (almost half the total student body at the time!) together with several gentlemen from the town. For some it meant standing room only, Burckhardt noted with satisfaction.[27]

Burckhardt taught the course at fairly regular two-year intervals for fourteen years thereafter—for the last time in the winter term of 1885–1886. He abandoned it only because he had made the decision, as of 1886, to confine his teaching to the history of art. During this entire period, he constantly revised his notes. Firsthand observation of the Parthenon Frieze in the British Museum, of the Winged Victory of Samothrace in the Louvre, and of the Pergamum altar in Berlin during visits to London, Paris, and Berlin in 1879 and 1882 are reflected in the manuscript. But even after that date, Burckhardt continued to make changes and additions—the latest in 1892, according to Felix Staehelin, an authority on Burckhardt's manuscripts.[28]

So far, we have spoken of *The Cultural History of Greece* as a lecture course. Burckhardt's plans for publication of a book on the topic were, and to some degree still are, a matter of speculation. It was suggested earlier that not long after the appearance of *The Civilization of the Renaissance in Italy* he essentially withdrew from the world of professional conferences and career-building, of books and publishing, in order to concentrate on what for him were the authentic goals of the scholarly life: the education or *Bildung* of his fellow citizens, his personal *Bildung*, and the well-being of the University of Basel. From the outset he was as coy and confusing as possible about whether he had a book in mind. "First of all, every moment of available leisure in the next two years must be devoted to my course," he wrote in the spring of 1872. "Then the thing must be offered again in the summer semester of 1874, if I am still alive and well by then. Only thereafter might it finally be ripe for definitive filling out and re-working. By that time, as Luther would say, the world will no longer be standing."[29] The course was offered in 1874, then again in 1876, and once more in 1878. In the fall of that year, Burckhardt began to toy with the idea of a trip to Greece but by the beginning of 1880 he told von Preen that he had "given up all travel plans and begun to envisage instead a major work—but one that can be done without drudgery."[30] It was around this time that he started to make a clean copy of the material for a history of Greek culture on folio sheets—the format he used for manuscripts intended for publication.[31] At the same time, however, he continued to revise his lecture notes (on quarto sheets) for the course, which was given again in the spring of 1880. A letter to the publisher Ludwig Ebner in 1880 reveals the same equivocation as in 1872: "As far as 'the history of Greek culture' is concerned, nothing is settled yet, and for reasons to do with the book itself, it would be such a risky venture for a publisher (over 1,000 pages in the format of your edition of Sybel) that I have already contemplated having it printed at my own expense. In any case not a single line of the final version has yet been written, and who knows what times are now approaching."[32]

A few months later von Preen was told that "the great literary undertaking" of which Burckhardt had spoken to him in the railway station at Karlsruhe during a visit in the previous spring, "has been begun but, after completion of 100 pages, wisely set aside, because I saw myself being led into a vast ocean."[33] Another publisher, E. A. Seemann in Leipzig, was told a similar story. "Large new ventures at my age have their questionable side. In the last few months I did begin work on something of the sort and then abandoned it when I realized that I would not be able to hold up if I were obliged to sacrifice every minute of leisure time over two full years."[34] Rumors of a new book by the author of the *Civilization of the Renaissance* and *The Cicerone* must have begun circulating among German publishers, however; for late in the summer of 1880, Burck-hardt wrote the famous publishing house of Cotta that he could not respond to their expression of interest and very much regretted that they had been misled by an idea that he had abandoned almost as soon as it had emerged.[35] Eight years later, pressed again by Seemann, he denied flatly that there was a book manuscript: "The erroneous idea that I have a completed *Cultural History of Greece* ready for publication," he wrote disingenuously, "comes from a passage in the writings of the unfortunate Herr Professor Dr. Nietzsche, who is presently resident in a psychiatric institution. He took a lecture course on that topic, which I taught several times, to be a book."[36] Evasive and even mendacious with publishers, Burckhardt confided his real ambivalence to his old friend from Berlin days, Eduard Schauenburg (still addressed in a warmly affectionate letter as *"liebster bester Ede"*): "Despite what I have said about my age, which is no protection from folly, I still live with literary projects, but I have experienced something that I had not experienced before, namely that one begins now this, now that, and then, after a time, puts it aside. One becomes careful and cautious."[37]

The facts behind all this equivocation are that Burckhardt had indeed prepared a manuscript of *The Cultural History of Greece* in the format he generally adopted for works that he intended to publish, that this manuscript runs to rather less than one-half of the manuscript of the entire course he taught between 1872 and 1886, and that physical evidence indicates he continued to work on both the projected book manuscript and on the course manuscript *after* he stopped teaching the course.[38] Further, neither the "book" manuscript of *The Cultural History of Greece* nor the manuscript of the lectures was included among the sets of lectures that he expressly instructed the executors of his will to destroy. (These included "Swiss history," "History of the Middle Ages," "History of the Fifteenth and Sixteenth Centuries," "History of the Seventeenth and Eighteenth Centuries," and "The Age of Revolution.")[39] On the contrary, Burckhardt stipulated in his will that both the lectures for the entire course and the reworking (in folio sheets), which was up to half completed, were to become the property of his nephew Jacob Oeri, a modest and conscientious classical scholar who taught at the *Gymnasium* in Basel and enjoyed the old man's confidence. He also stipulated, however, that nothing of either was to be published. Just before his death, Oeri claimed, Burckhardt relented and redefined his wishes orally as meaning only that his nephew was not to consider himself in any way *obligated* to publish the manuscripts. The work we have today was put together by Oeri from the folio manuscript already prepared by Burckhardt, the quarto lecture notes, and the notes of students in the course.

Burckhardt's hesitations and equivocations can be explained in large measure by his aversion to the world of scholarship and the literary marketplace as these had developed in the course of the nineteenth century. He knew that a book would not, in the first instance, reach or be judged by the audience for which he intended it—the lay audience made up of educated men and women, chiefly of the better classes (those referred to in Basel as the *Nichtstudirende*), for which he always claimed to write. Its first audience would inevitably be the *Fachleute*, the scholars and professionals, the men of *Wissenschaft*. He would become embroiled in controversies and polemics. There would be cutting reviews by scholars eager to score points and enhance their reputations by destroying someone else's reputation. And he would be expected to respond. He would thus, despite himself, contribute to the *business* of scholarship from which he had sought refuge decades earlier by returning to the University of Basel and concentrating on his role as a teacher.

Burckhardt had a clear insight into a dilemma that scholars as well as politicians at the end of the twentieth century can hardly fail to recognize. According to him, this dilemma was encountered as early as the fifth century B.C. In a fairly evenhanded discussion of the Sophists in the section of *The Cultural History of Greece* on the Greeks of the fifth century, he noted that in highly cultivated times a technique for creating effects and influencing opinions may be introduced that comes to constitute a power in itself and places an extremely efficient weapon in the hands of people of mediocre talent and standing, "like the press of the present day, an instrument that has produced very little good and is responsible for three quarters of what is bad." Soon, even the highly talented and those most qualified to speak are obliged to go along with the new technique or give up all expectation of getting a hearing.[40] Those too diffident to engage in the use of the technique must resign themselves to silence and exclusion. Silence and exclusion had in fact been Burckhardt's choice when he virtually ceased publishing new works or attending scholarly meetings and left the task of revising and promoting works already published to whoever cared to take it on. His refusal ever to review the work of other scholars was another consequence of his determined avoidance of noisy public debate. There should therefore be nothing unexpected about his constant equivocation concerning *The Cultural History of Greece.* "No, my dear Sir," he protested to Heinrich Gelzer when the latter—a former student, subsequently a colleague and friend—urged him to publish. "A poor stranger who stands outside the circle of the guildsmen dare not undertake such a thing; I am a heretic and an ignoramus and with my questionable views I would receive a cruel thrashing from the *viri eruditissimi.* Oh yes, yes, I would. Believe me. *Je connais ces gens!* In my old age I need peace and quiet."[41]

The reception accorded Burckhardt's work when it appeared in four volumes in 1898–1902 confirms in some measure the soundness of his instincts. As he predicted, the philologists were the most fierce, for in Jacob Oeri's words, Burckhardt "had permitted himself to sovereignly ignore the work of the classical philologists of our time" and to "build his knowledge of the Greeks on what *they* had written and not on what German professors in the last forty years had written *about* them." Wilamowitz's harsh condemnation—"This book is of no account for scholarship" ("Dies Buch existiert nicht für die Wissenschaft")—is notorious. Even though it was pronounced before Wilamowitz, or any one else, had been able to read the entire work and appeared not in a formal scholarly review but as a gratuitous observation in the preface to the second volume of a translation of Greek tragedies that appeared in Berlin in 1899, word of it spread like wildfire through the German universities and seemed to encourage others to add their mite. A student of Wilamowitz's, who was teaching at Zurich, picked up serious philological errors in Burckhardt's history (for instance, the use of a Byzantine source that recent scholarship had shown to date in fact from the sixteenth century), hauled Oeri over the coals for failing to correct them, and concluded that it would have been better if Burckhardt's wish that the manuscript not be published had been respected. This particular attack ended in a lawsuit.[42]

There were also some favorable reviews. Robert Pöhlmann, professor of Greek at Munich, took issue with his Berlin colleagues. Burckhardt's *Cultural History of Greece*, he declared, was "an important testimony to the deep-rooted transformation of historical judgment of the Greeks in the second half of the nineteenth century."[43] Among historians, in particular, the reputation of the Basel scholar who had twice been called to Berlin remained high. In the leading journal of the historical profession, the *Historische Zeitschrift*, Carl Neumann acknowledged the importance of Burckhardt's revision of the "canonical" view of the Greeks held by the neohumanists and consecrated in Ernst Curtius's history, and praised the unique combination in Burckhardt of "the purest enthusiasm for the beautiful, an extraordinary capacity to become inspired by his subject matter, and the most sober powers of observation." Similar favorable judgments were pronounced by an eminent disciple of Ranke, Alfred Dove, and by the classical philologist Gustav Billeter.[44] On the whole, however, it was not until the 1920s—in the chastened atmosphere of the collapse of German imperial ambitions—that Burckhardt's *History of Greek Culture* won widespread acceptance as a major and enduring historical and literary text.

If *The Cultural History of Greece* was at first rejected by the "philologists," that was understandable. Burckhardt did not disguise his disdain for much contemporary philological and historical scholarship and openly chose to write, as Nietzsche did, in a different mode. "Wir sind 'unwissenschaftlich' und haben gar keine Methode, wenigstens nicht die der anderen," he announced provocatively in the Introduction (8:5 *[7]*). ("We are 'unscholarly' and have no method; at least we do not follow that of others.") That Introduction, which Oeri took from the lecture notes, might well be Burckhardt's most programmatic statement about cultural history, as opposed to political history, and about *Bildung*, rather than *Wissenschaft*, as the proper goal of historical study. It reveals clearly both the deep seriousness of Burckhardt's ideal of the humanistically educated citizen and the idealist philosophical assumptions underlying it. There is no question that *Geist*, or spirit, is the ultimate reality for Burckhardt, even though he sees it as always connected to a material foundation; or that the essential function of cultural history is to put the spirit of the living in touch with the spirit of the dead, to attend to "those traits through which the . . . Greek spirit speaks to us" (8:6 *[8]*), and thus ensure, at least among an aristocracy of the spirit, the continuity and universality of human culture. It is not for nothing that Burckhardt's aesthetic views, broad and open as they are, are fundamentally classical. There is never any question for him that the particular, the material, the ephemeral are contained, explained, and redeemed—without ever being obliterated—by the general, the typical, the spiritual. Burckhardt's idea of cultural history is poles apart from present-day notions of cultural studies and Ernst Gombrich was not altogether wide of the mark when he insisted that there is, when all is said and done, a "Hegelian" side to Burckhardt.[45]

Cultural history—the history of states of mind, ways of thinking, or worldviews (*"Lebensauffassungen"* [views of life], *"Denkweisen und Anschauungen"* [habits of thought and mental attitudes] (8:2 *[4]*))—is quite distinct, according to Burckhardt, from both political history (narratives of discrete events in the histories of states) and the history of institutions or *"Altertümer"* (encyclopedic accounts of the various aspects of historical life). The history of events and institutions is external and factual, the product of positivist scholarship or philology. The history of culture, in contrast, aims to recover the inner spiritual forces of which particular events or institutions are scattered crystallizations; it relies on interpretation and hermeneutic. The former is of interest to specialists and is cumulative, the latter concerns all educated people (*"jeder Gebildete"*) and must be rediscovered anew by every age and by each individual. "In a period when a single investigation into the authenticity of a few external facts may take up an entire octavo volume" (8:2 *[4]*), narrative history—the sequence of singular events—requires an investment of time and effort disproportionate to the gain to be had from it, and in any case the results can be conveniently communicated in a manual. "We, for our part, wish to determine *points of view* from which the events can be considered. If what is truly worth knowing about ancient Greece is to be communicated to nonspecialist students (*"Nichtphilologen"*) in not much more than sixty hours, we cannot proceed otherwise than by way of cultural history. *Our* task, as we understand it, is to give the history of Greek ways of thinking and Greek views of life and to strive to achieve an understanding of the living *energies,* both constructive and destructive, that were active in Greek life" (8:2 *[4]*). While all cultures, presumably, are expressions of the human spirit and therefore of interest to the *"Gebildete,"* the special virtue of Greek culture, according to Burckhardt, is that it is virtually transparent and expresses the inner spirit directly and in immediately accessible form—unlike others (such as the Egyptian or the Indian) in which "the form is rebarbative, the outer husk impenetrable, the expression symbolic to the point of unintelligibility" (8:7 *[8]*). In other words, the human spirit appears in Greek culture in its most universal form.

Cultural history, to sum up,

> has as its object the inner life of past humanity and it describes how that humanity existed, desired, and thought, how it looked upon the world and how it was able to act on it. In so far as it thus engages with what remains constant [*"das Konstante"*], that constant element appears, in the end, greater and more significant than anything momentary, a character trait appears greater and more instructive than an action; for actions are only particular expressions of the corresponding inner power, which can produce any number of new expres-

sions. Desires and assumptions are thus as important as anything that actually happens, ways of looking at things as important as any actual undertaking. . . . Even when a reported act never in fact happened as reported or never happened at all, the way of looking at the world that underlies the representation of it as having happened retains its value for us through the *typical* character of the representation (8:3–4 *[5]*).

The materials of the cultural historian, in other words, are primarily those in which "spirit" or ways of thinking and views of the world are expressed most directly and most unselfconsciously, namely, works of art and literature. "What is living and important will be found not in the event that is narrated, but in the manner in which it is narrated and in the ethical and intellectual [*"geistig"*] assumptions from which the manner of narration springs" (8:7 *[8]*). As even fictions and forgeries can be a better source for learning about underlying assumptions and beliefs than the best authenticated facts, the data of the cultural historian turn out to be less vulnerable to historical criticism in fact than those of the historian of events or institutions (8:3 *[5]*).[46] Cultural history should also be distinguished from the internal history of particular cultural activities, such as art or literature or philosophy (8:7 *[9]*).[47] The historian of a particular activity is interested in the intrinsic conditions and traditions of that activity; the cultural historian draws on a wide variety of sources (8:8 *[10]*) in order to reach the "spirit" behind them all. (This distinction will be important when we consider Burckhardt's work as an art historian in the following chapter.)

The approach to be adopted in *The Cultural History of Greece* will thus "not be narrative, but it will be historical" (*"nicht erzählend, wohl aber geschichtlich"*) (8:2 *[4]*). Such an approach creates problems of exposition and representation or *Darstellung* for the cultural historian, for it is difficult to present what is "a simultaneous, powerful One," rather than a succession of discrete events, in language that is itself composed of successive discrete signs (8:5 *[7]*).[48] Particulars—events, personalities, institutions—will be retained only in so far as they illuminate the general way of thinking, the spiritual outlook of which they are manifestations. "The singular, and in the first instance, the so-called event, will receive mention here only as it bears witness to the general, not for its own sake" (8:2 *[4]*). Thus individuals will appear, but there will be no complete biographies of them; they will be invoked "only as illustrations and the highest possible testimony to the things of the spirit" (8:4 *[6]*). They will suffer no dishonor by being treated in this way, however, since they will be introduced because they are the highest expression and realization of some phenomenon, "prime witnesses in the great hearing" (8:4 *[6]*). *All* the facts of a life or career, in other words, do not have the same value. The historian *selects* those that are especially revealing of worldviews and mentalities.

As understanding, rather than positive knowledge, is the goal—insight rather than accumulation of information—cultural history does not aim to gather up all that can be known about a topic. "It proceeds by grouping items and placing emphasis according to the *proportional* significance of the facts." It thus "does not have to stamp out all sense of proportion as is so often the case in antiquarian studies and in critical-historical research" (8:4 *[6]*). Most significantly, it "highlights those facts which can establish a genuine inner connection with our own spirit, and to which we can relate in a real way either as a result of affinity or as a result of contrast and opposition. The rubbish is left aside" (8:4 *[6]*). Burckhardt insisted that works of cultural history have a continuous formative and educational function rather than the one-time function of adding to the store of scientific knowledge or of laying the groundwork for specialized studies. They can, indeed must, for that reason be constantly reread, like works of literature. He likewise disclaimed any intention of saying the last word or providing the final "truth" about the Greeks. The characteristic Burckhardtian modesty motif that we found in both *The Age of Constantine* and the *The Civilization of the Renaissance*—the insistence on the essayistic character of his work and the representation of the ideal reader as a cultivated layman (*"Nichtphilologe"*)—is taken up once more. The very first sentence proclaims that "this course has the character of an experiment [*"Probestück"*] and will never be anything else, and that the teacher here is and will always remain also a learner and fellow student" (8:1 *[3]*). In other words, there is no closure, no truth, but a constant rethinking and revising of views, an uninterrupted work of reappropriation. The teacher is a "*Nichtphilologe,*' who may well have made a few philological slips here and there" (8:1 *[3]*), and the intended reader is likewise a *Nichtphilologe,* "any humanistically educated layperson" (*"jeder humanistisch Gebildete"*) (8:6 *[8]*). It is one of the most important aims of the teacher, moreover, to inspire students with the desire to continue the investigation on their own, which all are capable of doing by simply reading and rereading the ancient sources. "Scholarship is well taken care of by our present-day historical and antiquarian literature; *we,* in contrast, advocate study as a means of cultivation and a source of joy for a lifetime" (8:8 *[9]*).

In the year 1872, as Prussia marked its military victories over the Austrians and then the French with the founding of the Second German Empire, Burckhardt's emphasis on "the constant" element in history, his undisguised disdain for the history of events, must have been understood by his audience as a repudiation of the Prussian national historians' emphasis on state power, a judgment of the inanity of patriotic celebrations of momentary triumphs, and a provocative reminder of the insignificance, over the long term, of individual events that in the eyes of contemporaries enjoy the semblance of world-shattering importance. (In *The Cultural History of Greece* itself, although the significance of both the Peloponnesian War and Alexander's conquests for the culture of the polis and for the future destiny of Hellenic culture as a whole is by no means overlooked, Burckhardt devoted not a line to narrating either.) Unlike political history, with its focus on acts and events, cultural history, as Burckhardt understood it, raises the reader (or listener) above the immediate and the momentary, opens up a wider and longer perspective, and effectively distinguishes the reflective man or woman of culture (*"der Bewusste"*) from the unreflective, un-self-conscious barbarian (*"der Barbar als ein Unbewusster"*) (8:11 *[12]*), imprisoned in his immediate world of beliefs, passions, and material needs. The implication that the historical awareness cultural history provides is an essential attribute of the educated and civilized citizen corresponds closely to the view prevalent in the Basel patriciate, that government cannot be entrusted to the mass of the people but must be the affair of those whom a broad humanistic education has taught to rise above the immediate and gain a larger and more general vision of the whole—those, Burckhardt would say, whom the striving to obtain "as full a vision as possible of the continuity of world history" (*"das Bild von der Kontinuität der Weltentwicklung in sich so vollständig zu ergänzen als möglich"*) (8:11 *[12]*) has released from the blinkers of preoccupation with the here and now. The kind of reading of the sources that cultural history requires, Burckhardt insisted, is beyond the power of anyone who does not have a sense of identity with them as well as of estrangement from them, who has allowed himself to be spoiled by newspapers and titillated by modern literature ("which speaks so much more directly to our *nerves*" (8:7 *[9]*)), and who can no longer "see with the eyes of the Greeks and speak with their expressions." For "everything that is of the present moment engages with the material in us, with our interests, whereas the past has at least the *potential* to engage with the spiritual in us, with our higher interest" (8:7 *[9]*).

Toward the end of his Introduction, having emphasized his own view that the study of antiquity means first and foremost reading and constantly rereading the ancient texts and drawing from them ever new understandings, Burckhardt turned a critical eye on the place occupied by the ancient Greeks in the contemporary world and, in particular, in contemporary German education:

> After Winckelmann, Lessing and the Voss translation of Homer the feeling arose that the German spirit and the Greek spirit are united by a *hieros gamos* (sacred marriage) in a special relationship and in a mutual understanding unknown to any other people of the modern West. Goethe and Schiller were classical in their being.
>
> As a result of this, in part, there was a renewal and deepening of philological study in schools and universities and also a conviction that classical antiquity is the indispensable foundation of any study whatsoever. This conviction was held differently and more deeply than had been the case since the Renaissance.
>
> Along with it, however, there occurred the enormous expansion of research and scholarship devoted to the ancient world with which we are now familiar. The monuments of Egypt and Assyria, the prehistoric remains of Europe, the constitution of a new science of ethnography, research into the origins of the

human species and of language, the rise of comparative language studies—all these things commanded attention; classical Greece found itself relegated to a corner of the larger field occupied by all those other interests.

In addition, this development was accompanied by a specialization of scholarly work, each ancillary branch of which required that many researchers dedicate their lives to it and that the state provide unconditional support for research institutions and collections.

In our *Gymnasiums* "higher education—so it is has been said—educates boys from the cultivated classes to be professors of philology."[49] One of the primary instruments of this education was and still is the Greek language.

After graduation from the *Gymnasium,* however, a familiar process regularly follows. Apart from the professional philologists, the others—we will not venture to say what percentage of them—abandon the ancient authors. First, within about three months, they forget the artful metrics of the tragic choruses, which they learned with so much effort, then one after another, the verb forms, and finally the vocabulary. Many are glad to get it all out of their minds and do so deliberately. Study and life make other demands on them.

From all this a distorted relationship has developed between the *Gymnasium* and the subsequent development of young people's minds as it actually occurs, and this could end one day in a catastrophe.

Let *our* entire effort aim, as far as our feeble means allow, at keeping the love of ancient Greek culture alive (8:9–10 *[11]*).

In sum, students—and readers—should not expect that the cultural history of Greece will provide them with a professional training or expertise, for the teacher's purpose is diametrically opposed to that of the majority of his colleagues in Germany. The aim of the course, and of the book, is not *Wissenschaft,* the accumulation of data about every aspect of the ancient world or the communication of critical methods of verifying and evaluating such data, it is not the creation of professors of philology, but *Bildung,* the formation of thoughtful and cultivated human beings and citizens through reconnection with a past that is part of who we presently are.

If we wish to learn from our study of the Greeks, however, we must strive to see them as they truly were, and not as we have imagined them. Honesty, as well as genuine piety, requires that we not construct an idealized antiquity adapted to our own current needs and desires. For that reason, the image of Greece propagated in schools since the end of the eighteenth century must, in Burckhardt's view, be firmly rejected. "There will be no transfiguring of antiquity and we intend to deal mercilessly with the prettifications of its devotees" (8:10 *[11]*). Burckhardt reiterated the position laid out in the Introduction to his course in the "General Evaluation of Greek Life," which sums up its first four major sections ("The Greeks and their World of Myth," "State and Nation," "Religion and Ritual," and "Telling the Future"):

Ever since the great development of German humanism in the previous century, people thought they knew all about the Greeks. In the bright glow of their warlike heroes and citizens, of their art and poetry, of their beautiful country and climate, they were held to have been happy. Schiller's poem "The Gods of Greece" gathered the whole supposed situation up in a single image, which has still not lost its magical power. At the very least, people were convinced that the Athenians of the Age of Pericles must have lived a life of pure delight, year in, year out. This is one of the greatest frauds ever perpetrated by the historical judgment and it was the more difficult to resist as it was put forward with innocent conviction. People simply did not hear the screaming protest of the entire literary tradition (9:343 [86]).[50]

In *The Cultural History of Greece* Burckhardt comes to terms both with the dreams and enthusiasms of his own education and youth, and with an idealized vision of the city-republic that was part of the ideology not only of his compatriots but of many of his contemporaries throughout Europe. All the issues that concerned him as a Baseler and a citizen of Europe at the end of the nineteenth century are taken up and examined through the lens of antiquity. Getting Greece "straight" meant at the same time getting history straight and doing away with the idea that it consists of a long journey from paradise lost to paradise regained; it meant casting a sober look on the repressive potential of the state as manifested in the ancient polis; it meant measuring the effects of democracy on the state, the individual, and culture. Above all, it meant reaffirming Herder's vision of the nation as "a distinctive civilization, which is the product of its unique history, culture, and geographical profile,"[51] and to which the state is, in some measure, incidental, even dangerous, against both the liberal-democratic understanding of the state as a civil polity based on consent and law and the prevailing Prussian view of the nation as finding its highest realization in the state.

Whatever his reservations about the views of his contemporary Fustel de Coulanges on the *origins* of the polis, Burckhardt was in basic agreement with his politically conservative French colleague on the role of religion and myth as the cement that binds the members of a political community together.[52] Though Fustel's now classic study of *La Cité antique* appeared in 1864, it came to Burckhardt's attention fairly late. Nevertheless, it was read attentively by him,[53] and it must have been read with sympathy. Hostile as he was to the radical Grote, Burckhardt can only have welcomed a history that not only did entirely without stories of battles, wars, and the actions of individual heroes—and that also virtually ignored contemporary academic scholarship in favor of the ancient texts[54]—but quite clearly rooted the state in a shared system of beliefs, rather than in a constitution, and linked the long process of its decline to the rise of democracy, rationalism, and critical philosophy. One of the leitmotifs of *The Cultural History of Greece* is identified in a remark the historian made in 1883 to Max Alioth: "With age I become more and more 'one-sided' in certain views, among them that in Greece the day of decline dawned with the arrival of democracy" and that it is only because "the great accumulated energy survived for a few decades longer" that it became possible to create "the illusion of its being the *product* of democracy."[55]

To Burckhardt, as to Fustel, demythologizing is not the beginning of culture but the beginning of the end of culture, or at least of a certain kind of culture; it is what destroys the unity of a culture and a political community. For it is myth, according to Burckhardt, that was the core of Greek life, the core of the polis, and the core of the culture. With the decline of myth came the decline of the polis and the decline of a culture that was sustained by and rooted in a political community. It was certainly by design that Burckhardt began his course, and his book, with an account of Greek myth—"the true spiritual Oceanus of that world" ("der wahre geistige Okeanos dieser Welt") (Introduction, 8:5 *[7]*), "the great spiritual foundation of national life" ("der grosse geistige Lebensgrund der Nation") (8:27 *[22]*), the "general precondition of Greek existence" ("eine allgemeine Voraussetzung des griechischen Daseins") (8:32 *[25]*).

For Burckhardt—who is faithful in this respect to the romantic tradition established by Herder and continued by Ranke—Greek myth is popular, profoundly anchored through "its 'voice,' the ancient epic" (8:26–27 *[21]*), in the minds and hearts of the people. It is not something prescribed for the people from the outside or imposed as a set of sacred statutes, it is not an ideology or a constitution or a religious dogma but "a product of the people's own creative power. The Greek gods arise out of the vision of the entire people and are, for that reason, an idealized mirror-image of the nation" (9:15, 22).[56] The Greeks did not think of them as remote from worldly life and experience. Some families even claimed to be descended from gods or epic heroes (8:41–42 *[32]*) and a quiet commerce with the gods never completely ceased (8:50 *[35]*). Certain nature gods were widely thought to be still active in the world. Theocritus's shepherds were afraid of Pan as of a power that was always close by and might manifest itself at any moment (a possibility vividly evoked in a number of paintings by Burckhardt's fellow citizen, contemporary, and—until they quarreled in 1869—friend and protégé, the artist Arnold Böcklin). There was great interest in identifying the geographical sites of episodes from myth and epic. The world of myth, in sum, is whole, and there is no division in it between the sacred and the profane, the transcendent and the immanent, the otherworldly and the worldly.

Because it remains popular and whole, myth is expressed only concretely, in works of visual and verbal art, and is innocent of the division into story and commentary, into belief and systematic theology, that occurred in Christianity, for instance—according to Burckhardt's colleague in theology at Basel, Franz Overbeck—after it lost its initial popular momentum (8:28–29 *[21–23]*). Correspondingly, myth has no priesthood to explain and interpret it (9:115, 140).

Arnold Böcklin, *Panischer Schreck* (*Panic Fright*), 1858. Öffentliche Kunstsammlung Basel, Kunstmuseum. Photo: Öffentliche Kunstsammlung Basel, Martin Bühler.

On the contrary, it is resistant to history, which it tends to absorb and reshape according to its own laws and traditions (8:34–36 *[26–28]*, 10:398–400), as well as to all attempts at interpretation. "At the peak of their powers, the Greeks did not want to interpret their myths but to preserve and glorify them" (9:59).[57] The shaping power of mythical construction was far more important to them than any factual, positive origin; the story or representation was what counted, not a particular reality or referent. It was only in the eyes of people who did not share in the world of myth that the story appeared as a covering or garment to be removed as quickly as possible so that the "facts" might be laid bare. Not until much later did interpretation creep into Greek culture, in the form of allegorical readings or of historicizing rationalizations, and that was a clear sign of myth's decline (9:60–61). For that reason, the efforts of Georg Friedrich Creuzer and Carl Otfried Müller to interpret the Greek myths with the help of modern scholarship defined, for Burckhardt, a domain of learning that he felt "not called upon to penetrate" and that he claimed would always be difficult to explore, in as much as ancient myth is the product of a people "which obviously *wanted* to forget the original meanings of its mythological figures, and whose symbolism thus became, or always was, a naive and unselfconscious one" (9:30). Between myth and its scientific interpretation, whether ancient or modern, rationalist or romantic, there is an unbridgeable gap. They belong to different worlds and different ways of thinking. In the world of myth, interpretation can only take the form of another myth.

Philosophy and scholarship are in fact "the enemies and rivals" of myth, for myth, to the Greeks, "offered a powerfully expressed vision of the world in place of philosophy" and took the place of knowledge in that it was itself the original form of knowledge and "contained in itself, in wonderfully symbolical garb, nature, geography, history, even religion and a cosmogony" (10:282).[58] Already in Heraclitus, according to Burckhardt, "we find a definite hatred of Homer and his world of gods" (10:297, 10:301). It is the artists and the poets—the "competitors and deadly enemies of exact knowledge"—who are the friends and allies of myth and it is "art and poetry that consistently give expression to myth and provide it with ever new offspring" (10:283).

Though history, along with philosophy, is here apparently opposed to myth, it is a certain *kind* of history, a kind of history with which Burckhardt himself has a quarrel. The sympathy with which myth is treated throughout *The Cultural History of Greece* and the author's relative coolness to philosophy (despite the engaging portraits of certain philosophers) call to mind Burckhardt's own frequently repeated protestations that he has no head for philosophy and that his bent is toward the concrete, the historical, the telling of stories. In fact, the discussion of myth and its relation to history, philosophy, and scholarship is closely related to the argument concerning cultural history developed in the Introduction. A major advantage Burckhardt claimed for cultural history, it will be remembered, was that its validity is not directly dependent on the kind of verification or criticism to which individual facts must be subjected, since its subject matter is the "constant," not the singular; the typical, not the particular; the values and ways of looking at the world that lie behind specific incidents or institutions, not those incidents and institutions themselves. The opposition of mythical and historical ways of thought and composition in the discussion of Greek culture corresponds closely to the opposition in the methodological Introduction between cultural history and the history of events and particular institutions. The greatest obstacle to exact historical science among the Greeks, we are told, was "their incorrigible imprecision and indifference to exactness." They are wonderfully objective; however, "their objectivity concerns not the materially exact establishing of individual facts but the inner significance of these, their general human or national content" (10:398–99). Thus their oral historical tradition was constantly being revised in the manner and direction of myth, that is to say, toward the *"charakteristisch-typisch"* rather than the "exact." That is the basis, Burckhardt observes, of the much discussed difference between Herodotus and Thucydides (a classic topos of historiographical reflection to which Creuzer had contributed an important essay at the beginning of the century). Whereas Herodotus creates out of oral stories that are sometimes quite far removed from the source they purportedly refer to, Thucydides works either from documentary evidence or from immediate eyewitness accounts (10:399).

Burckhardt goes on to offer a justification of the "mythicizing" historiography of Herodotus in terms that unmistakably recall the justification of his own practice of cultural history in the Introduction:

> Whoever has once come to know this typical-mythical form of narrative often gives up every attempt to recount what literally happened. . . . But the contempt with which contemporary critical erudition regards the anecdotal— which it declares completely without value and unworthy of scholarly attention in comparison with the communication of exact information—seems to us not very appropriate. For one is obliged, whether one wants to or not, to sift and sort through that very anecdotal material, and perhaps in the end it is the facts that are mere debris. Are all those histories, which are often all we have from a particular time, no longer to be viewed as history? History in the usual sense, they assuredly are not, since we cannot learn from them what happened at a particular time, in a particular place, as a result of the action of a particular person. But they do indeed constitute in some measure a *historia altera*, an imagined history that tells us what human beings were thought to be capable of and what was characteristic of them. *We* may well be directed by our education to value the exact and see no salvation outside of it; the Greeks, on the other hand, seek the typical and the expression of the typical is the anecdote, which is always true in general and yet never was true on any particular occasion. In that sense the first book of Herodotus, for instance, remains eternally true, even though not much of it would be left if one took away the typical from it (10:399–400).

To be sure, Burckhardt was well aware of the differences between the mythicizing history of the Greeks and modern cultural history, not least the fact that the ancient myths became the possession of an entire people, whereas modern cultural history remains the product of an individual vision of the past. Nevertheless, in important respects mythicizing history and cultural history sustain a common front against positive, scientific, or scholarly history. Both are closer, not only in their methods but in their goals, to poetry and art than to philosophy and science. Strikingly, the study of ancient myth as practiced by Burckhardt's fellow Baseler, Johann Jacob Bachofen, had also given rise, as we saw in chapter 8, not so much to "scientific" understanding of myth as to something like another version, or reenactment, of myth.

The power and unity of myth are inseparably related to the power and unity of the community whose members share that myth: the polis. As long as the polis is thriving, state, religion, and culture are virtually inseparable in it; only in its decline do they drift apart. The design of *The Cultural History of Greece* reveals Burckhardt's double intention of providing a *systematic* account of the polis (sections 1–4), culminating in the long eighty-page section 5 entitled "Toward a General Judgment of Greek Life" ("Zur Gesamtbilanz des griechischen Lebens"), and a *diachronic* account of its *"grandeur et décadence"* as we pass from the heroic age that preceded the polis to the Alexandrian and Hellenistic age by which it was overtaken.[59]

An epigraph from the inscription on the portal of Hell at the beginning of Book III of Dante's *Inferno*—*"per me si va nella città dolente"*—stands as a warning at the entrance to the section of volume I of Burckhardt's book entitled "The Polis," giving clear notice of the author's intention to avoid *"Schönfarberei,"* the whitewashing or prettying up of historical reality and the idealization of the ancient polis characteristic, in his view, in their different ways, of German neohumanists and English radicals, of Goethe and Grote. This will not, the reader is advised, be a celebratory account of the ancient polis. It will tell of the violence by which it came into existence as an organized state, of the violence it consistently—and increasingly—exercised both on its citizens and on its neighbors, and of the enormous sacrifice of human happiness and freedom it exacted, even in its heyday, as the price of its greatness and its achievements in art and literature. From the total picture will emerge a Schopenhauerian view of life as rarely happy, redeemed only by the seemingly inexhaustible creative energies of human beings and their realizations in art, and a dark, deeply un-Rankean view of history itself as a vale of tears, in which every achievement of culture is paid for by untold suffering and in which the conflicting values and claims of individual development and community cohesion, reflection and belief, personal freedom and state power, cosmopolitan humanism or universalism and intense national identification or patriotism are rarely, if ever, reconciled.[60] Implicitly, Burckhardt's account of the Greek poleis challenged Ranke's optimistic belief that the development of strong, unified national states as the repositories and champions of popular cultures ensured the enrichment and consolidation of all of them. War to the death, not the balance of power, was the norm for the poleis in Burckhardt's account of them. (See plate 4: Arnold Böcklin, *Kentaurenkampf.*)

The founding of the state, Burckhardt related, is always represented as instantaneous, not the result of an evolution (8:62 *[43]*). It is, in effect, a traumatic birth, "the decisive experience in the entire existence of a population" (8:69 *[49]*). The radical and painful transformation of traditional tillers of the soil into citizens marks the passage from a kind of prehistory to history.[61] By an act of will, loose, "natural" or "organic" communities are shaped into a single state which recreates its members as free and equal citizens, requires the identification of each individual will with that of the whole, and tolerates no deviation, no difference, no independence, within or without. It is at least arguable that the ancient polis, as described in *The Cultural History of Greece,* represents in many respects, for Burckhardt, the very essence of the state, the state in its perfect state, so to speak, and the focus, therefore, of his meditations on the state[62]—just as, shockingly no doubt from the standpoint of modern idealizers of the polis (but not from that of the Ancients themselves, Burckhardt claims), Sparta, where "the people is an army and the state an armed camp" (8:109), is represented as the essence or perfect model (*"die vollendetste Darstellung"*) of the polis (8:94).[63]

It was not unusual in Burckhardt's day, as we saw, to compare the Greek poleis and the Swiss cantons or the city-states of modern Europe. Burckhardt insisted, in contrast, that those seemingly similar political formations are fundamentally different. If anything, Burckhardt's poleis resemble the new nationalist states of Europe rather than the late medieval city-states or the Swiss cantons. Both in their origins and in their fundamental ideology the ancient poleis should be sharply distinguished, Burckhardt declared, from the city-republics of the Middle Ages, to which they bear only a superficial resemblance. The latter are "essentially something different—namely particular, more or less emancipated parts of previously existing empires" (8:76 *[55]*). They are individuated pieces broken off from larger wholes, whereas the polis is the culmination of a process of absorption, integration, and, where it encounters resistance, destruction of smaller units. Moreover, the Church, which hovered over all the European city-republics and empires, drawing them together like a cloak spread over them, has no equivalent in antiquity (8:76 *[55]*). On the contrary, religion is not an autonomous force in the polis; it is an integral part of it. In fact, the only religion in each polis is the religion of the polis. "The polis was basically the Greek's religion" (8:80 *[58]*). Similarly, there is no conception of a natural law claiming universal validity. "There are no human rights in antiquity, not even in Aristotle" (8:74 *[53]*). Law, like religion, is an integral part of each polis but it affects only the members of that polis, no one else—not members of other poleis and not those within the polis (such as slaves or residents) who are not citizens. "Nomos, which embraces both the laws and the constitution," is seen as "a higher objective instance that is not satisfied—as in the modern world—merely to protect and tax the individual and sustain military service, but instead claims to govern all individual existence and will, and to be the very soul of the whole. In the most elevated statements, law and constitution are praised as the invention and gift of the gods, the very character of the city and the preserver of its virtue" (8:82 *[59]*).

The laws of each polis, in sum, are viewed as part of the very being of that polis, and each one looks on others as an absolutely alien existence, a challenge and threat to itself. With neither a common religion, nor a notion of universal law, the Greek poleis are lined up more starkly and uncompromisingly against each other than the medieval city-republics ever were. It is virtually impossible for them to cooperate or confederate. "Since the polis is the highest power and the true religion of the Hellenes, the struggles of the poleis to promote or defend themselves have all the frightful horror of religious wars" (8:85 *[61]*).[64] Finally, among the inhabitants of the European city-republics the individual precedes the state. It cannot be said of the citizen of one of the modern city-republics (such as Basel) that he "realizes all his talents and finds occasion for the exercise of every virtue in and through the state" or that "all spirit and all culture stand in the strongest possible relation to the polis, so that the highest productions by far of the poetry and art of the age of greatest cultural flowering belong not to the domain of private enjoyment but to the sphere of public life" (8:77 *[55]*). Only of the citizen of the ancient polis could it be said without any reservation that "his *'Vaterstadt'* (patris) is not simply the home-town where he is happiest and to which he is drawn by homesickness, not simply the city to which, despite its faults, he feels proud to belong, but a higher, divinely powerful being" (8:77 *[56]*). Burckhardt subscribed explicitly to the radical distinction drawn by Benjamin Constant and, before him, by Montesquieu between the ancient and the modern worlds:

> In modern times, if we discount philosophical and other kinds of blueprints, it is essentially the individual who defines the state, and who demands that it be as he needs it to be. What he asks of it in fact is only security, so that he can develop his individual energies and capacities to the maximum. In order to achieve this goal, he is prepared to make well calculated sacrifices in return, but feels gratitude and loyalty to the state to the very degree that it leaves him alone to go about all his other business without interference. The Greek polis, in contrast, starts from the whole that is held to precede the part; that is, the whole is held to precede the individual human being and the individual family or clan (8:77 *[55]*).[65]

The most terrible birth pangs accompany the construction of this state that is to be the *"Eins und Alles"* (8:60 *[42]*, 9:314 *[64]*), the alpha and omega, of the lives of all its citizens, and that becomes "a fearful threat to any citizen the moment he no longer identifies totally with it," since it wields without any constraint the various instruments of coercion at its disposal (dishonor and public stigmatization [*"Atimie"*], exile, and death) (8:80). Burckhardt describes the rise of political man like a fall from innocence.

> The time when people lived according to country ways [*komedon*], sometimes in small districts [*Gauen*] of seven or eight villages, had been . . . more innocent; it had been necessary to defend oneself by arms against brigands and

pirates, but essentially people had lived a peaceful agricultural life. Now polis stood against polis as rivals for political power and for their very existence. . . . The whole of Greek life had been straining toward this final form, the polis, without which the highest achievements of Greek culture would be inconceivable. But examples from historical times about which we have clearer knowledge allow us to form an idea of the cost of this synoecism [welding together of different human groups into the polis]: namely the resettlement by violent means or the total elimination of all those who put up any resistance. What we can have but an inkling of, is the suffering of the many who went along with the new order but were forced to leave behind their old villages, settlements, and little towns. . . . Having to abandon the gravesites of their ancestors must have been experienced by the Greeks as a terrible misfortune. . . . In the entire course of history there is scarcely another example of such an accumulation of bitter suffering as we find in this Greek polis (8:64–65 *[45–46]*).[66]

As the *Eins und Alles* that brooks no rival and no otherness, the polis is engaged externally in bitter competition or open warfare with other poleis, the very existence of which is a threat to its absoluteness; internally, it oppresses its citizens mercilessly, promising death or banishment to all who deviate from total dedication to its purposes. The competition among the ancient poleis was quite unlike that among modern European cities, Burckhardt explains. Animosities among the latter, largely based on commercial envy and rivalry, convey no idea of the sometimes hidden, sometimes open animosity that the Greeks harbored against each other. "The exclusiveness of the polis, its hostility to all other poleis, especially those closest to it, is not just a dominant feeling but virtually an aspect of civic virtue" (8:279). And this relation to those on the outside repeats the polis's harshness to oppressed parties and groups within it, as well as its oppression of the ancient rural populations. As internal divisions developed apace in the course of the fifth century, the polis's external ventures became more frequent, the intervals of peace shorter, treaties less likely to be respected. "Each individual state became more and more aware that all other states were in a life or death struggle with it and behaved accordingly, so that the time of the highest flowering of culture was also that of the most horrific executions" (8:280). The motive for those struggles was not necessity or interest, no specific advantage, but "pure political hatred" (8:281). As no one can accept submission to a rival, or trust that a rival who has submitted will continue in submission, all enemies are potentially fatal threats and must be eliminated. The rules of war are of unexampled harshness: the victor kills off all the males and sells the women and children into slavery (8:284).[67] Burckhardt's judgment is unequivocal: "From time immemorial, worldly power has admitted of few restrictions on its actions whenever its interests were involved" (8:282). In large heterogeneous empires it is nonetheless held in check in some measure by competing interests and forces, and it aims in general at achieving external peace. That, however, was not the case with the Greek poleis. On the contrary, from the fifth century on, internal unrest propelled them into external adventures and as soon as war broke out, they believed no holds were barred and everything was permitted to them (8:282). The cruelty of the Spartans (8:97–98, 102) was not exceptional but typical.

Internally, the polis subordinated every aspect of individual life to its ends. Burckhardt is once again close to Benjamin Constant. Man in the polis is a citizen, never an individual. Though it does not itself run schools, the polis does favor traditional education: gymnastics to exercise the body and encourage boldness and effort; music to instill a sense of order and law. The polis forms and educates citizens, in short, through the theater, public architecture, and above all through the activities of daily life, such as participation in assemblies or the magistracy. In this way it creates "a unique product in world history—a general will that is immensely active and effective" (*"von höchster Tätigkeit und Tatfähigkeit"*) (8:79 [57]). But the corollary of the all-powerful state is "the lack of individual freedom in every respect. Religious rites, the festival calendar, myth, all are indigenous; in this way the state is at the same time a church empowered to hear and decide charges of impiety. To this combined power, temporal and spiritual, the individual is completely subordinate." He must provide military service throughout his life, and his property is entirely subject to the control of the state. "The polis exacted a high price for the modicum of security that it provided" and there was "absolutely no way of protecting life or property from the inroads of the state." (8:80 [57–58]). This servitude of the individual to the state is characteristic, Burckhardt argued, of all the constitutions of the polis, but it is at its worst, he insisted, under democracy. In Burckhardt's history, the democratic polis, the ideal model of modern radicals, is the most oppressively illiberal of all, the very model of the totalitarian state.

Like many accounts of the ancient city, at least since Montesquieu's *Grandeur et Décadence des Romains,* Burckhardt's has an underlying design, according to which the rot sets in virtually with the founding of the city, so that accompanying the description of the polis in its essential form there is a story that is almost exclusively one of decline. "The process of the gradual eating away of the polis, the result partly of internal, partly of external causes, is a logical one deriving inevitably from the very being of the polis" (8:260)[68]—that is to say, from its state of constant hostility toward all other poleis and from the tension within it between contradictory demands on its members. For if, on the one hand, the polis demands that each citizen develop his powers to the utmost in order to serve the state as effectively as possible, it requires, on the other, that each citizen renounce all personal gratification and subordinate himself entirely to the welfare of the state.

"It is an old rule of history," Burckhardt explained, "that capacities and talents can be developed self-consciously and to the full only through opposition and struggle with each other, but that, equally a strongly developed political power is the essential fundamental condition of all material and spiritual achievement, the indispensable support of culture, which can only grow out of that soil." The Greek poleis were remarkably successful in this respect and contributed greatly to human culture over a long period of time. At the same time, however, "we may truly say that, to the degree that it succeeded in developing its members both inwardly and outwardly, the polis must have made them, as time passed, overwhelmingly unhappy. It not only led the individual to form a personality, but drove him on as hard as possible and demanded complete renunciation on his part." Gradually, the desires and satisfactions of the highly developed individual came to replace the earlier communal ones, until under democracy the will of the polis as the highest value known to the citizen, the value to which he was required to subordinate his own will, was replaced by the whims of the popular mass, which "no longer represented a higher general will but only its own desires" (8:275–76).

The promotion of the individual for the sake of the polis, in short, produced personalities and desires that were less and less easily subordinated to the polis, and as these individual desires gradually permeated the polis, the latter in turn lost the objective character that had justified the sacrifices it required as well as the authority and credibility on which it depended to obtain them.[69] It must be emphasized that in Burckhardt's view this process was inevitable. The polis or the state was flawed from the start by the violence of its birth and by the continued exclusions and oppressions inseparable from its existence. "Firstly not all people are citizens. . . . Women, children and, most completely, residents and slaves are not, and yet they too required an ethic. But in addition to that, from the very time it demanded of all citizens [that they must strive to excel on its behalf], the polis developed in fact, along with great dedication to the common good in many cases, situations in which attack and defense among the citizens themselves aroused the most powerful passions and were excused" (9:314 *[64]*).

Burckhardt's sympathies, like those of his young friend Nietzsche, were deeply engaged by the heroic age of Greek civilization that preceded the polis. To that age, he believed, the later, more civilized Greeks were indebted for a treasury of human qualities and energies, a kind of moral and human capital, that they continued to draw upon long after they had lost the capacity to add to it. The ancient Greek hero is not the self-consciously "noble" character modern cultivated Europeans have often portrayed him as. He is a primitive—"in no way," Burckhardt insisted, "an ideal form of the human being." On the contrary, he is the opposite of "civilized" and stands in stark contrast to the sophisticated citizens of the mature, democratic polis. "Action and passion alike in the hero are stretched to the outermost limit. The ideal quality he possesses lies in his beautiful, pristine existence. He is not haunted by ideas of nobility, so-called dignity or moral perfection; he represents vividly the untainted, naive egoism of human nature, as unrepentant as it is possible to imagine it, but grand and benevolent" (11:32 *[140]*).

In a characteristically ironical move that relativizes his argument without disqualifying it, Burckhardt recognized that the modern "sentimental" sensibility (including, obviously, his own) is particularly inclined to look back on the qualities of this "naive" heroic age with wonder and nostalgia.

> For posterity, that is, for the sensibility of the later peoples of the West, all the ethics of the philosophical, literary and rhetorical age must indeed fade into the background compared with the noble and—despite all the passion and violence—extraordinarily pure Homeric world. Here a way of feeling is dominant that is still whole, undivided by self-reflection, here we find an ethic that has not been diminished by chatter about morality, a kindness and tenderness in comparison with which civilized Greece with all its intellectual refinement seems spiritually coarse and stunted. Whatever better qualities that later time still retained it owed at bottom to the survival of Homer and to his portrayal of mythical figures (9:316 *[65]*).

Within the polis too, Burckhardt's sympathy (though never uncritical) was for aristocracy and he frequently presented the resentment of privilege that he claimed motivated and mobilized the democratic mass as one of the elements most responsible for the decay of the polis as a whole. The ideal of *kalokagathia*, which combines outstanding attributes (*kalos*) and nobility of blood (*agathos*), dates back to the period of aristocratic government of the polis, but continued to inspire the Greeks, Burckhardt argued, long after many poleis had become democratic and in spite of the best efforts of the philosophers to eradicate it or at least give it a more moral meaning (8:163).

> In general, the time of the *agon* and of the founding of colonies is a time when the polis alternated between aristocracy and tyranny [the usual solution, according to Burckhardt (8:169), to the disorder brought about by rivalries among the leading families] and when, alongside a firm belief in the superiority of certain families, the peculiar ideal of *kalokagathia*, a combination of noble blood, wealth, and distinction, whose herald was Pindar, was widely accepted and held to be a distinguishing feature of the Greeks. The nobility governs at this time everywhere, even in those states that were not transformed by the Dorian invaders. The right to rule rests on superior blood, greater holdings of land, military experience, and knowledge of the sacrificial rites and the laws. All forms of labor—agriculture, artisanry, commerce, and the like—are despised. Only the making of weaponry is noble work and even then only when it serves the games and the state, not when it serves the needs of daily life. The masses striving to better themselves are encouraged to move to the colonies where they in turn become aristocracies (11:84–85).

The agonistic culture of the early polis—which in Burckhardt's eyes, as in the eyes of his young colleague Nietzsche, contrasted strikingly with the "plebeian" preoccupation with security of the late nineteenth century[70]—was tempered by a virtue that was at once the opposite and the complement of aristocratic *kalokagathia*, namely *sophrosyne*. *Kalokagathia* and *sophrosyne* work together in Burckhardt's vision of the ancient polis as Dionysian and Apollonian work together in Nietzsche's *Birth of Tragedy*. On the one hand, *kalokagathia* was "the inseparable fusion of a moral conviction, an aesthetic ideal, and a material view into a single concept that it is impossible for us now to communicate. At best we can try to define its boundaries. The moral and aesthetic weight falls on the *kalos* (noble), the material weight on the *agathos*, whom Homer already defines as the rich and distinguished in contrast to the lesser men" (8:163).[71] Despite the efforts of the philosophers in the age of democracy to give the term a new, "spiritual" meaning by substituting inner distinction for distinction of birth, the term retained its aristocratic meaning throughout (8:163), partly no doubt because, with respect to metics and slaves, citizens continued to constitute an ethnic aristocracy even in democratic times (11:86). *Kalokagathia* thus signified distinction and outstanding achievement.

If *kalokagathia* is the positive pole, the spur, in the culture of the ancient Greeks, *sophrosyne* or "measure" is, on the other hand, the popular (*"volkstümlich"*) foundation of Greek philosophical ethics, the negative pole that reins in the energies *kalokagathia* stimulates (9:315 *[65]*). It is thanks to the combination of the two that Greek art, in contrast to modern romantic art, for instance, is rarely arbitrary, whimsical, or idiosyncratic. And Greek art reflects in this respect the culture of the polis as a whole. "Athens always sought her highest in individuals," Burckhardt explained in a passage of his *Weltgeschichtliche Betrachtungen*. The strong local prejudice "that men must be able to do anything in Athens, and that there the best society and the greatest, or indeed the only stimulus was to be found" did in fact result in the city's producing "a disproportionate number of remarkable men." At the same time, while Athens might see herself embodied in an Alcibiades, she "knew all the time that she could not afford to suffer another one."[72] Everything depended on maintaining equilibrium between individuality and commonality, or between "genius" and "talent," as Burckhardt would put it elsewhere.[73]

> The great central quality of [the Greeks is] . . . the combination of freedom with restraint, which alone permits the creation of ideal yet living forms; it is the immediate respect art has not only for the gods and for men, but for itself; it is the urge to preserve and at the same time enhance everything that has already been achieved. It is that much praised sophrosyne that takes the form, in the better times of the polis, of obedience along with the energetic development of individual talents. . . . The preeminence of this quality is vividly vouched for by the length of the time during which art sustained itself at its highpoint. The great age was not immediately followed, as was the case with Raphael and Michelangelo, by a mannerist stage, marked by the laborious artistic constructions of eclectics and naturalists.

Without servile following of prescription but rather through free appropriation, art grows and develops from one generation to the next. Even in the
mythical period it manifests itself—in contrast to the Orient—as an affair of
great individuals. First we encounter families: the Cyclops, the Dactyli, the
Telchines; then, from the god Hephaestos on, the great heroes of art: Daedalus,
Trophonius, Agamedes. At a very early stage we come across the names of
historical artists with a tradition of students and disciples, until finally we meet
famous, totally free artists and their schools, whose activities are spread over
several cities. The mythical freedom and variety of the beginning is thus continued; but precisely because no single artist with his school draws all others
after him, art is protected from spurts of genius [*"vor dem genial Hingeworfenen
bewahrt"*]. The subjective is not permitted to thrust itself forward. The sensa-
tional, the arbitrary, the forced or excessively individual, the stroke of genius
are totally absent among the Greeks (10:11).

Individuality among the Greeks is thus sharply differentiated from the romantic cult of the individual genius. The individual artist of classical antiquity
does not seek "originality" at all costs—as the alienated romantic artist does—
by revolting against inherited and established norms, but works within the constraints set by a powerful and enabling traditional language of artistic forms,
which he may strive to enhance and even expand. Correspondingly, there is no
division in the heyday of Greek art and literature between popular and learned
or sophisticated. Tragedy, for example, was not an entertainment for a "cultivated" elite, but an essential element in the cult of the polis and the business of
the entire citizenry (10:190). In general, poetry, music, and dance "are understood to belong to the Greek nation or at the very least to an entire polis, and
not only to a class of educated people. They are public matters. . . . Poetry . . .
is a need of the people" (10:170).

Contemporary lyric poetry stands in the strongest possible contrast to that of
Greece. It knows absolutely no limits or laws other than those it sets for itself.
In addition, it has to reach out to the user from the printed page. Greek poetry,
in contrast, was bound to formal instruction and to public performance because
of its links to song, social life, musical instruments and dance. There was no
way for it to be simply scattered to the winds.

There was no separation of the educated and the uneducated where this
poetry is concerned. It was accessible as a matter of course to all free men. Just
as religious rites were every one's affair, rich and poor were equally well informed about the myths, which were the original basis of poetry. And yet, at
the same time, this was art of the highest order (10:150–51).

Thus, for example, every Greek was capable of putting together an appropriate
inscription for a gravestone. "Even ordinary people in Hellas had a way of expressing their grief in beautiful form; and every one could handle composition
and meter because every one had learned long passages of Homer by heart"
(10:161).

What Greek art represents is not the individual or the average, but the ideal

(11:3 *[127]*). Its rootedness in myth and the absence of an autonomous, institutionalized religion with a professional priesthood saved it from moralism, di-
dacticism, and the complex symbolism that afflicts "Oriental" and specifically
Egyptian art. Such symbolism was driven out of it at an early stage (10:6–9).
Equally, both its relation to myth and its relation to the polis ensure that Greek
art will not be realistic. The polis holds "the artist to the glorification of the
general, so that style remains unified without being uniform" (10:7). The fact
that sculpture, rather than painting, was dominant among the plastic arts reinforced the idealizing, antirealistic tendency imposed by the polis.

> To convey the essence of reality, it was necessary, not only in sculpture but in
> every genre, that representation leave aside the purely accidental, the common
> everyday reality, in which the life of the spirit can appear only in particular
> guises and broken up into innumerable individual instances, and that it neglect
> the countless accessory phenomena overgrowing it. But sculpture in particular
> is obliged by its very nature to engage in much more thoroughgoing simplifica-
> tion than painting. In painting, the illusion of reality is permitted: it may even
> be an important means of obtaining certain effects. But that is never so in
> sculpture. In sculpture the minute and laborious representation of bodily de-
> tails, as in fully naturalistic painting, is disturbing and repellent. In that sense,
> sculpture is the idealist art par excellence (10:18).

At the same time, the process of idealization, the abstracting of everything accessory, was prevented from resulting in a lifeless formalism by the urgent
Greek longing to achieve a concrete presence of the divine. "The gods are in
fact idealized human beings, and it was of critical importance here that the
elaboration of the figures of the gods took place in the plastic arts only after
the particular meanings of the gods had long been worked into the form of
individualities in the religious and poetic imagination" (10:19). For Burckhardt,
as for all the German neohumanists, Greek art realizes, in short, the miracle of
the concrete universal. For that reason, it is a mistake, to approach it realistically. Greek tragedy, for instance, should not be rationalized as punishment for
some sin or wrong (10:208–9).

True to his promise that he would not engage in whitewashing and to his
explicitly expressed conviction that good and evil, joy and suffering are inextri-
cably intertwined in all aspects of human existence at all times, Burckhardt did
not fail to report in considerable detail on the "dark side" of the agonistic culture. Not only did the athletic games at the heart of the agonistic culture often
result in horrible physical deformations (11:101–2 *[172]*, 106–7 *[175–76]*), but
"there was no positive happiness in directing the whole of life toward one moment of the most terrible tension, for in the intervals between such moments
the athletes must have been seized by extreme lassitude or acute anxiety about
the future" (11:106 *[175]*).[74] In addition, the exclusion of women from the
whole agonistic culture of the polis was deeply detrimental to their condition
in antiquity. The narrowness of their sphere of activity, their general cultural

impoverishment, and their oppression at the hands of men are directly attributable to it (11:141 *[199]*, 229–33 *[251–53]*, 240–41 *[258–59]*, 580–81 *[359]*). "To be born a woman was generally esteemed a misfortune" (11:581 *[359]*).

Closely related to the low status of women, homoeroticism was another, in no way accidental, aspect of the culture of the polis. It was, in Burckhardt's works, "an essential aspect of the Greek spirit and it presents itself moreover as a high ideal" (11:141 *[199]*). Homoerotic love, the historian was careful to point out, was a cultural phenomenon, not to be identified with what is now referred to as homosexuality. It neither excluded sexual relations with women, within and out of wedlock, nor did it constitute in any way a deviant form of behavior, nor was it regarded "medically" as a condition affecting a certain percentage of the population. On the contrary, in an agonistic culture, it was a socially recognized and respected feature of the education of citizens and was especially favored as a means of training brave and dedicated citizen warriors. Though the laws concerning it varied from polis to polis, only tyrannies—for fear of sedition—opposed it. Most poleis, however, permitted or encouraged only relations that were judged to be formative and educational; obtaining the favors of a youth by payment of money or by an act of violence was usually a punishable offence. Nevertheless, Burckhardt acknowledged that the high value placed by the Greeks on homoerotic relations adversely affected relations between men and women and he clearly considered this to be one of the darker sides (*"Schattenseiten"*) of the culture of the polis: "Marriage was as important an aspect of civic life as it is everywhere and at all times, since to be an authentic citizen a man had to be born from an authentic marriage; but one observes that there is no longer any trace of inwardness in the relation of husband and wife and that scornful and wanton talk about women becomes prevalent" (11:142 *[200]*).

The culture of the polis in its decline—which is closely associated, for Burckhardt, with the rise of democracy and the growing influence of philosophy—is considered and judged with the same evenhandedness and the same sense of the complexity of historical situations. If the unity and cohesion of the old polis were sacrificed, if the citizen was corrupted, the individual achieved emancipation, and there was an intense development of the private life and of private pleasures and sensibilities. The internal decay of the polis is counterbalanced by a far greater openness to the world beyond it and by a new spirit of cosmopolitan humanism. What ultimately resulted was not only a drastic decline in respect for the polis but "the great transformation of Greece from a political to a cultural force and the transformation of the citizen into the man of culture [*Bildungsmensch*] destined thenceforth to become the bearer of the values of Hellenism" (11:335 *[305]*). Ironically, the very decline of the polis—that is to say, of the *state*—ensured that the *culture* of Greece would become the heritage of all humanity.

As aristocracy degenerated into oligarchy and then into timocracy—the rule of the wealthy—it became simply a matter of time, according to Burckhardt, until those lower class people in whose hands money, moveable wealth, trade, and industry had been concentrated, entered into possession of the polis. Politics became a struggle between the well-to-do and the rest, with every one pursuing his own interest. By the time Aristotle came to write about aristocracy, the only kind he could have observed, Burckhardt claimed, was not the old aristocracy of blood but temporary oligarchies of wealth that had arisen in reaction to democracy and taken over the polis to protect their own interests. That type of oligarchy shifted the burden of the state on to the shoulders of others, while it itself sought not only the highest offices of the state but its own financial advantage (8:165–69).

The Cultural History of Greece is full of references to the harassment of the rich and talented by democratic regimes in which "popular assemblies have usurped the functions of the senate [*Rat,* in Burckhardt's text—the same term that is applied to the legislative and executive branches of the Swiss city-republic governments] and essentially taken over government" (8:227). The voice of the nineteenth-century Basel *Altbürger* and *Altliberal* is nowhere more audible. The equality of rights introduced by democracy, we are told, makes people keenly aware of inequalities they had hitherto accepted as part of the order of things. Inequality of wealth, in particular, becomes intolerable. But the contempt for most forms of labor (the so-called banausic occupations), which the Greek democracies inherited from their aristocratic predecessors, left few opportunities for remedying this situation through work (8:260–61). As a result, the poorer citizens first allow themselves to be rewarded for attending the assemblies and the courts, then they deliberately sell their votes, and begin to threaten the well-to-do, through the courts, with confiscations of property. The cancellation of debts is the next step. "Property ceases to be sacred and everyone measures his rights according to his so-called needs (i.e., desires). And for all that a momentary majority of votes was all that was required." Respect for the continuity of tradition, law, and culture is destroyed. "Everywhere we observe only revolution and counter-revolution" (8:248–49).

The process of corruption was already advanced by the fifth century, when "political organization had become predominantly democratic, individuality had been awakened and developed and was already in conflict everywhere with the state, and reasoning and argument were more and more the rule rather than simple fulfillment of one's duties" (11:264 *[273]*). A century later, the general character of Athenian life was that "every one was more concerned with his rights than his duties, with pleasures than with work" (11:329–30 *[301]*).

The state had ceased to be the *Eins und Alles,* the "higher self" of every citizen, and become a common property to be exploited by individuals bent on their own pleasure and interest. Burckhardt took the rhetor or demagogue and the sycophant or informer as typical products of democratic regimes. The man who has learned to speak well gets himself elected to lucrative positions in the state; the informer or investigator is necessary because too many elected officers have their hands in the till. Corruption is normal, not exceptional. The sycophant threatens everybody, however, the innocent as well as the guilty. No doubt with certain periods of the French Revolution in mind—today's readers could supply more recent instances—Burckhardt spoke of "public terrorism" (8:231–33). Fifth-century Athens, which most neohumanist scholars had taught generations of students to admire as a Golden Age, presents a bleak picture in Burckhardt's *Cultural History of Greece.* 'The real perils amid which any citizen lived who had distinguished himself in some way were so great that there was undoubtedly a decline in simple sociability [*die soziale Empfindlich-keit*]. The sycophants and the rhetors, the constant threat of legal prosecution by the state, especially on charges of venality and insufficient performance, along with the ever present danger of an accusation of impiety (*asebeia*), all of this taken together constituted an enduring state of terror" (*Gesamtbilanz,* 9:326 *[73]*).

By the fourth century the situation had become intolerable. The theater which had been at the core of the old polis now contributed to the breakdown of social solidarity. Aristophanes in particular used the stage as an instrument for slandering and discrediting individuals. "One might say in his defense," Burckhardt conceded, "that comedy was simply being made to stand in for an ineffective police force and justice system"—in which case, he observed unsympathetically, it took on a heavy responsibility rather lightly—and that it generally came out against demagogues and demagoguery. In fact, Burckhardt insisted, the comic dramatists ran few risks since, on the one hand, the demos enjoyed seeing its own leaders—or indeed anybody who, having emerged from its ranks, came to consider himself superior to the crowd—being made fun of, and, on the other, the objects of greatest mockery were always the rich, the influential, and those from old families (9:328 *[74–75]*). The overall judgment of fourth-century Athens is extremely negative:

> At all times and in all places there have been fiendish men, and the violence of all public life in Athens is not to be measured by our standards of security. The most repellent feature—because of which we look on the Athens of the public orators with horror—is this: that the public assembly and the court of justice, with all their official forms and procedures, had become the theater and the instrument of the worst forms of chicanery and persecution. When we envisage for ourselves the venal orators, the mass of resolutions and decrees that were never executed, the scandalmongers and slanderers,[75] the sycophants and false witnesses, the deliberate implicating of innocent people in criminal lawsuits, the silencing by means of murder of any one who is by right superior, we are taken aback by the enormous shamelessness with which evil exhibits itself publicly here (10:333).[76]

Finally Burckhardt comes out with it: "This situation has its equivalent in the French *Terreur* of 1793/4" (11:333 *[303]*). What Burckhardt conjures up in his description of the democratic polis is an ugly situation reminiscent of the worst days of the French Revolution, in which "men of original mind" are eliminated or intimidated into withdrawing from public life (8:276), while the mass of the citizens responds with resentment, suspicion, and hostility to the exploitation of the state by demagogues. "The permanent mood of the Athenians was as if something had been stolen from them. We are dealing here with a demos that has in part truly been betrayed and robbed by those in public office and in part been kept in a state of permanent angry distrust of the state authorities and that has become insatiably greedy for pleasures and handouts as a result" (11:187 *[229]*). Had modern Europeans not been so brainwashed about the glory of ancient Greece (11:189 *[230]*), they would have been forced to acknowledge that "no political power [*Potenz*] in the whole of world history ever paid such a frightful price for existence as the Greek poleis." It is childish, Burckhardt insisted, doubtless with Grote in mind, to imagine that it was the wicked Macedonians who came along one day and deprived the Greeks of their freedom and of every superior value. First, the Greeks never enjoyed freedom as we moderns understand it. And second, the polis was undermined by its own internal contradictions. The negative aspects of the polis "were old," as Burckhardt put it. "From the time democracy made inroads in the poleis, their internal life was dominated by constant persecution of all those individuals who were *capable* of amounting to something . . . ; by relentless attacks on talent, no matter how loyally and devotedly it tried to be of service; by periodical pursuit of those with possessions; and finally, by the fully developed conviction, among the persecutors, that . . . anyone of distinction must be so inwardly enraged that he would prove a traitor as soon as the opportunity arose" (11:484).

The trials of life in the democratic polis gave a new twist to the pessimism that Burckhardt—like his colleague Nietzsche—considered characteristic of Greek culture in general. That pessimism, according to him, was not a learned product of philosophical reflection but was deeply ingrained in the outlook of the entire people.[77] The Greeks were convinced, he claimed, that man is born to be unhappy and that it is far better not to be born or at least to die young (9:360 *[99]*). Hesiod's pessimistic account of the five ages of man reflects popular feeling (9:353 *[94]*). In *The Cultural History of Greece* many features of Greek life (such as the common view of sickness, the short period of mourning for the dead, the exposing of the newborn, the practice and justification of suicide) are grouped together and explained as aspects of the pessimism that is held to have pervaded the entire culture and to have been derived from a sober awareness of the fundamental facts of human existence (9:353–92 *[94–124]*).

In aristocratic societies, however, Burckhardt argued (again anticipating Nietzsche), pessimism is combined with a remarkable serene cheerfulness (*Heiterkeit*) and a striking eagerness to challenge life and do battle with it. This might take the form of dedication to a cause, heroism in battle, or the creation of works of art. "The remarkable peculiarity of the entire phenomenon of Greek pessimism becomes fully perceptible in the light of the strong optimism of the Greek temperament, which is thoroughly creative, plastic, turned toward the world and which, in addition, can appreciate—on the surface—the use and enjoyment of the passing moment" (9:358 *[98]*).

Taxing oneself to the utmost, struggling to reach the very limits of one's capacity, was not incompatible among the early Greeks with pessimism. On the contrary, it was the heroic response of a lively and gifted people—as, *mutatis mutandis,* it might be seen to have been Buckhardt's own response to the century of Blood and Iron.[78] Democracy, however, aggravated the hardships that human life itself invariably brings by undermining the ideals that had stimulated men to make enormous efforts, despite hardship, for the sake of goals they believed reached beyond themselves. As the old unity in the polis of state, culture, and religion disintegrated and as society fell under the sway of a greedy and resentful populace and the demagogues expert at manipulating its passions, gifted and noble-minded individuals withdrew in ever larger numbers from all participation in public life.

In contrast to most advocates of democracy, who envisage the individual in a democratic society as an active, participating citizen, Burckhardt held that disengagement from the polis and from politics—*Apolitie,* to use his own term, "the turning away from the state of many decent and in particular many talented citizens" (8:259)—is an inevitable, not a fortuitous feature of democracies.[79]

Two figures—both from the fifth century and both, significantly, described as "philosophers"—are evoked in a preliminary review of the phenomenon: Heraclitus of Ephesos and Timon of Athens—a philosopher and a "well-known, noble-minded, philosophically cultivated and at one time generous citizen who came to hate his city because of the ingratitude of friends and protégés" (11:200 *[233]*). Those two figures are emblematic, for Burckhardt, both of the citizen who withdraws from the polis and of the very force that destroyed the polis. For philosophy could not but be hostile to the pessimistic, agonistic worldview that characterized the polis in its heyday. Philosophy, Burckhardt held—like Nietzsche—is ultimately optimistic. With the help of its sister disciplines—sophistic, rhetoric, and science—it believes it can achieve mastery and control and it rejects the fatalistic, often tragic view of the world communicated in and through myth. Critical, abstract thought, corroding all naive belief and reverence, is understood in *The Cultural History of Greece* to both accompany and promote democracy and to be thus itself partly responsible for the descent into demagogy which led to aggravated persecution of philosophers.

With the exception of a very early period when they were advisers and wise men in the state, philosophers, we are told, had consistently been critics and enemies of myth (10:348), which, as Burckhardt never tired of repeating, is the heart and soul of the polis. The very earliest physical speculations already marked a "break with myth" (10:297). Heraclitus, as we saw, "did not disguise his hatred of Homer and his world of gods" (10:297). For it was clear that the advancement of philosophy was conditional on the destruction of myth. But if "philosophy is essentially the act of breaking through myth" (11:261 *[271]*), it is also at the same time the destroyer of the polis.[80]

Understandably, the polis was cool to philosophers. It "required of its citizens other things than knowledge," and no idea is more alien to the ancient Greeks than that the state should be involved in promoting knowledge. Pervading as it did every aspect of life, the polis in its heyday did not need to exercise "tyranny through the school" and left the education of citizens to be carried out in the home or in private institutions (10:342). Burckhardt's own sympathy for a form of education that reflects and communicates a culture rather than a state ideology, in modern times as well as in antiquity, is well documented, especially in his correspondence, and probably expressed the outlook of the Basel patrician, to whom *Bildung* or culture is not something to be systematically imparted or redistributed but something closer to a family inheritance. When it attempts to manipulate *Bildung* and subordinate it to its own ends, the state destroys it, according to Burckhardt, no less effectively than it destroys art when it attempts to turn it into an instrument of propaganda.[81]

The tension between the polis and the philosopher was such that from time to time the polis drove out or executed thinkers and researchers that the natural aptitude of the people had thrown up alongside poets and artists. By the fifth century, trials for impiety had become frequent (10:342). "When any one wanted to destroy a philosopher for political or social reasons, a charge of impiety was brought, which was always only a cover-up for some other hatred. . . . Thus the enemies of Pericles went after Anaxagoras on the grounds that he had presented the sun as a stone or a mass of molten metal, given naturalistic explanations of the signs produced at public sacrifices, proposed moral readings of the Homeric myths and interpreted the names of the gods allegorically" (10:299).

As aggravated internal tensions in the poleis as well as conflicts among them led to increasing tyranny and persecution, the rift between the philosophers and the polis grew deeper. *"Apolitia,"* Burckhardt observed at the conclusion of a portrait of Socrates in which it is almost impossible to doubt that he invested a good deal of himself, "is a common trait of all the philosophers and the natural reaction to the despotism of the polis" (10:358). "Few participate in the affairs of the concrete polis in which they reside, but reflect instead on the state as such, write theories of politics, and compose utopias. The world of thought offers them an inner happiness independent of the ruined polis, a refuge similar to religion in Christian times" (10:348). Many embrace poverty to signal their indifference if not disaffection (10:348, 358). "With few or no needs, they were able to despise the polis, the singular state, of which they are a living criticism" (10:358). Almost to a man, the philosophers are cosmopolitan and universalist. Already at the end of the sixth century and the very beginning of the fifth, Heraclitus had "turned away from the concrete polis to deal with larger problems and no longer with those of a single city; he is already a citizen of the world" (10:297).[82] Socrates, it is true, fulfills his civic obligations scrupulously, but in general is not actively engaged in political life (10:352–57). Plato is as remarkable for his *apolitia* as for his utopian laws and constitutions; the two in fact go together. In the *Theataetus* he has Socrates describe the philosopher as a man "whose body is in the polis but whose spirit moves freely everywhere" (10:365). The Cynics' embrace of poverty had "placed them, since Antisthenes, outside the polis, which they needled with their disdain. They are at home everywhere and everywhere strangers, a living critique of the despotic and decadent free city-state" (8:275). The Stoics notoriously have "no relation to the polis, but only to the world and deplore the division of mankind into states and cities with different laws" (10:367). Finally, Epicurus, who disclaimed any political ambition and notoriously recommended living in obscurity, far from the state, inverts the traditional relation of citizen and polis when he reduces it to a contract, the aim of which is to achieve the greatest possible measure of security for the individual citizen. "Man does not exist for the sake of the law; the law exists for the sake of man" (8:275, 10:367–68).

Burckhardt invoked the testimony of Diogenes Laertius: "The educated, who might have lent support to public life by their virtue, held back from the state and, out of fear, concentrated on their private lives, while the affairs of the state fell into the hands of the most wicked and presumptuous citizens" (8:260).[83] What began with some notable individuals in the fifth century, in sum, became a more and more general feature of the life of the polis.

> In earlier times the Greek could be understood only as a living part of his polis. The polis was the focus of all his efforts and of his moral life. But the development of the darker tendencies of democracy and the devastating moral and physical effects of the Peloponnesian War on the entire Greek people released the most able—even in Sparta—inwardly and even in some measure outwardly from their polis. Some seek now only to dominate the state and exploit the condition of Greece and feel themselves inwardly bound to nothing at all. Others live for the sake of spiritual or intellectual concerns that no longer have anything to do with the state. The majority desire only their own pleasure and satisfaction. Many belong as mercenaries to anyone who can afford to pay them (11:277 [282]).
>
> Obviously and notoriously, Greece was morally much diminished in comparison with the fifth century, not so much in private affairs as in everything regarding the polis. The highest idea of Greek life had at this point—as was clear for all to see—become bankrupt. The turning away of all thinking and

cultivated people from the state, their indifference to politics, and their cosmopolitanism were openly acknowledged phenomena (11:352 *[317]*).

As so often happens with Burckhardt, the historian's argument demonstrates
that good effects in history may spring from evil causes and that evil effects may
be produced by good intentions. *The Cultural History of Greece* shows that the
decline of the polis and the inward withdrawal from it of the noblest minds
resulted in an immense deepening of the inner life of the individual and in a
vision of solidarity among all human beings, not just the citizens of a single
polis. The very efforts of the polis to clamp down on the emigration of its unhappy citizens only aggravated the distance between an increasingly impoverished and repressive public life and the ever richer domain of private life.

> There was an old . . . idea that it was "not proper" to live outside of one's own
> city; . . . As in France in 1793 and 1794, every attempt to flee could still be
> punished by the all-powerful state [*Zwangsstaat*] . . . as a criminal offense. But
> even if flight could be prosecuted as avoidance of military service and de-
> nounced as a capital crime in intemperate speeches, like that of Lycurgus
> against Leocrates, that still was not enough to dam the stream of fleeing citi-
> zens. It was especially bad for the polis that the most distinguished of those
> who remained meticulously kept their distance from those sentiments of devo-
> tion and loyalty on which the polis counted. . . . For the very reason that the
> polis had screwed up its power to such an extent that it tyrannized all publicly
> expressed ideas, it could no longer touch the inner man; people's imaginations
> slipped from its grasp and sought out philosophy, the pleasures of life, and
> whatever else (11:376 *[324–25]*).[84]

The erosion of the polis as the *Eins und Alles* of the citizen is highlighted by
the pointed juxtaposition of the philosopher and the mercenary soldier, in the
section on "Fourth Century Man," as two sides of the same coin (11:311). The
emergence of both signals the death of the citizen and the rise of the private
individual.

If abstract thought reflected and contributed to the decay of the polis, poetry
and art, in contrast, as the audible and visible manifestations of myth, were
intimately bound up with the life and strength of the polis.[85] Inevitably, the
destruction of myth by philosophical rationalism resulted in the undermining
of the ideal character of Greek art. The rot began with literature. For Burckhardt, as for Nietzsche, the work of Euripides signals the decline of tragedy
into melodrama, the abandonment of the unquestioned and timeless mythical
view of the world for the views of contemporary scholars and philosophers,
the displacement of the language of poetry by a well-honed rhetorical practice
designed to produce strong emotional effects on the audience (10:227), and the
substitution of a trivializing realism for the heroic, idealized, larger-than-life
figures that represented humanity in the work of his predecessors. In Euripides,
according to Burckhardt, the monumental heroes and heroines of myth are re-

duced to the proportions of figures in genre painting. Whence Aristophanes's complaint that Euripides does not respect the generalizing, ideal character of tragedy. "There is indeed a quality in his work that recalls German painting of the fifteenth century," Burckhardt adds: "hideously realistic characters against the generalized golden background of tragedy" (10:228). The wonderful language of Euripides is that of the schools of rhetoric and the cultivated circles of Athens; it is much clearer and easier for us now to understand than that of his predecessors (10:232). "His plays are talking assemblies that echo the general Athenian rationalizing about divine and human affairs. Even in moments of highest emotion, Euripidean characters never miss an opportunity for a well-placed antithesis" (10:228–29). In general, the common reproach is that his work "does not proceed from inspiration but from the chatter of the time and the scraps and fragments of contemporary culture" (10:232).

In passages such as these it is not hard to hear the voice of the champion of the great Italian painters of the schools of Florence and Rome, the severe censor of Rembrandt and Caravaggio, as well as of nineteenth-century realism. The critic of the "neurotic frenzy" of life in the modern *Grossstadt* or metropolis is likewise audible in the account of growing sickliness and "nervousness" and increased preoccupation with medicine and doctors among late fifth-century Greeks, as the culture of the agon degenerates, thanks to the celebrated "development of the individual," into acute interpersonal competitiveness (11:214 *[241]*). The decline of literature under the Diadochan successors of Alexander is explicitly compared to a contemporary situation often denounced by Burckhardt: the invasion of literature by the values of the newspaper and the feuilleton. "The novel was missing from the literature of the age of the Diadochi. But only because the high cost of papyrus prevented the development of reading fodder, the industrialization of the publishing business, and the mass production of books for the reading masses" (11:606).

Burckhardt's account of the decline of the polis, which complements the systematic description of Greek culture in Books I and II, contains many harsh observations on the consequences of democracy and majority rule and on the displacement of a mythical and poetic worldview by a rationalist and philosophical one. Moreover, it is clear that Burckhardt fully expected his readers to make connections between the world of ancient Greece and their own contemporary world. "It is not the only time in the history of the world that envy has disguised itself as noble sentiment," he noted in a passage in which he claims that the "simplest explanation" of the strict sumptuary laws of the Spartans was not "a great resolution by the wisest members of the caste to practice abnegation" but was rather due to the envy of the "increasingly impoverished majority of the Dorians" who demanded "the satisfaction of knowing that large inheritors would not be able to enjoy their wealth" (8:104).[86] The historian's jaundiced view of developments that threatened the "culture of old Europe"—the growth of state power and the rise of fiercely competitive nationalist states, the spread of democracy and populism and the decline of individuality, the industrialization and rationalization of all areas of human activity, which he saw as the triumph of philosophy and of the rationalist, enlightened project to achieve domination of nature (including human nature)—can usually be sensed in his judgments of the ancient polis.

For while striving to achieve a degree of detachment from his *Krähwinkel* of a fatherland and even from "history" as a whole, Burckhardt had never aimed at indifference. The man who so often expressed his contempt for modern "newspaper culture" was in fact an avid and attentive reader of newspapers.[87] Even toward the end of his life when he declared, not for the first time, that he would "have no more of politics,"[88] he continued to discuss politics in Basel and in Europe in his letters to his many correspondents. Moeover, according to Kaegi, "as long as he was able to get out of the house he never missed a chance to vote."[89] *Apolitia* is not depicted in *The Cultural History of Greece* as a favorable development, even if it does not exclude a flowering of culture and is often accompanied by an enormous enrichment of the inner, private life of the individual. There may be something of Burckhardt himself in Diogenes's alleged combination of pessimism with *"Heiterkeit"* (which we might translate as something like "high spirits"), even more in the portrait of Socrates, who might seem to exemplify the historian's ideal of the "free personality." Like Burckhardt, Socrates forms men, not professionals, and fulfills his civic duties punctiliously even while retaining a critical distance that would have been alien to earlier citizens of the polis.[90] Diogenes and Socrates, however, represent courageous and admirable responses of "wounded humanity" to difficult historical conditions, not universal models. Fifth-century Athens resembles the last century of the ancien régime, the century of Enlightenment, more than it resembles the Renaissance with its teeming creative energies.

Nonetheless, Burckhardt's account of the decline of the polis is not a lament, in the style of Schiller or Hölderlin or, to some extent, even Hegel. The overall tone remains detached, often briskly satirical, rather than elegiac. One of the work's stated aims, after all, was to destroy the idealist view of the polis as a lost paradise, and to consider it instead as soberly and realistically as possible. Even in its heyday, as we saw, it was far from being an earthly paradise in Burckhardt's eyes. A realistic approach to all ages of the past was an essential part of the historian's effort to emancipate the study of history from *philosophies* of history. Judgment was thus bound to be complex and nuanced. It could not be deduced from ideas about the meaning and direction of the entire historical process. It had to be based on an unprejudiced examination of each situation from the purely human point of view of "suffering humanity."

Even when he enjoined the reader to look squarely at the Athens of Pericles and to recognize, beyond the transfigured image handed down by tradition, a bleak picture of repression and terrorism (9:355–56 *[96]*), even when he argued that there was probably still greater suffering than we know of, because many chose to suffer in silence and left no record of their distress, Burckhardt emphasized that "a large number of individuals nevertheless enjoyed whatever bliss the spirit can attain through the higher forms of art and poetry, thought and study, and, by reflecting it outward from their own being, communicated it to others" (9:356–57 *[96–97]*). The fortunes of culture, in short, do not necessarily correspond to those of politics and the state. Culture may even thrive—*pace* liberal optimists—in the midst of great suffering and in conditions of political corruption and oppression. "These creative powers have in some measure always been optimistic among the Greeks; that is to say, for artists, poets, and thinkers, it was always worthwhile to confront this world, however it may be, with mighty creative works. However dark their thoughts of earthly existence, the energy with which they struggle to bring to the light of day free and majestic images of what lives within them never flags" (9:357 *[97]*). As for Schopenhauer and for the Nietzsche of *The Birth of Tragedy,* art for Burckhardt was less a reflection of life than a counterbalance to it, an affirmation of human energy and joy, as well as a source of consolation in the face of the harshness of existence.

If there is no historical teleology, and if all historical phenomena have to be judged on their merits, rather than according to their place in a progressive evolution, "decadence" becomes an imprecise and questionable notion—as Ranke's idea that each age and each culture stands "in an immediate relation to God" already implied. A "decadent" culture may achieve great brilliance and even "decadent" political regimes may permit the development of important positive values, such as a rich inner life and even a highly developed personal ethics. After the greatness of Athens had become irretrievably a thing of the past and philosophy, with its disaffection from the state, had come to set the tone, no place in Greece, Burckhardt reminds us, was nearly as lively as Athens. The city was the center of the brilliant new art of eloquence—about which Burckhardt's judgment, though not favorable, was nuanced. "Eloquence heavily overshadows all the other talents of the Greeks by about 400 B.C.," he wrote, "and takes away the quality of naivete from everything they say. In the life of the state, it operates like the press today, a little for the good and 75 percent for ill" (11:255 *[267]*). Nevertheless,

> [i]t seems to us that the sophists have been taken altogether too tragically. People have paid too much attention to the voice of the Platonic Socrates. . . . Because of their doctrine that there are two sides to any question, they are supposed to have preached ethical indifferentism and thus hastened the process of decline. But there is nothing inherently objectionable about the idea that opposite opinions on any topic may be equally well defended and made to seem

plausible by good arguments: it simply articulates a fact and makes it a matter for the student's conscience that he defend only what truly seems right to him. On the matter of the application of this idea to law and morality, we would really have to have better sources than Plato, who was in competition with the Sophists (11:251–52 *[265]*).

As for the claim that the Greeks were corrupted by the Sophists, it is devoid of credibility. "The responsiblity belongs to the entire nation, which had fallen in love with talk. . . . Anyway, the Greeks had always been excellent advocates in everyday speech, long before Gorgias appeared on the scene" (11:253 *[266]*).

In addition, tragedy continued to be played and new works to be added to the repertory. Comedy was enriched by the new forms of the Middle and the New Comedy. "We have the impression of enormous intellectual and artistic energy" (11:336 *[305]*).

But it was not only rhetoric and the arts that thrived in the decadence of the polis; human behavior could still be marked by courage and nobility. Even at the lowest ebb of the city's fortunes, in the age of the Macedonians, there were, "despite everything, still two faces of Athens. Alongside the corrupt, shamelessly sycophantic city whose demagogues and *strategoi* do not deserve even a mention, there is a better one that holds out against Cassander (304 B.C.) until Demetrius appears as a liberator, frees itself from the Macedonians under the leadership of Olympiodorus, plays a significant part, albeit exaggerated by historical tradition, in the defense against the Celts, and wages the Chremonidean War (269–262 B.C.) against Antigonus Gonatas unsuccessfully but not without honor" (11:498).

In general, there is no necessary one-to-one correspondence between political conditions and the condition of culture or human behavior. Even within culture there may be wide variations. The *Zeitgeist* does not rule over all. While literature was inferior in the fourth century in comparison with the fifth, for example, the vital energy of the plastic arts was undiminished. As the latter had the good fortune, Burckhardt explained, to be considered banausic, only the most committed individuals were drawn to them in the first place and they were saved from being dissolved, like literature, in the chatter of rhetoricians and philosophers (11:383 *[330]*).

Two centuries later, the Pergamum altar offered an even more telling instance of the relative independence of culture with respect to politics. "Amid the indescribable wretchedness of Greece," we are told, a school of sculptors arose in Pergamum to produce some of the greatest works that have come down to us from antiquity. "Shortly before or after 197 B.C., hence under Attalos I or Eumenes II, there arose the famous altar, the astounding remains of which would in themselves be sufficient to make the Berlin Museum one of the chief pilgrimages in the world" for art lovers. "It is as though nothing had affected this art. With all the vigor, freshness and naivety of youth, and using means and techniques that are far closer to Phidias than one would ever have expected, it throws itself, like a lion on its prey, on the mightiest theme that myth can offer"—the struggle of the Titans and the Gods (10:54).

To Burckhardt both the Winged Victory of Samothrace in the Louvre and the great frieze from Pergamum were unquestionably major artistic achievements, despite the fact that they are works of the late, supposedly "decadent" period of Greek culture. Since it had been moved from the extremely unfavorable spot where it was exhibited before, he wrote to Max Alioth in the spring of 1882, the Victory, which was commissioned by one of the Diadochan kings, had been revealed as an outstanding work of sculpture. As for the Pergamum altar frieze, of which, he told Alioth, he had obtained large photographic reproductions, it challenged all the established patterns of art history and had sent the professionals scurrying to salvage their systems. "The professionals in the field of archaeology are already working at comparisons with Phidias in order to belittle it," he noted sarcastically. "They are not happy until they can demonstrate *decadence* somewhere."[91] Later the same year he wrote Robert Grüninger that he had been to Berlin to see the Pergamum altar, since "any one who practices my trade"—the history of art—"and has not seen these Pergamum things is a miserable worm." The discovery of this "overwhelmingly powerful work has wrought havoc in the systems of the archaeologists," he went on. "The pseudo-aesthetics of the academics [*die halbe Aesthetik*] has crumbled before it; everything that has been written about the emotional power of the Laokoon is for the waste-basket now that we have these terrific, glorious scenes."[92] One could no longer assume that whatever shows energy and simplicity is necessarily historically prior to what is more refined and sophisticated. In comparisons of the Laokoon with the Pergmamon altar frieze, "the extremely different standard of execution of the two works can lead to much confusion. With its broad and rapid execution technique, the frieze will give the impression of being the more original work in contrast to the unusual amount of knowledge and reflection that clearly went into the Laokoon. Imperceptibly the more 'original' acquires the meaning of the 'earlier' or of a 'precedent,' and that is a development one must be on guard against."[93]

Burckhardt's surprisingly positive assessment of the Hellenistic age—which was generally held in low esteem because of its association with the decadence of the polis—extended beyond the domain of the plastic arts.

The judgments of Philip of Macedon and of Demosthenes in *The Cultural History of Greece* are more nuanced than in Burckhardt's earlier writings. The Athenian orator now appears more as a characteristic figure of his time—that is to say, complex, morally equivocal, opportunistic, possibly less courageous than he might have been.

> As far as his political uprightness is concerned, that was already a matter of dispute in antiquity inasmuch as it was unclear whether he had accepted Persian gold, and if so, how much. Our affair is not to take sides *against* him inthat matter. Equally, however, we find it facile, simply on the basis of the

aesthetic effect he has on us, to make the great orator into a spotless model of patriotism and to describe the accusations of a Hyperides, a Theopomp, a Demetrios of Phaleron as mere hate-filled gossip. We cannot therefore go along unreservedly with modern efforts to salvage his honor. We have to admit that any one familiar with the Athens of that time will exercise extreme caution in deciding issues of that kind (11:343–44 *[310–11]*).

There are questions, according to Burckhardt, about Demosthenes's conduct on the battlefield, his loyalty and consistency, and his judgment (of Alexander, for instance). Philip of Macedon, in contrast, emerges from the pages of *The Cultural History of Greece* as a man of outstanding talent and sagacity, *"der geniale Mensch"* thanks to whom a state that had hitherto counted for little became the master of Hellas (11:284 *[288]*). Burckhardt admires his judgment and self-discipline and distinguishes carefully, for all his demonic power over other men (11:367), between *"der grosse Realpolitiker"* (11:363) and such *"ruchlose Outlaws"* as Lysander, who sought to profit personally from the polis's loss of aura and prestige in the aftermath of the Peloponnesian War (11:285–86 *[289]*). Even the Diadochi appear as gifted and in many respects extraordinary individuals, the first Greeks to wield power over large states (11:436–57). The decline of the polis, in other words, does not entail a totally negative judgment of those whose historical fate it was to emerge at that point on the stage of history.[94]

There is, in fact, something portentous and positive as well as something wretched and depressing about the decadence of the polis. The polis had never been perfect: even in its heyday it had been harsh, demanding, controlling, and unforgiving. Its decline marks the end of one era of history but is at the same time the condition of the preservation of the essential elements of Greek culture for the future. In the course of its slow disintegration as a total way of life—that is, as a complete, but unique, fusion of religion, politics, and culture—the Greek city-state came increasingly to represent an ideal of culture that was available to others beyond it in time and place. In Athens in particular it is possible to observe a historically momentous development by which Greek civilization was transformed from a political into a cultural power, and the Greeks themselves were transformed from citizens into men of culture (*"Bildungsmenchen"*) (11:335 *[305]*). As Burckhardt put it pithily at the opening of the section on "Fourth Century Man," "after the Peloponnesian War, the history of Greece becomes identical with the cultural history of Greece" (11:277 *[282]*). In this way, something essential of what might otherwise have simply faded from the earth was preserved for later ages to exploit and build upon.

It is clear that, no less than his former teacher Droysen, Burckhardt is deeply engaged by the role of Hellenistic Greece as the custodian and disseminator of Greek culture, the preserver of historical continuity, and ultimately the mediator beween West and East, the ancient world and Christianity. The Hellenistic Greek, he tells us, "is no longer a man of the polis but has acquired the new and grand mission of serving as an educative influence (*"Bildungselement"*) for the entire world (11:517). There is something "providential," he adds, about the role of Alexander the Great (11:407–8), the passion of the Romans for Hellas (11:535, 546–47), the continued place of Athens and subsequently the place of Alexandria as centers of culture in an expanding and rapidly changing world (11:594–97). The reader may be reminded of the "world-historical" role attributed to Constantine the Great. Alexander, we read, is the man "who is called upon to Hellenize the world" (11:407). Before this immensely gifted, larger-than-life "adventurer" and "discoverer"—who, "incommensurable" as he is, inevitably invites comparison with Bonaparte—it is impossible, we are told, to avoid the feeling that he was led by "an almighty hand" (11:410). Grote, for one, is roundly scolded for having been completely blinded by his liberal prejudices and his passion for the democratic polis to the "colossal, heroic necessity of Alexander" (11:499n).[95] To underline his point, Burckhardt conjures up the whole subsequent development of history before us, as in a scroll waiting to be unrolled:

> We cannot wish—and here we are beyond the mere curiosity of the historian— that instead of the Macedonian dominion over Greece and conquest of Persia there had been, let us say, a conquest of Greece, divided and splintered as it was, by some new barbaric, savage power [*Naturmacht*] from Asia or from the Scythian North. We cannot wish that Rome had remained untouched by Hellenistic culture, as would have happened in such a case; for we owe it entirely to the Philhellenism of the Romans, to their attachment to a still surviving Greece, that the culture of the entire ancient world was preserved. The Hellenistic civilization of Rome then became the indispensable basis for the spread of Christianity. And Christianity, quite apart from its qualities as a religion, was later to be the only bridge destined to unite the ancient world with its Germanic conquerors. In this entire chain of causes and effects the Hellenistic world is the most important link (11:277–78 *[282–83]*).

How should one interpret the apparent providentialism of a passage such as this? As an echo of Droysen, despite the severe criticisms of the latter's admiration for power in various places in Burckhardt's writing? Droysen, it will be remembered, had been convinced that "Providence had guided mankind along the path of Hellenism in order to produce Christianity." His *Geschichte Alexanders des Grossen* of 1833 had been republished in 1877–1878 as volume 1 of a revised *Geschichte des Hellenismus,* in which the *Geschichte des Hellenismus* of 1836–1843 appeared as volume 2—in time, therefore, for Burckhardt to consult it again.[96] However, the essential element in Burckhardt's version of providentialism, as his suggestion of alternative historical scenarios seems to indicate, appears to be not so much the discovery of an objective and demonstrable providential design, as a kind of reverential gratitude for the fact that the ancient world did not actually vanish, though it might have, and for the survival of the past and of some continuity of tradition, though neither was inevitable.

The argument appears to be less that history had to be the way it was and that we should therefore approve of the Macedonians because they are part of a providential plan, than that, on the whole, we should be thankful that history turned out as it did. Providence is not a predetermined program, in other words; divine agency, if such there is, remains free and ultimately inscrutable. "What do we know about purposes? And if they exist, could they not be fulfilled in other ways?"[97] Precisely because we do not know the full pattern of causes and effects in which any particular event is embedded, we should be willing to acknowledge that "we never know what would have happened if something else, however terrible it was, had not happened. Instead of one wave of history, which we know, another, which we do not know might have arisen; instead of one evil oppressor, perhaps one still more evil."[98]

That cautious and far from triumphant version of providentialism in no way implies that everything in history is justifiable simply because it happened, that is to say, on the grounds that it happened according to a supposed divine plan. "No good results can exculpate an evil past."[99] In fact, it is rarely the case that the stronger is the better. Burckhardt is unlikely to have been tempted by social Darwinism. "Even in the vegetable kingdom, we can see baser and bolder species making headway here and there," he noted in *Weltgeschichtliche Betrachtungen*. "In history, the defeat of the noble simply because it is in the minority is a grave danger."[100] Furthermore, even if historical agents acting from base motives (of greed, say, or ambition) sometimes turn out to "inaugurate a future of which they themselves have no inkling,"[101] it is anything but certain that all historical outcomes are "ultimately" good. "By no means every destruction entails regeneration. There are . . . absolutely destructive forces under whose hoofs no grass grows. . . . We must always be on our guard against taking our historical perspectives for the decree of history." Above all, no alleged decree of history, no putative historical teleology, can be used as a justification of suffering and it is unconscionable to hold out "ultimate good" as compensation to the sufferers.[102] Of "ultimate good" Burckhardt gave, in any case, an extremely modest definition. It is not progress toward a Utopian End or Consummation of History, but simply the "continuance of the life of wounded humanity with its center of gravity shifted." The most dangerous and reprehensible consequence of the belief that conformity with a putative historical plan is the criterion by which historical acts should be judged is, however, the license to perpetrate immoral acts that such a belief can be made to yield. Here Burckhardt is unshakable. "No man of power should imagine that he can put forward for his own exculpation the plea: 'If we do not do it, others will.'"[103]

The "philosophy of history" implied by *The Cultural History of Greece* seems to be consistent with Burckhardt's sense of his own role as a recorder of the great achievements of the past in the twilight of "the culture of old Europe." The collections and commentaries of the Alexandrians had preserved essential elements of Greek culture for later ages. In the same way, Burckhardt explicitly represented himself as preserving the old "aristocratic" culture for a time of reconstruction beyond the anarchy and barbarism toward which Europe was allegedly being propelled by modern democracy—or, in his own words, for a "continuance of the life of wounded humanity" in a later time and with a new center of gravity.

Burckhardt's tempered view of the Hellenistic age recalls in fact his modest justification of his own age as one of enormously expanded sensibility and receptiveness. Though he lamented the disintegration of the unified culture of the polis at its best, he recognized that the autonomization of the three *Potenzen* of the state, religion, and culture was not an altogether unfavorable development.

> One might well say that the earlier citizen of the polis had been a different kind of human being from the subject of the Diadochi; but he was gone forever and no power on earth could bring him back. The "unity of style" which had once held every expression of culture in art and in politics together in a single whole, had forever disintegrated. The former citizenry now had a private life, however, for which they had certainly paid a high price, but in which they finally began to find pleasure and benefit. Insofar as the individual enjoyed economic independence, he enjoyed independence in general and was free to engage in whatever activity appealed to him. As a result every one followed the path to which he was drawn by his own personal tastes and talents. Every one could travel, for instance, to the degree that he could afford it, without incurring dangerous suspicion, and every one could turn his energies to whatever end he wanted. There was a division of professional activities that was entirely new among the Greeks. Under the Ptolemaic emperors in particular the military was clearly distinguished from the civil service, while artists and scholars became professionals and no longer considered themselves bound to a particular state—a development already clearly pointed to by the *apoliteia* of the philosophers. What brings men together now is no longer their common political interest but their personal activities: the scholars gathered together in the Museum in Alexandria or the actors in their *synodoi,* are no less cosmpolitan than the mercenary armies of the time . . . (11:574–75 *[355]*).

There was certainly a downside to those changes. Scholarship in particular seems to anticipate some of the developments of the mid-nineteenth century that Burckhardt found distinctly unattractive, in particular careerism, the blind amassing of "facts" and documentation, and a high degree of division of labor and specialization:

> Culture was now a matter of interest and concern only in so far as a certain prejudice in its favor had been inherited from the Hellenic tradition [*"Hellenentum"*]. And even there a type of scholarship oriented mainly toward collecting and intended to win protection and stipends from above for its practitioners formed a distinct professional activity. The individual disciplines within this field of scholarship "were developed by means of a quite one-sided concentra-

tion on a particular practice, which the Ancients would certainly have considered banausic."[104] But it was now finally acceptable to be a whole-hearted specialist, that is a *Banausos*. . . .

Whereas formerly the common upbringing of the Greeks had produced something common to them all, they were now differentiated into many different character types. The New Comedy, Pastoral, and the plastic arts strove to impress those different types deeply in every genre and to bring them out in all their distinctiveness. One might say that the total humanity of the Greeks had been enriched by extensive specialization (11:576–77 *[356–57]*).

All in all, Burckhardt's nuanced judgment of Hellenistic Greece is strikingly similar to his judgment of his own time. Those who dream nostalgically of the Middle Ages, he once noted sharply, would have an unpleasant awakening if their dreams were ever to come true, for they would quickly find themselves out of their element and gasping for the free air of their own modern culture.[105] Modern men and women, in other words, are as different from the men and women of the Middle Ages as the subjects of the Diadochi were from the citizens of the old polis. And surprisingly perhaps, Burckhardt recognized that his own age had some of the same positive—if also, inevitably, ambiguous—features that he attributed to the Hellenistic age. The culture of the nineteenth century, he wrote in *Weltgeschichtliche Betrachtungen,* is "in possession of the traditions of all times, peoples and cultures, while the literature of our age is a world literature. . . . Even in straitened circumstances, a man of finer culture now enjoys his few classics and the scenes of nature much more profoundly and the happiness life has to offer much more consciously than in bygone times. State and Church now impose little restraint on such endeavors. . . . They have neither the power nor the desire to suppress them."[106] The same note was sounded in the introductory lecture to one of his courses on art history. The culture of his own age, he acknowledged, is fragmented and incapable of the "cohesion" he admired in the art of classical Greece or of the Renaissance. In compensation, however, "only our century has an inner and outer sense for everything and is capable of assimilating cultural values of every variety." Art history in particular belongs to that late moment of culture. "In the midst of our hurried age it is a domain of general contemplation, of which past centuries had little or no experience; a second dream existence, in which quite special spiritual organs are brought to life and consciousness."[107]

13

"A Second Creation"
The History of Art

When Paul Klee set out on a trip to Italy in the early years of the twentieth century, his future father-in-law presented him with a copy of Burckhardt's *Der Cicerone* to take along with him.[1] Once the standard vade mecum of travelers to the Peninsula, *The Cicerone* has receded into history and is now known chiefly to scholars. The last English edition dates back some ninety years. *Recollections of Rubens*, one of a small number of art historical writings from later life that the historian was prepared to publish, appeared in German in 1897, the year of his death, but was not translated into English until 1950 and has long been out of print. As for his copious lecture notes on art historical subjects, Burckhardt instructed that they should not be published after his death. Not surprisingly, in view of this scant output and in particular the dearth of material in English or French translation (in contrast, Middlemore's translation of *Die Cultur der Renaissance in Italien*, published within two decades of the German original, has been in print without interruption ever since), Burckhardt's reputation as an art historian has been eclipsed everywhere, with the possible exception of Italy, by his reputation as a cultural historian.[2]

Yet it was as an art historian that Burckhardt began and ended his career and won wide recognition during his lifetime. In the words of Heinrich Wölfflin, his most distinguished student, "the art historian was in all likelihood the essential Burckhardt."[3] Probably art came as close as anything in the historian's life to filling the place vacated by the religious faith he lost during his student years at Basel. Through it, he observed in one of his lectures, it was possible to obtain a "glimmer of light from our lost paradise" (*"Lichtschimmer aus dem verlorenen Paradiese"*), a "revelation similar to what was once vouchsafed through the Prophets" (*"Offenbarung, wie einst durch die Propheten"*).[4]

Apart from some short historical essays that grew out of his participation in Leopold von Ranke's seminar at the University of Berlin, Burckhardt's earliest writing was on art historical topics: articles on churches in Switzerland and Alsace and the "Bilder aus Italien" in the art periodical *Der Wanderer in der Schweiz* in the late 1830s and early 1840s; *Die Kunstwerke der belgischen Städte*

(*Art Works of the Cities of Belgium*)—a kind of Belgian *Cicerone*—in 1842; a book on romanesque churches in the Lower Rhine area in 1843; many articles on art and architecture for a new edition of the Brockhaus Encyclopaedia (1843–1846); an important review, in the Berlin *Kunstblatt* (1843) of a much discussed exhibition of Belgian historical paintings in the Prussian capital; and not least his immensely popular 1847 revision of Franz Kugler's *Handbuch der Geschichte der Malerei seit Konstantin dem Grossen* (*Handbook of the History of Painting since the Time of Constantine*), first published in 1837 and revised and reprinted many times both in Germany and in English and French translations and adaptations until the end of the century. Burckhardt continued to occupy himself with topics in the history of art throughout his life. His university courses on art history constitute a substantial manuscript archive; in the 1880s he wrote the studies of "The Collector," "The Altarpiece," and "The Portrait," which were published posthumously in German and are now, finally, beginning to come out in English translation; and in his last years he worked on the long essay on Rubens that was the only major piece of writing, after *The Civilization of the Renaissance,* that he intended for publication.[5]

Likewise a significant part of Burckhardt's career as a university teacher lay in the history of art. He was in fact one of the pioneers of art history as a scholarly and academic discipline. His first classes at the University of Basel were on the history of architecture and his first public lecture course was a hugely successful series on the history of painting given before a hundred or so subscribers in Basel in 1844–1846. At the time, art history was only beginning to win acceptance as a subject that could be taught at the university. Its earliest practitioners—Johann Joachim Winckelmann in the eighteenth century, Karl Friedrich von Rumohr and Karl Schnaase in the first part of the nineteenth— did not teach. G. D. Fiorillo gave lectures on the history of painting at Göttingen from a professorial chair established for him in 1813, but he was first and foremost a well-regarded painter and teacher of what we would call studio art. Though Aloys Hirt lectured on classical art at the new University of Berlin, it was not until 1844 that a lectureship in modern art history was created for Gustav Friedrich Waagen, the director, since 1830, of the painting gallery at the recently founded Altes Museum in Berlin. Hirt, Waagen, and Burckhardt's own teacher and mentor at Berlin, Franz Kugler, were all also, even chiefly, involved in the administration of the arts, so it is not surprising that when the Basel government opened the doors of its new public museum in the Augusti-nergasse towards the end of 1849, Burckhardt's mentor, the influential *Ratsherr* Andreas Heusler-Ryhiner, immediately thought of bringing the young scholar back to Basel to be its curator and of combining this post with some teaching.[6] In 1854, Ranke recommended his former student for a position at the University of Munich on the grounds that his exceptional knowledge of art history made his appointment particularly appropriate to an artistic center such as Munich, but the chair for which Burckhardt was recommended was a chair of history originally intended for Ranke himself, not a chair of art history.[7] Nevertheless, when Burckhardt did finally obtain a permanent academic appointment in 1855, it was to the first chair in art history in Switzerland, at the newly founded Federal Polytechnic (*Eidgenössische Technische Hochschule*) in Zurich. Burckhardt thus began his regular academic career as a teacher of art history. And it was also as a teacher of art history that he ended it.

After he returned from Zurich in 1858 to take up the chair of history at Basel, he continued to teach art history regularly. He was also elected almost immediately to the city-state's *Kunstcommission,* or Department of Fine Arts, which oversaw the museum and the commissioning and acquisition of works of art. Almost every summer term (sometimes in the winter term too) he taught one-hour-per-week courses, usually open to the public, on topics of art history: "Ecclesiastical Architecture," "The History of Painting," "Classical Architecture," "The Style of the Renaissance," "The Architecture of the Renaissance," "The Aesthetics of the Plastic Arts" (recently published from the manuscript in a modern edition), "The Aesthetics of Architecture." He was so eager that instruction in art history become a standard, not simply an occasional or supplementary subject of instruction at the University, that in December 1873, in the continued absence of funds for establishing a special chair in the subject, he proposed that he himself regularly teach a full academic course in art history as an addition to his normal teaching responsibilities, without any increase in salary. Until such time as the resources became available to appoint a special professor of art history, Burckhardt undertook to teach a sequence of courses that would meet three times a week over four semesters and that would cover the entire spectrum of art—from antiquity through the Middle Ages to the Renaissance and the seventeenth and eighteenth centuries.

The range of subjects covered in these courses is astounding. Burckhardt's present reputation, especially in the English-speaking world, rests largely on his work on the Italian Renaissance. As we saw in a previous chapter, however, his teaching of history ranged from ancient history to the history of revolutionary France. In his lecture courses on art history, he likewise dealt not only with Greek and Roman antiquity and medieval art (architecture, sculpture, woodcarving, stained glass, and so on) but with Flemish, Dutch, Spanish, German, and French art from the Middle Ages to the end of the eighteenth century.[8]

What started as a provisional, interim solution settled into a permanent arrangement. The art history course was expanded to five hours per week over four semesters and Burckhardt continued to teach it even after he retired from the chair of history in 1886. He gave it up only in 1893, when he was over seventy years old and in failing health. For almost twenty years, from 1874 until 1893, Burckhardt thus served in practice as professor of art history at the University of Basel.[9] A famous photograph shows him striding by the *Münster* on his regular brisk walk from his home on the St. Alban Vorstadt to the University, a slight wiry figure with a portfolio of engravings and photographs under his arm.

A fair amount of his later (not very copious) published writing was also devoted to art historical topics. The revised versions of Kugler's handbooks on the history of European painting and the history of world art were best-sellers that went through many editions. After a slow start, his own *Cicerone* enjoyed similar success. Even after he seemingly gave up interest in publishing his work, some of the material on art originally intended for *The Civilization of the Renaissance in Italy* went into print as the fourth volume of Kugler's *History of Architecture*. One of Burckhardt's last pieces of writing was the long, loving essay curiously entitled *Erinnerungen aus Rubens* ("Recollections of Rubens," literally "out of Rubens.")

The recently published *Skizzenbücher*—containing copious sketches and notations of painting, sculpture, architecture, and, occasionally, landscape from the late 1830s until the 1880s, which have been preserved in the Basel State Archives—also testify not only to a lifelong interest in art but to a skilled and practiced eye and hand. Burckhardt was an inspired dilettante in art as well as in poetry.

Drawing was not an idle supplement to education in the Basel of Burckhardt's day. Doubtless because of its importance to technicians and designers in the ribbon industry, it was one of the subjects regularly taught in the city-state's public schools after the educational reform of 1817. In addition, in the popular educational ideas and projects of Johann Heinrich Pestalozzi at the turn of the eighteenth and nineteenth centuries, drawing appears not as a luxury or an optional extra, not as an accomplishment of people of a certain social class, not even as a valuable practical skill, but as a critical part of the education of the child, promoting careful observation and a healthy relation between the subject and the object world.[10]

Strikingly, the key critical term in discussions of drawing by Pestalozzi and his followers was *Anschauung*, a term that also turns up frequently both in Goethe's writing on art and in Burckhardt's. To Burckhardt, the essential thing in approaching works of art, no less than the natural world, was to look at them as intensely and in as unprejudiced a way as possible—not to come to them with pre-established notions and conceptual categories in order to fit them into some currently fashionable intellectual pattern or story. "There was a time," he remarked sadly to Wölfflin toward the end of his life, in 1893, "when people traveled with a little sketchbook . . . in which they made architectonic sketches, copied elements of sculpture and noted the parts of a painting. In doing so, they looked at things carefully and precisely. Today people travel with some specialized study in mind and have only a fleeting glance to bestow on everything else."[11] In other words, they do not look. Concepts, theories, systems, the writings of critics, and the more or less widely disseminated narratives of art history itself get in the way of *Anschauung*—which is the educated but unprejudiced contemplation of independent individuals—rather as the philosophy of history and ideas of historical progress had made people less attentive to what was specific about the individual cultures and moments of the past, or as elaborate theological reasoning and philosophical interpretations seemed set to replace the simple, prayerful devotion traditionally preferred in Basel and well represented in the person of Burckhardt's father, the *Antistes*.[12]

Burckhardt might have sympathized with a remark by one of his younger contemporaries, the artist Hans von Marées, which the latter's patron and friend Conrad Fiedler took as his motto: *"Sehen lernen ist alles"* ("Learning to see is everything"). What Marées probably meant by that is that through an intense practice of looking, sight might free itself from subordination to ideas and concepts (that is, to preconceived notions of things) and recover its freshness and its autonomous powers of discovery.[13] The seemingly very modern idea of vision as an autonomous relation to the world, unmediated by concepts, had already been hinted at by one of the early art historians admired by Burckhardt. In 1827 Rumohr had maintained, perhaps under Kantian influence and certainly in opposition to Hegel, that "art is a thoroughly visual way of grasping and representing things . . . which is diametrically opposed to concepts and conceptual thinking."[14] A similar point had been made by the editor of the English translation of the first volume of Kugler's *Handbook of the History of Painting* (London, 1842), the painter and later president of the Royal Academy and director of the National Gallery in London, Sir Charles Eastlake. "The eye has its own Poetry," Eastlake affirmed. If he ever read Eastlake's preface to Kugler's work, Burckhardt must surely have agreed with its basic argument. "With the cultivated observer," Eastlake noted, considerations such as "the influence of religion, of social and political relations, and of letters, the modifying circumstances of climate and of place, the character of a nation, a school and an individual, and even the particular object of an individual painter . . . are in danger of superseding the consideration of the Art as such." For that reason, he himself proposed to "invite his [reader's] attention more especially to the Art itself."[15] That was also a major concern of Burckhardt as a teacher of art history. "The essential condition" for viewing works of art, he told the students in his art history classes, "is that the eye must still be capable of seeing and must not yet have been dulled in relation to the visible world by overexertion or have become incapable of reacting to anything but the world of writing and print."[16] According to Wölfflin, Burckhardt believed that "some element of beauty is to be found wherever the eye experiences delight. Thus there are for him beautiful surfaces, beautiful cubes, beautiful spaces, which need no further justification than the pleasure they provide for the eye."[17]

Not surprisingly, Burckhardt often referred to the difficulty of evoking pictorial values and experiences in words. As early as his public lecture courses at Basel in 1844–1846, he noted that we can never really describe (*"beschreiben"*) the innermost essence of a style or a work of art; we can only hope to suggest it by talking around it (*"umschreiben"*).[18] Even Hegelians distinguished between conceptual thinking and an original, more comprehensive, "poetic" grasp of reality from which conceptual thinking gradually disentangled itself.

By the middle of the century, the deleterious effect of learning and scholarship indicated by Eastlake—not least that of art history itself—on public appreciation of the visual arts had become a fairly common theme of artists and art critics. The claim was made more and more insistently, especially by critics sympathetic to the modern movements in the arts, such as the neo-Kantian Conrad Fiedler in the 1870s and 1880s and the doughty Julius Meier-Graefe at the turn of the century, that the visual is sui generis, nonconceptual, like smell or taste.[19] "Painting," Vlaminck would write later, "is like cooking—it cannot be explained, only tasted."[20] Art history was even held responsible by some people for the alleged inability of the new educated middle-class public in Germany, the expanded *Bildungsbürgertum* of the Wilhelminian Empire, to respond to the specifically visual qualities of the plastic arts. "We have to learn to see with our eyes again," the painter Max Liebermann declared in 1897. "If understanding of the plastic arts is less developed in Germany than in other countries, it is the Lübkes who are mainly to blame."[21] (The allusion is to Wilhelm Lübke, Burckhardt's successor in the chair of art history at the Swiss Federal Polytechnic and the author of many frequently revised, re-edited, and translated standard art histories.)[22]

Recent art historical scholarship appears to bear out Liebermann's assessment. "What the educated middle class expected from art," a contemporary art historian has observed, "was more easily satisfied by the systematic literary writings of art historians than by paintings and sculptures. . . . The educated middle class of the late nineteenth century was not a public with a trained eye but a public accustomed to the written word, a public that concealed its inability to appreciate the visual by appropriating formulas found in art periodicals, exhibition reviews, and art historical handbooks. . . . Art history itself had done everything to incapacitate the public in matters of art. Art had to undergo the serious scholarly scrutiny of the discipline before it could be passed on to the public; by the time it reached the public it had become something non-visual, a mere literary derivative."[23]

The testy hero of one of Thomas Bernhardt's novels, who takes up position every other day in the Bordone room of the Kunsthistorisches Museum in Vienna on a bench opposite Tintoretto's *White-Bearded Man,* denounces with particular relish a distinguishing feature of German visitors to the museum: They "look at their catalogue all the time while they go through the rooms, and scarcely at the originals hanging on the walls; . . . as they walk through the museum they crawl deeper and deeper into the catalogue until, having reached the last page of the catalogue, they have thereby reached the exit from the museum."[24] Ironically enough, Burckhardt's own *Cicerone*—even though it offered highly personal judgments—may well have contributed to this development. G. P. Gooch observed that the book became a publishing success only after the expansion of the railways and increasing affluence made leisure travel to Italy accessible to large numbers of the German middle classes.[25]

Burckhardt's own artistic experience and competence, though hardly sufficient to make an artist of him, may well have played a role in determining his approach to works of art.[26] That approach is sometimes contrasted with the approach of the Hegelian Karl Schnaase, the author of two pioneering works in the history of art—a study of Flemish and Dutch art (*Niederländische Briefe,* 1834) and a general history of art (*Geschichte der bildenden Künste,* 1843–1864). To Schnaase and his fellow-Hegelian Heinrich Gustav Hotho, the editor of Hegel's posthumously published lectures on aesthetics, the new discipline of art history was part of general history; and as they saw in the latter more than a mere chronicle of events, they expected art history to be more than a succession of empirical notations of artists and schools. The Hegelian philosophy of history, or their version of it, offered a foundation and a framework for the new discipline. "Art," Schnaase declared, ". . . is the most complete and most reliable expression of the *Volksgeist*" and the greatest individual artist is the one who "immerses himself most deeply into the spirit of his time and his people." Thanks to art history, "in the most brilliant periods of art we perceive through the works of individual artists the spirit of the nation." The history of art thus became the history of the various peoples among whom it was produced, demonstrating the same meaning and order as political history. If anything, art history revealed the essential movement of history more directly than political history, since art expresses the "spirit of the time" more immediately than acts and events.[27]

The belief that it is the fortuitous presence or absence of talented individuals that determines whether art flourishes or not, and therefore that "the task of art history is simply to tell the story of such individuals and schools," corresponds—according to Schnaase—to the "old-fashioned" but tenacious view that history is a series of accidents. In contrast, the scholar who can discern the *"geistiges Wesen"* or spiritual reality of history and its "inner order and connectedness" understands that the history of art also has an inner connectedness, since great individual works of art give direct expression to the spirit of a people or nation and of an age. In fact, the greatness of works of art is in direct proportion to their ability to represent the essence of an age and not simply its surface accidents. Philosophy of history thus provides the order and meaning of both political history and art history. All historical phenomena—political events, wars, institutions, works of art—are to be interpreted as more or less mediated manifestations or realizations of spirit in its movement through history toward complete self-realization.[28] The inner connectedness of the history of art is thus to be found not in the evolving traditions or forms of art themselves but in the evolution of the spirit that is expressed through those forms.

In contrast to Schnaase's generalizing and systematic version of art history, which had more to say about the philosophy of art and the philosophy of history than about individual works of art, Burckhardt and his teacher, Franz Kugler, are usually seen as having adopted a more empirical approach and focused their attention on the visible forms of the artwork itself.[29] Burckhardt, in particular, often spoke disparagingly of the idealist philosophers, notably Hegel and Schelling.[30] The contrast between the idealist approach of the Hegelian Schnaase and the more "empirical" approach of Kugler and Burckhardt should not be overdrawn, however. There was much communication and common ground as well as quite sharp disagreement among leading artists, writers, and philosophers in the Berlin of the 1820s and 1830s. Alois Hirt, Gustav Waagen, and the architect Friedrich Schinkel—who were all involved both in the planning of the new museum in Berlin and in a lengthy polemic on Schinkel's conception and design of it—were all three also friends of Hegel, though neither Hirt nor Waagen (who disagreed with each other on the museum) can be considered Hegelians.[31]

It seems highly likely, moreover, that passage by way of some form of philosophy of history, in the sense of an overarching view of universal history, was an essential stage in the transformation of what Burckhardt referred to as *"Künstlergeschichte"* ("the history of artists," or art history as chronicle) into *Kunstgeschichte* ("the history of art," or art history as organized narrative).[32] In one of the earliest modern art-historical monographs (*On Hubert and Jan van Eyck*, 1822), Waagen, who had taken classes with Hegel at Heidelberg but was not one of the philosopher's disciples, acknowledged that it was "a major error of most works on the history of postclassical art that they regard art as an isolated phenomenon instead of viewing it in relation to its time and place. For every emergence of an art, every alteration of a tradition can be understood only by taking those factors into consideration. So it is indispensable to take account of political history, the political constitution of a people, its character, the situation of the church and of literature, and finally the nature of the country itself in so far as all these are elements that may be favorable or unfavorable to art and may lead to its assuming one form rather than another."[33]

In addition, Kugler and Schnaase entertained friendly relations, dedicated books to one another, and reviewed one another sympathetically, if not uncritically.[34] Burckhardt, for his part, refers respectfully to Schnaase's *Niederländische Briefe* in the text of his *Kunstwerke der belgischen Städte* of 1842 and recommends it in the foreword as "the best guide."[35] Kugler's comments on the history paintings by the Belgians Louis Gallait and Edouard Bièfve, which created a stir when they were exhibited in Berlin in the fall of 1842, are themselves quite Hegelian in tone and spirit,[36] as were parts of Burckhardt's review of the same works, published at Kugler's instigation in the then recently founded *Kunstblatt*. Burckhardt did not simply compare contemporary German history painters unfavorably with the Belgians, he noted that without a public life and public participation in national history, history painting can never be other than contrived and abstract, faithful at best to the external costume of history, but not to its life and spirit, like the Nibelungen frescoes commissioned in 1830 by Ludwig I of Bavaria from the Nazarene school painter, Julius Schnorr von Carolsfeld: "Since German governments, especially that of King Ludwig of Bavaria, have commissioned so many representations of scenes from national history, how does it come about that we lag so far behind our neighbors? In the first place, because it is not enough to have a history. If history painting is to be produced, people must be able to participate in that history and in a genuine public life."[37]

A similar judgment might have come from any of the philosophers associated with the early Hegel—Schelling, for instance, who declared in 1804, before his break with Hegel, that "[w]here public life degenerates into the particularity of private life, poetry is also more or less drawn down into this insignificant sphere. . . . Genuine and universal poetry can arise only out of the spiritual unity of a people and a truly public life";[38] or Friedrich Theodor Vischer, who was to become Burckhardt's colleague at the Federal Polytechnic, and whose writings of the 1830s and 1840s not only stipulated the political and social conditions necessary for the flourishing of different literary and artistic genres but called for action to achieve the freedom and national unity in which alone a great public art comparable to that of antiquity might thrive on German soil.[39] In a valuable study of Vischer's aesthetics, Willi Oelmüller has shown that after 1848 Vischer came to adopt many of the positions we associate with Burckhardt.[40] What seems equally true, however, is that until the late 1840s Burckhardt seems to have shared the general view that art is grounded in the *Volksgeist*. No doubt the popular uprising that had led in 1830 to the secession of the southern provinces from the United Netherlands and the creation of a new nation-state in Belgium constituted the kind of participation in public life that Burckhardt called for in his review of the 1842 Berlin exhibition and—at a time when he was closely associated with Gottfried Kinkel as well as Kugler— still believed might be realized in Germany. "Only since the uprising of 1830 has a great new historical spirit entered the [modern Flemish] school," he declared in *Kunstwerke der belgischen Städte* (1842). "As a result, in ten years of national enthusiasm, that school has created works that make it worthy to stand alongside the very greatest schools of painting." Burckhardt singled out for special praise Bièfve's *Compromise of the Netherlands Nobility* and Gallait's *Abdica-*

tion of Charles V. While their subject matter was historical, the liveliness of the execution ensured, he said, that these two paintings will be *"unsterblich für alle Zeiten"* ("immortal for all time").[41] As late as 1854 Burckhardt helped to launch an appeal for a public subscription to commission a historical painting for the new museum in the Augustinergasse from the successful Basel artist Albert Landerer, then living in Paris. The work that was delivered in 1855 depicted a key moment in the city-state's history: *Entry of the Swiss Delegates into Basel to Take the Oath of Confederation.*[42] In subject matter and style, this work differs strikingly from the tapestry-like treatment of the past in an earlier *Entry of King Rudolf von Habsburg into Basel in 1273* by Franz Pforr, a painter of the Nazarene school like Schnorr. (See illustrations at the end of this chapter.)

The Schnaase–Kugler contrast does hold in some measure, nonetheless. In his *Niederländische Briefe,* for instance, Schnaase made little attempt to describe individual works, discuss them in any detail, or convey his own response to them. His objective, he declared in the foreword, was to contribute to the theory of art and to the philosophy of history. Thus we find long reflections on the inner connection, by way of history, between seemingly unrelated genres such as landscape painting and genre painting.[43] The entire sixteenth letter (a substantial fifty-page essay in itself) deals with general questions of the theory and philosophy of art in a style reminiscent of Hegel's *Aesthetics.*[44]

Kugler, in contrast, paid more attention to specific formal features and to the effect on the viewer of individual works of architecture, sculpture, or painting. Burckhardt even more so. One of the ways in which Burckhardt contributed to art history in fact was by renewing its vocabulary and style, as Winckelmann and Diderot had done in the previous century. Where many writers still wrote on art like inventory-takers or philosophers, either not discussing individual works at all or talking "through" them to the general style they were said to exemplify and to the alleged historical significance of that style (for example, the three historical period styles outlined by Schnaase: essentially the highly codified style of the Middle Ages, the plastic style of the "high Renaissance," and the painterly style of the "Baroque"), Burckhardt invented a language of evocation and suggestion that aimed not only to conjure up a mental image of the work but to recreate in the reader the viewer's response to it.[45]

Burckhardt and Franz Kugler became close friends and collaborators. The student remained devoted to his teacher, as well as to his family, throughout his life. Both the Belgian and the Italian *Cicerones* were dedicated to Kugler, who returned the compliment by dedicating his *Kleine Schriften und Studien* (3 vols., 1854) to his "student and friend in Basel, Dr. Jacob Burckhardt." The first course Burckhardt taught as a lecturer at the University of Basel—on the history of architecture—was modeled on the course Kugler taught at Berlin in 1839–1840. Like Kugler, Burckhardt began with Carnac and Stonehenge, advancing by way of the Egyptian and Mexican pyramids, then the Babylonians and the Phoenicians, to the Greeks, and like Kugler—or, for that matter, the Hegelians—he emphasized the close relation between architecture (notably temples and graves) and religion in early societies.[46]

Burckhardt's practice of art history and his attempts to define appropriate objectives for it reveal tensions among the three perspectives he was inclined to adopt and doubtless hoped to unify in his encounters with particular works: that of the cultural historian, that of the historian of art in particular, and that of the art lover or dilettante. If he never quite resolved those tensions, he was no different in that respect from many others—his Zurich colleague F. T. Vischer, for instance. And if his stance appears to have shifted in response partly to the experience of the history and politics of his time, so did that of many others. Certain characteristic features of Burckhardt's style of thinking and of his persona as a scholar, moreover, allowed him to pursue and advocate a variety of approaches to art which, taken together, do not necessarily constitute a theoretically unified or coherent system.[47] In this respect he was, of course, extremely un-Hegelian, though curiously similar to a great French predecessor, Denis Diderot. He professed an aristocratic disdain for the tunnel vision of the systematizer; disavowed all philosophical ambition by reason of his—somewhat disingenuously protested—ineptitude in such matters; dismissed philosophical aesthetics as futile, on the grounds that the beautiful can be apprehended only in and through works of art[48] (a conviction sometimes shared even by F. T. Vischer, arguably the most prominent philosopher of aesthetics of his day);[49] claimed to distrust all abstract theoretical formulations, even of basic concepts like "Renaissance" or "baroque" style; and in characteristically Basel manner refused to let himself be boxed into dogmatic corners. He teased Vischer about the latter's work on a systematic aesthetics. "How much luckier you are," he wrote him ironically in 1854 as he sent him a copy of the newly published *Cicerone.* "You deal with eternally valid *laws* and not with transportable and destructible *things.*" Because he, in contrast, had to consider so many heterogeneous *things,* he complained—different artists, styles, periods, and a huge variety of individual works—his *Cicerone* had turned into a "little monster . . . a book which had been horribly 'clobbered together,' and into which thousands of things had had to be bent or pressed so that, one way or another, they could all be included."[50] In Burckhardt's lectures, his student Wölfflin reported, there was no systematic presentation and not a trace of art-historical method; everything arose out of the lecturer's response to individual works.[51]

One might, for instance, find in Burckhardt the stimulus for certain ideas that we associate with the aesthetics of Alois Riegl and the Vienna school: that art history is properly a history of artistic styles (*"Kunstwollen"* in Riegl's terminology)[52] rather than an account of outstanding individual artists and their works or an exercise in the *"philologisch-historische Methode"* of determining the exact authorship and date of individual works; that the art of so-called decadent ages ought not to be condemned for extraneous political or philosophical reasons but deserves to be looked at and judged for its artistic qualities (Burckhardt's receptiveness to the art of late antiquity and the baroque is well known);[53] that there are formal connections across history between styles whose proximate contexts, causes, or preconditions may be quite distinct, such as Roman imperial portraiture and the portraits of the Spanish and Dutch seventeenth century (Velasquez and Frans Hals).[54] In the aftermath of 1848 many writers besides Burckhardt distanced themselves from Hegel's subordination of aesthetics to history. Vischer, for example, tried to establish an autonomous logic of aesthetics and asserted that there was only an "approximate and partial" correspondence between the idea of the beautiful and history.[55]

At the same time, however, Burckhardt is a prime example of the kind of connoisseurship that Riegl rejected. According to the editor of Riegl's papers, "the best art historian, to Riegl, was the art historian who had no personal taste."[56] The aim of the art historian, Riegl himself wrote, is not to judge the works of other times and cultures by *our* interests and desires, but to inquire what the artists and publics of those times and cultures wanted to achieve, what their specific *Kunstwollen* was. The goal of art history, he explained, is "not to seek in works of art what appeals to our contemporary taste but to read out of them the artistic intent that produced them and that gave them the form they have and no other."[57] Only by so doing can we arrive at a proper esthetic judgment of the art of other ages.

At times Burckhardt made strikingly similar claims. He was no less passionately opposed than Riegl to judging the work of other periods by modern interests and values. In his lecture course on the aesthetics of the plastic arts, he spoke of the role of the viewer's imagination when confronted with incomplete or defective works of art—architectural ruins, faded frescoes, sketches, works whose artistic ambitions surpass the means available to the artist. In all such cases, *"die Phantasie muss ergänzen* ("imagination must complete the work of the eye")—and knowledge of cultural history (the artist's *"Gedanken- und Geschichtenwelt"*),[58] along with knowledge of art history itself, becomes a training of the imagination, a means of countering the danger of "projecting our own spirit" into the work of art. Though Burckhardt was clearly thinking here of patently unfinished or fragmentary works, what is true of them can be said to hold true, in some measure, also of finished works. Art history can thus be viewed, as Riegl was later to propose, as an indispensable propaedeutic training in imaginative response to the art of other times and places.[59]

Nevertheless, the taste and personal judgment of the experienced art lover or connoisseur remained essential components of Burckhardt's art historical writing.[60] These were in fact the qualities that enabled the viewer to transcend the tastes and preferences of his own time and place. Thus we find Burckhardt arguing in his course on the "Aesthetics of the Plastic Arts" (prepared between 1851 and 1863) that all true art has what he calls *"Idealität"*—that is to say, that what is beautiful about it may be rooted in but is not limited to a particular time and place; that it is not Dutch or French, for instance, but European, not local or even national, but universal; that it should not simply illustrate a particular historical event but should be accessible in principle to anyone at any period of historical time without detailed foreknowledge of the subject matter.[61] It is essential for the purposes of art, he claimed in 1884, in a lecture on history painting (*"Über erzählende Malerei"*), that it not be dependent on historical or any other kind of knowledge but be "immediately intelligible to all."[62] According to the art historian Emil Maurer, Burckhardt had held that view from the time of his encounter with Rubens in the early 1840s, when he was preparing *Die Kunstwerke der belgischen Städte.* That encounter had so overwhelmed him, Maurer claimed, that he came to question the liberal art-historical categories in which he still thought at the time. The essence of Rubens' work, he then argued, could be grasped without any biographical, cultural-historical, or iconographical detour by any viewer capable, on his or her side, of rising above the interests and prejudices of his or her time. "Das Sichtbare," in Maurer's words, "soll sich aus sich selbst erklären und seinerseits auch nichts anderes erklären helfen" ("The visible should be explained in its own terms; correspondingly, it should not be used to explain something else").[63] As Burckhardt was to put it himself almost four decades later, "the work of art must make its impression on the viewer independently of the content. There will always be time later to inquire what specifically it purports to represent."[64]

There was also room in Burckhardt's art history for the material elements— "function, materials, and technique"—that in the eyes of another of his colleagues at Zurich, the architect Gottfried Semper, played a major role in artistic production and that Riegl considered secondary to the more cultural or psychological *Kunstwollen.*[65]

Finally, it is worth recalling that though Burckhardt promoted *Kunstgeschichte,* as distinct from traditional *Künstlergeschichte,* it did not occur to him to repudiate the latter altogether. On the contrary, in a draft preface for his *Kunstgeschichte der Renaissance* he stated that "the art history of the Renaissance broadly conceived will have to follow the chronologically arranged, narrative history of artists. In trying to present art history in terms of types and genres [*"nach Sachen und Gattungen"*], my aim is simply to add a second, systematic part to the already existing narrative history of art."[66]

It is not clear that Burckhardt ever satisfactorily worked out the relation between cultural history and the history of art. His most famous work, *The Civilization of the Renaissance in Italy,* bears the mark of a crucial decision to forgo integrating the history of Italian Renaissance art into a book on the history of

Italian Renaissance culture. There was, in addition, as already suggested, a further potential tension between the history of art viewed as an autonomous inquiry distinct from the history of culture—including even the version of it he was to elaborate himself: the so-called history of art *"nach Aufgaben,"* that is, in terms of artistic traditions and commissions—and the understanding and *Genuss* or enjoyment of individual works of art, to which Burckhardt was no less dedicated.[67] Of that last activity his copious *Notizen*—notes taken on individual paintings or sculptures as he encountered them on his way through galleries and museums, written up later in his hotel room, and used ultimately as the basis of his lectures—bear ample witness.[68] According to one modern scholar, this unresolved tension between art history and art experience resulted in the end in Burckhardt's gradually giving up all publication in the field of art history: "What Burckhardt demanded of art history led him into an insoluble dilemma: he welcomed art history as one of the most important educational elements of his age and yet, at the same time, he wanted it to facilitate *direct* access to beauty, and thereby to make itself superfluous."[69] About the growing popularity of museums and the increasingly widespread view of art as a piece of *Bildung* or culture to be acquired rather than as an object of delight or solace to be enjoyed he had very mixed feelings. He even tried to discourage people from going to museums out of duty.[70] As his Zurich colleague F. T. Vischer once observed despairingly, "We have no need of scholarly analysis when we find ourselves before a beautiful object: we desire only *Genuss.* All scholarship achieves is that instead of *Genuss,* we have work."[71]

After the sobering experiences of the late 1840s, Burckhardt was not, it seems, in two minds about the relation of art to political history. Artistic achievement, he repeatedly pointed out, was not dependent on the successful realization of the *Volksgeist* or national spirit in the form of a national state; in general, it had only a very mediated relation to political power. In distancing himself from romantic-liberal views of the relation between the political development of a nation and the achievement of its artists, Burckhardt was not alone. F. T. Vischer, who had been a committed Hegelian, underwent a similar change as he came to judge as illusory and utopian his earlier hope that political change would solve the problem of art in the alienated modern world. If anything, Vischer came to believe, political action had aggravated the situation of art. The attempt to incarnate a people's culture in a politically powerful state was not only no more than a beautiful dream; it was a potential nightmare—one of the modern ideologies that was driving the world to *"Despotie"* and to *"Blut und Schrecken"* ("blood and terror"). The likely political consequence of utopian ideologies and the permanent danger of the current revolutionary age was dictatorship, for as it becomes apparent, Vischer held, that society cannot fulfill its general desire for change and improvement through its own efforts, it will call on a dictator to realize the impossible in the name of all.[72]

For Burckhardt, the art historian's map of Europe did not correspond in any way to Ranke's map of a continent dominated by five great powers (England, France, Prussia, the Habsburg Empire, and Russia).[73] The great European art powers, in Burckhardt's view, were Italy and the Low Countries, followed by Spain and then, at a considerable distance, by Germany and France. England hardly counted at all. Nor did artistic achievement necessarily correspond to economic prosperity or political freedom. In Spain, for instance, the incomparable artistic flowering of the seventeenth century occurred during a time of economic as well as political decline, while the achievement of Italy in the same period, a period of political and economic decadence in the Peninsula also, is hailed as "splendid testimony to the power and autonomy of the spirit with respect to the external destinies of peoples."[74] Religion and a certain tradition of culture and learning were more important for the production of art, Burckhardt claimed, than the achievement of political freedom or power, economic prosperity, or the successful incarnation of the *Volksgeist* in a national state.[75] He even rejected the widely held view that a marked decline of German art in the early seventeenth century was attributable to the devastation of the Thirty Years' War.[76] One is reminded of Voltaire's defiant declaration of the independence of art in his pioneering *Essai sur les moeurs:* "It may seem surprising that so many great geniuses arose in Italy in the midst of dissension and wars and without either protectors or models; but among the Romans, Lucretius produced his beautiful *De Rerum Natura,* Virgil his *Bucolics,* and Cicero his philosophical writings amid the horrors of civil wars. Once a language begins to take on its own form, it becomes an instrument which is ready to be used by great artists and which they exploit without paying any attention to who is governing the world and who is disturbing its peace."[77]

Burckhardt's ideas concerning the relation of art history to cultural history also appear to have evolved in the light of the "lessons" of 1848. In the early 1840s he seems to have thought of art history chiefly as a branch of cultural history. Art was one of the most important sources for the cultural historian. This was the approach of some of the most imaginative historians of the time, including the French historian Jules Michelet, whose work Burckhardt admired.[78] In 1841–1843, Burckhardt's correspondence indicates a conception of art history as—in Emil Maurer's words—"knowledge of verifiable, source-like monuments." Works of art are seen as created objects "out of which it is possible to read the structures of thought and representation of a given time."[79] "You can't imagine," he tells his friend Karl Fresenius, how, if you keep working at them, "the facta of history, the works of art, the monuments of all ages, gradually acquire meaning as witnesses of past stages of the development of the spirit."[80] In his revision of the article *"Kunstgeschichte"* for the Brockhaus Encyclopaedia, Burckhardt took over the opening sentence unchanged: "The history of art constitutes a major part of cultural history."[81] In *Die Kunstwerke der belgischen Städte* of 1842, the struggle between a realist and an idealist tendency is said to inform art "in all periods of its history." In one period the realist tendency dominates, in another the idealist tendency, but it is never the arbitrary act of will of an individual artist that determines the shift from one to the other, but "great laws of cultural history."[82] The integration of art history into cultural history had been, after all, the means by which art history was elevated by scholars such as Schnaase and Kugler from a mere chronicle of the lives of artists into a genuine form of historical knowledge, the companion and interpreter of the history of customs and manners (*"Begleiterin und Erklärerin der Sittengeschichte"*).[83] "A great deal of what is only dimly understood hieroglyphs in the written sources becomes clearly interpretable through works of art."[84] Conversely, art history occupied a privileged place in the historicist conception of history, since art was considered the only direct historical manifestation of the very principle of history—the human spirit.[85]

In the manuscript notes for the public lecture course given at Basel in 1844–1846, art history is again seen as a branch of cultural history, as *"gestaltete Geschichte."* To the loyal student of Ranke, it appeared as part of the pattern of universal history. "As in universal history, nothing here is arbitrary or accidental. Everything is deep historical currents, intimations of universal ideas." Works of art are *"Zeugen ihrer Zeit"* ("witnesses to their time").[86] Rubens, for example, is *"das Form und Farbe gewordene Belgien seiner Zeit"* ("the Belgium of his time in form and color").[87]

In these early lectures, the historical vision is more important than the aesthetic. Aesthetic judgment, we are told, is not part of art history. "It is not in any way the task of art history to judge artists and their work, but rather to understand them as witnesses to their time." Aesthetic judgment itself is historicized: "It is left to aesthetics to apply to each artist and his work the criteria of the idea that inspired him and the artistic means of his age and to judge him accordingly."[88] In an essay of 1843 on Murillo, which circulated in manuscript among the members of the Bonn *Maikäferbund*, Burckhardt expressed the same historicist view: *"Lassen wir doch jeder Epoche ihren Wert"* ("Let us grant to every age its own value")[89]—an unmistakable reminiscence of Ranke's teaching as summed up later in the celebrated phrase from the first of the lectures to Maximilian II of Bavaria in 1854: *"Jede Epoche ist unmittelbar zu Gott."*[90] This is still the position taken in a letter to Kinkel in 1847: "How is the spirit of the fifteenth century expressed in painting? Once you have formulated that question, everything becomes clearer."[91]

By the 1850s, however, Burckhardt was having second thoughts about a variety of things—among them his view of art history as a branch of cultural history. This is the time of the letter to Paul Heyse, cited in an earlier chapter, which announced a general shift in his ideas after the political and social upheavals of the late 1840s. In fact, that letter was a reflection on art history in particular: "Some time ago, I gradually altered my view of art (taken en bloc). . . . I would never have believed that such a rotted through old cultural historian as myself, who imagined that the value of every standpoint and every age had to be respected, could finally become as one-sided as I am now. But it is as if the scales had fallen from my eyes. I tell myself what Saint-Remy told Chlodowig: incende quod adorasti, et adora quod incendisti. . . . It is high time for me to free myself from the general, would-be objective respect for each and all and to become really intolerant."[92] According to Werner Kaegi, *The Cicerone,* the first great product of the new outlook, marks a decisive stepping back, on Burckhardt's part, from his romantic youth, a withdrawal from his romantic vision of Germany, and at the same time a reconnecting with another Germany, that of Winckelmann and Goethe.[93] Without rejecting the use of art as a source of cultural history, Burckhardt now argued that cultural history is not the only approach to the study of art.

In 1851, in the introductory lecture of a course on the history of architecture, he appears to have tried to work out his position on the relation of art history and cultural history with as much clarity as possible. In what seems like a reaffirmation of Gustav Waagen's cautious view of art as *conditioned* by history rather than as the incarnation or manifestation of history,[94] Burckhardt now declared that there are two ways of doing art history: "Either art history aims to be essentially a servant of history, and especially of cultural history, and it treats the beautiful as a shifting historical element; or it starts out from the beautiful and brings in cultural history only as an auxiliary."[95] Either works of art are to be regarded as silent "witnesses to their time" or there is an autonomous logic to the working of artistic forms, which may well be affected by historical conditions but is not reducible to them.

From this post-1848 perspective, cultural history can be perceived as an auxiliary science of art history, rather than the other way round. Nevertheless, Burckhardt did not abandon the idealist and historicist view of art as an expression or repository of the human spirit—though there was less talk now of the *Volksgeist* or national spirit and greater emphasis on the contribution of the individual. "Our principal theme will be: *approaches to the spirit in the works of art themselves,*" he noted in the manuscript of his course on "The Aesthetics of the Plastic Arts," given at Basel in 1863. That is to say, the beautiful work of art is to be seen as an expression in visual form of the artist's *"Vision der Welt."*[96] There is little doubt that Burckhardt continued throughout his life to regard works of art as offering more reliable and direct testimony to past moments of human culture, experience, and above all to what human beings in the past have dreamed of and aspired to, than any other documentation. The great moments

364 • CHAPTER THIRTEEN

of past religious architecture, he writes, "are often the only witnesses to an existence that would otherwise have become totally mute."[97] In conversation and correspondence with Wölfflin and others in later life, he continued to hold that works of art embody or "express" a *Vision der Welt* and that the scholar's aim is to discern that vision, even while he also insisted that the origin of great art remains "inexplicable" and that it cannot be regarded simply as the "product" of its age.[98] On the one hand: "My task in art history, as I conceive it, is to explain the imagination of earlier times; to say what kind of worldview underlies the work of this or that master or school. Others describe chiefly the techniques and means of the art of the past; my business is with the artist's intent."[99] On the other: the production of art is no less determined by a human drive to create beautiful objective forms (*"Kunsttrieb"*), as well as by specific artistic traditions and the demands and expectations of a given culture or clientele; works of art are not therefore to be seen only as "illustrating" or "manifesting" some state of culture. In sum, "We no longer look in the work of art for an idea that we take to be the key to it. We now know that the nature and origin of the work of art are highly complex."[100]

The uncoupling of art history and cultural history seems to have produced uncertainty in Burckhardt's mind about both. He continued to practice cultural history, as *The Cultural History of Greece* with its strong, programmatic introduction demonstrates, and he continued to make use of the conceptual categories that were part of the general heritage of German historicism. The basic assumption of cultural history—that the "inner life of humanity" and "points of view" are more fundamental than mere "events," that the "living *energies,* both constructive and destructive," that animate a society and find "expression" in particular actions are more fundamental than those actions themselves[101]— was, after all, essential to both neohumanism and historicism, the major influences on Burckhardt's intellectual development. But he had learned to be more wary of associating cultural history too closely with the philosophy of history than he had been in the days of his collaboration with Kinkel, and even then, it will be recalled, he had been more guarded than some of his friends. Cultural history provided understanding of what our human ancestors had suffered, dreamed of, and striven to achieve; it allowed us to connect with their "inner life"; but it offered no key to human destiny. "I have not completely lost faith in a law that governs history," F. T. Vischer had written in the aftermath of 1848. "But we cannot embrace in a single view the ways in which that law operates."[102] Burckhardt was certainly no less skeptical. His skepticism did not diminish with the years. Near the end of his life, in 1882, he told Wölfflin that he considered cultural history "a vague concept" (*"ein vager Begriff"*).[103]

In fact, Burckhardt pursued a variety of art historical paths. One pointed toward an autonomous history of art: art history *"nach Sachen und Gattungen"* or *"nach Inhalt und Aufgaben,"* that is to say, in terms of the major generic divisions of art, the particular artistic problems the artist was called on to solve with each work or commission, and the subject matters the artist had to work with.[104] Another, closely related to the first, pointed toward a more empirical, less abstract and philosophical sociology of art—a historical sociology of patrons and collectors, for instance—than that of Hegelians, such as Schnaase.[105] And a third focused on detailed commentary and interpretation of individual works, on that encounter of the viewer with the work from which a special form of delight or joy, usually referred to as *Genuss,* might be expected to result. The last named, about which we shall have more to say shortly, was not the least important. "The main thing," Burckhardt declared in his lecture course "On the Aesthetics of the Plastic Arts," "is always the impact of the work of art on the individual, the stimulation of a responsive (*entgegenkommenden*) imagination."[106] That position was restated in the lectures later published as *Weltgeschichtliche Betrachtungen:* "All high art arises when the soul is set mysteriously vibrating. What is released as a result of those vibrations no longer belongs to a particular individual or a particular time but functions as a symbol and acquires everlastingness."[107] Even at the time when he appeared most willing to view art history as part of cultural history, Burckhardt never overlooked *Genuss.* Suggesting different approaches to art history to the audience at his public lecture series at Basel in the mid-1840s—such as treating the work of art as an object of scholarly investigation concerning authorship, provenance, iconography, and so on, or as a piece of cultural history—he still asked what room such a discipline would leave for *Genuss.*[108]

In the projected *Kunstgeschichte nach Aufgaben,* artistic creation is conditioned by an artistic impulse (a *"zu Grunde liegender Wille"*)[109] that is universal but takes specific forms in particular cultures, by *"Präzedentien"* or particular traditions and "languages" of artistic production, by the expectations and demands of clients, and by the efforts of artists to explore and develop inherited forms and techniques and to find answers to particular artistic problems. Burckhardt wanted to teach art history, he once said, in a new way, "as a pure history of styles and forms."[110] As has been noted, that ambition is sometimes seen as an anticipation of the Riegl of the *Stilfragen.* Characteristically, however, Burckhardt never achieved or sought the systematic rigor of Riegl, and as a result never exercised an influence remotely comparable with that of the leading representative of the Vienna school. Though a succession of distinguished scholars have taught art history at Basel, beginning with Burckhardt's own student and friend Heinrich Wölfflin, there is no identifiable Burckhardtian school either of historians or of art historians, and that, of course, is how Burckhardt wanted it to be. He observed more than once that he did not intend to found a method or form a school. Like history, the history of art was—and ought to be, in his view—no less than art itself, the work of an individual mind and sensibility.

It is by no means obvious that Burckhardt would have been any more willing to devote himself to the mere *"Wissenschaft"* of art history than he had been willing to devote himself to the *"Wissenschaft"* of history. Nor was he essentially interested in methodology. His primary goals were always education, *"Bildung,"* forming the well-rounded, independent-minded, and harmonious human being that was the ideal of the German neohumanists; ensuring the continuity of human culture through constant reappropriation of the culture of the past rather than "scientific" knowledge of it; and encouraging the continued production of the highest art. "There is nothing more precarious than the life of books on history and the history of art," he declared. "Art and poetry do far more for human understanding than history."[111] The best history, he had once noted, is "always mostly poetry" (*"immer grösstenteils Poesie"*).[112]

There was thus no question ever, for Burckhardt, of a positivistic art history centered on the biographies of artists and on external facts about individual works. The student of Kugler and *Kunstgeschichte* did not intend to retreat to the *Künstlergeschichte* of the past. He even came to judge his own *Cicerone* too close to the latter,[113] and though he considered works of art the expression of individual artistic personalities as well as moments of culture, he consistently refused to see them as communicating particular personal experiences[114] or reflecting specific events in the artist's life. Even in one of his earliest essays, on Murillo, he provided in a couple of lines the artist's date of birth, the names of his teachers, the places he lived in, and the place and date of his death. "These are (by God!) the only documented facts I know about him," he declared. "Yet in his pictures, the history of this great soul lives for us to see, and with it the history of his time."[115] The much later book on Rubens sketched the artist's biography in a few rapid strokes before moving on quickly to commentaries on the paintings. Moreover, just as cultural history in its search for "constants" turned away from the particular events that dominated traditional political history, Burckhardt highlighted in the few pages devoted to the artist's biography Rubens's general character and the public aspects of his life (his many talents as artist, businessman, diplomat; his broad linguistic, literary, and artistic culture; his relation to Italy and the Italian masters), neither providing a detailed chronicle of events nor investigating essentially unknowable and, in the historian's view, irrelevant private experiences. Where biographical interpretations of individual works had been proposed, Burckhardt, who was himself notoriously jealous of his privacy, tended to reject them. It was commonly asserted, for instance, that in the *Madonna with Saints* over Rubens's tomb in the chevet chapel of St. Jacques in Antwerp the artist had represented his own family—grandfather, both wives, sons, daughters, and himself as St. George. This common view had been accepted by Eugène Fromentin, whose study of Rubens in *Les Maîtres d'autrefois* (1876) Burckhardt often referred to admiringly. Fromentin had claimed that the entire life story of Rubens could be read in this painting. Burckhardt at first followed Fromentin, then wrote into his manuscript: "I no longer believe in such precise family portraits."[116] The final text of *Recollections of Rubens* is categorical: Rubens's canvas, Burckhardt acknowledged "is obviously intended to convey some special message to us, and was also painted with special devotion, probably during the master's last years, but whether for his own tomb is doubtful. Some happy interpreter may one day penetrate its secret meaning, but the first condition would be that he should cease to interpret the heads as 'Rubens and his Family.'"[117]

The author of *The Cicerone* had already noted that in the case of many portraits by Titian, "we shall always be uncertain how far they were painted as portraits, how far out of pure artistic impulse, and whether we are looking at some particular beauty, or a problem of beauty grown into a picture." Through the artist's vision and the requirements of pictorial composition, empirical reality is raised to a level at which the individual is subsumed in an ideal type. Thus in two well-known paintings by Titian of ostensibly different subjects (*La Bella* [Florence, Palazzo Pitti] and *Flora* [Florence, Uffizi]), it is obvious, Burckhardt claimed, that the same woman has been represented. But "whatever the beauty of the woman who gave the impulse to these two pictures may have been Titian raised it to a plane on which it can be seen as the counterpart to the Venetian type of the head of Christ."[118]

As an art historian no less than as a general historian, Burckhardt was contemptuous of fact-grubbing erudition. *"Eitele Gleissnerei"* ("vain show"), he called it.[119] Following his neohumanist teachers, he thought of historical understanding as resulting from concentrated and sympathetic attentiveness, an *"Ahnden"* or divination, as Wilhelm von Humboldt wrote in his essay "On the Task of the Historian," rather than a product of inductive science. The mere accumulation of information (*"Materialsammlungen"*) was a task that scholars with no historical or artistic sensibility were quite capable of executing, he held, whereas it took a special, indefinable talent to penetrate to the heart and principle of things. This does not mean that Burckhardt was opposed to research and scholarship. Though he did not confuse scholarly research with the writing of history, it would not have occurred to him that there could be history without scholarly research. In art history as in other areas of history, he was a scholar of vast learning—*"einer der letzten gebildeten Europäer"* in Wölfflin's words.[120] Even if he did not keep up with the latest publications of modern research as assiduously as more "professional" historians, he possessed an unparalleled command of the published documentary and literary sources contemporary with the art works he discussed and he made more effective use of those than most art historians of his time.[121] The great artists of the past were themselves men of learning, Burckhardt liked to emphasize, not least his hero Rubens. There was a certain coquettishness, an aristocratic pose, about Burckhardt's repeated protestations of professional ignorance and his disdain of "mere"

scholarship. The fact remains that in preparing his book on Rubens, he spent
absolutely no time rummaging in the archives and a lot of time traveling all
over Europe to view the paintings.[122]

Burckhardt's rejection of a "science" or body of knowledge about art, which
is unrelated either to an understanding of the inner laws and processes of art
or to the viewer's life-enhancing experience of individual works, is of a piece,
moreover, with his acute awareness that even while vast museums were being
developed as repositories of the most heterogeneous works of art, the actual
environment of the large numbers of people for whose edification the collections were presumably intended was being progressively degraded by the relentless advance of contemporary commercial and utilitarian interests. The art museum began to seem at times like a mausoleum of stranded beautiful objects in
an increasingly unlovely modern world. Writing from London in 1879, Burckhardt described the astounding wealth of objects in the South Kensington
Museum—the present Victoria and Albert—and reflected both on the absence
of any principles guiding the collections and on the destruction of the living
urban landscape of the city in which the collections were housed. Far from
leading to a new age, in which art would enhance the life of the city as in
classical antiquity—the dream of early art critics and historians like Winckelmann and Diderot—the development of museums and of art history itself
seemed to go hand in hand not only with artistic disarray but with the crassest
indifference to beauty in the world around us. The specter that Burckhardt
glimpsed in London in 1879 and that haunted him in his later years was the
figure he was to call "the American man of culture," that is to say the modern
individual "who has rejected the historical and a large part of spiritual community," who has broken with cultural tradition "but would like to keep art and
poetry as a luxury item."[123]

> What does it mean for our art history when art is collected in this way and no
> one any longer has a comprehensive overview? If I had a year to spend here, I
> would . . . get on with the job of articulating in the clearest possible terms the
> living laws of form. . . . As matters stand, however, I cannot alter what remains
> of my career for the sake of those marvelous works. As for the Londoners,
> what good is all this high aesthetic stimulation to them, when purely utilitarian
> considerations are bringing about a colossal degradation of the city's appear-
> ance. Our new bridge in Basel [the Wettsteinbrücke] seems truly harmless in
> comparison. To be specific, a hideous, high standing, dead straight bridge of
> steel girders has been driven right through the exceptionally beautiful leading
> prospect of the city and a main line railway laid across it to a newly constructed,
> monstrously ugly ladies' trunk [the Charing Cross terminus]. As I was walking
> last night under a full moon on Waterloo Bridge, which lies just beyond the
> new bridge, I found the once wonderfully picturesque view of the Houses of
> Parliament, Westminster Abbey, and Lambeth Palace cut in two. I could have
> howled for grief. The twilight and the rising full moon made it all truly painful.
> Further down river, near London Bridge, there is another similar horror of a

steel bridge, which also leads to a colossal rail terminus. God, what else will we have to sacrifice to the "practical sense" [in English in Burckhardt's text] of the 19th Century?[124]

Burckhardt's shifting relation to the Italian scholar Giovanni Morelli provides a vivid illustration of his attitude to positivist scholarship. At first he had been drawn to Morelli because the Italian's sharp eye seemed to him more appropriate to genuine understanding of art than the "cultural-historical" chatter—*"eitler Kulturbrei"*[125]—of many art historian colleagues. He welcomed Morelli's closeness to old-fashioned connoisseurship as a counterweight to the cultural historians' approach to works of art. The section on "The hands" in the Rubens book, for instance, may well reflect the influence of Morelli. (In determining attributions Morelli often relied on careful characterization of the way individual artists represent particular, often seemingly minor features, such as hands or ears.)[126] Morelli, on his side, appreciated what he took to be Burckhardt's determination not to conflate the two talents for which he was equally famous: that of the connoisseur and that of the cultural historian. As we noted earlier, however, in refusing to subordinate art history to cultural history as it was currently practiced, Burckhardt in no way renounced the basic historicist interest in the work of art as the expression of an inner, spiritual vision. Morelli's interest, in contrast, seemed to center on identifying characteristic formal features of individual artists. In the end, as he came to believe that Morelli's method of meticulous observation of forms and unconsciously repres   d details exhausted itself in mere *"Attribuzzlertum"*—the obsessive, ultimately unaesthetic preoccupation with correct attributions—Burckhardt, here once again anticipating Riegl, turned away from it. Not long after the two men finally met in Basel in 1882 Morelli suddenly appeared in a short satirical poem of five verses (*"Klagen des alten Cic"* ["Complaint of the old Cicerone"]) as *"der schreckliche Morelli,"* whose works the old Cicerone leaves unread in his trunk while he wanders freely among the paintings themselves and announces that

> Das Beste, was in Bildern steckt,
> Ist doch am Ende, was uns schmeckt.
> (In painting the greatest treasure
> Is after all what gives us pleasure.)[127]

In the end, *knowledge about* painting was not Burckhardt's top priority. He wanted paintings to be loved "for the sake of their beauty," not for what they tell us about an artist or a culture or even, perhaps, about the history of art. "Identification of the special characteristics of particular schools and particular masters has made rapid progress and continues to do so," he declared in a public lecture "On the Authenticity of Old Paintings" at the Basel Museum in February 1882. But "this hunting of famous names has its downside; it would be much more appropriate to love pictures for the sake of their beauty. To be sure, it is a wonderful thing to be able to get to know a great master in his [authenticated] works and to enter thus into his mind and spirit. But the other approach also has its justification and its advantages—not to be concerned whether the painting has been correctly identified, provided it arouses in us the reverberations that always accompany the truly beautiful as soon as it captures our inner ideal sense and appears to us as a symbol of the all-highest." The lecturer then recalled the words of a "charming old Milanese," who owned a valuable private collection of paintings, but always turned down every request to investigate their authorship: "Purchè la roba sia buona, non mi cura di saperne l'autore" ("Provided the merchandise is good, what need do I have to know who made it").[128]

In fact, the bulk of Burckhardt's writing on art historical topics, whether published texts or unpublished lectures, consists principally of commentaries on individual works or the *oeuvre* of individual artists rather loosely connected by chronology, genre, or school. In *The Cicerone* he had avoided a rigorously systematic arrangement of the material. The work is not simply a travel guide; it is an art history. But if its organization is not geographical, it is not purely chronological either; nor is it generic, or stylistic, or topical. It is partly generic (architecture, sculpture, painting, and so on), partly chronological (fifteenth-century painting, sixteenth-century painting, and so on), and partly arranged by artist and school and, within the sections devoted to individual artists, again arranged according to generic or thematic categories (under Titian, for instance: portraits, nudes, historical paintings [sacred and profane], mythological subjects, frescoes, and so on). Wilhelm Waetzoldt writes of an "unpedantic compromise among biographical, topographical and aesthetical and technical approaches," to which is due, he claims, the "indestructible literary charm" of the book. "The point of view of a developmental history of art, the actual narrative of the history of Italian art, retreats here before the magic of personal judgments of artists and artworks, suggestive but by no means exhaustive characterizations of period styles, the powerful sensuousness of the experience of art, and an urbane freedom of tone."[129]

Likewise Werner Kaegi discovered that the lecture notes for the course on "Italian Art after 1400" (on which he relies heavily for his account of Burckhardt's views on Italian art in volume six of his great biography) do not constitute a continuous narrative but a *"Notizensammlung,"* or collection of notes and comments on individual art works. This material was classified simply according to four broad chronological categories: "Early Renaissance," "High Renaissance," "Period from 1540–1580," and "Baroque after 1580." By the 1870s, Kaegi acnowledged, Burckhardt was an experienced lecturer and no longer felt the need to write out his lectures in full.[130] Nevertheless, he claimed, the form of these lecture notes seems to point to something fundamental in Burckhardt's approach to art history, and not simply to his skill at improvising from notes.

The art historian Emil Maurer made the same point when he described Burckhardt's method as one *"des konglomerierenden Sammelns"* (of cumulative collecting).[131] As he wrote up the notes he took after viewing a number of paintings, Maurer explained, Burckhardt sometimes introduced reflections on general topics such as "Composition," or "The Hands" (as in the notes on Rubens), and as he made order in his material, he might later group various individual commentaries under such headings. Whereas the headings are quite "labile," however, the actual texts of the commentaries are remarkably stable and persist with few changes from the *"Notizen"* through later rewritings to eventual publication. This suggests to Maurer "that Burckhardt's aim was far less to develop an 'idea' than to communicate a visual experience."[132] Burckhardt, Maurer concluded, was "a gifted empiricist. . . . The generalizing reflections [in *Recollections of Rubens*] are not the product of abstract thinking but of a process of classifying similar kinds of observations." The most casual reader is indeed struck by the heterogeneous, unsystematic, ad hoc character of the classifications or headings in this decidedly personal, aristocratically essayistic work— "Rubens' Engravings," "The Hands," "The Putti," "Ideal of Female Beauty," "Religious Feeling," "Relation to Italian Masters," *"The Last Supper,"* "Gods and Goddesses," "Marie de'Medici," and so on. As Maurer noted, "The Professor of Art History never quite freed himself from the method of the 'Collectionneur.'"[133] The Rubens book still had something of the quality of the earlier *Cicerone:* into it "thousands of things had had to be bent or pressed so that, one way or another, they could all be included."[134]

An intense preoccupation with the individual object and uneasiness about subordinating it to general cultural or even art historical categories have been seen recently as the underlying motive for Burckhardt's decision to exclude art history from *The Civilization of the Renaissance in Italy* and thus abandon the original project for a cultural history of "The Age of Raphael." From this perspective, the later art historical writings on relatively circumscribed topics, such as the portrait, the altarpiece, or the collector, appear to mark a retreat from the more ambitious unifying structure of *The Civilization of the Renaissance* to the looser structure of the earlier writings up to and including *The Cicerone.* It was precisely in those late works, it has been claimed, that Burckhardt, having freed himself from the constraints of his plan for a comprehensive "art history of the Renaissance," was able to rediscover the pleasure of writing out of pure delight in the object at hand.[135]

In the end, the narrow positivism and individualism of the *Attribuzzler* was undermined by the very empiricism and concreteness of Burckhardt's *Kunstgeschichte nach Aufgaben,* with its emphasis on artistic traditions and on the conditions of art production. If the organization of artists' studios in the early modern period is taken into consideration, Burckhardt suggested, the modern mania for establishing authentic authorship—works that were painted by the author's own hand—may well seem inappropriate and foolhardy. Rubens, for instance, turned out over fifteen hundred pictures from his studio. But only the early works, painted before he became famous, and a number of relatively small-scale works painted for relaxation and private pleasure, such as the famous *Chapeau de paille* (London, National Gallery), are entirely by the master's hand. In all other cases, according to Burckhardt, the master and his students and associates contributed in varying proportions to the finished product. Sometimes Rubens provided the overall design and supervised its execution closely, dividing out the labor according to the special talents of his students (so that one painted the heads and flesh, another architectural elements, another flowers and fruits, yet another landscape settings) and going over the entire work himself only at the end. Sometimes we are looking at pure studio pictures, designed and outlined in chalk by the master, but executed by his students. These, Burckhardt insisted, are still authentic Rubens, since Rubens's students were so thoroughly trained in his style that they painted entirely in his spirit, and some even surpassed the master in particular techniques, like Jordaens in the painting of flesh tones. Then again, besides copies of Rubens originals made by other artists and other studios, copies were also made in Rubens's own studio.[136] It is sometimes extremely difficult, Burckhardt insisted, to distinguish a really well-executed copy from the original. He cited the example of one of the "most splendid and attractive creations of Raphael" (the *Bridgewater Madonna,* at the time in the Bridgewater Gallery, London, now in the National Gallery of Scotland), of which there is another version in Naples. Only the closest scholarly comparison of the two paintings would make it possible to determine which is the copy and which the original, he maintained. The *Madonna del passeggio* (also formerly in the Bridgewater Gallery, London, and now in the National Gallery of Scotland) is another superb painting of the Virgin, the authenticity of which has been questioned on account of a flaw in the drawing of the head of the child.[137] Why not simply assume, Burckhardt asked, that Raphael painted most of the picture?

In view of the whole method of production of painting in the early modern period, authentication cannot be the simple matter that a poorly informed public takes it to be. And aesthetically, Burckhardt insisted, it is irrelevant. Even art dealers now value some works by the students of a great master as highly as those by the master himself. A work by Marco Basaiti, a disciple of Bellini, may fetch as much on the art market, Burckhardt claimed, as a work by Bellini himself. What sense does it make then to demote a painting that has always been loved and admired simply because its authenticity as a work of this or that master has been questioned on scholarly grounds? In the end, the work of art is far more important to Burckhardt than its authorship; the judgment of taste is preferred to the *"wissenschaftlich"* knowledge of the scholars. He refused to accept the authority of a commission of fourteen "experts" who determined in

1871 that the Dresden Madonna (the *Madonna of Bürgermeister Meyer*) attributed to Holbein is a copy and that the Darmstadt Madonna is the authentic one. No doubt four eyes are better than two, Burckhardt conceded, but it is by no means clear that twenty-eight are. In matters of art, questions are not resolved "by majority vote" and external evidence does not deserve to carry more weight than the judgment of the connoisseur. Anyone who looks at the Dresden Madonna will not be persuaded that it is a late copy. In view of the utter incompetence of Holbein's imitators, "it is an odd assumption that a painter of such pure and powerful inner strength could have developed in complete silence and isolation, quickly painted the Dresden Madonna, and disappeared just as quickly without leaving a trace. We might just as well assume that he was killed, in order to prevent him from ever painting another picture and that we are dealing with a veritable Caspar Hauser of painting."[138]

The art history toward which Burckhardt was feeling his way was clearly not a matter of accumulating facts about artists and paintings. It involved, on the one hand, paying attention to the artistic forms and traditions developed by each art and, on the other, looking closely at the concrete relations between the artist and society. "How did the pattern of Italian family life actually determine the shape of palaces, did the Italian desire to *fare una bella figura* actually influence decoration more than the desire not to spend too much money? How did the Confraternities decide to build, what did they require of their architects, and how did they finance the work?" These, according to the British art historian Peter Murray, are the kinds of questions raised by Burckhardt's *Architecture of the Italian Renaissance.*[139]

Burckhardt's failure to integrate art history into *The Civilization of the Renaissance in Italy* did not at all mean that art history was not still closely associated with cultural history.[140] But the cultural life of the Renaissance was now seen as the *condition* of the flowering of Renaissance art. And that condition was now defined with greater precision and differentiation. The discovery of the world and of man, the desire for fame and glory, the love of antiquity, the "worldview" of the Italian Renaissance courts were all vitally important influences on the production of art works, especially as these influences were mediated by the desires and expectations of patrons and clients. But so too were the organization of artists' studios and their relation to patrons and collectors, both institutional and individual (the *"Besteller,"* in Burckhardt's terms). The themes and styles of artistic production and the scope of artistic experimentation and invention are decisively affected, in Burckhardt's view, by the composition of the artist's clientele and by the latter's education, expectations, and worldview. Thus, as long as the church was the principal patron and art was still closely linked to religion, art was characterized, he explained, by respect for tradition and the use of conventional symbolism. When wealthy private persons became patrons, there was greater emphasis on the rich presentation of immediately experienced reality. The emergence of powerful individuals in the Italian Renaissance—both as clients and as artists—together with the rivalries among neighboring cities (reminiscent of the agon of antiquity) and the growing wealth and worldly power of the church, created a situation for the artist totally unlike the situation that had obtained during the Middle Ages. "There is a large increase in commissions for profane works of art from private individuals. . . . Architecture must help to express not only the power of the church and the state but also that of wealthy private individuals."[141]

Entire pictorial genres might be affected by such changes in the composition of the artist's clientele and in the latter's expectations. In Holland, for instance, the House of Orange showed no particular interest in the arts, and the Calvinist Church, for theological reasons, had no direct connection with painting. "Private wealth had to come to an understanding with painting and to set objectives for it or accept those set by painting itself. The collective pictures of guilds and governing boards [a topic to which Riegl was to devote one of his most important art historical studies—L.G.] were semiofficial but at the same time they were private commissions, in that they came about through each individual's paying for his own portrait in the composition. Everything else produced by painting—sacred or mythological subjects, portraits, genre paintings, landscapes and marine landscapes, still lives of every kind—was intended only for the private home. . . . The general love of collecting among the Dutch was a great boon to art, as was the climate which forced people to stay indoors for a good part of the year: the adornment of the interior of the home, which on the outside was extremely modest, became a dominant preoccupation."[142] In the art of other cultures there are similar representations of daily life and labor (Egyptian wall paintings from the third millennium B.C., for instance), but the *"zu Grunde liegender Wille"* of the artists who created those representations was different from that which motivated a David Teniers in seventeenth-century Holland.[143] Similarly, there are examples of something like still life in Hellenistic art and in the art of Pompeii, long before the Dutch painters of the seventeenth century. But if the Dutch developed the still life into an original and at the same time immensely popular genre, that success was attributable to the historical conditions of seventeenth-century Holland: a deeper feeling for nature in the Dutch painters than in those of the age of the *diadochi* or of Pompeii, and a different outlook on the world among the well-to-do "Mynheers." "Alongside portraits, genre paintings, battle scenes, pastorales, and landscapes, a corner of their consciousness remained open to a thoroughly neutral pleasure, one that aimed to be completely independent of the human world and everything that goes with it." This capacity for finding delight not only in traditional narrative and symbolically significant subjects but in the particularity, the form and texture of the object world, was not unrelated, Burckhardt claimed, to the enjoyment of a high material culture: "the most perfectly created and maintained gardens; the finest fruit from greenhouses or from distant lands; the most refined tools and instruments; curtains and marble tables and carpets as rich as one could desire; the most beautiful bales of every kind of material. To these things it was worth raising monuments."[144] The genres in which the Dutch painters excelled were thus largely determined by the culture of the Netherlands in the seveenth century as reflected in the desires and worldview not only of the country's artists but—perhaps especially—of the latter's clients. Burckhardt appears to have attributed to the wealthy mercantile cultures of Flanders and Venice a similar influence on the Flemish and Venetian painters.

It was among the latter that he found the greatest incidence of what he called the *"Existenzbild."* The term is nowhere precisely defined. It seems clear, however, that it was intended to designate a type of painting that aims to capture on canvas and celebrate the sensuous qualities of the real world and the beauty of the human figure in their earthly reality— *"das schönste Dasein"* or *"das bloss wonnevolle Dasein,"* in Burckhardt's words—rather than point to some narrative or symbolic meaning. What one should look for in a painting, he had told his audience at the 1844–1846 public lectures in Basel, was "not symbolism, but an ennobled naturalism, deep individuality, distinctiveness of character, and yet, at the same time, beauty."[145] Later, in *The Cicerone* (1855), we read that among the Venetians biblical scenes "were not painted for church or private devotion, but sprung only from the impulse to represent a rich and beautifully colored existence. They show ... how ... the incident is but the pretext for the representation of pure existence." With Veronese's pictures of festivals, in particular, painting "shakes off the last fetters of the historical picture [i.e., history painting—L.G.] and only requires the remains of a pretext to celebrate all the splendour and glory of the earth in unrestrained rejoicing; above all, a beautiful and free human race in full enjoyment of their existence."[146] Only a culture free of theological constraints and scholastic dogmatism, Burckhardt appears to argue, could produce such a "representation of pure existence" (*"Darstellung der blossen Existenz"*).[147]

The meaning of the term *Existenzbild* can be better grasped if we consider the terms to which it might be opposed, such as *Ideenbild* and *Gedankenkunst*. In a standard history of German painting first published in Munich just over half a century ago, *Gedankenkunst* was used to describe the great graphic (as opposed to the painterly) tradition of German art and its strong moral and literary emphasis. In particular, *Gedankenkunst* evoked the programmatic and allegorical painting of the school of German artists of the first half of the nineteenth century known as the "Nazarenes."[148] Anticipating in some ways the English pre-Raphaelite Brotherhood, the founding members of this school (Johann Friedrich Overbeck [1789–1869] and Franz Pforr [1788–1812]) had bound themselves into a quasi-religious order, the *Lukasbrüder,* with the aim of regenerating German art by renouncing the worldly, profane, and in their view decadent development of painting after Perugino and the early Raphael. Overbeck and Pforr were joined in Rome, where they began painting in 1810, by other German painters. Soon the Nazarenes were a major force in German painting, especially in the schools of Munich and Düsseldorf.[149] The static character, harmonious composition, well-defined contours, flat colors, absence of chiaroscuro, and religious subject matter that were the hallmark of their work hark back to the art of the late Middle Ages and early Renaissance. If the heyday of art, for Burckhardt, began with the Italian Renaissance—the theme of a wall painting of 1877, *Das Erwachen der Kunst in der Renaissance* (*The Awakening of Art in the Renaissance*), in the staircase of the Basel Kunsthalle by Ernst Stückelberg, a young Basel artist whose career Burckhardt helped to guide—Overbeck had taken a decidedly different view in 1840 in his *Der Triumph der Religion in den Künsten* (*The Triumph of Religion in the Arts;* Städelsches Kunstinstitut, Frankfurt), as had Philipp Veit in his *Einführung der Künste durch das Christentum* (*The Arts Introduced by Christianity;* also in Frankfurt) (see illustrations at the end of this chapter). The strongly favorable reviews that both Burckhardt and Kugler wrote of the work of Gallait and Bièfve and their evident endorsement of the demand inspired by the 1842 exhibition, that German art should free itself from the dominance of the graphic and literary and strive to achieve painterly effects of color and light comparable to those of the Belgians, leave little doubt that the two friends intended the *Existenzbild* to define an artistic style opposed to the *Gedankenkunst* or *Ideenbild* of the Nazarenes.

Burckhardt's praise of the *Existenzbild* thus marks a crucial intersection in his work of art history with art criticism, of interest in the past with concern for the present and the future. The *Existenzbild* did not simply designate Venetian painting of the sixteenth century; it was seen by Burckhardt as a model for painting and painters in his own time, an alternative to what he considered the excessive idealism and "spiritualizing" (*"Kunstpietismus"*) of the Nazarenes and, later, to the excessive anti-idealism of the French.[150]

The term *Existenzbild* itself may have been borrowed from or suggested by Kugler. In his *Handbuch der Geschichte der Malerei* (*Handbook of the History of Painting*) of 1837, which Burckhardt revised in the mid-1840s at his teacher's request, the work of Titian was described as "life in its full presence, the transfiguration of earthly existence without halos or sacrificial blood." It marked "the emancipation of painting from the bonds of religious dogma." Titian's figures, Kugler went on, "reflect the fullest consciousness and the highest enjoyment (*Genuss*) of being. Everywhere they convey blissful contentment, calm satisfaction, a balanced, harmonious existence, and that is why they have such a beneficent effect on the viewer, that is why they impart to the viewer a purer, ennobled state of mind."[151] Even where the subject matter has been borrowed from the Christian repertory, Kugler adds, it has been humanized by the painter, who has transformed religious motifs into purely aesthetic elements. Already at that time Kugler's remarks seem to have implicitly targeted the Nazarenes. In a manuscript note on Titian's *Martyrdom of St. Peter* (destroyed in a fire in 1867) Burckhardt later hinted that his and Kugler's praise of the Venetians was just such an implied citicism. "Thank Goodness, Titian has not sentimentalized the matter in the style of the Nazarenes," he noted.[152]

What seems to be evoked by Kugler's and Burckhardt's category of the *Existenzbild* is the view of art and of human life developed in the circles of neohumanist poets, critics, and philosophers in late-eighteenth- and early-nineteenth-century Germany. The world in which Kugler moved in Berlin, and into which, as Burckhardt related, he was received like a son, was still inspired by the ideals and generous enthusiasms of the Age of Goethe and Hegel. An accomplished amateur poet and musician and the author, in later years, of a successful biography of Frederick the Great, Kugler counted among his friends Friedrich Schinkel, who was also a friend of Hegel's and was the outstanding architect of the day, the painter Adolf Menzel, who provided illustrations for the book on Frederick, and the poet Paul Heyse. In addition, as advisor to the Prussian *Kultusministerium* he played a role in state policy in the arts and he had an abiding interest in the work of his contemporaries. "We are whole only in the presence of art that is actually being created," he wrote. "Where there is no production of art, there is also no full understanding of it, and it is only through the work of today that we are led to that of yesterday."[153] Kugler had himself, in short, something of that Goethean all-roundedness, inner completeness, and harmoniousness that the German neohumanists and most of the idealist philosophers admired in the Greeks and in their own greatest poet, something of the *uomo universale* held up as an example of ideal humanity by Burckhardt in his accounts of artists he deeply revered, such as Leonardo da Vinci or Rubens. And he seemed to rise above the specialism that all the neohumanists deplored as the worst consequence of modern civilization, technology, and the division of labor required by an advanced economy. Burckhardt, as is well known, never concealed his contempt for narrow specialism,[154] associating it with the *"Banausen"* or lower-class artisans of the ancient world or with the narrow-minded guildsmen and "purse-proud" merchants of his own native city. Specialization, like provincialism and popular nationalism, was the sign of a falling-away from full humanity.

The neohumanism of Goethe, Wilhelm von Humboldt, Hegel, and Georg Friedrich Creuzer did not at first exclude romantic elements.[155] At Heidelberg in the late 1820s Kugler had been an enthusiastic student of medieval art and had held the view that both Greek architecture and "German" (or Gothic) architecture were superior to that of the Italian Renaissance on account of their "organic" and "popular" character, and that German architecture surpassed even that of the Greeks on account of its greater and purer spirituality.

However, by the time of Burckhardt's association with him in the early 1840s and the collaboration of the two men on the revision of Kugler's art history handbooks (the *Handbuch der Geschichte der Malerei* of 1837 and the impressively comprehensive *Handbuch der Kunstgeschichte* of 1842[156]), Kugler had taken his distance from romanticism, much as Goethe had earlier distanced himself from his youthful denigration of Renaissance architecture and from the preference expressed in the prerevolutionary essay *"Von deutscher Baukunst"* (1772) for the "creative" over the "beautiful." The classical turn taken by Burckhardt's ideas in *The Cicerone* and his sharp denunciations of willful "subjectivism," even in great Italian Renaissance artists like Michelangelo and Tintoretto, should probably be viewed in the context of the increasingly critical stance adopted by many neohumanists toward romanticism—both the backward-looking, religious-sentimental romanticism of the Nazarenes and the revolutionary romanticism of the progressive liberals, with its emphasis on the real and the contemporary. It has been suggested that Kugler's decision to revise his handbooks was itself a sign of this antiromantic turn.[157]

Above all, though he was fairly conservative politically, like Burckhardt (or for that matter, Goethe and Hegel), Kugler shared the neohumanists' generous if idealistic vision of a society and a humanity transformed and ennobled by art. He considered that art was a proper object of government (*"Über die Kunst als Gegenstand der Staatsverwaltung"* was the title of one of his essays) and he liked to quote Humboldt's view that "the enjoyment of art [*Kunstgenuss*] is an essential capacity in any people that . . . aspires to higher things."[158]

By adopting this statement as his own, Kugler aligned himself with the ideas of art and beauty and their place in modern life that had been developed in works like Schiller's *Über die ästhetische Erziehung des Menschen (On the Aesthetic Education of Man)* or Goethe's *Der Sammler und die Seinigen (The Collector and His Circle)*. In the beauty of works of art, which are the product of a fundamental human "play impulse," Schiller had argued, seemingly irreconcilable opposites are harmonized: freedom and order, subjectivity and objectivity, spontaneity and law, nature and reason, particularity and universality, the private individual and the citizen—"life" or the "sense impulse" and "form" or the "form impulse" in Schiller's own terms. In the poet's rather abstract formulation: "The sense impulse requires variation, requires time to have a content; the form impulse requires the extinction of time, and no variation. Therefore the impulse in which both are combined (allow me to call it provisionally the *play impulse*, . . .), this play impulse would aim at the transcendence of time *in time* and the reconciliation of becoming with absolute being, of variation with identity.[159] Kugler's friend, the architect Friedrich Schinkel, expressed similar ideas in a somewhat more concrete way: "It is a natural inclination of man to try to find Heaven already on this Earth and to weave something eternally enduring into his earthly activities, to plant and cultivate the imperishable in the ephemeral, not simply in an imperceptible way, inaccessible to mortal vision, separated as it is from the eternal by an unbridgeable gulf, but in such a way that it is visible even to moral eyes.[160]

So too for Burckhardt, "[w]hat one expects of art is that it give eternity to the singular, to what was valid for only particular moods, times, peoples, and interests."[161] While being rooted in time and place, art also overcomes them: "A people that has reached . . . the highest point of artistic creation transmits its last word to humanity as something that is no longer national, no longer of a particular religion, but universal and everlasting."[162] In the face of the transitoriness, the fragmentation, and the suffering of actual historical existence, art offers a consoling transfiguration. "Die Kunst aber will ewig sein" ("Art aims to be eternal").[163] In contrast, works of art that have merely served passing ideas and interests quickly become unintelligible or at best objects of historical curiosity. "True art . . . seeks to endure. It is one of those glorious bonds that bind peoples and centuries together into a commonality. And even if that commonality is composed of an elite, fortunately it need not be an elite of the rich and powerful. Any person who has not been spoiled by a false education can respond to public works of art, even if he or she is uneducated. Both the viewers and the subjects of art have a common ideal citizenship that acknowledges no boundaries of nation or time."[164]

To Burckhardt, the ex-student of theology, art binds those who love it, artists and viewers alike, in a community that is both historical and transhistorical—in history, yet beyond any particular historical time. The choice of the subtitle of *The Cicerone*— "*Einleitung zum Genuss der Kunstwerke Italiens*" ("*Introduction to the Enjoyment of the Art Works of Italy*")—was probably not random.[165] The term *Genuss* (enjoyment or delight) was part of the vocabulary of neohumanism, of Schiller and Goethe, Kugler and Schinkel. Schiller described what he called "true art" as "that alone which procures the highest *Genuss* and the highest *Genuss* is the freedom of the spirit in the lively play of all its capacities."[166] To Schinkel, *Genuss* is the "necessary consequence of the production of beauty" and it is "the aim of the artist to enable every one to experience such *Genuss* or delight in the highest things with him." This he should do, not by slavishly copying reality, but by recreating it in such a way that the viewer "intuits and appreciates a higher form in the individual phenomenon."[167] To Burckhardt, *Genuss* is experienced as the viewer of art enters "a world of beauty, strength, intense feeling and happiness"[168] and makes contact with "a second creation, the only imperishable and universal thing on this earth."[169]

For the earlier generation of neohumanists, the beautiful and the *Genuss* that it engendered had a significant moral and political dimension. The emancipation from all constraint—the constraint of law and reason as well as that of nature—that Schiller's esthetic education was supposed to achieve was intended as the first essential step in the emergence of a creative, nonrepressive morality and a free yet orderly polity. Beauty, Schiller emphasized, has no particular purposes, prescribes no particular laws, and communicates no particular truths. Rather it releases us from the narrowness, exclusiveness, and oppressiveness of all particular purposes, laws, and dogmas and restores the ability to think and act freely, without constraint.[170] In the shadow of the French Revolution and the Jacobin Terror, Schiller's "aesthetic education" could thus be seen as leading to a social and cultural order founded on a more nobly humane basis than either the violence of passion or the cold inhumanity of reason, just as it proposed a more harmonious form of ethical behavior than the rigors of Kantian morality. The beautiful and the *Genuss* that accompanied it were in some measure justified and vindicated, in other words, by larger ethical and political considerations. The aesthetic was a crucial moment in the process of an education toward the good and the true.[171]

On this essential point Burckhardt diverged from Schiller and may have been closer to Goethe. The beautiful, he insisted, was not a means to an end; it was an end in itself. It needed no justification, and it did not have to be thought of "as an antecedent phase of, or an education for, the true. . . . Art exists mainly for its own sake."[172] As Burckhardt explained clearly, art was "a second creation," in which humanity's deepest experiences and highest aspirations are preserved for all time, a source of solace for the pain and imperfection of historical existence. This view of art, though by no means new with Burckhardt, must have been reinforced by his chastened sense, after the mid-1840s, of what lay in store for the "culture of old Europe," as he liked to say. It had become difficult to accept even Schiller's moderately optimistic expectations of what the aesthetic education of man might achieve in the public sphere, let alone Hegel's far more radical view that in modern conditions art has been overtaken by philosophy and, as the central vehicle of humanity's highest truths, has become for ever more "a thing of the past" (*"ein Vergangenes"*).[173] For Burckhardt, in contrast, art was and must remain something eternally present and timelessly consoling. The transcendence of contradictions that Hegelian philosophy held out as the final homecoming of the spirit after its journey through the desert of history must have seemed to him, in contrast, cold, remote, abstract, and fantastical.

In the end, all Burckhardt's art historical teaching and writing was aimed at making his audiences and readers capable of experiencing those moments of *Genuss*—of an immediate, joyful, liberating transcendence of life's contradictions and contingencies—such as he himself had experienced in the contemplation of works of art. In this view of art, the *Existenzbild* occupied a privileged position. It represented, in the words of the art historian Wilhelm Schlink, quoting from Burckhardt, a "universe of quiet, insouciant joy (*Genuss*), such as 'ought to exist,'" and in which a noble humanity celebrates and rejoices in itself. As Schlink observes somewhat severely, no concrete or realistic political reference intervenes to disturb an inspiring and consoling image of happiness. "In Veronese's 'dream existence,'" Schlink concludes, "the modern viewer finds himself raised above history to a higher plane and discovers 'a tranquil well-being,' untroubled by the threatening forces and figures which viewers sought to avoid not only in painting but in the real life of the nineteenth century—the 'nervous and agitated vitality' of a Correggio or the 'intense physical power, . . . already demonic' of a Michelangelo."[174] Wölfflin's definition of the art of the Italian Renaissance comes to mind: "The mind apprehends this art as the image of a higher, free existence in which it may participate."[175]

Nevertheless, the acute sense of the historicity of everything, including art, which so fundamentally marked the experience and thinking of the postrevolutionary generation and to which, as we saw, was due the acceptance of art history as a field of intellectual inquiry and academic instruction, made it impossible not to recognize that art had not always provided in the same degree the *Genuss* that Burckhardt expected from it and that not all historical ages had been equally favorable to the production of art. No less than the pioneer art critics and historians of the previous century—Diderot and Winckelmann—or his own teacher Franz Kugler, Burckhardt was preoccupied by the conditions and prospects for artistic creation in his own time. If facilitating the *Genuss* of art was one important aim of art history, obtaining a clear understanding of the ways in which social, political, cultural, and economic factors might affect art and artists, and guiding artists and the public, as far as that was possible, in a desirable direction—a direction that would be productive of *Genuss*—was another hardly less important aim. A century before Burckhardt, Diderot had criticised Boucher and the fashionable rococo artists of his time for their complicity in the commercialization of art and the "corruption" of taste; Winckelmann's *History of the Art of Antiquity* had also been intended to combat current taste and redirect artists toward the great models of classical antiquity. The goal of neohumanist and early romantic art history was likewise not simply to record the achievements of the past, but to discern and help achieve the art of the future, to give guidance to artists, and to promote the conditions, as Wilhelm Schlink put it, that might produce a new Periclean age.[176]

Burckhardt's active career as an art historian coincided with the end of the climate of moderate optimism that marked the early decades of the nineteenth century. By the late 1840s, as we observed in preceding chapters, he had begun to regard the increasingly democratic, utilitarian, market-driven culture of his age with apprehension as fundamentally inimical to the production of great art in the humanist tradition. "Artists, poets and philosophers have a dual function," he declared later: "to give ideal form to the inner content of time and the world and to transmit it to posterity as an imperishable heritage." But "our age is driving the most competent artists and poets into money-making. We can see this by the fact that they meet the 'culture' of our time half-way and illustrate it, submit to any kind of material patronage, and lose their ability to hearken to the inner voice."[177] It was an essential goal of art history, as Burckhardt practiced it, to combat this situation. Art history thus became one of the ideological battle-grounds of the age. "We interrogated the past in order to promote the future," the art critic and art historian Wilhelm Bürger (known, after 1848, as Théo-phile Thoré) observed in 1835 in an essay on Winckelmann.[178] Bürger was a modernist. History, for him, showed that each age must have its own art and that the past cannot and should not prescribe the art of the future. Burckhardt, in contrast, retained a strong commitment to the ideal and the normative, even while recognizing—in fact drawing attention to—the impact and perva-siveness of historical change. The issue was not the central importance of his-tory; it was the way each responded to the ineluctable fact of historical change.

Despite Burckhardt's well-advertised reservations with regard to Hegel, a grand narrative can be constructed from his writings on art and cultural history that bears a certain resemblance to that traced in Hegel's *Aesthetics.* He shared with Hegel, for instance, the view that in the heyday of the ancient polis art had been the natural medium for the expression of the ancient community's highest truths. It was the growing influence of rationalist philosophy, he argued in *The Cultural History of Greece,* resulting in the undoing of myth and the dis-tinguishing of myth, religion, and history, that broke the charmed unity of truth and beauty. Nevertheless, the art of classical Greece enjoyed the unique privi-lege of being virtually transparent, a continuous unbroken unity of material form and spiritual content—in contrast to that of other cultures (such, no doubt, as the Egyptian or the Indian, to which Hegel and Schinkel also refer in this context) in which "the form is rebarbative, the outer husk impenetrable, the expression symbolic to the point of unintelligibility."[179]

Greek art—above all, the sculpted human form—thus always retained for Burckhardt, as for Hegel and everyone who had been influenced by neohuman-ism, a highly normative character. His attention to painterly qualities and his later openness to the baroque coexisted with a notion of ideal beauty (*das Schöne*) that seems always to have been closely linked to the representation of the human form in classical sculpture.[180]

With the coming of Christianity, in Burckhardt's narrative, the highest truths are independent of art. Art now signifies or points to a truth beyond itself. In the Middle Ages, it is subordinate to religion. As late as the fourteenth century, "the means of representation—drawing, color, perspective—are still quite primitive." Much therefore remained beyond the reach of this art: notably the representation of energetic action and of man in his purely human and worldly aspects.[181]

The Renaissance marks the emancipation of art. "Though still employed in the service of the church," we are told in *The Cicerone,* "its principles were henceforward developed without reference to merely ecclesiastical purposes. A work of art now gave more than the church requires."[182] The princes, prelates, and wealthy merchants of the fifteenth and sixteenth centuries did not dictate to the artist in a blunt way but delighted in artistic effects and were happy to gain renown as patrons and sponsors.

In some ways the change from the classical period was of great benefit to art, in Burckhardt's narrative, in that art attained greater freedom in the modern world than it had known in either the Middle Ages or antiquity. The Age of Raphael, the Swiss art historian Emil Maurer observed, represented for Burckhardt an absolute high point of artistic achievement: it was *vielseitiger, ja tiefsinniger als die griechische Blütezeit* ("more varied and profound than ancient Greek art in its fullest flowering"). The quattrocento, Burckhardt himself noted, achieved "here and there in the beauty of its sculpture a sweetness such as had not been achieved since antiquity and had not even been achieved in quite the same way in antiquity—the beauty of the soul"[183]: that is to say, the beauty of a richer, more inward humanity and subjectivity than was known to antiquity. If that was so in sculpture, it was far more so in painting, which the Ancients had completely subordinated to line and volume. When pressed, Burckhardt gave line and composition primacy over the painterly qualities of color and light—he liked to quote Ingres's remark that "le dessein est la probité de l'art"[184]—but basically he insisted on the value and importance of both. "It is not the case," he declared in a lecture on Rembrandt in 1877, "that the representation of light and air. . . is incompatible with careful execution. It is not the case that *Lichtmalerei* dispenses the artist from paying attention to the beauty and truthful representation of the human body."[185] In the later part of his career, in fact, he came to think of life and movement not as attributes of an "ideal" body but as integral to that body, filling it with a "beautiful liveliness."[186] While admiring Poussin's draftsmanship, for instance, he considered his emphasis on line and drawing responsible for stifling the desire to "yield to the immediacy of the moment and to a joyful and agreeable existence" (*Hingebung an den Moment oder an irgendeine heitere und gemütliche Existenz*") in an entire generation of French painters, thus foreclosing until the Flemish-born Watteau the possibility of *Existenzbilder* of the kind produced by the great Venetians.[187]

The Renaissance made it possible to conceive and pursue purely artistic goals with considerable freedom. The viewer likewise became aware of a specifically aesthetic pleasure, distinct from worship, understanding, or edification. "A free consciousness of visual effect . . . gradually developed," Burckhardt wrote, "and the eye [became] ready to respond to it."[188] Art became "emancipated from its dependence on any existing types, without even a tendency to imitate exactly any of the models of antiquity."[189] In architecture, for instance, architectural forms were released from their "organic" connection, in ancient and medieval building, to specific functional structures, such as religious temples, and could be freely and imaginatively recombined for essentially aesthetic purposes.[190] The rise of easel painting, as distinct from fresco, also pointed to the growing autonomy of art and its emancipation from the strictly public sphere. Burckhardt contrasts the independence of Rubens in his studio, "where the master was surrounded by a select group of assistants unique at the time" and from which "the paintings, rolled up, were sent all over Europe," with the far more dependent, itinerant life of the "fresco painter, who moved about from church to church, from palace to palace."[191]

Burckhardt obviously delighted in the independence enjoyed by Rubens, which he saw as inseparable from the existence of an incipient art market of informed and educated clients. Rubens himself was described, with admiration rather than criticism, as an entrepreneur, watchful of his own and his associates' interests, notably those of the master-engravers of Antwerp, whose fine work allowed the artist to "appeal to a large purchasing public all over Europe." In fact, the demand for engravings was so great, Burckhardt related, that in order to expedite matters, they were sometimes made "not after the completed picture, but after early or preliminary sketches."[192] As a citizen of one of the great Renaissance centers of fine engraving, paper manufacture, and book production, Burckhardt clearly appreciated the energy and freedom, and even the commercial initiative manifested by all this activity. Art and commerce could still collaborate as equals in seventeenth-century Antwerp; commerce did not yet dictate terms to art. On the contrary, by serving as a counterweight to the influence of the church and the prince or the state, it helped to ensure a considerable degree of freedom for the artist. Rubens, in Burckhardt's words, "was a king without lands or subjects."[193]

Finally, though he never subscribed to a strict formalist aesthetics of the kind developed by Johann Friedrich Herbart in the early decades of the century or Robert Zimmermann in his own time, Burckhardt emphasized that the *Gegenstand,* or subject matter, of a work of art is only the point of departure of an imaginative artistic construction— *"der Anlass, dessen die Kunst bedarf, um das Ihrige zu geben"* ("the occasion that art needs in order to produce what belongs to it alone"). Art, as Burckhardt often noted, should not serve simply to illustrate ideas or literary subjects. It has a language and meanings of its own.[194] There are "glorious Venetian paintings, for instance, whose most probable origin lies primarily in the artist's delight in tackling a beautiful problem of color, atmosphere, and the distribution of light and shadow. . . . In general, much of what occurs in the act of looking at paintings cannot be communicated in words. In fact, as a whole, art offers something in forms and tones that cannot be articulated in words."[195]

In many respects, therefore, despite his veneration of the art of antiquity, Burckhardt welcomed the growth of artistic freedom and the new possibilities presented by painterly values of light and color in modern times. Even before

The Cicerone and *The Civilization of the Renaissance in Italy*, he had emphasized that the Renaissance cannot be understood simply as a revival of antiquity, but must be seen as an original modern culture. "A good Florentine of the cinquecento believed in all conscience and to the best of his knowledge that he was reproducing the work of the Ancients, when in fact he was creating something new and infinitely beautiful," he had declared in the *Kunstwerke der belgischen Städte* as early as 1842. That view was reaffirmed twenty-five years later in his *Geschichte der neueren Baukunst* (*The Architecture of the Italian Renaissance*), which appeared as volume four of Kugler's general *Geschichte der Baukunst:* The term *rinascità* "remains one-sided, because it stresses only half the facts. The freedom and originality with which the rediscovery of classical antiquity was received and assimilated, the sheer extent of the modern spirit revealed in the great movement is not fully expressed by it."[196] Burckhardt draws back, however, when the newly won freedom begins to degenerate, as in his judgment it was doing in his own time, into revolutionary rejection of all ideal norms, of order, tradition, and historical continuity. Extreme idealism that ignores temporality and sensuous experience and extreme realism that refuses to seek the ideal or universal in the passing, transient experience ("strict following of nature as it is") are equally harmful, he holds, to artistic production. But whether a fruitful tension between the two poles of idealism and realism—and that tension defines, for Burckhardt, the whole history of art[197]—can be preserved or not appears to depend on larger social and cultural influences. It is at this point that Burckhardt's interest in art history intersects with his critique of contemporary society and his conviction that democracy and industrialization have provoked a crisis in European culture.

The commodification of art and literature in the France of the bourgeois monarchy had been a major theme of the reports that as a young correspondent for the *Basler Zeitung* in Paris in the mid-1840s he had sent home to his editor. Their message had been similar to that of the painter Ingres in a notorious denunciation of the commercializing effect of the annual Salon and the magazine reviews that accompanied it. "The Salon," Ingres had declared, "stifles and corrupts the sense of grandeur and beauty; artists are driven to exhibit by the desire to make money and to draw attention to themselves at any price. . . . The Salon is, in truth, nothing more now, literally, than a warehouse full of pictures for sale, a bazaar where one is overwhelmed by the enormous quantity of objects, and where industry calls the tune instead of art."[198] That vision of the industrialization of art was to haunt Flaubert's *L'Education sentimentale* of 1869.

To the old-style Basel republican it must have seemed that the balance struck in the early modern period among the various forces contributing to the production of art—the freedom and interests of the artist as artist, the influence of artistic tradition, the requirements of ecclesiastical or secular powers or of well-to-do, cultivated individual patrons—had been upset in the new postrevolutionary democracies. The development of a large, anonymous art and literary market had turned the relative autonomy art had achieved in the Renaissance into the alienation of art. "The whole of Dutch art [in the seventeenth century]," Burckhardt noted, "was the very opposite of ours today in that it existed only for connoisseurs and amateurs, not for the general public, exhibitions and newspaper critics. No one needed to beat the big drum and cry louder than anyone else." At a time when "like everything else on earth, art cannot avoid entering into relation with public opinion and specifically with the press,"[199] the "quiet art of quiet enchantment"[200] created by the Dutch is no longer conceivable. Burckhardt was every bit as contemptuous as his young colleague Nietzsche of the way modern art resorted to "exciting little traits of 'naturalisme,'" in Nietzsche's words, in order to "sweep the reader away" and force the attention of "gross minds exhausted by work and hungry for violent emotions."[201] Curiously, Delacroix, whom Burckhardt considered party to this disastrous development, held not dissimilar views.[202]

To the poet Paul Heyse, who had expressed concern about the fate of the arts in the modern world, Burckhardt wrote in 1884 that his own view was extremely bleak, "not only because art seeks in the most dubious way to entwine its own fate with the general fate of the world"—that is to say, because art was increasingly willing to participate in contemporary business and politics, instead of representing the ideal and the beautiful—but "because those who might commission works of art or purchase them had become a far too mixed class of people ("ein gar zu melirtes Corps," in Burckhardt's characteristic Swiss German) and because the church and the superior ranks of society no longer set the tone."[203]

Emancipation from tradition and from traditional patrons, in short, has placed the artist at the mercy of the market. "There is a difference between a sixteenth century prince, a religious order, a seventeenth century guild or corporation that commissions a work on the basis of distinction or celebrity or prior achievement, or a paterfamilias who wants a devotional painting (Andachtsbild), on the one hand, and the public that attends nineteenth century art shows and distributes laurels and commissions . . . on the basis of newspaper reviews, on the other." Work produced for that modern public will not be able to draw on traditional subject matter but will have to rely on the subjects in fashion with the public at any given moment, and those might well include, along with historical scenes, aspects of "reality" that art has previously avoided as artistically unsuitable or intractable. The work produced in those conditions will be ephemeral, "caught up in excessive servitude to content and in contingencies that are incapable of giving life to art but must be dragged along as dead weight after it."[204] Works of art, moreover, are increasingly treated as commodities, the new art collectors being mainly concerned not with aesthetic value but with external, measurable indicators of market value, such as authorship. Even as the *"Modeleute"*—fashionable people—drive up prices because they "believe it is impossible to live elegantly except in the company of authentic old masters," they reveal their lack of any real love of art by exposing the works they compete with each other to acquire to the dangerous wear and tear of a wandering, nomadic existence; for wealth in the modern world is constantly shifting, and pictures can thus no longer be guaranteed a secure home. Where they had once been locked up for hundreds of years in some castle or palace, "the poor paintings pass rapidly from hand to hand and rarely know a moment's repose."[205]

Along with pressure from the market and an artistically uneducated clientele, art was also now subject to a new kind of pressure from the state. Burckhardt never imagined that art had ever been or could ever be independent of the rest of history. On the contrary, he held that it was often dominated by religion (he usually gave Byzantine art as the supreme example of this) or politics and made to serve ends other than its own. "At many different epochs, and in many different civilizations, art has been expected or compelled to take upon itself the representation of all kinds of past events that had in some way . . . been of importance to the ruling power. Power conceived this to be the best way of achieving immortality. Art, as a rule, obeyed, if only because power, on such occasions, tends to be rather more open-handed than at other times; besides, these were times and conditions when obedience was the rule, and not even the artist attempted to evade it."[206]

But it is always a perilous situation for art to be directly under the thumb of politicians or priests and it is especially perilous when, as in the modern age, art is expected "to serve a prevailing opinion, patriotic, political or religious, in great historical pictures, and to instill that opinion, in the form of feeling, into the faces and lineaments of the principal figures." For "those opinions are in no case enduring; they constantly change with the times, and it may not take long for monstrous, overcrowded pictures to become unintelligible."[207] Art, Burckhardt told the audience at one of his public lectures in Basel, "is not there to illustrate what has happened, however noteworthy the event in question may be." The "historically significant" should not be confused with the "artistically significant." By becoming the servant of the ideas and politics of a particular party or moment (*"Zeittendenzdienerin"*), art "loses its oecumenical or universal character and makes itself unintelligible or even hateful to entire nations, religions or parties."[208] In art's better times, Burckhardt added later, "patriotism consisted in paying for something beautiful to be placed on an altar or in a city hall; the content did not have to be a direct exhibition of patriotism or political commitment." Burckhardt's simple principle is that art is degraded when it is used primarily to illustrate historical events that a particular party or regime considers important. "Painting (and art in general) is too good for the mere singular event if it is nothing more than that."[209] Burckhardt's judgment of history painting is entirely consistent with his view of historiography itself.

In the great series of allegorical paintings commissioned by Marie de' Medici for the gallery of the Luxembourg Palace (now in the Louvre), Rubens offers an example, according to Burckhardt, of the kind of balance of influences that makes great history painting possible: the artistic tradition itself; the expectations of the public or of a particular patron; the vision of the individual artist. Though intended to glorify the patroness, these paintings are not subject to the dangers of mutability and incomprehensibility, Burckhardt claimed, because art has here thoroughly infused its subject matter. "The brilliant moments of time here depicted are, spiritually and materially, clearly self-sufficient in the theme and details of each picture; they move us in themselves, without suggesting to the spectator that reading-matter on the subject is awaiting him outside. Whatever his response may be today to the factual content of the series, art has still remained art, even in this kind of royal servitude."[210]

Unfortunately, Rubens' good fortune was not likely to be experienced by nineteenth century artists.

> There is no question that our century would have presented the historical painter of Antwerp with a different programme. First he would have been expected to paint the whole past history of Brabant and the rest of the Netherlands realistically, in historically accurate costume, with the old battles, rebellions, festivals and so on, and all that not on account of its artistic quality, but in the name of patriotism and even progress, since what matters in such things is not what actual epochs of the past may have felt, but the present-day notion of what they felt, which is, of course, drawn from such books and other writings of the day that people happen to be reading.[211]

When he wrote those lines, Burckhardt may well have been thinking of the artistic projects of Ludwig I of Bavaria, about which both he and Kugler had expressed their reservations in the early 1840s. At that time Burckhardt had still been romantic enough to make a distinction between the official history paintings celebrating the medieval German past, which had been commissioned by the Bavarian royal house, and the patriotic works of the Belgian school (Wappers, Bièfve, and Gallait), which had been inspired by the popular uprising in favor of Belgian independence in 1830. In addition, there was an influential movement to promote patriotic painting in the new federal Switzerland[212] and, as late as 1854, as noted earlier, Burckhardt himself had encouraged the Basel Museum to commission Landerer's *Entry of the Swiss Delegates into Basel to Take the Oath of Confederation.* Two decades later, however, after the Austro-Prussian and Franco-Prussian wars, he had a less rosy view of such patriotic history painting. "In modern times," he told his Basel audience at a public lecture on history painting in 1884, "the arrogance of entire nations demands that monuments be erected and whole cycles of frescoes painted.[213] In their essential nature these are far more inimical to art and even destructive of it than anything that the dynasties of the old regime ever commissioned. The reason is that the trumped up political and specifically patriotic passions [of the present] have to be projected back into the historical figures represented in the painting." In other words, the artist does not try to grasp and represent in his work the authentic spirit of past historical reality, or an authentically living idea of it that has become part of a culture's tradition and beliefs. What officially sponsored history painting conveys is an image determined by bookish historical scholarship and by a completely unartistic interest in stimulating particular political sentiments in an artistically ignorant mass public. Art, Burckhardt continued, "is entitled to defend itself against this kind of violation of the truth of things by every means at its disposal, since only by so doing will it be able to justify itself (in some measure at least) before future centuries, which will find all that vanished passion for power (*"das vergangene Machtpathos"*) either meaningless or ridiculous."[214]

In his lecture notes, Burckhardt pointed to the absence of historical-patriotic themes among the Dutch painters of the seventeenth century, despite the fact that many of them were active during the period of the emancipation struggle against Spain. If their paintings expressed "Dutchness," that was not achieved directly by representations of political patriotism. "Quite slight, even trivial occasions (*Anlässe*) were enough to stimulate their immense artistry, provided these permitted the expression of their inner energies."[215] And in an 1877 lecture on Rembrandt, he took pains to underscore the Dutch artist's healthy indifference to "patriotic" themes. Though he was almost always critical of Rembrandt and regarded him as a sort of artistic *Gewaltmensch,* a dangerous self-taught rebel determined to go his own way without regard to tradition or the expectations of clients or even in defiance of them, Burckhardt defended him for not having "created great paintings"—as his "latest enthusiastic biographer (Lemke)" would have liked him to do—"on themes from the glorious recent or contemporary history of Holland, such as Admiral Tromp on the deck of his ship in the moment of victory, enveloped in smoke from the ship's canon." Here is Burckhardt's comment to his Basel audience on Lemke's wish: "It is impossible to imagine a deeper misunderstanding of Rembrandt's entire being. . . . Rembrandt would have been . . . unwilling to lend himself to such an ephemeral topic, . . . to such a prescribed emotion, to a so-called great moment. . . . And he would have been right. . . . It was left to the so-called history painting of the nineteenth century to produce work of this kind. Fortunately, the Holland of Rembrandt's day knew nothing of it."[216]

The crudeness with which the modern state acted as patron and source of commissions thus combined with the ignorance of the new middle-class clientele and a prosaic, positivistic view of reality, past and present, to produce exceptionally unfavorable conditions for nineteenth-century artists. The counterpart

in art of the political and constitutional climate of "endless revision" (in Burckhardt's words) created by the French Revolution was a situation in which tradition no longer informed the imagination and artists were subject to the public's
demand for constant innovation or to the state's opportunistic exploitation of
their talents. The art of ancient Grece had never been revolutionary, Burckhardt noted. No Greek artist had ever felt he had to radically reinterpret traditional tasks or commissions (*"Aufgaben"*) or to revolutionize artistic practices for
the sake of creating an effect, as current conditions virtually required contemporary artists to do—though, according to Burckhardt, a few early modern artists
like Michelangelo and Rembrandt had begun to move in that direction.[217] The
effect of such artistic practices was to further blunt people's sensibilities: to
make viewers demand violent and startling effects and find all traditional art
insipid.[218] But the true *Genuss* of art, Burckhardt insisted, results neither from
"Abspannung" ("excitement") nor from *"Zerstreuung"* ("distraction"),[219] the two
essential requirements of the modern public.

A striking contrast drawn in the Rubens book between the conditions of art
production in the sixteenth and seventeenth centuries and in the nineteenth
makes Burckhardt's vision of the historical changes affecting art vividly clear.

> The material situation of European art as Rubens found it is a matter of com-
> mon knowledge. Yet we shall always feel the need of recalling in detail his
> world of patrons and artists as a contrast to our own. Above all, the ground
> from which art sprang was not that of our great cities of today, with their mo-
> bile and . . . fluctuating wealth. There was no public opinion feeding on perpet-
> ual novelty; no press to serve as the voice of that public opinion, and to cast its
> net even over . . . art . . . and make artists subservient to it. And no novel with
> its goal of representing the people and events of the day, whatever they may be,
> and its programme of constant invention. . . . No sudden fashions sweeping
> away the so-called "cultured" classes of the great cities until another fashion
> takes hold of them soon after. In a word, no public on which everything and ev-
> erybody, including artists, depends, and no exhibitions in our sense of the word.
> What still existed to furnish Rubens with the matter of his art was an estab-
> lished stock of ideas, forming a single whole, blended of the ideal world and a
> recognized sphere of the real world, and predominantly southern in character.
> The Bible, vision, legend, mythology, allegory, pastoral, history, and even a
> piece of the everyday world, figures as well as scenes, still formed a whole, and
> a mighty naturalist, inspired by his own fullness of life, undertook to maintain
> all these things at the right temperature. Rubens never really broke through
> this horizon, which he had absorbed in his early years in Antwerp, and still
> more in Italy. He was no willful dreamer of strange fantasies, but only the
> mightiest herald and witness of the great tradition. His vast power of invention
> was essentially occupied in an ever-fresh response to it and an ever-new expres-
> sion of it.[220]

Next to Raphael, and increasingly in the historian's later years, Rubens emerges
in fact as the hero of Burckhardt's history of art: "one of the most powerful and
blessed personalities the world has ever known, building on the achievement of

the last healthy Italian school, the Venetians, to enter into full and steady possession of all the means of his art."[221] Rubens appears to have represented the mature Burckhardt's ideal of the modern artist—perhaps even an idealized image of himself, of the artist he would have liked to be. Certainly no philosopher or historian arouses quite the same degree of enthusiasm in him. What Burckhardt seems to have admired particularly in the Flemish artist was an unusual ability, as he saw it, to harmonize within himself conflicting but, to the Basel patrician, equally valid and desirable characteristics: urbanity and worldliness; delight in both the here and now and the enduring forms behind immediate experience; bold originality and disciplined submission to cultural tradition; intense feeling for the movement and energy of life and determination to capture and represent it in a balanced and orderly composition.

Just as Rubens, working within tradition, came to represent for Burckhardt the right road for art, Rubens's contemporary Rembrandt, working against tradition (in Burckhardt's view), came to represent the wrong road. The contrast between the historian's judgments of the two great seventeenth-century artists gradually emerges as an implicit theme of his writings on art and an indicator of his position in the artistic debates and controversies of his day—in which, with characteristic caution, he refrained from participating publicly. He himself made the connection between his negative reaction to Rembrandt and his later negative reaction to Delacroix. (In the early 1840s, at the time of his enthusiasm for the Belgian romantics, he had been somewhat more favorably disposed.)[222] Both, he declared in a letter to his cousin, the architect Max Alioth, offended his sense of the beautiful.[223] Presumably he was not impressed by Delacroix's open veneration of Rubens or—if he was aware of it—by Baudelaire's description of the French artist as "le Rubens français."[224]

As is well known, Burckhardt repudiated the admiration for *Gewaltmenschen*—individuals of extraordinary willfulness, energy, and artistry, "beyond good and evil"—that was sometimes attributed to him, notably by Nietzsche, on the basis of his portrayal of the tyrants of the Italian Renaissance. He may well, in truth, have contributed to an international movement (it seems to have begun in France with Stendhal and Gobineau) referred to in Germany as *Renaissancismus,* which glorified Renaissance *virtù,* energy, and "selffashioning," to borrow the expression made famous by Stephen Greenblatt, as a form of protest against the mediocrity and utilitarianism of the nineteenth century and which later received further impetus from Nietzsche's vision of the *Übermensch.*[225] Nevertheless, Burckhardt explicitly distanced himself from this movement. "I have never been an admirer of *Gewaltmenschen* and *Out-laws* in history," he protested toward the end of his life, "and have, on the contrary, held them to be *Flagella Dei* [scourges of God]."[226] What he admired about the Renaissance, he remarked in similar vein, was not its brilliant and ruthless captains, but its art and its artists.

Within art itself, however, beginning at least with the Renaissance, Burck hardt recognized a tension between those artists who respect artistic tradition and work within it, and the rebellious artist of demonic, exceptional talent—Diderot's and Goethe's "genius," the "Titanic" or "Promethean" artist, in the terms Burckhardt himself used referring to Michelangelo.[227] The historian acknowledged that uncommon energy and capacity for innovation were necessary both to initiate the Renaissance—"the decision in favor of the new could only be taken through a great act by an extraordinary individual," he wrote of the dome Brunelleschi designed for Florence Cathedral[228]—and then to keep the humanist tradition, once established, from atrophying into mannerism. Burckhardt always admired the energy, the imagination, the powerful sense of life and movement in artists about whom, in other respects, he expressed misgivings: Donatello, Michelangelo (as sculptor), and Correggio. He even showed some sympathy for the artist fated to serve as an agent of challenge and change, pointing out that that role often entailed the sacrifice of qualities such as grace, harmony, and beauty that remained within the reach of lesser artists.[229] Still, as genius, by definition, is inimitable, the "Titanic" artist, necessary and salutary as he may sometimes be, often infects his fellow artists with a kind of "madness" ("Betörung"),[230] seducing them into attempts at imitation with disastrous consequences not only for their own work but for the ensemble of traditions and practices elaborated over generations to guide and nurture younger artists and ensure the continuity of culture.[231] Genius, in short, is a dangerous and, fortunately, uncommon gift. It cannot be acquired, inherited, or shared, and no one should strain after it. "Originality is something one has," in Burckhardt's pithy phrase, "not something one strives to achieve."[232]

The most fortunate and beneficent artists are those who see through custom and routine to the "eternal and divine"[233]—the fundamental order of things—without rebelling or falling prey to excessive subjectivism. Far from neglecting the achievements of their predecessors, these artists build on them.[234] Similarly, they do not allow themselves to be dominated by their imagination, but discipline it in order to have it serve the goals of their art.[235] Brunelleschi's achievement was grounded in a thorough mastery of the laws of mechanics.[236] In Leonardo, "a wonderfully gifted nature, always an originator and discoverer, whether we take him as architect, sculptor, engineer, physiologist, or anatomist," were "united the beautiful soul of the enthusiast with the strongest power of thought and the highest understanding of the conditions of ideal composition."[237] The achievement of Raphael was due less to "genius" than to a disciplined will to beauty, a powerful artistic conscience.[238] "At the core of his being is his faithful sense of obligation (Pflichttreue)," his commitment to his art.[239]

The tension Burckhardt evoked between the genius and the disciplined artist reflects a tension in his own culture, in his own city, and in some measure in his own mind: between unrestrained individual enterprise ("Manchesterism," as it was called by continental writers on economic issues) and community order and well-being; rebellious romantics and classicising traditionalists; Delacroix (*"le chef de l'école moderne,"* as his champions thought of him, *"le vrai peintre du XIX-ème siècle," "la dernière expression du progrès dans l'art,"* according to Baudelaire) and Ingres (*"l'adorateur rusé de Raphael"*).[240] Like Goethe, Burckhardt finally came down on the antiromantic side, but the art historical writing reveals a fairly prolonged effort to define a classicism or traditionalism more suited to the changed conditions of the postrevolutionary era than the style of the pure and serene Raphael. If Raphael dominated the imagination of the younger Burckhardt, the outstanding example, for the later Burckhardt, of a dynamic imagination reined in and controlled by dedication to an ideal of beauty is Rubens. But it took time for Burckhardt to come around to that view of Rubens.

In the early 1840s—the *Kunstwerke der belgischen Städte* appeared in 1842—Rubens is considered a "Titan," a *"Riesenseele"* ("gigantic force"),[241] owing little to his teacher Otto Venius and going far beyond even his Venetian models. "In painting after painting," Emil Maurer has written, "Burckhardt finds 'ideal' beauty and a powerful sense of movement locked in struggle with one another. This basic tension is the essence of his early experience of Rubens. Classical reserve . . . and acknowledgment of the power of genius coexist without being reconciled with each other." In the relatively optimistic period preceding the *Sonderbundkrieg* and the Revolutions of 1848, the accent in Burckhardt's comments on Rubens falls above all on "the fiery pulsing life" of the paintings and on Rubens's ability to represent "with great intensity the power of life" and "the most blessed moments of man's physical existence."[242] In the historian's own words, Rubens is the painter of action, the master of "the clear representation of the moment,"[243] but he is not simply a narrator of particular actions. It is action and life in themselves that are the true subject of his work. In that sense Rubens is a counter-model to the Nazarenes.

As Maurer noted, Burckhardt was in two minds about Rubens at this time. He defended him against those who measured him against an ideal model ("the paintings of Raphael, for instance") and inevitably found his style "impure" and his imagination "common."[244] Nonetheless, he still judged the baroque by the standard of the high Renaissance. He reproached Rubens—as a decade later in *The Cicerone* he would reproach Michelangelo—with having let himself be carried away by his own enormous talent. "He often exaggerates what is in nature," he notes in *Kunstwerke der belgischen Städte,*[245] his sacred characters have nothing holy about them, and in some cases "there is not a single noble figure in the entire painting."[246] The "diagonal movement" in the *Elevation of the Cross* in the transept of the Cathedral in Antwerp is "too violent."[247] His "gigantic powers of imagination and representation"[248] are contrasted, moreover, with the more calm, rounded off, finished art of Van Dyck. "Rubens is the painter of action. For that reason his composition lacks equilibrium and finish (*Abrundung und Gleichgewicht*). . . . . Rubens aims to express above all the energy of nature. . . .

Van Dyck, in contrast, returns to the beauty of nature."[249] In Rubens's later works, the composition is even weaker and the drawing even sketchier.[250] In the public lecture course on art history given at Basel a couple of years later, in 1844–1846, what the lecturer admired was the depiction of the "brilliance of earthly existence," the "magic of reality," "worldly feeling and desire." What he found lacking was the ideal element, "the higher nobility of form."[251] For that, he said, one must still look to Raphael. "One could say that Rubens possessed more the gift of expressing the moment than an immanent sense of the ideal."[252] Rubens at this stage in Burckhardt's experience is the "Shakespeare" of painting, he is "dramatic" in the highest degree.[253] He has some, but not all the qualities required of a painter of *Existenzbilder*.

In later years, focusing on the later works of Rubens in the Munich Pinakothek rather than on those he had seen in the early 1840s in Belgium, Burckhardt began completely revising his (and Kugler's) view of these later works and reversing the preference both men had expressed in the 1840s for the early, supposedly more Italianate works.[254] Burckhardt had in fact visited the museum in Munich in 1839 and again in 1856, but it was not until he was in his sixties, according to Maurer, that he discovered there the Rubens who was to be the model artist of his last years: the master of composition, the lawmaker (*"Gesetzstifter"*) rather than rebel, the incomparable narrator drawing on the culture's vast store of mythology, the provider of solace.[255] The deepest artistic affinity of this painter, as he appears in the *Recollections of Rubens,* is with Veronese.[256] He is no longer the "Shakespeare" but is now the "Homer" of painting.[257]

There is a new desire to see Rubens as more than simply a northern "realist," and to present his image of beauty as truly an ideal, even if it is not the familiar ideal of the Italian quattrocento. Above all, there is a new sense of Rubens's mastery of composition, an appreciation of the powerful structure and organization that order and contain the painting's dynamic energies.

"The bounds of the beautiful . . . for him," we are now told, "were set wide." The features, especially in the female, "which were his ideal . . . were certainly bodied forth out of his own most inward imagination, and they are by no means those which Europe had long regarded as the highest attainable, namely those of the holy women of Leonardo, Raphael, Fra Bartolommeo and so on, which so many Flemish artists had admired, and had been struggling to imitate for a hundred years. Nor are they those of the Venetians." Nor are they borrowed from "living Italian women he encountered in Italy," like the Madonnas of Van Dyck (according to Burckhardt). Nor does "the new and living creation which impresses us even today . . . in its actual features represent a native Flemish type." Rubens' human figures are not copied either from other painters or from "reality." They are neither "mannerist" nor "realist." They are truly an original ideal construction that his imagination has created from the real—nothing less than that *"charakeristisch-typisch"* which the ancient Greeks saved from history and incorporated in their enduring myths: "By virtue of a mysterious divination," that ideal construction "corresponds to the inward feeling of his race." Burckhardt quoted approvingly from Fromentin's *Les Maîtres d'autrefois:* "Rubens established the Flemish type of the Virgin, the Redeemer, the Magdalen and the Disciples."[258]

The powerful presence of an ideal element is now affirmed not only in Rubens's individual figures but in his composition. He was superior in composition to all the Italian artists of his time, we are told, "by the mighty double gift of his nature . . . the delight in living invention and representation and the premonition of laws which, while setting bounds to them, supremely enhanced the appeal of the picture. . . . Only in Rubens do we find the richest symmetrical manipulation of a variety of elements of equal value, of equivalents, in the picture, combined with a most animated or even agitated incident to produce an effect which triumphantly captivates both eye and mind. The horses of his sun chariot are fiery creatures, but he would not let them run away with him."[259]

It was Rubens's ability to achieve deep order in the midst of agitation that aroused Burckhardt's unbounded admiration. "In Rubens's very great picture of momentary action, what the spectator enjoys, at first unconsciously, is the combination of dramatic movement with a mysterious visual restfulness, and it is only later that he becomes aware that the separate elements cohere by a furtive symmetry, or even by a mathematical figure." Thus in *The Rape of the Daughters of Leucippus* (Munich Pinakothek), "the two female figures form an almost uniform mass of light exactly in the lower center of the picture, round which the rest is disposed like a cloud—that is, the Dioscuri, Castor and Pollux, the two horses and the two putti. These eight beings fill out the exact square of the picture on the background of a bright, lush landscape. But it can further be seen that the two magnificently developed female figures are precisely complementary, that the one presents exactly the view not presented by the other, and that the artist has isolated them by an intervening space, so that they nowhere overlap. And all this is fused in the incredible fire of the moment. No other artist, at any time or of any school, could have created just this."[260]

Similarly, in *The Battle of the Amazons* (also in Munich) the "tumult" of the scene is dominated by the "restful mathematical figure" of the stone arch of the bridge in the center of the picture. In *The Lion Hunt* (another Munich picture), "that incredibly instantaneous moment composed of seven men, four horses and two lions, the heads of the helmeted man in the act of striking, of one lion and of the falling Arab . . . lie in one and the same vertical, while the helmeted man . . . forms an equilateral triangle with the two lying on the ground—one dead, the other still warding off the lioness with his dagger." Such underlying symmetries, Burckhardt emphasized, "can be seen only if . . . looked for." As a rule, "nobody realizes anything." But they are what "secretly dominates and lends repose" to the most varied and turbulent compositions (see illustrations at the end of this chapter).[261]

The tensions in Rubens's art are thus now seen as fully integrated in a new harmony. The "Titanic" artist, who seemed at first to threaten tradition, ends up preserving and enriching it. But if the power of artistic tradition was still strong enough in Rubens's time to absorb the most dynamic and original talent, the need to find original thematic material and "invent new topoi," Burckhardt observed in an aside in his course on "Art of the Seventeenth and Eighteenth Centuries," "is notoriously the chief misfortune of contemporary art."[262] The modern artist is thereby deprived of the common language that had been the condition of the most original creations of past art. "The value of uniformity for the development of styles is incalculable," we read in the *Weltgeschichtliche Betrachtungen*. "It challenges art to remain eternally youthful and fresh" while developing traditional themes. Thus it comes about that Madonnas and descents from the cross, repeated a thousand times, are not the feeblest, but the best productions of the best period of art.[263]

Burckhardt's harsh judgments of Rembrandt, whom he associated with romanticism, rejection of tradition, and rebellious, anarchic individualism—"plebeian, Protestant, republican" was how he once described him, in contrast no doubt to the worldly, courtly, and Catholic Rubens—strike us today as shocking, almost incomprehensible.[264] Rembrandt, he told the Basel public in a notorious lecture in 1877, cannot draw, in particular he cannot draw the human body; he gets the slightest foreshortening of an arm wrong; his forms are not only incorrect, they are ugly; he makes mistakes in perspective; he has no sense of composition or proportion and does not know how to arrange masses or to group figures; his subjects are vulgar, his Christ figures particularly "hideous" and "plebeian"; in general, far from celebrating *"die Wonne des Daseins,"* he is drawn to gloom and darkness, to the ill-fated and the outcast. And he is not interested in the inner form or objective character of men or things, but uses subject matter only as a pretext for his own experiments with light and air and for the expression of his own subjectivity.[265] In most respects Rembrandt's work represented for Burckhardt the polar opposite of the *Existenzbild*.

Burckhardt had sensed the challenge Rembrandt's art posed to the classical ideal of *"das Schöne"* from the beginning. "Its basis is a harsh and violent naturalism bordering on vulgarity, hostility to beauty of form," he told his Basel audience in 1844–1846. "Poetry and character have taken refuge in color and chiaroscuro, the fantastical beauty of which runs through the paintings like some wild music." Rembrandt deliberately chose ugly models in order to highlight "the master's own subjectivity" and bring out the "poetry of ugliness." In the article on Rembrandt that Burckhardt wrote for the ninth edition of the Brockhaus Encyclopedia in 1847 (vol. 12, p. 58), the artist is attacked personally: "He was and remained a sordid unconventionalist, comfortable only in low company."[266] Revising Kugler's *Handbook,* Burckhardt cut back on his teacher's moderately sympathetic comments.[267]

In the 1840s, this severe judgment of Rembrandt was not yet exceptional, especially in Germany. It belonged to a tradition reaching back to Rembrandt's contemporary, Joachim von Sandrart (*Teutsche Akademie,* 1675), and continued after the artist's death by Italian and French critics and by a younger generation of Dutch painters who had turned away from Rembrandt to seek inspiration in Italian models and in antiquity.[268] Even the moderately sympathetic German romantic view of Rembrandt—reflected in some measure in the first edition (1837) of Kugler's *Handbook*—highlighted the "fantastic" and the "bizarre" as the chief characteristics of the Dutch artist.[269] By the 1870s, however, Rembrandt had been made over into an icon of romanticism and modernism, and general critical evaluation of his art had become overwhelmingly favorable, not to say reverential.

The process had begun in France and had been closely associated, as Burckhardt was well aware, with the revolutionary movements of 1830 and 1848.[270] In *Notre Dame de Paris* (1831), Victor Hugo had compared Rembrandt to Shakespeare. Théophile Gautier had proclaimed him a *"génie romantique dans toute la force du mot,"* a companion-in-arms of Delacroix, "an alchemist of color" and a "magician of light" and atmosphere. Delacroix's *Christ descendu au tombeau,* he noted in a newspaper review, could easily be mistaken for a lost Rembrandt.[271] Delacroix himself confided to his journal for 6 June 1851 that Rembrandt might be discovered to be "a far greater painter than Raphael" and "more of a natural painter than Perugino's studious pupil." Whereas in the art of the Ancients, as in that of Renaissance painters such as Titian and Veronese, external, plastic form takes precedence over expression, he continued, with Michelangelo, Correggio, and Rembrandt there is a willingness to sacrifice correctness and perfection of form in order to achieve greater expressivity. That is what establishes them as pioneers of the modern.[272] Though Delacroix's journal was not published until 1893, some of the ideas expressed in it had been put forward with fewer nuances three decades earlier in the second volume of Théophile Thoré's *Musées de la Hollande* (1860), which Burckhardt had almost certainly read. Thoré made of Rembrandt and Burckhardt's idol Raphael a Janus head, with the Italian artist looking backward and the Dutch artist forward. "One," he declared "is the past of art, the other its future." In the introduction to the first volume, Thoré had already announced provocatively that the Dutch school had no link with tradition but marked a completely new and modern art: *Prolem sine matre creatam.*[273]

Less than a decade after the appearance of Thoré's book, the learned Dutch art historian Carel Vosmaer published—in French—the first major scholarly monograph on Rembrandt. Refuting the old prejudice that Rembrandt was a vulgarly realistic, self-taught *peintre sauvage* and emphasizing his deeply reflective approach to his art, the austerely disciplined imaginative recreation of reality in almost all his works, and—as if to answer the charge of plebeian vulgarity—his social ties to the most distinguished patrician families in Leiden and Amsterdam, Vosmaer nevertheless presented his countryman as a romantic painter *avant la lettre*, a unique, revolutionary artist, and at the same time the most perfect expression of the Dutch national spirit ("bourgeois, republican, vigorous in the struggle for freedom, bold, active, and enterprising"). To critics who claimed, as Burckhardt did and continued to do, that Rembrandt's drawing was "defective and deliberately ignoble," Vosmaer responded that the classical idea of draftsmanship is not the only one and that there are different ways of drawing. "Is there only one way of drawing? That which sets down the forms of objects in correct and precise contour? I do not think so. Even the artist who draws with the greatest exactness . . . is not content to give a flat outline. He aims to model his figures. So even he tends to transcend line itself. But as art has infinitely many forms of expression, so there are many different ways of drawing, just as there are many different ways of painting. Rembrandt's drawing is as indisputable as Raphael's color. It is extremely precise, but it is not to be found in contours. Rembrandt was to highlight not contour, but relief, color, light, life, and precisely because of that, he had to eliminate line."[274]

Vosmaer made much of the very feature that troubled Burckhardt and that the latter interpreted as a sign of arbitrariness and rebellion: Rembrandt's independence of patrons and of the traditional topoi of painting. "No commissions; no requirement to paint heroic and historical subjects; no dominance of a great leader, of the directors of an academy, of powerful protectors. Taste and selection of topics remain entirely free. . . . Only the great civic paintings can be regarded as resulting from imposed subjects."[275]

Hegel's lectures on aesthetics which appeared posthumously in the late 1830s may also have contributed to the growing reputation and popularity of Rembrandt as the first truly "modern" painter. Dutch art, according to Hegel, had brought about the fullest emancipation of the painterly, the triumph of light and color over sculptural form, the fully realized pleasure of the eye—even if, to Hegel, that very achievement meant that Dutch painting was both the culmination and, in a way, the end of art.[276]

One final observation on the matter of Burckhardt's judgment of Rembrandt: With the erection of a statue of Rembrandt in Amsterdam in 1852 and the construction of the Rijksmuseum, opened to the public in 1885, as a monument to the national art of the Dutch and a shrine for their greatest artist, Vosmaer's interpretation of Rembrandt as the national painter of Holland was integrated into the popular nationalist ideology of the age.[277] The statue was almost certainly a response to the Belgians' unveiling of a statue of Rubens in

Antwerp in 1840, no doubt intended itself as a symbol of national identity and the independence Belgium won from Holland in 1830. Romanticism in art thus appeared to go hand in hand with romantic populism and nationalism in politics. The high point of the appropriation of Rembrandt for the purposes of romantic cultural politics was probably the appearance, in 1890, of Julius Langbehn's immensely popular *Rembrandt der Erzieher,* which presents Rembrandt as a truly "Germanic" artist and the inspiration for a future purely "Germanic" art.

All that can only have been deeply repugnant to Burckhardt. His idea of art, as we saw, was that, while conditioned by time and place, by nationality and history, it transcended these. "The term 'art of the fatherland' ['*vaterländische Kunst*']," he wrote to a friend in 1874, "is one about the value of which I have gradually come to have very negative thoughts."[278] In addition, the patrician, humanistically educated citizen of Basel looked with apprehension on the blurring of boundaries and the smudging of distinctions in modern art as well as in modern politics. In Emil Maurer's words, Burckhardt could not avoid "establishing parallels between the artistic uprising" represented by the romantic nineteenth-century cult of Rembrandt "and the political and social uprising of his time. . . . Just as he understood revolutionary democracy to be the granting of complete license to the lower instincts, so the cult of Rembrandt signified to him a plebeian tide sweeping through contemporary, so-called higher culture [*Eindringen einer Pöbelwoge in die jetzige sogenannte höhere Bildung*'] and the triumph in art of the lackey's view of the world."[279] It is not surprising to find Burckhardt comparing Rembrandt to Wagner in the 1877 lecture. What he perceived—and disliked—in both was a complete dissolution of the forms and hierarchies he believed essential to any civilization.

By 1877, then, it was no longer Rembrandt who was the odd man out, but—increasingly—Burckhardt. The vehemence of the historian's tone in the 1877 lecture, the withering sarcasm of his comments about the "fantastical" interpretations to which Rembrandt's romantic devotees were prone, and the rhetorical, programmatic character of the concluding paragraph, each sentence of which begins "*It is not true that* . . ." make it clear that the lecturer knew he was now taking on not simply an individual artist but an entire artistic and cultural movement. Rembrandt was now being judged as the herald of modern art's break with the great models and the humanist tradition of the Renaissance, the symbol of the entire modernist movement in art and of modernity in general.[280]

It was thus as the icon of modernity, the artist represented by the champions of the modern as having come to revolutionize painting and dissolve the humanist tradition inherited from the Italian Renaissance, that Rembrandt provoked Burckhardt's ire. It is not surprising that in these conditions the patrician scholar of Basel found in the humanistic artist from mercantile Antwerp the perfect representative in art of the values he liked to associate with the traditions of his native city-state: independence of mind, energy, resourcefulness, commercial flair, but at the same time respect for learning and the accumulated cultural heritage, recognition of the value of order, and a deep conviction that human life is enhanced by reverential contemplation or *Anschauung* of an ideal and beautiful existence glimmering through the imperfect apppearances of a shared objective world, rather than by self-indulgent subjectivism or concentration on the raw fragments of experience. The *Existenzbild* gave a sense of the blissfulness of that ideal existence— *"die Wonne einer idealen Existenz,"* as he put it in a letter to the artist Ernst Stückelberg.[281]

Thirty years after Burckhardt's death, in 1926–1927, Aby Warburg, the well-to-do citizen of another old commercial city-state and the son of a well-established family of Jewish bankers, directed a seminar at the University of Hamburg on the Basel historian. Warburg looked to Burckhardt, as Burckhardt had looked to Rubens, as the model of a scholar and artist who had seen in beauty and the sense of form a means of reining in and subordinating demonic and irrational energies. To Warburg, living through a time of social, political, and cultural upheaval and uncertainty, and recovering from his own personal breakdown, art was an instrument of sanity and civilization, as it had been to Burckhardt, and not, as it often appears in the writings of Thomas Mann, a force of dissolution. "Artistic production and artistic *Genuss* require the combination of two actions of the soul which are normally mutually exclusive," he noted: "a passionate giving up of self to the point where one becomes identical with the impression produced on one by the object at hand, and a bold, distancing self-consciousness in the ordering contemplation of things." If Rubens was Burckhardt's answer to Rembrandt and romanticism, Burckhardt appeared to have been Warburg's answer to the late romanticism of Nietzsche. In contrast to Nietzsche, in Warburg's view, Burckhardt had succeeded in reconciling and combining the two actions of the soul. Burckhardt, he wrote, "seeks measure or heightened form, . . . a form that is at once life and limitation: Rubens."[282]

In an age that has invented the "instant classic," it is not hard to sympathize with Burckhardt's negative judgment of the modern infatuation with "originality" and "the new" or with his conservative view that "style means . . . that a degree of perfection once achieved is retained in opposition to the popular taste persisting beside it (which may always have had a bias toward the pretty, gaudy, ghastly, etc.)."[283] At the same time, the historian's apparent failure to respond to most of what we now consider the best art of his own time suggests that the perspective he adopted had its limitations. He did appreciate and encourage fine classicizing Swiss artists, like the Baseler Ernst Stückelberg, a distant relative, whose *Marionetten* (1869) he urged the Basel Museum to acquire—"a beautiful, calm, clear *Existenzbild* of antiquity," as one critic described it in 1904, possibly repeating a judgment heard from Burckhardt's own lips[284]—or

Charles Gleyre, from whom the Basel Museum commissioned a handsome *Pentheus Pursued by the Maenads* in 1865 (see illustrations at the end of this chapter). And he continued to support his fellow Baseler Arnold Böcklin by encouraging the Museum to buy his work. But his few comments on the most radically modernizing French painters of the time, such as Manet or Courbet, were consistently negative.[285] And his later break with Böcklin resulted, if only in part, from Böcklin's feeling that the influential professor was imposing his artistic norms on him.[286] Hunkering down in Basel allowed Burckhardt to preserve his independence of judgment and provided him with a lookout remarkably close to that Archimedean point outside events about which he wrote in the *Weltgeschichtliche Betrachtungen*. But it also exacted a price. With so much learning, sensitivity, and insight, he has surprisingly little to say to and about the modern artist trying to respond to the modern world.

Certainly, his diagnosis of a portentous shift in the relation between the artist and the public in the age of bourgeois democracy seemed to be borne out by developments. By the later years of the century it had even become a commonplace of art criticism. In 1874, for instance, the young Munich art historian Adolf Bayersdorfer—whose portrait by Böcklin is currently in the Basel Kunstmuseum—pronounced the German public completely insensitive to the art of painting and incapable of responding to anything except narrative or didactic moralizing:

> Their comprehension is based on the childish position that every picture should tell them a little story or provide a . . . description of some historical or genre scene or of a landscape. They also understand didactic, moralizing intentions and delight in recognizing them. They find no less pleasure in having their emotions aroused, and consider emotional effect to be unequivocal evidence of the presence of art. They would not know where to begin if confronted by an untitled picture representing a simple unchanging state of something, with no pragmatic, novelistic content or striving for effect, . . . by the pure solution of a problem of painting, by a landscape in which nature does not play theatrically with mood and effect, and in general by any painting which does not declaim its meaning rhetorically in easily intelligible language.[287]

Confronted with an undiscriminating and ignorant public, some of the best German artists had responded by withdrawing from the public sphere altogether. Hans von Marées, for instance, spent the most productive half of his short life as an exile in Italy, hardly exhibited his paintings, refused even to admit any but a chosen few to see them in his studio, and expressed equal contempt for the Berlin salon public and for the state as patrons of art. The best that could happen, he held, would be the complete destruction of the entire art establishment. "Almost the only hope for a better future would be if art were to be completely snuffed out by the corrupt taste and stupid dilettantism of the present day."[288] As for the state, the most useful thing it could do would be to pension off 99 percent of living artists (the *"Künstlerpöbel,"* in his own words), on condition that they stop painting. "Art is thoroughly aristocratic. Nobility of spirit is the *sine qua non* for any one practicing or promoting it."[289] Marées had withdrawn from the *"Getümmel des modernen Wirrwarrs"* ("the tumult of the modern pandemonium") and was determined to swim against the tide,[290] even while acknowledging the negative consequences for art of the artist's alienation from modern society: "One's total lack of any relation to the outside world has a disabling enough effect and undermines any creative energy one might have."[291] Marées went on to criticize even Böcklin, one of his few friends and a fellow exile in Italy, for being too rhetorical, too concerned with producing an effect on the viewer.

Marées's views of contemporary art and the situation of the contemporary artist, as well as his own efforts to develop a new pictorial idiom consonant with the classical tradition, seem not at odds with Burckhardt's. Yet there is no evidence that Burckhardt took an interest in him or in other artists pursuing similar goals—such as Marées' friend, the sculptor Adolf von Hildebrand. Burckhardt's silence in the face of the work of his most interesting contemporaries, and his seeming failure to respond to it, is mirrored in the limitations of his understanding of the problems and opportunities of the modern artist. Beyond denouncing the conditions of modern artistic production, he has little or nothing to say on this topic—far less, for instance, than his somewhat younger contemporary Conrad Fiedler, the critic and philosopher of aesthetics and the patron of Marées.

In a magisterial essay on "Modern Naturalism and Artistic Truth" that appeared in the *Leipziger Zeitung* in 1881—three years before Burckhardt shared his pessimism about the fate of art in the modern world with Paul Heyse—Fiedler placed himself squarely in the situation of the modern artist. Fiedler agreed with Burckhardt that the contemporary artist is no longer sustained and guided by the institutions, the shared culture, and the artistic conventions and traditions that sustained and guided the artists of earlier times; he agreed that the modern artist is confronted instead by a society with little genuine understanding or love of art, but with high demands for titillation and immediate gratification. Fiedler went on to review the various options open to the modern artist. One was what Burckhardt in effect recommended: to remain loyal to past traditions that he truly admires. Fiedler represented this option as honorable, but noted that it would effectively remove the artist from the public sphere altogether; he would end up as an epigone without any impact on his time or relation to it. A second option was to try to follow fashion and give the public what it appears to want at any given moment; that choice meant renouncing any serious attempt to forge an authentic artistic vision. Finally, said Fiedler, the artist can embrace the principles of naturalism, that is to say, he can reject the authority both of tradition and of an undiscerning public and accept only that of reality itself, committing his art to the most rigorously truthful representation of reality, not ennobled by the "ideal," but as he perceives or experiences it. Fiedler himself strongly favored such a declaration of independence from the public, on the one hand, and from tradition, on the other. The French naturalists and impressionists, he claimed, have done for art what Hume, according to Kant, did for philosophy: they have "awakened art from its dogmatic slumbers." At the same time, Fiedler warned that realism, the goal of faithfully "representing reality," which contemporary painters claimed as their justification, is philosophically naive and, if left unexamined, would ultimately lead art into a new and more wretched servitude. At most, it would achieve the emancipation of art from rhetorical conventions—but that would be "truly a dismal experience of disenchantment, after all the noble goals that earlier times have attributed to art."[292] Fiedler thus called for a complete rethinking of the aesthetics of the visual arts.

Burckhardt, in contrast, offered no clear vision of the future. He remained chiefly focused on what he perceived as the breakdown of artistic tradition: drastically altered conditions of patronage and artistic support, willfulness and subjectivism among artists, indifference to traditional artistic subjects and practices, and a self-regarding preoccupation with artistic processes. Compared with his hero Rubens—who was not only a magisterial practitioner of his craft but an *uomo universale,* an artist whose work communicated a supreme vision of human energy reconciled with form—the modern artist cut a poor figure indeed in Burckhardt's eyes. His alienation and his exacerbated self-consciousness had turned the subject matter of painting (the *Gegenstand*) into little more than an occasion for experimenting with the technical possibilities of color and light. Burckhardt had consistently protested both against the overwhelming of aesthetic form by subject matter, the dominion of the *"Was, das stets neue Sujet, über das Wie"* ("the What, the ever new subject, over the How"), as he put it,[293] and against the reduction of subject matter to a mere occasion for the exploration or display of artistic technique. For four centuries the humanist tradition had upheld the balance of content and form, real and ideal, modern experience and traditional themes and topoi, individual invention and established norms and conventions, and painterly execution and narrative or intellectual conception. Now, in Burckhardt's own time, that balance seemed almost unsustainable.

In the context of his concern about the fate of art, as he understood it, the study of art history may well have represented for Burckhardt both an acknowledgment of the fragility of tradition and an attempt to shore it up. If the *Genuss* of works of art was no longer something that occurred naturally and spontaneously in a public familiar with the tradition, if the immediate pleasure was now usually insufficient and superficial (pleasure at the "cleverness" of a representation, for instance, or at the recognition of a subject matter), providing viewers with some understanding of the tradition might well seem to be a necessary condition for restoring contact with works of art and thus ensuring the cultural continuity that was so important to the historian. Equally, if the public itself could no longer guide and orient the artist, it became the task of the art historian who had familiarized himself with artistic traditions to do so.

Burckhardt wrote art history, one might perhaps conclude, as a way of campaigning not only against the "retrograde" idealism of the Nazarenes but against the realism of the moderns, both of which he appears to have seen as aspects of romanticism. The goal of his work as an art historian was essentially conservative: to awaken or reawaken in the readers and audiences—as well as in the artists—of his own "hurried age," or at least in a devoted elite of them, a love and understanding of art in the humanist tradition. The *Genuss* of individual works was as much a part of that project as was the narrative of the tradition, with its heroes—Da Vinci, Raphael, Rubens, Titian—and its dangerously talented *Gewaltmenschen,* such as Michelangelo, Tintoretto, or Rembrandt. Whether directly, through the *Genuss* to which he invited them, or indirectly, through the "story" of art which he told them, Burckhardt, it seems, intended to facilitate his readers' and audiences' participation in humanist culture and to lead artists themselves back from the wilderness of the marketplace and an untutored public to the traditions of humanist art.[294] In the modern artists he supported, it has been said, he believed he recognized a continuation and adaptation of the great artists of the Renaissance and the baroque: in Konrad Grob, a contemporary Murillo; in Charles Gleyre, a descendant of Raphael; in Böcklin a successor of Rubens.[295]

Burckhardt knew that the political restoration of 1815 had failed to halt the dynamics of revolutionary change and that the old Europe could never be reconstituted. To the man who had always been more interested in the "recurrent, constant, and typical," and to whom underlying cultural continuities had always mattered more than ephemeral events, what was required, as Josef Mali has argued, was "not a political restoration, but a cultural renaissance."[296] He may well have seen his role, in art history no less than in his other writings, as that of a latter day St. Severin, salvaging what could be salvaged of the "culture of Old Europe" so that it could be handed on, beyond a harsh immediate future of decline and decay, to later, more fortunate generations. In an age of fragmentation and dissolution, art remained for the citizen of old Basel—as he thought it ought to be for everyone—harmonizing and unifying. "A golden glow of reconciliation must lie over things before they can be handled [by the artist]," he told the aspiring poetess Emma Brenner-Kron in 1851, in words that seem to echo Goethe, as he warned her not to try to make poetry out of inner pain and frustration.[297] "In the highest painting," we read in *The Cicerone,* "we do not want the real, but the true. . . . We wish to be reminded of what is best in us, of which we expect it to give us the living expression." A few pages later

Titian is praised because "[w]hat in real life is broken, scattered, limited, he represents as complete, happy, and free."[298] Art, in short, is an opening on to a "higher" world of beauty and harmony. "In the midst of our hurried age, it is a domain of general contemplation, of which past centuries had little or no experience, a second dream existence, in which quite special spiritual organs are brought to life and consciousness."[299]

Friedrich Overbeck, *Der Triumph der Religion in den Künsten* (*The Triumph of Religion in the Arts*), 1840. Städelsches Kunstinstitut, Frankfurt am Main.

Philipp Veit, *Einführung der Künste durch das Christentum* (*The Arts Introduced by Christianity*), 1834–1836. Städelsches Kunstinstitut, Frankfurt am Main.

Franz Pforr, *Der Einzug König Rudolf's von Habsburg in Basel* (*Entry of King Rudolf von Habsburg into Basel in 1273*), 1808–1810. Städelsches Kunstinstitut, Frankfurt am Main.

Albert Landerer, *Der Einzug der eidgenössischen Gesandten in Basel* (*Entry of the Swiss Delegates into Basel to Take the Oath of Confederation in 1501*), 1855. Öffentliche Kunstsammlung Basel, Kunstmuseum. Photo: Öffentliche Kunstsammlung Basel, Martin Bühler.

Louis Gallait, *L'Abdication de Charles V* (*The Abdication of Charles V*), 1841. Musée royal des beaux-arts de Belgique, Brussels.

Ernst Stückelberg, *Das Erwachen der Kunst in der Renaissance* (*The Awakening of Art in the Renaissance*), 1877. Kunsthalle, Basel.

Peter Paul Rubens, *Die Löwenjagd* (*The Lion Hunt*), 1621. Alte Pinakothek, Munich.

Ernst Stückelberg, *Die Marionetten* (*The Marionettes*), 1869. Öffentliche Kunstsammlung Basel, Kunstmuseum. Photo: Öffentliche Kunstsammlung Basel, Martin Bühler.

Marc Charles Gabriel Gleyre, *Pentheus von den Mänaden verfolgt* (*Pentheus Pursued by the Maenads*), 1865. Öffentliche Kunstsammlung Basel, Kunstmuseum. Photo: Öffentliche Kunstsammlung Basel, Martin Bühler.

PART FOUR

"The Sulking Corner of Europe"

If I had any assurance that my work here would continue as undisturbed in
the next few years as in the past I would not even fleetingly contemplate giving up my obligation to be active on German soil, particularly as an educator
of the nation in matters of politics. On the other hand, . . . would it not be infinitely instructive to observe Germany for a while from the outside, and yet
from such a proximate look-out post? . . . Perhaps it is only by writing out of
Basel that I can communicate what I have to say about the political problems
of the present time.

—Gerhard Ritter (1934)

Some day a book should be written on the topic: Berlin and Basel in the age
of the founding of the Bismarckian Reich. It should show how the modern
German study of history as a history of the spirit culminated in these two
places in two different positions that came into conflict with one another. The
two positions should be shown to have resulted from their historical backgrounds and contexts—Prussian-German on one side; Swiss (but still closely
related to the spiritual life of Germany as a whole) on the other. Pride and satisfaction at the rise of Germany as a strong nation-state on one side; criticism,
suspicion, and anxiety in the face of that very achievement on the other.
Droysen, Treitschke, and Dilthey joining their voices with that of Ranke; the
young Nietzsche, Overbeck, and Bachofen joining theirs with that of Burckhardt. A book such as this could become a symbol of our spiritual destiny.

—Friedrich Meinecke (1948)

Friedrich Nietzsche. Universitätsbibliothek Basel, Porträtsammlung.

Franz Camille Overbeck and his wife, Ida. Universitätsbibliothek Basel, Porträtsammlung.

14

Friedrich Nietzsche and Franz Overbeck

In 1869 Friedrich Nietzsche, then a twenty-four-year-old student of the Leipzig philologist Friedrich Ritschl, was called to the chair of Greek language and literature at the University of Basel, from which the previous occupant, Adolf Kiessling, had resigned in order to accept a position in Hamburg. A year later he was joined by another young German, the thirty-three-year-old Franz Camille Overbeck, who was appointed to the chair of New Testament theology and church history. Neither man could have hoped for a comparable appointment at a German university, especially Nietzsche, who had not yet defended a dissertation or been properly authorized to teach at a German university ("*habilitiert*"). In fact the University of Leipzig, to maintain a semblance of academic form, had to hurriedly award him a doctorate on the basis of a couple of learned articles that had been published, on Ritschl's recommendation, in the scholarly *Rheinisches Museum*. In the letter in which he proposed Nietzsche to Wilhelm Vischer-Bilfinger, then chairman of the Basel Education Committee, Ritschl asserted that in thirty-nine years of teaching he had never come across "a young man who has matured to such an extent at such an early age," pronounced him "a phenomenon," predicted that he would stand in the front rank of German philologists, and declared himself "willing to stake my whole academic reputation on the appointment's turning out to be a success." He conceded, however, that he had "not yet encountered the committee on appointments that would have the courage and the confidence in such a case to overlook the formal deficiencies of the candidate." Basel was probably the only university willing to do so at the time. Since the *Kantonstrennung* the University of Basel had fallen on hard times. The situation had improved somewhat since the 1830s and 1840s, but the authorities still pursued a policy of bringing in bright, promising younger men from whom their institution and the city as a whole could hope to benefit for a few years before they moved on to more prestigious—and better paid—positions in Germany.[1]

While they were always in some sense "foreigners" in the close-knit society of Basel—"I have always been a foreigner in this land, even after living here as a guest for twenty-five years," Overbeck wrote to his old friend, the historian Heinrich von Treitschke, on the eve of his retirement[2]—the destinies of both Nietzsche and Overbeck are indissolubly linked to the old city-state on the

Rhine. Overbeck was by temperament extremely reserved, but he slowly built a circle of friends and admirers in Basel. His colleagues at the University several times elected him rector. Characteristically, he was far less close to Burckhardt than Nietzsche was, and his relation to Bachofen appears to have been even more distant and formal, but notes in his recently published *Nachlass* indicate that he knew his colleague Burckhardt well enough to have an acute sense of the older man's personality. He was "attached" to the city, he explained to Treitschke, even though he had remained a "foreigner." Above all, he appreciated the freedom he enjoyed in Basel. Though his theological views had turned out to be unorthodox, and he had disappointed the expectations of some and shocked the religious sensibilites of others, he had not once in twenty-five years been subjected to interference, criticism, or attack, he declared, and had no reason to suspect that any one had ever even contemplated trying to have him removed from his professorship.[3] "Basel was and has remained the refuge of my *Theology*," he wrote shortly before his death in an afterword to a re-edition of his provocative short book of 1873, *Über die Christlichkeit unserer heutigen Theologie,* "and I have never ceased to experience it as such from the moment I first arrived. For that reason it has earned my enduring gratitude."[4] Overbeck never left his adopted city and died there in 1905.

Nietzsche—at the time of his appointment "a quiet, serious, retiring man of neat appearance and fine manners, with a great love of music," in the words of his recent biographer[5]—seems to have been more capable of forming attachments and, partly no doubt because of his musical talent, quickly became a much appreciated figure in Basel social circles. After some months of loneliness—"I am forgetting the very use of speech," he wrote his friend Erwin Rohde, a fellow student of Ritschl's, in early 1870[6]—he began receiving invitations to the Heuslers, the La Roches, the Sarasins, the Thurneysens, and the Vischers.[7] In the early years especially, he was a frequent guest of the Bachofens. Bachofen's wife Louise Bachofen-Burckhardt had a particular fondness for him. They were about the same age. Sometimes Nietzsche would accompany her to a concert; sometimes they played the piano together in the handsome house on the Münsterplatz. "I shall always be glad that I got to know Nietzsche in those early years," Louise Bachofen wrote later to C. A. Bernoulli, when the latter was preparing his book on Nietzsche and Overbeck. "That was the time of his passionate enthusiasm for Wagner, and *how* passionate it was! Every Sunday he would travel to Lucerne and each time he came back full of his idol and told me of all the splendid things he had seen and heard. . . . But you know all that better than I, though perhaps you are not so familiar with that most sunny, friendly time in Nietzsche's life, at least not from personal experience, since you are far too young."[8]

Nietzsche quickly got to know his senior colleague Jacob Burckhardt, whom he came to revere, and with whom he believed he had a deep intellectual affinity. As early as May 1869, he told his sister that he had lunch every day at a restaurant near the central railway station with three other colleagues and that his closest acquaintance was Jacob Burckhardt, "the famous teacher of aesthetics and art history and a very smart man."[9] "We have discovered that our aesthetic paradoxes are wonderfully congruent," he wrote happily to Rohde.[10] In the fall of 1870, Nietzsche sat in on Burckhardt's lectures on the study of history and expressed his satisfaction at finding them marked by "the spirit of Schopenhauer."[11] At weekends the two colleagues often walked the three miles or so to a village on the other side of the border in neighboring Baden, where they would drink a glass of wine at one of the local inns regularly patronized by Burckhardt.

Nietzsche had a heavy teaching load. In his first semester he lectured on Greek lyric poetry on Mondays, Tuesdays, and Wednesdays, and on Aeschylus on Thursdays, Fridays, and Saturdays; in addition he had a seminar on Mondays and he taught two classes at the *Pädagogium* on Tuesdays and Fridays, and one class on Wednesdays and Thursdays. Often enough, however, he lectured to only two or three students. *"Die gesamte Philologenschaft"* ("The entire company of philologists") at the University consisted of eight students, he reported in 1869.[12] After the beating *The Birth of Tragedy* took from some scholarly reviewers in Germany, the numbers seem to have diminished further. Nietzsche expressed concern. "I am so decried among my professional colleagues that our little University is suffering for it," he told Wagner toward the end of 1872.[13]

Adding to Nietzsche's discomfort were his doubts about continuing to pursue a career in philology. "I live in complete estrangement from philology," he wrote to Rohde in 1871.[14] That same year he presented himself as a candidate for the chair of philosophy at the University of Basel. This time the university authorities were more circumspect and Nietzsche, who had no formal training in philosophy, was turned down. Despite his heavy teaching load, his sense of being imprisoned in philology, and a growing feeling that Schopenhauer's scathing attacks on the universities were well founded and that "a truly radical pursuit of truth is not possible here," Nietzsche loyally carried out his professional obligations as professor of Greek language and literature. He was grateful for the freedom his position allowed him. "I value Basel," he told Rohde in 1872, "because it allows me to live in peace."[15]

He had already begun to feel the effects of the illness that was to destroy him within a little more than a decade, however,[16] and in 1876–1877 he was granted an unpaid leave on grounds of ill health. More and more severe bouts of physical sickness and mental depression finally made it impossible for him to continue, and in 1879 he resigned from the University. But he never sought another position, nor, thanks to the University's generosity, did he need to. Though it was not rich, the University of Basel granted its now seriously ailing young professor an annual pension of three thousand francs, and that, together with some other sources of private income, was enough to support him for the rest of his life. After a decade of restless wandering, during which he produced his most powerful work even while his condition continued to deteriorate, Nietzsche ended his days in a mental institution. His professorship at Basel was the only regular post he ever held.

If the two young Germans were fairly quickly integrated into Basel society, without ever becoming real Baselers (that would have taken several generations at least!), they were virtually wedded to the University. Their earliest published works were such that it would have been difficult for either of them to move from Basel to an academic position in the new Bismarckian Empire, even if that had been their wish.[17] Thus it came about that the immigrants contributed almost as much as their native-born colleagues, Bachofen and Burckhardt, to defining the strikingly original intellectual character nineteenth-century Basel has assumed for us as we look back upon it at the turn of the twenty-first century. While Bachofen challenged the German philological establishment and the prevailing academic orthodoxy in the study of classical antiquity, and Burckhardt the progressivist, nationalist historiography dominant in the Germany of the *Gründerzeit,* along with the entire worldview that that historiography reflected and promoted, Nietzsche challenged the academic philosophy of his time and Overbeck the popular liberal theology that had made religion an integral part of the culture of the nineteenth-century German national state. Compared with Zurich, where the role of leading local intellectual played in Basel by Burckhardt was played by the liberal-minded Gottfried Keller, and where the immigrant and refugee scholars were mostly progressive liberals (Gottfried Semper, Francesco De Sanctis, Gottfried Kinkel, Hermann Köchly, Theodor Mommsen),[18] the intellectual physiognomy of Basel bears the imprint of the thoroughgoing critique of modern liberalism and progressivism carried out by Bachofen, Burckhardt, Nietzsche, and Overbeck.

Between the two young Germans—Overbeck and Nietzsche—a close friendship quickly developed, based on their common dislike of comforting "Philistine" pseudo-solutions to hard philosophical and moral problems.[19] The newcomers took rooms in the same house at 45 Schützengraben—the *"Baumannhöhle,"* as they described it after the name of their landlady and with a playful allusion to a famous scene in Goethe's *Faust.* The *"Höhlenbären"* (den bears), as they called themselves, took their meals together, made music together, discussed their work, and talked together until far into the night, Nietzsche almost certainly confiding in Overbeck more than the other way around. The year 1873 must have been one of the happier high points of their friendship, for it saw the publication, with the same publisher, of the first of Nietzsche's *Unzeitgemässe Betrachtungen* attacking David Strauss and of Overbeck's stinging critique of liberal theology, *Über die Christlichkeit unserer heuti-*

Lodgings of Nietzsche and Overbeck, Schützengraben 45.

gen Theologie. The two friends, colleagues, and housemates had both little works bound together in two single volumes, and each presented one of the volumes to the other. (A third volume was prepared for their mutual friend Erwin Rohde—the author of the influential *Psyche* [1896], one of the chief sources of E. R. Dodds's classic *The Greeks and the Irrational* [1951].) Nietzsche and Overbeck might have been speaking of themselves when they referred to the two short works as *"die Zwillinge"* ("the twins").

The "contubernium" of Nietzsche and Overbeck lasted until 1875 when Overbeck married and moved out of the *Baumannhöhle* into a townhouse a couple of minute's walk away in the Eulerstrasse. But the friendship of the two men endured. Overbeck's wife, Ida Rothpelz, was brought into it and in 1880 the *"eheliche Mitheidin"* or "fellow-pagan spouse," as Nietzsche called her,[20] translated Sainte-Beuve's *Causeries du lundi* into German for Nietzsche. After Nietzsche resigned from the University and left Basel in 1879, Overbeck oversaw his finances for him, advised him on how best to invest the pension he received from the University, and forwarded money to him as he needed it. He also acted as his literary agent, purchasing and mailing the books Nietzsche asked him to procure. Above all, he gave Nietzsche whatever support he could as his illness took an ever greater toll mentally and physically.

In 1889, it was to Overbeck that an alarmed Burckhardt brought a demented letter he had received from Nietzsche, and it was Overbeck who set out immediately for Turin, took matters in hand, and brought the now gravely ill Nietzsche back to Basel, where he arranged for him to be cared for in a local mental clinic known as *"Friedmatt."* Scrupulous and relentlessly analytical as always, Overbeck agonized over his part in a process that ended with Nietzsche's infantilization and loss of control over his own life. Even though he and his wife had long before taken the measure of their friend's sister, Elisabeth Förster-Nietzsche, who had kept house for Nietzsche at various times during his years in Basel, he was bitterly offended by her insinuation that he had completely misdiagnosed her brother's malady and failed to ensure that he received the right treatment in time. The inevitable estrangement caused by Nietzsche's mental condition was aggravated by Overbeck's distrust and dislike of the ambitious, self-promoting, and domineering Förster-Nietzsche—*"eine Nähmamsell,"* as he called her contemptuously[21]—who began gathering together everything relative to her brother for a planned Nietzsche Archive in Weimar, through which she proposed to develop the already burgeoning Nietzsche cult. Such an "industrial exploitation"[22] of Nietzsche's legacy distorted it, in Overbeck's view, brought out what was worst in it, and obscured what was truly valuable. Though he resisted making his friendship with Nietzsche an object of public discussion and refrained for many years from speaking out against Förster-Nietzsche, Overbeck strove for the rest of his life and beyond it, through the work of his student Carl Albrecht Bernoulli, to preserve a different picture of Nietzsche from that propagated, unfortunately with considerable success, by *"die Dame Förster,"* as he insisted on calling her. On her side, Elisabeth Förster's hostility to the Overbecks was relentless; she sensed that Nietzsche had at times spoken unfavorably of her to them and she knew that they shared Nietzsche's disdain for her husband's rabid, loudly proclaimed anti-Semitism.[23]

Unlike Bachofen and Burckhardt, both of whom had deep roots in their native city, Franz Overbeck was a rootless, thoroughly modern individual. He was born in St. Petersburg of a French Catholic mother and a German Lutheran father. His paternal grandfather held British citizenship, having lived and worked for a number of years in England. Raised multilingually (French, Russian, English, and some German) in a society of exiles (his father was employed by an English store in the Russian capital) and educated internationally in Russia, France, and Germany, he was neither rich nor well connected. His prospects of finding academic employment in Germany were not bright when he received an invitation to join the theology faculty at Basel. He accepted, as many Germans accepted offers from Swiss universities, thinking that it would tide him over until something better turned up in Germany. In the event, he never returned to Germany and spent his entire career at Basel.[24]

Overbeck was invited to Basel in response to local pressure on the University authorities to hire a scholar who could represent the influential liberal tendency in modern Protestant theology. Without anyone to teach the new currents in theology, the University had become isolated theologically and was losing students to other institutions.[25] Overbeck was a compromise candidate, the choice of the ruling elite, and only grudgingly accepted, from the outset, by the more committed reformers.[26] A quiet, unremarkable man who, externally, led a thoroughly bourgeois existence, Overbeck was in almost every respect a complete outsider, a man of everywhere and nowhere, and of no clear religious confession or conviction, though of extraordinary personal integrity and moral uprightness.[27] He himself related that without any strong religious background in his family—only his paternal grandmother was a devout Lutheran—he had simply drifted into the study of theology, vaguely motivated by a desire to pursue a scholarly career and by diffuse feelings of humanitarianism. Among his fellow students in theology at the University of Leipzig, he recounted, he felt like a Hottentot[28] and that is exactly how he was viewed by many for years to come. According to his successor in the chair of practical theology and church history at Basel, "he was cosmopolitan and interconfessional by birth. Highly gifted, sharp-witted, and intensely curious, he had absolutely no experience of the everyday life of a German Evangelical family, no church affiliations or churchgoing habits, no feeling for any homeland, community or congregation. . . . His entire outlook was that of a scholar—theoretical, critical and skeptical."[29]

Overbeck's extreme detachment—a detachment in no way identical with indifference, particularly to other human beings—was the dominant trait of his personality. Because of it, he succeeded in maintaining, as few other associates of Nietzsche could, his intellectual independence and the ability to criticize important aspects of Nietzsche's thought and work. At the same time, his sense of detachment made his life as a theology professor difficult. "I did not teach what I believed, that is to say, what I wanted to," he later confessed, "but what I considered appropriate, that is, what I took it to be my duty to teach." Inevitably, he came to find his "role as a teacher disagreeable" and saw himself as a scholar, a researcher, and a learner, rather than a teacher.[30]

Within barely three years of his arrival in Basel and on the morrow of the intercantonal concordat of 1872, which opened up Basel's well-guarded parishes to liberal ministers from other cantons, Overbeck demonstrated his independence of mind by publishing a work that turned out to be a scathing critique of the very theology he had been brought to Basel to represent. As in the case of Nietzsche's attack on David Strauss, however, the satisfaction of the local Pietists and orthodox Calvinists must have been tempered by the sobering thought that the divinity had made use of an apostate to smite His enemies. For Overbeck's work was not only a rejection of liberal theology. It was a challenge to all theology and to the very possibility of reconciling authentic Christianity with authentic modernity. Shortly after the appearance of *On the Christian Character of our Present-Day Theology* in 1873, Overbeck announced publicly that he and his wife were no longer members of any church. It was now generally understood in Basel that the new professor of theology and church history might not be a believing Christian.[31]

In his student days at Leipzig, under the influence of his close friend, the future nationalist historian Heinrich von Treitschke, Overbeck had strongly supported the cause of German unity under the leadership of Prussia. Newly arrived in Basel on the outbreak of the Franco-Prussian war in 1870, he at first participated in efforts to mobilize support for the Prussian cause among Germans resident in Switzerland. As in the case of Nietzsche, however, his enthusiasm rapidly turned to disillusionment and finally to outright hostility toward the new German Empire as he reassessed the character of the war and reached the conclusion that the effect of the Prussian victory was going to be the complete subordination of German culture, in particular of the universities and the church, to the interests of the state and the new economic moguls. As early as 1866, at the time of the Austro-Prussian War, he had confessed to "an invincible and bothersome feeling of political uneasiness" at seeing goals with which he was in complete sympathy "being pursued by Prussia in a manner that constantly ran counter to my convictions"—so much so, in fact, that he began to be concerned lest, "as a result, these goals might themselves be endangered for a considerable time to come."

What these goals were, as well as his misgivings about them, Overback made clear. He could not altogether "suppress an anxious feeling that no one has quite measured the extent of the misfortune it would be if the issues of national unity and freedom were to be treated as separate."[32] Years later he confided to his notebooks that what united him to the nineteenth century was not its nationalism, not its love of power, but "that which was most youthful in all its struggles," its "striving for freedom and everything it achieved for mankind through that striving."[33] Freedom to develop all one's capacities, complete emancipation from all intellectual and historical phantoms—that is what Overbeck sought for himself and that is the right he demanded for all who wished to make use of it. The strength of this commitment to freedom is highlighted by the contrast between Overbeck's position on Bismarck's nationalist policies and the far more typical position of Bachofen's former friend, the law professor Rudolf Jhering, who had left Basel for an appointment at Rostock in the late 1840s. At the time of the Austro-Prussian War in 1866 Jhering spoke out, in the name of liberal principles, against Bismarck's decision to expand the army without the consent of Parliament. "Never, perhaps, has a war been planned with such outrageous shamelessness and such horrifying frivolity. One is inwardly revolted by such a criminal attack on the most fundamental principles of law and morality." Two months later, however, after the brilliant Prussian victory over Austria, the enthusiasm of the nationalist drowned out the moral indignation of the liberal. "I bow before the genius of a Bismarck. I have forgiven the man everything he has done hitherto. . . . For one such man of action, I would give a hundred men of powerless honor."[34]

On the Christian Character of Our Present-Day Theology accused German liberal theology of betraying Christianity by turning it into a state religion for the new imperial Germany. It was a provocative declaration of independence. By publishing such a work Overbeck was fully aware that he had "embroiled himself," as he put it, "in an unresolvable conflict with the dominant theological current in the German Empire and in consequence was condemned to exile."[35]

In Overbeck's view, early Christianity was an eschatological religion premissed on the prophetic announcement of the imminent end of the world. In other words, it was a religion of crisis and immediate and dramatic decision. No thought was given to codifying and institutionalizing the teaching of Christ because there would be no future for the world, and thus no need for any codification. A theology was elaborated only when it became necessary to take account of the fact that the world was not coming to an end, at least not immediately, and to sustain the faith of the disciples in face of that realization. The task of the early theologians was thus to facilitate the survival of religion and its accommodation to the changing world of history, to mediate between spontaneous religious experience and the historical world of culture, philosophical reflection, and practical interests and politics. Theology and religion, however, were polar opposites. All he himself got out of his first year of theological study at Leipzig, Overbeck related, was the loss of what still remained of the faith of his childhood.[36] The corruption of religion by theology is evoked in striking phrases that bring to mind the Grand Inquisitor chapter in Dostoievsky's *The Brothers Karamazov* (1881). "Theology is the Satan of religion," we are told, and theologians are "traitors to the cause they are to defend," "panderers coupling Christianity and the world," "the Figaros of Christianity," "old washerwomen drowning religion for us in the endlessly flowing stream of their chatter."[37] Moreover, their commitment to the worldly survival of Christianity has made them "craven worshippers of power in all its forms."[38] All theologians, in Overbeck's pithy phrase, are Jesuits, in the sense that "Jesuitism is Christianity that has become worldly wise."[39] An obvious thread connects these ideas with Burckhardt's view of power as inherently evil. Just as Burckhardt dissociated himself from the Prussian nationalist historians' project of combining culture and power in a new national state, which was supposed to provide the necessary material and political clout to protect the German *Kulturvolk,* Overbeck denounced the effort to combine religion and power through a Church that was intimately, too intimately, associated with the national state.

In stark contrast to the project of "modernizing" religion—which in nineteenth-century Germany meant downplaying the Jewish roots of Christianity and suggesting, like Droysen and Harnack, that Christianity owed more to Hellenism than to Judaism—Overbeck's project was to emphasize how essential the original (Jewish) religious impulse in Christianity is and how different the "cultural" Christianity of the modern liberal theologians was from the Christianity of Christ and the early disciples. "Those fruits are too high for you to reach," he warned his friend Treitschke, when the latter began trying to enroll Christianity in the service of his nationalist politics.[40] Similarly, he regarded with suspicion the efforts of David Strauss and Paul Lagarde to found new religions. Lagarde's plan to introduce a new theology to be taught in the universities as the forerunner of a future "German religion" seemed especially dubious to Overbeck. "Theologies," he noted drily, "have always followed their religions. That a theology should precede a religion is unheard of and it is scarcely to be expected that something like that could happen in the future."[41] The attempts of some theologians, such as the "Nietzschean" theologian Arthur Bonus, to seek out "a new logic-free domain of truth" and to base religion on a new "concept of truth" provoked his undisguised contempt. Such men were nothing but "clever priests," "Protestant Jesuits."[42]

Overbeck's critique of liberal Christianity did not, however, lead him into the camp of religious conservatism. On the contrary, for those who had been touched by worldliness and modernism or whose faith had been shaken, he advocated a dramatic leap into an unprecedented new condition (*"sich in die Luft stellen,"* in his own words), a condition genuinely of their own time and experience, a true *modernity* beyond the half-hearted compromise position represented by *modernism.*[43] In a striking comparison, he likened the situation of modern man to that of the original Christians, for whom there could be no going back but only a bold pressing forward on new and untrodden paths. "Our defection from the old and our falling away from it are irreparable, as we learn from Hebrews 6, 4–8. . . . There is nothing for it: having come so far, we have no option but to press on further. . . . If our falling away has truly extinguished all light for us, we can least expect to receive new illumination by turning back, and we can be sure that it can only lie ahead of us. We find ourselves faced with the same *adinaton* [impossibility] as the early Christians."[44]

Overbeck was unmoved by the pleas and protests of former friends and fellow students who had embraced the new liberal theology.[45] He had no sympathy with attempts to shore up religion by turning it into an ideological support of the state and the bourgeois social order. In a disenchanted world the genuinely modern, free individual must learn to do without all such supports. "Whoever stands truly and firmly on his own two feet in the world must have the courage to stand on nothing," wrote the professor of practical theology and church history at the University of Basel. "The thorough individualist must be able to do without God. . . . Only without God can he live as a free individual. If he cannot bid farewell to God, either his individualism is not genuine or it has not yet developed to its fullest point of freedom."[46]

The Nietzschean strain in these remarks is evident. However, there were significant differences between the two men, which Overbeck himself tried to articulate as the Nietzsche cult gathered strength in the years after the philosopher's breakdown.

The works Nietzsche published at the beginning of the decade during which he occupied the chair of Greek at Basel are certainly less radical, original, and complex than those that appeared after he resigned his post in 1879. Perhaps their more accessible style reflects not only an earlier stage in Nietzsche's development—Nietzsche in these years was still, like his older colleague Burckhardt, under the spell of Schopenhauer as a teacher and thinker, even if he had begun to note down some serious criticisms of his thought[47]—but a degree of congruence between an author of unconventional views and a somewhat eccentric, independent-minded society that was ready to lend him a sympathetic ear. Nevertheless, these early writings lay out many of the central themes of Nietzsche's work. In particular, they set forth with great clarity a number of positions that he shared with Schopenhauer, notably rejection of nineteenth-century liberalism, of modern democratic politics and education, of the growth of state power, and in general of the rationalist, scientific optimism inherited from the Enlightenment.

On the whole, these early works were well received in Basel. Some people were no doubt shocked by the young professor's unorthodox account of Greek antiquity. Nonetheless, a preview of his ideas, presented to the Basel public in his inaugural lecture on "Homer and Classical Philology" in the Aula of the city museum in the Augustinergasse on May 28, 1869, and in two subsequent lectures at the museum in January and February of 1870, had attracted "a packed audience," as Nietzsche reported to his sister.[48] In addition, Bachofen, Burckhardt, and the chairman of the Basel Education Committee, Wilhelm Vischer-Bilfinger all later expressed their pleasure at *The Birth of Tragedy*. The five public lectures on education (published as *The Future of Our Educational*

Institutions) drew and held an audience of more than three hundred over several months. Nietzsche reported to Rohde that they had been a huge "success," a "sensation."[49]

In Germany, in contrast, as is well known, the philological establishment pronounced its anathema on *The Birth of Tragedy* through its spokesman Ulrich von Wilamowitz-Moellendorff—who was also to declare Burckhardt's posthumously published *Cultural History of Greece* totally "worthless for scholarship." "I am denounced by every one," Nietzsche wrote to Richard Wagner. "Even those who 'know me' will not do more than express pity on account of this 'absurdity.' A professor of classical philology at Bonn, for whom I have great respect, has informed his students that my book is 'complete nonsense' and that it is impossible to do anything with it. Any one capable of writing such a thing, he says, has ceased to exist for scholarship [*sei wissenschaftlich todt*]."[50] Even Nietzsche's old teacher Ritschl received the work coolly, responding to the complimentary copy his old student had sent to him with only a noncommittal thank you note. When Nietzsche pressed him for a fuller response, Ritschl answered with kindness, affection, and respect, but with obvious reticence. "I am too old to be looking for completely new ways of life and thought," he replied. "With my whole being, I belong so completely and decisively to the historical approach and the historical view of all human affairs, that I could never imagine finding the answer to the enigma of the universe in one or another philosophical system. . . . At the age of 65 I no longer have the time or the energy to study the philosophy of Schopenhauer, which is an indispensable guide through your arguments. . . . That your views might be abused to form the basis of a new kind of education, that the vast mass of our young people might be led along such a road only to arrive at an immature contempt for learning, without the compensation of an enhanced artistic sensibility, that instead of an expansion of poetry we might be in danger of opening the gates to widespread dilettantism—these are some of the anxious thoughts that must be allowed to occur to an old philologist."[51]

Years later, in a section of *Ecce Homo*, Nietzsche himself defined the central argument of *The Birth of Tragedy*. It proposed, he wrote, "in defiance of all the known prejudices of our democratic age, that the great optimistic-rationalist-utilitarian victory, together with democracy, its political contemporary, was at bottom nothing other than a symptom of declining strength, approaching senility, somatic exhaustion—*it*, and not its opposite, pessimism."[52] This thesis was articulated through a critique of the modern interpretation of antiquity which shares much common ground with that already articulated in Bachofen's work and which was being put forward in those very years by Burckhardt in his course on Greek cultural history. Like Bachofen, whose books we know he borrowed from the Basel University library, Nietzsche claimed that the antiquity admired by contemporary classical philologists was a prettified version of the real thing, adapted to the needs and capacities of an "enlightened" age that could no longer face the truth of life freely and honestly, as the ancient Greeks had done. "The Apollonian determinacy and lucidity" of Greek tragedy, "the luminous images of the Sophoclean heroes" are not normal, easy, natural features of a beautiful, calm, and serene existence, which is in fact a complete invention of modern classical scholars. They are, on the contrary, "the necessary productions of a deep look into the horror of nature, luminous spots, as it were, designed to cure an eye hurt by the ghastly night."[53] The "serenity" that resulted from the victorious struggle to give artistic form to a terrifying vision of reality—"an Apollonian culture blossoming over a somber abyss"[54]—is "totally misinterpreted nowadays as a condition of undisturbed complacence,"[55] a "counterfeit serenity" which—already in late antiquity—was "in utter contrast to the naivete of the older Greeks."[56] It is "the serenity of the slave, who has no difficult responsibilities, no high aims, and to whom nothing, past or future, is of greater value than the present."[57]

The essential contrast in *The Birth of Tragedy* is not between the Dionysian and the Apollonian—these are inseparably linked, complementary, and rooted in the very origins of antiquity—but between both and the late-developing, "decadent" Socratic spirit. "The real antagonism," in Nietzsche's own words, "was to be between the Dionysiac spirit and the Socratic, and tragedy was to perish in the conflict."[58] For the essence of the new spirit is "optimism which believes itself omnipotent," confidence in reason and dialectics, the perception, as Nietzsche wrote contemptuously, "of a triumph in every syllogism," "the illusion that thought, guided by the thread of causation, might plumb the farthest abysses of being and even *correct* it." This "radically new prestige of knowledge and conscious intelligence" is "the grand metaphysical illusion" that *The Birth of Tragedy* seeks to destroy. For it is the illusion in which the entire modern age is stuck, without even the undoubted element of grandeur that attended it on its first appearance among the Greeks. "Our whole modern world is caught in the net of Alexandrian culture and recognizes as its ideal the man of theory, equipped with the highest cognitive powers, working in the service of science, and whose archetype and progenitor is Socrates. All our pedagogic devices are oriented toward this ideal."[59]

The antinomies developed in Nietzsche's essay can be grouped around the two poles of the "Dionysian" and the "Apollonian" on the one hand, and the "Socratic" on the other: heroic pessimism versus complacent optimism; life and nature versus ethics ("my vital instincts turned against ethics," he would explain in *Ecce Homo*)[60]; the creative artist versus the man of theory; reverence and awareness of the mystery of being versus "a dubious enlightenment"[61]; a critical and challenging sense of the transcendent (that is, of the past and the future, of the eternal, of the possibility of difference), versus complacent imprisonment in a narrow, journalistic culture focused on the "modern" and contemporary—

426 • CHAPTER FOURTEEN

"the miserable rationalism and ephemerism of the American way of feeling," as the celebrated neohumanist scholar Friedrich Welcker had phrased it as early as 1834.[62] In the end, Nietzsche's goal was to force a choice between art, poetry, and imagination, which promote life, according to him, and "asceticism, high intellect, duty,"[63] which alienate from life and distract from its mystery, between "the 'I' dwelling truly and eternally in the ground of being"—and reached by "a process of un-selving"—and "that of the waking man," the autonomous and, in Nietzsche's view, superficial individual self that was the goal and the ideal of Enlightenment.[64] Reality, according to Nietzsche, is the harshness of existence, the heroic character of choice, the necessity and permanence of crisis and trag-edy, as opposed to the comforting "belief that nature can be fathomed, . . . knowledge [is] the true panacea . . . and all moral and sentimental accomplish-ments—noble deeds, compasssion, self-sacrifice, heroism . . . —[are] ulti-mately derived from the dialectic of knowledge, and therefore teachable."[65]

Nietzsche's essay is more than an attack on the "optimist-rationalist-utilitarian" outlook of his time. It is a call—in line with the ideas of his friend Wagner—for a reawakened German spirit to take the lead in countering that outlook and in bringing about through the "rebirth of tragedy" a new *"ger-manisches Hellenentum"* ("Germanic Hellas").[66] "For the coming age of culture, fighters will be needed: it is for that struggle that we have to hold ourselves ready," he had told his friend Carl von Gersdorff at the time of the Franco-Prussian War.[67] *The Birth of Tragedy* suggested that the time had now come: "Socratic man has run his course; crown your heads with ivy, seize the thyr-sus. . . . Dare to lead the life of tragic man and you will be redeemed."[68] In a passage that Bachofen must have read with the warmest sympathy, Nietzsche called likewise for restoring myth to its proper place in culture: "Only a horizon ringed about with myths can unify a culture. . . . Nor does the commonwealth know any more potent law than that mythic foundation which guarantees its union with religion and its basis in mythic conceptions."[69] In line with a prevail-ing opinion among German neohumanists Nietzsche claimed that the German people was uniquely qualified to carry out this new Reformation. Though it might seem to have succumbed, in 1871, "to mediocrity, democracy and 'mod-ern ideas'—in the pompous guise . . . of empire building," it preserved "under-neath the hectic movements of our civilization . . . a marvelous ancient power, which arouses itself mightily only at certain grand moments," such as the Lu-theran Reformation.[70]

Finally, by evoking the specter of proletarian revolution as the inevitable out-come of liberalism, Nietzsche gave his exalted meditation on the meaning of tragedy and myth in ancient culture an urgent realism and relevance that cannot have been lost on his Basel readers. "One thing should be remembered: Alexan-drian culture requires a slave class for its continued existence, but in its opti-mism it denies the necessity for such a class; therefore it courts disaster once the effect of its nice slogans concerning the dignity of man and the dignity of labor have worn thin. Nothing can be more terrible than a barbaric slave class that has learned to view its existence as an injustice and prepares to avenge not only its own wrongs but those of all past generations."[71] The pessimistic and tragic view of life has the obvious advantage, from the point of view of the ruling class, of providing no justification whatsoever for the slaves to feel that they should be recognized as the equals of their masters.

The lectures on education were, if anything, more polemical than *The Birth of Tragedy*. The object of attack is identified in the introduction: the enlightened "striving to achieve the greatest possible extension of education" and its inevitable consequence, "a tendency to minimise and to weaken it" and to "compel [it] to renounce its highest and most independent claims in order to subordinate itself to the service of the State."[72] The idea of education defended by Nietzsche, in contrast, is essentially that of German neohumanism as articulated by Friedrich August Wolf and Wilhelm von Humboldt and represented in Basel by the generation of young men who immigrated to the city at the time of the repressive Carlsbad Decrees and became the teachers of Bachofen and Burckhardt. To the neohumanists, as to Nietzsche, education meant above all the development in the individual, to the highest degree possible, of a free and creative spirit, and it was best achieved through study of the Greek language and literature. The idea was not to copy the Greeks in a servile way but, through study of their language and literature, to appropriate their free, original, and creative spirit (thus circumventing the secondary and dependent classicism of the French). In this way, the young German student might in turn create a free, original, and authentic culture. The critical, utopian character of early neohumanism remained essential to Nietzsche's view of education and underlies his repeated attacks on the state's subordination of education to its own ends. Characteristically, in the last lecture Nietzsche evoked the *Burschenschaften,* the student fraternities of the Restoration period, and praised the "most memorable of bloody acts, the murder of Kotzebue,"[73] in striking contrast with Treitschke, the apologist of *Realpolitik* and of the new imperial Germany, who was to mock the *Burschenschaften* mercilessly in his *German History in the Nineteenth Century* (1879).

Nietzsche emphasized that the erosion and abandonment of the original neohumanist ideal were directly related to the rise of the modern state and of a modern industrial economy in Germany, especially since the founding of the empire in 1871. In the rather backward Germany of his own student days, he told his audience, "the . . . exploitation of youth by the State for its own purposes—that is to say, so that it may rear useful officials as quickly as possible and guarantee their unconditional obedience to it by means of excessively severe examinations—had remained quite foreign to our education."[74] With the passing of those simpler times, it became clear that the neohumanist ideal was threatened by three forces: the modern nation-state, the modern economy, and the ideology of the modern. As the need of the state is for trained and loyal administrators or executors of its will, it cannot tolerate the critical perspective and the potential for deviance that a true classical education, a genuine immersion in the life of antiquity brings. The state will therefore promote "the greatest possible expansion of education" only to the degree that it is confident it can "bring the most determined emancipation, resulting from culture, under its yoke." It will support every extension of culture in so far as such extension is "of service to its officials or soldiers, but in the main to itself, in its competition with other nations."[75]

Modern economies likewise require a well-prepared, disciplined, and unquestioning workforce to carry out their functions, and that is "the quarter in which the cry for the greatest possible expansion of education is most loudly raised."[76] Nietzsche conceded—and the concession must have been welcomed by his audience of Basel businessmen and industrialists—that one can have nothing against a practical education in modern subjects like the sciences and modern languages, such as is offered by the *Realschule*. "For the great majority of men such a course of instruction is of the highest importance." He even advocated admitting graduates of the *Realschule* to the universities.[77] The *Realschule*—he acknowledged—performs honestly the task it professes to do. It is the classical *Gymnasium*, claiming to promote culture or *Bildung*, rather than provide a practical education, and to form men and leaders rather than efficient workers or cogs in a bureaucratic machine, that is the problem: this is so because the *Gymnasium*, which ought to be a constant challenge to the prevailing culture of the market and of modernity, has opted to become their servant. Its students no longer expect of it that it will assist them to develop their minds in freedom from all prejudice and constraint but that it will provide them with a passport to material success and social preferment. In addition, the *Gymnasium* has taken over the methods of commerce and industry and applied them to its own central activity, the study of classical antiquity. "A specialist in scholarship comes to resemble nothing so much as a factory worker who spends his whole life turning one particular screw or handle on a certain instrument or machine, at which occupation he acquires the most consummate skill."[78] Finally, his own modern methods and labors come to interest the scholar far more than the "fallen statue of Greek antiquity which for centuries philologists have been trying, with ever-failing strength, to re-erect. . . . Consciously or unconsciously, large numbers of [philologists] have concluded that it is hopeless and useless for them to come into direct contact with classical antiquity. . . . This herd has turned with much greater zest to the science of language. . . . where the most mediocre gifts can be turned to account."[79] The students of antiquity, in other words, now wish to forget their un-modern, un-comfortable vocation and to engage in a modern comfort-bringing business like everybody else. The distinction between leaders and led, the elite and the general, is being erased.

Finally, the ideology of the modern, which is associated with both the power and prestige of the state and the power and influence of trade and industry, spreads unbounded self-satisfaction at the achievements of modern civilization; a smug unwillingness or inability to acknowledge or entertain any interest in what is radically other and, for that reason, challenging and potentially subversive; and a willing submission to the mind-deadening, distracting culture of the ephemeral and immediate—the latest news, the latest fashion, whatever will facilitate "flight from one's self" and the annihilation of genuine individuality.[80] In this ideology, in Nietzsche's own words, "the journalist, the servant of the moment, has stepped into the place of the genius, of the leader for all time, of the deliverer from the tyranny of the moment"[81]—that is, of the true man of culture.

The result of the enormous expansion of the education apparatus together with the *Gymnasium's* abdication of its proper role is the corruption of the sources from which true culture grows. For though true culture is always a matter for a small handful of people, it is important that a far larger number, "led on by an alluring delusion," should seek it. Even if only a few are chosen, many must petition.[82] "The rights of genius are being democratized in order that people may be relieved of the labor of acquiring culture. . . . What! . . . Do you suppose you can reach at one bound what I ultimately won for myself only after long and determined struggle."[83] It is not hard to understand that Nietzsche's audience of Basel "patricians" responded favorably to a vision of meritocracy that corresponded so closely to what they perceived their own situation to be. As in *The Birth of Tragedy*, the corruption of contemporary German culture is denounced with special vehemence because it is in the German spirit that the hope of a revival of genuine culture, as opposed to the pseudo-culture of modern democratic and industrial societies on the English, French, or American model, lies. Only the German spirit can "join with the genius of Greece" to achieve this revival.[84] The final image evoked in these lectures is arresting, to say the least, but at the same time, in the wake of the success of fascist ideologies in the 1930s, disturbingly ambiguous to the modern reader.

> Have you ever, at a musical rehearsal, looked at the strange, shriveled-up, good-natured species of men who usually form the German orchestra? . . . What noses and ears, what clumsy, *danse macabre* movements! Just imagine for a moment you were deaf. . . . Undisturbed by the idealizing effect of the sound, you could never see enough of this . . . comical spectacle, this harmonious parody on *homo sapiens*. Now . . . assume that your musical sense had returned and that your ears are opened. Look at the honest conductor at the head of the orchestra performing his duties in a dull, spiritless fashion; you no longer think of the comical aspect of the whole scene, you listen—but it seems to you that the spirit of tediousness spreads out from the honest conductor over all his companions. . . . But set a genius—a real genius—in the midst of this crowd; and you instantly perceive something almost incredible. It is as if this genius, in his lightning transmigration, had entered into these mechanical, lifeless bodies,

and as if only one demoniacal eye gleamed forth out of them all. . . . You can divine from my simile what I would understand by a true educational institution, and why I am very far from recognizing one in the present type of university.[85]

Just as in *The Birth of Tragedy* the high tenor of the essay as a whole was interrupted by a sharp, thinly veiled warning of the perils of proletarian revolution, the lectures on education contain a sardonic allusion to the danger to which universal education exposes the privileges of the liberal bourgeoisie itself—"the great and awful danger that at some time or other the great masses may overleap the middle classes and spring headlong into this earthly bliss."[86] Or, as Nietzsche had put it in his notes for these lectures: "universal education is the stage prior to communism . . . the condition for communism."[87]

No doubt it was a rhetorical ploy directed toward his audience of well-meaning Basel citizens, a traditional *captatio benevolentiae,* when the newly arrived young professor from Germany allowed in his opening remarks that the criticisms he was about to make of modern German education in his lectures might not apply to his adopted city "which is striving to educate and enlighten its members on a scale so magnificently out of proportion to its size that it must put all larger cities to shame."[88] But his audience—and even to some extent Nietzsche himself—could have taken it seriously. The Baselers, as we saw, liked to think their schools were distinctive, and in some measure they probably were. German academics, for instance, looked down on the study of the classics at Basel, which they judged old-fashioned and unprofessional, and which *was* directed more toward the general education of the *Nichtstudierende* than to the formation of future scholars. As the last refuge of the neohumanist ideals of the early years of the century, the conservative city-republic might well have had some grounds for thinking itself exempted from the sins of modern culture.

Yet the exemption Nietzsche allowed it remains ambiguous. For Nietzsche, as for Bachofen, Burckhardt, and Overbeck, Basel itself was ambiguous. It had offered him sanctuary from the modern world, certainly, and an almost "Archimedean" perspective from which to look out on it critically. At the same time, it *was*—increasingly—the modern world. The scandal surrounding the publication of *The Birth of Tragedy* in Germany, Nietzsche told both Erwin Rohde and Richard Wagner in 1872, had caused him extreme distress "because I am truly dedicated, as well as grateful, to our little University, and the last thing I would want would be to cause it harm."[89] He was grateful to Basel in general, he wrote Rohde, "because it has let me live in peace, as on a country estate" whereas "the sound of Berlin vocal organs, in contrast, is as hateful to me as the clanging of steam-driven machinery."[90] But in that very same year, Burckhardt complained that the railroad center and mill town Basel had become "gives you a feeling of emptiness and sadness" punctuated by the "ceaseless whistling and wailing" of steam locomotives.[91] It was only the formerly despised but now nostalgically remembered Biedermeier Basel of his youth that Burckhardt might have been willing to compare to a peaceful "country estate."[92] Alongside Nietzsche's view of Basel as a refuge we must place his later bitter remark to Overbeck that Basel had been "the accursed breeding ground of all my ills." He himself wrote of his "Basileophobia."[93]

The Basel elite's historical experience, their interest in preserving both their anachronistic polity and their privileged position within it, and the apprehension they felt as they observed the development of expansionist nationalistic states on their very borders had made them sympathetic to dissidents and heretics critical of the dominant ideas of the age. Taking an independent stand or tolerating the independence of others, moreover, was an old Basel tradition. The genius loci, as Michelet put it, was Erasmus. But independence had customarily been moderated by modesty and prudence. Writing of religion, Karl Barth observed that

> [t]he Basel theologian is from the start and in all essentials conservative, a basically shy man of the *quieta non movere*, and that will always emerge somewhere in his person. At the same time, however, he has his secret, almost sympathetic delight in the radicalism and the extravagances of others, e.g. of all kinds of excited foreigners, whom from David Joris to Nietzsche and Overbeck he has eagerly welcomed within his walls for the contrast they provide. While finding them frightfully interesting, however, he will hesitate to make them his own. A mildly humanistic skepticism that is, so to speak, inborn inoculates him against both Catholicism and a too strict [Calvinist] orthodoxy. A practical wisdom acquired by careful observation protects him from excessive digression to the left. So he will settle somewhere in the middle of these extremes, perhaps quietly devoting himself to a certain amount of freethinking, perhaps equally quietly indulging in a certain amount of pious enthusiasm, while outwardly in all circumstances presenting the picture of a sound union of freedom and moderation, outwardly and in all circumstances affirming and striving for nothing impractical, assuming ironically the presence of eccentricity in instances of excessive insistence on principle, always inclined to seek the heart of all discussions in a mere dispute about words, victorious in the method of always leaving the first and last words to others and thus thinking one's own thoughts without having openly compromised oneself in action.[94]

Consciously or unconsciously, the elite had sought to justify and strengthen their position through their control and support of the city's institutions of high culture. They cared about the standing of "their" University. At the same time, these merchants and manufacturers remained practical and worldly men. "Study for study's sake," Bachofen once complained, "is something that is not understood by a people whose character is distinguished by practical concerns."[95] As businessmen, they continued to regard profit as their top priority, and they had a remarkable capacity for the pragmatic compromises necessary for economic success. It was they who presided over the transformation of an essentially eighteenth-century merchant economy into the modern industrial one that ultimately helped to undermine their political hegemony and that Burckhardt saw as the ruin of traditional bourgeois culture. When push came to shove, the Basel elite accepted that they had to adapt to the world that they themselves had helped to bring into existence. An acute observer, who had lived in Basel in the last decades of the nineteenth century and had known Burck-hardt, recalled as late as 1922 how he had been struck by the "remarkable mix-ture of tranquillity and energy in the air of Basel. The street scene itself," he wrote, "displays both a delight in antiquity and its vivid preservation and a reso-lute commitment to progress that shrinks from no invasion by the new, no re-construction or new construction. In this respect the street is exactly like the proud old mansions of the patricians, which one might think had been built purely for a distinguished and elegant way of life, but which are full of counting rooms and spaces for transacting business. Social and domestic life in particular is still marked by an unmistakable and distinctive historical character. It re-mains dominated by echoes of the past, despite the fact that, being a center of trade and industry, the city has not withdrawn from the generally homogeniz-ing current of modern life."[96]

In contrast to the elite itself, the intellectuals it supported refused accommo-dation, on principle, to the end. The four we have discussed were uncompro-misingly critical of modern culture—and their presentiment of a coming mass culture destined to displace the humanist culture in which they themselves had been raised seems not less relevant today than a century and a quarter ago—but the grounds for their criticism varied. Bachofen's antimodernism is not identical with Burckhardt's or Overbeck's or Nietzsche's. Moreover, the style of their refusal of the modern also varied. In this respect Basel left a greater im-print on its native sons than on at least one of the two gifted outsiders. However challenging their ideas, Bachofen and Burckhardt—and in considerable mea-sure Overbeck also—were in practice cautious men with little confidence in the power of individuals to affect historical processes. None of the three actively sought to promote revolutionary change or to disturb violently the beliefs of the majority of their fellow citizens. Overbeck appears to have believed with Pascal—the only theologian he respected, and, typically, an amateur rather than a professional—that the "simple" whose faith had not been shaken were best let alone. When Anna Baumann, the landlady of the house on the Schüt-zengraben, expressed an interest in reading the work of her other former lodger, Professor Nietzsche, Overbeck advised her to hold to her faith as strongly as she could, since doubt does not bring happiness. As for the writings of his colleague, he told her, he did not recommend that she read them.[97]

Nor does it appear that Bachofen, Burckhardt, or Overbeck believed much could be done to stem the tide of barbarism they saw approaching. Bachofen and Overbeck wrote for an audience of a few scholars and sedulously avoided publicity; in fact, after his 1873 tract on contemporary theology, Overbeck's most challenging work was kept in his desk drawer. "He who would not be misunderstood by the plebs should not venture into its dense thickets," he wrote of Houston Stewart Chamberlain.[98] Burckhardt's caution, skepticism, and evasiveness—which Nietzsche interpreted, wrongly in the view of most scholars, as a prudent and polite cover laid over truly dangerous and subversive thoughts—discouraged rushing to radical conclusions or entertaining utopian fantasies. Moreover, Burckhardt also published very little after *The Civilization of the Renaissance*. Only Nietzsche carried his ideas to provocative extremes and aspired to prophetic influence. It is not surprising that of the four he was the only one who could not reconcile himself to Basel—or that the other three all sooner or later distanced themselves from him intellectually in varying degrees.

The most conservative of the group, Bachofen was the first to detach himself from the enormously talented but increasingly restless scholar who was his junior by twenty-nine years. "My dear husband liked him," Bachofen's widow, Louise Bachofen-Burckhardt, told Carl Albrecht Bernoulli. "And I know that on his side Nietzsche admired my husband very much. He often told me so. That was around the time when *The Birth of Tragedy* appeared. My husband was absolutely delighted with the book and expected great things from Nietzsche. Then came his later writings. My husband judged them very severely as he was bound to do, given his convictions. Thereafter, little by little our extremely pleasant relationship became clouded and broke off."[99]

Even before the publication of the cuttingly anti-Christian *Menschliches-Allzumenschliches* in 1878, Nietzsche's second *Unzeitgemässe Betrachtung* "On the Use and Abuse of History" had outlined a critical and aestheticizing approach to history that can only have filled the pious Bachofen with dismay. What Bachofen shared with Nietzsche was opposition to the professionalization of historical studies, to the bland optimism of classical studies in particular, to the focus of modern historians on "progress" and national power as manifested in the development of the economy and the state, and to the critical, positivistic methods and ideals of much historical study in the second half of the nineteenth century. But whereas Nietzsche's critique of historical studies implied a critique of modern (historical) culture in general as harmful to "Life," to human energy and creativity, Bachofen's critique of historical studies implied a critique of the modern break with the traditional world of myth and symbol. History, properly understood, was still for the devout Bachofen meaningful: it was a sacred story of fall and redemption. The study of history, he declared, "leads us up to the divine."[100] Every "truly serious historical inquiry necessarily leads to the truths of Christian revelation."[101] History binds human beings together in communities and it binds humans and the rest of creation to the sacred and divine. Nothing could have been further from Nietzsche's view that history is simply time, directionless movement, change; and it did not take

Bachofen long to realize that whereas he saw history as a road back to the true life, Nietzsche saw it as an obstacle to his conception of the true life.

While sharing many of his fellow citizen's misgivings about the practice of history in his own time, Burckhardt's position was considerably less conservative than Bachofen's. As we noted earlier (chapters 3 and 5), Bachofen looked on Burckhardt as an aesthete, to whom history was no longer a providential experience of sin and redemption but simply the theater and spectacle of human action and of the development of human culture. As Overbeck observed, Burckhardt was remarkably free and open ("*unbefangen*") in his thinking, especially as regards Christianity, given his background and education. More free, in fact, Overbeck held, than Nietzsche, since he did not feel impelled to constantly attack Christianity and religion. On the contrary, he acknowledged and respected the beneficent effect of Christianity on human behavior. "In the matter of Nietzsche's immoralism, the two men were in complete disagreement," Overbeck observed in his notebooks. "Nietzsche's denunciation of pity was particularly horrifying to Burckhardt."[102] This, as it happens, was a point on which Overbeck was in agreement with Burckhardt. "Christianity," he wrote, "tries to help us humans, and for that reason alone it deserves not to be hated by us, even if it does not in fact have the means to help us."[103] Likewise, Overbeck reported, Burckhardt was offended by Nietzsche's attacks on scholars and book learning.[104] Burckhardt's "growing antipathy to Nietzsche" was thus "fully understandable."[105] The story of Nietzsche's veneration of Burckhardt, of Burckhardt's increasing coolness as he began to grasp the explosive character of Nietzsche's ideas, of his evasiveness and protestations of incompetence in philosophical matters as Nietzsche pressed him to respond to his increasingly provocative writings, of Nietzsche's frustration at the older man's polite reserve, and of his thinly veiled criticism of him in the portrait of the scholar in the second of the *Unzeitgemässe Betrachtungen* has been told often and need not be repeated. What should be noted here is that, while recognizing Nietzsche's extraordinary gifts, Burckhardt was put off by the violence of the younger man's nature and the excessiveness of his ideas. As we have already observed in several contexts, Burckhardt was fearful of "geniuses" and "*Gewaltmenschen*" of all kinds, even when he admired their enormous talent and energy.

Finally, even Overbeck found it necessary to establish a certain intellectual distance from Nietzsche. The two friends were united in their critical attitude to history. For both, history had no lessons to teach. It justified neither optimism nor pessimism, according to Overbeck.[106] "Asking about the meaning of history is a bad habit that people acquired during the long period when human thought was dominated by Christianity and was not yet, in that respect, 'enlightened.' The Enlightenment is still too young to have ensured that we have completely put that habit aside."[107] Both also prized intellectual freedom—in the sense of freedom not only from external constraints but from internal, mental phantoms—and the individual's absolute right to that freedom. To Overbeck, the exercise of such freedom was the true heroism of the individual,[108] but it was a completely undramatic, untheatrical heroism—nothing more than the courage to reason honestly and to face facts, one of which was the relative unimportance of the individual in the universe.[109] It was on this point—his refusal to hypostatize the individual—that Overbeck parted company with his former housemate. Nietzsche's extreme individualism seemed to Overbeck a hangover from what his friend had consistently denounced: religious enthusiasm and philosophical idealism.

In notes on P. J. Moebius's book on Nietzsche's illness (*Über das Pathologische bei Nietzsche*, 1902), Overbeck took issue with the doctor's identification of "irreligious individualism" as one of the characteristics of the age and one of the prime causes of Nietzsche's mental illness. On the contrary, Overbeck suggested, Nietzsche's difficulties and contradictions were aggravated by the survival of a religious element in him.

> One might well wonder whether it is not completely wide of the mark to speak with Moebius of "irreligious individualism" in connection with Nietzsche, rather than *religious* individualism. For *worship* of self was a basic feature of Nietzsche's individualism from the very start and that is something that Moebius surely cannot fail to recognize. One of the most unambiguous symptoms of Nietzsche's mental derangement was his megalomania, which was grounded psychologically in his case, and not only pathologically. Nietzsche was already inhabited by Zarathustra, whom Moebius sees as the product of his progressive paralysis, in the first period of his apostolic literary activity, and even at that time all his striving was directed toward projecting a Zarathustra, that is to say an Alter Ego, out of himself, to whom he could attribute his ingenious oracular sayings. . . . Nietzsche always really took himself with religious seriousness as an individual and that explains the otherwise incomprehensible phenomenon of the two faces he presented to those who knew him: the wild, tempestuous nature, the fanatic (which he himself from time to time acknowledged he was), and the model human being. His immoralism is also understandable in this connection. It is related to his religious fanaticism far more than to any laxness of morals.[110]

Likewise, the idea of the "superman" or *"Übermensch"* was attributed by Overbeck to a residue in Nietzsche of the very philosophical idealism he repeatedly denounced. Humanity is marked by its "solidarity," according to Overbeck. It arose only as a species, and the idea that a single human being, as an individual, could have achieved human status "is an undemonstrable fantasy that cannot be grounded in any reality." Equally, however, "whatever humanity has accomplished has been accomplished and could be accomplished only through individuals. . . . With that antinomy, namely that he is at once Everything and Nothing, modern man finds himself cast rudderless, without the guidance of religion, on the ocean of the cosmos."[111] He can find reassurance only in looking backward and reflecting that what could be accomplished before can probably continue to be accomplished.

> For man did not create and cannot alter the very conditions of existence. And least of all, for modern man, can these conditions be altered by an idea, including the idea of the "superman," since modern man has given up belief in the "creative power" of ideas. There can be no other ground, in the end, for belief in the "superman" than the fact that nothing ever did happen without supermen and that, for that reason, the superman is not a being that is still to be created in the future. For such an act of creation never occurred before, either by means of an idea or by means of a word. And what an idea cannot achieve, the idea of an idea is even less able to achieve. . . . What heroes could not do, hero-worship is even less likely to do.[112]

A more simple objection to Nietzsche's idea of the "superman" arose out of Overbeck's modest and humane vision of human life. "However we humans think of ourselves . . . humanity [*Menschlichkeit*] is still our highest title to glory. I do not believe in Nietzsche's '*doctrine*' of the superman, not at least in so far as it claims more for the powers by which we are to be helped than Goethe ascribed to the heavenly powers when he wrote:

> Wer immer strebend sich bemüht
> Den können wir erlösen."[113]

Finally, Overbeck had reservations about Nietzsche's aphoristic style, which he also referred to sometimes, ironically, as "oracular." He saw it as intimately connected with the philosopher's excessive, "religious" individualism. Overbeck's analysis of the aphorism conveys clearly his strong sense of intellectual responsibility and of the limitations set on human thought. What caused him to have misgivings about aphoristic writing, he noted, is its "idealizing or, if I may be permitted the expression, its cosmetic power."

> Through its form and its concision, the aphorism lends the paradox expressed in it an unearned appearance, exaggerates its effect, or rather draws off to the effect far too much of the attention that ought to be paid to the truth of what is being said. . . . [The aphorism's] genuine validity would be more simply and securely appreciated if the author had taken more time and granted the reader more time to ground it with care. Nietzsche's aphorism "Morals are as immoral as everything else on earth: morality itself is a form of immorality" can also be calmly and seriously grounded, though obviously to do so would require a far greater expenditure of time. But then it would also be done more surely and with a far more enduring, albeit less powerful *initial* effect. . . . The possibility of refutation, the sword of Damocles that hangs over everything one has tried to found by argument, is less dangerous than the fundamental criminal violence attending the entry into the world of whatever lacks proper grounding, however meteorically the firmament is illuminated on its entry. Furthermore, in aphoristic writing, the individual must rely far more on his own powers than he is generally in a position to do in his activity in the world. It is true that

whatever man achieves in the world can be achieved only through individuals and through individual powers, but it is just as certain that no effect produced in this way will be taken up and made use of without the assistance of like accessory powers . . . , without [the individual's] drawing his fellows into collaboration with him. In Nietzsche's hands, the aphorism is only another instrument of his limitless individualism. Whoever writes in aphorisms should at least be conscious of the enormity of his presumption, as Nietzsche assuredly was.[114]

15

Burckhardt and Ranke
Basel and Berlin

Bachofen, Burckhardt, and the thoroughly European Overbeck may have had greater affinity with the outlook and the dominant traditions of the city in which they spent the greater part of their lives and careers than did Nietzsche. In the context of their own time, however, all four together represented a minority, oppositional current in German thought.

In what must be one of the best short appreciations of Burckhardt in any language[1]—it runs to fewer than twenty pages—the English historian Hugh Trevor-Roper defined that current of opposition above all as it concerned history; but in theology and philosophy the points at issue were similar. Trevor-Roper begins his essay by contrasting the emphasis on culture of the German Enlightenment and its respect for all cultures, including those of the past, with the French Enlightenment's emphasis on reason, progress, and modern civilization. To Herder or Goethe, he reminds us, the unity of Germany, the element that made it more than a geographical expression, was not politics—"politics only divided and weakened it"—but culture. After the experience of revolution and Napoleonic imperialism, however, it became clear, especially in Prussia, which had contributed most to the ultimate victory over Napoleon, that Germany as a culture could hold its own in the modern world only if it had the protection of a powerful state apparatus, "if, from a *Kulturvolk,* [Germany] became a *Kulturstaat.*" "It was against this background," Trevor-Roper explains, "that the school was formed which was to dominate German historical writing for over a century, from the earliest works of Leopold Ranke, in 1825, until the last work of Friedrich Meinecke, in 1948."[2]

Though the best historians of the new school did not forget the teaching of the German Enlightenment, their emphasis shifted more and more from culture to the state.

> They believed that history was the history of culture, that culture was indivisible, organic, that the past was to be respected on its own terms, not judged by the present. . . . But they also, increasingly saw the power of the state not as an irrelevance (as it had been in eighteenth century Germany), but as an essential part of the same organism, the protective carapace which society created out of

its own substance, and which was therefore no less valid, no less autonomous, than the culture which it protected. If differing forms of culture were all equally valid and not to be criticized by absolute standards, so were differing states. States too, like cultures followed their own rules, their "reason of state," which was thus legitimized, and not to be criticized from a standpoint of morality or natural law.[3]

Developing an argument that pervades the work of the great German historian of the early twentieth century, Friedrich Meinecke, Trevor-Roper presented Burckhardt as the only effective challenger of this set of ideas, which quickly became an orthodoxy among German historians.

It was in the years of revolution from 1846 to 1852 that Burckhardt's historical views crystallized, resulting in a "decisive break" with German historiography. "It was a break on both sides," Trevor-Roper declares,

> a great divide. After the failure of the revolution in Germany, the German historians forgot any liberal views they may have held and invested their hopes and actions (for most of them were active in politics) in the authoritarian Prussian state. The German *Kulturvolk,* they declared, could not now be welded into a viable state by its own efforts. Like ancient Greece, it must be united by a "Macedonian" military monarchy. . . . When Bismarck came to power, the classically and historically trained intellectuals of Germany were ready for him. They could welcome him as the necessary agent of *Weltgeschichte.* Nor would they demur at his methods, his *Realpolitik.* Why should they? . . . The state, Hegel had said, was the march of God on earth. The state, Ranke had written, was a . . . spiritual substance, a thought of God. The state, wrote Droysen, was "the sum, the total organism of all ethical communities, their common purpose"; it was a law to itself—a moral law: in following its "real interests," it could not be wrong.[4]

"Against this whole philosophy," Trevor-Roper writes, Burckhardt, the patrician citizen of the old city-republic of Basel, "now declared himself a rebel." While standing back from liberalism as it was developing in the 1840s—to Burckhardt the liberals of 1848, "by their individualism and their patronage of the masses, were destroyers of culture"—he denounced the opportunist conservatism of Prussia, "which was not defending German culture, as an earlier generation had supposed, but distorting, if not destroying it." He differentiated himself in every possible way from the professional toadies of power. "He made himself as different as he could from a German professor. The German professors were pompous, omniscient, magisterial. Burckhardt affected a deliberate informality, a self-mocking insouciance, a Socratic affectation of ignorance. The German professors were bureaucrats, or satraps, in an academic empire. With their hierarchy of patronage and their organized seminars they trained a professional class. Burckhardt remained an individual, an amateur," and declared that his aim was not to train scholars and disciples "in the narrower sense" but to teach his students to "'appropriate those aspects of the past which appealed to them'" and to "'find happiness in so doing.'" It was, Trevor-Roper insisted, "a deliberate breach with the methods as well as with the philosophy of Ranke, an emphatic repudiation of the German academic world."[5]

After the revolutions of the middle of the century, the Prussian victories of 1866 and 1870 deepened the divide between Burckhardt and the historiographical orthodoxy of the Germany of his day. To

> the Prussian historians at whose feet Burckhardt himself had once sat, . . . the military victories of Prussia and the foundation of the Empire were the realization of their dream, the corroboration of their philosophy. The liberals of 1848 had failed to unite Germany, failed to convert the atomized *Kulturvolk* into a viable *Kulturstaat.* Now Bismarck had done it. . . . How right Droysen had been to extol Macedon and Alexander. . . . How right Ranke was to emphasize the historic function, and the divine right, of the state, the primacy of foreign policy, the salutary function of war! It is true, Ranke, the old legitimist, had at first been uneasy about Bismarck, but by now he had swallowed his doubts. His disciples had no doubts. War, they declared, was the proper function of the state, its healthy exercise.[6]

Trevor-Roper emphasizes that "it was in opposition to this gradual perversion of the ideas of Herder and Goethe that Burckhardt formulated his own views of history—his antipathy to the state and state power, his insistence on the totality of culture, his refusal to identify state and culture, his distrust of the demiurgic 'great men' of history, his rejection of a metaphysical World Plan."[7]

To Trevor-Roper, the reception of the *Weltgeschichtliche Betrachtungen* on their posthumous publication in 1905 confirms his account of an ever-deepening opposition of Burckhardt and the Prussian establishment, Basel and Berlin. "The spokesman of the historical establishment at that time, its Wilamowitz, was Friedrich Meinecke," Trevor-Roper writes, simplifying Meinecke's position for the sake of his argument.[8] "Meinecke had been young in the days when Bismarck created the German Empire. He had accepted with enthusiasm the historical philosophy of the Prussian school. Now, reviewing Burckhardt's lectures, less ferociously indeed than Wilamowitz [had reviewed the *Cultural History of Greece*], he lamented 'the great gulf which divides his historical outlook from that of his German contemporaries.'"[9] Trevor-Roper traces this story to its tragic conclusion: the German historians' enthusiastic support of the Kaiser in 1914 ("Wilamowitz and Meinecke among them"), and then again, though with some admirable defections, of Hitler. "The rise of Hitler did indeed at first disturb Meinecke, as that of Bismarck had at first disturbed Ranke; but like Ranke, he would come around, and by 1940 he was openly exulting in the military victories of Hitler as Ranke had done in those of Bismarck. Historical necessity, it was admitted, chose surprising instruments, but after an unfortunate interruption it was back on course and working according to plan." During this time, that is to say, the years of National Socialist military adventurism, "the dissenting voice of Burckhardt was heard in Germany only in whispers, or silenced by official disapproval. He was regarded as defeatist, parochial, unable to rise to the great events of history."[10]

Those were the very failings for which Overbeck and Nietzsche had been reproached by the nationalist historian Heinrich von Treitschke in 1873, just after the appearance of Overbeck's *Über die Christlichkeit unserer heutigen Theologie*. Overbeck's critique of theology and of modern Christianity led nowhere, Treitschke complained, and would have "no positive result." He rejected Overbeck's criticism of his own attempt to enroll Christianity in the service of "his religion, patriotism." What he most admired about Christianity, he wrote Overbeck, was exactly what Overbeck disliked about it, about modern Christianity at least—its political and historical cunning, its capacity to survive and adapt to changing historical circumstances, its success in providing itself with an institutional framework and with political clout. By settling into their "sulking-corner" ("*Schmollwinkel*") in Basel, Treitschke concluded, Overbeck and Nietzsche had cut themselves off from the historical development of the fatherland: "The two of you sit there in your corner and see nothing, absolutely nothing of what is now moving the nation."[11]

Burckhardt's opposition to the Prussian historical school and Bachofen's deep-seated, almost pathological hostility to Theodor Mommsen have their counterpart in Overbeck's relentless attacks on Adolf von Harnack, the leading representative of modern theology in Berlin and, like the classical scholar Mommsen, a prominent member of the Prussian Academy. Harnack, in Overbeck's words was "the supreme salon professor," "the protestant abbé," "happy with the well-being provided by the present-day Reich," "the principal friseur of His Majesty's theological wig."[12] Nietzsche had made no secret of his hostility to the new imperial Germany in his lectures on education. "I consider present-day Prussia a power that is extremely dangerous for culture," he had told his friend Carl von Gersdorff at the time of the German victory in the Franco-German war.[13]

The struggle between Overbeck and Förster-Nietzsche over the Nietzsche *Nachlass* and Nietzsche's legacy in general is yet another moment in the same broad conflict outlined by Trevor-Roper. Overbeck's principal aim was to save Nietzsche from what he saw as Förster-Nietzsche's brazen plan to flatten out an extraordinary complex, mobile, and ironic work in order to place it in the service of the very elements that—Overbeck insisted—Nietzsche hated and despised. Overbeck's Nietzsche—the "Basel Nietzsche," as opposed to the Nietzsche being promoted by Förster-Nietzsche's Nietzsche-Archive in Weimar—was the unrelenting foe of the vulgar jingoistic nationalism to which Förster-Nietzsche wanted to hitch her brother's name and work.

In the years following Germany's defeat in the First World War and more particularly after the National Socialists came to power in 1933, Basel was again set up, this time by the enemies of the Weimar Republic and the League of Nations, as the arch-foe of Berlin, the general headquarters of an international conspiracy of the weak against the strong, the weary and wavering against the young and vigorous. From Switzerland to the Netherlands, from the land of Burckhardt to the land of Johan Huizinga, along the entire valley of the Rhine and beyond, to the Hansa towns, it was alleged, an over-ripe patrician culture and an entrenched commercial civilization had produced a spirit of skepticism and accommodation profoundly opposed to the powerful German national state that was essential, according to the nationalist historians, for the protection and preservation of German culture. The anachronistic old patrician city on the Rhine in particular—*"die stolze Basilea"*—was said to be the rallying point of neutrals who preferred sitting on the fence to active engagement and whose aim was to subvert every attempt to shape Germany politically and historically into a major European and world power. Such was the central thesis of *Das Reich und die Krankheit der europäischen Kultur* (*The Reich and the Sickness of European Culture*), a rambling and repetitious 770-page diatribe published on the eve of the Second World War (1938; reprinted in 1940). Its author was a young Nazi historian, Christoph Steding, who had spent some time studying in Basel under Werner Kaegi, Burckhardt's successor and future biographer. Steding's mentor, however, was not Kaegi or Huizinga, to whom Kaegi recommended him and with whom he also studied briefly, but Carl Schmitt, the political philosopher who articulated a drastically "realistic" version, more appropriate to the politics of the interwar years, of the philosophy of the German national historians, and who became a leading intellectual spokesman for the National Socialists.[14] Against the background of politics and international affairs in the 1920s and 1930s—the humiliation of Germany at Versailles, the weakness of the Weimar republic, the growing intensity of class conflict in the parliamentary democracies in general, the efforts of the beneficiaries of the peace to maintain the post-Versailles order through the League of Nations— Schmitt developed the notion of the *"Ernstfall,"* the moment of decision, the moment when talk and negotiation end and the harsh reality of unresolvable conflict is revealed and confronted, the moment when interlocutors discover each other as simple foes, engaged in a life-and-death struggle for power.[15] To Steding, Basel had come to stand for the insidious resourcefulness and sophistication with which the weak fend off such situations. Almost every German scholar who had settled in Basel—De Wette and Overbeck in theology, Wackernagel in literature, Steffensen in philosophy—had been corrupted, *"baselianisiert"* ("baselized") by the experience, he maintained. *"Sich verbaseln"* had been their common fate. Steding did not make an exception even for Nietzsche, despite the efforts of idealogues in the National Socialist movement to enlist him in their cause. All Germany was threatened, Steding warned, with *"Baselianisierung,"* as with a malignant disease.[16]

The great historian Friedrich Meinecke cannot have appreciated the learned but half-crazed rantings that Steding presented as history. Professor successively at Strasbourg (1901–1906), Freiburg (1906–1914), and Berlin (1914 until his retirement in 1932), and editor for more than four decades (1893–1935) of the *Historische Zeitschrift,* the leading journal of historical scholarship in Germany (there is no review of Steding's magnum opus in the *HZ*), Meinecke was internationally respected. His major works—*Cosmopolitanism and the National State* (1908), *The Age of German Liberalism* (1913), *Machiavellism: the Doctrine of Raison d'État and its Place in Modern History* (1924), *The Rise of Historicism* (1936)—are classics of the historiography of the first half of the twentieth century and all have been translated into English. Writing about German historiography, however, Meinecke was no less persuaded than Steding of the existence of two competing traditions: a major one, which he associated with Prussia, and a minor or dissident one, centered in Basel. Unlike Steding, who had no doubt where he stood, Meinecke always recognized the force of the dissident tradition and felt caught between the two.

Meinecke's work is traversed from beginning to end by a meditation on the relation of ethics to power and on the relative weight that should be accorded to what he discerned as the two major tendencies within the mainstream or "Prussian" historiographical tradition—a more liberal and universalist tendency, rooted in the idealism and romanticism of the great days of the struggle for national independence against Napoleon, and still formative in the work of Ranke, and a narrower, more statist, and far more *"realpolitisch"* tendency in the historians of the post-1848 and imperial periods who followed Ranke: Gustav Droysen, Treitschke, Heinrich von Sybel. While praising the achievement of the latter, who were his teachers, and generally aligning himself with them, Meinecke continued to express some regret at the narrowing of historical focus in the later historiography and at the weakening of the older, more broadly European, pluralistic, and cosmopolitan outlook, still strong in Ranke himself, in which homeland and humanity, national independence and international order, were not considered incompatible. In fact, his first major work (1896–1899), a biography of Field-Marshal von Boyen, the friend of Stein, Gneisenau, and Wilhelm von Humboldt, drew attention to ideals more ethical than political, which the *Realpolitik* of Bismarck had all but erased from the consciousness of German historians.[17]

As Trevor-Roper suggested, however, Meinecke inclined strongly in the early part of his career to the Prussian tradition. Whether promoting the interests of the national state was seen optimistically as a harmonizing of culture and ethics with power or in a more hardheaded way as an immediate and necessary objective to which it might be necessary to subordinate other considerations, it remained the goal that the writing of history in Germany ought to serve. Correspondingly, the history of the state, political history, was "the proper field of historical research," as the political historian Dietrich Schäfer had maintained in the 1880s in a polemical debate with the cultural, social, and economic historian Eberhard Gothein, a staunch admirer of Burckhardt.[18] The Schäfer-Gothein debate had been a prelude to the virulent *Methodenstreit* of the 1890s, in which the champions of "cultural history"—an umbrella term used to shelter not only Burckhardt's version of *Kulturgeschichte* but social and economic history as advocated by Karl Lamprecht and Kurt Breysig—unsuccessfully challenged the professional hegemony in Germany of the academically entrenched "statist" or political and national historians. Meinecke's position in the *Methodenstreit* had been unambiguous. He had been an ardent defender of political history. Nor did he moderate his judgment of the "materialist" and allegedly left-leaning social and economic historians until after the Second World War.[19] From early on, however, he demonstrated a respectful and reflective awareness of the alternative tradition, the *via altera* as he himself defined it, represented by Burckhardt.

In the years after the First World War, Meinecke's sympathy for that tradition grew stronger. Finally, some time into the Second World War, his private correspondence with colleagues shows that the Burckhardtian strain had become dominant in his mind, though there was never a total abandonment of the nationalist position. The shift was made public in a short work entitled *Die deutsche Katastrophe* (1946), which was immediately translated into English and gave rise to lively discussion, and in a celebrated lecture on "Ranke and Burckhardt" delivered before the German Academy of Sciences a year later, on May 22, 1947.

In his 1906 review of Burckhardt's *Weltgeschichtliche Betrachtungen,* Meinecke noted that quite apart from its "pleasantly old-fashioned," idiosyncratic manner, the matter of the book is not what "a member of the German historians' guild would have proposed," since "it does not offer an introduction to scholarly research and method or a philosophical foundation for historical method" but consists only of observations that are "intended to arouse a sense of the historical." Even the argument about the three *Potenze*—state, religion, and culture—and their interrelations is not laid out systematically. The accent falls on contemplation rather than research. This is rightly considered a sign of dilettantism, Meinecke continued, though it might not be a bad thing, he added, if young German students retained a measure of dilettantism, of intelligent love of the subject, while undergoing the strenuous training in the critical methods of historical scholarship for which the German universities were famous.[20]

Meinecke insisted on the *"Sonderstellung"*—the exceptional position—of Burckhardt in German historiography. Burckhardt followed an independent path, he claimed, with little concern for what his German colleagues considered the requirements of rigorous historical scholarship. Still, it is not superficially in his use of sources or his unsystematic, essayistic manner but in the Basel historian's relation to the great historical events and processes of his own time that "one can measure the gulf separating his historical standpoint from that of his German contemporaries."

> Our historical thinking was by and large developed in the course of the struggle for state and nation. Burckhardt did not go through this school of political struggle with us. . . . He refrained from participating in it even to the extent of his fellow countryman, Conrad Ferdinand Meyer [the Zurich writer], who lived through the changing destinies of the German nation with great sympathy and concern. With that it becomes clear that a quantity of experiences, impressions, and aspirations which have nourished our historical concepts and judgments simply do not exist for Burckhardt. He neither breathes the air of great international political relations, as Ranke did, nor has he any emotional investment in the realization of the state in general. On the contrary, like Schlosser [an historian of the late eighteenth and early nineteenth centuries] only in a larger and more provocative sense, Burckhardt considers that power, which is the very essence of the state, is "in itself evil."[21]

Unlike the German historians, Meinecke continued, Burckhardt as a citizen of Basel had no strong commitment to the large and powerful state, such as the newly founded German Reich. Large and powerful states exist, "in his characteristically cool judgment," only to fulfill, in Burckhardt's own words, "large external purposes." He has far greater sympathy with the small state, which exists, as he put it himself, so that there might be a spot on earth where the greatest possible number of subjects can be citizens in the fullest sense. To Burckhardt (quoted by Meinecke) the real, concrete freedom of the small state "far outweighs as an ideal the mighty advantages of the large state, even the latter's power"; and the current tendency to regard the small state with contempt as a scandalous anachronism, to value membership in a large and powerful state as alone desirable, signals clearly that power is now considered society's primary goal and culture at best a secondary one. To Burckhardt, in short, as Meinecke saw it, Ranke's idea of a reconciliation of the two objectives of culture and power, individual freedom and a strong national state was an illusion, which was bound sooner or later to be displaced by the increasingly "realistic" interest in power for its own sake displayed by the historians of the Bismarck era. Though power and culture are always in a relation to each other, in sum, they are heteronomous and even incompatible. That is the fundamentally pessimistic conviction that distinguishes Burckhardt from his German contemporaries, the genially optimistic Ranke no less than the more frankly nationalistic Treitschke. Seen from Basel, the entire enterprise that the German historians had rallied behind—the fusion of *Kulturvolk* and *Nationalstaat*—was doomed from the outset.

In addition, unlike the German historians, Burckhardt had no optimistic expectations of what history as a whole would bring, according to Meinecke. In contrast to Ranke, he was convinced that the old Europe had been irreparably transformed by the forces that culminated in the French Revolution and did not believe an accommodation of the values of the ancien régime and those of the postrevolutionary era was possible. As far as culture (the arts and morality) is concerned, there is no such thing as "progress": the human spirit, in Burckhardt's view, reached its full capacity at a very early stage. The man of genuine culture is not therefore impressed by a so-called culture that boasts of progress and expansion; on the contrary, he is alarmed by it, since he sees that the true goal of such a culture is power—the regulation and coercion of the individual.[22]

Finally, there was no doubt in Meinecke's mind that it was Burckhardt's Swiss perspective that underlay his unusually free and unprejudiced view of the entire cultural life of the present and the past.

In 1906 Meinecke could present this minority view respectfully, tolerantly, even in some measure sympathetically—perhaps because it was a distinctly minority view. German historians should not ignore it, he argued, but should attend carefully to what they can learn from it, since it too is part of the larger German tradition. At the same time, the German historical school need make no apologies. "Many aspects of things can be discerned only by those who have been actively engaged in the struggle to realize them. Pure contemplation is not everything. It may even lead to a kind of egoistic self-satisfaction," to which some (Meinecke claimed not to be one of that number) may believe that Burckhardt himself succumbed.[23]

A quarter of a century later, in an important reevaluation of Droysen published in the aftermath of the First World War, Meinecke again alluded to the symbiosis of scholarship and politics that he claimed underlay both North German Protestant historiography and West and South German Catholic historiography in the second half of the nineteenth century. Once again, while praising the achievement of those who dedicated themselves to the political project of establishing the national state, like the later Droysen, he expressed regret at the narrowing of historical focus that resulted from it and the weakening of the more cosmopolitan, universalist strain in the German tradition, associated with Ranke. But if Meinecke continued to feel torn between Ranke and Droysen, he clearly still did not believe that a historiography free of *both* the moderate optimism of Ranke *and* the extreme political realism or "Machiavellism" of the nationalist historians was an option for Germany. Once again he underscored Burckhardt's *Sonderstellung*. "Only Jacob Burckhardt represents a completely different kind of historiography. But Burckhardt lived beyond the frontiers of Germany and did not share our aspirations."[24]

As the tide of battle turned in the Second World War and initial elation over German victories in Poland and France turned to dismay and indignation at the devastating loss of life on the eastern front, the prospect of German defeat, and the "more and more brutal . . . conduct of the war by the Anglo-Saxons"— accused of "contributing basically to the decline of bourgeois culture" and thus having "no more grounds for holding morality over us"[25]—Meinecke's thoughts again apparently turned to Burckhardt. "I am turning back now from Mommsen to Burckhardt," he wrote Siegried Kaehler, his former student who had become professor at Göttingen, in the spring of 1943. "One has the feeling that he is looking on us with irony and compassion, even warm compassion."[26] He began to sketch out again his recurrent "parallel" of Burckhardt, with his "pessimistic realism," and Ranke, with his "harmonising optimism."[27] A year later, amid the ruins and in the certainty of coming disaster for Germany, Meinecke told Heinrich Ritter von Srbik, that "in the last few months I have been busy with Burckhardt, in particular the *Historische Fragmente*. . . . Despite many points of detail on which I disagree with him, he is becoming steadily more and more important to me."[28] To Kaehler he confesses that he has moved "further and further from Ranke's far too easily achieved comfortable feeling about the world and closer and closer to Burckhardt's admittedly somewhat egocentric delight in culture for itself as well as his acid verdict on grand historical interpretations that purport to hold together the rest of world history."[29]

In *Die deutsche Katastrophe*, published immediately after the end of the war, Meinecke tried to come to terms with German historiography's support of the Bismarckian state. The dark side of Bismarck's *Realpolitik* and of what it achieved was clearly recognized and Burckhardt's criticism pronounced justified. In a letter to Gustav Mayer, written about the same time, Meinecke considered his own burden of responsibility. The letter seems to signal a somewhat forced and reluctant but definite shift of allegiance toward a Burckhardtian view of history:

In addition to the immeasurable general disaster, every German must also feel the weight of a particular and personal one. . . . As to the causes of this indescribable catastrophe, I am sure we will see eye to eye. I see them overwhelmingly in a century-old decadence of the German bourgeoisie and of German national thought. At the beginning [of my career], I tried to move from cosmopolitanism [*Weltbürgertum*] to the national state [*Nationalstaat*], without losing sight of the former. Today I am traveling the opposite road, except that the national state is now completely kaput and the only possibility remaining to us is to be a *Kulturnation* dedicated exclusively to preserving its spirit—and we do not even know whether that possibility can be a reality.[30]

A year later, Meinecke addressed the Ranke–Burckhardt, Berlin–Basel theme for the last time. He was clearly deeply preoccupied with it, since in addition to selecting it as the topic of his German Academy of Sciences lecture in the late spring of 1947, he made it the subject of a summer course he taught in that year. The correspondence for the months preceding contains countless references to the preparation of both. "Ranke's and Burckhardt's visions of history," he told Gustav Mayer, is a "powerful topic that stirs me deeply."[31] A few days later, he wrote Kaehler that "it is an uncommonly moving topic for me.

Ranke took on the priestly task of trying to explain God through history; Burckhardt played rather the role of the moral, thinking individual who looks the evil world unflinchingly in the eye, in order to observe how the most marvelous creations of beauty—for which he had a religious reverence—emerge against this sombre background. I think you will agree with me that Burckhardt saw this wicked world of today in far sharper focus than Ranke."[32] Even now, however, there was no complete break with the ideals of the national historians. "Burckhardt has more important things to tell us at this time [than Ranke], but we must learn from both," he told another correspondent.[33] Just as he had once tried to hold in equilibrium the two strains within German historiography—the older, more idealist strain of Ranke and the newer, more aggressive and "realistic" strain of Treitschke and Sybel—he now dreamed in letters to Gustav Mayer and the English historian G. P. Gooch of reconciling Burckhardt and Ranke in a "higher synthesis."[34]

That was also the final word of the remarkable lecture he gave to the Academy of Sciences in Berlin on May 22, 1947.[35] Meinecke's characterizations of Ranke and Burckhardt in this lecture are more rhetorically pointed and brilliant than ever. Ranke's simple faith and confidence in divine Providence is contrasted with Burckhardt's skepticism and from that basic difference flow the two historians' well-known differences on essential issues, such as the relation of power and culture, with Ranke including "religion, the state, and in general, whatever is human in the noble sense" in a comprehensive notion of culture, while Burckhardt insisted that "the three forces [of religion, state, and culture] are highly heterogeneous and cannot be coordinated"; the question of continuity, with Ranke emphasizing "the bridge leading from the Roman Empire and Christianity to the Germans, and Burckhardt . . . the incredible *good fortune* that the conquering Romans admired, and were permeated by, Greek culture"; and the fundamental question with which each approached history: "If we may state this perhaps too sharply we may say that one asks, 'What does man mean for history?' and the other, 'What does history mean for man?'"[36]

But Meinecke did not decide between the two positions to which, for rhetorical purposes, he assigned the names "Ranke" and "Burckhardt." He called instead for a "synthesis" in which "the spirits of Burckhardt and Ranke would live on." It cannot be an "eclectical merging," he declared vaguely, but must "result from a new, more profound orientation to the relationship of power and culture, of the elemental and the spiritual in life and history."[37]

Such a call for a Hegelian "higher synthesis" to reunite, at a "superior" level of understanding, what had entered into dialectical opposition at an earlier stage of development is itself anything but Burckhardtian. Clearly, its explicit intent is to "transcend" the alleged one-sidedness of the Burckhardtian position. The most catastrophic moment in German history could thus be considered not the disastrous consequence of an unprecedented intensification of the desire for power, as Burckhardt would almost certainly have taken it to be, but a necessary stage in the advance of the "spirit" to a new and more complete understanding, as in a tragedy by Friedrich Hebbel.

Die deutsche Katastrophe displays virtually no awareness in fact of the untold suffering inflicted on the victims of the Third Reich and it is disappointingly silent on the persecution of the Jews and the Holocaust. Meinecke's few expressions of regret or pain are evoked by the plight of the German people under attack and in defeat. The focus of the work is—in a most un-Burckhardtian way—the German national state and the lessons to be learned by the state from the disaster that has befallen it, not the evils the state perpetrated and the human misery it brought on. It is hard to avoid the impression that, as far as Meinecke was concerned, there would have been no *Katastrophe* had Germany been victorious. That such an outcome might have been an even greater *Katastrophe* is a thought that appears not to have occurred to him. His perspective remained resolutely that of the *Nationalstaat* and only quite secondarily that of *Weltbürgertum*. Despite repeated criticism of Bismarck and his *Realpolitik,* Meinecke even managed to summon up a last reproach to Burckhardt and a curiously defiant restatement, in the noblest terms of course, of the goals of the nationalist historians:

> Even a Germany such as we today must live with—a Germany broken up and robbed of its independence as a national polity—is permitted to reflect with pride as well as grief on its former unity and power. Its previous struggle to achieve unity and power was not only a blind mass struggle, unconcerned with culture, as Burckhardt views it in his *Weltgeschichtliche Betrachtungen*. No, it was borne along by something that Burckhardt failed to understand—the great idea of an inner alliance of spirit and power, of humanity and nationality. . . . Through our own fault, that alliance has been shattered. The question that arises now is whether we should once again immediately resume working to restore it.[38]

Meinecke's answer was: not yet. Partly because the objective world power relations were unfavorable and any effort to regain the degree of power that such an alliance requires would result only in "impotent convulsions." And partly for "internal" reasons, because the very idea of power must first be "cleansed in Germany of the filth with which it became encrusted during the Third Reich, before it can once again be a suitable partner for spirit and culture."[39] In all of this, despite the dramatic contrasting of Ranke and Burckhardt, Berlin and Basel, despite the announcement that Burckhardt has "more to say to us today than Ranke," Meinecke remained essentially faithful to the position that he had always occupied.

To that position, not only Burckhardt but the three other Basel critics—Bachofen, Overbeck, and Nietzsche—were unalterably opposed. They feared the expansion of state power that Meinecke and his teachers considered necessary and desirable for the preservation and promotion of German culture. In fact, they were convinced that far from promoting culture, the alliance of power and culture was a threat to genuine culture and had already resulted in the contamination of culture by power, both directly as a result of state patronage of the arts and control of the institutions of culture, such as the schools and the universities, and indirectly through the mechanisms of the market, the media, and fashion. Beset by such powerful forces, culture, they held, would be unable to maintain the freedom and spontaneity that were its essential conditions. They even opposed social legislation that we today might consider humane and progressive (and the Bismarckian state, it should be remembered, was among the first to introduce such legislation) because it expanded the range of state power and conflicted with their ideal of individual freedom and responsibility. "The State will be most likely to remain healthy," Burckhardt declared in the *Weltgeschichtliche Betrachtungen*, "when it is aware of its own nature (and maybe of its essential origin) as an expedient."[40]

The likely source of the Basel scholars' ideal of individual freedom and independence from the state is the liberal neohumanism of the turn of the century in Germany, particularly in the writings of Wilhelm von Humboldt. To all liberals "society is a blessing, government even in its best state but a necessary evil."[41] To the neohumanists, in particular, culture in the sense both of the free life of civil society and the fullest possible development of the individual is the only true value, while the state is at best a necessity to be tolerated. To Humboldt there was no question that the true starting point of any reflection on political questions was the individual in his particularity and variety. Man's true end, he stated, is *Bildung*, the fullest and most harmonious development of his faculties. To assist him in achieving that end, the state should be guided by the principle that "reason cannot desire for man any other condition than that in which each individual not only enjoys the most absolute freedom to develop himself, as an individual, by his own energies, but in which physical nature itself is worked and shaped by human hands only in so far as each individual works and shapes it himself and by his own free will, in accordance with his needs and inclinations and with no restriction except that imposed by the limitations of his own powers and rights."[42]

From that premise, Humboldt drew the conclusion that "any state interference in the private affairs of citizens, where there is no immediate problem of violence done to the rights of one by others, is to be rejected." The state, in Humboldt's argument, is not an end in itself, but merely a means "to raise the culture of the citizen." If it has an ultimate end, it is "security," that is, the ensuring of freedom from arbitrary violence. Security had no other meaning: above all it did not mean exercising "benevolence toward the people, like the governance of a father over his children."[43] Kant had already judged that such "paternalistic government, in which the subjects, like minors who cannot distinguish between what is good and what is bad for them, are forced to adopt a passive role, and must look to the sovereign to determine the nature of their happiness," is "the worst possible despotism one can imagine."[44] In the same vein Humboldt argued against the "providential state" that manifests excessive solicitude for the "well-being" of its citizens on the ground that when government intervenes outside its allotted sphere of action—the maintenance of internal and external order—the result is to create uniformity of behavior, discourage the development of capacities, and stifle the natural variety of character and temperament. And variety and free activity are, according to him, goals that man naturally has and should pursue.[45] In fact, conflict and competition should be encouraged. It was the view not only of Adam Smith but of Kant and Humboldt that "the invidious and vainglorious spirit of emulation" promotes the development of human capacities that would otherwise lie dormant.[46]

When Overbeck said that what he most loved about the nineteenth century was its striving for freedom, it was this idea of freedom as emancipation from the condition of being a minor, as personal responsibility, and as the possibility of developing one's capacities to the full that he had in mind. When Burckhardt emphasized the agonistic character of Greek civilization rather than its harmoniousness, or showed how the competitiveness and rivalry of individuals and cities during the Italian Renaissance contributed to the development of a high culture, he was likewise being faithful to the notion of freedom that was dominant during his most formative years. And when Burckhardt and Bachofen (or Nietzsche, for that matter) railed against democracy, it was because they feared that democracy would result in the use of state power not to secure and promote freedom but to secure and promote the material well-being they believed to be the goal of the masses, at the expense of freedom. "It is because I love freedom," Bachofen declared, "that I hate democracy."[47] Both he and Burckhardt saw a connection between popular suffrage and the establishment of the Second Empire in France and both were convinced that freedom had as much to fear from universal suffrage as from the ambitions of tyrants; in fact, they believed that these two would play into each other's hands.[48] The only equality the Basel scholars could approve of was equality of the right to liberty. That is why the "commonality" constituted by those who have developed their capacity to respond to works of art, though an elite, according to Burckhardt, "need not, fortunately, be an elite of the rich and powerful." On the contrary, "any person who has not been spoiled by a false education can respond to public works of art, even if he or she is uneducated."[49]

When Burckhardt described culture as "the sum total of those developments of the spirit that take place spontaneously and lay no claim to universal or compulsive authority,"[50] it is clear that the spheres of culture and human freedom are coterminous for him. Does that mean that, apart from the external constraints on freedom (notably the state and the laws which it is the state's function to enforce) there are no other constraints? At least for the two native Baselers, Burckhardt and Bachofen, the answer to that question is probably no. An early romantic strain in their thought, deriving from Herder, Humboldt, Grimm, and Savigny, comes into play here. Bachofen saw the moral and legal tradition as part of the living culture of a people, like its language. That culture, he held, provides the opportunity for individual moral behavior, just as the common language provides opportunity for individual expression. Genuine moral behavior is thus not arbitrary, but both limited and rendered possible by tradition; at the same time, it is also individual, free, and creative, not uniform or mechanically imposed by codes of law and state legislation. "In all ages, whatever is truly great," Bachofen wrote unequivocally, "was the work of individuals."[51] In practical terms this can only mean that the proper response to social problems such as poverty, for instance, is voluntary or charitable action (old Basel style), not social welfare legislation (Bismarck [and modern Basel] style). In Burckhardt's case, we might look to his vision of the role of artistic tradition in the work of the individual artist. The greatest artists, as we saw in chapter 13, are not for him the rebels, the radical individualists (Michelangelo, Rembrandt), but those who take over and enhance tradition by their original and creative use of it (Raphael, Rubens). Or we might consider his view of the creative transformation of the Greek myths as they are handed down from generation to generation.

Burckhardt's obvious but rarely expressed lack of sympathy for English society (Nietzsche was notoriously more outspoken) may help to define a position that seems to have been common to the Basel scholars. On one hand, they could surely only applaud a liberal society whose members, in Matthew Arnold's words, "have not the notion, so familiar on the Continent and to antiquity, of *the State*—the nation in its collective and corporate character, entrusted with stringent powers for the general advantage, and controlling individual wills in the name of an interest wider than that of individuals." On the other, they could not admire a culture in which individual energies were not or were no longer directed toward the fullest development of the individual personality but were turned instead to the pursuit of power and material gain. The Englishman's democratic "right to do what he likes . . . march where he likes, meet where he likes, hoot as he likes, threaten as he likes, smash as he likes," in the harsh and hostile terms used by Arnold,[52] was a far cry from the freedom that the Basel scholars advocated and in the name of which they carried out their remarkable, prophetic critique of the modern—in classical philology and *Altertumswissenschaft*, in historical scholarship, in art, in religion, and in politics.

NOTES

Introduction

Author's note on translations and quotations: As this book is intended for the English-speaking reader, I quote from and refer to standard English translations wherever these are available, even when they are old, as is often the case, and do not reflect the latest scholarship. (A good deal of recent Burckhardt scholarship, for instance, has been devoted to establishing philologically more accurate texts than those available to Burckhardt's translators.) Where no translations exist, I have myself translated the passages I quote, both in the text and in the notes. I much regret that I could not take advantage of two new English translations of works by Burckhardt—one of *Die Cultur der Renaissance in Italien,* scheduled for publication in late 1999 or 2000, and one of the *Griechische Kulturgeschichte* in a handsome new one-volume abridgment, which appeared in England in late 1998.

1. On Roman civilization in the Rhineland, especially cities and trade, see Jean Colin, *Les Antiquités romaines de la Rhénanie* (Paris: Les Belles Lettres, 1927), pp. 76–151, 262–84; Matthias Riedel, *Köln: ein römisches Wirtschaftszentrum* (Cologne: Greven, 1982).

2. On the horizontal trading routes cutting the corridor of the Rhine at Basel, Mainz, Cologne, see Etienne Juilland, "L'Espace rhénan," in *Une Histoire du Rhin,* ed. Pierre Ayço-berry and Marc Ferro (Paris: Ramsay, 1981), pp. 57–58.

3. The figure of twenty thousand, given in Robert E. Dickinson's "Basle: A Study in Urban Geography," ch. 5 of *The West European City* (London: Routledge & Kegan Paul, 1951), p. 67, is undocumented, but probably reflects the calculations of Felix Plattner, the Basel city doctor, who in 1610 estimated the population of the city at 16,160. As 4,049 people had just died of the plague, Plattner judged that the population at the beginning of the century must have been around twenty thousand. Other estimates set the number of inhabitants of Basel toward the end of the fifteenth century as high as thirty thousand (Paul Doppler, *Organisation und Aufgabekreis der Stadtgemeinde Basel 1803–1876* [Ingenbohl: Theodosius-Buchdruckerei, 1933]). Modern historical demographers apparently do not accept Plattner's figure. In his *European Urbanization 1500–1800* (Cambridge: Harvard University Press, 1984), pp. 269–78, Jan de Vries set the population of Basel in the year 1600 at ten thousand.

4. Ayçoberry and Ferro, *Une Histoire du Rhin,* pp. 227–49.

5. Ibid., p. 139.

6. Ibid., p. 65.

7. Albert Demangeon and Lucien Febvre, *Le Rhin: Problèmes d'histoire et d'économie* (Paris: A. Colin, 1935), pp. 81–82.

8. Ibid., p. 83.

9. J. de la Tynaa, *Almanach du Commerce* (Paris: J. de la Tynaa, 1806), pp. 824–25. See also Franz Lerner, ed., *Das Tätige Frankfurt im Wirtschaftsleben dreier Jahrhunderte (1648–1955)* (Frankfurt am Main: Gerd Ammelburg, 1955), p. 26. Basel appears not to have been a primary asylum for religious refugees. Often it was the second generation of refugee families that was drawn to Basel, as the most active trading center in Switzerland; see Andreas

Staehelin, "Gold aus Seide," in *Schaffendes Basel: 2000 Jahre Basler Wirtschaft*, ed. Hansrudolf Schwabe (Basel: Birkhäuser, 1957), pp. 102–35.

10. Demangeon and Febvre, *Le Rhin*, pp. 74, 80. Most of Basel's business was with the plain and the river valley, with Frankfurt and Strasbourg; contacts with the inner Swiss cities were less important (Dickinson, "Basle: A Study in Urban Geography"). As late as 1870, it was Basel that initiated the massive evacuation of elderly people, women, and children from beleaguered Strasbourg during the Franco-Prussian War. Many other Swiss citizens contributed to this enterprise, but according to Werner Kaegi, it was the brainchild of the Basel statesman Gottlieb Bischoff and was chiefly supported by the population of Basel. *Jacob Burckhardt: eine Biographie* (Basel: Schwabe, 1947–1982), 7:144–45.

11. And possibly suggested by him. See Michelet's *Journal*, ed. Paul Viallaneix and Claude Digeon (Paris: Gallimard 1959–1976), 1:529: "La noble et passionnée figure d'Amerbach à trente ans. . . ."

12. Demangeon and Febvre, *Le Rhin*, pp. 96–97. Febvre recognized shadows in the brilliant culture of the Rhenish cities—the internal oppression of the poor by the rich, the narrowness of the guilds, the fierce and blinkered local patriotism. He might have added the massacres of Jews in Frankfurt, Strasbourg, and Basel in the mid-fourteenth century, at the time of the Black Death.

13. Christoph Steding, *Das Reich und die Krankheit der europäischen Kultur* (Hamburg: Hanseatische Verlagsanstalt, 1939), pp. 57–60 *passim*. See also Heinrich von Treitschke, *History of Germany in the Nineteenth Century*, trans. Eden and Cedar Paul (New York: McBride, Nast, 1917), 3:90–93 *passim*.

14. See Anthony Giddens, *The Nation-State and Violence* (Berkeley and Los Angeles: University of California Press, 1985), p. 107.

15. Friedrich Metz, "Die Reichsstädte," in *Beiträge zur Wirtschafts- und Stadtgeschichte: Festschrift für Hektor Ammann* (Wiesbaden: Franz Steiner, 1965), pp. 29–54; Christopher R. Friedrichs, "The Swiss and German City-States," in *The City-State in Five Cultures*, ed. Robert Griffeth and Carol G. Thomas (Santa Barbara: ABC-Clio, and Oxford: Clio, 1981), pp. 109–42.

16. Demangeon and Febvre, *Le Rhin*, pp. 184–89; Ayçoberry and Ferro, *Une Histoire du Rhin*, pp. 65–66.

17. Lerner, *Das tätige Frankfurt*, p. 45.

18. Ibid. The adjutant was John Trumbull.

19. On the architecture of Basel, see *Das Bürgerhaus in der Schweiz*, published by the Swiss Union of Architects and Engineers (Zurich, Leipzig, and Berlin: Art Institute Orell Füssli), vols. 17 (1926), 22 (1930), 23 (1931); on Basel art collections, Daniel Burckhardt-Werthemann, "Die Baslerischen Kunstsammler des 18. Jahrhunderts," *Basler Kunstverein: Berichterstattung*, 1901, pp. 3–69, 1902, pp. 71–116; on Basel as a source of capital, Hans-Conrad Peyer, "Basel in der Zürcher Wirtschaftsgeschichte," *Basler Zeitschrift für Geschichte und Altertumskunde* 69 (1969): 223–37, and Maurice Lévy-Boyer, *Les Banques européennes et l'industrialisation internationale dans la première moitié du XIX siècle* (Paris: Presses universitaires de France, 1964).

20. *Dichtung und Wahrheit*, pt. III, bk. 12, *Goethe's Werke*, ed. Ernst Beutler (Zurich: Artemis Verlag, 1948–1971), 10:520–21.

21. Alexis de Tocqueville, "Voyage en Suisse, 1836," *Oeuvres complètes*, ed. J.-P. Mayer (Paris: Gallimard, 1951–1995), 5 (pt. 2): 171–88, at p. 176. Cf. the judgment of Abraham Stanyan, a British envoy to the Swiss cantons in the early eighteenth century:

The close alliances by which the Thirteen Cantons are linked to one another, their manner of acting, as members of one body, in their diets, and the many treaties they have jointly entered into with several foreign princes and states, have given grounds for an opinion, which is generally received in the world, that these Thirteen Cantons make but one Commonwealth, like the states of the United Provinces; yet whoever will take the pains to inquire into the formulation of their union will find them so many independent commonwealths, joined indeed by very strict alliances for their mutual defence, but so far from making but one sovereignty, or one body, that there is not so much as any one public act or instrument by which they are bound together, and wherein the Thirteen Cantons are reciprocally engaged to each other. . . . So far are they from making one body, or one commonwealth, that only the Three old Cantons are directly allied with every one of the other twelve. There is indeed such a connection established between them, that, in case any one Canton were attacked, all the other twelve would be obliged to march to its succour; but it would be by virtue of the relation that two cantons may have to a third. . . . For example, of the Eight old Cantons, Lucerne has a right of calling but five to its succour, in case of attack; but some of these five have a right of calling others, with whom they are allied, tho' Lucerne be not; so that at last all must march by virtue of particular alliances, and not of any general one among them all. . . . The truth of it is, that they have nothing in common, which proves any dependence of one on the other: there is no common judicature in being, that has the right of obliging all the Cantons by its decisions; there is no common treasure, no common coin. . . . Each exercises the right of making particular treaties with foreign princes and states . . . and if the Thirteen Cantons send any ambassadors abroad, they never choose one or two to represent them all, but each Canton sends its own representatives, to shew its right of sovereignty.

Anon. (Temple Stanyan), *An Account of Switzerland, Written in the Year 1714* (Edinburgh: Hamilton, Balfour, and Neill, 1756), pp. 111–12, 116–17.

22. See Martin Alioth, "Geschichte des politischen Systems bis 1833," in *Das politische System Basel-Stadt: Geschichte, Strukturen, Institutionen, Politikbereiche*, ed. Lukas Burckhardt et al. (Basel and Frankfurt: Helbing & Lichtenhahn, 1984), pp. 17–36, at p. 27. See also Rudolf Wackernagel, *Geschichte der Stadt Basel* (Basel: Helbing & Lichtenhahn, 1907–1924), 4:5; Paul Burckhardt, *Geschichte der Stadt Basel von der Zeit der Reformation bis zur Gegenwart*, 2nd ed. (Basel: Helbing & Lichtenhahn, 1957 [1942]), p. 1.

23. As a "Low Alemanic island," Basel is separated from the High Alemanic dialects of the rest of German-speaking Switzerland. "Linguistically, it belongs to the Rhineland plateau, to Alsace, Mulhouse, Colmar, and Strasbourg" (Emil Steiner, *Abriss der Schweizerdeutschen Mundart* [Basel: B. Wepf, 1937], pp. 13, 40). In addition, as the most international city in German-speaking Switzerland, Basel always looked outward rather than inward. Gottlieb Bischoff, one of those progressive members of the Basel patriciate who decided to embrace the new, more centralized Swiss Confederation of 1848 and to work within it, used to complain of a *"Mangel an Grenzsinn"*—a lack of a sense of the world beyond the frontiers—in the federal administration in Bern. Kaegi, *Jacob Burckhardt*, 7:142, 146. The Swiss writer Gonzague de Reynold summed up the common view of the city: "Carrefour de trois grandes civilisations auxquelles elle participe sans jamais se donner tout entière à l'une d'elles, [Bâle] se défend sans trève contre l'absorption morale ou politique, contre le cosmopolitisme, en conservant ses traditions et son esprit municipal" (Gonzague de Reynold, *Cités et pays suisses* [Lausanne: Editions de l'Age d'homme, 1982], p. 178).

24. Likewise the distinctive *"Basler Mundart"* or *"echtes Baseldeutsch,"* of which Burckhardt

was once a master, was still spoken in the mid-twentieth century by a small number of "old Baselers" who made up the city's upper class or elite—the *"Altbasler Oberschicht"*—and who alone had successfully resisted the tide of *"Schweizerdeutsch"* or Swiss German swept into the city by massive immigration from other parts of Switzerland. See Robert Schläpfer, *Die Mundart des Kantons Basellaud* (Frauenfeld: Huber, 1956; Beiträge zur schweizerdeutschen Mundartforschung, 5), pp. 217–18.

25. On the free cities' acquisition of contiguous territories, see Friedrichs, "The Swiss and German City-States," pp. 122–25.

26. Gottfried Keller's Martin Salander welcomes the new Swiss Constitution of 1848 as particularly timely: "All around us, in the great unified nations, the world has enclosed itself as within four iron walls" (*Werke* [Zurich: Atlantis, n.d.], 2:806).

27. Kaegi, *Jacob Burckhardt*, 7:124.

28. See Hans Mauersberg, *Wirtschafts- und Sozialgeschichte zentraleuropäischer Städte in neuerer Zeit* (Göttingen: Vandenhoek & Ruprecht, 1960), pp. 297–303.

29. For a good overview of Bachofen's impact in the German-speaking world, see the collection of articles in Hans-Jürgen Heinrichs, *Materialien zu Bachofens "Das Mutterrecht"* (Frankfurt am Main: Suhrkamp, 1979). For a briefer survey of Bachofen in both the German- and English-speaking worlds, see Lionel Gossman, *Orpheus Philologus* (Philadelphia: American Philosophical Society, 1983; Transactions, vol. 73, pt. 5), notes 1–16.

30. Walter Muschg, "Bachofen als Schriftsteller," *Basler Universitätsreden*, Heft 27 (Basel: Helbing & Lichtenhahn, 1949).

31. Josef Pieper, *Leisure the Basis of Culture*, trans. Alexander Dru, with an introduction by T. S. Eliot (New York: Pantheon Books, 1952), p. 65.

32. Introduction to Isaiah Berlin, *Personal Impressions*, ed. Henry Hardy (London: Hogarth Press, 1980), p. xv.

Chapter One

1. Friedrich Engels, *Wanderings in Lombardy* [1841] in Karl Marx and Friedrich Engels, *Collected Works* (New York: International Publishers, 1976), 2:170–71.

2. See *Das Bürgerhaus in der Schweiz*, published by the Swiss Union of Architects and Engineers (Zurich, Leipzig, and Berlin: Art Institute Orell Füssli), vol. 22 (1930), pp. xxii–xxiii.

3. See, for instance, L. Simond, *Switzerland: Journal of a Tour or Residence in that Country in the Years 1817, 1818, and 1819*, 2 vols. (Boston: Wells and Lilly, 1822), 1:54; Samuel Irenaeus Prime, *Letters from Switzerland* (New York: Sheldon and Co.; Boston: Gould & Lincoln, 1860), p. 10. On the other hand, a German traveler visiting Basel in 1786 found the setting unattractive and the city itself, "with the exception of a few *palais*, poorly built, with steep, narrow, unlighted streets." He especially disliked the "grotesque" frescoes on the exteriors of many buildings. Christian Gottlieb Schmidt, *Von der Schweiz: Journal meiner Reise vom 5 Julius 1786 bis den 7 August 1787*, ed. T. and H. Solfinger (Bern and Stuttgart: Paul Haupt, 1985), p. 192).

4. "The Civil War in Switzerland," in Marx and Engels, *Collected Works*, 6:369.

5. See François Walter, "Von der vorindustriellen Siedlung zur Industriestadt," in *Alltag in der Schweiz*, ed. Bernhard Schneider (Zurich: Chronos Verlag, 1991), pp. 238–46.

6. For a good account of the events of 1830–1833, as well as an overview of the abundant literature on the topic, see *Basellaud vor 150 Jahren: Wende und Aufbruch* (Liestal: Jubiläums-verlag, 1983), especially the following articles: Roger Blum, "Für Volkssouveränität und Fortschritt: Die Volksbewegungen der Jahre 1830–33" (pp. 11–28); Heinrich Staehelin, "1830–33: Basellaud und Aargau—zwei Revolutionskantone" (pp. 29–44); Fritz Grieder, "Die Landschaftler Revolution: von der Petition zur Trennung" (pp. 45–66); and Dorothea

Roth, "Die dreissiger Wirren—bedeutendste Krise der Basler Stadtgeschichte im 19. Jahrhundert" (pp. 67–84).

7. Emil Dürr, ed., *Burckhardt als politischer Publizist* (Zurich: Fretz & Wasmuth, 1987), p. 103 (article of 3–4 April 1845).

8. Basel's reserved relation to the new federal state is the context of a playful comment by Bachofen after Burckhardt decided, in 1858, to return to Basel and accept a position at the city's University after a three-year stint at the newly founded Federal Polytechnic in Zurich. Burckhardt, Bachofen wrote to Wilhelm Henzen, a German philologist resident in Rome, *"will doch lieber cantonal als eidgenössisch sein"* ("has decided he would rather be cantonal than federal") (letter of 31 March 1858, *Gesammelte Werke,* ed. Karl Meuli [Basel: Schwabe, 1943–1967; publication interrupted at vol. 10], 10:179).

9. Lukas Gloor, "Die Geschichte des Basler Kunstvereins von 1839 bis 1908," in *Die Geschichte des Basler Kunstvereins und der Kunsthalle Basel 1839–1988,* ed. L. Gloor, T. Kellein, and M. Suter (Basel: Kunsthalle Basel; Schwabe & Co., 1989), pp. 11–74, at pp. 43–46.

10. As late as the mid-1830s, when the population of Basel stood at around twenty-four thousand, that of Zurich was only fourteen thousand. Paul Burckhardt, *Geschichte der Stadt Basel* (Basel: Helbing & Lichtenhahn, 1957 [1942]), p. 202.

11. *Schweizerische National-Zeitung,* 27 August 1842 (hereafter *SNZ*).

12. See the figures of deaths from the plague and new citizens in the fourteenth, fifteenth, and sixteenth centuries given by Markus Lutz, *Baslerisches Bürger-Buch, enthaltend alle gegenwärtig in der Stadt Basel eingebürgerte Geschlechter, nebst der Anzeige ihres Ursprungs, Bürgerrechts-Aufnahme, so wie ihrer ersten Ansiedler und beachtenswerthen Personen, welche aus denselben zu Dienste des Staats, der Kirche und der Wissenschaften hervorgegangen sind* (Basel: Schweighauser'sche Buchdruckerey, 1819), pp. 7–9.

13. Hans Mauersberg, *Wirtschafts- und Sozialgeschichte zentraleuropäischer Städte in neuerer Zeit* (Göttingen: Vandenhoek & Ruprecht, 1960), pp. 130–31.

14. Ratsbeschluss of 1546, cited in Andreas Staehelin, "Gold aus Seide," in *Schaffendes Basel: 2000 Jahre Basler Wirtschaft,* ed. Hansrudolf Schwabe (Basel: Birkhäuser, 1957), pp. 101–2; see also Peter Stolz, *Basler Wirtschaft in vor- und frühindustrieller Zeit* (Zurich: Schulthess Polygraphischer Verlag, 1977), p. 150; Heinz Polivka, *Die chemische Industrie im Raume von Basel* (Basel: Helbing & Lichtenhahn, 1974), p. 29 (Basler Beiträge zur Geographie, 16).

15. In 1610 the city doctor Felix Plattner estimated there were 16,160 inhabitants, and 4,049 persons had just died of the plague. See Paul Doppler, *Organisation und Aufgabekreis der Stadtgemeinde Basel 1803–1876* (Ingenbohl: Theodosius-Buchdruckerei, 1933). Mauersberg (*Wirtschafts- und Sozialgeschichte,* p. 26) gave a figure of twelve thousand.

16. Paul Burckhardt, *Geschichte der Stadt Basel,* p. 80; Mauersberg, *Wirtschafts- und Sozialgeschichte,* p. 29.

17. William Coxe, *Travels in Switzerland and in the Country of the Grisons in a Series of Letters to William Melmoth, Esq.,* 4th rev. ed., 4 vols. (London: Cadell & Davies, 1801 [1st ed. 1778]), 1:152–76.

18. See engravings of the sixteenth and seventeenth centuries reproduced in *Dictionnaire historique et biographique de la Suisse* (Neuchâtel: Administration du Dictionnaire, 1921–1934), art. "Bâle"; townplans in various nineteenth-century guidebooks; see also Robert E. Dickinson, *The West European City* (London: Routledge & Kegan Paul, 1959), p. 69, fig. 16, illustrating the historical development of Basel; Schmidt, *Von der Schweiz,* p. 192.

19. See also Lutz, *Baslerisches Bürger-Buch,* pp. 17–18.

20. Mauersberg, *Wirtschafts- und Sozialgeschichte,* p. 102; Paul Burckhardt, *Geschichte der Stadt Basel,* p. 81; Lutz, *Baslerisches Bürgerbuch,* pp. 13–14.

21. Lutz, *Baslerisches Bürgerbuch,* p. 15.

22. Mauersberg, *Wirtschafts- und Sozialgeschichte,* p. 102, table and note 1. Between 1600 and 1700 Frankfurt admitted 415 persons to citizenship, Hamburg 1,000, Basel 45.

23. Coxe, *Travels in Switzerland,* 1:167, 169.

24. These occurred in the years 1691, 1803, 1814, 1833, 1846, 1852; see Paul Burck-hardt, *Geschichte der Stadt Basel,* pp. 30, 72, 141–42.

25. Mauersberg, *Wirtschafts- und Sozialgeschichte,* pp. 181, 220–23. In this important re-spect Basel appears to have differed from many cities in France, Spain, and Germany. In the outstanding chapters devoted to the European city in the period between the Black Death and the Age of Enlightenment (*After the Black Death: A Social History of Early Modern Europe* [Bloomington: Indiana University Press, 1986], chs. 2–4), George Huppert notes that dur-ing the sixteenth century the old close tie between craft guilds and city government had begun to loosen in cities such as Beauvais and Frankfurt. In Basel, as elsewhere, the mer-chants had effectively gained control of the city from the artisans, but they did so through their domination of the guilds and their members and without ever ceasing to be themselves actively engaged in business.

26. Mauersberg, *Wirtschafts- und Sozialgeschichte,* p. 222.

27. Ibid., p. 22.

28. Traugott Geering, *Handel und Industrie der Stadt Basel: Zunftwesen und Indus-triegeschichte bis zum Ende des 18. Jahrhunderts* (Basel: Felix Schneider, 1886), p. 606.

29. Paul Burckhardt, *Geschichte der Stadt Basel,* p.142. In 1798 an English visitor gave the population of the entire canton as forty thousand and that of the city itself as fifteen thou-sand, made up of eight thousand citizens and seven thousand noncitizens. Helen Maria Wil-liams, *A Tour in Switzerland, or a View of the Present State of the Government and Manners of those Cantons,* 2 vols. (London: G. G. & J. Robinson, 1798), 1:96–97.

30. Mauersberg, *Wirtschafts- und Sozialgeschichte,* p. 119. See also the detailed study by Martin Maurer, *Die soziale Differenzierung in Stadt und Landschaft Basel als Ursache der Kan-tonstrennung 1833* (Liestal: Kantonale Schul- und Büromaterialverwaltung, 1985. Quellen und Forschungen zur Geschichte und Landeskunde des Kantons Baselland, vol. 22).

31. Geering, *Handel und Industrie der Stadt Basel,* pp. 612–13; Andreas Staehelin, "Gold aus Seide," pp. 102–17, at pp. 11–112; Mauersberg, *Wirtschafts- und Sozialgeschichte,* p. 222; Maurer, *Die soziale Differenzierung,* p. 26; P. Fink, *Vom Passementerhandwerk zur Bandindus-trie* (*Basler Neujahrsblatt,* 1979) and *Geschichte der Basler Bandindustrie, 1550–1800* (Basel: Helbing & Lichtenhahn, 1983). According to Geering, the *Kleiner Rat* spelled out in its report that the aim of manufacturing was not to do little work with many workers, but to do as much work as possible with as few workers as possible. At the same time, however, the report tried to reassure the passementerie workers by reminding them that they would still have most of the local market, since the production of the merchants was almost exclu-sively exported.

32. Staehelin, "Gold aus Seide," pp. 113–14; Maurer, *Die soziale Differenzierung,* pp. 24–26.

33. Staehelin, "Gold aus Seide," p. 114.

34. Maurice Lévy-Boyer, *Les Banques européennes et l'industrialisation internationale dans la premièrre moitié du XIX siècle* (Paris: Presses universitaires de France, 1964), p. 135.

35. Staehlin, "Gold aus Seide," p. 112. Staehelin gives figures of 2,268 looms in 1786, 3,000 in 1800.

36. Ibid., pp. 114–15. In 1806 a trade directory for the city listed twenty-four such firms. *Basler Handlungs-schema oder Verzeichnis aller in Basel befindlichen Kaufleute, Fabrikanten, Künstler, Commercial-Professionisten, u.s.w.* (Basel: Heinrich Haag, 1806).

37. *La Suisse économique et sociale,* ouvrage publié par le Département Fédéral de l'Econo-mie Publique (Einsiedeln: Etablissements Benzinger, 1927), 1:187.

38. Emil Walter, *Soziale Grundlagen der Entwicklung der Naturwissenschaften in der alten Schweiz* (Bern: Francke, 1958), p. 234 note 3.

39. Mauersberg, *Wirtschafts- und Sozialgeschichte*, p. 328.

40. In one of his public lectures—given in 1822–1823—Wilhelm Martin Liebrecht De Wette outlined what seems to have been the official conception of the guilds in those years. They constitute a legitimate form of "sociality," so De Wette argued, and as such are one of the foundations of the entire polity, but they must remember that this is their true raison d'etre and resist the inevitable temptation to act out of self-interest. "The natural and permanent distinction of classes lies in profession or calling; and every calling should be pursued, in the spirit of love, to the general good, so, however, that the advantage of each individual may not suffer thereby. But even professional public spirit may become selfish and unjust, if the associates of a calling, united in privileged guilds, make these privileges their object more than the happy, and, generally, useful pursuit of their business" (*Human Life, or Practical Ethics*, trans. Samuel Osgood, 2 vols. [Boston: James Munroe, 1842], 2:253–54). By the 1840s at least, however, there was open criticism of the guilds from fairly conservative businessmen. Karl Sarasin, who by his own account was "happy to be counted a member of the conservative party," contributed a series of articles entitled "Das Innungswesen oder das Noli me tangere" to the *Allgemeines Intelligenzblatt der Stadt Basel* (November and December, 1846) in which he attacked the guilds as economically counterproductive. See Philipp Sarasin, "Sittlichkeit, Nationalgefühl und frühe Ängste vor dem Proletariat: Untersuchungen zu Politik, Weltanschauung und Ideologie des Basler Bürgertums in der Verfassungskrise von 1846/47," *Basler Zeitschrift für Geschichte und Altertumskunde* 84 (1994): 52–126, at p. 111.

41. Mauersberg, *Wirtschafts- und Sozialgeschichte*, pp. 119–20. On the government's consideration of the vital economic concerns of the artisans and *Handwerker*, see also *Basler Wirtschaft in vor- und frühindustrieller Zeit* (Zurich: Schulthass Polygraphischer Verlag, 1977), p. 152.

42. As late as 1847, every butcher, smith, and painter-decorator in Basel was still a citizen. Paul Burckhardt, *Geschichte der Stadt Basel*, p. 206.

43. The noncitizens of Basel constituted a class that "is in a state of complete degradation," according to the English radical Helen Maria Williams, a staunch champion of the French Revolution. It is "excluded from all political rights, can exercise no trade, and the individuals of which it is formed are considered merely as strangers, to whom the privilege is granted of living in the town, placed for the most part under the immediate responsibility of the manufacturer or artizan by whom they are employed, and who is bound to take such measures respecting them, as shall prevent their becoming burdensome to the state. When persons of this class are born in Basil, when even their parents have been natives of the city for several successive generations, they acquire not one further prerogative from these circumstances; and the admission of a few of these individuals to the right of burghers is always attended with so many obstacles, that the instances in which it takes place are extremely rare" (*A Tour in Switzerland*, 1:97–98).

44. Lutz, *Baslerisches Bürger-Buch*, p. 16. See also Maurer, *Die soziale Differenzierung*, p. 49. (Lutz's figures are slightly at variance with those of the *"Basler Volkszählung"* of 1779 found in the *"Ratsherrkasten"* of Emanuel Burckhardt-Sarasin and reproduced by Carl Burckhardt-Sarasin, "Untergang und Übergang," in *Schaffendes Basel: 2000 Jahre Basler Wirtschaft* [Basel: Birkhäuser, 1957], pp. 118–35, though they appear to have been derived from this source.) In 1798, Helen Williams placed the number of citizens at eight thousand and the number of noncitizens at seven thousand, remarking also, however, that "the last class increases in the same proportion that the first diminishes from year to year" (*A Tour in Switzerland*, 1:96–97).

45. Lutz, *Baslerisches Bürger-Buch*, p. 16.

46. Paul Burckhardt, *Geschichte der Stadt Basel*, p. 206.

47. Mauersberg, *Wirtschafts- und Sozialgeschichte*, pp. 130–33, 328.

48. In addition to the considerable financial resources and the leisure required to exercise public office, when the exercise of public office was unremunerated, eligibility was restricted by formal minimum property conditions. These drastically reduced the number of "active" citizens to about 20 percent of the male citizen population. As late as 1837 there were only about eighteen hundred "active" citizens out of a total population of twenty-two thousand. See Paul Burckhardt, *Geschichte der Stadt Basel*, pp. 130, 142, 202. Similar restrictions on the franchise obtained, of course, in other representative or parliamentary regimes, such as Britain and France. The Great Reform Bill of 1832 effected the first major breach in those restrictions in Britain.

49. January 2, 4, 9, 11, 16, 23, February 8, 10, 22, March 2, 5; this from the article of January 11. Cf. Wolfgang Köllmann, "The Merchants and Manfacturers of Barmen," in *The Urbanization of European Society in the Nineteenth Century*, ed. Andrew Lees and Lynn Lees (Lexington, Mass.: D.C. Heath, 1976), pp. 117–31, and the same author's *Sozialgeschichte der Stadt Barmen* (Tübingen: J.C.B. Mohr, 1960).

50. *SNZ*, 4 January 1844.

51. See the analysis of household wealth in the St. Johann-Vorstadt in the eighteenth century in Stolz, *Basler Wirtschaft*, p. 148.

52. Coxe, *Travels in Switzerland*, 1:173. Coxe's optimistic account was explicitly challenged by the radical Helen Williams. Writing in 1798, she described the government of Basel as "thirty thousand seven hundred inhabitants of the canton of Basil . . . being governed by three hundred self-elected individuals" (*A Tour in Switzerland*, 1:112). Nor according to Wiliams was the citizen of Basel the well-rounded, educated individual, the reader of Virgil and Horace, as portrayed by Coxe. "Whatever were the Halcyon days of taste and learning at the period of Mr. Cox's visit, it is a melancholy fact, that this literary spirit has entirely evaporated since his departure" (1:114–15).

53. Rudolf Hanhart, "Rede bei der Promotions-Feyerlichkeit den 13 Weinmonat, 1817" (Basel, 1818), p. 5. Basel University Library, K.Ar.F.V.4.

54. The relative decline of the artisan population would probably be even more noticeable if the manufacturers and industrialists, printers, artists, pensioned officers, and city employees, many of whom were placed by custom in the artisan guilds, could be subtracted from the artisan guild rolls.

55. Mauersberg, *Wirtschafts- und Sozialgeschichte*, p. 183; see also Paul Burckhardt, *Geschichte der Stadt Basel*, p. 206.

56. Paul Burckhardt, *Geschichte der Stadt Basel*, pp. 202–3.

57. *SNZ*, 20 October 1842.

58. Ibid., 11 January 1844.

59. Paul Burckhardt, *Geschichte der Stadt Basel*, p. 207.

60. *SNZ*, 11 January 1844; see also Paul Burckhardt, *Geschichte der Stadt Basel*, pp. 206–7, and Köllmann on the similar plight of the artisans of Barmen, *Sozialgeschichte der Stadt Barmen*, p. 128.

61. *La Suisse économique et sociale* (Einsiedeln: Etablissements Benzinger, 1927), vol. 1, p. 198; Werner Kaegi, *Jacob Burckhardt: eine Biographie* (Basel: Schwabe, 1947–1982), 7:117–18, 120–21.

62. W. Bickel, *Bevölkerungsgeschichte und Bevölkerungspolitik der Schweiz seit dem Ausgang des Mittelalters* (Zurich: Büchergilde Gutenberg, 1947), pp. 168–69.

63. Paul Burckhardt, *Geschichte der Stadt Basel*, p. 206.

64. F. Föhr, *Basel's Bürgerschaft unter besonderer Berücksichtigung der Wirkungen der in diesem Jahrhundert erlassenen Bürgerrechtsgesetze* (Basel: Schwabe, 1886), p. 7.

65. The emancipation of the Jews, grudgingly conceded by Switzerland in 1866 in response to strong pressure from France and, to a lesser degree, the United States and Great Britain, must have been experienced by many in this social class as another blow to their once privileged status. In the referendum at Basel, the measure passed by a margin of only 482 citizens' votes, 1,278 votes having been cast against it. Throughout the period from the fifteenth to the eighteenth century, the city had a policy of strict exclusion as far as the Jews were concerned. A few managed to settle in the villages of the *Baselbiet,* but none were admitted into the city itself. Apart from the antisemitism endemic throughout northern and central Europe, there may have been fear of competition from the Jews. (Helen Williams, who devoted several indignant pages to Basel's "uniformly zealous" opposition to Jewish settlement and to commercial dealings with Jews, scoffed at such fear: "No person of discernment will put in competition the fine commercial intelligence of a burgher of Basil, with the rude cunning of the miserable outcast of his proscription" [*A Tour in Switzerland,* 1:108].) Not till the time of the revolutionary Helvetic Republic were Jews permitted to settle in a city that had once been celebrated for its Hebrew scholars and printers. And that liberal policy was short-lived. In 1814, as it celebrated the city's liberation from the Napoleonic yoke, the *Stadtrat* lost no time in declaring that Basel was no longer obliged to suffer "this wandering and troublesome people" within its walls. Laws were passed restricting residence to the eldest son in each family after marriage. By 1837, the thirty-five Jewish families in Basel in 1815 had dwindled to thirteen. Characteristically, what support the Jews found in Basel came from members of the merchant elite. *Ratsherr* Peter Merian, a solid conservative, and *Ratsherr* Samuel Köchlin-Burckhardt, a prosperous ribbon manufacturer, reminded their fellow citizens that "though the Jews are treated as if they were not even human, there are in fact worthier men among them than many Christians can claim to be," and introduced legislation to provide them with a minimum of security. It was also, most likely, pressure from the merchant elite that led the city to open its gates to Jewish refugees fleeing the pogroms that, in neighboring Alsace, accompanied the revolutionary enthusiasms of 1789 and 1848. That generosity won the city a fine poetic tribute from the Hebrew poet Hartwig Wessely, a student of Moses Mendelsohn; in addition, a prayer was read regularly in Hebrew and German in all the synagogues of Alsace for *"die Wohlfarth der loblichen Stadt Basel und ihrer Angehörigen."* Basel, as is well known, was selected by Theodor Herzl as the site of the first Zionist Congress in 1897, partly no doubt because of the city's neutral status, but partly also, perhaps, in recognition of its readiness to serve as a place of refuge for Jews, if not as a place of residence. Moreover, the Zionists returned to Basel for several subsequent congresses. See Theodor Nordmann, *Geschichte der Juden in Basel: Jubilaeumsschrift der Israelitischen Gemeinschaft Basel aus Anlass des 150-jährigen Bestehens 5565-5715, 1805-1955* (n.p., n.d.)

66. *SNZ,* 6 May 1843. As reported in the Paris weekly *L'Illustration* (3 January 1846), the Strasbourg-Basel line was the first of a series of railway lines that the Basel merchant class intended to finance. It was to be completed by the Central line, "linking the south with the north and west, the railways of Italy with those of Germany and France." The arrival of the first train was the occasion, according to *L'Illustration* of a citywide celebration, in the course of which "M. le Bourguemestre Burckhardt" made a speech, in French, calling for consolidation of the bonds between Basel and the cities of Alsace. There were receptions, a banquet at the Casino, and a concert in the theater.

Chapter Two

1. Paul Burckhard pointed out that between 1529 and 1798 only four genuine artisans held any significant public office. Not one was ever mayor. *Geschichte der Stadt Basel* (Basel: Helbing & Lichtenhahn, 1957 [1962]), p. 72. That the names of the leading families were

well known to all the citizens is born out by a speech at the *Pädagogium* in the first half of the nineteenth century. The rector quotes the names of students in the "modern" track at the school, in order to show that the administration could have no interest in favoring the "classical" track, the sons of the *Herren* being equally distributed over both tracks. *Lehrplan des Pädagogiums für das Schuljahr 1840 auf 1841*, "Jahresbericht," pp. 18–20.

2. The British envoy to the Swiss cantons in the early years of the eighteenth century distinguished between six "democratical," predominantly rural cantons and seven that were "aristocratical" and urban. Government in the latter had also been originally in the hands of the citizens, but having made "great acquisitions of territory," they were seen to have become "aristocratical." Among the seven, there were differences: "In the cantons of Zurich, Bazil and Schaffhausen, the meaner sort of citizens, and companies of tradesmen, who are divided into tribes [guilds], have their part of the government, and are elected by their tribes into the Sovereign Council; but in those of Berne, Lucerne, Fribourg and Soleurre, the little council have the sole right of filling up vacancies in the Sovereign Council . . . ; and as these persons always choose their relations and friends to supply these vacancies, the common tradesmen and citizens are, by that method, almost excluded from having any share in the sovereign power" (Abraham Stanyan, *An Account of Switzerland. Written in the Year 1714* [Edinburgh: Hamilton, Balfour & Neil, 1756], pp. 64–66). The author conceded, however, that this difference "is not very essential" and that seems to be a fair judgment, for in the guild cities also, the *Ratsherren*, who were elected for life, filled whatever vacancies occurred by selecting replacements from the leadership of the guilds of which they themselves were prominent members. That leadership, in turn, was not elected by all the members of the guilds, but replaced itself. See René Teuteberg, *Basler Geschichte* (Basel: Christoph Merian Verlag, 1986), pp. 235–40.

3. This has been amply demonstrated in a prosopographic study by Douglas Forsyth, *Basler Gross- und Kleinräte 1814 bis 1846* (unpublished seminar paper at University of Basel).

4. *Human Life, or Practical Ethics*, 2 vols. (Boston: James Munroe, 1842), 2:235, 247, 252–57.

5. Ibid., pp. 258–59, 269. Writing from an earlier liberal perspective, Montesquieu had also criticized Roman patriotism as essentially aggressive.

6. Forsyth (see note 3 above) has shown that these *Juristen*, of whom Karl Burckhardt and Andreas Heusler are typical examples, were considerably younger than the majority of the *Kaufleute* and the few *Handwerker* in the Senate. Heusler in turn appears to have had a hand in preparing the young Bachofen for what was to have been a career in public service, since Bachofen followed in Heusler's footsteps by studying in London and Cambridge.

7. Cf. Eduard His, *Basler Handelsherren des 19. Jahrhunderts* (Basel: Schwabe, 1929), p. 179:

> A peculiar trait of the Basel merchants may have been that from earliest times they were not as politically ambitious as the leading commercial citizens of other cantons. All the representatives of the Basel business class we have discussed here did serve the community in various positions and offices; but they did not typically strive to enhance economic influence with political power. That may be due to the fact that the canton of Basel-City, geographically the smallest canton in Switzerland, never had much of a say in the democratic majority system of the Confederation and did not weigh much in the political scales, resembling in this respect the city-canton of Geneva, which, not much bigger, was important economically and culturally. . . . When the Basel merchants spoke out on Confederation issues, they did so chiefly as pure businessmen, without much emphasis on party politics. This also protected them from

the destructive political activity, which we often observe among the unhesitating practitioners of power politics from large cantons, and which has done much damage to Switzerland and to peaceful relations among the members of the Confederation.

This is obviously not a mere description of the Basel *Handelsherren;* it also echoes, in the 1920s, the indifference to politics that it purported to describe.

8. This appears to have been the case of the Passavants, for instance, who were converted to the Reformed faith *after* they came to Basel.

9. See Andreas Staehelin, "Gold aus Seide," in *Schaffendes Basel: 2000 Jahre Basler Wirtschaft,* ed. Hansrudolf Schwabe (Basel: Birkhäuser, 1957), pp. 102–17; Heinz Polivka, *Die chemische Industrie im Raume von Basel* (Basel: Helbing & Lichtenhahn, 1974), pp. 29–30; Peter Stolz, *Basler Wirtschaft in vor- und frühindustrieller Zeit* (Zurich: Schulthess Polygraphischer Verlag, 1977), p. 150.

10. Werner Kaegi, *Jacob Burckhardt: eine Biographie* (Basel: Schwabe, 1947–1982), 7:112–13.

11. See Christopher R. Friedrichs, "The Swiss and German City-States," in *The City-State in Five Cultures,* ed. Robert Griffeth and Carol G. Thomas (Santa Barbara: ABC-Clio, and Oxford: Clio, 1981), p. 125.

12. *Das Bürgerhaus in der Schweiz,* published by the Swiss Union of Architects and Engineers (Zurich, Leipzig, and Berlin: Art Institute Orell Füssli), vol. 17 (1926), p. ix. Vols. 17, 22, 23 are devoted to Basel-Stadt.

13. Alfred Bürgin, *Geschichte des Geigy-Unternehmens von 1758 bis 1939* (Basel: Kommissionsverlag Birkhäuser, 1958), p. 116. According to Eduard His, the Basel elite remained open to *homines novi* right into the nineteenth century (*Basler Handelsherren,* pp. 182–83).

14. On this episode, see Kaegi, *Jacob Burckhardt,* 3:233–49. In the consolidation of family fortunes through marriage, there were inevitably personal tragedies, exceptional and memorable cases that had the effect of confirming the rule. Benjamin Constant told of hearing one such story, which occurred shortly before his visit to Basel in 1811, from a relative of one of the parties, Marguerite-Elisabeth Faesch-Passavant. A daughter of Samuel Ryhiner, the cotton manufacturer, fell in love at the age of nineteen with a Passavant, but her father had other plans for her. The daughter tried to submit to her father's wishes and was engaged to the man he had in mind for her. But she soon fell sick and began to pine away. The engagement had to be broken off and within a short time she died. Many people believed she had taken poison. Ryhiner was so affected by his daughter's death that the following year he declined the office of *Bürgermeister.* Benjamin Constant, *Journeaux intimes,* in *Oeuvres* (Paris: Pleiade, 1957), p. 677 and note, p. 1548. (Constant's editor remarks that in 1957 the story was still part of the Ryhiner family's oral history.)

15. Marcel Godet *et al., eds., Dictionnaire historique et biographique de la Suisse,* 7 vols. and supplement (Neuchâtel: Administration du Dictionnaire, 1921–1934), 1:540–41.

16. Quoted by Eduard His, *Geschichte der Historischen und Antiquarischen Gesellschaft zu Basel, 1836–1936* (Basel: Karl Werner, 1936), p. 3.

17. J. R. Schinz, *Die vergnügte Schweizreise* (1773), quoted in Eugen A. Meier, *Freud und Leid: kuriöse und seriöse, erheiternde und erschütternde Geschichten aus dem alten Basel und seiner Umgebung von den Anfängen der Stadt bis zum Untergang des Ancien Regime (1798),* 2 vols. (Basel: Birkhäuser, 1983), 2:228.

18. Christian Gottlieb Schmidt, *Von der Schweiz: Journal meiner Reise von 5 Julius 1786 bis den 7 August 1787,* ed. T. and H. Solfinger (Bern and Stuttgart: Paul Haupt, 1985), pp. 199–200.

19. Daniel Scherer, *Verzeichnuss dessen, was seith Anno 1620 in E. Ehren Burgerschafft*

dieser Lobl. Statt Basel und dero Gebieth under den Underthanen Denckwürdiges erhebt und zuge-tragen, quoted in Meier, *Freud und Leid,* 2:57–58. On the high point and the decline in student enrollment, see Edgar Bonjour, *Die Universität Basel 1460–1960,* 2nd ed. (Basel: Helbing & Lichtenhahn, 1971), pp. 242–44. Professor Andreas Staehelin, archivist of Basel State and the author of several studies of the University and its professors, told me in an interview with him on June 18, 1984, that public concern about the University dated only from 1833, when the survival of the institution came into question. "Before that, the merchants were not very interested in it."

20. C. G. Küttner, *Briefe eines Sachsen aus der Schweiz* (1785), in Meier, *Freud und Leid,* 2:66. Cf. Schmidt, *Von der Schweiz,* pp. 199–200: "You are hardly aware that there is a university here, though it is one of the oldest in Europe. It has eighteen professors and about a hundred students, who are lost among the inhabitants like a drop of wine in a large pitcher." Similarly, one reads in J. G. Zimmermann's *Letters to Haller:* "Je n'ai point vu d'université où il y ait moins d'activité que dans ce Bâle. Les professeurs l'avouent eux-mêmes et ils ne sont point surpris si pendant cinq ans ils n'ont point de disciple" (quoted in Bonjour, *Die Universität Basel 1460–1960,* p. 253). On the long-standing relation between the University of Basel and Hungarian Protestants, see Bonjour, pp. 230–31.

21. On salaries, see Bonjour, *Die Universität Basel 1460–1960,* pp. 250–51.

22. See Andreas Miller, *Struktur und soziale Funktion der Universität Basel* (Winterthur, P. G. Keller, 1955), p. 15. C. G. Küttner reported in 1785 that selection of professors by lot (from the three top candidates), introduced to prevent nepotism, resulted in a lowering of standards, since decisions were made by chance rather than according to merit. Maier, *Freud und Leid,* 2:66. Edgar Bonjour has pointed out that the decline of the institution had little to do with this appointment procedure. Competition from newer universities, the extension of Catholicism in the population, and the cost of living in Basel all contributed to reducing the number of students; that in turn led to a reduction in course offerings, which further reduced the attractiveness of the University to students. Bonjour, *Die Universität Basel 1460–1960,* p. 249.

23. J. H. Campe, *Aus einer Reise von Hamburg in die Schweiz in August 1785* (1886), in Meier, *Freud und Leid,* 2:73–74.

24. Helen Maria Williams, *A Tour in Switzerland, or The Present State of the Government and Manners of those Cantons,* 2 vols. (London: J. G. & G. Robinson, 1798), 1:115, 1:9. It is not clear how Helen Williams obtained her information about what went on in Basel's all-male smoking clubs. It is corroborated, however, by the German traveler Christian Gottlieb Schmidt, who reported in 1786 that, though he had met a few outstanding personalities, "the general tone of social life must be considered extremely dull. The men go every day to their *Kämmerli,* abandoning their womenfolk to boredom or at best weekly social visits. These *Kämmerli* are private societies of twenty to thirty people. They usually meet in one of the guild houses, between five and eight in the evening, smoke, and drink tea and wine" (*Von der Schweiz,* pp. 198–99).

25. Emil J. Walter, *Soziale Grundlagen der Entwicklung der Naturwissenschaften in der alten Schweiz* (Bern: Franke, 1958), p. 233; see also Paul Burckhardt, *Geschichte der Stadt Basel,* pp. 82–86.

26. H. C. Peyer, "Zürich und Übersee um die Wende von 18. zum 19. Jahrhundert," in *Beiträge zur Wirtschafts- und Stadtgeschichte: Festschrift für Hektor Ammann,* ed. Hermann Aubin et al. (Wiesbaden: F. Steiner, 1965), pp. 205–19; also id., "Basel in der Zürcher Wirtschaftsgeschichte," *Basler Zeitschrift für Geschichte und Altertumskunde* 69 (1969): 223–37.

27. Thus in 1808 Johann Jacob Bachofen senior, the father of the philologist, was em-

ployed by the Bergamo silk spinning firm of Angelo Riccardi; in the 1830s and 1840s his sons Carl and Wilhelm served apprenticeships in London and New York, respectively. R. Forcart-Bachofen and F. Vischer-Ehinger, *Chronik der Familie Bachofen in Basel* (Basel: Birkhäuser, 1911).

28. Frau Adeline Bischoff-Buxdorff, quoted by Gertrud Lendorff, *Kleine Geschichte der Baslerin* (Basel and Stuttgart: Birkhäuser, 1968), p. 150.

29. From Thurneysen's press, in the last decades of the eighteenth century, came fine editions of Blair (*Lectures on Rhetoric*), Bolingbroke (*Letters on the Study and Use of History, Remarks on the History of England*), Burke (*Of the Sublime and the Beautiful*), Clarendon (*History of the Rebellion*), Ferguson (*Essay on the History of Civil Society* and the less-well-known *History of the Progress and Termination of the Roman Republic*), Hume (*Essays, History of England*), Kames (*Elements of Criticism, Sketches of the History of Man*), Millar (*Origin of the Distinction of Ranks*), Robertson (*History of the Emperor Charles V, History of America, History of Scotland*), Smith (*Wealth of Nations, Theory of Moral Sentiments*), Sterne (*Tristam Shandy, A Sentimental Journey*), Sir James Stewart (*Inquiry into the Principles of Political Economy*), the complete plays of Shakespeare in 23 volumes and the complete works of Pope in 9, and above all, the Thurneysen press's great success, Gibbon's *Decline and Fall of the Roman Empire*. See Martin Germann, *Johann Jakob Thurneyesen der Jüngere 1754–1803* (Basel and Stuttgart: Helbing & Lichtenhahn, 1973).

30. Emil Walter, *Soziale Grundlagen der Entwicklung der Naturwissenschaften in der alten Schweiz* (Bern: Francke: 1958), p. 217.

31. Ibid., p. 233; see also Staehelin, "Gold aus Seide," p. 117.

32. Cited in Miller, *Struktur und soziale Funktion,* pp. 15–17.

33. Paul Fink, *Geschichte der Basler Bandindustrie 1550–1800* (Basel and Frankfurt am Main: Helbing & Lichtenhahn, 1983), p. 64 (Basler Beiträge zur Geschichtswissenschaft, 147).

34. Lévy-Boyer, *Les Banques européennes et l'industrialisation internationale dans la première moitié du XIX siècle* (Paris: Presses universitaires de France, 1964), p. 61.

35. Ibid., p. 135. Basel had a virtual monopoly of the production of spun silk from waste; no other center in Switzerland approached it in volume or value.

36. See *The Economic Organisation of Early Modern Europe,* ed. E. E. Rich and C. H. Wilson, vol. 5 of *The Cambridge Economic History of Europe* (Cambridge: Cambridge University Press, 1977), p. 520.

37. C. G. Küttner (1785), in Meier, *Freud und Leid,* 2:71–72.

38. Lévy-Boyer, *Les Banques européennes,* pp. 51–61.

39. The Bachofens' choice of Roslin indicates that they were well informed as well as ambitious. The Swedish-born artist was highly prized for society portraits. Diderot related that he beat out Greuze for a commission to paint the La Rochefoucauld family and that the completed work was valued at fifteen thousand francs at the Salon of the Paris Académie Royale in 1765. Diderot judged it severely—"Jamais composition ne fut plus sotte, plus plate et plus triste. . . . L'on donneroit toute chose à un homme de goût pour l'accepter, qu'il n'en voudroit point" (*Salons,* ed. J. Seznec and J. Adhémar, 4 vols. [Oxford: Clarendon Press, 1957–1967], 2:124)—objecting that Roslin was far more interested in rendering silks, satins, and embroidery than in representing human situations. In that domain, however, he conceded that Roslin was outstanding: "Il faut avouer qu'il y a des étoffes, des draperies . . . de la plus grande vérité. Ce satin, par exemple . . . est on ne peut mieux de mollesse, de couleur, de reflets et de plis. . . . Roslin est aujourd'hui un aussi bon brodeur que Carles Vanloo fut autrefois un grand teinturier" (pp. 125–26). He ought to limit himself "aux étoffes, aux broderies, aux dentelles" (p. 127). Diderot summed up his judgment of Roslin in the "Etat

actuel de l'Ecole française" at the end of the "Salon" of 1767: "Assez bon portraitiste; mais il ne faut pas qu'il sorte de là. Il excelle dans l'imitation des étoffes" (*Salons*, 3:317). The portrait of Margaretha Bachofen-Heitz, presently in a private collection in Basel, is reproduced in Staehelin, "Gold aus Seide," p. 113.

40. Daniel Burckhardt-Werthemann, "Die Baslerischen Kunstsammler des 18. Jahrhunderts," *Basler Kunstverein: Berichterstattung*, 1906, pp. 75–7.

41. Kaegi, *Jacob Burckhardt*, 7:114.

42. As the *Herren* owned the looms, however, and rented them out to the cottagers, there was some fixed capital investment, even before the introduction of factory production in the city in the 1840s.

43. *"Commissions- und Speditionshandel"* in German. On these, see Herman van der Wee in *The Cambridge Economic History of Europe*, 5:354–56.

44. Fink, *Geschichte der Basler Bandindustrie*, pp. 74–75.

45. Ibid., pp. 76–77. See also Heinz Polivka, *Die chemische Industrie im Raume von Basel* (Basel: Helbing & Lichtenhahn, 1974), p. 37 (Basler Beiträge zur Geographie, 16).

46. August Püntener, *Das schweizerische Bankwesen* (Bern and Suttgart: Paul Haupt, 1977), p. 14.

47. *Murray's Handbook for Travellers in Switzerland*, 7th ed. (London: John Murray, 1856), p. 4.

48. *Journal*, ed. Paul Viallaneix (Paris: Gallimard, 1959), 1:529.

49. Lévy-Boyer, *Les Banques européennes*, p. 454 note, about the year 1837.

50. Ibid., pp. 349–50, 450–51, 454–55, 469, 471, 592, 705 note; see also Max Ikle, *Die Schweiz als internationaler Bank- und Finanzplatz* (Zurich: Orell Füssli, 1970), pp. 21–23; H. C. Peyer, "Basel in der Zürcher Wirtschaftsgeschichte," *Basler Zeitschrift für Geschichte und Altertumskunde* 69 (1969): 223–37.

51. See "Neue Zeit, Neue Wirtschaft" in *Schaffendes Basel*, pp. 136–53.

52. E. Fueter, *Die Schweiz seit 1848: Geschichte, Politik, Wirtschaft* (Zurich and Leipzig: Orell Füssli, 1928), p. 16.

53. He defined these as citizens worth from ten thousand to fifty thousand pounds.

54. *Freimüthige Gedanken über die Entvölkerung unserer Vaterstadt*, Basel, 1758, pp. 14–15. Basel University Library, E. J. IV 31.

55. Stolz, *Basler Wirtschaft in vor- und frühindustrieller Zeit*, pp. 147–48.

56. C. G. Küttner, a traveler from Saxony, marvelled at the wealth of Basel's merchants. "You have hardly any idea of the wealth in Basel," he tells his fictional correspondent. "There are several families here whose fortune is generally held to be a million Basel gulden . . . about 600,000 Saxon thalers . . . or more. . . . A considerable number of families have fortunes of 200,000–300,000 gulden and nobody with 100,000 gulden would even be considered rich" (C. G. Küttner [1785], in Meier, *Freud und Leid*, 2:73).

57. Ibid.

58. *Das Bürgerhaus in der Schweiz*, 22:viii, xix.

59. The late-eighteenth-century author (Hentzi) of *Promenade pittoresque dans l'évêché de Bâle* regretted that in Basel all the handsome new buildings were not grouped together in a single elegant section of the city as in Genoa or Amsterdam. "Nevertheless," he conceded, "there are a few parts of Basel that are rich in fine houses, among them the Rittergasse, the Sankt Johannsvorstadt, the Sankt Albanvorstadt, the Münsterplatz and the Petersplatz. If it were possible to assemble in one place all these large and comfortable houses, with their *portes cochères*, their coach houses, their fountains and beautiful gardens, they would constitute a whole that would merit comparison with the Faubourg Saint-Germain in Paris, the former quarter of the *haute noblesse* and of millionaires" (quoted in *Das Bürgerhaus in der Schweiz*, 22:xxii).

60. Samuel von Brunn, *Chronik vieler merckwürdiger Geschichten . . .* , in Meier, *Freud und Leid,* 2:56.

61. *Das Bürgerhaus in der Schweiz,* 22:viii, xiii.

62. Ibid., pp. vii, xiii, xix.

63. The Bachofens, for instance, also owned many properties in the city and the surrounding countryside.

64. On houses as a form of investment in this period, see Herman van der Wee in *The Cambridge Economic History of Europe,* 5:355.

65. Thus, for instance, the Augustinerhof, acquired by J. J. Merian-de Bary, passed, doubtless through a daughter, to J. J. Bischoff-Merian, then through a daughter of Bischoff-Merian to Martin Berneshardt-Bischoff; the Haus Zum Delphin, sold to Franz Christ-Frey in 1815, passed by way of a daughter to Emanuel Ryhiner-Christ in 1828, then to Eduard His-Heusler in 1860 and in 1905 to Karl Vondermühll-His.

66. In this way the Ritterhof on the Rittergasse, built by Remigius Frey around 1748, was sold three years later to Franz De Bary. Sandgrube, built for Achilles Leissler in the mid-century, was sold in 1795 to J. J. Burckhardt-Keller and again in 1804 to J. J. Merian-Wieland. Samuel Burckhardt's Holsteinerhof of about 1752 was sold in 1767 to Albert Ochs, who had just returned to Basel from Hamburg. In 1801, it was sold again to J. C. Burckhardt-Ryhiner. The palace-like Zum goldenen Löwen on the Aeschenvorstadt was renovated and modernized by the Legrands in 1775 and sold four years later to Christoph Burckhardt-Frey. The Haus zum Delphin on the Rittergasse, rebuilt by J. A. Huber in the late 1760s, was sold to Christoph Merian-Hoffmann in 1803 and sold again twelve years later to Franz Christ-Frey. Even the most sumptuous of all the Basel townhouses, the Weisses Haus and the Blaues Haus, built by Lucas and Jacob Sarasin on a prime site on the Rheinsprung in 1763–1769, were subject to sale. The Weisses Haus was sold on Jacob Sarasin's death in 1805 and resold in 1811 to J. J. Bachofen and Son.

67. Burckhardt-Werthemann, "Die Baslerischen Kunstsammler," 1901, pp. 3–69 and 1902, pp. 71–116.

68. Forcart-Bachofen and Vischer-Ehinger, *Chronik der Familie Bachofen,* 73–89; see also Burckhardt-Werthemann, "Die Baslerischen Kunstsammler," 1902, pp. 73–88.

69. As the first really rich member of the family, Martin Bachofen, for example, is said to have collected more out of desire to establish his standing than out of any love of painting. Burckhardt-Werthemann, "Die Baslerischen Kunstsammler," 1902, p. 80. In his "Salon of 1767," Diderot described the financial considerations motivating contemporary art patrons and collectors: "Here is how most of the wealthy men who keep artists busy reason: 'The money I am investing in drawings by Boucher, paintings by Vernet, Casanove, and Loutherbourg will have been invested at the highest possible rate of interest. Throughout my life I shall be able to enjoy a first-rate work of art. The artist will die; and my children and I will be able, if we wish, to realize twenty times the sum originally paid for his work.' This reasoning is thoroughly sound. That is why heirs have absolutely no objection to this way of making use of the wealth they can barely wait to inherit." The work of art is thus "an object that [wealthy individuals] can leave to their children, their heirs, just like any other valuable asset in their estate" (*Salons,* 3:53–54). In the same "Salon," which, like all his other annual reviews of the Paris Academy's exhibitions, appeared in Grimm's privately circulated *Correspondance littéraire,* Diderot himself strongly recommended a Vernet: "A father, who has children to think of and is moderately well-to-do, would make a wise investment by purchasing it. He would be able to enjoy it in his own lifetime and thirty years from now, when Vernet is no more, he will have invested his money at a very good rate of interest" (p. 161).

70. Burckhardt-Werthemann, "Die Baslerischen Kunstsammler," 1901, pp. 29, 32, 40–41, 43, 59.

71. Ibid., 1902, pp. 81–87.
72. Schmidt, *Von der Schweiz*, p. 197.
73. Coxe, *Travels in Switzerland and in the Country of the Grisons in a Series of Letters to William Melmoth, Esq.*, 4th rev. ed., 4 vols. (London: Cadell & Davies, 1801 [1st ed. 1778]), 1:163.
74. See articles on both Mechel and Birmann by D. Burckhardt in *Schweizerisches Künstlerlexikon*, ed. Carl Brun (Frauenfeld: Hubner, 1905–1917).
75. According to the art historian Lukas Gloor, twenty-five hundred people paid to visit this exhibition, which ran for three weeks. "Die Geschichte des Basler Kunstvereins von 1839 bis 1908," in *Die Geschichte des Basler Kunstvereins und der Kunsthalle Basel 1839–1988*, ed. L. Gloor, T. Kellein, and M. Suter (Basel: Kunsthalle Basel, Schwabe & Co., 1989), pp. 21–22. The total population of the city at the time was twenty-five thousand.
76. See Burckhardt-Werthemann, "Die Baslerischen Kunstsammler," 1901, pp. 3–69, 1902, pp. 71–116.
77. On this episode, see Margarethe Pfister-Burkhalter, "Böcklins Basler Museumsfresken," in *Arnold Böcklin 1827–1901* (Basel and Stuttgart: Schwabe, 1977), pp. 69–80.

Chapter Three
1. Werner Kaegi, *Jacob Burckhardt: eine Biographie* (Basel: Schwabe, 1947–1982), 1:80–81.
2. See René Teuteberg, *Basler Geschichte* (Basel: Christoph Merian Verlag, 1986), pp. 266–70. On the service in the Cathedral on January 22, 1798, which opened the Festival of Brotherly Unity and which was followed that evening by a great ball given by "citizen" Lucas Sarasin in the Blaues Haus, see Gertrud Lendorff, *Kleine Geschichte der Baslerin* (Basel and Stuttgart: Birkhäuser, 1966), pp. 127–28. Even the radical Helen Williams, otherwise so critical of the narrowness of the Baslers, reported that "Mr. Le Grand, member of the great council, an ardent and enlightened friend of the French Republic, had taught his infants to lisp the cherished sounds of liberty, and chaunt its favorite airs with such fond enthusiasm, that his house seemed a chapel worthy of William Tell" (*A Tour in Switzerland, or a View of the Present State of the Government and Manners of those Cantons*, 2 vols. [London: G. G. & J. Robinson, 1798], 1:117–18).
3. See Lendorff, *Kleine Geschichte der Baslerin*, p. 174. According to Lendorff, "It was the women themselves who jealously stood guard to prevent marriages between persons belonging to different circles."
4. For an excellent portrait of Sarasin, see Alfred Bürgin, *Geschichte des Geigy-Unternehmens von 1758 bis 1939* ((Basel: Kommissionsverlag Birkhäuser, 1958), pp. 37–39. A contemporary German traveler reported that Sarasin was a devotee of Cagliostro, whom he credited with having saved the life of his ailing wife, and that he had instructed his London banker to provide Cagliostro with whatever funds he might need during his stay in England. Christian Gottlieb Schmidt, *Von der Schweiz: Journal meiner Reise von 5 Julius bis den 7 August 1787*, ed. T. and H. Solfinger (Bern and Stuttgart: Paul Haupt, 1985), p. 195.
5. Williams, *A Tour in Switzerland*, 1:115–18.
6. Paul Siegfried, *Geschichte der Gemeinnützigen Gesellschaft in Basel 1777–1926* (Basel: Schwabe, n.d.). Merchants—and their wives—sometimes attended lectures in history or the sciences at the University, even if their interest was not usually deep. Schmidt, *Von der Schweiz*, p. 200.
7. *Vorträge welche bey den öffentlichen Prüfungen der Zöglinge der Bernoullischen Lehranstalt am 6. und 7. April 1807 gehalten wurden* (Basel University Library, Ki. Ar. G.IV.11, no. 14). See also Bürgin, *Geschichte des Geigy-Unternehmens*.

8. *Notices sur la Ville et le Canton de Basle pour l'instruction des Voyageurs* (Basel: Samuel Flick, n.d. [probably 1811]), pp. 11–13 (Basel University Library, Falk 3177).

9. To everyone's surprise, the popular vote at Basel (that is to say, the direct vote of the citizens) turned out to be strongly in favor of the new Constitution (1,364 for, 186 against). In the *Rat,* or Great Council, it was a somewhat different story. Almost half of the members stayed away on the day of the decisive vote. According to Paul Burckhardt, the Constitution was accepted by the *Ratsherren* "without enthusiasm, in weary resignation, and with the feeling that the long-established independence of Basel was now coming to an end" (*Geschichte der Stadt Basel* [Basel: Helbing & Lichtenhahn, 1957], p. 253). See also Teuteberg, *Basler Geschichte,* p. 324.

10. Maurice Lévy-Boyer, *Les Banques européennes et l'industrialisation internatioinale dans la première moitié du XIX siècle* (Paris: Presses universitaires de France, 1964), p. 451, note.

11. Burckhardt, *Geschichte der Stadt Basel,* pp. 213–24.

12. On the "liberalism" of the students in the *Burschenschaften,* see Golo Mann, *The History of Germany since 1789* (Harmondsworth: Penguin Books, 1974 [orig. German 1958]), p. 103.

13. See De Wette, *Human Life, or Practical Ethics,* trans. Samuel Osgood, 2 vols. (Boston: James Munroe, 1842), lecture XVIII ("Sociality and Public Spirit"); see also translator's preface, 1:xvii. Osgood surmised that De Wette had ruffled some feathers at Basel: "Basel is nominally republican in its government. . . . Yet, unless that city is much misrepresented by travelers, the sentiments expressed in these lectures must have attacked some of the prejudices and rebuked many of the pretensions of certain classes in Basel." The most conservative circles at Basel may well have been alarmed by De Wette's public expression of his "liberal" views, but as "a conservative reformer" (Osgood's description), De Wette was in fact completely in tune with the ideology of the Basel governments of the time. "So far as respect for law and the great civil, domestic, and religious institutions, is concerned, our author is strenuously conservative" (ibid.).

14. Albert Teichmann, ed., *Die Universität Basel in den fünfzig Jahren seit ihrer Reorganisation im Jahre 1835* (Basel: Schultz'sche Universitätsdruckerei [L. Reinhardt], 1885). On Snell and Follen, and on the "liberals" of the time in general, see Heinrich von Treitschke, *History of Germany in the Nineteenth Century,* trans. Eden and Cedar Paul (New York: McBride, Nast, 1917), 3:68–76, 170–74.

15. Teichmann, *Die Universität Basel in den fünfzig Jahren seit ihrer Reorganisation,* pp. 62–63. On Freiburg, see Erwin Schombs, "Von der Landesuniversität zum tertiären Bildungssystem," in *Stadt und Hochschule im 19. und 20. Jahrhundert,* ed. Erich Maschke and Jürgen Sydow (Sigmaringen: Jan Thorbecke Verlag, 1979), p. 13, note 20. According to Burckhardt, there were only twenty-eight students at the University of Basel when he began to teach there in 1843 (letter to Kinkel, 24 November 1843). Kaegi noted that even in the year when Burckhardt returned to Basel after a stint at the Federal Polytechnic in Zurich (1858), only eleven students were enrolled in the philosophical faculty, which, at that time, included the natural sciences. Kaegi, *Jacob Burckhardt,* 2:332, note 101.

16. Cited by Andreas Staehelin, *Geschichte der Universität Basel 1818–1835* (Basel: Helbing & Lichtenhahn, 1959), p. 129.

17. Treitschke, *History of Germany in the Nineteenth Century,* 3:176–78. In addition, some German states, particularly the southern ones, regarded the Carlsbad Decrees as incompatible with their sovereignty and did not carry them out. Mann, *History of Germany since 1789,* p. 105.

18. In fact, Basel's defense of Snell and Follen rested on shaky ground. The two men had not told the whole truth. Follen at least had been working with various secret societies from

the safety of Swiss soil. Fearing that the Basel authorities might get wind of this and yield to the pressure of Prussia, Austria, and the Confederation itself, he fled the city in late 1824, with the help of some Basel friends, and embarked for America, where he became the first professor of German at Harvard College in 1830. See Staehelin, *Geschichte der Universität Basel 1818–1835*, p. 49. Treitschke painted a portrait of Follen as a sinister Svengali figure, far more cynical and politically shrewd than the enthusiastic and misguided young students he manipulated. Treitschke, *History of Germany in the Nineteenth Century*, 3:69–79, 170.

19. The anecdote is reported by C. A. Bernoulli, *Franz Overbeck und Friedrich Nietzsche: eine Freundschaft*, 2 vols. (Jena: E. Diederichs, 1908), 1:41.

20. "Die religiöse Physiognomie Basels in der ersten Hälfte dieses Jahrhunderts," *Basler Nachrichten*, 4, 6, 11–13 June 1873; issue of 6 June.

21. See Hagenbach, "Die religiöse Physiognomie Basels"; see also Samuel Taylor, "The Enlightenment in Switzerland," in *The Enlightenment in National Context*, ed. Roy Porter and Mikulas Teich (Cambridge: Cambridge University Press, 1981), pp. 72–89.

22. On the Eglise française as "Kirche der beau monde" etc., see C. G. Küttner, *Briefe eines Sachsen aus der Schweiz* (1785), in Eugen A. Meier, *Freud und Leid: kuriöse und seriöse, erheiternde und erschütternde Geschichten aus dem alten Basel und seiner Umgebung von den Anfängen der Stadt bis zum Untergang des Ancien Regime (1798)*, 2 vols. (Basel: Birkhäuser, 1983), 2:176; on the membership, see L. Junod, *Histoire de l'Eglise française de Bâle* (Lausanne: Bridel, 1868), p. 43.

23. A collection of sermons from the period 1803–1805 in the university library at Basel (Ki. Ar. G.iv.11) contains pieces by a Faesch, a Falkeisen, a Merian, and a Von Speyr. Among the Basel pastors listed by Karl Gauss in his *Basilea Reformata* (Basel: Verlag der historischen und antiquarischen Gesellschaft, 1930), there are Battiers, Bernoullis, Berris, Bischoffs, Burckhardts (at least twenty-four), Faesches, Freys, Heuslers, Hoffmanns, Iselins, Jungs, La Roches, Merians (at least fifteen), Meyers, Paravicinis, Passavants, Preiswerks, Respingers, Ryhiners, Sarasins, Socins, Staehelins (thirteen), Thurneysens, Von Speyrs, Werenfels, and Wettsteins.

24. G. P. H. Normann, *Geographisch-statistische Darstellung des Schweizerlandes*, Hamburg, 1786, quoted by Lendorff, *Kleine Geschichte der Baslerin*, p. 125. Similarly, according to Schmidt, *Von der Schweiz*, p. 200: "Most of the preachers are Herrnhuter, so they do not study, but rely on inspiration."

25. According to Professor Andreas Staehelin, State Archivist of Basel, pietism was not confined to separatist sects but had penetrated the church itself. In addition, many of the manufacturers and merchants had been touched by it and contributed to various pietist foundations. See "Das geistige Basel," in *Basel: eine illustrierte Stadtgeschichte*, ed. Eugen A. Meier (Basel: Helbing & Lichtenhahn, 1969), pp. 51–72, at pp. 62–64.

26. Thomas Burckhardt-Biedermann, *Geschichte des Gymnasiums zu Basel* (Basel: Birkhäuser, 1889), pp. 202–3.

27. *Basler Nachrichten*, 4 June 1873. Cf. Traugott Geering, *Handel und Industrie der Stadt Basel: Zunftwesen und Industriegeschichte bis zum Ende des XVII Jahrhunderts* (Basel: Felix Schneider, 1886), pp. 593–95. Geering argues that the leading families reinforced their economic domination through their control of the University and of the community's theologians.

28. Hagenbach, "Die religiöse Physiognomie Basels," *Basler Nachrichten*, 6 June 1873.

29. In *Buddenbrooks*, Thomas Mann represents this change vividly as the passage from the worldly irreverence of old Johann (Jean) Buddenbrook, with his skepticism, his courtly ways, and his French phrases, to the earnestness, religious concerns, and faith in Providence of his son, Consul Johann Buddenbrook, Jr.

30. In his Annual Report for 1819, the Director of the Missionsschule gave thanks for the support of "our dear friend Herr Benedikt Laroche"—apparently a member of the wealthy La Roche family, if not the Benedikt La Roche who later organized the federal postal service. Basel University Library, Falk. 3185.

31. Article "Basel," in *Allgemeine Encyclopädie der Wissenschaften und Künste*, ed. J. S. Ersch and J. G Gruber (Leipzig: J. D. Gleditsch, 1818–1819), 8:16–21.

32. Hagenbach, "Die religiöse Physiognomie Basels," *Basler Nachrichten*, 11 June 1873.

33. Quoted by Wilhelm Pauck, *The Heritage of the Reformation*, rev. ed. (Glencoe: Free Press, 1961), p. 119.

34. Hagenbach, "Die religiöse Physiognomie Basels," *Basler Nachrichten*, 4 June 1873.

35. Ibid., 12 June 1873.

36. Friedrich Engels recounts that at Barmen Pietism had likewise made deep inroads among manufacturers and artisans. The son of a prominent textile manufacturer, he himself had been "brought up in the most extreme orthodoxy and piety" (letter to W. Graeber, 30 July 1839, in Karl Marx and Friedrich Engels, *Collected Works* [New York: International Publishers, 1975], 2:466). His collected works include a fervent poetic outpouring of religious sentiment composed at the age of seventeen (ibid., pp. 555–56). Only a few years later, however, in his *Letters from Wuppertal*, Engels gave a scathing account of the effects of Pietism in the Lutheran and Reformed communities of Barmen and Elberfeld in the late 1830s (letters 1 and 2, ibid., pp. 7–22; see also letter to Graeber, April 1839, ibid., pp. 446–47). According to Engels, the merchant elite of the Hanseatic city of Bremen appears to have been as troubled as the Basel elite by the excessive factionalism of the religious groups; after a particularly provocative sermon the fiery preacher W. F. Krummacher was prohibited from engaging in any further missionary activity in the city (ibid., pp. 121, 126–27).

37. Cited in Jenny, "Wie De Wette nach Basel kam," *Basler Jahrbuch*, 1941, pp. 51–78, at p. 61.

38. Letter of 1807, quoted by Kaegi, *Jacob Burckhardt*, 1:130–31.

39. The complete separation of church and state was carried through only at the end of the first decade of the twentieth century.

40. *Schweizerische National-Zeitung* (hereafter *SNZ*), 22 April 1843. In his *Letters from Switzerland* (New York: Sheldon & Co.; Boston: Gould & Lincoln, 1860), Samuel Prime notes with the satisfaction of a New England Puritan that "Basel is a goodly town, and if the people has some rigid notions of morality in the judgment of travellers of easy virtue, it is refreshing to come into a city where the shops are closed of a Sunday, and every one is required to be at home by eleven o'clock at night" (p. 10).

41. *SNZ*, 4 January 1844.

42. *Murray's Handbook for Travelers in Switzerland*, 7th ed. (London: John Murray, 1856).

43. See Lorenz Stucki, *The Secret Empire* (New York: Herder & Herder, 1971 [orig. German 1968]), pp. 121–25.

44. *SNZ*, 22 November 1842.

45. Burckhardt, *Geschichte der Stadt Basel*, pp. 228–30.

46. A well-known painting by Sebastian Gutzwiller in the Kunstmuseum (*Basler Familienkonzert*, dated 1849) provides some evidence that this tradition continued into the nineteenth century and penetrated well beyond the circles of the very well-to-do. Jacob Burckhardt, who did not come from a wealthy branch of the Burckhardt family, wrote many musical compositions in his youth and remained an ardent music lover all his life.

47. Lendorff, *Kleine Geschichte der Baslerin*, p. 116.

48. Burckhardt, *Geschichte der Stadt Basel*, p. 87. On Basel musical life, see the delightful

study by Max F. Schneider, *Musik der Neuzeit in der bildenden Kunst Basels* (Basel: Holbein Verlag, 1944).

49. *Louis Spohrs Lebenserinnerungen,* ed. Folker Gothel, 2 vols. (Tutzing: Hans Schneider, 1968), 1:223–24. See also Paul Meyer, "Basels Concertwesen 1804–1875," *Basler Jahrbuch,* 1890, p. 83.

50. Meyer, "Basels Concertwesen," p. 82.

51. Ibid., p. 89.

52. To Eduard Schauenburg, 3 October 1880, *Briefe,* ed. Max Burckhardt, 10 vols. plus index vol. (Basel: Schwabe, 1949–1994), 7:195; and to Friedrich von Preen, 2 December 1880, ibid., p. 203.

53. Burckhardt, *Geschichte der Stadt Basel,* p. 230. Eighteenth-century travelers reported that musical performances were virtually the only public events, apart from church services, attended by both men and women, and that audiences chattered constantly throughout the performances, to the annoyance of the few genuine music lovers. Schmidt, *Von der Schweiz,* p. 199.

54. To von Preen, 2 December 1880, *Briefe,* 7:203.

55. Lukas Gloor, "Geschichte des Basler *Kunstvereins von 1839 bis 1908,*" in *Die Geschichte des Basler Kunstvereins und der Kunsthalle Basel 1839–1988,* ed. L. Gloor, T. Kellein, and M. Suter (Basel: Kunsthalle Basel; Schwabe & Co., 1989), p. 15.

56. Before coming to Basel, Gerlach, who was to be a major influence on Bachofen in particular, had taught briefly at the *Kantonschule* in Aarau, one of the most thoroughly neo-humanist institutions in Switzerland. In a provocative address in 1807 on "Education to Bestiality" (*"Über die Schulbildung zur Bestialität"*), the director of the Aarau school—the fanatical Ernst August Evers, who like Gerlach had studied in Göttingen—launched a passionate attack on the ideal of vocational education. Evers distinguished sharply between "the political freedom and rational self-determination characteristic of republics and the education aimed exclusively at contentment, peace, and bourgeois success, at the mere satisfaction of need, that is to say at 'bestiality,' which he claimed was characteristic of monarchies. He identified this kind of education, which orients people only toward 'profit' and making a living, as the condition of the existence of states populated by subjects and slaves. Such an education resembled [Benjamin] Rumford's soup kitchens. With the 'yoke of authority' and the education designed to produce 'humility and poverty of spirit,' which authoritarian regimes require and in which the pursuit of knowledge can never be more than a recipe for material well-being . . . Evers contrasted the rational state, which is grounded in freedom, and the education to 'humanity,' which necessarily produces and promotes such a state" (Karl-Ernst Jeismann, *Das preussische Gymnasium in Staat und Gesellschaft* [Stuttgart: Ernst Klett, 1974], p. 233). Like Evers, Gerlach appears to have believed that the chances of recreating the culture of the classical Greek polis were greater in Switzerland than in Germany. Similarly, in his 1822–1823 public lecture series (published in English translation as *Human Life, or Practical Ethics*), De Wette gave an impassioned account of Greek and Roman patriotism, which he hoped might be revived and in some respects improved upon in Switzerland. Lamenting that, unlike the Greeks and early Romans, "we do not live in the free, sunny air of public life, which exalts and strengthens the mind" he called for "institutions and points of public union" and an awakening of "the spirit of community" (2:267–69).

57. On Müller-Burckhardt, see Kaegi, *Jacob Burckhardt,* 1:456–60.

58. See Eduard His, *Geschichte der historischen und antiquarischen Gesellschaft zu Basel, 1836–1936* (Basel: Karl Werner, 1936); on Heusler, see the useful notice in Max Burckhardt's edition of Jacob Burckhardt's *Briefe,* 2:320–21.

59. To Heinrich Meyer-Ochsner, 8 December 1867, *Gesammelte Werke* (hereafter *GW*), ed. Karl Meuli Basel: Schwabe, 1943–1967; publication interrupted at vol. 10), 10:396.

60. Letter of J. J. Bachofen, as member of the University *Curatel* or Governing Board, to J. Burckhardt offering him the chair of history, 24 January 1858, *GW,* 10:172. *"Ein gemischtes Publikum"* meant a mixed audience of men and women. As Helen Williams noted with indignation in her *Tour in Switzerland,* many social activities in Basel were exclusively male (1:7–14). The public lecture series was thus distinctive in being designed for a mixed audience.

61. Among the notables: *Ratsherr* Andreas Heusler, *Ratsherr* Felix Sarasin (a future *Bürgermeister*), *Stadtrat* J. J. Burckhardt-Ryhiner (another future *Bürgermeister*), Hieronymus Bischoff (a partner in his father's banking business, "Bischoff zu St. Alban," and future president of the Central Railway), Achilles Bischoff (owner of a textile mill in Lombardy, founder—in 1843, with J. J. Speiser—of a "Giro- und Depositenbank," and future *Nationalrat*). Among the professors: De Wette, Hagenbach, Müller, Wackernagel, Vischer-Bilfinger, Girard (Alexandre Vinet's replacement).

62. See Burckhardt's *Briefe,* letter of 1 November 1845, 2:182–84, and editor's notes.

63. To Meyer-Ochsner, 26 December 1858, *GW,* 10:184–85.

64. Williams, *A Tour in Switzerland,* 1:14.

65. To Meyer Ochsner, November 1861, *GW,* 10:248. "Pater Hebich" is Bachofen's humorous description of Samuel Hebich, a fervent missionary preacher—"a thick-nosed Swabian," according to Burckhardt, "who has been preaching to the Hindus for 25 years" and whom an extreme religious group brought to Basel in the hope of "hatching an *Erweckung* or Revival in the North American style" (letter to Paul Heyse, 12 February 1860, *Briefe,* 4:51–52). Both Basel "patricians"—the deeply religious Bachofen and the freethinking Burckhardt—regarded popular religious movements with undisguised disdain. The "vile popular balls at Carnival" refer to the lively Basel tradition of *Fastnacht* or *Fasnacht,* a popular, satirical *fête des fous* that—uniquely—survived the Reformation and continues right down to the present time—much to the dismay of the upper classes and earnest Reformers from Erasmus on. See note 3 of chapter 5.

66. To Anita Bachofen, 8 and 15 April 1887, *GW,* 10:543, 547. The same tone is heard in a letter to Rudolf Müller in Rome seven years earlier. "Boredom as always. In a town like Basel absolutely nothing happens, except what happens wherever men have congregated together—baptisms and burials." On the subject of burials, he added, two good old Baselers—the merchant Leonhard Respinger and the ribbon manufacturer Daniel Burckhardt-Forcart—had recently gone to their deserts, "two men endowed with many fine qualities, but without the slightest trace of feeling for anything artistic, authentic Baselers, knowing nothing but their businesses." As for himself and his family, "We get up, have breakfast, watch the . . . schoolboys playing noisily on the Cathedral Square, see to our daily affairs, and go betimes to bed, in order that we may grow old. So we count the days of the month, the months, the years . . ." (letter of 7 November 1879, *GW,* 10:495).

Chapter Four

1. See Edgar Bonjour, *Die Universität Basel von den Anfängen bis zur Gegenwart 1460–1960* (Basel: Helbing & Lichtenhahn, 1960), p. 646; on the appointment of Werner Jaeger, see William M. Calder III and Christhard Hoffmann, "Ulrich von Wilamowitz-Moellendorff on the Basel Greek Chair," *Museum Helveticum* 43 (1986): 258–63.

2. Paul Burckhardt, *Geschichte der Stadt Basel* (Basel: Helbing & Lichtenhahn, 1957), pp. 155–56.

3. "The possession and enjoyment of material goods, with which Providence has blessed our city and the city of our fathers, would become a perilous snare if it were not accompanied by a desire to promote and nurture the feeling for higher spiritual activities" (quoted in C. F. Burckhardt, *Geschichte der Freiwilligen Akademischen Gesellschaft der Stadt Basel während der ersten 100 Jahre ihres Bestehens* [Basel: Helbing & Lichtenhahn, 1935], p. 50).

4. "Our fathers have nobly manifested their love and respect for the culture of the spirit in countless worthy foundations, and the supreme authorities of our state have recently proved that they regard the memory of that noble past as sacred. For that reason we must continue to build on what our fathers have left us, so that our beloved Basel shall become more and more a place of spiritual cultivation and activity. If its prosperity is advanced by trade and industry and its piety is manifested in so many religious foundations and charitable institutions, let us also devote our energies to the task of making art and science bloom among us in an ever more propitious climate" (ibid., p. 42).

5. Burckhardt, *Geschichte der Stadt Basel*, pp. 155–56.

6. See Lionel Gossman, "The 'Two Cultures' in Nineteenth Century Basel," *Journal of European Studies* 20 (1990): 95–133.

7. Quoted in Werner Kaegi, *Jacob Burckhardt: eine Biographie* (Basel: Schwabe, 1947–1982), 1:334.

8. Theophil Burckhardt-Biedermann, *Geschichte des Gymnasiums zu Basel* (Basel: Birkhäuser, 1889), pp. 209–31, 319–28.

9. Bonjour, *Die Universität Basel*, p. 435, note 8.

10. See Gossman, "The 'Two Cultures' in Nineteenth Century Basel."

11. *Schweizerische National-Zeitung* (hereafter *SNZ*), 16 January 1844.

12. Christoph Bernoulli, *Über die Entbehrlichkeit des Lateinlernens für Nicht-Studirende* (Basel: Neukirch, 1825), pp. 33–34; *Über zweckgemässe Behandlung des mathematischen Elementarunterrichts* (Basel: Wieland, 1828), pp. 4–6.

13. In his 1822–1823 public lectures, De Wette summed up the prevailing view of the Basel moderates when he declared that the absence of particular selfish interests is the condition of whatever "calling is connected with the commonwealth, like that of magistrates and soldiers." De Wette also implied that an academic training promotes such emancipation from particular interests. "The more selfishness is kept in the background in a calling, as in that of scholars and artists, the purer and more vital such a public spirit becomes" (*Human Life, or Practical Ethics*, trans. Samuel Osgood, 2 vols. [Boston: James Munroe, 1842], 2:254–55).

14. Bernoulli, *Über die Entbehrlichkeit*, p. 14.

15. Ernst Jenny, "Wie De Wette nach Basel kam," *Basler Jahrbuch*, 1941, pp. 51–78, at pp. 64–66; On Faesch's *Bemerkungen über einige Lehrgegenstände des Gymnasiums* (1827), see Burckhardt-Biedermann, *Geschichte des Gymnasiums zu Basel*, p. 223, note 2, and p. 265.

16. The radical *SNZ* had conducted a campaign in which it accused the administration of favoring classical studies and theology at the University at the expense of more modern and "useful" subjects like political economy and foreign languages. In its number of 27 April 1841, the paper reported that a conservative reply to these articles had described them as "venomous and hate-filled attacks on the University and on humanism," equivalent to attacks "on the State and God knows what else."

17. Friedrich Paulsen, *Geschichte des gelehrten Unterrichts auf den deutschen Schulen und Universitäten*, 3rd ed. revised by Rudolf Lehmann (Berlin and Leipzig: Walter de Gruyter, 1921), 3:313–15.

18. The opposition of *Zivilisation* and *Kultur,* a cliché of German ideology—*Zivilisation*

being a kind of artificial, material culture, an *external* polishing, *Kultur* a kind of *inner*, organic development, a "natural" culture, so to speak—conveys very well the terms in which a generation of patriotic and idealist Germans rejected the "artificial" Latin tradition, both in the form of the aristocratic French culture that was identified with the absolutist courts and ruling classes of Germany in the seventeenth and eighteenth centuries, and in that of the bourgeois emphasis on analytical reasoning, the value of science, and the goal of technical domination of nature. On the social underpinnings and ideological significance of neohumanism, see Ralph Fiedler, *Die klassische deutsche Bildungsidee. Ihre soziologischen Wurzeln und pädagogischen Folgen* (Weinheim: Beltz, 1972); Karl-Ernst Jeismann, *Das preussische Gymnasium in Staat und Gesellschaft* (Stuttgart: Ernst Klett, 1974); and Paulsen's classic *Geschichte des gelehrten Unterrichts.*

19. It has been pointed out that the factious urban *"Kleinstaaterei"* of the Greek city-states soon came to seem less appropriate than early pre-imperial Rome to German scholars, with Niebuhr, of course, in the forefront, as a model for the *"gesunde Bauerngemeinde"* ("healthy community of free peasants") that they hoped a still predominantly rural Germany would become. Later, as many historians rallied to the idea of national unification under Prussia (seen as a modern Macedonia), Droysen wrote contemptuously of the *"schwatzhaft, unkriegerisch, banausisch gewordene Bürgertum Athens"* ("the chattering, unmilitary, unheroic citizenry of Athens"). Zwi Yavetz, "Why Rome? Zeitgeist and Ancient Historians in early 19th Century Germany," *American Journal of Philology* 19 (1976): 276–96. In addition, there was a progressive retreat, in Germany, from the high-water mark of neohumanism in the repressive climate that followed the assassination of Kotzebue. A close adviser of Friedrich Wilhelm III of Prussia, Georg Philipp Beckendorff, rejected the idea of *Nationalerziehung* (the development of all talents and capacities in all individuals) as "appropriate to republics with democratic constitutions" but "not compatible with monarchical institutions." Quoted by Manfred Botzenhart, "Von den Preussischen Reformen bis zum Wiener Kongress," *Handbuch der deutschen Geschichte,* ed. Otto Brandt, Arnold Oskar Meyer, and Leo Just, vol. 3, pt. 1 (Wiesbaden: Athenaeion, 1988), p. 461.

20. *Über die Bildung von Staaten und Bünden, oder Centralisation und Föderation im alten Griechenland* (Basel: Schweighauser, 1849), p. 9.

21. See his *Die oligarchische Partei und die Hetairen in Athen,* an address given at the graduation exercises of the *Pädagogium* in 1836 (Basel: Wieland, 1836), and *Über die Bildung von Staaten und Bünden, oder Centralisation und Föderation im alten Griechenland,* given at the graduation of 1849. Many ideas commonly associated with Burckhardt are expressed in these two essays by Burckhardt's teacher at the *Pädagogium* and the University of Basel, the first in the aftermath of the *Kantonstrennung,* the second in the aftermath of the passing of the Swiss Federal Constitution of 1848. In particular, Vischer-Bilfinger argued that if the principle of the Greek polis was that the individual exists only in and through the state and that the will of the individual must be identical, on pain of severe punishment, with the will of the state, "this outlook survived only as long as the old customs and the old beliefs." At a certain point the individual's desire for distinction and glory, which Vischer-Bilfinger claimed was strong at all levels of Greek social life, entered into conflict with the old outlook. The tension between these two claims of individual and community, whether as conflict between individual cities in confederations or leagues of cities or as conflict within individual cities between the individual citizen and the community, was what made Greek life so rich and full, according to Vischer. Soon each city wanted to rule, and the *Gesamtvaterland* became simply the instrument of each city's own aggrandizement. Likewise, for the individual within a given city: "The principle that the individual has his existence within the state was

retained, but the meaning was reversed. For instead of the individual will subordinating itself to the general will and vanishing in it, the state becomes the instrument of the glory and power of the individual" (*Die oligarchische Partei*, p. 4).

22. Letter to Arnold von Salis, 29 November 1871, *Briefe*, ed. Carl Burckhardt, 10 vols. plus index vol. (Basel: Schwabe, 1949–1994), 5:144.

23. Wilhelm Riehl's recollections of the German *Gymnasium* in the 1850s evoke something of this enthusiasm but are already tinged with elements not present in classical neohumanism:

> We regarded Greece as our second homeland; for it was the seat of all nobility of thought and feeling, the home of harmonious humanity. Yes, we even thought that ancient Greece belonged to Germany, because of all the modern peoples, the Germans had developed the deepest understanding of the Hellenic spirit, of Hellenic art, and of the harmonious Hellenic way of life. We thought this in the exuberance of a national pride, in virtue of which we proclaimed the German people the leading culture of the modern world, and the Germans the modern Hellenes. We announced that Hellenic art and nature had been reborn more completely in German poetry and music than in the poetry and music of any other people of the contemporary world. . . . Our enthusiasm for Greece was inseparable from our enthusiasm for our fatherland. With all that, we remained good Christians. . . . We looked back with longing to classical antiquity as to a lost paradise.

Kulturgeschichtliche Charakterköpfe (1891), quoted in Fritz Blättner, *Das Gymnasium* (Heidelberg: Quelle & Mayer, 1960), pp. 161–62. See also Klaus Sochatzy, *Das Neuhumanistische Gymnasium und die rein-menschliche Bildung* (Göttingen: Vandenhoek & Ruprecht, 1973), pp. 146–47: "Von der Griechenbegeisterung zum christlichen Germanizismus."

24. Quoted by Kenneth Atwood, *Fontane und das Preussentum* (Berlin, 1970), p. 267.

25. As part of the settlement of the conflict with the country districts in 1833, Basel-City had to transfer two-thirds of its assets to the new half-canton of Basel-Countryside. The University was desperately short of funds and for several decades offered only a limited course of instruction, which students were expected to complete at another German university. Bachofen went to Berlin and Göttingen.

26. Thus, according to Wolf, the study of the Ancients ensures "the elevation and enhancement of all our mental and spiritual energies; for in order to represent to ourselves the long vanished life of an outstandingly well organized and richly developed Nation [i.e., the Greeks] we have to summon up all our own talents and capacities and employ them in concerted action" (quoted by Blättner, *Das Gymnasium*, p. 107). In other words, in order to understand the Ancients, we have to imaginatively *become* them again, to rediscover in ourselves the unspoiled creative powers that made them what they were. Likewise to Wilhelm von Humboldt the study of antiquity is not a grammatical and rhetorical exercise; it is not a study of finished products or literary works but an attempt to enter into and reappropriate the creative spirit that engendered them; it is a study of *energeia*, not *ergon*. If anything, then, far from the study of the ancient languages' being an approach to the study of texts, the study of the ancient texts was a way of getting to the creative "spirit" of the language and culture that produced them. Cf. the fragment "Concerning the Laws of Development of Human Forces" (1791), quoted by Paul R. Sweet, *Wilhelm von Humboldt: A Biography* (Columbus: Ohio State University Press, 1978), 1:105: "True reality consists not in . . . events, but in the physical, intellectual, and moral energies that produce them. Events are the mere effect of these *Kräfte.*" From Humboldt to Heidegger, this idea of language as the most immediate

manifestation of the spiritual energy, "life," or "spirit" of a people has proved remarkably resilient in Germany. See, for example, Heidegger's short essay *Hebel der Hausfreund* (Pfüllingen: Günther Neske, 1958) on the Basel-born Baden poet, Johann Peter Hebel.

27. "Verschiedene Ansichten über höhere Bildung: Einladungsschrift zur Eröffnung der Sommervorlesungen" (Basel: Wieland, 1822), p. 4. In similar vein R. B. Jachmann, first director of the innovative *Conradinum* near Danzig in 1812: "Die Schule soll weder eine Copie der gemeinen Welt seyn, noch überhaupt im Dienste der Welt stehen und ihre Schüler für den gemeinen Weltdienst abrichten, sondern sie soll eine heilige Schirmstätte seyn, in welcher die aufblühende Generation, vor den Zerstreuungen und Gefahren der Welt gesichert, an der Wissenschaft, Kunst und Natur ihre noch bildsame Geistes- und Körperkraft entwickelt, nährt und vervollkommnet" (quoted by Sochatzy, *Das Neuhumanistische Gymnasium und die rein-menschlich Bildung,* p. 88).

28. Though he does not address the question of neohumanist education, Treitschke's chapter on the *Burschenschaften* or student societies in his *History of Germany in the Nineteenth Century,* trans. Eden and Cedar Paul (New York: McBride, Nast, 1917), 3:3–76, still offers an invaluable analysis of the youth movements of the Restoration period.

29. Karl Bücher, *Die Bevölkerung des Kantons Basel-Stadt am 1. Dezember 1888* (Basel: H. Georg, 1890), p. 46; see also Hans Mauersberg, *Wirtschafts- und Sozialgeschichte zentraleuropäischer Städte in neuerer Zeit* (Göttingen: Vandenhoek & Ruprecht, 1960); F. Föhr, *Basels Bürgerschaft* (Basel, 1866), p. 7, quoted in Paul Doppler, *Organisation und Aufgabenkreis der Stadtgemeinde Basel 1803–1876,* Ingenbohl, 1933.

30. The categories of citizen and foreign-born are not mutually exclusive. As in Germany and Switzerland even today, many inhabitants who were born in the city were not citizens; and some who were born abroad were citizens because they were children of citizens or were able to acquire citizenship. Broadly speaking, however, citizens tended to be Basel-born, while noncitizens were immigrants or the children of immigrants who were not well enough off to acquire citizenship.

31. Bücher, *Die Bevölkerung des Kantons Basel-Stadt,* p. 83; see also Burckhardt, *Geschichte der Stadt Basel,* p. 299.

32. Bücher, *Die Bevölkerung des Kantons Basel-Stadt,* Table XXVII; *The Cambridge Economic History of Europe,* vol. 5, ed. E. E. Rich and C. H. Wilson (Cambridge: Cambridge University Press, 1977), p. 503.

33. Article "Basel," in *Allgemeine Encyclopädie der Wissenschaften und Künste,* ed. J. S. Ersch and J. G Gruber (Leipzig: J. D. Gleditsch, 1818–1819), 8:21.

34. See Paul Siegfried, "Basel im neuen Bund," *Neujahrsblatt* of the Gesellschaft für das Gute und Gemeinnützige, 1925, no. 103, pt. 3, 'Das Basler Gesundungswerk'; see also Othmar Birkner, "Bauen und Wohnen in Basel (1850–1900)," *Neujahrsblatt,* 1981, no. 159, pp. 9–10.

35. Alfred Bürgin, *Geschichte des Geigy-Unternehmens von 1758 bis 1939* (Basel: Kommissionsverlag Birkhäuser, 1958), pp. 114–15.

36. Burckhardt, *Geschichte der Stadt Basel,* p. 209.

37. Kaegi, *Jacob Burckhardt,* 7:121.

38. Ibid., p. 122.

39. Burckhardt, *Geschichte der Stadt Basel,* p. 213.

40. Letter to Bachofen of 15 February 1847, Basel University Library, Bachofen-Nachlass 93, no. 122; see also Albert Brückner, ed., "Unbekannte Briefe R. von Jherings aus seiner Frühzeit 1846–1852," *Zeitschrift für schweizerisches Recht,* n.s., 53 (1934): 34–71.

41. Cf. De Wette's view, expressed in the early 1820s, that "in a city without public spirit charity, industry, education, culture of the arts and sciences . . . will be left to the care of

government, which must carry them on by force, and at great cost, and often not without great mistakes, only through its officers, who lack impulse and insight, and who must be remunerated; and even then, the affairs are not made the cause of the people. But, if public spirit unite those, to whose hearts such matters are peculiarly dear, into an associate prosecution of them from free impulse and their own resources, then everything will succeed better, and the people receive the beneficent gift with grateful hearts, as a free boon." The model of all such associations "is presented by this city [Basel], in the Society for the Promotion of Virtue and the Public Good [Iselin's *Gemeinnützige Gesellschaft*]" (*Human Life, or Practical Ethics*, 2:256).

42. Paul Leonhard Ganz and Georg Germann, *Das Museum in der Augustinergasse in Basel und seine Porträtgalerie* (Basel: Verlag der Historischen und Antiquarischen Gesellschaft, 1979).

43. Burckhardt, *Geschichte der Stadt Basel*, p. 148.

44. Letter of 24 January 1858, *Gesammelte Werke* (hereafter *GW*), ed. Karl Meuli (Basel: Schwabe, 1943–1967; publication interrupted at vol. 10), 10:173. Floto had been felled by a stroke, which had left him incapable of ever resuming his teaching functions, but his chances of physical survival were still unclear. See also Bachofen to Meyer-Ochsner, 2 June 1867, *GW*, 10:162–63.

45. Burckhardt, *Geschichte der Stadt Basel*, p. 211.

46. Gertrud Lendorff, *Kleine Geschichte der Baslerin* (Basel and Stuttgart: Birkhäuser, 1966), pp. 161–64.

47. Burckhardt, *Geschichte der Stadt Basel*, p. 210.

48. Cf. Wolfgang Köllmann, *Sozialgeschichte der Stadt Barmen* (Tübingen: J.C.B. Mohr, 1960), p. 222 *et passim*, on the efforts of one of the more conservative members of the manufacturing elite in Barmen to restrict the number of working hours and limit what he saw as the "Triumph des krassen Materialismus" in the uncontrolled expansion of industry.

49. Burckhardt, *Geschichte der Stadt Basel*, pp. 210–11 *et passim*. On Adolf Christ as the incarnation of the *"alte Baslerische Einheit von Staat und Kirche"* in an increasingly secular and competitive society, see Andreas Staehelin, "Das geistige Basel," in *Basel: eine illustrierte Stadtgeschichte*, ed. Eugen A. Meier (Basel: Helbing & Lichtenhahn, 1968), pp. 51–72, at p. 64.

50. Quoted by Bürgin, *Geschichte des Geigy-Unternehmens*, p. 145, from a text of 1852.

51. Quoted by Bürgin, *Geschichte des Geigy-Unternehmens*, p. 145. On the struggle for factory legislation, see ibid., pp. 144–46.

52. Burckhardt, *Geschichte der Stadt Basel*, p. 210.

53. To Meyer-Ochsner, 27 December 1868, *GW*, 10:416. Earlier that year, reporting the death of Andreas Heusler, Bachofen had expressed the same bitter disenchantment with the *juste-milieu* policies he had himself once supported: "Yesterday we laid former *Ratsherr* A. Heusler to rest. . . . His time was that of the old Confederation [i.e., prior to the 1848 federal Constitution—L. G.]. Since then he tried in vain to ingratiate himself with the new world by making ill-fated moves in the direction of liberalism, which only resulted in his ruining his credit with the champions of the old ways" (to Meyer-Ochsner, 15 April 1868, *GW*, 10:403). An extremely influential figure in the 1830s, Heusler prided himself on his pragmatism and adaptability (see Burckhardt's account of his dealings with him in chapter 5). In the constitutional crisis of 1846–1847 he explained his position in the *Basler Zeitung*, which he owned and directed: "I have no system to propose. I am not the man for that. I am far too much of a Baseler and I know my native city too well to come forward with anything of that kind. We Baselers have never modeled our community relations according to any doctrine, we have always sought in a practical spirit to seize on whatever might seem appropriate

to our situation and then put the pieces together in the best way we could . . ." (*Basler Zeitung*, 28 October 1846, quoted by Philipp Sarasin, "Sittlichkeit, Nationalgefühl und frühe Ängste vor dem Proletariat: Untersuchungen zu Politik, Weltanschauung und Ideologie des Basler Bürgertums in der Verfassungskrise von 1846/47," *Basler Zeitschrift für Geschichte und Altertumskunde* 84 (1994): 52–126, at p. 92, note 49).

54. Quoted by Bürgin, *Geschichte des Geigy-Unternehmens*, p. 145. For a succinct account of the changing social and economic situation in Basel, see Edmund Wyss, "Aus der Frühgeschichte des sozialen Basel," in *Basel: eine illustrierte Stadtgeschichte*, ed. Meier, pp. 165–74.

55. To Meyer-Ochsner, 26 October 1860, *GW,* 10:216. The word *"Bauer"* also means "builder," used here deliberately by Bachofen no doubt to distinguish Stehlin from a "genuine" architect such as Berri, who had received a classical education at the Basel *Pädagogium*, whose work is indeed marked by the classical influence of his teachers and models, Weinbrenner, Hittorff, Schinkel—and who came from a good Basel family. Stehlin's father, also a builder, had been employed by the Bachofens in 1825 to execute a remodeling plan drawn up for one of their properties by Berri. See my article, "Basel, Bachofen, and the Critique of Modernity in the Second Half of the Nineteenth Century," *Journal of the Warburg and Courtauld Institutes* 47 (1984): 136–85, at p. 155. On the *homines novi* who came up in the nineteenth century, see Eduard His, *Basler Handelsherren des 19. Jahrhunderts* (Basel: Schwabe, 1929), p. 183, and note.

56. See Bücher, *Die Bevölkerung des Kantons Basel-Stadt*, pp. 71–72. By 1888 almost half the bakers and butchers in the city, for instance, had come from Germany, and nearly a third more from other parts of Switzerland. Fewer than a quarter were native Baselers. Table XXII (pp. xxxii–xxxviii) lists ninety-eight *"Fabrikbesitzer und Theilhaber"* as born in Basel, thirty-five as natives of other parts of Switzerland, seventeen from Alsace, four from France, and no less than thirty-three from Germany (excluding Alsace). On the acquisition of citizenship by foreigners, mostly from Baden, but after 1870 increasingly from other parts of Germany and from Alsace, see Willy Pfister, *Die Einbürgerung der Ausländer in der Stadt Basel im 19. Jahrhundert* (Basel: Friedrich Reinhardt, 1976).

57. Eduard His, *Basler Handelsherren*, pp. 180–81.

58. A fair number of old Baselers might well have reacted as old Jean Buddenbrook does, in Mann's novel, when he hears his son, the consul, praise "with serious zeal" the *"enrichissez-vous"* philosophy of the July monarchy and "the new practical interests and ideals of the time." "Practical ideals, well—h'm—they don't appeal to me in the least. . . . We have trade schools and commercial schools springing up on every corner; the high schools and classical education suddenly turn out to be all foolishness, and the world thinks of nothing but mines and factories and making money. . . . That's all very fine, of course. But in the long run pretty stupid, isn't it?"

59. On this difference of generations, see Bürgin, *Geschichte des Geigy-Unternehmens*, pp. 37–43, 153–55; Wolfgang Köllmann on a similar situation among the merchants of Barmen, in "The Merchants and Manufacturers of Barmen" (extracted from *Sozialgeschichte der Stadt Barmen*) in Andrew Lees and Lynn Lees, eds., *The Urbanization of European Society in the Nineteenth Century* (Lexington, Mass.: D.C. Heath, 1976) pp. 117–31, at pp. 125–30; and Lorenz Stucki, *The Secret Empire* (New York: Herder & Herder, 1971 [orig. German 1968]), on the collapse of the Swiss watch industry in the early 1870s in the face of more technically advanced American mass production methods. Stucki quoted the author of a history of the watchmaking industry: "The golden age of the Genevan watchmaking industry, where the *établisseur* had nothing more to do than sell the watches assembled by his workers at double the cost price, and for the rest of the day amuse himself riding around in a carriage or sailing on a ship in the magnificent environs of Geneva was now at an end." See also, in Thomas

Mann's *Buddenbrooks*, the increasing strain of competition on Thomas Buddenbrook, as compared with his father or grandfather.

60. Before 1864–1865, the Historical Society tried to restrict membership to people who would really contribute learned papers; penalties were written into the statutes for failing to deliver a paper on the day set aside for it, for instance. The new statutes of 1864–1865 declared all who shared the general aims of the Society and could pay the membership dues eligible for membership. The Antiquarian Society had had this larger public character from the beginning. The circular announcing the establishment of the new *Gesellschaft für vaterländische Alterthümer* that was sent out in 1842 invited not just scholars, but the participation of the general public. "We hope thereby," it was said, "to render a service to many men who have a taste for historical research and an interest in it, but who do not have the time to undertake it themselves" (Rudolf Thommen, "Die Geschichte unserer Gesellschaft," in *Basler Zeitschrift für Geschichte und Altertumskunde* 1(1962): 202–47, at p. 215).

61. To von Preen 3 July 1870, *Briefe,* 5:98.

62. To von Preen, 26 April 1872, *Briefe,* 5:161.

63. *SNZ,* 11 December 1842, 6 May 1843.

64. Jacob Maehly, *Byrsopolias,* 1860, quoted by Paul Siegfried, "Basels Entfestigugng," *Basler Jahrbuch,* 1923, pp. 81–146, at pp. 88–89; see also Othmar Birkner, "Bauen und Wohnen in Basel 1850–1900," *Neujahrsblatt,* no. 159 (entire volume), Basel, 1981. The poem translates roughly as follows: "Every one thinks only of the good of the state, no one has any axes of his own to grind. The landowner would be glad to see a railway station arise on his property, but not out of interest—the heart of the matter is pure love of fatherland. The shopkeeper, the tradesman fight with genuine passion for the heart of the city, out of civic duty and not because of the haulage business. The shareholder, the speculator are free of self-interest; they think of themselves, but also of the country, out of pure patriotism."

65. Rolf Brönnimann, *Villen des Historismus in Basel: ein Jahrhundert grossbürgerlicher Wohnkultur* (Basel, Berlin, and Stuttgart: Birkhäuser, 1982), p. 70.

66. John Cuenod, "Die herumlungernde Bevölkerung und die Klassen, die Genf bedrohen," quoted by François Walter, "Von der vorindustriellen Siedlung zur Industriestadt," in *Alltag in der Schweiz seit 1300,* ed. Bernhard Schneider (Zurich: Chronos Verlag, 1991), pp. 243–44.

Chapter Five

1. Letter to Heinrich Schreiber, 18 December 1852, *Briefe,* ed. Max Burckhardt, 10 vols. plus index vol. (Basel: Schwabe, 1949–1994), 3:172.

2. Louis Spohr, *Lebenserinnerungen,* ed. Folker Göthel, 2 vols. (Tutzing: Hans Schneider, 1968), 1:223. John Russell quoted a French traveler in the 1830s: "At Basel every shutter is closed at the sound of a traveling coach and every woman hides herself. Everything is dead and deserted. A city to let, one might say" (*Switzerland* [London: Batsford, 1950], p. 139).

3. For the radicals' view, see *Schweizerische National-Zeitung* (hereafter *SNZ*), 17 February 1844. From the sixteenth century on, the upper classes and many earnest Reformers expressed dismay at the continuation of this boisterous and satirical *fête des fous.* As late as the 1920s, in two sermons, "Jesus weeps over the city" (1920) and "The lament of the creature at Fasnacht time" (1925), Ernst Staehelin, a professor of theology, warned the humble and downtrodden against seeking redemption from their condition in the *Fasnacht* festivities. "Seek what you desire in St. Augustine," he admonished, "not where you are presently seeking it." See Alfred Berchtold, *Bâle et l'Europe: une histoire culturelle,* 2 vols. (Lausanne: Payot, 1990), 1:186–87. By the early nineteenth century, however, the character of *Fasnacht* seems already to have changed. It had become a more organized and officially sanctioned form of

civic festivity. In the section of his novel *Jean-Christophe* entitled "The Burning Bush" (composed around 1911), Romain Rolland wrote that in Basel (unnamed, but evident)

> the carnival had preserved up to the time of the events narrated in this history—(it has changed since then)—a character of archaic license and roughness. In accordance with its origin, by which it had been a relaxation for the profligacy of the human mind subjugated, wilfully or involuntarily, by reason, it nowhere reached such a pitch of audacity as in the periods and countries in which custom and law, the guardians of reason, weighed most heavily upon the people. . . . The more moral stringency paralyzed action and gagged speech, the bolder did action become and speech the more untrammeled during those few days. Everything that was secreted away in the lower depths of the soul, jealousy, secret hate, lewd curiosity, the malicious instincts inherent in the social animal, would burst forth with all the vehemence and joy of revenge. Every man had the right to go out into the streets, and, prudently masked, to nail to the pillory, in full view of the public gaze, the object of his detestation, to lay before all and sundry all that he had found out by a year of patient industry, his whole hoard of scandalous secrets gathered drop by drop. . . . This cloud of public insult, constantly hanging over their heads, did not a little to help maintain the apparently impeccable morality on which the town prided itself.

In the parenthesis at the beginning of this passage, Rolland implied that some of the original asperity and liveliness had gone out of *Fasnacht*. In modern times, mass tourism and self-conscious cultivation of local tradition have further softened the satiric and aggressive power of the Basel *Fasnacht*. Berchtold, *Bâle et l'Europe*, 1:193.

4. Fritz Liebrich, *J. P. Hebel und Basel* (Basel: Helbing & Lichtenhahn, 1926), pp. 35–36.

5. To Friedrich Salomon Vögelin, Jr., 14 January 1866, *Briefe*, 4:213 (letter 440).

6. See Werner Kaegi, *Jacob Burckhardt: eine Biographie* (Basel: Schwabe, 1947–1982), 1:293. "Burckhardt day"—October 14—was celebrated with a large dinner party and music; see Katherine Sim, *Desert Traveller: The Life of John Lewis Burckhardt* (London: Gollancz, 1969). Helen Williams related that at the end of the eighteenth century it was customary for mothers and fathers of families to hold a family day once a week when "all the offspring assemble at the house, sometimes to the fourth, fifth, and even sixth generation" (*A Tour in Switzerland, or a View of the Present State of the Government and Manners of those Cantons*, 2 vols. [London: G.G. & J. Robinson, 1798], 1:15).

7. To Eduard Schauenburg, 24 January 1846, *Briefe*, 2:192–94 (letter 166).

8. To Peter Merian-Thurneysen, 9 February 1858, *Gesammelte Werke* (hereafter *GW*), ed. Karl Meuli (Basel: Schwabe, 1943–1967; publication interrupted at vol. 10), 10:176.

9. Letter to his father, dated early 1867, in *Der junge Dilthey: ein Lebensbild in Briefen und Tagebüchern 1852–1870*, ed. Clara Misch, 2d ed. (Stuttgart: B. G. Teubner; Göttingen: Vandenhoek & Ruprecht, 1960), p. 237.

10. In the 1840s Bachofen was recommending his younger fellow citizen to friends in classical studies in Rome and in Naples as *"mein geschätzter Freund"* ("my valued friend"). See letters to Emil Braun, Wilhelm Henzen, Agostino Gervasio, *GW*, 10:57, 58, 59. He also reported on "Köbi"—as Burckhardt was familiarly known in the small world of the Basel elite—to former colleagues like Rudolf Jhering in Rostock (*GW*, 10:63, 78) and, after Burckhardt left for Zurich in the mid-1850s, he would send greetings to him via their mutual friend, Heinrich Meyer-Ochsner. After Burckhardt's return to Basel in 1858, he transmitted greetings to him from Meyer-Ochsner (*GW*, 10:152, 161, 224–25). The two scholars also met occasionally at the *Antiquarische Gesellschaft* (*GW*, 10:375). But they appear to have seen

less of each other after Burckhardt's move to Zurich (*GW,* 10:171–72, 378), and relations, probably never very warm, cooled considerably. Bachofen did not like Burckhardt's enthusiasm for art or his artistic tastes—"I distrust his passion for painting, for he finds the filthiest things beautiful" (*GW,* 10:376, also 184–85)—but most of all he was suspicious of Burckhardt's politics (*GW,* 10:192).

11. To Meyer-Ochsner, 3 November 1866, *GW,* 10:378.

12. To Meyer-Ochsner, 18 March 1866, *GW,* 10:364.

13. Ibid.

14. To Meyer-Ochsner, 13 January 1860 and 18 March 1866, *GW,* 10:202, 364.

15. To Meyer-Ochsner, 21 June 1856, *GW,* 10:148.

16. Letter to Meyer-Ochsner, 3 November 1866, *GW,* 10:378.

17. Albert Teichmann, ed., *Die Universität Basel in den fünfzig Jahren seit ihrer Reorganisation im Jahre 1835* (Basel: Schultze'sche Universitätsbuchdruckerei [L. Reinhardt], 1885), pp. 62–63.

18. To von Preen, 2 December 1880, *Briefe,* 7:202.

19. The figures are in Charles E. McClelland, *State, Society, and University in Germany 1700–1914* (Cambridge: Cambridge University Press, 1980), p. 208.

20. See *SNZ,* 16 January 1844: "Regarded with hostility by the artisan class and a large part of the merchant class, [the professors] gather around those who run the government and set its tone, those whom we have already identified as the more intelligent part of the merchant class. [No doubt the reference here is to figures like Peter Merian and Andreas Heusler—L.G.] Here they find support and protection even if these are not always given purely for love of science, and in gratitude they adopt the outlook and attitudes of their patrons. . . . An unhappy fate, which first became evident at the time of the Revolution [of 1830–1833], placed the scholars between the people who did not respect them and was even hostile to them and the ruling class, which did in some respects understand and value them correctly, but in return for that embezzled their palladium, the free and open pursuit of knowledge, the gospel of spiritual leadership."

21. *SNZ,* 8 June 1843.

22. *SNZ,* 16 January 1844.

23. Letter to Bachofen of 22 June 1846, in "Unbekannte Briefe R. von Jherings aus seiner Frühzeit 1846–1852," ed. Albert Brückner, *Zeitschrift fur Schweizerisches Recht,* n.s., 53 (1934): 38.

24. William M. Calder III and Christhard Hoffmann, "Ulrich von Wilamowitz-Moellendorff on the Basel Greek Chair," *Museum Helveticum* 43 (1986): 258–63. This kind of recommendation, hedged with reservations, was quite common when the candidates were Jewish.

25. Basel retained a surprising degree of distinctiveness, however. In particular, the celebrated "classical" Baseldeutsch, which Burckhardt apparently used with great effectiveness, was carefully cultivated among "Old Baselers" conscious of their background and social position. Many traditions—linguistic, political, religious—survived into the 1930s. A further, more serious erosion of the old traditions occurred in the aftermath of the Second World War. See Hans Trümpy, "Vom Wesen der Basler," in *Das politische System Basel-Stadt: Geschichte, Strukturen, Institutionen, Politikbereiche,* ed. Lukas Burckhardt et al. (Basel and Frankfurt: Helbing & Lichtenhahn, 1984), 145–55.

26. By 1889, the population of the Zurich urban area was 91,187, that of Basel 70,481 (*Statistisches Jahrbuch der Schweiz,* [Berne, 1891; Zurich: Orell Füssli, 1891], p. 146). Banking at Zurich was organized and conducted almost from the start on modern lines, whereas at Basel the transition from the old family banks—relying on a network of wealthy individu-

als and businessmen who were personally known to each other—to modern enterprises with publicly traded shares was slower, perhaps because the Basel elite was loath to relinquish one of its chief sources of power in the city, its control of capital.

27. The number of enrolled students at Basel in 1887 reached 342, but at Zurich it was 526, with a further 580 students at the Federal Polytechnic. Foreign students were markedly more drawn to Zurich than to Basel. Basel outclassed Zurich only in the number of theology students. In all other fields Zurich had an overwhelming lead. In addition, women students made up more than 10 percent of the student body at Zurich, whereas at Basel the first woman student was not admitted until 1890. In general, Zurich emerges from the first volume of the *Statistisches Jahrbuch der Schweiz* (1891, pp. 187–95) as by far the more modern institution. On the other hand, Basel-City spent more per head of population on education than any other canton in Switzerland and had proportionately more students in technical schools and commercial schools than all the other cantons, including Zurich.

28. To von Preen, 17 March 1872, *Briefe*, 5:154.

29. To Meyer-Ochsner, 14 (15) January 1863, *GW*, 10:265.

30. To Meyer-Ochsner, 2 February 1863, *GW*, 10:268.

31. To Meyer-Ochsner, 27 December 1868, *GW*, 10:416.

32. To Joseph Marc Hornung, professor of jurisprudence in Geneva, 7 June 1881, *GW*, 10:513. Bachofen translated the old Roman-style motto, Senatus Populusque Basiliensis (S.P.Q.B.)—"the Senate and People of Basel"—inscribed on most of the public buildings in Basel into what seemed to him one more appropriate to the Basel of the second half of the nineteenth century: Sentina Populi Quondam Basiliensis—"The Scum of the People, once Citizens of Basel." The "*héros de Saint-Jacques*" are the Swiss soldiers who defended Basel against the Burgundians in 1444.

33. *Human Life, or Practical Ethics*, trans. Samuel Osgood, 2 vols. (Boston: James Munroe, 1842), 2:261–62.

34. To Carl von Speyr, 15 January 1839, *GW*, 10:12–14.

35. On Engels, see Karl Marx and Friedrich Engels, *Collected Works* (New York: International Publishers, 1977), 8:138–53, especially 139–49 on the poor quality of public speaking in the Swiss National Council (report of 6 December 1848, in *Neue Rheinische Zeitung*, 10 December 1848): "Philistinism, which lends a certain originality to the *physique* of this assembly, because it is rarely seen in this classic form, here too remains *au moral* flat and tedious. There is little passion and no question at all of wit." On Gobineau, see extracts from his reports in D. Biddiss, *Father of Racist Ideology: The Social and Political Thought of Count Gobineau* (New York: Weighbright & Talley, 1970), pp. 82–89.

36. *Dr. Wilhelm Theodor Streuber. Nekrolog. November 1857* (Basel: Schweighauser'sche Buchdruckerei), p. xi.

37. To Kinkel, 11 September 1846, *Briefe*, 3:36.

38. Gerlach to Bachofen, 15 September 1851, Basel University Library, Bachofen-Archiv, Nachlass 272, no. 65.

39. "Die Verfassungsrevision von Basel" (Supplement to the *Augsburger Allgemeine Zeitung*, 31 October 1857), *GW*, 1:436–39.

40. To Meyer-Ochsner, 15 April 1868, *GW*, 10:402–3.

41. Bachofen to Meyer-Ochsner, 27 December 1868, *GW*, 10:416: "Das Schlimmste ist, dass wir noch nicht am Ende sind, sondern noch tiefer sinken müssen, ehe das Verlangen nach ganz andern Grundlagen der Gesellschaft sich Befriedigung verschafft."

42. To Bernhard Kugler, 9 August 1874, *Briefe*, 5:237.

43. See, for instance, *The Age of Constantine the Great*, trans. Moses Hadas (New York: Pantheon Books, 1949), pp. 69–70.

44. Emil Dürr, *Jacob Burckhardt als politischer Publizist,* ed. from Dürr's manscripts by Werner Kaegi (Zurich: Fretz & Wasmuth, 1987), p. 40.

Interlude

1. Romain Rolland, *Jean-Christophe. La Fin du Voyage* (Paris: P. Ollendorff, 1910–1912), 3:186–91.

Chapter Six

1. Marriage into an existing ribbon making family was apparently by far the easiest way to enter the business. Only occasionally was a specially talented employee made a partner. Paul Fink, *Geschichte der Basler Bandindustrie, 1550–1800* (Basel: Helbing & Lichtenhahn, 1983), p. 64. On the rapid rise of the Bachofen firm and Johann Jakob Bachofen's increasing share in it even during Strub's lifetime, see ibid., pp. 65–66. Tables of the taxes and duties paid by the Basel ribbon manufacturers in the eighteenth century show the Bachofen firm rising from one of the smallest contributors in 1729–1730 to be one of the four largest by the end of the century. Ibid., pp. 161–69.

2. Karl Meuli, "Bachofens Leben," in *Gesammelte Werke* (hereafter *GW*), ed. Karl Meuli (Basel: Schwabe, 1943–1967; publication interrupted at vol. 10), 3:1015.

3. J. J. Bachofen-Merian, *Kurze Geschichte der Bandweberei in Basel* (Basel: Schultz, 1862), pp. 69, 86, quoted in Meuli, "Bachofens Leben," *GW,* 3:1015. Meuli also quotes (p. 1016) a passage from Bachofen-Merian's unpublished *Lebenserinnerungen* in which Bachofen senior reported with satisfaction that among the country people at Sissach, where the family had their country house, they "continue to enjoy the respect of all. There is a way of relating to these people that is kindly without excess and that upholds the difference in rank." In Meuli's optimistic judgment, Bachofen-Merian "undoubtedly ruled his numerous city and country workers as their master, from a proper distance, but did not fail to take a wise and benevolent interest in them."

4. Ibid., 3:1015.

5. A good idea of these "patrician" buildings, which served both as business premises and as the residence of the owners, can be had from Thomas Mann's *Buddenbrooks.*

6. On the Bachofen family properties, see R. Forcart-Bachofen and F. Vischer-Ehinger, *Chronik der Familie Bachofen in Basel* (Basel: Birkhäuser, 1911).

7. Letter from Berlin to Dorothea Hartmann-Brodtbeck, 22 March 1840, *Briefe,* ed. Carl Burckhardt, 10 vols. plus index vol. (Basel: Schwabe, 1949–1994), 1:147.

8. Meuli, "Bachofens Leben," *GW,* 3:1023. On Herr Munzinger's school and on the teachers and curriculum at the *Gemeindeschule* and the *Gymnasium* in Basel, see the detailed account in Werner Kaegi, *Jacob Burckhardt: eine Biographie* (Basel: Schwabe, 1947–1982), 1:10–18. Bachofen emerged only gradually as an outstanding student: in his first year at the *Gymnasium* (1826) he placed twenty-first in Latin, eighth in German, third in geography, and fourth in arithmetic out of a class of fifty-five; the following year, he placed fourteenth overall in a class of fifty-one—sixteenth in Latin, seventeenth in German, ninth in geography, nineteenth in arithmetic. At least he did better than his younger brother Karl. *Collocations* of the Basel *Gymnasium* for 1826, 1827, in Basel University Library, Ki. Ar. F. V.4.

9. There has been much reflection on the relation between Bachofen's Christian faith and his glorification of primitive societies in which erotic relations were free of the Christian burden of sin and guilt. The view that Bachofen's work emerges from his Christian faith is represented by Karl Schefold, *Die Religion des Archäologen J. J. Bachofen* (Munich: Bayerische Akademie der Wissenschaften, 1987); Sitzungsberichte der Bayerischen Akademie der Wissenschaften, Philosophisch-Historische Klasse, 1987, no. 5.

10. Kaegi, *Jacob Buckhardt,* 1:146–47.

11. *Das Lykische Volk,* in *GW,* 5:12. See also a note scribbled into a book, quoted in *GW,* 10:229, note 1 (letter to Savigny, 16 August 1854): "We should not seek God in nature, but in ourselves, where He speaks in grander, deeper, and more audible tones." A letter to Meyer-Ochsner of 6 February 1861 (*GW,* 10:229) is in the same vein: "I agree with Socrates that stones and trees have nothing to teach me." The idea that man can understand history better than nature recalls the eighteenth-century Italian philosopher Giambattista Vico. According to Vico, our knowledge of history is surer than our knowledge of the natural world because we ourselves make history and are thus intimately familiar with it, whereas nature is the creation of God.

12. Nachlass, in *GW,* 8:493–94.

13. The curriculum or *Lehrplan des Pädagogiums,* which was printed each year (copies in Basel University Library), shows little variation throughout the 1830s and 1840s. In the first two years, humanists had eight hours per week of Latin, six of Greek, three of German, three of French, four of mathematics, and four of history. In the third year, French, mathematics, and history were reduced to two hours per week, while two hours of physics and two of logic were added. Greek, Latin, and German remained constant. The modern or "technical" track, as it was sometimes referred to, covered only two years: in the first year, five hours per week of mathematics, three of physics and chemistry, four of natural history, and six of French, together with four of history, three of Italian, and three of German; in the second year, five of mathematics, three of chemistry, three of mechanics and technology, three of psychology, five of French, four of history, and three each of German, Italian, and English. An interesting feature of the program was that humanists and modernists shared some classes in German, French, history, and mathematics, so that an absolute segregation of the two groups was avoided.

14. Max Burckhardt, "Die politischen Betrachtungen über das Staatsleben des römischen Volkes," *GW,* 1:478–89, at p. 489.

15. Three years later, in 1854, Gerlach dedicated his essay on "Die aetiologischen Mythen als Grundlage der römischen Geschichte" to "Herrn Johann Jacob Bachofen."

16. See the letter to Franz Overbeck (16 November 1876, *GW,* 10:474), then serving as rector of the University, requesting that some funds be paid out of a University charity for indigent professors and their families to supplement the small pension of widow Gerlach.

17. The words are Gerlach's, quoted in *GW,* 1:1026.

18. Kaegi, *Jacob Burckhardt,* 1:448.

19. "Mein Lehrer gesegneten Andenkens" (*GW,* 1:1025).

20. On Müller, see Kaegi, *Jacob Burckhardt,* 1:456–57. The quotations are from Burckhardt's notes on Müller's lectures.

21. Albert Teichmann, ed., *Die Universität Basel in den fünfzig Jahren seit ihrer Reorganisation im Jahre 1835* (Basel: Schultz'sche Universitätsdruckerei [L. Reinhardt], 1885), pp. 62–63.

22. Konrad H. Jarausch, *Students, Society and Politics in Imperial Germany* (Princeton: Princeton University Press, 1982), p. 30.

23. "My Life in Retrospect" (much abbreviated English version of *Selbstbiographie* [see note 27 below]), in *Myth, Religion, and Mother Right: Selected Writings of J. J. Bachofen* (hereafter *MRMR*), trans. Ralph Mannheim, introduction by Joseph Campbell (Princeton: Princeton University Press, 1967; Bollingen Series, 84), p. 9.

24. Günther Rose, "Karl Marx und Friedrich Engels an der Berliner Universität," in *Forschen und Wirken: Festschrift zur 150-Jahr-Feier der Humboldt-Universität zu Berlin,* 3 vols. (Berlin: Verlag der Wissenschaften, 1960), 1:133–63. On Marx as a student of Savigny's, see Boris Nicolaievsky and Otto Maenchen-Helfen, *Karl Marx: Man and Fighter* (Philadelphia and London: J. B. Lippincott, 1936), pp. 29–31. In later years, Marx studied Bachofen

carefully. See Lionel Gossman, *Orpheus Philologus: Bachofen versus Mommsen on the Study of Antiquity* (Philadelphia: American Philosophical Society, 1983; Transactions, 73, 5), p. 2, note 4.

25. See Karl Meuli in Bachofen, *GW,* 1:1030–31.

26. Gossman, *Orpheus Philologus,* note 20.

27. J. J. Bachofen, *Selbstbiographie und Antrittsrede über das Naturrecht,* ed. Alfred Bäumler (Halle/Saale: Max Niemeyer, 1927), p. 13. (The so-called *Selbstbiographie* was first published by Hermann Blocher in 1916.) During his stay in London, Bachofen noted in similar vein, he was equally fascinated by the law courts and by the British Museum and dreamed of a way "to combine the two aspects, to cultivate them both, side by side" ("My Life in Retrospect," *MRMR,* p. 7).

28. Review of F. L. Keller, *Semestrium ad M. Tullium Ciceronem libri sex* (Zurich, 1842), in *Kritische Jahrbücher für deutsche Rechtswissenschaft,* VI, 12 (Leipzig, 1842), p. 962, quoted in Andreas Cesana, *Johann Jakob Bachofens Geschichtsdeutung: Eine Untersuchung ihrer geschichtsphilosophischen Voraussetzungen* (Basel, Boston, and Stuttgart: Birkhäuser, 1983), p. 26. See also Meuli, *GW,* 1:1033–34.

29. Cesana, *Johann Jakob Bachofens Geschichtsdeutung,* pp. 27–28.

30. Savigny, "Vom Beruf unserer Zeit für Gesetzgebung und Rechtswissenschaft" (Berlin, 1814; 3rd ed. Heidelberg, 1840), p. 11, quoted in Cesana, *Johann Jacob Bachofens Geschichtsdeutung,* p. 28.

31. Savigny, p. 117, quoted in Cesana, *Johann Jacob Bachofens Geschichtsdeutung,* p. 29.

32. See the excellent summary in Cesana, *Johann Jacob Bachofens Geschichtsdeutung,* pp. 29–30. Cesana observes aptly that the historical school was not in fact asking or answering a properly historical question, but rather a philosophical question—namely, the question of the foundation of law. That it found the answer to that question in history, rather than in reason, does not alter the essentially philosophical nature of the question.

33. Eugène Lerminier, *Introduction générale à l'histoire du droit* (Paris, 1829), p. 270, quoted in Donald R. Kelley, *Historians and the Law in Postrevolutionary France* (Princeton: Princeton University Press, 1984), p. 115.

34. Basel University Library, Bachofen-Archiv, Nachlass 93, no. 288, letter from Julius Zschokke to Bachofen, 20 September 1839. Zschokke, son of the then-celebrated liberal novelist, publicist, and statesman Heinrich Zschokke of Aarau, had been a student at Göttingen at the same time as Bachofen. (He addressed Bachofen as "Du"—one of very few correspondents to do so). An Anglophile (he declared that he liked Britain a hundred times better than Germany or France), he had traveled directly from Hamburg to Edinburgh and recommended that Bachofen spend at least two to three months in the Scottish capital, since, despite differences between Scottish and English law, the peculiar characteristics of British law, notably the jury system, were more easily and less expensively studied in Edinburgh than in London.

35. Letter to Carl F. Burckhardt, 18 March 1866, *GW,* 10:365.

36. Pellegrino Rossi, "De l'étude du droit dans ses rapports avec la civilisation et l'état actuel de la science," *Annales de législation et de jurisprudence* 1 (1820): 357–428. See Kelley, *Historians and the Law,* pp. 87, 124–25.

37. Letters to Bachofen from Julius Zschokke. Basel University Library, Bachofen-Archiv, Nachlass 93, no. 288, letter of 20 September 1839.

38. "My Life in Retrospect," *MRMR,* p. 7.

39. This custom seems to have been common in the German merchant cities; see, for instance, Thomas Mann's *Buddenbrooks.*

40. *Neue Basler Zeitung,* 18 March 1841, 23 March 1841, 10 April 1841, 17 April 1841, 27 April 1841.

41. Letter to Savigny, 26 March 1841, *GW,* 10:20. In the autobiography he later composed for Savigny, he described his situation more succinctly with a quotation from Cicero: "Thy lot is Sparta!" ("My Life in Retrospect," *MRMR,* pp. 8–9).

42. Basel University Library, Bachofen-Archiv, Nachlass 90, no. 7. Invitation from Freiburg i. B., 9 February 1850.

43. 8 May 1867, *GW,* 10:382.

44. See Lionel Gossman, "Basel, Bachofen and the Critique of Modernity," *Journal of the Warburg and Courtauld Institutes* 47 (1984): 136–85, at p. 164.

45. A letter to Rudolf von Jhering, dated 22 May 1850, is fairly typical of these local satires. It begins by congratulating Jhering on his marriage, then goes on to give news of people in Basel whom Jhering got to know during his stint as professor of law at the University.

> Your other friends from here are also still the same as ever. Gerlach robust and cheerful as always. Yet I am wrong. Manny [Emanuel Burckhardt-Furstenberger] who serves us as *Paiazzo* [Pagliaccio or buffoon], has entered on a quite new stage of his life. You know how eagerly he busied himself with scholarly jurisprudence even as a young lad, and you doubtless still have a vivid recollection of his three volume work on *furtum* [thievery]. His lectures attracted extraordinary numbers of people. This brilliant career has now been brought to a sudden halt. Manny has been elected to the government of the great state of Basel by the sovereign people he so often delighted with his noble affability. *Spe magis quam meritis* [more in hope than on the basis of merit], I believe. He who attains to such heights looks down on the profession of the teacher. Manny, however, has shown himself to be made of finer stuff. He insists that it is only with great pain and difficulty that he has sacrificed his natural intellectual bent to the public weal. However that may be, he has devoted himself ever since, body and soul, to government affairs, and was delighted when the census of the state of Basel was entrusted to him recently. Twenty secretaries were set up in his house and he asserted that he did not rest day or night. The end result was to show that a population of 30,000 souls obeys his orders. People say that Manny represents the interests of scholarship in the heart of the highest offices of government, and he himself gives himself such an air. But there has been no improvement in the condition of the University. To help out in this area, Manny has now decided he will resume lecturing himself. Governing, he says, does not satisfy him. But lecturing, I fear, will not satisfy his audience. Music shares his attention with scholarly concerns. In the Manny home there are musical evenings. Only *enragés* are admitted. Bachelors [Bachofen was still unmarried] are in principle never invited. Manny has it in for such people ever since the census. There has been no improvement yet in the character of his wife. Her tongue is sharp and its lashes are harsh. Only a preferred few are in any case admitted to her presence. Bachofen has not yet been seen in her house. . . .

GW, 10:103.

46. Letter to Meyer-Ochsner, 16 December 1864, *GW,* 10:336; letter to Meyer-Ochsner, 26 December 1858, *GW,* 10:184–85.

47. Letter to Meyer-Ochsner, 24 December 1862, *GW,* 10:251.

48. Letter to Meyer-Ochsner, 4 June 1865, *GW,* 10:342.

49. Letter to Anita Bachofen, 15 April 1886, *GW,* 10:543.

50. Letter to Meyer-Ochsner, 2nd half of October 1869, *GW,* 10:433; letter to Joseph Marc Hornung (in French), 2 December 1870, *GW,* 10:455.

51. J. J. Bachofen, "Über Herkommen und Zucht. Rede gehalten am Grütlifest vor der Section Basel des Zofingervereins," in *Zofingia: Centralblatt des schweizerischen Zofinger-vereins* (Basel, February 1958), 98:145.

52. Letter to Emanuel Schneider, August or early September 1837, *GW,* 10:7–8.

53. Letter to Carl von Speyr, 15 January 1839, *GW,* 10:13–14. Bachofen's dislike of "roy-alist" Oxford with its "glacial air of aristocracy, the hollow splendor, the immobility that lay over everything, the countryside, the people, and particularly men's minds" ("My Life in Retrospect," *MRMR,* p. 7) and his preference for traditionally more liberal Cambridge may be another sign of his political sympathies at this time.

54. *Letters of Jacob Burckhardt,* selected and trans. Alexander Dru (London: Routledge & Kegan Paul, 1955), letter 91, 21 April 1844.

55. Bachofen's *Das Lykische Volk* is dedicated to Leonidas Sgoutas, the editor of *Themis,* a Savigny school legal journal, in the new kingdom of Greece. The two scholars met at various times in Paris, in Switzerland, and also in Greece at the time of Bachofen's visit to that country in 1851, and they maintained a lifelong exchange of scholarly ideas and infor-mation. They may originally have met when both were students of Savigny's in Berlin. See *GW,* "Nachwort," 10:563.

56. Kelley, *Historians and the Law,* p. 86.

57. See ibid., p. 87, *et passim.*

58. Letter to Carl von Speyr, 15 January 1839, *GW,* 10:13.

59. Letter to Leopold August Warnkönig, 4 April 1844, *GW,* 10:43.

60. Similarly on his journey to Scotland Bachofen sought out Sir William Hamilton, the eminent Edinburgh philosopher whose liberal sympathies were well known. See Gossman, "Basel, Bachofen, and the Critique of Modernity," p. 159.

61. Basel University Library, Bachofen-Archiv, Nachlass 93, no. 178, Michelant to Bachofen, 27 December 1865. The tone of this correspondence is throughout friendly and playful.

62. Aurelio Saffi, *Ricordi,* vol. 1 (1892), p. 74, quoted in *GW,* "Nachwort," 10:565. In an invaluable study of Bachofen's reports from Rome at the time of the 1848 revolutions, Giam-piera Arrigoni questions my characterization of Bachofen as "moderately liberal" in the late 1830s and early 1840s. His frequentation of the gatherings at Greene's are not evidence of moderately liberal views, she claims; he went there primarily to meet and talk with scholars on scholarly topics. While one should use the word "liberal" with caution, especially at this time ("liberal-conservative" would probably be a better term), his frequentation of the gath-erings at Greene's is not the primary evidence for the young Bachofen's relatively liberal, *juste-milieu* political views. See Giampiera Arrigoni, *La fidatissima corrispondenza: un ignoto reportage di Johann Jakob Bachofen da Roma nel periodo della Rivoluzione romana (1848–1849)* (Florence: La Nuova Italia, 1996), pp. 21–22.

63. *GW,* 1:12–13.

64. Introduction to *Mother Right, MRMR,* pp. 97, 113, 115.

65. *GW,* 1:19–20.

66. Ibid., pp. 19–20, 22–23. Years later, in his autobiographical letter to Savigny, Bach-ofen developed this theme once more in a striking critique of English law which, he claims, despite its many qualities, is condemned to disappear without a trace because it never appro-priated the generalizing and universalizing character of Roman law but remained bogged down "in innumerable precedents which are scattered in hundreds of volumes and a gigantic mass of parliamentary acts, making a patchwork of details, with one amendment burying another." The English spirit, according to Bachofen, lacks a sense of "those grand propor-

tions, in which the particular finds its appropriate but subordinate place. It remains stuck fast to the ground, buried in the dust, and allows the whole to disappear in the richness of the details. . . . I envy England's legal scholars the advantage of being able to elevate the history of their own people and their own law into the object of their study and their affection, instead of having to devote themselves to the history of a foreign people and a foreign law, as is the case with us. But in considering Roman law, they could have learned what is lacking in their own, and in what way that lack could be made up . . . English law will disappear with as little trace as that of Carthage. For, unlike Roman law, it contains no creative and formative element that could inspire later times with a desire to appropriate it or that could serve future generations as a point of departure for new development" (*Selbstbiographie*, pp. 19–20; this important section was omitted from the English translation, "My Life in Retrospect," in *MRMR*). See also the passage on the greatness of Roman law and the Roman idea of the state in the introduction to *Mother Right, MRMR*, pp. 116–18.

67. *Historische Fragmente*, edited from the Nachlass by Emil Dürr (Stuttgart: Koehler, 1957), p. 270.

68. On Basel's role, see René Teuteberg, *Basler Geschichte* (Basel: Christoph Merian Verlag, 1986), pp. 323–24.

69. Letter to Adolf Friedrich Rudorff (profesor of law in Berlin), 21 March 1840, *GW,* 10:17.

70. Both Bachofen and Burckhardt would probably have subscribed to the definition of tyrant proposed by their conservative (but Republican) French contemporary, Numa Denys Fustel de Coulanges, both in his doctoral thesis of 1858 on Polybius (*Polybe, ou la Grèce conquise par les Romains* [ed. Bertrand Hemmerdinger, Naples: Jovenet, 1984], pp. xvi–xvii, 11, 77) and in *La Cité antique* of 1864 ([Paris: Flammarion, 1984], preface by François Hartog, pp. 324–27).

71. Paul Burckhardt, *Geschichte der Stadt Basel von der Zeit der Reformation bis zur Gegenwart,* 2nd ed. (Basel: Helbing & Lichtenhahn, 1957 [1942]), p. 236.

72. Emil Dürr, ed., *Jacob Burckhardt als politischer Publizist* (Zurich: Fretz & Wasmuth, 1937), p. 21.

73. Letter to Agostino Gervasio, 6 January 1848, *GW,* 10:80.

74. *Selbstbiographie*, p. 36. The same ideas, and some of the same phrases, can be found in an article written for the *Augsburger Allgemeine Zeitung,* October 1850 (*GW,* 1:419):

> The true sovereign is the people: the councilors on the Great Council are only its highest servants, with no will of their own in relation to their master, like all servants. That is truly 'pure democracy,' but democracy that has been carried to that extreme is the end of every people. A government that derives its authority only from the mandate of the people does not deserve the name of a government. For it should stand *above* the people, and as a mandatary it stands *below* it. How should the pot be placed above the potter? How shall the pot rule over pots? Whatever form it may have, government comes not from the people, but only from God. That is the cornerstone of all political wisdom, the eternally true word of our Savior, the lesson of the Old and the New Testaments, the outlook of the whole of antiquity, the Roman no less than the Judaic. Government is a divine, not a human institution. Only my appointment comes from the people, the office comes from God. Only this doctrine guarantees true and authentic democracy, and society in general. For it alone ensures an eternal divine foundation for society.

Similar ideas of the sacred character of the magistracy, around the same time (1850), are to be found in *Politische Betrachtungen über das Staatsleben des römischen Volkes* (*GW,* 1:25–62), in the chapter on "Die Weihe der Magistratur." "The Roman people," Bachofen wrote, "venerated in its magistrates the representatives of the divine on earth" (p. 35).

75. Quoted by Teuteberg, *Basler Geschichte*, p. 322.

76. *Selbstbiographie*, p. 37. See also the letters to Bachofen from Rudolf von Jhering, the great legal scholar. (Jhering's appointment to a chair at Basel had been strongly advocated by Bachofen, and the two men remained friends for years after Jhering left Basel for Rostock, where Bachofen appears to have visited him.) Having lost both his wife and child in 1848, Jhering wrote that for him it had been a year both of great personal loss and of public disaster. "The spectacle of the horrors that the giddy idea of freedom has brought us will convince all right-thinking men that lawfulness, respect for the state and its authorities, moderation, and restrictions on freedom are the inseparable conditions of true freedom, and that the freedom we presently enjoy is nothing but the delirium of a body racked with fever" (Albert Brückner, ed. "Unbekannte Briefe R. von Jherings aus seiner Frühzeit 1846–1857," *Zeitschrift für Schweizerisches Recht*, n.s., 53 [1934]: 34–71, letter of 7 July 1848). Jhering had already expressed sympathy with Bachofen's dismay at the turn of affairs in Switzerland. "If a caricature of the state is to be seen anywhere today it is in Switzerland. When cobblers, tailors, and other such riff-raff get caught up in such doings, I am not surprised, though I regret that a sense of order and respect for authority, which they do not possess a priori, cannot be imposed upon them a posteriori" (letter of 14 December 1846).

77. *Selbstbiographie*, pp. 17–18.

78. Letter to Meyer-Ochsner, 15 April 1868, *GW*, 10:403.

79. Letter to Wilhelm Henzen, 3 March 1850, *GW*, 10:94.

80. Letter to Wilhelm Henzen, 21 May 1850, *GW*, 10:98.

81. Letter to Meyer-Ochsner, 27 December 1868, *GW*, 10:416.

82. Letter to Meyer-Ochsner, from Paris, 29 August 1864, *GW*, 10:321–22.

83. Letter to Meyer-Ochsner, 6 September 1863, *GW*, 10:285.

84. Letter to Meyer-Ochsner, end of September 1866, *GW*, 10:376. Gerlach was expressing disenchantment with Berlin as early as 1851, when he wrote to Bachofen of his plans to attend the Congress of German Philologists at Erlangen: "I am . . . glad that it is not to be once again in the loathesome city of Berlin [*dem eckelhaften Berlin*], where every new sprout is already withered. Prussia has never sunk lower than at the present moment . . ." (Basel University Library, Bachofen-Archiv, Nachlass 93, no. 65, letter from Gerlach to Bachofen, 15 September 1851).

85. Letter to Joseph Marc Hornung (professor of sociology at the University of Geneva), 9 February 1871, *GW*, 10:461: "Je ne touche plus à journal allemand. Rien de plus dégoûtant que le cynisme d'esclaves."

86. Letter to Meyer-Ochsner, 15 September 1870, *GW*, 10:447–48. See also letter of 5 December 1870, *GW*, 10:455–56.

87. Letter to Meyer-Ochsner, 26 December 1870, *GW*, 10:457.

88. Letter to Marc Hornung, 2 December 1870, *GW*, 10:453–55.

89. Letter to Meyer-Ochsner, 27 December 1868, *GW*, 10:416.

90. *Selbstbiographie*, p. 37.

91. Letter to Meyer-Ochsner, 25 May 1869, *GW*, 10:428.

92. See Cesana, *Johann Jakob Bachofens Geschichtsdeutung*, pp. 57–58.

93. *Selbstbiographie*, p. 37.

94. *Dr. Wilhelm Theodor Streuber. Nekrolog. November 1857* (Basel: Schweighauser'sche Buchdruckerei), pp. viii, xxxvi.

95. *Griechische Reise*, ed. Georg Schmidt (Heidelberg: Richard Weissbach, 1927), p. 8. The quotation from Tertullian is taken from *De Pallio*, 5: "One must of course live for one's

country, the Empire, a successful career. That was once the reigning opinion. But no one is born for another, since we shall all die for ourselves alone."

96. Letter to Savigny, 18 May 1855, *GW,* 10:142; see also letter to Savigny, 16 August 1854, *GW,* 10:136: "In the end, the highest goal is to work on oneself." On the idea of self-cultivation in German thought and letters, see W. H. Bruford, *The German Tradition of Self-Cultivation: Bildung from Humboldt to Thomas Mann* (Cambridge: Cambridge University Press, 1975).

97. *Streueber Nekrolog,* pp. vi–xi.

98. "My Life in Retrospect," *MRMR,* p. 15 (translation revised).

99. On the two strains in Savigny's work, see Gossman, *Orpheus Philologus,* pp. 61–62, where there are also references to scholarly literature on the topic.

100. Letter to Andreas Heusler-Ryhiner, 7 March 1845, *GW,* 10:51.

101. *Selbstbiographie,* p. 14.

102. Ibid., p. 13.

103. ". . . auch am römischen Recht zu dogmatisiren, so viel ich kann, wenn ich darüber auch bei Ihnen in die Acht fallen sollte" (Brückner, "Unbekannte Briefe R. von Jherings aus seiner Frühzeit 1846–1852," letter of 7 July 1848).

104. "Eine glückliche äussere Lebensstellung, um die ich Sie beneiden mochte, setzt Sie, mein lieber Bachofen, in Stand, sich ganz in dieser Art der historischen Studien zu vertiefen, und ich hoffe, dass es der Welt zu Gute kommen wird" (ibid., p. 67, letter of 26 October 1852). In an earlier letter of 15 February 1847, Jhering had divided the Basel scholarly world into three groups: those like Künzli or Völlmy, who are nothing, those like Merian, Bachofen, Vischer, and Passavant whose names "have to be written with six or seven zeros after them," and those like Brommel, Staehelin, and Emanuel Burckhardt, after whose names one can write only one zero, but who are as distinguished scientifically as the others are financially.

105. *GW,* 2:373, note 1: "Jhering, Geist des Röm. Rechts 2, 2 [1875], 565 gibt die wenig geistreiche Erklärung, der Sklave habe die Bedeckung nötig, weil man ihm nicht auf den Kopf sehen dürfe, und sagt von der Sitte des Haarscherens, ihr liege der Gedanke zu Grunde, dass der Freigewordene damit alles, was ihm aus der Zeit der Gefangenschaft anklebt, gründlich abtue. Man kann hienach beurteilen, wie tief jener 'Geist' in den wirklichen Geist des Altertums eingedrungen ist."

106. *Selbstbiographie,* pp. 15–16.

107. Ibid., p. 16. See "My Life in Retrospect," *MRMR,* pp. 5–6.

108. On Savigny's view of the French, see Kelley, *Historians and the Law,* p. 78. As early as 1847, recommending a legal scholar (Bernhard Windscheid) to Andreas Heusler, Bachofen had singled out for special praise Windscheid's considerable knowledge of modern law and his familiarity with French jurisprudence and the Napoleonic Code, which had been adopted in his home city of Düsseldorf. These were "qualities, the importance of which is enhanced by the special circumstances of our city" (letter to Andreas Heusler-Ryhiner, 12 March 1847, *GW,* 10:72–74).

109. *Selbstbiographie,* p. 16. Bachofen's views appear to reflect his experience in Paris, for the so-called Germanist school (going back to Dumoulin in the sixteenth century and including Boulainviller, Montesquieu, Grosley, and Boucher d'Argis) was very much alive in France in the Restoration period, which also saw much scholarly work on the indigenous French legal tradition and on the legal monuments of the Middle Ages. Kelley, *Historians and the Law,* pp. 65–67.

110. See Kelley, *Historians and the Law,* pp. 51, 63–71 on Henrion de Pansey (1742–1829), minister of justice in the first Restoration government in 1814, premier président of

the Cour de Cassation in 1828, and a strong supporter of "judicial discretion" or "judicial authority" and of the Germanic inclination to judicial decisions. Bachofen's suspicion of all attempts to routinize legal practice is well expressed in the letter to Savigny:

> I felt an increasing distaste for all modern systems. . . . I was also dissatisfied with the current method of resolving controversies. The use of every means of juridical sophistication and cleverness, of the most forced kind of criticism, of the most arbitrary distinctions, to arrive at a reconciliation of contradictory judgments in the writings of the Ancients could only correspond to the need for a firm practically applicable maxim or rule. The whole procedure struck me as no better than Justinian's fantasy of a jurisprudence free from doubt and contradiction. It seemed to me much more worthy, fruitful and desirable to communicate the basis and the thought processes that had led equally distinguished jurists to come to entirely different conclusions. For strange as it may seem, . . . in questions of jurisprudence opposite views can often have an equal degree of justification. I was glad that Justinian had not succeeded in erasing all trace of these disputes, which are always the consequence of free and creative thinking. I myself was convinced that it was the golden age of Roman law that must have been richest in deviations and disagreements in every branch of legal practice.

Selbstbiographie, p. 14; abbreviated in "My Life in Retrospect," *MRMR.*

Chapter Seven

1. Letter to Meyer-Ochsner, 16 December 1864, *Gesammelte Werke* (hereafter *GW*), ed. Karl Meuli (Basel: Schwabe, 1943–1967; publication interrupted at vol. 10), 10:336.
2. *Geschichte der Römer,* in *GW,* 1:270. In the introduction to *Mother Right,* Bachofen acknowledged the repetitive character of his writing, attributing it to what he liked to call his "empirical" approach, his respect for the specificity of the materials at hand, and his refusal to impose his own ideas on them, in the manner, according to him, of modern critics of the school of Niebuhr and Mommsen. "Historical investigation . . . must everywhere stress the particular and only gradually progress to comprehensive ideas. Success depends on the most complete investigation and unprejudiced, purely objective appraisal of the material. . . . The very nature of this method precludes a logical progression in our exposition of the ideas related to matriarchy; instead, we shall have to follow the documents regarding each people. . . . Moreover, we shall have to deal repeatedly with one and the same question" (*Myth, Religion, and Mother Right: Selected Writings of J. J. Bachofen* (hereafter *MRMR*), trans. Ralph Mannheim, introduction by Joseph Campbell (Princeton: Princeton University Press, 1967; Bollingen Series, 84), p. 119.
3. Bachofen frequently referred to the fascination Rome had for him and was fully aware of its central role in his thought: see Letters 162, 179, 185, 188, 190, 202, 204, 315 in *GW,* vol. 10; *Geschichte der Römer* in *GW,* 1:129, 268–69.
4. Introduction to *Mother Right, MRMR,* p. 92.
5. "De la vie future chez les Anciens: Lettre à Mr. J. J. Bachofen fils, à propose des 'Römische Grablampen' de feu son père," serving as introduction to *Römische Grablampen* (Leipzig: Hiersemann, 1912), pp. i–xxix, at p. ii.
6. "Das Altertum des Altertums" (*Griechische Reise,* ed. Georg Schmidt [Heidelberg: Richard Weissbach, 1927],p. 93).
7. "Die Grundgesetze der Völkerentwicklung und der Historiographie," *GW,* 6:435.
8. Letter from Lewis Morgan to Bachofen, 4 June 1878, *GW,* 10:482. See also letter from

Bachofen to Morgan, 14 May 1878, *GW*, 10:480: "The point I am presently taking under special observation is the relation of brother and sister, brother and nephew or niece by the sister, the question therefore of maternal uncle, the Roman *avunculus*, so nearly related to the system of exclusive maternal relationship." Likewise *Antiquarische Briefe*, in *GW*, 8:47 *et passim* (letters 13–15 on sister's son, letters 26–30 on family and social structures based on matrilinear descent via "sister's son," and letters 45–61 on the terms *avus* and *avunculus* and on the "*Avunculat*" in various traditions, notably classical antiquity and India). The relation of brother and sister's children is raised in the section on Lycia in *Mutterrecht*; see *MRMR*, p. 141.

9. In a letter to Meyer-Ochsner in October 1869 (*GW*, 10:434), he requested that the latter's son, then in London, obtain for him a copy of MacLennan's *Primitive Marriage* (Edinburgh, 1865). Before the young man could respond, Bachofen had already found a copy and in December he outlined MacLennan's thesis enthusiastically to Meyer-Ochsner (letter of 6 December 1869, *GW*, 10:435–36). A year later, he was asking a Geneva friend to get him Lubbock's "Origin of Civilization" [probably *Prehistoric Times*, 1865] and Tylor's "Primitive History of Mankind" [*Researches into the Early History of Mankind*, 1865] (letter to Marc Joseph Hornung, 2 December 1870, *GW*, 10:454). A little later still, he was in correspondence with Adolf Bastian (letter from Bastian to Bachofen, 10 May 1872, *GW*, 10:462–65). By 1874 he was obviously familiar with Morgan's work, for he sent him a copy of *Tanaquil.* It was Morgan's letter of thanks (dated Rochester, 25 December 1874, *GW*, 10:468–69) that initiated an important scholarly correspondence between the two men that ended only on Morgan's death.

10. Fritz Krämer, *Verkehrte Welten: zur imaginären Ethnographie des 19. Jahrhunderts* (Frankfurt am Main: Syndikat, 1977).

11. Letter to Joseph Marc Hornung, 17 January 1870, *GW*, 10:452.

12. Bachofen did make an attempt to interest the publisher Cotta in this text. In February 1857 he sent Cotta a sample section from it—the section on Megara (pp. 37–56 of the 1927 edition)—which Cotta published in his review *Das Ausland* later that year (no. 30, pp. 209 ff., 236 ff.). See letter to Johann Georg von Cotta, 11 February 1857, *GW*, 10:157. In this letter he also made the first of several attempts, unsuccessful as it turned out, to interest Cotta in publishing his "Gynaikokratie," as he then called *Das Mutterrecht*.

13. Letter to Savigny, 18 May 1855, *GW*, 10:142.

14. This view of historical scholarship was common among romantic historians. On Jules Michelet, for instance, see my essays in *Between History and Literature* (Cambridge: Harvard University Press, 1990), pp. 152–224; see also "The Go-Between: Jules Michelet 1798–1874," *MLN* 89 (1974): 503–41, at pp. 528–29; the foreword to the special issue on Michelet of *Clio* (vol. 6, no. 2 [1977]: 121–25); and the entry on Michelet in the new *Oxford Companion to French Literature*, ed. Peter France. Georg Friedrich Creuzer, admired and studied by Bachofen and Michelet alike, objected to the suggestion that he take refuge in scholarship from a passionate and destructive love affair with the poetess Karoline von Gunderode and claimed it was pure bourgeois "philistinism" to drive a wedge between the personal life and the scholarly life, between eros and sophia. See Erwin Rohde's edition of the correspondence between Creuzer and Karoline, *Friedrich Creuzer und Karoline von Gunderode: Briefe und Dichtungen* (Heidelberg: C. Winter, 1896), pp. 18, 69.

15. Letter to Meyer-Ochsner, 6 December 1869, *GW*, 10:435.

16. In his very last work, *Die römischen Grablampen*, Bachofen again devoted many pages to this theme. "Der Mutter höchste Wonne," he wrote, "ist die Wiedervereinigung mit der Tochter" ("The highest joy of the mother is being reunited with her daughter") (*GW*, 7:261).

17. Mommsen's article appeared in the classical journal *Hermes* (1870, no. 4). Bachofen

responded in a separately published appendix to *Tanaquil:* "Theodor Mommsens Kritik der Erzählung von Cn. Marcius Coriolanus" (1870). See on this episode Emanuel Kienzle's afterword to *Die Sage von Tanquil,* in *GW,* 6:453.

18. *Griechische Reise,* pp. 7–8.

19. *Selbstbiographie und Antrittsrede über das Naturrecht,* ed. Alfred Bäumler (Halle/Saale: Max Niemeyer, 1927), p. 34. "I no longer desired to embrace not the goddess hereself, but her airy, deceptive image. As a consequence of this spiritual revolution, it was impossible for me, on my return from Italy, to announce the old course on the history of Roman law."

20. Introduction to *Mutterrecht,* in *MRMR,* p, 83.

21. *Griechische Reise,* p. 50.

22. Ibid., p. 94.

23. "My Life in Retrospect," *MRMR,* p. 13.

24. Letters to Meyer-Ochsner, 16 March 1862, *GW,* 10:255 ("Ich kann gar nicht sagen, welche Sehnsucht nach dem 'vagari' wieder in mir tobt"); 21 February 1863, *GW,* 10:269 ("Reiselust, m. l. Freund, rinnt in allen meinen Adern. Ich gestehe Ihnen, dass es mir hier oft zu enge wird und ich manchmal den Sack nehmen möchte"); and 12 July 1861, *GW,* 10:235 ("Ich musste in 35 Wärme herumlaufen, zog mir Durchfall und Magenerhitzung zu, wurde bettlägerig, und kam noch halb krank in mein liebes regnerisches Schützenvaterland zurück").

25. *Griechische Reise,* p. 7.

26. "So standen auch die Phallen . . . als bleibende Zeichen des Lebens und des *Bestehens;* Stand- und Bestandbilder in jedem Sinne, Unterpfänder der physischen und bürgerlichen Wohlfahrt" (Georg Friedrich Creuzer, *Symbolik,* 2nd ed., 6 vols. [Leipzig and Darmstadt: Heyer & Leske, 1819–1823], 2:670).

27. On this question, see Fritz Krämer, *Verkehrte Welten,* pp. 31–32, 34–36. "In his Mythology, Creuzer brought up and exhibited the oppressive images of his 'inner life,' to which he could not give expression in the 'bourgeois world.' Consciously or unconsciously, many of his texts, including texts not identified as having symbolic meaning, have a secret meaning; even in their countless footnotes and references, his learned texts conceal feelings and images that the reader who is on the look-out for them cannot fail to detect" (p. 35). Krämer added, however, that Creuzer also intended thereby to challenge the prettified Hellenism of his contemporaries. "Creuzer was aware that his theory of symbols made explicit what his idealist and classicizing contemporaries knew very well, but did not wish to acknowledge. 'Aesthetic and poetic spirits,' he wrote in the introduction to the third edition of the *Symbolik,* 'do not like to be reminded that the noblest and most deeply spiritual poetic and allegorical constructions of the Ancients proceeded from the most profound sense of mankind's degeneration and helplessness. To inquire into the underlying causes of these doctrines and poetic productions and to delve into the eternally unsatisfiable needs of the human soul through the study of the history of myth and religion would be considered by those aesthetes and students of the fine arts an attack on the noble life'" (Krämer, p. 35, quoting *Symbolik,* 3rd ed., 1:x). Bachofen's intentions were identical: to reveal the dark underside of classical culture and thus attack the complacent classicism of neoclassical artists and *Gymnasium* professors.

28. *MRMR,* pp. 40–43 ("Sanctum" and "Sacrum"), and pp. 44–47 (Amor and Psyche).

29. *MRMR,* pp. 203–7.

Chapter Eight

1. *Friedrich Creuzer und Karoline von Günderode: Briefe und Dichtungen* (Heidelberg: C. Winter, 1896), p. 44.

2. Foreword to *Gräbersymbolik,* in *Myth, Religion, and Mother Right: Selected Writings of*

J. J. Bachofen (hereafter *MRMR*), trans. Ralph Mannheim, introduction by Joseph Campbell (Princeton: Princeton University Press, 1967; Bollingen Series, 84), p. 21.

3. *Griechische Reise*, ed. Georg Schmidt (Heidelberg: Richard Weissbach, 1927), p. 137.

4. *"Politische Betrachtungen über das Staatsleben des römischen Volkes"* (1850), in *Gesammelte Werke* (hereafter *GW*), ed. Karl Meuli (Basel: Schwabe, 1943–1967; publication interrupted at vol. 10), 1:27–29.

5. *MRMR*, p. 23.

6. *Griechische Reise*, p. 117. "Antiquity is at its greatest in its graves. For the graves were, after all, eternal dwelling-places, whereas the houses of the living were mere overnight accommodations on the stages, constantly changing from one day to the next, of man's earthly journey. The thinking of the Ancients in this respect had extraordinary dignity and grandeur. It is easy to understand why so many spent their lives laying plans for a grave." Cf. "My Life in Retrospect," *MRMR*, p. 11:

> All the treasures that fill our museums of ancient art were taken from tombs, and in general human civilization owes them more than is usually supposed. In nomadic societies the tomb was the first and only stable edifice. Building was done more readily for the dead than for the living; perishable wood was held to be sufficient for the life span allotted to the living, but the eternity of man's ultimate dwelling place demanded the solid stone of the earth, In all essential things the earliest men thought soundly and correctly, as we may expect of those who were still so close to their eternal origin. The oldest cult is bound up with the stone that designates the burial place; the earliest temples were related to the burial site, while art and ornament originated in the decoration of the tombs. It was the tombstone that gave rise to the concept of the *sanctum*, of the immovable and immutable. This concept also applies to boundary posts and walls, which along with tombstones constitute the *res sanctae*. In them ancient man saw an image of the primordial power that dwells in the earth, and consequently all three bear its symbol. The earth sends forth tombstones, boundary posts and walls from its womb, where, as Plato says, they previously slumbered; the phallus is its mark.

7. "My Life in Retrospect," *MRMR*, p. 12; *Griechische Reise*, pp. 5, 99, 100.

8. Foreword to *Gräbersymbolik, MRMR*, p. 22.

9. *Griechische Reise*, pp. 162–63.

10. On Burckhardt's preoccupation with death and the transitoriness of things, see Werner Kaegi, *Jacob Burckhardt: eine Biographie* (Basel: Schwabe, 1947–1982), 1:21, 269–86.

11. *Verschiedene Ansichten über höhere Bildung. Einladungsschrift zur Eröffnung der Sommervorlesungen* (Basel, 1822), p. 9.

12. *Griechische Reise*, p. 170.

13. Ibid., p. 106.

14. Ibid., p. 120.

15. Ibid., p. 135; "Die Grundgesetze der Völkerentwicklung und der Historiographie," *GW*, 6:435–37.

16. *Griechische Reise*, p. 191.

17. Ibid., p. 190.

18. The landscape "appears here still in the full grandeur of earliest beginnings, pure and untouched as on the first day when the Creator beheld his completed work and was pleased with it." ("Erscheint sie hier noch in der ganzen Grösse voller Ursprünglichkeit, so rein und unberührt, wie am ersten Tage, da der Schöpfer sein vollendetes Werk mit Wohlgefallen

betrachtet.") Likewise animal life, notably the herds of goats that wander freely over the landscape, evokes an Edenic time infinitely remote from the present age. "As you observe the delicate dignity of those goats picking their way rapidly and unobtrusively among the rocks and scrub, you understand how antiquity could imagine that Amalthea the most beautiful of women was transformed into one of these animals" (*Griechische Reise*, p. 59).

19. Ibid., pp. 59, 71, 134, 161–62.

20. Ibid., p. 136. See also on this topic, *Geschichte der Römer, GW,* 1:270–71.

21. Letter to Wilhelm Henzen, 4 October 1850, *GW,* 10:107. See likewise the introduction to *Mother Right:* "The scholar must be able to renounce entirely the ideas of his own time, the beliefs with which these have filled his spirit, and transfer himself to the midpoint of a completely different world of thought. Without such self-abnegation no real success in the study of antiquity is thinkable. The scholar who takes the attitudes of later generations as his starting point will inevitably be turned away from an understanding of the earliest time. . . . True criticism resides in the material itself and knows no other standard than its own objective law, no other aim than to understand the alien system . . ." (*MRMR,* pp. 81–82).

22. *Griechische Reise,* p. 37.

23. Ibid., pp. 119–20.

24. Ibid., p. 189.

25. "My Life in Retrospect," *MRMR,* p. 16.

26. Ibid., p. 10.

27. Letter to Meyer-Ochsner, 2nd half of October 1869, *GW,* 10:433. Cf. *Griechische Reise,* p. 23 on the joy of leaving "der Nord mit seinem trüben Himmel."

28. See especially the introduction to *The Myth of Tanaquil, MRMR,* pp. 242–46. "The capital offense consists in injecting ourselves into the objects of observation, carrying our own ideas into a foreign subject matter instead of apprehending the ideas inherent in the things themselves, and approaching nature in a carping, argumentative frame of mind instead of subordinating ourselves to the phenomenon and seeking to discern its special character" (p. 245).

29. Among many places where this point is made, see *Geschichte der Römer, GW,* 1:169–70, 173, 182; *MRMR,* p. 83.

30. *Griechische Reise,* p. 94 ("Die Wölfe des Nordens").

31. Ibid., p. 111.

32. *GW,* 1:147.

33. Writing of the Lions of Mycenae, Bachofen called them "remnants of an older culture, of an age that the Hellenes themselves already looked upon from a distance, as on something long vanished and overtaken. They stand there, like Homer, isolated rocks in the sea, with nothing before them, and nothing after them for a long time either. Their whole being is Asiatic, they belong to the Orient, they do not belong to Hellenic Greece" (*Griechische Reise,* p. 105). While it is clearly the Lions of Mycenae that are being described as Oriental, the allusion to Homer is not inconsistent with Bachofen's general view of the poet as at once the inheritor and the destroyer of the "Oriental" tradition.

34. *Griechische Reise,* p. 111.

35. Letter to Meyer-Ochsner, 29 December 1865, *GW,* 10:355–56.

36. Letter to Meyer-Ochsner, 16 January 1851, *GW,* 10:114–15.

37. On Ross, see the article by A. Baumeister in *Allgemeine Deutsche Biographie;* also Otto Gruppe, *Geschichte der klassichen Mythologie und Religionsgeschichte* (Leipzig: B. G. Teubner, 1921), p. 171. Ross had spent many years in Greece and had written abundantly about both ancient and modern Greece. He had supplied Böckh with a large number of inscriptions. In

his correspondence C. O. Müller refers to "der treffliche Ross" and both he and Böckh continued to treasure the man and his friendship even though they could not share his extreme opposition to Niebuhrian criticism. See Max Hoffmann, *August Böckh. Lebensbeschreibung und Auswahl aus seinem wissenschaftlichen Briefwechsel* (Leipzig: B. G. Teubner, 1901), pp. 192, 342, 373. It was this opposition, however, that was the basis of Ross's relation to Bachofen. Thanking the latter for his dedication of *Die Gräbersymbolik* to him, Ross confesses to having been surprised as well as touched by it, since, as he put it pointedly, he had no gift for speculation, was a stranger to symbolic interpretations, and could not follow him in his intricate arguments. In the same letter, however, he confirmed his view of Niebuhr as one of the "*grosse Irrlichter*" who have misguided the youth of Germany and corrupted the study of antiquity. There is also a ringing denunciation of the "*Bodenlosigkeit der Mommsenschen Hallucinationen über die Vorgeschichte und die Königzeit Roms*" which must have been music to Bachofen's ears (Basel University Library, Bachofen-Archiv 272, item 243, letter of 2 February 1859).

38. Letter of 17 January 1859, *GW,* 10:186. See also letter to Count Giovanni Gozzadini, a historian and archaeologist from Bologna, 8 April 1870, *GW,* 10:443 (in French): "Pour comprendre une tradition, il faut commencer par l'accepter."

39. Letter to Lewis Morgan, 4 January 1881, *GW,* 10:508.

40. "Das Naturrecht und das geschichtliche Recht in ihren Gegensätzen" (Bachofen's inaugural lecture as professor of law at Basel in 1841), *GW,* 1:18.

41. "My Life in Retrospect," *MRMR,* p. 16; introduction to *Mutterrecht, MRMR,* pp. 76, 119–20.

42. Letter to Emil Braun, Secretary of the Istituto di corrispondenza archeologica in Rome, 9 January 1844, *GW,* 10:36.

43. Letter to Meyer-Ochsner, 4 June 1865, *GW,* 10:342: "History is not to be found only in books"; letter of 19 October 1865 to Wilhelm Henzen, *GW,* 10:347: "You can understand that I leave Rome unwillingly and look forward with sadness to the end of my stay here. In the north, books are everything, and for that reason everything stays pallidly abstract, colorless, and cold." See also *Griechische Reise,* p. 67; and *Geschichte der Römer, GW,* 1:98–99, on the Roman Campagna.

44. *Griechische Reise,* pp. 46–48, 50, 85.

45. Ibid., pp. 98, 157–58. See also *Politische Betrachtungen,* sec. IX, *GW,* 1:47–52; "My Life in Retrospect," *MRMR,* p. 10.

46. *Griechische Reise,* pp. 89–90, 94–95, 163.

47. Ibid., p. 33.

48. Ibid., p. 84.

49. This idea had been crucially important to Winckelmann, who used it to criticize Christianity. By outlawing homoerotic relations and restricting love to the domestic sphere of marriage and the family, Winckelmann argued, Christianity had undermined the political life of the ancient world.

50. *Politische Betrachtungen,* sec. XII, *GW,* 1:60; see also ibid., sec. X (1:54), where this view is carried to an extreme of conservatism: "I consider it criminal to undermine superstition, not only because it becomes no one to release the human mind from subordination to the divine, but because superstitious belief is so entwined with belief in general that the undermining of the one prepares the way for the collapse of the other."

51. Introduction to *Tanaquil, MRMR,* pp. 238–39.

52. Ibid., *MRMR,* pp. 241–42.

53. *Griechische Reise,* p. 98.

54. Ibid., p. 104.

55. Ibid., p. 173. Though such ideas were not uncommon among romantic writers, Bachofen might have heard them expressed in De Wette's lectures. Convinced that all the phenomena of nature and human history—"from the beauty of the flower to the sublime grandeur of the glacier, from the laughter of the infant to the nobility of Cato and Socrates"—point to the higher, eternal ideas which infuse them and which "we cannot grasp with concepts and measurements," De Wette liked to evoke those "sacred instants in which, as in a fleeting vision, we catch a reflection of the divine glory itself, either in the great spectacles of nature or in the grand acts of destiny" (De Wette, *Über Religion und Theologie*, 2nd ed. [1821], p. 12; quoted by Kaegi, *Jacob Burckhardt*, 1:449).

56. "My Life in Retrospect," *MRMR*, pp. 15–16, and note p. 16. Schelling was a visitor to Bad Ragaz in Canton Sankt Gallen toward the end of his life, in the 1850s, and it was there that he died in 1854. A letter from Savigny to Bachofen from Ragaz informing him of the death "*des würdigen Schelling*" seems to indicate that Bachofen had met with the philosopher during one of his visits to Savigny. Letter from Savigny to Bachofen, 27 August 1854, *GW*, 10:137–38.

57. *Griechische Reise*, p. 121.

58. Ibid., pp. 98–99. See also ibid.,p. 118: "I thought the pencil would allow me to retain at least the outlines of that miraculous scene. But what is that sheet of paper to me now? No more than the last of the little oil lights that glows at the end of the spectacle and now, as it peters out, fills the air with its acrid smell. At the time, however, all the glory of the moment had attached itself to those lines drawn on the page."

59. *Gräbersymbolik, MRMR*, p. 48.

60. Letter to Heinrich Brunn, who replaced Emil Braun as Secretary of the Istituto di corrispondenza archeologica, 20 December 1860, on the interpretation of some terra-cotta vases in Salzburg, 20 December 1860, *GW*, 10:219: "*Ma domandono un vero Edipo*"; on the same day the same phrase is used in a letter to Meyer-Ochsner (*GW*, 10:220). See also letter to Meyer-Ochsner, 24 March 1864, *GW*, 10:311: "*Oedipo indiget*"; letter of 27 May 1885 to Enrico Stevenson, the archaeologist and Scriptor of the Vatican Library, on a grave-lamp that he cannot understand (*GW*, 10:538): "Pour moi tout est énigme. Vous en devez être l'Oedipe." Jules Michelet, the great romantic historian, whose historical hermeneutic has many resemblances to Bachofen's, also referred frequently to the historian as an Oedipus. Obviously, we are dealing here with a common enough rhetorical figure; nevertheless, it is not unimportant that Bachofen and Michelet do not refer to themselves as Newtons—as eighteenth-century historians were happy to do—but look for their model in the world of myth itself.

61. *MRMR*, pp. 166–71, 180, 182.

62. Letter to Count Giovanni Gozzadini, 8 April 1870, *GW*, 10:443.

63. *MRMR*, p. 241.

64. *Selbstbiographie und Antrittsrede über das Naturrecht*, ed. Alfred Bäumler (Halle/Saale: Max Niemeyer, 1927), p. 29. Cf. *Dr Wilhelm Theodor Streuber. Nekrolog*: "In the decisive moments of our lives we seldom freely determine our own actions. What appears to be our work has its origin in a higher design. We believe we choose our vocation, but in fact we are chosen by it. Therein lies its justification, therein the source of the joy with which we carry it out and the blessing it brings us" (pp. vi–vii).

65. See Josef Pieper, *Leisure the Basis of Culture*, trans. Alexander Dru, with an introduction by T. S. Eliot (New York: Pantheon Books, 1952), p. 32.

66. "My Life in Retrospect," *MRMR*, p. 16; introduction to *Mutterrecht, MRMR*, p. 76.

67. Letter to Meyer-Ochsner, 22 December 1864, *GW*, 10:337.

68. Letter to Meyer-Ochsner, 5 December 1863, *GW*, 10:296.

69. Letter to Meyer-Ochsner, 1 August 1861, *GW,* 10:239.

70. Letter to Meyer-Ochsner, 5 December 1863, *GW,* 10:296. See also letter to Meyer-Ochsner, 10 November 1870, *GW,* 10:451: "Interminable discussion of the marble busts here destroys all one's pleasure in the end. How utterly baseless and almost ridiculous all that aestheticizing prattle is."

71. Letter to Meyer-Ochsner, 10 November 1870, *GW,* 10:451: "A few conjectures, some nonsense about ancient Rome or scraps of inscriptions" would have been more welcome to the Royal Prussian Academy than the heretical suggestion [made by the Africanist Heinrich Barth] that classicists should broaden their horizons. "How little feeling there is now for what is truly great."

72. Letter to Wolfgang Menzel, a historian, literary historian, and editor of *Literaturblatt* (in which he reviewed several of Bachofen's essays), 5 July 1859, *GW,* 10:199.

73. Letter to Meyer-Ochsner, 13 June 1860, *GW,* 10:211–12. The reference is to Theodor Panofka, *Bilder antiken Lebens* (Berlin: Reimer, 1843).

74. Letter to Morgan, 29 October 1880, *GW,* 10:502–3.

75. Letter to Meyer-Ochsner, 26 September 1860, *GW,* 10:214.

76. Ibid.

77. Letter to Elie Reclus, a student of mythology and anarcho-communist, brother of the geographer Elisée Reclus, 29 October 1880, *GW,* 10:504.

78. Bachofen's Genevan disciple, Alexis Giraud-Teulon—trained in law and philosophy and professor of classcal studies and aesthetics at the University of Geneva—reported in a letter to a colleague that Bachofen is grateful to him for having undertaken to translate his work. "Il espère que par moi des études qui sont presque restées inaperçues par le monde savant, seront enfin introduites dans la discussion publique, évitée en Allemagne par un silence calculé. Là, on n'aime pas les choses nouvelles, surtout quand on n'a pas le mérite d'être dans l'intimité des académiciens prussiens. Malheur à qui ose être indépendant et ne suivre que son chemin" (letter from Giraud-Teulon to J. M. Hornung, professor of jurisprudence at the University of Geneva, 22 January 1868, *GW,* 10:398). See likewise a letter from Bachofen to Albrecht Weber, professor of Sanskrit at the University of Berlin, outlining the argument of *Das Mutterrecht* and the *Antiquarische Briefe,* 13 December 1875, *GW,* 10:473; and a letter to Josef Kohler, a legal scholar in Würzburg, subsequently professor of the history of law and of comparative law in Berlin, 23 October 1881, *GW,* 10:517.

79. Letter to Meyer-Ochsner, 4 April 1870, *GW,* 10:442. The reference to the Augustenburgs is to Christian von Augustenburg's claim to the throne of Denmark. When Schleswig-Holstein revolted against Danish rule in 1848, the German liberals supported Augustenburg's claim. On the death of Frederick VII of Denmark in 1863, Christian's son revived his father's claim, but Bismarck dropped his support of the Augustenburgs after a joint Austro-Prussian force occupied the disputed border province in 1864. Following Austria's defeat by Prussia in 1866, the bipartite Austro-Prussian administration of Schleswig-Holstein came to an end and the province was annexed to Prussia. The German liberals at first opposed war against Denmark, but soon rallied in support of Bismarck. The Schleswig-Holstein affair (and, by association, the career of the province's celebrated son) thus confirmed, for Bachofen, the slide of pragmatic and materialistic modernists from liberalism toward an opportunistic and even militaristic nationalism.

80. Letter to Meyer-Ochsner, 16 January 1851, *GW,* 10:114–15.

81. Letter to Meyer-Ochsner, 12 March 1868, *GW,* 10:400.

82. Letter to Meyer-Ochsner, 4 April 1870, *GW,* 10:442.

83. Letter to Meyer-Ochsner, 18 February 1869, *GW,* 10:420.

84. Letter to Meyer-Ochsner, 13 December 1862, *GW,* 10:262.

85. See Lionel Gossman, *Orpheus Philologus: Bachofen versus Mommsen on the Study of Antiquity* (Philadelphia: American Philosophical Society, 1983; Transactions, 73, 5), pp. 25–26.

86. Letter to Meyer-Ochsner, 4 March 1849, *GW,* 10:85. In German: "Ich schmiere, wie man Stiefel schmiert." German *"schmieren"* means "to spread" or "to smear," and by extension "to scrawl or scribble," "to spread grease," "to flatter," "to bribe." The range of meanings is similar, though wider, than English "daub" (*OED,* 1c and 4). Normally in German one would use *"putzen"* of boots. *"Stiefel schmieren,"* which allows Bachofen to pun richly, is South German or Swiss.

87. *Selbstbiographie,* p. 30; letter to Eduard Gerhard, 7 October 1862, *GW,* 10:261; letter to Meyer-Ochsner, 21 June 1856, *GW,* 10:147–48. The Zurich friend with whom Bachofen told Savigny he had had a heated dispute about Mommsen (see letter to Savigny, 16 August 1854, *GW,* 10:136) may well have been Meyer-Ochsner. Mommsen held a chair at Zurich between 1852 and 1854.

88. *GW,* 1:450.

89. Letter to Meyer-Ochsner, 12 July 1861, *GW,* 10:234.

90. Cf. *Discours sur les Sciences et les Arts,* in Jean-Jacques Rousseau, *Oeuvres Complètes* (Paris: Editions de la Pléiade), 3:19–20: "Les anciens Politiques parlaient sans cesse de moeurs et de vertu; les nôtres ne parlent que de commerce et d'argent. . . . Selon eux, un homme ne vaut à l'Etat que la consommation qu'il y fait. Ainsi un Sybarite aurait bien valu trente Lacédémoniens."

91. Letter to Meyer-Ochsner, 24 January 1862, *GW,* 10:252–53.

92. Letter to Meyer-Ochsner, 16 March 1862, *GW,* 10:254–55.

93. Letter to Meyer-Ochsner, 13 December 1862, *GW,* 10:261–63.

94. Letter to Meyer-Ochsner, 16 March 1862, *GW,* 10:255.

95. Letter to Meyer-Ochsner, 10 November 1870, *GW,* 10:451.

96. Letter to Meyer-Ochsner, 4 April 1869, *GW,* 10:422; a similar judgment is found in an earlier letter to Meyer-Ochsner, 13 February 1866, *GW,* 10:359.

97. "Antwort auf Harnacks Antrittsrede" at the Royal Prussian Academy of Sciences, 3 July 1890, in *Reden und Aufsätze* (Berlin: Weidmann, 1905), p. 209.

98. Introduction to *The Myth of Tanaquil, MRMR,* p. 245.

99. According to the poet Carl Spitteler, who was his student (Spitteler, "Jacob Burckhardt und der Student," *Gesammelte Werke,* 10 vols. [Zurich: Artemis, 1945–1958], 6:387).

100. Letter to Andreas Heusler-Ryhiner, 17 August 1847, *GW,* 10:73.

101. "Burckhardt is like Socrates: he likes cobblers and carpenters best. None of his colleagues finds favor in his eyes" (letter to Meyer-Ochsner, 13 January 1860, *GW,* 10:202). Later the same year he returns to this theme. The entire populace took part in the celebrations marking the jubilee of Basel University ("Der ganze Demos hat mitjubiliert"), he tells Meyer-Ochsner. But it remains to be seen whether learning has anything to hope for from the populace. Socrates—with his preference for "brother cobbler, tailor, and carpenter" appears to be the new model for scholars, but "to me every connection with the populace is more disagreeable than an oppressive *Föhn*" (letter to Meyer-Ochsner, 26 September 1860, *GW,* 10:214). The *Föhn* is a psychologically debilitating wind—the central European equivalent of the mistral or sirocco.

102. *Griechische Reise,* pp. 111, 135.

103. "My Life in Retrospect," *MRMR,* p. 10; letter to Meyer-Ochsner, end of May 1868, *GW,* 10:406.

104. Letter to Meyer-Ochsner, 6 February 1861, *GW,* 10:230—a year after the publication of Burckhardt's *Die Cultur der Renaissance in Italien.*

105. Letter to Joseph Marc Hornung, 9 February 1871, *GW,* 10:461.

106. Letter to Meyer-Ochsner, 28 September 1864, *GW,* 10:324.

107. Quoting from a section in Mommsen's *Roman History* where the absence of an efficient bureaucracy is presented as having prevented Rome from successfully managing the transition from city-state to world empire within the framework of its republican institutions, Burckhardt approved the Romans' lack of a bureaucracy and, with an unmistakable nod in the direction of Mommsen's Prussia, their unwillingness to turn education "with the help of an examination system, into a monopoly, and little more than the foundation of the state bureaucracy" (*Historische Fragmente,* ed. Emil Dürr [Stuttgart, Köhler, 1957], p. 24).

108. Letter to Meyer-Ochsner, 29 August 1864, *GW,* 10:320.

Chapter Nine

1. "Beside the primordial female egg stands a chthonian male god who works in the moist depths of matter. He represents the awakening principle and is hidden in the darkness of the earth, a true Zeus Arcanus . . . a god of hidden counsels, a demon of the phallic power from which Murcia awaits fecundation. Subterranean is his altar, Neptunian his nature; his physical foundation is the moisture that permeates the depths; the animal sacred to him is the horse, image of the generative waters; the games consecrated to him are real horse races, *hippocrateia* or Equiria. Murcia, an Aphroditean primal mother, had her shrine in the damp valley between the Aventine and the Palatine. In the rich meadowland lay the divine stone, the *metae Murciae* (goal posts of Murcia), and the nearby Aventine itself bore the name of Murcus. Beside the mother stood Consus, a chthonian demon, just as Eros stood beside Aphrodite, who in Virgil addresses him as *mea magna potentia.* He is the darling and fructifier, without whom Murcia can do nothing; he dwells by her in the depths, rests in her bosom, 'by the goal posts under the earth she keeps him hidden' [Tertullian, *De Spectaculis,* 8]" (*Gräbersymbolik* ["An Essay on Ancient Mortuary Symbolism"] in *Myth, Religion, and Mother Right: Selected Writings of J. J. Bachofen* (hereafter *MRMR*), trans. Ralph Mannheim, introduction by Joseph Campbell [Princeton: Princeton Univ. Press, 1967; Bollingen Series, 84], p. 36; see also introduction to *Mother Right, MRMR,* p. 92, and *Mother Right, MRMR,* pp. 123–24). The fructifying of the land by the waters of the Nile, represented by Isis and Osiris, is seen as another image of chthonic phallic power that is contained in the *gremium matris* (*Gräbersymbolik, MRMR,* pp. 59–60). Dionysus represents the next stage in the process by which the male principle detaches itself from the female, but he still remains bound to the latter. "The phallic God striving toward the fertilization of matter is not the original datum; rather he himself springs from the darkness of the maternal womb; he stands as a son to feminine matter; bursting the shell of the egg, he discloses the mystery of phallic masculinity that had hitherto been hidden within it, and the mother herself rejoices in him as in her own demon" (ibid., p. 30).

2. *Gräbersymbolik, MRMR,* pp. 60–61; on the rope of Ocnus, the weaving of Penelope, the egg, the circus games as symbols of "tellurian creation as . . . eternal becoming and eternal passing away," "images of the eternally vain labors of nature, which through eternal destruction brings about the eternal rejuvenation of the race," see ibid., pp. 26–28, 33–34, 38–39; on the myth of Bellerophon as expressing "the identity of life and death" in "tellurian creation," see *Mother Right, MRMR,* pp. 126–27.

3. Aristotle, *Metaphysics,* 986a (*Works,* ed. J. A. Smith and W. D. Ross [Oxford: Clarendon Press, 1908], vol. 8).

4. *Griechische Reise,* ed. Georg Schmidt (Heidelberg: Richard Weissbach, 1927), p. 54.

5. *MRMR,* pp. 46, 148.

6. *MRMR,* pp. 114–15, 128–29; *Mutterrecht,* in *Gesammelte Werke* (hereafter *GW*), ed. Karl Meuli (Basel: Schwabe, 1943–1967; publication interrupted at vol. 10), 3:647.

7. *MRMR,* p. 139.

8. *Mutterrecht, GW,* 3:631, 641.

9. It is almost impossible to refer the reader to particular passages in Bachofen's work where these themes are articulated, since they appear on almost every page; however, the following page references to the Bollingen volume will guide the reader to some of the most explicit statements or elaborations: *MRMR,* pp. 25, 40–50, 59–60, 79, 92–100, 109–119, 134–39, 223–41.

10. *MRMR,* pp. 161–62.

11. "Die Grundgesetze der Völkerentwicklung und der Historiographie," *GW,* 6:435.

12. Introduction to *The Myth of Tanaquil, MRMR,* pp. 234–35.

13. Introduction to *Mother Right, MRMR,* pp. 115–16.

14. "Bemerkungen zu Livius," *GW,* 1:70.

15. *MRMR,* p. 230.

16. Ibid., p. 213.

17. Ibid., pp. 75–76, 87, 213.

18. Ibid., p. 75.

19. "Die Grundgesetze der Völkerentwicklung und der Historiographie," *GW,* 6:417–18.

20. *Mother Right, MRMR,* pp. 160–61.

21. *Griechische Reise,* p. 195

22. Introduction to *Tanaquil,* in *MRMR,* p. 239.

23. *MRMR,* p. 224.

24. This is another major theme that runs through all Bachofen's work from the *History of the Romans* to *Tanaquil,* the original title of which was to have been "Italy and the Orient" (letter to Meyer-Ochsner, 27 December 1868, *GW,* 10:417) and the subtitle of which is still "A Study of Orientalism in Rome and Italy." The following are simply some points of reference to assist the reader: *Geschichte der Römer* in *GW,* 1:165–70; *MRMR,* pp. 211–46 (the whole of the introduction to *Tanaquil*); letter to Meyer-Ochsner, 29 August 1864, *GW,* 10:320–21, recounting a visit to the Campana museum in Paris: "I have retained an ineradicable impression of the oldest age of Etruria before the refinements introduced by Greek influence. I would have thought it impossible that clay pots could produce an effect on the viewer comparable to that produced by Assyrian sculptures. The finest Greek vases belong to a perfect but much narrower world. A German walked by me. 'Pure Greek, everything!' In contrast, I say: Greece emerged out of Asia, like Etruria, but each developed in a different way. In Etruria the Asiatic form remained purer. Greece overcame it and then tried to reform Etruria too, but without complete success. That is what distinguishes Italy: it preserved the ideas and forms of the most ancient world more faithfully than Hellas." See also letters to Meyer-Ochsner, 26 February 1864 (*GW,* 10:306) and 12 March 1868 (*GW,* 10:400).

25. The harmony and simplicity of the life he enjoyed at the inn run by the Epaminonda family in Megara, Bachofen noted, made him feel the equal of any monarch on earth. "And yet all that is not enough to satisfy the endless longing of the human soul. Like everything that draws us into a contemplative mood, the tranquil grandeur of the south only stirs up even more deeply that dark inclination to dream that draws sustenance from every ray of light" (*Griechische Reise,* p. 53). Likewise ancient Greece, for Bachofen, is not the land of the "*so-genannte Classicität,*" which he considered an invention of the Germanic West, but the home of obscure terrors and longings that found expression in the mystery cults.

26. *MRMR,* p. 75.

27. *Griechische Reise,* p. 109.

28. Introduction to *Mother Right, MRMR,* p. 87.

29. *Mother Right, MRMR,* p. 142.

30. Introduction to *Mother Right, MRMR,* pp. 94–95.

31. *Mother Right, MRMR,* pp. 142–43. See also ibid., p. 144: "Woman was the source of the first civilization"; and *Antiquarische Briefe, GW,* 8:28–30: "In Indian legend it is woman in whom a mighty longing for a higher condition first awakens. . . . How else can we interpret woman's weeping, her burning thirst for the pure waters of the Ganges, her tears mingling with the sacred waters? How else than as the expression of woman's profound misery at the overwhelming burden wild Indra's law places on her sex?"

32. Introducton to *Mother Right,* in *MRMR,* p. 107. "From the banks of the Nile to the shores of the Black Sea, from Central Asia to Italy, Amazonian names and deeds are interwoven with the history of the founding of cities that later became famous" (ibid., p. 106).

33. *Mother Right, MRMR,* p. 144.

34. Introduction to *Mother Right, MRMR,* p. 91.

35. Letter to Wilhelm Henzen, 11 November 1850, *GW,* 10:110.

36. Introduction to *Mother Right, MRMR,* p. 79.

37. Ibid., pp. 80–81.

38. *Selbstbiographie und Antrittsrede über das Naturrecht,* ed. Alfred Bäumler (Halle/Saale: Max Niemeyer, 1927), p. 29. The phrase about "pain and joy and the true meaning of things" reappears in somewhat different form in *Griechische Reise,* p. 173: "What one enjoys, one enjoys more deeply but one is also more sharply conscious of the soul's pain and its insatiable longing."

39. *Mutterrecht, GW,* 3:587.

40. Letter to Meyer-Ochsner, 10 June 1863, *GW,* 10:279; letter to Meyer-Ochsner, 11 December 1865, *GW,* 10:353. See also letter to Meyer-Ochsner, 4 June 1865, *GW,* 10:342–43 (written from Rome): "I feel how difficult it must be to come to any kind of real and right vision [of antiquity] when one is far from this soil, in the cold north, in a smoke-filled room, among crabbed and crippled rationalists."

41. *Griechische Reise,* p. 202.

42. Ibid., p. 62.

43. Ibid., p. 85.

44. Ibid., pp. 59–60.

45. *Römische Grablampen, GW,* 7:270–71.

46. *Griechische Reise,* p. 54.

47. Ibid., pp. 30–31.

48. Ibid., p. 99.

49. Ibid., p. 200.

50. Ibid., pp. 201–2. Wilhelm Vischer-Bilfinger, the professor of Greek at Basel, and the person most responsible for bringing Nietzsche to Basel to be his successor, made a strikingly similar contrast between Greek and Gothic—this time in relation to the Parthenon—in his otherwise rather dry *Erinnerungen und Eindrücke aus Griechenland* (Basel: Schweighauser, 1857):

> We do not have here that majesty striving upward toward infinity, which seizes us at the aspect of the great Gothic cathedrals, with their flying buttresses, their high vaulting, and their lofty spires, and which fills our minds with obscure intuitions and feelings of mysterious awe. Rather the spirit is made calm and at the same time elevated by the all-pervasive idea of a whole raised to its purest form and manifested organically in every particular. This idea produces in us the impression of a calm and unforced grandeur. That is what constitutes the essence of the Greek spirit in general, and what we encounter in every aspect of Greek life and creation—not a striving toward the infinite and the unattain-

able but the most complete possible representation within a limited scope and in appropriate form of that which the human mind is capable of grasping, the imparting of intelligible outward form to clearly conceived ideas. The work of art conceived in this spirit, the Parthenon above all, appears as something necessary. Every part seems an organic part of the whole and it is as though nothing could be otherwise.

P. 159, quoted by Werner Kaegi, *Jacob Burckhardt: eine Biographie* (Basel: Schwabe, 1947–1982), 1:337–38, note 108. It is not surprising that Vischer read a commemoration address on Winckelmann to the Basel Antiquarian Society in 1867 and instituted regular celebration of Winckelmann's birthday.

51. *Griechische Reise*, pp. 221–22.
52. Ibid., pp. 222–23.
53. *Geschichte der Römer, GW,* 1:102–3.
54. Ibid., p. 110.
55. Ibid., p. 113.
56. Ibid., p. 126.
57. *Griechische Reise*, p. 33.
58. Ibid., p. 40.
59. See Kaegi, *Jacob Burckhardt*, 1:337–38.
60. "My Life in Retrospect," *MRMR*, p. 10.
61. Ibid., p. 12.
62. It is the writer's difficult task, Bachofen held, to preserve and communicate through his writing the immediate flashes of insight vouchsafed to him in his encounters with the landscapes, texts, and artifacts of antiquity. Bachofen had no doubt that the image of antiquity produced by those encounters in the imagination was superior to anything that reasoning alone could provide; the question was "how to preserve it" and "that," he wrote, "is what escapes me. The best of what we feel and experience is incommunicable" (*Griechische Reise*, p. 98). It was not that the insight or experience is ever lost. "Great and rich are those moments when the classical scholar feels himself one with his object! Though they cannot last for long, the image that remains behind never pales. . . . In the interior of our soul the image it has received lives eternally" (ibid., pp. 120, 164). The challenge for the scholar and writer was to find a way of calling up that image, exteriorizing it, and communicating it to others.
63. For a succinct, sympathetic discussion of the deleterious effect of Bachofen's method on his scholarly contribution, see P. G. Bietenholz, *Historia and Fabula* (Leiden, New York, and Cologne: E. J. Brill, 1994), pp. 350–68. See also the essential essay of the Zurich classical scholar Ernst Howald, "Wider Johann Jacob Bachofen" (1924), reprinted in his *Humanismus und Europäertum* (Zurich and Stuttgart: Artemis Verlag, 1957), pp. 63–75. On Bachofen's place in the history of anthropology, see Lionel Gossman, *Orpheus Philologus: Bachofen versus Mommsen on the Study of Antiquity* (Philadelphia: American Philosophical Society, 1983; Transactions, 73, 5), pp. 1–3 and notes.
64. See, for instance, on the one hand, Georg Schmidt, *Johann Jacob Bachofens Geschichtsphilosophie* (Munich: C. H. Beck, 1929) and, on the other, Ludwig Klages, *Vom kosmogonischen Eros* (Munich: Georg Müller, 1922). On the "undeniable discrepancy in Bachofen's vision of history," see also Karl Schefold, "Die Religion des Archäologen J. J. Bachofen," Sitzungsberichte der Bayerischen Akademie der Wissenschaften (Philologische-Historische Klasse), 1987, Heft 5.
65. *De la Religion*, ed. Pierre Deguise (Lausanne: Bibliothèque romande, 1971), pp. 65–66.
66. Letter to Johann Georg von Cotta, 11 February 1857, *GW,* 10:157.

67. "Die Grundgesetze der Völkerentwicklung und der Historiographie," *GW,* 6:409–10.

68. Introduction to *Mother Right*, in *MRMR*, p. 74.

69. Introduction to *Tanaquil*, in *MRMR*, p. 232.

70. Ibid., pp. 242–43.

71. *Antiquarische Briefe, GW,* 8:41.

72. Introduction to *Mother Right*, in *MRMR*, p. 76.

73. Letter to J. M. Hornung, 2 December 1870, *GW,* 10:454.

74. "Die Grundgesetze der Völkerentwicklung und der Historiographie," *GW,* 6:410–16.

75. Ibid., *GW,* 6:436–37.

76. Some Bachofen scholars emphasize the direct contribution of ancient sources such as Plutarch to the elaboration of his philosophy of history. German philosophy of the early decades of the nineteenth century—not only the classic philosophical writings of Hegel and Schelling, but the speculations on universal history and religion of Görres, Creuzer, and Friedrich Schlegel—was shot through with Platonic and neo-Platonic influences.

77. Introduction to course on "German History to the Reformation," from student notes taken by Eduard Winkelmann, in Leopold von Ranke, *Vorlesungseinleitungen,* ed. V. Dotterweich and W. P. Fuchs (Munich and Vienna: R. Oldenbourg, 1975), p. 274. (Ranke, *Werke und Nachlass,* ed. W. P. Fuchs and T. Schieder, vol. 4.) Cf. Burckhardt's notes from the early 1840s on Ranke's course on German history: "A nation must participate in the general spiritual development of mankind. Peoples, like individuals, cannot isolate themselves. Only such peoples [i.e., as do so participate] have a prospect of eternity" (quoted by Kaegi, *Jacob Burckhardt,* 2:59).

78. Ranke, *Über die Epochen der neueren Geschichte* [lectures given before King Maximilian II of Bavaria, 1854], ed. Hans Herzfeld (Schloss Laupheim: Ulrich Steiner Verlag, n.d.), p. 30.

79. Introduction to *Mother Right, MRMR*, p. 116.

80. Introduction to *Tanaquil, MRMR*, pp. 231–32. See also letter to Meyer-Ochsner (*GW,* 10:320–21), cited in note 24 above.

81. Introduction to *Mother Right, MRMR*, p. 116. This passage should be compared with the comments on English common law in the *Selbstbiographie* or letter to Savigny of 1851.

> The study of English law is made difficult by the absolute contrast between its basic outlook and that of continental jurists, especially those steeped in Roman law, by the division of its courts and jurisprudence into equity and common law, and especially by its evolution through countless precedents that lie scattered in hundreds of volumes, by the immense quantity of acts of parliament, constantly patching up details and burying one amendment under another, and finally by the style and manner of English legal writers, who always have practice in mind, assume that the reader has a knowledge of whatever is more general, begin their exposition, on the very first page, with particular case studies, and seldom submit to logical order or the setting out of principles. Such material is normally accessible to a foreigner only after long familiarity and years of practice. To make order in it, discern its leading principles, and put these together into a *jus civile* would require the labor of a lifetime. The English spirit seems unsuited ever to carry out such a task. . . . It stays close to the ground and allows the whole to vanish in the wealth of details. . . . England's legal scholars . . . might have learned from the study of Roman law what is lacking in their own and how that lack might be corrected, how to sort and order material, how

to arrive at a *jus civile*, how to substitute a direct *formula petitoria* for clumsy fictions, . . . how to combine *jus* and *aequitas* into a unified practice of law, how to rise above the many species of tenure to a grasp of the higher concept of property itself, and how to clarify the nature of the judicial in contrast to the obligatory [*das Dingliche in seinem Gegensatz zu dem Obligatorischen durchführen*]. These are all benefits that English law must now do without and which cannot therefore improve either its theoretical understanding or its practice. The former in any higher sense simply does not exist, and the creative life has long vanished from the latter. I therefore predict for English law the fate that awaits all political institutions that have been rendered incapable of development appropriate to the times: they ultimately become the object of violent transformation—first the target, then the victim of advancing democracy. At that point, English law will disappear without trace in the way that the law of Carthage did. For, unlike Roman law, it contains in itself no creative and formative element that could inspire later times with a desire to appropriate it or that could serve future generations as a point of departure for new development. . . . The entire Germanic world has produced nothing capable of instructing, establishing or stimulating other worlds.

Selbstbiographie, pp. 19–21; this important passage was omitted from the English translation in *MRMR*. See note 67 to chapter 6.

82. Introduction to *Mother Right*, MRMR, p. 117.

83. Ibid., p. 118.

84. Introduction to *Tanaquil*, MRMR, p. 237.

85. "Die Grundgesetze der Völkerentwicklung und der Historiographie," *GW*, 6:411–12; *Geschichte der Römer*, *GW*, 1:131. Also the inaugural lecture on "Natural Law and Historical Law," *GW*, 1:19–23. Bachofen's view that the individual nation is not an end in itself but contributes, through its contacts, friendly or hostile, with others to the evolution of humanity—so that the isolated, self-sufficient nation would be historically sterile—was that of his teacher Ranke.

86. *Die Staatshaushaltung der Athener*, 3 vols. (Berlin: G. Reimer, 1817–1840), 1:1.

87. *Griechische Reise*, p. 134.

88. Most strikingly perhaps, in *Tanaquil*, Bachofen questioned that the general plan and the perfection of the state to which it appears to lead is the last word in the history of mankind. In the efforts of the Jews to preserve their original revelation pure of later accretions and in the Romans' decision to burn the old books and thus make any return to the simple and grandiose ideas of the earlier religious tradition impossible, he discerned an important contrast between "the preference of the city on the Tiber for the point of view of the state" and the preference of Israel for religion. "The former founded the most enduring empire that ever existed, the latter never achieved a lasting state formation." But in the end, he recalled, "Bethlehem overthrew the universal empire!" *Tanaquil*, *GW*, 6:177–78.

89. "Die Grundgesetze der Völkerentwicklung und der Historiographie," *GW*, 6:433.

90. *Antiquarische Briefe*, 57, *GW*, 8:387.

91. *Über die Epochen der neueren Geschichte*, p. 30.

92. *Gräbersymbolik*, MRMR, pp. 29–30.

93. Ibid., pp. 28–29; introduction to *Mother Right*, MRMR, pp. 101–3.

94. Introduction to *Mother Right*, MRMR, p. 194.

95. Ibid., pp. 102–3. Cf. in *Mutterrecht* (*GW*, 3:593), the praise of a way of life, associated with the cult of Dionysus, which combined "abandonment without reserve to the most luxu-

riant life of the senses and fidelity to that best Hope that reaches beyond the grave" and in which "no idea of struggle, of self-discipline, of sin and repentance disturbs the harmony of a life at once sensual and transcending sensuality."

96. Introduction to *Tanaquil, MRMR,* p. 236.

97. *Griechische Reise,* p. 135.

98. Introduction to *Tanaquil, MRMR,* p. 236. The female figure represented in Arnold Böcklin's *Das Drama* (plate 2) combines the matronly and underlying chthonic or phallic aspects of Bachofen's Tanaquil.

99. Ibid., p. 232.

100. Jules Michelet, *Journal,* ed. Paul Viallaneix and Claude Digeon, 4 vols. (Paris: Gallimard, 1959–1976), 1:378 (30 January 1842).

101. *Histoire de France,* Préface de 1869, in *Oeuvres complètes,* ed. Paul Viallaneix (Paris: Flammarion, 1971–), 4:18.

102. Franz D. Gerlach, *Über den Geschichtschreiber C. Salustus Crispus. Einladungsschrift zur Promotionsfeier des Pädagogiums und zur Eröffnung des Jahreskurses 1831* (Basel: August Wieland, 1831), pp. 7, 16.

103. Letter to Morgan, 24 February 1879, *GW,* 10:489; letter 298*, Morgan to Bachofen, 13 March 1879, *GW,* 10:493.

104. See the passages from the introduction to *Mother Right,* from *Mother Right,* and from the introduction to *Tanaquil, MRMR,* pp. 117–18, 132–33, 140, 191–93, 231–37.

105. Letter to Morgan, in English, 24 February 1879, *GW,* 10:489.

106. Letter from Morgan to Bachofen, 13 March 1879, *GW,* 10:492.

107. Letter from Morgan to Bachofen, 21 June 1880, *GW,* 10:501.

108. Letter to Morgan, 29 October 1880, *GW,* 10:502–3.

109. Letter from Morgan to Bachofen, 12 November 1880, *GW,* 10:505.

110. Letter to Morgan, in English, 4 January 1881, *GW,* 10:509.

111. *Griechische Reise,* p. 26.

112. Ibid., pp. 64–65.

113. Weavers are exclusively male in some societies, exclusively female in others. In the classical tradition Bachofen was most familiar with, weaving is the invention and the activity of the female, and it is as a female art that he presented it in the essay "Oknos der Seilflechter" (*GW,* 4:360–65). In the competition between Aphrodite and Athena over weaving, he saw a representation of the passage from primitive hetaerism or communism (Aphrodite and her unskilled, crude handiwork, the most primitive kind of production) to the earliest cultures, which are also the creation of women (Athena and her highly skilled, refined handiwork). Among the many myths referred to in these pages is that of Arachne, a woman of Lydia (hence an "Oriental"), who dared to challenge Athena herself and who provocatively depicted in the corners of her work various episodes in which Athena's father Zeus exploited and violated mortal women. When her work turned out to be flawless, Athena destroyed it and threw the spindle at Arachne's head. Arachne hanged herself but Athena transformed her into a spider-woman perpetually and patiently spinning and weaving. This myth was popular at the time. Creuzer discusses it in *Symbolik,* 2nd ed., 6 vols. (Leipzig and Darmstadt: Heyer & Leske, 1819–1823), 2:748. To Bachofen it was of particular interest in that it represented mythically—in the conflict between the "Oriental" woman and the Western goddess born only of a father—the struggle between "East" and "West," the community and the state, the law of nature and the law of the spirit, and the effort of the "West" to subordinate the "East," the effort of the state to subordinate culture without destroying it. In another version of the myth the goddess gives the gift of arms to Phalanx and that of weaving to his sister Arachne.

114. "Oknos der Seilflechter," ch. 2 ("Bedeutung des Flechtens und Webens, der Gespinste und des Seils"), *GW,* 4:359–69.

115. *Kurze Geschichte der Bandweberei in Basel* (Basel: Schultze, 1862), pp. 68–69.

Chapter Ten

Author's note: The epigraph that opens part 3 is from Carl Spitteler, *Gesammelte Werke* (Zurich: Artemis-Verlag), 6:379–82. The poet, novelist, and essayist Carl Spitteler (1845–1924), winner of the Nobel prize for literature in 1919, hailed from Liesthal in Basel-Country and studied at the University of Basel, with Burckhardt among others. He often visited the old scholar in his modest apartment. The German *mysterisch,* translated here as *mysterical,* is an invention of Spitteler's; probably he meant by it: "ready to accept a certain mysteriousness of things, albeit not in a Christian sense." Karl Lamprecht's judgment of Leopold von Ranke evokes a similar philosophical reticence in Burckhardt's teacher: "Ranke is no philosopher, even though he has a strong philosophical streak in him. . . . He is loath to articulate the sacred core of his convictions. He will go only up to a certain point in expressing them. The innermost depths remain concealed, like those groves in which the ancient Germans placed their ruling gods. . . . [He] is by no means alone in adopting this stance toward the highest philosophical questions. It is Goethe's attitude, for example. We do them all an injustice when we try laboriously to derive a . . . philosophical system from individual statements they have made. At best we can aim at an approximate description of what is essential in their outlook" ("Alte und neue Richtungen in der Geschichtswissenschaft," in Karl Lamprecht, *Alternative zu Ranke: Schriften zur Geschichtstheorie,* ed. Hans Schleier [Leipzig: Philipp Reclam jun., 1988], pp. 161–62).

1. Werner Kaegi, *Jacob Burckhardt: eine Biographie* (Basel: Schwabe, 1947–1982), 1:35.
2. Tagebuch Isaak Iselin (MS), 27 August 1755, quoted by Kaegi, ibid., p. 38.
3. Quoted by Kaegi from J. J. Oeri-Burckhardt, *Aus meinem Leben,* ibid., p. 151.
4. Quoted by Kaegi, ibid., p. 47.
5. Ibid., p. 36.
6. On Johann Lucas and Lucas Gottlieb Burckhardt, see ibid., pp. 293–300.
7. Letter to Max Alioth, 4 February 1883, *Briefe,* ed. Max Burckhardt, 10 vols. plus index vol. (Basel: Schwabe, 1949–1994), 8:107–10.
8. Burckhardt's performance at the *Gymnasium* appears to have been somewhat better than Bachofen's. In his first year there (1827), he already placed eighth overall in a class of 61: second in Latin, seventh in German, fourth in history, and thirty-ninth in arithmetic! (*Collocations* of the Basel *Gymnasium,* Basel University Library, Ki. Ar. F. V.4).
9. Kaegi, *Jacob Burckhardt,* 1:380.
10. Letter to Gottfried Kinkel, 20 August 1843, *Briefe,* 2:35.
11. Jacob Burckhardt, *"Lebensrückschau"* (a brief curriculum vitae traditionally prepared by members of patrician families in Basel for recitation at their graveside), in *Jacob Burckhardt: Die Kunst der Betrachtung. Aufsätze und Vorträge zur bildenden Kunst,* ed. Henning Ritter (Cologne: Dumont, 1984), pp. 15–18.
12. Quoted by Kaegi, *Jacob Burckhardt,* 1:383, from the inscription in a copy of one of his Dante Studies that the eighty-two-year-old Picchione presented to his former student.
13. Letter to Heinrich Schreiber, 15 July 1836, *Briefe,* 1:49.
14. A letter to his sister Louise, 29 March 1840, in which he practices his English, demonstrates a decent level of accomplishment. *Briefe,* 1:151–52.
15. See Kaegi, *Jacob Burckhardt,* 1:422.
16. See Kaegi's biography for many illustrations of these sketches, which are preserved in the Bachofen Archives at the University of Basel.

17. Examples of Jacob Burckhardt the Elder's poetic compositions are in Kaegi, *Jacob Burckhardt,* 1:538–42.

18. Letter to Friedrich von Tschudi, 16 March 1840, *Briefe,* 1:145.

19. See Kaegi, *Jacob Burckhardt,* 1:549–53.

20. Schreiber was subsequently removed from the theological faculty at Freiburg on account of his continued outspokenness on these issues, joined the nationalist *"deutsch-katholisch"* movement of Johannes Ronge, and was finally excommunicated.

21. "Gedanken Gottes" (Leopold von Ranke, *Die Grossen Mächte; Politisches Gespräch,* with an afterword by Theodor Schieder [Göttingen: Vandenhoek und Ruprecht, 1955], p. 61).

22. Kaegi, *Jacob Burckhardt,* 1:396.

23. See his notes on Wackernagel's lectures in Kaegi, *Jacob Burckhardt,* 1:492–93.

24. Quoted from Burckhardt's notes by Kaegi, ibid., p. 496.

25. See ibid., pp. 442–43.

26. Letter of 21 May 1807, quoted by Kaegi, ibid., p. 131.

27. Letter to Johannes Riggenbach, 26 August 1838, *Briefe,* 1:84.

28. Ibid.

29. Ibid.

30. Kaegi, *Jacob Burckhardt,* 1:474–75.

31. Letter to Johannes Riggenbach, 9 October 1838, *Briefe,* 1:91–92.

32. Ibid. Cf. a comment many years later in a letter of 3 July 1870 to his friend Friedrich von Preen, a government official in Baden, at the time of the Franco-Prussian War: "If the German spirit can still react with its deepest and innermost energies against this terrible violence, if it can set up against it a new poetry, art, and religion, then we are saved; if not, then we are not. I say: religion, because without some desire for what transcends the world, which can counterbalance the frenzied pursuit of money and power, nothing will do any good" (*Briefe,* 5:97).

33. *Griechische Kulturgeschichte,* ed. Felix Stähelin, in Jacob Burckhardt, *Gesamtausgabe,* ed. Emil Dürr et al., 14 vols. (Stuttgart, Berlin, and Leipzig: Deutsche Verlagsanstalt, 1930–1934), 8:78 (hereafter *Gesamtausgabe*).

34. Ibid., 1:4. Quoted by Kaegi, *Jacob Burckhardt,* 1:522.

35. See a letter to Willibald Beyschlag of 14 January 1844 (*Briefe,* 2:60): "I have broken with the Church forever, from quite personal motives, because I quite literally can't make sense of it. My moral life . . . marches forward without the help of the Church, and retreats without the sting of ecclesiastical conscience. The Church has lost all power over me, as over so many others, and in a period of dissolution that is no more than is to be expected" (text from *Letters of Jacob Burckhardt,* ed. and trans. Alexander Dru [London: Routledge & Kegan Paul, 1955], p. 88).

36. Letter to Heinrich Schreiber, 15 January 1840, *Briefe,* 1:136: "I was very well received by Droysen and visit and talk with him quite often, but his influence passes entirely through the medium of the intelligence."

37. Letter to Heinrich Schreiber, 4 March 1842, *Briefe,* 1:193.

38. Johann Wenzel, *Jacob Burckhardt und die Krise seiner Zeit* (Berlin: VEB Verlag der Wissenschaften, 1967), p. 17.

39. Letter to his sister Louise Burckhardt, 29 January 1842, *Briefe,* 1:189. On Bettina von Arnim and Marx, see Fritz Boettger, *Bettina von Arnim: Ihr Leben, ihre Begegnungen, ihre Zeit* (Bern, Munich, and Vienna: Scherz, 1990), pp. 271–72.

40. *Gottfried Kinkels Selbstbiographie 1838–1848,* ed. Richard Sander (Bonn: Friedrich Cohen, 1931), p. 98.

41. Letter to Heinrich Schreiber, 15 January 1840, *Briefe*, 1:132. At this point Burckhardt was determined to resist the appeal of the Germanic and Romance Middle Ages and to specialize in the history of the Near East!

42. "Zur eigenen Lebensgeschichte" (*Sämtliche Werke*, vol. 53/54 (Leipzig, 1890), pp. 45, 56), quoted by Kaegi, *Jacob Burckhardt*, 2:55. The peace of Basel, between France and Prussia, was signed in 1797.

43. Kaegi, *Jacob Burckhardt*, 2:55. See also Leopold von Ranke, *Über die Epochen der neueren Geschichte*, ed. Hans Herzfeld (Schloss Laupheim: Ulrich Steiner Verlag, n.d. [1955?]), p. 191: "The reconciliation of monarchy and national sovereignty, hereditary authority from above and self-government from below—that was the watchword in Europe"; pp. 194–95: "In my view the leading tendency of our time is the struggle between two principles, that of monarchy and that of popular sovereignty. All other oppositions and conflicts are related to that one. . . . But any one who would conclude from that that universal history is moving in the direction of the triumph of national sovereignty over everything has not understood the tolling of the bell. For so many destructive tendencies are connected with those popular aspirations that, if they were to gain the upper hand, culture and Christendom would be endangered. Thus monarchy also recovers its roots in the world, in that it becomes necessary for the eradication of the destructive tendencies borne in on the huge tide of popular principles."

44. This echo of Ranke is in a letter to Gottfried Kinkel, 13 June 1842, *Briefe*, 1:202.

45. Kaegi, *Jacob Burckhardt*, 2:65, quoting from Burckhardt's lecture notes.

46. See ibid., p. 58. Cf. Ranke, *Über die Epochen der neueren Geschichte*, p. 30: "As no Time stretches before it, I imagine that the divinity surveys all historical humanity in its entirety and finds value everywhere. The idea of the progressive education of mankind contains indeed an element of truth, but in the eyes of God all the generations of man appear equally justified, and that is how the historian too should see things."

47. Quoted from *Historisch-Politische Zeitschrift*, I (1832), p. 375, in Wolfgang Hardtwig, *Geschichtsschreibung zwischen Alteuropa und moderner Welt: Jacob Burckhardt in der Krise seiner Zeit* (Göttingen: Vandenhoek & Ruprecht, 1974), p. 31. See also letter to his brother Heinrich, 24 December 1826 (*Neue Briefe*, ed. Bernahrd Hoeft and Hans Herzfeld [Hamburg: Hoffmann & Campe, 1949], pp. 89–90): "Is not the deciphering of past actions an inspiring goal? You know my old ambition—to discover the plot of universal history, that course of the events and developments of our species that we should consider history's true content, center, and essence."

48. Ranke, *Die grossen Mächte; Politisches Gespräch*, p. 59. "Friedrich" responds, however: "In fact, you will not be able to name me many wars, which could not be shown to have resulted in the victory of the true moral force."

49. Such an assumption, according to Ranke, would be tantamount to imputing "an injustice to the divinity." "What I hold, however," he explained, "is that every age stands in an immediate relation to God and that its value does not reside in what came after it, but in its own being. . . ." ("Ich aber behaupte: jede Epoche ist unmittelbar zu Gott, und ihr Wert beruht gar nicht auf dem, was aus ihr hervorgeht, sondern in ihrer Existenz selbst. . . .") (*Über die Epochen der neueren Geschichte*, pp. 29–30). See Herder, "Auch eine Philosophie der Geschichte" (1774), in *Herder on Social and Political Culture*, ed. F. M. Barnard (Cambridge: Cambridge University Press, 1969), pp. 206–14.

50. Kaegi, *Jacob Burckhardt*, 2:61.

51. Quoted by Kaegi, ibid., p. 40. On Droysen, see Hardtwig, *Geschichtsschreibung zwischen Alteuropa und moderner Welt*, pp. 81–87.

52. Quoted by Kaegi, *Jacob Burckhardt*, 2:42.

53. See Christopher Parker, *The English Historical Tradition* (Edinburgh: John Donald, 1990), p. 115.

54. Letter to Friedrich von Tschudi, a fellow theology student in Basel, 16 March 1840, *Briefe,* 1:145.

55. Letter to Karl Fresenius, 19 June 1842, *Briefe,* 1:206–7.

56. Letter to Kinkel, 7 December 1842, *Briefe,* 1:224.

57. Reported in Heinrich Gelzer, "Jacob Burckhardt als Mensch und Lehrer," *Zeitschrift für Kulturgeschichte* (1899) and quoted by Kaegi, *Jacob Burckhardt,* 2:44–45. The view of Demosthenes in Burckhardt's lectures on the cultural history of Greece was considerably more nuanced and the great orator and statesman does not emerge from those lectures as a heroic or even particularly admirable figure. See chapter 12.

58. See Kaegi, *Jacob Burckhardt,* 2:47, quoting Droysen's *Grundrisse der Historik* (Leipzig, 1868), p. 33, and Burckhardt, *Weltgeschichtliche Betrachtungen,* ed. Albert Oeri and Emil Dürr, in *Gesamtausgabe,* 7:2, quoted here from the English translation by Mary Hottinger, *Reflections on History* (London: George Allen & Unwin, 1943), p. 16 (hereafter *Reflections on History*). Kaegi pointed out that at the time he was composing the *Weltgeschichtliche Betrachtungen,* Burckhardt did not know Droysen's work, which was only then being printed from the manuscript.

59. Quoted in Introductory Note to *Reflections on History,* p. 7. The original text of the letter, dated 25 February 1874 (*Briefe,* 5:222), reads: "Vor Allem ist mein armer Kopf gar nie im Stande gewesen, über die letzten Gründe, Ziele und Wünschbarkeiten der geschichtlichen Wissenschaft auch nur von ferne so zu reflectiren wie Sie dieses vermögen. Als Lehrer und Docent aber darf ich wohl sagen: ich habe die Geschichte nie um dessentwillen gelehrt was man pathetisch unter Weltgeschichte versteht. . . ." ("Above all, my poor head has never been able even remotely to reflect, as you can, on the ultimate causes, goals and desiderata of historical study. Nevertheless, I can say this: as a teacher and college instructor I have never taught history for the sake of that thing referred to dramatically as Universal History. . . .").

60. Note of 15 January 1883, in *Jacob Burckhardt und Heinrich Wölfflin: Briefwechsel und andere Dokumente ihrer Begegnung 1882–1897,* ed. Joseph Gantner, 2nd enlarged ed. (Basel: Schwabe, 1989 [1948]), p. 29. Shortly afterwards, Wölfflin softened his position. In a conversation with the young philosophy teacher Hans Heussler, the two came to discuss Burckhardt: "Resolute enemy of all efforts to make history a science," Wölfflin noted, adding "Perhaps rightly" ("Vielleicht mit Recht") (ibid., pp. 31–32). For a thorough analysis of Burckhardt's equivocal position between providentialism and agnosticism, a normative ethics and historical relativism, and so on, see Hardtwig, *Geschichtsschreibung zwischen Alteuropa und moderner Welt.* According to Hardtwig, Burckhardt's dilemmas are inherent in any fully developed historicism.

61. The passages from Cousin and Célestine Lefèbvre's letter to Michelet are quoted in Gabriel Monod, *La Vie et la pensée de Jules Michelet. 1798–1852,* 2 vols. (Paris: Champion, 1923), 1:189, 192. On Michelet's response to the "optimism" of Cousin, see ibid., pp. 187–95. The Barante passage is in *Histoire des Ducs de Bourgogne,* 2 vols. (Brussels: Wahlen, 1838), 1:26.

62. Kaegi, *Jacob Burckhardt,* 2:134.

63. Ranke, *Über die Epochen der neueren Geschichte,* pp. 28–29.

64. Letter of 13 June 1842, *Briefe,* 1:201.

65. Letter to Eduard Schauenburg, 28–29 January 1844, *Briefe,* 2:78.

66. Letter to Kinkel, 21 April 1844, *Briefe,* 2:86.

67. On these, see the detailed analysis in Kaegi, *Jacob Burckhardt,* 2:331–77.

68. See especially ibid., pp. 344–46. Burckhardt's view of the relative roles of the West and of Islam corresponds also to that of Ranke (*Über die Epochen der neueren Geschichte*, p. 28).

69. Quoted from the manuscript by Kaegi, *Jacob Burckhardt*, 2:350. Cf. Ranke, *Über die Epochen der neueren Geschichte*, p. 28: "But there is only one system of peoples who take part in this general historical movement. Others, in contrast, are excluded from it. . . ."

70. Quoted from the manuscript by Kaegi, *Jacob Burckhardt*, 2:346.

71. Quoted from the manuscript by Kaegi, ibid., p. 345.

72. Ranke, *Über die Epochen der neueren Geschichte*, "Schlussgespräch," p. 195.

73. See Hardtwig, *Geschichtsschreibung zwischen Alteuropa und moderner Welt*, pp. 31–33. Hardtwig has argued that Ranke never really doubted either the unity and continuity of history or its legibility. He quotes in this regard from Rudolf Vierhaus's *Ranke und die soziale Welt* (Münster, 1957): "At no point does he [Ranke] mention that the old feudal society of orders has reached its end and that a new one, the industrial class society, is taking its place. An observation of that kind supposes a questioning that never takes place in Ranke" (Hardtwig, p. 33 note). Hardtwig adds that Ranke's historical methodology—his confidence in the objectivity of historical knowledge based on the critical evaluation and interpretation of sources—is also related to his confidence in the reconciliation he believed had been effected by the Restoration. "The simultaneous difference and identity of past and present made possible both critical distance from the historical object and an appropriating identification with it" (ibid., p. 33).

74. "Die Bildung Alteuropas." Letter to Hermann Schauenburg, 5 March 1846, *Briefe*, 2:210.

75. Letter of 30 December 1841. He gave his passion for Germany poetic expression:

> In deines Rheines Prachtgelände,
> Da zogst du eng ans Herze mich;
> Zum Himmel hob ich meine Hände
> Und schwor zu leben nur für dich.
> Dort möcht' ich vor dein Antlitz treten
> Zu blauen Bergen hingewandt,
> Und mit des Dankes Tränen beten
> Zu dir, mein deutsches Vaterland.

Quoted by Wilhelm Waetzold, *Deutsche Kunsthistoriker*, 2nd unrevised ed. (Berlin: Bruno Hessling, 1965), 2:176. Roughly translated: "On the splendid banks of your Rhine, you drew me close to your heart. I raised my hands to heaven and swore to live only for you. Oh, might I appear before you, turned toward blue mountains, and with tears of gratitude pray to you, my German fatherland." See note 116 below for complete text.

76. Letter to Kinkel, 26 November 1843, *Briefe*, 2:52.

77. Letter to Eduard Schauenburg, 30 November 1843, *Briefe*, 2:54.

78. Letter to Kinkel, 24 November 1843, *Briefe*, 2:51. See also another letter to Kinkel of 1 November 1845 (*Briefe*, 2:183–84) on the "Geschäftigkeit, welche man hier verlangt . . . dazu noch der politische Satan, der in diesen engen Hexenkesseln helvetischer Kantonalität viel beengender wirkt" ("the activity that is demanded of you here . . . and added to that, the Satan of politics which results in even worse narrow-mindedness when it operates in the narrow confines of the witches' cauldrons of Helvetic cantonal existence").

79. Letter to Eduard Schauenburg, 30 November 1843, *Briefe*, 2:54.

80. Letter of 24 November 1843, *Briefe*, 2:50.

81. Letter to Johanna Kinkel, 29 January 1844, *Briefe*, 2:81.

82. Letter to Kinkel, "All Saints' Day" (1 November 1845), *Briefe*, 2:182–84.

83. Letter to Kinkel, 20 August 1843, *Briefe*, 2:34–35. See, among many others on this topic, a letter to Karl Fresenius of 21 January 1844, *Briefe*, 2:72: "I see few people, have virtually no companionship, and never have a genuine exchange with any one in which there is a mutual expression of feeling." See also another letter to Kinkel dated All Saints' Day, 1845, *Briefe*, 2:184, in which Burckhardt relates that his favorite companions are "one of my former friends from 1838–39, a bit rambunctious after studying in Heidelberg and an arch-radical to boot" and "Professor Jhering, the merriest and most droll of East Frisians," except that he is engaged to be married, hence "out of commission." As for his old teacher Wacker-nagel, he is too much of a paterfamilias to accept an *"enfant perdu,"* as Burckhardt claimed to be inwardly, as a friend of the family.

84. Letter to Johanna Kinkel, 29 January 1844, *Briefe*, 2:80.

85. Letter to Eduard Schauenburg 30 November 1843, *Briefe*, 2:55.

86. See Burckhardt's own succinct account of the events leading up to the *Freischaren* in a letter to Willibald Beyschlag, 6–9 January 1845, *Briefe*, 2:150–55.

87. Letter to Kinkel, 19 April 1845, *Briefe*, 2:158.

88. Letter to Kinkel, 11 June 1845, *Briefe*, 2:166–67. The hymn—"Behut' uns, Herr, vor Pofelsgrimm"—was in the *Christliches Gesangbuch*, 1743, frequently reprinted.

89. Letter to Hermann Schauenburg, 5 March 1846, *Briefe*, 2:210.

90. Letter to Hermann Schauenburg, 28 February 1846, *Briefe*, 2:209.

91. Letter to Karl Fresenius, 16 August 1845, *Briefe*, 2:179. On Burckhardt's articles in the *Basler Zeitung* at the time of Lucerne's recall of the Jesuits—the occasion of the dispute between the liberal and conservative cantons—see Emil Dürr, ed., *Jacob Burckhardt als politischer Publizist* (Zurich: Fretz & Wasmuth, 1937).

92. Letter to Hermann Schauenburg, 28 February 1846, *Briefe*, 2:208. In German: "der Geschichte abgestorben ist"—"which has dropped out of history" or "which is dead to history," rather than "where history is dead" in Alexander Dru's excellent but unfortunately highly restricted selection and translation of Burckhardt's letters, *Letters of Jacob Burckhardt*, selected, edited, and translated by Alexander Dru (London: Routledge & Kegan Paul, 1955), p. 96 (hereafter *Dru*).

93. Letter of 27 February 1847, *Briefe*, 3:55.

94. Letter to Hermann Schauenburg, 22 March 1847, *Briefe*, 3:60–61. The following is a rough translation of the poem: "Receive, oh passionately beloved South, the stranger, weary of wandering. Fill his soul full of your joyful sunlight. Let the wondrous round of the old gods rise in glory around him. Show him figures of eternity from ancient and modern times." Not surprisingly, when he returned to Italy a year later, Burckhardt made a point of stopping off at Trieste to visit the grave of Winckelmann, who had met a tragic death there over half a century earlier. Winckelmann was not only, as Burckhardt noted, the father of modern art history, he had been a founder of the neohumanism on which Burckhardt was nourished at the Basel *Gymnasium* and *Pädagogium* and had anticipated the feelings of alienation from the conditions of life in Germany and of longing for the more beautiful, essential, and harmonious existence represented by Italy, which now filled Burckhardt. See Burckhardt's description of Winckelmann's tomb in *Cicerone, Gesamtausgabe*, 3:81.

95. Letter to Andreas Heusler-Ryhiner, 19 January 1848, *Briefe*, 3:94. Given Burckhardt's judgments of the people around this time, it may seem strange to find him advocating the "popularization" of historical knowledge. The "people" he has in mind to write for, however, was not the "Volk," which he had warned Hermann Schauenburg can turn easily and without warning into a *"barbarisches Pöbel"* (letter of 5 March 1846, *Briefe*, 2:210); it was not, probably, the demi-cultured public of the newspaper feuilletons; most likely, it was the

"populus" referred to in the official Basel inscription, "Senatus Populusque Basiliensis," that is to say, serious, educated, responsible individuals, who might theoretically be drawn from any class, but most probably belong in fact to the upper class—in other words, those *"Nicht-studierende"* (male and female) to whom Burckhardt explicitly addressed all his writings.

96. Letter to Heusler-Ryhiner, 19 January 1848, *Briefe,* 3:94.

97. Henning Ritter, "Burckhardt as Journalist" (unpublished paper presented at the Princeton Colloquium on Burckhardt, October 18–19, 1997), p. 7 (to appear in *Beiträge zu Jacob Burckhardt* [Basel: Schwabe; Stuttgart: Christian Metz]).

98. Ibid., p. 10. See also Josef Oswald, ed., *Unbekannte Aufsätze Jakob Burckhardts aus Paris, Rom un Mailand* (Basel: Schwabe, 1922), especially the essay "Hat Jakob Burckhardt Pariser Feuilletons für die *Kölnische Zeitung* geschrieben" (pp. 43–59) and Burckhardt's feuilleton "Die französische Literatur und das Geld," which appeared in the *Kölnische Zeitung,* no. 255, 12 September 1843 (pp. 60–68).

99. Letter of 8 January 1848, quoted by Kaegi, *Jacob Burckhardt,* 3:169 note 32a.

100. See Max Burckhardt, "Rom 1848: Berichte von Jacob Burckhardt," *Corona* 9, no. 2 (1939): 112.

101. Ibid., pp. 115, 119.

102. Ibid., p. 215; cf. Kaegi, *Jacob Burckhardt,* 3:183.

103. Letter of 4 March 1848, *Briefe,* 3:102. "Lacus Curtius" refers to a chasm that is said to have suddenly opened up in the forum toward the beginning of the period of the Kings. It could be closed, according to the soothsayers, only by the sacrifice of that *"quo plurimum populus Romanus posset."* Whereupon a youth named Curtius jumped in and the opening closed. The connection of the site with the underworld made it sacred and coins were later thrown in, no doubt to propitiate the gods. See Samuel Bell Platner, *A Topographical Dictionary of Ancient Rome,* revised by Thomas Ashby (London: Oxford University Press, 1929), pp. 310–11.

104. Report to *Basler Zeitung* of 23 March 1848, in Max Burckhardt, "Rom 1848," p. 225.

105. Report of 27 March 1848, in ibid., p. 228. Burckhardt may have had ambivalent feelings about the events in Rome. It was to be expected that in letters to the conservative Heusler and articles for the latter's newspaper, the *Basler Zeitung,* he would emphasize his fear and horror—which were probably real enough. On the other hand, the old liberal in him might have felt some exhilaration. He certainly stood by his old friend Luigi Picchioni when the latter went off to fight the Austrians in Lombardy, and a decade later Bachofen still suspected him of harboring sympathy for the cause of the Italian patriots. Letter from Bachofen to Wilhelm Henzen, 1 June 1859, *Gesammelte Werke* (hereafter *GW),* ed. Karl Meuli (Basel: Schwabe, 1943–1967; publication interrupted at vol. 10), 10:192.

106. Johann Gottfried von Herder, *On World History. An Anthology,* ed. Hans Adler and Ernest A. Menze, trans. Ernest A. Menze and Michael Palma (Armonk, N. Y. and London: M. E. Sharpe, 1997), p. 44.

107. *Griechische Kulturgeschichte, Gesamtausgabe,* 8:2.

108. Hardtwig, *Geschichtsschreibung zwischen Alteuropa und moderner Welt.*

109. *Reflections on History,* p. 19.

110. Quoted by Kaegi, *Jacob Burckhardt,* 3:201. "No one can hold it against you that you all want to leave for America," Burckhardt wrote Schauenburg, 23 August 1848 (*Briefe,* 3:105).

111. On Kinkel, see Kaegi, *Jacob Burckhardt,* 3:204–14; see also Kinkel's own *Selbstbiographie* (Bonn, 1931), and the *Lebenserinnerungen* (Berlin, 1906) of Carl Schurz, whose career has an even more epic character than Kinkel's. After securing Kinkel's escape, Schurz

emigrated to America. He was appointed U.S. minister to Madrid, served with courage as a brigadier general on the Union side in the Civil War (he fought at the second Bull Run, at Chancellorsville, and at Gettysburg), won election as senator for Missouri in 1869, and had an outstanding career as a journalist first for Horace Greeley's *New York Tribune,* then for the New York *Evening Post* and the *Nation.* Schurz was a brilliant orator in the struggles against slavery, oppression, and—in his later years—imperialism (he opposed both Grant's plans to annex Santo Domingo and the war with Spain). He spoke his mind freely to President Lincoln on the latter's administration. Lincoln, on his side, wrote Schurz toward the beginning of their exchange of letters that "to the extent of our limited acquaintance, no man stands nearer to my heart than yourself" (letter of 18 June 1860, *Collected Works of Abraham Lincoln,* ed. Roy P. Basler, 8 vols. [New Brunswick: Rutgers University Press, 1953], 4:78).

112. Letter of 23 August 1848, *Briefe,* 3:104–5.

113. Ibid.

114. Letter to Wilhelm Henzen, 1 June 1859, *GW,* 10:192.

115. See, for example, a letter to von Preen, 17 November 1876, *Briefe,* 6:113–16, in which he referred to "das regno d'Italia, wo die Demokratie im besten Zuge und die Widerstandskraft sehr gering ist" ("where democracy is in full swing and the forces of resistance are slight"). There are many other scathing references in the correspondence to the influence of newspapers and politics in Italy, the substitution of the cheap images of modern politics for the old religious images, and so on. A public lecture of 1855 on Manzoni's *I Promessi Sposi* communicates both Burckhardt's early sympathy with the national aspirations of the Italians and his rejection of revolutionary means to realize them. "It is a national novel in the highest degree and also symptomatic of the decade in which it was written: a book of pain and consolation for an Italy reduced to passivity and still under the partial domination of foreigners. The model: the time around 1630 in Lombardy; a harsh and oppressive Spanish administration; men of violence; public affairs in a miserable state; no respect for law. Manzoni shows how even in such conditions, the individual can resist and save himself, and how revolution and subversion of the laws are false means. . . ." (from an Italian translation of the text, published from the manuscript in the Basel State Archives, in Ezio Raimondi, "Un lettore a Basilea," *Un Romanzo senza idillio: Saggio sui "Promessi Sposi"* [Turin: Einaudi, 1974], pp. 309–18).

116. Letter to his sister, Louise Burckhardt, 5 April 1841, *Briefe,* 1:165. See also the poem "An Deutschland" of summer 1841:

> Du hast mir Freuden viel bereitet
> Du heilig grosses Vaterland,
> Hast deine Pracht mir ausgebreitet
> Vom Alpenschnee zum Meeresstrand.
>
> . . . .
> Und dich verschmäht' ich, ach, wie lange!
> Doch ward zuletzt die Liebesglut
> Der Mutterbrust, an der ich hange,
> Gewalt'ger als mein Übermut.
>
> . . . .
> In deines Rheines Prachtgelände,
> Da zogst du eng ans Herze mich;
> Zum Himmel hob ich meine Hände
> Und schwor's, zu leben nur für dich.
>
> . . . .

Dort möcht' ich vor dein Antlitz treten,
Zu blauen Bergen hingewandt,
Und mit des Dankes Tränen beten
Zu dir, mein deutsches Vaterland!

Quoted from J. Burckhardt, *Gedichte*, ed. Emil Hoffmann (Basel: Schwabe, 1926), p. 54.

117. Letter to Eduard Schauenburg, 31 July 1844, *Briefe*, 2:122.

118. Letters to Hermann Schauenburg, September 1849, *Briefe*, 3:112.

119. The cooling of the friendship between Burckhardt and Kinkel that had begun at the time of the 1848 Revolutions had not led to a radical break and after Kinkel was appointed to Burckhardt's old chair of art history at the Federal Polytechnic in 1866, there was something like a resumption of relations. That did not prevent Burckhardt from reaffirming his deep political disagreement with Kinkel. On the issue of Bismarck and the Austro-Prussian war, which Kinkel supported, Burckhardt wrote: "Geh Du Deine Wege und lass mich meine gehen" ("You go your way and let me go mine") (letter to Kinkel, 7 September 1866, *Briefe*, 4:225). See also Kaegi, *Jacob Burckhardt*, 5:460 note 38.

120. See Martin Warnke, "Jacob Burckhardt und Karl Marx," *Neue Rundschau*, 81 (1970):701–23; reprinted in *Umgang mit Jacob Burckhardt*, ed. Hans R. Guggisberg (Basel: Schwabe & Munich: C. H. Beck, 1994), pp. 135–58. In Warnke's suggestive rapprochement of Burckhardt and Marx both are seen as realists who were never deluded by the radical posturing of 1848 but on the contrary were acutely aware—and contemptuous—of its inner weakness. Both therefore turned against the romantic revolutionaries. The implication of Warnke's argument is that in some way—different perhaps from Marx, but not completely opposed—Burckhardt remained faithful to the essence of his early liberal convictions. However, it is difficult to gainsay the intensity of Burckhardt's rejection of all aspects of social democracy.

121. See Kaegi, *Jacob Burckhardt*, 3:195–96.

122. Letter to Heusler-Ryhiner, 4 March 1848, *Briefe*, 3:103. Severin was an ascetic who founded monasteries, preached the gospel, and ministered to his flock along the Danube from Vienna to Passau amid the violence and turbulence of the barbarian invasions of the late fifth century. The reference is to *Corpus des Hieronymus Pez* (Vienna, 1743), 1:62–92. Burckhardt seems to have become interested in Severin during his stay in Berlin. Willibald Beyschlag, a friend from that time, related that "one of my best poems, the ballad *St. Severinus . . .* was suggested by reading the remarkable *Vita Sancti Severini* from the fifth century, which Burckhardt brought to my attention" (W. Beyschlag, *Aus meinem Leben* [Halle, 1896], p. 135, quoted by Kaegi, *Jacob Burckhardt*, 3:385 note 369). In the winter of 1854–1855 Burckhardt gave one of his public lectures at Basel on Severin (the twelve-page manuscript, preserved in the *Nachlass*, is discussed briefly in Kaegi, *Jacob Burckhardt*, 3:536–37); in a letter to the student Albert Brenner of 11 February 1856, he again alluded to "this marvelous story" (*Briefe*, 3:243); and toward the end of his life he told Otto Markwart that Severin—"one of the greatest of mortals"—had been the object, for him, of a private cult (see Otto Markwart, *Jacob Burckhardt; Persönlichkeit und Jugendjahre* [Basel: Schwabe, 1920], pp. 44–45).

123. Letter to Hermann Schauenburg, 22 March 1847, *Briefe*, 3:59.

124. Letter to Paul Heyse, 13 August 1852, *Briefe*, 3:161.

125. *The Age of Constantine the Great*, trans. Moses Hadas (New York: Pantheon Books, 1949), pp. 262, 124.

126. Ranke, *Über die Epochen der neueren Geschichte*, p. 196. Ranke had added: "If, according to one's conscience and best knowledge, one thinks one can go along with the currents of the time, one should do so; but if one is not in agreement, one ought not to submit to them" (p. 196).

127. Letter to Hermann Schauenburg, 5 March 1846, *Briefe,* 2:210. Cf. Count Hermann Kayserling, *The Travel Diary of a Philosopher,* trans. J. Holroyd Reece (New York: Harcourt, 1925), 2:286–87: "It is no doubt painful to think that the historical function of the traditional cultured classes of old Europe is at an end; but at some time or another every one must make room for the younger generation. And this abdication does not imply death; in noble leisure, unconcerned with worldly ideals, the Western man of culture may yet continue to flourish for a long time and thus experience a sublimation which would never have fallen to his lot in active life. . . . We should remember, when despondency overtakes us, that it is the Jews and the Greeks, not the Goths and the Vandals, to whom the Germanic world owes the impulses which have given it direction ever since."

128. Letter to Wilhelm Schmidlin, rector of the *Gewerbeschule,* 31 May 1852, *Briefe,* 3:156.

129. Kaegi comments on this episode that Burckhardt "did not want to be transformed from a free member of the faculty into an overburdened and overstressed educational employee" (Kaegi, *Jacob Burckhardt,* 3:449). At stake were two conceptions of the teacher which have still not been fully reconciled, especially in societies with strong bourgeois and commercial values similar to those of nineteenth-century Basel. On the one hand, the teacher as a free spirit dedicated to the pursuit of learning as well as to the transmission of culture—a conception more in tune with patrician or aristocratic values and entertained, at Basel, by the old elite; on the other, the teacher as a worker performing the specialized task of preparing young people for life in contemporary society and accountable, like any worker, for the quality of the product. Burckhardt himself appears to have seen the champions of the *Gewerbeschule* as less than fully committed to the University: "I haven't the least doubt that those gentlemen who decreed the *Gewerbeschule* will also decree us, as a University, out of existence, as soon as some kind of Federal Institution is in place" (letter to Heusler-Ryhiner, 13 February 1854, *Briefe,* 3:186).

130. Kaegi, *Jacob Burckhardt,* 3:305, 329.

131. Letter to Emma Brenner-Kron, 21 May 1852, *Briefe,* 3:150. Cf. a letter to Paul Heyse of 13 August 1852: "Oh, if only I could get away from our zone of endless rain" (*Briefe,* 3:160).

132. Letter to Emma Brenner-Kron, 5 November 1852, *Briefe,* 3:167.

133. Letter of 18 December 1852, *Briefe,* 3:172.

134. On the conditions of appointment, see Kaegi, *Jacob Burckhardt,* 3:561.

135. Letter to Heusler-Ryhiner, 31 October 1853, *Briefe,* 3:180.

136. The letter in which Burckhardt puts forward his candidacy includes a list of publications and of relevant courses he has taught. To Johann Conrad Kern, President of the Swiss Education Committee, 18 November 1854, *Briefe,* 3:195–97.

137. Letter of 27 January 1855, quoted in Kaegi, *Jacob Burckhardt,* 3:562.

138. Letter from the Governing Board of the University to the Education Department, 10 July 1854, quoted by Kaegi, *Jacob Burckhardt,* 3:561 note 94. After his son's departure for Zurich, *Antistes* Burckhardt noted bitterly that he heard many people in Basel regretting that the young teacher could not be retained. "But what prevented them from finding him a better post than one that did no more than keep hunger away from his door," he wrote (quoted by Kaegi, ibid., p. 570).

139. Letter of 25 January 1855, quoted in Kaegi, *Jacob Burckhardt,* 3:567.

140. For a lively account of mid-nineteenth-century Zurich, see Gordon A. Craig, *The Triumph of Liberalism: Zurich in the Golden Age, 1830–69* (New York: Charles Scribner's Sons, 1988).

141. "Lebensrückschau," in *Jacob Burckhardt: Die Kunst der Betrachtung,* ed. Ritter, pp. 15–18, at p. 17.

142. *Jacob Burckhardt und Heinrich Wölfflin,* ed. Gantner, p. 116, from some notes of conversations with Burckhardt that Wölfflin listed under the rubric "Köbiana."

143. See Craig, The *Triumph of Liberalism,* pp. 148–49.

144. Quoted by Craig, ibid., p. 148.

145. Letter to Johann Heinrich Frey, 29 November 1855, *Briefe,* 3:231.

146. Letter of 6 May 1855, *Briefe,* 3:217.

147. Hartwig Floto, author of a two-volume work on the Emperor Henry IV and his age, which he dedicated to Ranke. Ranke must have been consulted on his appointment, for he wrote a (fairly routine) letter of recommendation for him to the Basel University authorities. Leopold von Ranke, *Neue Briefe,* ed. B. Hoeft and H. Herzfeld (Hamburg: Hoffmann & Campe, 1949), p. 369, letter of 5 December 1855. Floto lived for another twenty-six years.

148. Letter to Burckhardt of 24 January 1858, in *GW,* 10:174.

149. From the brief account of his life that Burckhardt prepared, according to Basel custom, to serve as his obituary, *Gesamtausgabe,* 1:viii. Also in *Jacob Burckhardt: Die Kunst der Betrachtung,* ed. Ritter, p. 17.

150. Letter to *Ratsherr* Peter Merian, Head of the Basel Education Department, 7 February 1858, *Briefe,* 3:276.

151. Letter of 16 November 1860, *Briefe,* 4:76.

152. According to Wölfflin, he was twice invited to Berlin. See *Jacob Burckhardt und Heinrich Wölfflin,* ed. Gantner, pp. 31–32. Other students of Ranke's who were sounded out, and who also turned down the invitation, included Georg Waitz and Heinrich von Sybel. In the end the chair was accepted by Karl Wilhelm Nitzsch together with Heinrich von Treitschke. See Kaspar Elm, "Mittelalterforschung in Berlin: Dauer und Wandel," in *Geschichtswissenschaft in Berlin im 19. und 20. Jahrhundert* (Berlin and New York: De Gruyter, 1992), pp. 211–59, at p. 215. On the whole episode, see Fritz Kaphahn, "Jacob Burckhardt und die Wiederbesetzung von Rankes Geschichtsprofessur an der Universität Berlin," *Historische Zeitschrift* 168 (1943): 113–31; also Kaegi, *Jacob Burckhardt,* 4:30–33.

153. Letter of 28 June 1872, *Briefe,* 5:170.

154. Letter of 9 August 1874, *Briefe,* 5:237. Kugler was to be professor of history at Tübingen.

155. "Lebensrückschau," in *Jacob Burckhardt: Die Kunst der Betrachtung,* ed. Ritter, pp. 17–18. Cf. letter to Emanuel Geibel, 10 October 1863, *Briefe,* 4:138: "I will not publish any more books. I believe the time is better spent on my lectures"; letter to Paul Heyse, 3 April 1864, *Briefe,* 4:142: "I consider my slight literary career ended and am much happier and more content reading in the sources, for I am now studying and taking notes only for my classes, not for any scribbling of books."

156. "I see crowds of them in the galleries, etc. The majority belong to the modern class of penitent pilgrims. These no longer wend their way around every one of the indulgence churches in Rome with stones in their shoes and weals on their backs; instead they do penance by boring themselves to death in front of works of art that mean nothing to them" (letter to Robert Grüninger, a member of the *Grosser Rat* and former student, 13 April 1875, *Briefe,* 6:26). Burckhardt himself refers familiarly to the "Tschitsch" in this letter.

157. "Jacob Burckhardt zum 100. Geburtstag," in Heinrich Wölfflin, *Gedanken zur Kunstgeschichte,* 3rd ed. (Basel: Schwabe, 1941), p. 156.

158. Ibid., p. 161.

159. Reported in a letter of December 1882 from Eduard Wölfflin to his son Heinrich in *Jacob Burckhardt und Heinrich Wolfflin,* ed. Gantner, p. 24. See also H. Wölfflin, "Nachruf auf Jacob Burckhardt," ibid., p. 177.

160. Ibid., pp. 28 and 28 note 12.

161. Ibid., p. 116.

162. "Nachruf," ibid., p. 177.

163. "Köbiana," ibid., p. 116.

164. Letter of 3 December 1869, *Briefe*, 5:61–62.

165. A new German edition appeared in 1982: *Über das Studium der Geschichte*, ed. Peter Ganz (Munich: C. H. Beck).

166. See Werner Kaegi, "Avant-Propos" to the French translation by Sven Stelling-Michaud, *Considérations sur l'histoire universelle* (Geneva: Droz, 1965), pp. xvii–xxi. The main body of this foreword is a translation from the text Kaegi prepared as an introduction to a new German edition published in Switzerland in 1941. To this, Kaegi added a brief note for the 1965 French edition. The French translation originally appeared with Felix Alcan in Paris in 1938, but no copies survive. On the *Weltgeschichtliche Betrachtungen* as "el testamento de Burckhardt, la última proyección que dibuja sobre todas sus generalizaciones históricas, en un esfuerzo sintético parecido al de Montesquieu," see the fine essay of Alfonso Reyes, "Prólogo a Burckhardt," which served as introduction to the 1943 Spanish translation of the *Weltgeschichtliche Betrachtungen* by W. Roces (Mexico: Fondo de Cultura Económica, 1943) in Reyes's *Obras Completas*, 26 vols. (Mexico: F.C.E., 1955–1993), 12:100–29.

167. Letter to Heinrich Schreiber, 18 December 1852, *Briefe*, 3:172.

168. Letter to von Preen, 23 December 1871, *Briefe*, 5:149. The term *genussvoll*, translated here as "enjoyable," had a special meaning for Burckhardt. It evoked the "higher" epicurean pleasures, at once sensuous and spiritual, similar to those obtained from the contemplation of works of beauty. The subtitle of *Der Cicerone*, it will be remembered, was *Anleitung zum Genuss der Kunstwerke Italiens*.

169. "Ein ewiges Pfeiffen und Heulen," letter to von Preen, 17 March 1872, *Briefe*, 5:154.

170. Letter to Rudolf Oeri, 23 December 1871, *Briefe*, 5:146–48.

171. Letter to Bernhard Kugler, the son of Franz Kugler, of 9 August 1874, *Briefe*, 5:237.

172. Letter to von Preen, 31 May 1874, *Briefe*, 5:224–25.

173. Letter to Max Alioth, 6 May 1884, letter 1054, *Briefe*, 8:201.

174. Letter to von Preen, 25 March 1890, in *Dru*, p. 223.

175. Letter to von Preen, 31 May 1874, *Briefe*, 5:225.

176. Letter of 4 March 1848, *Briefe*, 3:103.

177. Letter to von Preen, Sylvester 1870, *Briefe*, 5:118–20. Cf. another letter to von Preen of 14 September 1890 (*Briefe*, 9:264) in which Burckhardt predicted an era of authoritarian regimes in the twentieth century to provide an answer to the social problem: "Oh, how will it go with so many interests that are dear to us? Scholarship among other things. . . . How little store the new authority will set by it."

178. Letter to von Preen, 13 April 1882, *Briefe*, 8:31–33.

179. Letter to von Preen, 27 December 1890, *Briefe*, 9:280.

180. Letters to von Preen, 20 July 1870, *Briefe*, 5:103–5; 26 April 1872, *Briefe*, 5:159–61.

181. Letters to von Preen, Sylvester 1870, *Briefe*, 5:119; 26 April 1872, *Briefe*, 5:160–61.

182. Letter of 25 August 1843, *Briefe*, 2:43.

183. Letter to Hermann Schauenburg, 27 February 1847, *Briefe*, 3:55.

184. Reports of 18 Sepember and 30 November 1844, quoted by Kaegi, *Jacob Burckhardt*, 2:432–33.

185. Report of 23 September 1845, quoted by Kaegi, ibid., p. 435.

186. Report of 8 October 1845, quoted by Kaegi, ibid., p. 435.

187. Letter to Hermann Schauenburg, 22 March 1847, *Briefe*, 3:59. Cf. Diderot on "the tiresome uniformity produced by our education, our social conventions, and our proprieties" (*Le Neveu de Rameau*) and on the way "education in the first place, and then social man-

ners, . . . flatten people out, like coins rubbed down by being passed from hand to hand" (*Jacques le fataliste*) (*Oeuvres* [Paris: Bibliothèque de la Pleiade, 1951], pp. 426, 663). In *Le Neveu*, Diderot had also directly attacked the press ("the great judges of literature: l'*Avant-Coureur*, les *Petites-affiches*, l'*Année littéraire*, l'*Observateur littéraire*, le *Censeur hebdomadaire*, the entire clique of scribblers" (p. 469).

188. Letter to Heinrich Schreiber, 2 October 1842, *Briefe*, 1:216.

189. Letter to von Preen, 26 September 1890, *Briefe*, 9:269.

190. See Alan S. Kahan, *Aristocratic Liberalism: The Social and Political Thought of Jacob Burckhardt, John Stuart Mill, and Alexis de Tocqueville* (New York: Oxford University Press, 1992).

191. *Historische Fragmente*, ed. Emil Dürr (Stuttgart: Köhler, 1957), p. 275.

192. See, for instance, letter to von Preen, 13 April 1882, *Briefe*, 8:32.

193. "Our charming 19th century has . . . accustomed people to the idea that every novelty, even the most questionable, is justified . . ." (letter to von Preen, 25 March 1890, *Briefe*, 9:238).

194. Letter to Karl Fresenius, 21 April 1846, *Briefe*, 3:16. Cf. letter to Johanna Kinkel of 9 March 1846: Evoking "Elberfeld, that horrible factory country!" he announces that he "really long[s] to be in Italy, because there is so much begging there and so little industry" (*Briefe*, 2:216).

195. Letter to Robert Grüninger, 13 April 1875, *Briefe*, 6:25-26.

196. Letter to Max Alioth, 15 August 1878, *Briefe*, 2:261. Burckhardt described *La Stella* as an "inflammatory socialist rag" ("*sozialistisches Hetzblatt*").

197. Letter to von Preen, 9 December 1878, *Briefe*, 6:290.

198. Letter of 13 January 1890, *Briefe*, 9:233.

199. Letter to Heinrich von Geymüller, an engineer and architect who had become an enthusiastic student of the Italian Renaissance, 8 May 1891, *Briefe*, 9:299.

200. Letter to Max Alioth, 24 July 1875, *Briefe*, 6:42. On Burckhardt's antisemitism, see the excellent observations in Wenzel, *Jacob Burckhardt in der Krisis seiner Zeit*, pp. 167-68.

201. Letter to Johanna Kinkel, 25 August 1843, *Briefe*, 2:43.

202. Letter to Heinrih von Geymüller, 8 May 1891, *Briefe*, 9:299.

203. Letter to Jacob Oeri Jr., 3 March 1867, *Briefe*, 4:241. Burckhardt's nephew and literary executor, Oeri was appointed professor of classics and German literature at the Schaffhausen *Gymnasium* in 1871 and at the Basel *Gymnasium* in 1882. He was the editor of the posthumously published *Griechische Kulturgeschichte* and *Weltgeschichtliche Betrachtungen*. Cf. Franz Overbeck's comment in *Christentum und Kultur*, ed. C. A. Bernoulli (Basel: Schwabe, 1919), p. 260: "Naturally one can still learn a great deal in Berlin and from Berlin. But one can do so equally well in and from other places."

204. Letter to the poet Emanuel Geibel, 10 October 1863, *Briefe*, 4:138.

205. *Historische Fragmente*, p. 267.

206. Jacob Burckhardt, *The Civilization of the Renaissance in Italy*, trans. S. G. C. Middlemore, with an introduction by Benjamin Nelson and Charles Trinkaus, 2 vols. (New York: Harper Colophon Books, 1975), 1:148.

207. To von Preen, 3 July 1870, *Briefe*, 5:98.

208. Europe, Burckhardt declared, is "the home of an infinitely varied life," where "everything spiritual attains expression in words or in other ways. . . . What is European is . . . the manifestation of *all* energies, including the individual ones, in the form of monuments, plastic representations, words, institutions, parties; the personal experience of every tendency of spiritual life; the aspiration of the spirit to make known everything it contains, never surrendering without protest to world monarchies or theocracies, as they do in the East. If we occupy a sufficiently high and distant vantage point, as the historian should, we find that all

the bells in all the towers are ringing in harmony, even though up close we hear dissonances: *Discordia concors*" (*Historische Fragmente*, no. 142). This point of view is very close to that of Ranke. Cf. Ranke's lecture course on modern history, winter semester 1833–1834: "Only the Christian European peoples of Germanic-Romance origin, who emerged in the course of the great migrations but were limited to a small area, were able to comprehend and develop all aspects of culture in themselves . . . and even to transfer it to the newly discovered American continent, while all the other parts of the globe lay sunk in lethargy . . ." (notes taken by Siegfried Hirsch, in Ranke, *Aus Werk und Nachlass*, 4:106). Cf. also "A Few Pages on Bosnia" (translation of "Die letzten Unruhen in Bosnien,") in *History of Servia*, trans. Mrs. Alexander Kerr (London: Henry G. Bohn, 1853), p. 364: "The vitality of the human race is at this day centered in the nations of the Roman and Germanic stocks, and in those which they have incorporated and assimilated with themselves. However manifold may be our internal discords, however various and often hostile our tendencies, we yet constitute one whole in contrast with the rest of the world."

209. Letter of 20 July 1870, *Briefe*, 5:104–5. Burckhardt could have learned from Schopenhauer, one of the few modern philosophers he deeply admired, that "constructive philosophies, guided by a positive optimism, always ultimately end in a comfortable, rich, fat state, with a well-regulated constitution, good justice and police, useful arts and industries, and, at the most, intellectual perfection; for . . . what is moral remains essentially unaltered. But it is the moral element which, according to the testimony of our inmost consciousness, is the whole concern" ("On History," in *The World as Will and Representation*, trans. R. B. Haldane and J. Kemp, 3 vols. [London: Routledge & Kegan Paul, 1957; orig. 1883], 3:225).

210. To von Preen, 17 November 1876, *Briefe*, 6:115.

211. Letter to Otto Markwart, a former student who became professor of history at the Zurich *Gymnasium*, 15 November 1893, *Briefe* 10:137: "St. Severin, for me, is one of the greatest of mortals, and his altar tomb in Naples has been a holy place for me." See note 122 above.

212. Letter to von Preen, 17 November 1876, *Briefe*, 6:115.

213. Letter of 30 May 1877, *Briefe*, 6:133. Cf. Burckhardt's claim in his "Lebensruckschau" that the years spent in Basel after 1858 were "the happiest years of my life" (*Jacob Burckhardt: Die Kunst der Betrachtung*, ed. Ritter, p. 17).

214. Letter to Robert Grüningen, 4 September 1876, *Briefe*, 6:110. The theme was a familiar one in a deeply religious city like Basel. Some time around 1842–1843 De Wette, for example, had chosen Hebrews 13:14 ("For here we have no permanent city, but we seek the one to come" ["Wir haben hier keine bleibende Stadt, sondern die zukünftige suchen wir"]) as the topic of a sermon in which he justified patriotism, even while reminding his listeners of the Christian's view of life as a pilgrimage. Paul Handschin, *Wilhelm Martin Leberecht De Wette als Prediger und Schriftsteller* (Basel: Helbing & Lichtnenhahn, 1957), Appendix, pp. 162–70.

215. *Griechische Kulturgeschichte, Gesamtausgabe*, 8:260.

216. Letter of 14 June 1842, *Briefe*, 1:204–5.

217. Letter of 19 June 1842, *Briefe*, 1:206–8.

218. Letter to von Preen, Sylvester 1870, *Briefe*, 5:119–20.

Chapter Eleven

1. "I would like to make known what human society was like at that time [thirteenth and fourteenth centuries], what family life was like, what arts [in the sense also of crafts and techniques] were cultivated, rather than recount again the tale of so many disasters and wars—those commonplaces of man's cruelty to man that are the usual sorry objects of

history. . . . The artisans and merchants who are protected by their very obscurity from the furious ambition of the great and powerful are ants quietly digging out homes for themselves while the eagles and vultures above them tear each other to pieces" (*Essai sur les moeurs*, ch. 81, *Oeuvres complètes*, ed. Louis Moland 52 vols. [Paris: Garnier, 1877–1885], 12:53–54). In his overview of traditional academic disciplines in the *Discourse on Method*, Descartes had already rejected history on the grounds that "even the most faithful histories, those that do not change or enhance the value of things to make them more worthy of being read, almost always leave out the most humble and least illustrious conditions" ([Paris: Garnier-Flammarion, 1966], p. 37).

2. The words *histoire universelle*, which directly invite comparison with Bossuet, were dropped only from later editions (as of 1756).

3. Quoted by Wolfgang Hardtwig, *Geschichtsschreibung zwischen Alteuropa und moderner Welt: Jacob Burckhardt in der Krise seiner Zeit* (Göttingen: Vandenhoek & Ruprecht, 1974), p. 164, from Thomas Nipperdey, "Kulturgeschichte, Sozialgeschichte, historische Anthropologie," *Vierteljahrshefte für Sozial- und Wirtschaftsgeschichte* 55 (1968): 145–64.

4. Leopold von Ranke, *Über die Epochen der neueren Geschichte. Vorträge dem König Maximilian II von Bayern gehalten*, ed. Hans Herzfeld (Schloss Laupenheim: Ulrich Steiner Verlag, n.d.), 1st lecture, p. 30.

5. On Germany as a *Kulturvolk*, see the excellent pages in Hagen Schulze, *Staat und Nation in der europäischen Geschichte* (Munich: C. H. Beck, 1994), pp. 126–50, 170–72.

6. Ranke, *Über die Epochen der neueren Geschichte*, ed. Herzfeld, p. 30.

7. Leopold von Ranke, *Die grossen Mächte; Politisches Gespräch*, with an afterword by Theodor Schieder (Göttingen: Vandenhoek und Ruprecht, 1955), p. 42. See also ibid., p. 59, on the importance of *"die auswärtigen Verhältnisse"* ("external affairs"). In "The German Constitution" (1799–1802) Hegel had written of the formation of the modern European nation-states, of the Treaty of Westphalia as an obstacle to the development of Germany, and of the revelation, thanks to the Revolutionary and Napoleonic Wars, that "[s]tates stand to one another in a relation of might; illusions on this matter have vanished. If a Republic like Geneva behaved as a sovereign state and boasted . . . of being the first to send an ambassador to the French Republic and give it formal recognition, still, the relation of Geneva to France, as soon as it was taken seriously, was speedily determined differently" (*Hegel's Political Writings*, trans. J. M. Knox [Oxford: Clarendon Press, 1964], p. 227). Geneva was not made part of the Helvetic Republic, but was annexed by France.

8. On the German confederation, see Golo Mann, *History of Germany since 1789* (Harmondsworth: Penguin Books, 1985), pp. 97–105; Theodore S. Hamorow, *Restoration, Revolution, Reaction: Economics and Politics in Germany, 1815–1871* (Princeton: Princeton University Press, 1958), pp. 56–74.

9. In his article on "The Old Cultural History," *History of the Human Sciences* 9 (1996): 101–26, Donald R. Kelley discusses the work of German historians exclusively (Adelung, Eichhorn, Hegewisch, Herder, Meiners, Pölitz).

10. Quoted in George E. Iggers, "The Dissolution of German Historicism," in *Ideas in History: Essays presented to Louis Gottschalk*, ed. Richard Herr and Harold Parker (Durham: Duke University Press, 1965), pp. 288–329, at p. 293.

11. "Über die Behandlung der Angelegenheiten des deutschen Bundes durch Preussen" (30 September 1816), quoted by Franz Herre, *Nation ohne Staat* (Bergisch Gladbach: Gustav Lübbe, 1982 [orig. Cologne, 1967]), p. 262; see also Schulze, *Staat und Nation*, pp. 182–83.

12. To Goethe, culture was incompatible, in particular, with nationalism that takes the form of hatred of other nations. No cultured person can be a nationalist in that way. *Gespräche mit Eckermann*, 14 March 1830 (Basel: Birkhäuser, 1945), 2:685. In the *Italian Journey*,

Goethe's interest in art, in the Italian people and in Italian popular culture, and his indifference to politics anticipate Burckhardt's, and Denis de Rougemont's formulation of Goethe's views could be applied to Burckhardt's: "What has created Europe's true unity is her culture, and what destroys it is the ideological politics which has been adopted by the masses" (*The Idea of Europe*, trans. Norman Guterman [New York: Macmillan, 1966], p. 229). Even at the end of the century, Eberhard Gothein, arguing against the political historian Dietrich Schäfer for the primacy and the comprehensiveness of cultural history, still maintained that the exercise of power cannot be the goal of the state but only the precondition of its productive influence. When power overrides all other concerns as the goal of the state, according to Gothein, that is the surest sign that the state has taken the wrong road. *Die Aufgaben der Kulturgeschichte* (Leipzig: Duncker & Humblot, 1889), p. 9.

13. While "nation" cannot be identified with "society," Werner Conze's reflections on the relation of state and society in Germany in the period from 1815 to 1848 are extremely suggestive. "Das Spannungsfeld von Staat und Gesellschaft im Vormärz," in Werner Conze, ed., *Staat und Gesellschaft im deutschen Vormärz 1815–1848* (Stuttgart: Klett, 1962), pp. 207–69, at pp. 208–12. Conze distinguishes between England and France. In England the tension between society and state was resolved after 1689, government or the state becoming, through Parliament, the executive organ of "society," so that the very term *the state* never acquired in England the meaning and importance it had on the Continent. In France the opposition between society and state or government was to have been resolved by the Revolution of 1789, and the attempt was repeated with each successive nineteenth-century revolution. To Conze, therefore, the situation in France as well as England, can be contrasted with that in Germany. See also Jean L. Cohen and Andrew Arato, *Civil Society and Political Theory* (Cambridge, Mass. and London: MIT Press, 1992), p. 89: "In England after the Glorious Revolution, Locke's ambiguous separation of society from government was slowly eroded. What counted as 'society' was now organized as a state that involved a gradual fusion between parliamentary representation and the executive. The term 'society' as distinct from 'the state' came to be reserved for high or polite society, a custodian of manners and influence, but not of any kind of political project. In general, the term 'civil society' preserved its traditional identification with political society or the state."

14. "Préface de 1869," *Histoire de France*, 19 vols. (Paris: Calmann-Lévy, 1898–99), 1:iii.

15. Felix Gilbert, *History: Politics or Culture? Reflections on Ranke and Burckhardt* (Princeton: Princeton University Press, 1990), p. 46.

16. Quoted from notes taken by a student in Hüllmann's class, and preserved among Hüllmann's papers in Bonn University Archives, in ibid., pp. 46–47.

17. *Staedtewesen des Mittelalters*, 4 vols. (Bonn: Adolph Marcus, 1826–1829).

18. The first number appeared in 1858. Germany was not the only country where culture served to create or confirm national identity. As is well known, the publication of dictionaries, folk poetry collections, and histories of literature was one of the main instigators of nationalist feeling and nationalist independent movements throughout Europe in the nineteenth century. Even solidly established nation-states like England and France sought to identify a national "culture." Michelet's *Introduction to Universal History* (1830) is an early attempt to define the principal national cultures of Europe, with France at their head.

19. Quoted in Jost Müller, *Mythen der Rechten: Nation, Ethnie, Kultur* (Berlin and Amsterdam: Edition ID-Archiv, 1994), pp. 40–41.

20. On Riehl, see the fine but not uncritical tribute by Eberhard Gothein, "Wilhelm Heinrich Riehl," *Preussische Jahrbücher* 92 (1898): 1–27. Gothein presented Riehl as a traditional conservative, distrustful of the power of the state and its bureaucracies, and distinguished him from those whose fear of revolution had led them to seek salvation in a strong

military and a strong bureaucracy. At the same time, he pointed out the contradiction in Riehl's appeal to the state to intervene in order to preserve traditional rural life from decay (pp. 4, 9–10). For a less benign view of Riehl, see Hermann Strobach, "'. . . aber wann beginnt der Vorkrieg?' Anmerkungen zum Thema Volkskunde und Faschismus (vor und um 1933)," in Helge Gerndt, ed., *Volkskunde und Nationalsozialismus* (Munich: Münchner Vereinigung für Volkskunde, 1987), pp. 23–38, at pp. 26–27, 31–32.

21. *Zeitschrift für deutsche Kulturgeschichte* 1 (1858): 281–82.

22. Dietrich Schäfer, *Das eigentliche Arbeitsgebiet der Geschichte* (Jena: Gustav Fischer, 1888). This was Schäfer's inaugural lecture at Tübingen. On the development of cultural history in Germany in the nineteenth century, from romanticism to the "Methodenstreit" and beyond, see Stefan Haas, *Historische Kulturforschung in Deutschland, 1880–1930* (Cologne, Weimar, and Vienna: Böhlau, 1994). On the "Methodenstreit," see Hans Schleier, "Der Kulturhistoriker Karl Lamprecht, der 'Methodenstreit' und die Folgen," introduction to a collection of essays by Lamprecht, entitled *Alternative zu Ranke: Schriften zur Geschichtstheorie* (Leipzig: Philipp Reclam jun., 1988), pp. 7–45. Lamprecht, for his part, was no less ardently nationalist than his opponents, but he considered that the *"Kleindeutsch"* ambitions of the earlier generation had been realized and that Germany's goal must henceforth be to make a wider, more general impact on the world. In some respects his attempt to alter the emphasis of historiography in Germany could be seen as an adaptation to the new Imperialist age. See his "Alte und neue Richtungen in der Geschichtswissenschaft," in *Alternative zu Ranke*, pp. 143–207, at p. 146.

23. According to Dietrich Schäfer, cultural history is favored by "small peoples"—he mentions the Dutch and the Danes—"which in our age of dominant great powers either do not have or have renounced a historical vocation requiring the application of all their energies" (*Das eigentliche Arbeitsgebiet der Geschichte*, pp. 6–7).

24. *Voltaire's Correspondence*, ed. T. Besterman, 107 vols. (Geneva: Institut et Musée Voltaire, 1953–1965), 107 vols., letter 1914, 8 May 1739. Cf. a letter to Shuvalov, the Russian general (letter 7090, 17 July 1758): "The great difficulty of this work [the projected history of Peter the Great] will be to ensure that it is of interest to all nations. That is the crucial point." Another observation of Voltaire's in a letter to Hénault (letter 3980, 7 September 1751)—"it is of very little consequence to posterity whether a man called Nicolas Fouquet [the superintendant of finance arrested by Louis XIV as the first major act of his personal government in 1661] died in 1680 at Pignerol or on an estate belonging to his wife"—anticipates Burckhardt's no less caustic criticism of fact-grubbing Philistines who confuse the discovery of trivial information with genuine history (letter to Gottfried Kinkel, 17 April 1847, *Briefe*, ed. Max Burckhardt, 10 vols. plus index vol. [Basel: Schwabe, 1949–1994], 3:68).

25. Burckhardt accepted the importance Enlightenment and neoclassical historians attributed to the selection of an appropriate topic. One should select one's *"sujet"* carefully, he advised, and it should be an episode or situation capable of interesting large numbers of people. Letter to Bernhard Kugler, 11 April 1870, *Briefe*, 5:78 ff.

26. On German "particularism" (attachment to the multiplicity of small German states) as the foundation of a larger German national feeling in conservative thought in the period between 1815 and 1848, see Theodor Schieder, "Partikularismus und Nationalbewusstsein im Denken des Vormärz," in Conze, ed., *Staat und Gesellschaft im deutschen Vormärz*, pp. 9–38. According to Schieder, the particularity of the individual German states was often thought of as an essential characteristic of the German nation as a whole. The unity of the nation was thus inseparable from its multiplicity; the latter could not therefore be resolved in a single unified state-formation. Schieder refers to the *Oldenburgische Blätter* of 1828,

where "the idea of a glorious Germany united and strong in a common language, in science and scholarship, in customs, in loyalty and respect for law, and in the preservation of its particular customs is represented as entirely compatible with the multiplicity, particularity, and originality of the individual branches of the people. 'This Germany, as it lives in the mind and heart of every individual German cannot be unified by empty formulas'" (p. 32). Even the liberal Georg Gottfried Gervinus described particularism as a feature of the Germanic, as opposed to the Romance peoples (notably France and Spain). Where the latter strive toward *"einheitlich regierten Staatsgebieten,"* (state territories governed as a single unit), the individualistic drive (*"Trieb"*) of the Germanic peoples is toward smaller states or, at most, federations. "This organization into small states everywhere imparted to the life of the Germanic nations, in contrast to the expansionist, outward-striving Romance states, a strong strain of inwardness and an inclination toward peace" (*Einleitung in die Geschichte des neunzehnten Jahrhunderts*, ed. Walter Boehlich [Frankfurt am Main: Insel Verlag, 1967], p. 44). To Hegel, writing his essay on "The German Constitution" (1799–1802) during the French revolutionary wars, particularism seemed so ingrained in the German mentality and way of life that he could envisage "the making of Germany into one state" as something that would be achieved only by force. *Hegel's Political Writings*, pp. 238–42.

27. The "European" idea is itself, of course, not at all incompatible with the racism and the ideological disguising of social conflict often associated with narrower forms of nationalism.

28. Like Riehl, Bachofen was drawn to enduring, fundamental patterns of culture. However, Bachofen found these not so much in the historical world as in *pre*history, the world of myth and of the Mothers. History, for him, was already the world of violence, repression, and paternal law—preeminently the sphere of the state rather than the community.

29. "Einleitung," *Griechische Kulturgeschichte*, ed. Felix Stähelin, in Jacob Burckhardt, *Gesamtausgabe*, ed. Emil Dürr et al., 14 vols. (Stuttgart, Berlin, and Leipzig: Deutsche Verlagsanstalt, 1930–1934), 8:2 (hereafter *Gesamtausgabe*).

30. *Histoire de France*, 19 vols. (Paris: Calmann-Lévy, 1898–1899), 1:iii.

31. Letter from Wölfflin to his parents, 5 July 1884, in *Jacob Burckhardt und Heinrich Wölfflin: Briefwechsel und andere Dokumente ihrer Begegnung 1882–1897*, ed. Joseph Gantner, 2nd enlarged ed. (Basel: Schwabe, 1989 [1948]), p. 41. In view of the high regard in which Riehl was held as a historian of culture, it is striking that Burckhardt appears to have had very little to do with him. In his massive and detailed biography of Burckhardt, Kaegi mentioned only a couple of rather indirect and unimportant contacts (Werner Kaegi, *Jacob Burckhardt: eine Biographie* [Basel: Schwabe, 1947–1982], 3:664, 6:420–21), and there is only one mention of Riehl in the entire ten volumes of Max Burckhardt's recent edition of his ancestor's correspondence.

32. "Einleitung," *Griechische Kulturgeschichte*, *Gesamtausgabe*, 8:2.

33. Cf. Hans Herzfeld's judgment of Ranke in the introduction to his edition of Ranke's *Über die Epochen der neueren Geschichte*, pp. 24–25: "Ranke remained to the end a representative of that Christian and humanistic education by which he had been formed and in which he had been steeped since his early school days at Schulpforta. State, Church, and Culture—which, as autonomous and competing forces, developing through interaction with each other, had shaped the history of that group of peoples [the European, Germanic, and Romance peoples] and imparted to it the rich and colorful variety of its diverse cultures—always remained for him the great forces that shaped the course of world history."

34. Until well into the second half of the nineteenth century, the bulk of the Basel ribbon industry was still essentially organized on a putting-out basis. That is to say, the merchant-manufacturers supplied the materials, designs, and sometimes the looms themselves to indi-

vidual artisans in the city or, more frequently, to country people in the surrounding areas, and paid them for their labor by the piece. The merchant-manufacturers consistently supported the introduction of new techniques and new types of loom in opposition to the artisans, who resisted them. Ultimately, the merchants reorganized production on a factory basis. See chapters 1 and 2.

35. Jacob Burckhardt, *Aesthetik der bildenden Kunst*, ed. Irmgard Siebert (Darmstadt: Wissenschaftliche Buchgesellschaft, 1992), pp. 93, 164.

36. "Einleitung," *Griechische Kulturgeschichte, Gesamtausgabe*, 8:3–4. See also Jacob Burckhardt, *Reflections on History*, trans. Mary Hottinger (London: George Allen & Unwin, 1943), p. 17 (hereafter *Reflections on History*).

37. Letter to Bernhard Kugler, 30 March 1870, *Briefe*, 4:76.

38. "Einleitung," *Griechische Kulturgeschichte, Gesamtausgabe*, 8:2.

39. Letter to Edwin von Manteuffel, 29 November 1882, in Leopold von Ranke, *Neue Briefe*, ed. B. Hoeft and H. Herzfeld (Hamburg: Hoffmann & Campe, 1949), p. 706.

40. "Über die Verwandschaft und den Unterschied der Historie und der Politik"; see introduction to Ranke, *Über die Epochen der neueren Geschichte*, ed. Herzfeld, p. 20.

41. Ranke, *Über die Epochen der neueren Geschichte*, ed. Herzfeld, p. 30. On Ranke's interest in and contribution to cultural history and Burckhardt's acknowledgment of it, see Gilbert, *History: Politics or Culture?*, pp. 97–101 *et passim*.

42. *Reflections on History*, p. 55.

43. Ibid.

44. Albert Demangeon and Lucien Febvre, *Le Rhin: problèmes d'histoire et d'économie* (Paris: A. Colin, 1935), pp. 96–97.

45. Both Burckhardt and Bachofen were members of the Basel Antiquarian Society and of the Historical Society, both contributed papers, and both regarded these societies with condescension. They were pleased that the business community still retained enough of the old humanistic ideal to want to engage in any kind of scholarly or intellectual activity, but they had no illusions about the quality or significance of the work presented by the members; though both of them were patriotic Baselers, they also saw themselves as citizens of a larger European cultural community and their own work far transcended any purely local pride and curiosity.

46. On Burckhardt and the French historians, see Niklaus Röthlin, "Burckhardts Stellung in der Kulturgeschichtsschreibung des 19. Jahrhunderts," *Archiv für Kulturgeschichte* 69 (1987): 389–406, at pp. 397–98. On the historian's educative mission, see Prosper de Barante, preface to *Histoire des Ducs de Bourgogne de la Maison de Valois*, 2 vols. (Brussels: Wahlen, 1838), 1:8: "What we seek in studying the past is solid information and full knowledge of things, moral examples, political wisdom, comparisons with the present time." This general humanist idea of *historia magistra vitae* is more concrete in Augustin Thierry who, even after renouncing his earlier, polemical use of history in the liberal cause, still expressed the hope—in 1834, in the less than brilliant aftermath of the July Revolution—that his work would help to "combat the sort of moral lethargy that is the affliction of the new generation; . . . and to lead back on to the right path some of those over stimulated spirits who complain that they have lost faith and don't know what to hold on to, and who go seeking everywhere, never finding it anywhere, something to admire and devote themselves to" (*Dix Ans d'études historiques* [Paris: Garnier, 1867], p. 24). On Michelet's view of the historical text as an instrument of conversion, a kind of eucharist that will recreate the national community, see my article "Michelet's Gospel of Revolution," in Lionel Gossman, *Between History and Literature* (Cambridge: Harvard University Press, 1990), pp. 201–24, especially p. 221.

47. Barante, *Histoire des Ducs de Bourgogne*, 1:9.

48. To Breysig's suggestion that his practice of cultural history had marked a radical new departure in historiography, Burckhardt responded: "What about the French!" and mentioned "by name Guizot and Thierry . . . as well as several other French historians" (Kurt Breysig, *Aus meinen Tagen und Träumen: Memoiren, Aufzeichnungen, Briefe, Gespräche,* ed. Gertrud Breysig and Michael Landmann [Berlin: de Gruyter, 1962], p. 79).

49. See Peter Ganz's introduction to Jacob Burckhardt, *Über das Studium der Geschichte: der Text der 'Weltgeschichtlichen Betrachtungen' . . . nach den Handschriften herausgegeben,* ed. Peter Ganz (Munich: C. H. Beck, 1982), pp. 24–25. Burckhardt was probably following the example of his teacher Ranke, who often preceded his courses with one or several lectures on topics such as "Über die Idee und das Studium der allgemeinen Historie" (summer semester, 1831), or "Über das Studium der Geschichte" (winter semester 1831–1832); see "Vorlesungseinleitungen," ed. V. Dotterweich and W. P. Fuchs, vol. 4 of Leopold von Ranke, *Aus Werk und Nachlass,* ed. W. P. Fuchs and T. Schieder (Munich and Vienna: R. Oldenbourg, 1975), p. 72.

50. Quoted in Kaegi, *Jacob Burckhardt,* 3:371. Original text now published in *Über das Studium der Geschichte,* ed. Ganz, pp. 83–103.

51. Kaegi, *Jacob Burckhardt,* 3:371. In the introduction to his highly popular *Histoire de la conquête de l'Angleterre par les Normands* (1826), Thierry acknowledged that "no matter how superior one's intelligence, one cannot transcend the horizon of one's time; thus each new age provides history with new points of view and a form particular to that age" (4 vols. [Paris: Garnier, 1867], 1:9). In the preface to his *Dix Ans d'études historiques* (1834) he admitted that an earlier hope of constructing "the true history of France, the history that would never need to be redone and would belong to no particular writer," by compiling authentic chronicles and memoirs, had proved illusory ([Paris: Garnier, 1867], p. 20). Michelet described his aim as "winning a few moments from the whirlwind that is hurrying us all along, only as much as is required to observe it and describe it" ("Je voudrais dans ce rapide passage, obtenir quelques moments du tourbillon qui nous entraîne, seulement ce qu'il en faut pour l'observer et le décrire; qu'il m'emporte après, et me brise s'il veut") (*Introduction à l'histoire universelle,* in *Oeuvres complètes,* ed. Paul Viallaneix [Paris: Flammarion, 1971–], 2:228).

52. "Einleitung in die Geschichte des Revolutionszeitalters," *Gesamtausgabe,* 7:426: "We would dearly love to know the wave that is carrying us over the ocean, but we *are* that wave" ("Wir möchten gerne die Welle kennen, auf welcher wir im Ozean treiben, allein wir sind diese Welle selbst"). See Hardtwig, *Geschichtsschreibung,* pp. 25, 219–24. See also Michelet, *Introduction à l'histoire universelle* (1831), opening statement on the role of the historian of France at a time when France has become the "world-historical nation" in Hegelian terms, "the pilot of the ship of humanity" ("le pilote du vaisseau de l'humanité"), as Michelet himself put it. "But today that ship is hurtling forward in the hurricane; it is moving so fast, so fast, that the steadiest are seized with vertigo and every one is gasping for breath. What is there for me to do in this beautiful and terrible moment? One thing only: understand it" ("Mais ce vaisseau vole aujourd'hui dans l'ouragan; il va si vite, si vite, que le vertige prend aux plus fermes, et que toute poitrine en est oppressée. Que puis-je dans ce beau et terrible mouvement? Une seule chose: le comprendre) (*Oeuvres complètes,* 2:227–28).

53. Kaegi, *Jacob Burckhardt,* 3:371–72; *Über das Studium der Geschichte,* ed. Ganz, p. 84.

54. Letter of 21 March 1842, *Briefe,* 1:197.

55. The object of study was "not so much political life as culture," "not so much princes and dynasties as peoples and their development in a single common spirit," and the lectures were to be arranged "not by countries or chronologically, but according to the pervasive spiritual and cultural currents" (*"nach den geistigen Strömungen"*). See the quotations from the maunscript of the lectures on the Middle Ages (winter term 1849–1850) in Kaegi, *Jacob Burckhardt,* 3:327.

56. *The Age of Constantine the Great,* trans. Moses Hadas (New York: Pantheon Books, 1949), p. 10 (hereafter *Constantine*).

57. Ranke considered only those peoples "historical" who had contributed to the elaboration of culture, and culture, as he understood it, was essentially European culture. Cf. the notes taken by Eduard Winkelmann of Ranke's course on "German History until the Reformation with an Overview of the Period to 1815" (winter term of 1857–1858): "All nations are not equal and not all have a history which is worth our trouble. There is no point in speaking of peoples who let centuries pass by as if they were days; there are peoples who have a literature but no history. It is permissible to distinguish between peoples, the description of whom might belong in a natural history of mankind, and historical nations. The latter become historical by playing a part in the development of the human race, in culture. Since culture has been developed, peoples have entered into contact with each other through it. Being cut off from it would be equivalent to being plunged into eternal barbarism" ("Nicht alle Nationen sind gleich, und nicht alle haben eine Geschichte, die sehr der Mühe wert ist; es ist nicht zu reden von Völkern, die Jahrhunderte vergehen lassen wie Tage, es gibt viele Völker, die wohl Literatur haben, aber keine Geschichte. Man darf wohl einen Unterschied machen zwischen Völkern, die in der Naturgeschichte des Menschen beschrieben werden, und historische Nationen. Historisch werden sie durch ihre Teilnahme an der Entwicklung des Menschengeschlechtes, an der Kultur. Seitdem diese gepflegt wird, ist ein Volk mit dem andern dadurch in Berührung gekommen. Sich abschliessen hiesse, sich in ewige Barbarei stürzen") (Ranke, *Aus Werk und Nachlass,* 4:274).

58. Letter of 13 August 1852, *Briefe,* 3:161.

59. Ranke, *Die grossen Mächte; Politisches Gespräch,* ed. Schieder, pp. 59–60.

60. *The World as Will and Representation,* trans. R. B. Haldane and J. Kemp, 3 vols. (London: Routledge & Kegan Paul, 1957; orig. 1883), bk. 3, ch. 38 ("On History"), 3:220–30, at pp. 227–29.

61. Letter from Wölfflin to his parents, 19 October 1882, in *Jacob Burckhardt und Heinrich Wölfflin: Breifwechsel und andere Dokumente ihrer Begegnung,* p. 22.

62. Lectures on "Neuere Geschichte von 1450 bis 1598," *Gesamtausgabe,* 7:283.

63. Letter to Karl Fresenius, 19 June 1842 *Briefe,* 1:206–07.

64. Kaegi, *Jacob Burckhardt,* 3:310–11.

65. Ibid., p. 316.

66. *Constantine,* p. 124. Similar hints can be found in the agnostic Fustel de Coulanges, who declares in his thesis on Polybius (1858) that the social struggles in Athens were "a mysterious means by which the peoples succeeded in uniting" (*Polybe, ou la Grèce conquise par les Romains* [Naples: Jovene, 1984]) and in Ernest Renan, for whom "the world is a comedy, at once divine and infernal, a strange round, led by a choragos of genius, . . . with a view to the fulfillment of a mysterious end" (*Vie de Jésus* [Paris: Gallimard, 1974], p. 50).

67. On this, see Hardtwig, *Geschichtsschreibung,* pp. 224–31.

68. Gilbert, *History: Politics or Culture?,* p. 53, citing Kinkel's *Selbstbiographie 1838–1848,* ed. Richard Sander (Bonn: Friedrich Cohen, 1931), p. 29.

69. In the preface to the second edition of *Die Zeit Konstantins des Grossen* (1880), Burckhardt described his objective in this work as "not so much a complete historical account as an integrated description, from the viewpoint of cultural history, of the important transition period named in the title."

70. *History and Historians in the Nineteenth Century* (London: Longmans Green, 1935; orig. 1913), p. 580.

71. In the aftermath of the *Sonderbundkrieg* and the Revolutions of 1848, Burckhardt rejected Ranke's optimistic conviction that the Revolution had been integrated into the continuity of European history and insisted, on the contrary, that it had inaugurated a new era

of crisis in which everybody and everything would finally be swept up. *Historische Fragmente,* ed. Emil Dürr (Stuttgart: Koehler, 1957), p. 270.

72. *Constantine,* pp. 260–61.

73. *Essai sur les moeurs,* ch. X, cited in Kaegi, *Jacob Burckhardt,* 3:382.

74. *Constantine,* pp. 260–61. On the history of the image of Constantine from the Middle Ages to Burckhardt, see Kaegi, *Jacob Burckhardt,* 3:379–83.

75. *Constantine,* p. 262.

76. *Reflections on History,* p. 16 (translation slightly amended).

77. See chapter 10 on Burckhardt and Droysen.

78. *Reflections on History,* p. 215.

79. "Einleitung in die Geschichte des 17. und 18. Jahrhunderts (1598–1673)," dated May 1869, *Gesamtausgabe,* 7:370. Cf. *Weltgeschichtliche Betrachtungen,* section 5 ("Das Individuum und das Allgemeine"), *Gesamtausgabe,* 7:180: "The fate of peoples and states, the direction of entire civilizations, may depend on the ability of one extraordinary soul, at a certain moment in history, to sustain a high degree of tension and effort." Cf. *Reflections on History,* pp. 191–92.

80. *Reflections on History,* p. 16 (translation amended to conform more closely to German original).

81. Ibid., p. 20.

82. Albert Salomon, "Jacob Burckhardt: Transcending History," *Philosophy and Phenomenological Research* 6 (1946): 225–69, at p. 237.

83. Ibid., p. 234.

84. Ibid., p. 260.

85. See Gerhard Oestreich, *Neostoicism and the Early Modern State,* ed. B. Oestreich and H. G. Koenigsberger, trans. David McLintock (Cambridge: Cambridge University Press, 1982).

86. Letter to Arnold von Salis, 29 November 1871, *Briefe,* 5:144, in reaction to further saber rattling in Germany in the wake of victory in the Franco-Prussian war.

87. *Constantine,* p. 164.

88. Ibid., p. 164.

89. Ibid., p. 183.

90. Ibid., p. 184.

91. Ibid., p. 199.

92. Ibid., p. 213.

93. Ibid., pp. 207, 212.

94. Ibid., p. 185.

95. Alfred von Martin, *Die Religion Jacob Burckhardts* (Munich: Erasmus-Verlag, 1947; 1st ed. [confiscated by the Gestapo] 1942). See in particular the section on Kierkegaard and Burckhardt, pp. 216–55.

96. Letter to Friedrich von Preen, 2 July 1871, *Briefe,* 5:130.

97. Manuscript of lecture notes by Arnold von Salis from Burckhardt's course of 1870–1871 (posthumously published as *Weltgeschichtliche Betrachtungen*); quoted by Kaegi, *Jacob Burckhardt,* 6(1):80.

98. Letters to Willibald Beyschlag, 14 January 1844, *Briefe,* 2:60, and Gottfried Kinkel, 29 June 1845, *Briefe,* 2:172. Willibald Beyschlag recalled in his memoirs that as early as the 1840s Burckhardt was convinced that the heyday not only of theology but of the church itself was past (Willibald Beyschlag, *Aus meinem Leben* [Halle, 1896], quoted by Kaegi, *Jacob Burckhardt,* 2:211). See also von Martin, *Die Religion Jacob Burckhardts,* pp. 20, 52.

99. *Constantine,* p. 224.

100. Ibid., p. 225.

101. Ibid., pp. 226–27.
102. Ibid., p. 228.
103. Ibid., p. 229.
104. Ibid., p. 229.
105. Ibid., p. 232.
106. Ibid., p. 234.
107. Ibid., p. 235.
108. Ibid., p. 237.
109. Ibid., p. 238.
110. Ibid., p. 240.
111. Ibid., pp. 238–39.
112. Ibid., p. 242.
113. Ibid., p. 366.

114. Describing the Arian conflict and the Council of Nicaea which was called to resolve it (325), Burckhardt noted that "a host of . . . interests, in part very worldly, attached themselves to the conflict and were concealed in it, so that it assumes the aspect of a merely hypocritical pretext. For the sake of this quarrel, the Church made itself inwardly hollow; for the sake of orthodox dogma it suffered the inward man to be famished, and itself demoralized, it completely forfeited its higher moral effect upon the individual. And yet this business, so distasteful in itself, was of supreme importance in world history. This Church, with its collateral sects, grown rigid and cut off from all development, was for another millennium and a half to hold nationalities together against the pressure of alien barbarians, even to take the place of nationalities, for it was stronger than state or culture, and therefore survived them both" (*Constantine*, p. 313).

115. Christianity could not save the state, according to Burckhardt, but it did "so far prepare the Empire's Germanic conquerors that they did not wholly tread its culture underfoot" (*Constantine*, p. 216).

116. Ibid., pp. 242–43.
117. Ibid., pp. 368–69.
118. Ibid., pp. 323–24.
119. Ibid., pp. 324–25.

120. See notably William Kerrigan and Gordon Braden, *The Idea of the Renaissance* (Baltimore: Johns Hopkins University Press, 1984), chs. 1 and 2. Criticism of Burckhardt's vision of the Renaissance focuses on the allegedly too radical break he established between "Middle Ages" and "Renaissance" (Huizinga, Ortega y Gasset) and on his view of culture as almost exclusively "high" culture. Nevertheless, in contrast to Bachofen's work, Burckhardt's remains astonishingly relevant today. See Paul O. Kristeller, "Changing Views of the Intellectual history of the Renaissance since Jacob Burckhardt," in *The Renaissance: A Reconsideration of the Theories and Interpretations of the Age*, ed. Tinsley Helton (Madison: University of Wisconsin Press, 1961), pp. 27–52: "After a hundred years, this book still dominates the debate on the Renaisssance, and although it has been criticized and supplemented in a variety of ways, it has hardly been replaced. . . . This great book is not merely well written; it reflects a mastery of the historical and literary sources of fifteenth century Italy that has been rarely equaled by later scholars. It is also full of subtle qualifications and observations which should be quite surprising to those who like to make contemptuous remarks about 'Burckhardtian views'" (p. 29).

121. Victor Hugo's expression in *L'Année terrible*.

122. David Norbrook, "Life and Death of Renaissance Man," *Raritan*, spring 1989, pp. 89–110, at pp. 91, 99.

123. *The Civilization of the Renaissance in Italy* (hereafter *CRI*), trans. by S. G. C. Middlemore, with an introduction by Benjamin Nelson and Charles Trinkaus (New York: Harper & Row, 1958), pp. 58, 56, 54, 102. By basing the last edition of his English translation on the fifteenth edition of the German original, "with slight additions to the text and large additions to the notes by Dr. Ludwig Geiger and Professor Walther Götz," Middlemore no doubt intended to serve the ends of historical *Wissenschaft*. He does mark off those places "where Dr. Geiger's and Professor Götz's views differ from those taken by Dr. Burckhardt." Nevertheless, readers of Burckhardt, as opposed to scholars of the Renaissance, require access in English to what Burckhardt wrote and not to what is no longer the latest scholarly account of the Renaissance. The beautiful Phaidon Press edition (Vienna, n.d.) restores the early text.

124. Ibid., pp. 442–43 *et passim.*

125. Ibid., p. 26.

126. When Burckhardt described the state as a *Kunstwerk* and war as a *Kunstwerk* (*CRI*, pt. 1, ch. 9), there is no doubt an "aesthetic" dimension to the term *Kunstwerk*. Above all, however, Burckhardt was emphasizing that the modern state and modern warfare are not natural, but products of artful calculation, as he himself made abundantly clear. It is a misunderstanding to argue from this term, as one scholar did in 1959, that, in contrast with others who "have regarded the state as an engine of repression, and war as a scourge of mankind, beauty-loving Burckhardt saw them as works of art" (Edward Rosen, "Renaissance Science as seen by Burckhardt and his Successors," *The Renaissance: A Reconsideration*, ed. Helton, p. 80).

127. The Bavaria, Baden, and Württemberg that emerged from the Napoleonic period bear the marks of that period, according to Theodor Schieder ("Partikularismus und Nationalbewusstsein," in Conze, *Staat und Gesellschaft im deutschen Vormärz*). What later came to be referred to with disdain as 'particularism,'" Schieder writes,

> was in fact the will to modern statehood, the statist orientation of each particular state. The legal privileges and special status, grounded in historical tradition, of particular provinces and territories were to be thoroughly rooted out, while—as the charter of the Bavarian Constitution of 1818 put it, for instance—"a single, indivisible, and unalienable total state" was to be created "out of a sum of constituent parts, in the form of various lands, peoples, authorities, properties, prerogatives, and revenues, with all their appurtenances." This principle was enacted chiefly by dividing the old territory into new administrative units, with no basis in history, and with the aim of erasing all memory of the old traditional territories and estates. That is exactly what happened not only in Bavaria but in almost all other states. In the state of Count Montgelas [i.e., Bavaria]—but also in that of the Minister of Baden, Reitzenstein, the historical is sacrificed to the "rational idea of the state," the rational organization of administration. The elimination of the old privileges, the annexation of the old Imperial cities and Imperial principalities had as its objective the extension of the state and the solidification of the state's undisputed role as the single repository of public authority (p. 16; see also pp. 22–23).

128. *CRI*, pp. 250–51.

129. Ibid., p. 104.

130. Quoted by Karl Joachim Weintraub, "Jacob Burckhardt: The Historian among the Philologists," *American Scholar*, spring 1988, pp. 273–82, p. 276.

131. Ibid., p. 279.

132. See the invaluable comments of Peter Ganz on Burckhardt's "triple layering" of temporal references (Middle Ages, Renaissance, and the contemporary world of the nineteenth century) to produce what he calls a "diachronic depth" in *The Civilization of the Renaissance*. "Jacob Burckhardts *Kultur der Renaissance in Italien:* Handwerk und Methode," *Deutsche Vierteljahrsschrift für Literaturwissenschaft und Geistesgeschichte* 63 (1988): 24–59.

133. *CRI,* p. 143, opening of pt. 2.

134. Ibid., p. 26 *et passim.*

135. Ibid., pp. 22, 36, 429, 437 *et passim.*

136. Ibid., p. 36.

137. Ibid., p. 107.

138. Ibid., p. 110.

139. Ibid., p. 143.

140. Ibid., p. 142. For discussion of the concept and term *individualism* in Burckhardt, see Richard Koebner, "Zur Begriffsbildung der Kulturgeschichte. II: Zur Geschichte des Begriffs 'Individualismus,'" *Historische Zeitschrift* 149 (1933): 253–93. Koebner points to the origins of the concept in different traditions, such as the Saint-Simonian critique of social and economic individualism, on the one hand, and the Humboldtian ideal of harmonious development of the autonomous individual on the other.

141. *CRI,* pp. 474, 480.

142. Ibid., p. 301.

143. Ibid., pp. 353, 354, 43.

144. Ibid., p. 176.

145. Ibid., pp. 171–72.

146. Ibid., p. 428. I have amended Middlemore's translation in two places.

147. Ibid., p. 428.

148. Ibid., p. 428.

149. Ibid., p. 476.

150. Ibid., p. 110 (italics added).

151. Ibid., p. 143.

152. Quoted by Ganz, "Jacob Burckhardts *Kultur der Renaissance in Italien,*" p. 29.

153. *CRI,* p. 431.

154. Ibid., p. 104.

155. Ibid., p. 229: "The age in which we live is loud enough in proclaiming the worth of culture, especially the culture of antiquity. But the enthusiastic devotion to it, the recognition that the need of it is the first and foremost of all needs, is nowhere to be found but among the Florentines of the fifteenth and the early part of the sixteenth century."

156. Ibid., p. 474.

157. Ibid., p. 148.

158. *History and Historians in the Nineteenth Century,* pp. 582, 584.

159. *CRI,* p, 176.

160. Ibid., p. 348.

161. Ibid., pp. 355–57.

162. Ibid., pp. 399–400.

163. Ibid., pp. 389–91.

164. Ibid., p. 168.

165. Ibid., p. 88.

166. Ibid., pp. 103–04.

167. Ibid., p. 144.

168. See the acute comments of Hans Baron in a beautiful essay entitled "The Limits of

the Notion of 'Renaissance Individualism': Burckhardt After a Century" (1960; revised 1973), in his *In Search of Florentine Humanism,* 2 vols. (Princeton: Princeton University Press, 1988), 2:155–81, at pp. 168–72.

169. "He utters his scorn of the incessant changes and experiments in the constitution of his native city; he addressed his home in words of defiance and yearning which must have stirred the hearts of his countrymen. But his thoughts ranged over Italy and the whole world" (*CRI,* p. 96).

170. Ibid., p. 104.

171. Ibid., pp. 220–23.

172. Ibid., p. 276.

173. Ibid., pp. 330–31.

174. Ibid., p. 332.

Chapter Twelve

1. Translated by Palmer Hilty (New York: Frederick Ungar, 1963). See the reviews by M. L. Finlay, *New Statesman and Nation,* 18 September 1964, p. 409, and Oswyn Murray, *Classical Review* 79 (1965): 209–12; see also *Times Literary Supplement,* 15 October 1964.

2. A new translation and abridgment entitled *The Greeks and Greek Civilization,* expertly translated by Sheila Stern, the widow of the highly respected British Germanist, J. P. Stern, and edited, with a beautiful introduction by the British classical scholar Oswyn Murray, appeared with Harper Collins in England in 1998 and has now appeared in the United States with Macmillan. It is infinitely superior to the earlier translation. Unfortunately, it reached me only in the fall of 1998 as I was making final revisions to this book after its publication had been approved by the Editorial Board of the University of Chicago Press. I have not retranslated the passages that I had already translated fairly literally myself, but for the benefit of the reader I have added page references to the new edition wherever the passage in question has been included in it. These appear in square brackets in italics after the references to the *Gesamtausgabe.*

3. Its relative inaccessibility may account for the fact that *The Cultural History of Greece* is not referred to in popular English (or French) comprehensive studies of the Greeks, such as André Bonnard, *La Civilisation grecque* (Lausanne, 1959), Engl. trans. R. C. Knight (London: Allen & Unwin, 1961); C. M. Bowra, *The Greek Experience* (London: Weidenfeld & Nicholson, 1957); G. Lowes Dickinson, *The Greek View of Life* (London: Methuen, 1904); M. I. Finley, *The Ancient Greeks* (Harmondsworth, Middlesex: 1977); George Thomson, *Studies in Ancient Greek Society* (London: Lawrence & Wishart 1949–1955). Two pages—essentially a review of the excellent comprehensive study by E. M. Janssen, *Jacob Burckhardt und die Griechen* (Assen: Van Gorcum, 1979)—are devoted to Burckhardt in Hugh Lloyd-Jones's *Blood for the Ghosts: Classical Influences in the Nineteenth and Twentieth Centuries* (London: Duckworth, 1982; Baltimore: Johns Hopkins University Press, 1983), pp. 153–54. Even in a recent scholarly study of republican societies and constitutions (Paul A. Rahe, *Republics Ancient and Modern* [Chapel Hill and London: University of North Carolina Press, 1992]), which is extremely detailed (it runs to 1,200 pages of fairly small type) and develops an argument, familiar to readers of Burckhardt, about the polis as illiberal and oppressive, I found no mention of *The Cultural History of Greece.* Like Burckhardt, the author of this work also takes the Ancients at their word in viewing Sparta as the very model of the polis. Even on more specific points—the political character of homoeroticism and its consecration by the laws in the heyday of the polis, its increasingly private and simply sexual character and the erosion of the laws upholding it as the polis declined—he is extraordinarily close to Burckhardt. It is curious that an author who acknowledges having had the benefit

of advice from numerous classical scholars and political theorists seems to have been un-aware of Burckhardt's *Cultural History of Greece.* Characteristically, the one fairly popular study of the Greeks in German that I consulted—Egon Friedell's *Kulturgeschichte Griechen-lands* (London: Phaidon, 1949)—does refer to Burckhardt's work in several places, in partic-ular on the question of Greek pessimism. By emphasizing the pessimism and unhappiness of the Greeks, according to Friedell, who was expressing a view common among German scholars on this point, Burckhardt radically revised the prevailing view of antiquity. In the English- and French-speaking worlds, it is usually Nietzsche who is credited with having effected that change.

4. Letter to Otto Ribbeck, 16 October 1865, *Briefe,* ed. Max Burckhardt, 10 vols. plus index vol. (Basel: Schwabe, 1949–1994), 4:197. See Werner Kaegi, *Jacob Burckhardt: eine Biographie* (Basel: Schwabe, 1947–1982), 7:5, 33–34.

5. Letter of 25 March 1847, *Briefe,* 3:63.

6. Letter of 3 March 1867, *Briefe,* 4:243.

7. Kaegi, *Jacob Burckhardt,* 7:6–7.

8. See ibid., p. 21, and Werner Rihm, *Das Bildungserlebnis der Antike bei Johannes von Müller,* Basler Beiträge zur Geschichtswissenschaft, vol. 7 (Basel, 1959).

9. The first volume of William Mitford's whiggish *History of Greece,* a glorification of Greek freedom and a heroization of Demosthenes in particular, appeared in 1784; the three volumes of John Gillies's antidemocratic *History of Ancient Greece, its Colonies and Conquests,* which included "the history of literature, philosophy and the fine arts," in 1787; Connop Thirlwall's *Greek History* began to appear in 1835; the first volume of George Grote's more radical and prodemocratic twelve-volume *History of Greece* in 1846. Ernst Curtius's three-volume *Griechische Geschichte,* in contrast, did not appear until 1857–1867. See Arnaldo Momigliano, *George Grote and the Study of Greek History* (London: University College, 1952), pp. 4–8 (Momigliano's inaugural lecture at University College, London).

10. George Grote, *Seven Letters on the Recent Politics of Switzerland* (London: T. C. Newby, 1847), pp. iii–iv.

11. Quoted by Kaegi, *Jacob Burckhardt,* 7:31. By adopting the generic term *Kleinstaat-erei*—which the upholders of the *Machtstaat* used to convey their contempt for the "anachro-nistic" remnants of a weak and flawed political order—in order to designate the source of *"unendlich reiches Geistesleben,"* Vischer underlined what to him, and no doubt many of his fellow Baselers, was the deeply questionable character of the preoccupation of German histo-rians such as Droysen and Mommsen with power and political success.

12. See Felix Gilbert, *J. G. Droysen und die preussisch-deutsche Frage* (Munich and Berlin: R. Oldenbourg, 1931), and Arnaldo Momigliano, "J. G. Droysen between Greeks and Jews," in his *Quinto Contributo alla storia degli studi classici e del mondo antico* (Rome: Edizioni di storia e letteratura, 1975), pp. 109–26.

13. Hagen Schulze, *Staat und Nation in der europäischen Geschichte* (Munich: C. H. Beck, 1994), p. 180.

14. *Die Briefe der Frau Rath Goethe,* ed. Albert Koster, 2 vols. (Leipzig: Insel-Verlag, 1908), 2:40, 144 (letters 268, 12 January 1798, and 373, 19 August 1806).

15. See Schulze, *Staat und Nation in der europäischen Geschichte,* pp. 182–85. The editors of the *Archiv für deutsche Kulturgeschichte* announced in their prospectus that "cultural history follows with intense interest every struggle of the *Volksgeist* to incarnate itself in the form of a state" ([1858], 1:23). Cf. John Hutchinson, *The Dynamics of Cultural Nationalism* (London: George Allen & Unwin, 1987): "In terms of its own communitarian goals, cultural national-ism is a failure, and it regularly shifts into a state politics to institutionalize its program in the social order. In doing so, it paves the way for its suppression by political nationalism" (p. 41).

16. *Über die Bildung von Staaten und Bünden, oder Centralisation und Föderation im alten Griechenland* (Basel: Schweighauser'sche Universitaets-Buchdruckerei, 1849). Basel University Library, E.bb.I.36.

17. Ibid., p. 14.

18. *Griechische Kulturgeschichte*, ed. Felix Stähelin, vols. 8–11 of Jacob Burckhardt, *Gesamtausgabe*, ed. Emil Dürr et al., 14 vols. (Stuttgart, Berlin, and Leipzig: Deutsche Verlagsanstalt, 1930–1934), 9:343. Further references to *The Cultural History of Greece* will be given in parentheses in the text. The number indicates volume number and page of this edition. The number in italics is to the new English translation described in note 2 above.

19. "Die Hellenen waren im Glanze der Kunst und in der Blüte der Freiheit unglücklicher als die meisten glauben" (*Die Staatshaushaltung der Athener* [Berlin: G. Reimer, 1817], 2:159).

20. Ibid., 1:2. Quoted by Kaegi, *Jacob Burckhardt*, 7:24–25 note 70.

21. Johann Wolfgang von Goethe, *Werke*, Artemis-Ausgabe, *Gespräche*, 20 November 1813, 1:703. Quoted by Kaegi, *Jacob Burckhardt*, 7:25. Cf. Burckhardt's remark: "Die Tyrannis ist eine der ganz unvermeidlichen Formen der griechischen Staatsidee und in jedem begabten und ehrgeizigen Griechen wohnte ein Tyrann und ein Demagog" (8:169).

22. On the situation at Basel, see Kaegi, *Jacob Burckhardt*, 7:28–30. The passage from Böckh is in *Staatshaushaltung der Athener*, quoted by Kaegi, 7:30.

23. See Kaegi, *Jacob Burckhardt*, 7:44–50.

24. Kaegi recalls (*Jacob Burckhardt*, 7:42–43) that the famous damaging review by Wilamowitz-Moellendorff (Nietzsche hardly knew Homer, had never read Euripides, was a disgrace to his venerable old humanistic college, *Schulpforta*, and so on) was the work of a young and ambitious scholar, himself a product of *Schulpforta*, who was not yet even a *Privatdozent*. "Das Ganze war in der Tat im Grunde ein Hochmutsstreit unter ehrgeizigen Primanern" (7:43).

25. Letters to Erwin Rohde and Richard Wagner, mid-November 1872, *Briefwechsel*, ed. G. Colli and M. Montinari (Berlin: De Gruyter, 1975–1984), in three sections and sixteen volumes, sec. 2, vol. 3, pp. 85, 88.

26. Ibid., p. 89. What most bothered him, Nietzsche explained, was that the attack on his scholarly reputation had badly damaged an institution that had placed its trust full in him and to which he was "devoted and grateful."

27. Kaegi, *Jacob Burckhardt*, 7:9, 44–45. See also the postscript in a letter from Burckhardt to Jacob Oeri, 17 May 1872, *Briefe*, 5:162–63.

28. Kaegi, *Jacob Burckhardt*, 7:13, 15.

29. Letter to von Preen, 17 March 1872, *Briefe*, 5:153.

30. Letter of 2 January 1880, *Briefe*, 7:130.

31. On Burckhardt's manuscripts, see Kaegi, *Jacob Burckhardt*, 7:15.

32. Letter of 14 March 1880, *Briefe*, 7:145. The Sybel work in question was the *Geschichte des Revolutionszeitalters von 1780 bis 1800*.

33. Letter of 2 August 1880, *Briefe*, 7:171.

34. Letter to Ernst Arthur Seemann, 19 July 1880, *Briefe*, 7:167.

35. Letter to Cotta Verlag, 22 August 1880, *Briefe*, 7:178.

36. Letter to Seemann, 29 November 1889, *Briefe*, 9:224. Five years later, shortly before his death, Burckhardt repeated the same story to Seemann, though he spoke less harshly this time of Nietzsche. "I must explain again, as I have done several times to different parties in recent years, that no *Greek Cultural History* by me exists and that poor Nietzsche confused a notebook containing my lectures with a fully elaborated work" (letter of 7 December 1894, *Briefe*, 10:194–95).

37. Letter of 3 October 1880, *Briefe*, 7:195.

38. See Kaegi, *Jacob Burckhardt,* 7:12, 15.

39. See ibid., p. 16.

40. *Griechische Kulturgeschichte, Gesamtausgabe,* 11:255–56 *[267–68].* To avoid encumbering the notes, most subsequent references to these volumes in this chapter will be given in parentheses in the text.

41. Heinrich Gelzer, "Jacob Burckhardt als Mensch und Lehrer," *Zeitschrift für deutsche Kulturgeschichte,* vol. 8, 1900, quoted by Kaegi, *Jacob Burckhardt,* 7:15.

42. See Kaegi, *Jacob Burckhardt,* 7:101–2. The critic, Leo Bloch, went on to accuse Oeri of having pressured Burckhardt on his deathbed to relax his formal prohibition against publication. Oeri brought suit against Bloch and his publisher, the eminent B. G. Teubner Verlag, in Leipzig. The relevant documents are to be found in Jacob Burckhardt Archiv (Staatsarchive des Kantons Basel Stadt) 207 (Nachlass), 181.

43. "Griechische Geschichte im neunzehnten Jahrhundert," *Festrede* on the 143rd anniversary of the founding of the Royal Bavarian Academy of Sciences in Munich, Munich 1902. See Kaegi, *Jacob Burckhardt,* 7:100.

44. See Kaegi, *Jacob Burckhardt,* 7:99, 103, 106.

45. Ernst Gombrich, *In Search of Cultural History* (Oxford: Clarendon Press, 1969) (the Philip Maurice Daneke Lecture of 1967).

46. The argument Burckhardt developed here can be traced back at least as far as seventeenth- and eighteenth-century French scholars who were arguing for the *historical* value of medieval romances. See my *Medievalism and the Ideologies of the Enlightenment: The World and Work of La Curne de Sainte-Palaye* (Baltimore: Johns Hopkins University Press, 1968), pp. 153, 247–53.

47. See also *Gesamtausgabe,* 10:279, 10:351–52. This distinction had been made clearly by the editors of the *Archiv für deutsche Kulturgeschichte* in their prospectus ([1858], 1:23–25) and was developed with great clarity by Eduard Gothein, an admirer of Burckhardt, in his *Die Aufgaben der Kulturgeschichte* (Leipzig: Dunker & Humbolt, 1889), pp. 34–49.

48. This is an old problem. Among Enlightenment philosophers such as Hume, Rousseau, and Diderot, there was an acute sense of the discrepancy between the fluidity and continuity of the world of inner experience and the discontinuity of the language by means of which that experience is represented and even comprehended. A famous passage from Diderot's *Lettre sur les sourds et muets* comes immediately to mind: "Autre chose est l'état de notre âme, autre chose le compte que nous en rendons, soit à nous-mêmes, soit aux autres. . . . Notre âme est un tableau mouvant d'après lequel nous peignons sans cesse; nous employons bien du temps à le rendre avec fidélité; mais il existe en entier et tout à la fois: l'esprit ne va pas à pas comptés comme l'expression" ("What is actually going on in our minds and the way we conceptualize it for ourselves as well as for others are two quite different things. . . . The mind is a moving picture, which we are constantly trying to paint; we devote a lot of time to representing it as faithfully as possible; but it is present in complete fullness at any given moment; the spirit does not proceed with the measured tread of our vehicles of expression").

49. The source of this statement is identified in a note as Mommsen, *Römische Geschichte,* 5:336.

50. Burckhardt might have found inspiration for this revised idea of antiquity, some time before Nietzsche and even before Bachofen, in Goethe's essay "Der Sammler und die Seinigen." Goethe here introduced an art historian (Aloys Hirt [1759–1839]), who had challenged his view of the Ancients, and allowed him to express the opinion that "Lessing foisted on us the principle that the Ancients created only beauty. Winckelmann lulled us to sleep with his 'quiet grandeur, simplicity and calm' instead of telling us that the art of antiquity

appears in every conceivable form. But these gentlemen only concentrate on Jupiter and Juno, the Genii and the Graces, and they do not talk about the ugly bodies and heads of barbarians, the disheveled hair and dirty beards, the scrawny physiques, wrinkled skin, protruding veins and sagging breasts of old age" (Goethe, *Essays on Art and Literature*, ed. John Geary, trans. Ellen and Ernest H. von Nardroff [New York: Suhrkamp, 1986], p. 139).

51. Hutchinson, *The Dynamics of Cultural Nationalism*, pp. 12–15.

52. Cf. *Gesamtausgabe*, 8:55 (opening page of section on the polis): "Through the cult of ancestors the family is held together. . . . Likewise the right to property in land is causally related to the veneration of the hearth and of grave sites." Cf. Numa-Denys Fustel de Coulanges, *La Cité antique*, preface by François Hartog (Paris: Flammarion, 1986), pp. 39–89.

53. See Kaegi, *Jacob Burckhardt*, 7:77–78. Kaegi's source is the commentaries or *"Nachträge"* which Jacob Oeri appended to the first volume of *Griechische Kulturgeschichte*.

54. "La plupart de nos jeunes érudits, depuis 15 ans, commencent par *se mettre au courant*. On entend par là se faire des listes bibliographiques et parcourir les ouvrages les plus récents. C'est le contraire de la méthode, qui consiste à lire avant tout les textes" ("Fragments inédits de Fustel de Coulanges," *Revue de synthèse* 2 [1902]: 257, quoted by Bertrand Hemmerdinger, introduction to his edition of Fustel's thesis of 1858, *Polybe, ou la Grèce conquise par les Romains* [Naples: Jovene, 1984], p. xviii).

55. Letter of 16 December 1883, *Briefe*, 7:170.

56. The contrast between a natural, popular (often polytheistic and immanentist) religion and a priestly religion founded on a set of written prescriptions and a radical separation of the human and the divine is found throughout nineteenth-century German culture—in the early Hegel and in Heine, as well as in Nietzsche and Burckhardt, and in most cases it is the former that is regarded with sympathy. In the 1880s, it was applied to Judaism by the great Biblical historian Julius Wellhausen who distinguished between an early "natural" religion of the Israelites, which was similar to the religions of other peoples in the region, and the later religion of the Mosaic law. The creation story allegedly reflected the new nonpopular, priestly religion in that it completely emptied the world of the old immanent powers and demons.

57. Burckhardt reflected a great deal on the development of theologies and churches—that is, on the institutionalization and regulation of religion and its alienation from its sources in popular imagination and creativity. On the whole, but not unequivocally, he considered institutionalization—in the form of the *ecclesia triumphans*, which turns the church into an accomplice of the state, "a police institution," and makes religion into an *instrumentum imperii*—destructive of authentic religion (*Reflections on History*, 52–55, 88 [on Islam], 120–24). The oldest religions, those that are free of dogmas and priesthoods, according to Burckhardt, are the cradle of culture, even if culture later gave rise to a criticism of religion (p. 124). "There is no original divergence between religion and culture. On the contrary, they are to a great extent identical" (p. 125).

58. On philosophers as "enemies and rivals of myth," see also *Gesamtausgabe*, 9:60.

59. Section 9 ("Hellenic Man in his Temporal Development"). Sections 6–8, on the arts, with a section on philosophy and oratory, occupies an intermediary position, since it considers each art form and each genre both in its relation to Greek life in general and in its relation to the historical evolution of Greek life.

60. In his courageous *Nietzsche und Burckhardt*, 2nd ed. (Munich: Ernst Reinhardt, 1942), the sociologist Alfred von Martin highlighted Burckhardt's insistence on history as a domain of human suffering and victimization. See especially, section 16, "Die Leidenden" (pp. 121–25).

61. "Until then, people had been 'tillers of the soil,' now, as all came to live together,

they became 'political beings'" (*"Bisher waren es 'Landwirte' gewesen, nun, als alles beisammen wohnte, wurden es, 'Politiker'"*) (*Gesamtausgabe*, 8:69 *[49]*).

62. During a brief discussion of Burckhardt's *Griechische Kulturgeschichte* with P. Vidal-Naquet at Princeton on October 11, 1994, in the course of which I expressed the view that a good part of the interest of Burckhardt's work lies in the fact that his reflections on the polis are in truth reflections on the state as such, the great classical historian replied that Burckhardt would have done better not to treat the polis as a state. Respectfully, I continue to believe that Burckhardt's interpretation of the polis as the pure form of the state, whether historically accurate or not, produced some of his morally and politically most deeply engaging pages. Perhaps only the citizen of a small city-state could have presented such a concrete and sobering picture of Leviathan.

63. For a modern consideration of Sparta as the very type of the polis, see Paul H. Rahe, *Republics Ancient and Modern* (Chapel Hill and London: University of North Carolina Press, 1992), pp. 134–85.

64. According to Paul H. Rahe, "The polis was akin to a party of zealots" (ibid., p. 134).

65. On Burckhardt's awareness of the difference between the Italian cities of the Renaissance and the Greek poleis, see also Kaegi, *Jacob Burckhardt*, 7:78–79.

66. Burckhardt's account of the birth of the polis is considerably more pessimistic than Droysen's. Momigliano has referred to a paper of 1847 on "Die attische Communalverfassung," in which Droysen argued that Solon and Cleisthenes "allowed freedom in religious, patrimonial, and administrative matters to the villages of Attica. They created a characteristic balance between the Athenian polis and its individual components, which eliminated any rivalry 'zwischen Staat und Commune'" ("J. G. Droysen between Greeks and Jews," p. 118). "No doubt Droysen had in mind contemporary problems of the Prussian state in speaking of the balance '*zwischen Staat und Commune*,'" Momigliano added, underlining the contemporary relevance of Droysen's optimistic view of the state. See also *Reflections on History*, pp. 35–36: "We cannot share the optimistic view according to which society came into being first, and the state arose as its protector, its negative aspect, its warden and defender. . . . Human nature is not like that. . . . There are two probable theories: (a) Force always comes first. . . . In many cases, the state may have been nothing more than its reduction to a system. Or (b) we feel that an extremely violent process, particularly of fusion, must have taken place. A flash of lightning fuses several elements into one new alloy. . . . In this way, the three Dorian races and the three Gothic tribes may have fused for the purpose or on the occasion of a conquest. . . . An echo of the terrible convulsions which accompanied the birth of the state, of what it *cost*, can be heard in the enormous and absolute primacy it has at all times enjoyed. We see this primacy as an established indisputable fact, while it is assuredly to some extent veiled history."

67. Could Burckhardt have had in mind the custom of the Swiss soldiers of the heroic days of the Confederation to take no prisoners? In his *Imagined Battles: Reflections of War in European Art* (Chapel Hill: University of North Carolina Press, 1997), Peter Paret cites in a note the War Orders of the Confederation of 1476 and the Lucerne Decree of March 1499, "which states: 'Every community should have its men swear not to take prisoners when we have a battle . . . but to kill everyone as our pious ancestors always did'" (p. 11 note 1).

68. Fustel's account of the transformations of the polis in *La Cité antique* of 1864 (Paris: Flammarion, 1984) also described a seemingly inevitable trajectory.

69. As he developed this point, Burckhardt could well have had in mind an address given by his former teacher and colleague, Wilhelm Vischer-Bilfinger, at the graduation ceremony from the *Pädagogium* in 1836. "At an early stage, the striving of the individual for prestige and distinction entered into conflict with the old customs and beliefs [i.e., 'that the individ-

ual is to be regarded only as a part of the state, that he can exist only in and through the state']. That striving was unusually intense among the people of Hellas and found expression both in the relations among states and in each individual community. This is the source of the infinitely rich abundance of life of that people and at the same time the obstacle to any lasting union of the various individual states and the origin of the jealous ambition that led the Hellenes to consume their noblest energies in mutual struggles. . . . Within each state, we find the same phenomenon as among the states. Each citizen seeks to win respect for his own individual character; when that cannot be done by legal means, illegal means are not disdained. The principle that the individual exists only in and through the state is indeed maintained, but inverted. So that instead of the individual will subordinating itself to the general will and losing itself in it, the state becomes the instrument by which the individual will achieves power and prestige. In the original way of looking at things, the community was the end; now it becomes the means. The Greek can win recognition only through the state; for that reason he continues to be attached to it, even after it has become simply a means of fulfilling his own ambitions. He remains ready to make great sacrifices for it and he considers exile the most frightful of punishments . . ." (Wilhelm Vischer, *Die oligarchische Partei und die Hetairien in Athen von Kleisthenes bis ans Ende des peloponnesischen Krieges* [Basel: August Wieland, 1836], pp. 3–4).

70. See *Reflections on History,* p. 62: "For we judge everything by that standard of security without which *we* could no longer exist. . . . We need not wish ourselves back in the Middle Ages, but we should try to understand them. Our life is a business, theirs was living."

71. On *Kalokagathia,* see also *Gesamtausgabe,* 11:86–88 *[161–63].*

72. *Reflections on History,* p. 109.

73. "The Great Men of History," *Reflections on History,* pp. 202–3.

74. See also ibid., p. 109, on the terrible strains that the ambition to distinguish themselves imposed on the Athenians.

75. *Auspocher,* literally "beaters," those who drive the animals out of their habitat and force them within range of the huntsmen.

76. See also *Gesamtausgabe* 11:187 *[228–29],* 484–85.

77. To the Greeks, "it is not accident that explains why the world is as it is, but the envy of the gods." As a result, they have a "low estimation of the value of life" (ibid., 9:84; see also 9:87–88, 104–5).

78. There is no need to belabor the point that the combination of *"das heitere Temperament"* with pessimism was the patrician Burckhardt's own form of wisdom or *sagesse.*

79. Distinguishing between ancient and modern republics, Benjamin Constant had already identified the rise of the private domain and the decline of the public domain, the displacement of the citizen by the bourgeois, as features of modern liberal and individualistic societies. See *De l'Esprit de conquête et de l'usurpation* (1814) and *De la Liberté des anciens comparée à celle des modernes* (1819).

80. Burckhardt nevertheless acknowledged that there is an intimate connection between Greek culture as such and philosophy and, following Curtius, attributed to the structure of the Greek language itself—as opposed to most others, especially no doubt Hebrew—the capacity to rise above the content of thought to its form. In addition, the typically agonistic Greek approach to philosophy (as to everything else) ensured, he claimed, that there would be no enslavement to a particular terminology or a particular school and that the word would never be sacralized or venerated in stony fixedness. *Gesamtausgabe,* 10:279–82. Likewise the fact that the Greeks had no institutionalized religion and therefore no priesthood to claim and try to impose a monopoly on knowledge and thought left the field open to free speculation. Ibid., pp. 282, 298, 343.

81. "The great centers of intellectual exchange, such as Athens, Florence, etc.," Burck-hardt observed in the *Weltgeschichtliche Betrachtungen*, ". . . produced from among their own citizens a disproportionate number of great individuals, through whom they continue to act on the world. That is not the result of 'great educational facilities,' as in the big or even middle-sized cities of our day." All such "great educational facilities" can produce is "inflated nonentities, monopolizing leading positions by dint of waiting and their own social claims" (*Reflections on History*, pp. 60–61).

82. Heraclitus of Ephesus and Timon of Athens are in fact the first "milestones" on what would be a progressive disengagement of the philosopher from the polis: "The former gener-ally full of contempt for everything around him, old poets as well as living philosophers, deliberately obscure in his chief work, scornful of the Ephesans, especially when they solic-ited laws from him for their wretched polity, holding his tongue 'so that you may all chatter!' The latter a well-known figure in Athens who could on no account be left out of a picture of the cultural history of the city in the fifth century" (*Gesamtausgabe*, 8:259–60).

83. The reference Burckhardt gives is Diogenes Laertius, IX, 1 ff.

84. On the displacement of the center of gravity of life from the public to the private domain in the fourth century, see M. M. Austin and P. Vidal-Naquet, *Economic and Social History of Ancient Greece: An Introduction* (Berkeley and Los Angeles: University of California Press, 1977), p. 144.

85. Though the fate of poetry and art are seen as inseparable from that of the polis, Burckhardt allowed that the two forms of expression may follow independent trajectories, so that sculpture, for instance, remained lively and creative long after literature had passed its prime. *Gesamtausgabe*, 11:265 *[273–74]*, 383–84 *[330–31]*, 588–91, 607. Burckhardt insisted on this relative autonomy of the arts and it is one of his most original contributions to the history of art and literature. There is a continuous tension—of which he was fully aware— in his writing, especially on art, between the approach of the cultural historian and that of the art historian.

86. Comparisons of ancient and modern situations are usually implicit in Burckhardt, but from time to time they are explicit. Some examples: "The tyrant represents the polis approximately as Napoleon represents the Revolution" (*Gesamtausgabe*, 8:169n); "This situa-tion has a parallel in that of the Terror in 1793–94" (11:333 *[303]*); "One particular way in which the tendency to withdraw from the state in democratic Athens expressed itself was through praise of what had been long established and remained unchanged and unaffected by the development of democracy, above all through praise of Egypt. . . . This Egyptophilia is found not only in Plato. . . . Isocrates also speaks in the same vein. One is reminded of the special affection for China of some thinkers and writers of the Enlightenment" (11:377–78 *[326]*); "One is reminded [by certain responses of the diadochi rulers] of the tone in which Napoleon used to handle his admirals" (11:474); "One is reminded [by the Stoic conception of virtue as permanent, once acquired] of the Pietists's doctrine that 'it is impossible to fall from grace'; indeed, again and again the Stoics appear as the Pietists of the declining ancient world" (11:613). Alternatively, a comparison will be invoked in order to underline a differ-ence: "Philip of Macedon's relation to Greece was quite unlike that of Napoleon to the Con-federation of the Rhine; the Macedonians were in part fellow Greeks" (11:408n).

87. See Kaegi, *Jacob Burckhardt*, 5:548, 557.

88. "Politisiren will ich nicht mehr . . ." (letter to von Preen, 28 December 1891, *Briefe*, 9:331, quoted by Kaegi, *Jacob Burckhardt*, 7:191).

89. Kaegi, *Jacob Burckhardt*, 7:182; see in general, on Burckhardt's alleged *apolitia*, ibid., pp. 127–93.

90. "He was a most dutiful citizen and soldier, even if he did not take an active part in

politics, and he believed that the state would be saved by the education of its citizens. . . . For the rest, he and his followers were strong critics of the state and mostly kept out of its way" (*Gesamtausgabe*, 10:352–53).

91. Letter of 6 and 7 March 1882, *Briefe*, 8:23.

92. ". . . diese fürchterlich herrlichen Evenements" (letter of 17 August 1882, *Briefe*, 8:67).

93. Letter to Adolf Trenelenburg, Basel, 25 March 1884, *Briefe*, 8:206.

94. It is possible that Burckhardt's judgment of Philip was influenced by his judgment of Bismarck. Like Bachofen, Burckhardt condemned the conduct of the German states in the Schleswig-Holstein affair in 1864, was deeply disturbed by the Austro-Prussian War of 1866, and deplored the Franco-Prussian War of 1870. He wrote to Otto Ribbeck, who had come around to supporting Bismarck, that the treatment of Denmark in the Schleswig-Holstein affair had sent shock waves through southern Germany and Switzerland. "You have no idea how sensitive a nerve this matter has touched among the South Germans. Bismarckophobia has broken out everywhere" (letter of 17 October 1865, *Briefe*, 4:198). Switzerland, he told Theodor Vischer, the philosopher of aesthetics, was being pushed since 1866 toward alliance with France. Letter of 17 February 1867, *Briefe*, 4:238. Burckhardt himself, however, seems to refrain from condemning Bismarck. His judgments are extremely nuanced. In April 1872, he wrote to von Preen: "I am not unreasonable. Bismarck only took into his own hands what with time would have happened anyway, only without him and against him. He saw that the expanding democratic social wave would one way or another provoke a violent situation, whether through the democrats themselves or through the governments; and he said: *ipse faciam* [let me do it myself], and so initiated the three wars: 64, 66, 70" (letter of 26 April 1872, *Briefe*, 5:160). A much later letter to von Preen confirmed this view of Bismarck as a statesman who attempted to control and structure dangerous energies: "I completely approve of your subscribing to the monument to Bismarck, even though the man himself is unattractive and his activity has had quite negative effects on us in Switzerland. . . . For Germany, however, Bismarck was the great supporter and standard-bearer of the mystery of *Authority* and you, in your position, can well have learned to appreciate the considerable value of such an *Imponderabile* in all areas" (letter of 26 September 1890, *Briefe*, 10:268–69).

95. Grote had already been criticized on this point by Freeman in a review of the former's *History of Greece* in the *Edinburgh Review* of April 1857. See Edward A. Freeman, *Historical Essays*, 2nd series (London and New York: Macmillian, 1873), pp. 161–206, especially pp. 174–83 on the "Greekness" of Macedonia, Philip's goal "not to macedonize Hellas but to hellenize Macedonia," and on Alexander as a Greek in the eyes of the Greeks themselves.

96. Momigliano, "J. G. Droysen between Greeks and Jews," pp. 109–26, especially pp. 116–19.

97. *Reflections on History*, pp. 39–40.

98. Ibid., p. 215.

99. Ibid., p. 39.

100. Ibid., p. 213.

101. Ibid., p. 213.

102. "The theory of compensation is . . . generally the theory of desirability in disguise, and it is and remains advisable to be exceedingly chary in the use of such consolation as is to be gained from it, since we cannot finally assess these losses and gains" (ibid., p. 217).

103. Ibid., pp. 214–17. There is some tension between this unequivocal rejection of "immoral acts" and the defense of Bismarck referred to above (note 94).

104. A note gives Nietzsche's friend Erwin Rohde as the source of this quotation.

105. *The Civilization of the Renaissance in Italy,* trans. S. G. C. Middlemore, with an introduction by Benjamin Nelson and Charles Trinkaus (New York: Harper & Row, 1958), p. 104.

106. *Reflections on History,* p. 64.

107. "Über die Kunstgeschichte als Gegenstand eines akademischen Lehrstuhls" (Introductory lecture to the course on Ancient Art, ed. Felix Stähelin), *Gesamtausgabe,* 13:23–28, at p. 23.

Chapter Thirteen

1. See Paul Klee, *Briefe an die Familie 1893–1940,* (Cologne: DuMont, 1979), 1:153, letter to Lily, 11 October 1979. Klee criticized Burckhardt's blind worship of Raphael (*"Burckhardt bleibt an Raffael wie eine Dame haengen . . ."*) and his misunderstanding of Donatello. Nevertheless, Burckhardt remained for Klee the standard by which all art critics are measured. Bayersdorfer on the arts, he wrote, is "better than Burckhardt, I maintain; and that says everything" (ibid., pp. 165, 188, 223, 233, 391, letters to Lily in 1901, 1902, 1904).

2. Francis Haskell's substantial treatment of Burckhardt in his recent *History and its Images: Art and the Interpretation of the Past* (New Haven: Yale University Press, 1993), together with the publication in London in 1985 of a handsome first translation into English of *The Architecture of the Italian Renaissance,* and in 1988 of a translation of the essay on the altarpiece, and the forthcoming publication by the Getty Center in Los Angeles of *The Aesthetics of the Plastic Arts* and other art historical texts should create a greater awareness of Burckhardt as art historian.

3. Heinrich Wölfflin, "Jacob Burckhardt und die Kunst," in his *Gedanken zur Kunstgeschichte: Gedrucktes und Ungedrucktes,* 3rd ed. (Basel: Benno Schwabe, 1941; 1st ed. 1940), p. 136. Hugh Trevor-Roper is one of the few general historians to recognize the central importance of art history in Burckhardt's work and thought; he does so at the very beginning of the superb British Academy "Master-Mind" lecture of 11 December 1984, which he devoted to Burckhardt. See *Proceedings of the British Academy* 7 (1984): 359–78.

4. Quoted from manuscript of the lectures on the history of painting, given in Basel in 1844–1846, in Emil Maurer, *Jacob Burckhardt und Rubens* (Basel: Birkhäuser, 1951), pp. 193–95.

5. See *The Altarpiece,* ed. P. Humfrey (Oxford: Phaidon, 1988). As for the Rubens book, Burckhardt believed that, like the essays on the altarpiece, the collector, and the portrait, it would not be easy to publish it in prevailing business conditions. "General business conditions are unfavorable for such undertakings," he wrote to a young friend, "and won't be any better by the time I have come to the end of my road, which is no longer far distant. Apart from handbooks, the sales of art historical writings are poor. To ask you to see to publication, would be to place far too great a burden on you, even assuming a modest subsidy from my estate." He then suggested that manuscripts of the four texts be deposited in the University library. "But if you are game to do more than your due, you can publish the fourth and most readable of them, the *Erinnerungen aus Rubens,* as a single small volume. The necessary help should be provided by the estate. This little book would at least have a limited sale here in Basel as a gift book" (to Carl Lensdorff the Younger, 3 July 1897, *Briefe,* ed. Max Burckhardt, 10 vols. plus index vol. (Basel: Schwabe 1949–1994), 10:328–29).

6. See Werner Kaegi, *Jacob Burckhardt: eine Biographie* (Basel: Schwabe, 1947–1982), 3:168–70. Waagen enjoyed a European reputation as an arts administrator and was invited to testify before various Select Committees of the British Parliament about art museums and art education.

7. Ibid., p. 135.

8. Ibid., 6:449–50.

9. See Felix Stähelin, introduction to his edition of Burckhardt's course on ancient art, in Jacob Burckhardt, *Gesamtausgabe*, ed. Emil Dürr et al., 14 vols. (Stuttgart, Berlin, and Leipzig: Deutsche Verlagsanstalt, 1930–1934), 13:9–11.

10. Clive Ashwin, *Drawing and Education in German-speaking Europe, 1800–1900* (Ann Arbor: UMI Research Press, 1981), pp. 2, 23. Also *Wie Gertrud ihre Kinder lehrt* (1801) in Heinrich Pestalozzi, *Sämtliche Werke* (Berlin and Leipzig: Walter de Gruyter, 1927–1935), vol. 13, ed. H. Schönebaum and K. Schreinert, pp. 287–89. The leading post-Kantian champion of formalist aesthetics in the first half of the eighteenth century in Germany, Johann Friedrich Herbart, was also a strong supporter of Pestalozzi; see his *Pestalozzi's Idee eines ABC der Anschauung* (Göttingen: J. F. Röwer, 1804). Herr Munziger, the director of the primary school attended by Burckhardt, was not, however. As conservative pedagogically as he was politically, Munziger was opposed to Pestalozzi and his doctrines, and drawing did not figure in the curriculum of his school; see Kaegi, *Jacob Burckhardt*, 1:13. Probably Burckhardt received private lessons in drawing, like other members of the elite families; see Yvonne Boerlin-Brodbeck, *Die Skizzenbücher Jacob Burckhardts* (Basel: Schwabe; Munich: C. H. Beck, 1994), p. 14.

11. "Köbiana," in *Jacob Burckhardt und Heinrich Wölfflin: Briefwechsel und andere Dokumente ihrer Begegnung 1882–1897*, ed. Joseph Gantner, 2nd expanded ed. (Basel: Schwabe, 1989; 1st ed. 1948), p. 113. In the introductory lecture ("Art History as an Academic Discipline") to his course on ancient art (1874), Burckhardt had already warned his students that in viewing works of art, "one must not be preoccupied by other things; otherwise the eye wanders from the greatest creations and no longer attends to their outward appearance" ("Über die Kunstgeschichte als Gegenstand eines akademischen Lehrstuhls," *Gesamtausgabe*, 13:27).

12. On the faith of Antistes Jakob Burckhardt, see Thomas A. Howard III, *Historicist Thought in the Shadow of Theology: W. M. L. De Wette, Jacob Burckhardt, and the Shaping of Nineteenth Century Historical Consciousness* (Ph.D. diss., University of Virginia, 1996), pp. 291–304. (Forthcoming from Cambridge University Press.)

13. See Gottfried Boehm, "'Sehen lernen ist alles': Conrad Fiedler und Hans von Marées," in Christian Lenz, ed., *Hans von Marées* (Munich: Prestel-Verlag, 1987), pp. 145–50. Cf. Diderot in "Salon de 1765": "Il faut apprendre à l'oeil à regarder la nature, et combien ne l'ont jamais vue et ne la verront jamais" (*Salons*, ed. Jean Seznec and Jean Adhémar [Oxford: Clarendon Press, 1957–1967], 2:58).

14. Quoted from *Italienische Forschungen* (1827) in Gert Schiff, ed., *German Essays on Art History* (New York: Continuum Books, 1988), p. 90. See also Michael Podro, *The Critical Historians of Art* (New Haven and London: Yale University Pess, 1982), p. 28.

15. C. L. Westlake, editor's preface to *A Handbook of the History of Painting*, vol. 1, by Franz Kugler (London: John Murray, 1842), pp. xii, xvi.

16. "Über die Kunstgeschichte als Gegenstand eines akademischen Lehrstuhls," *Gesamtausgabe*, 13:28.

17. Wölfflin, "Jacob Burckhardt und die Kunst," pp. 139–40.

18. Quoted by Maurer, *Jacob Burckhardt und Rubens*, p. 184. Wölfflin reported Burckhardt as saying that "the better a picture is, the harder it is to speak about it adequately" ("Je besser die Bilder sind," pflegte er zu sagen, "um so schwerer hat es der Redner, daneben aufzukommen") ("Jacob Burckhardt und die Kunst," p. 137).

19. See Gottfried Boehm, introduction to vol. 1 of *Schriften zur Kunst*, by Konrad Fiedler, 2 vols. (Munich: Wilhelm Fink, 1971; reprint of Munich 1913–1914 ed.), pp. xxi–lxi, and Fiedler's essay "Moderner Naturalismus und künstlerische Wahrheit," ibid., 1:135–82 (originally in *Leipziger Zeitung*, 1881); Julius Meier-Graefe, *Entwicklungsgeschichte*

der modernen Kunst . . . Beitrag zu einer neuen Aesthetik, 3 vols. (Stuttgart: Julius Hoffmann, 1904). For a helpful overview of the long-lasting discussion of the autonomy of the various arts, see Peter Zima, "Ästhetik, Wissenschaft und 'wechselseitige Erhellung der Künste,'" in *Literatur Intermedial: Musik, Malerei, Photographie, Film,* ed. Peter Zima (Darmstadt: Wissenschaftliche Buchgesellschaft, 1995), pp. 1–28.

20. Maurice de Vlaminck, *Portraits avant décès* (Paris: Flammarion, 1943), p. 179.

21. Max Liebermann, *Die Phantasie in der Malerei: Schriften und Reden,* ed. G. Busch (Frankfurt am Main: S. Fischer, 1978), quoted by Wilhelm Schlink, "'Kunst ist dazu da, um geselligen Kreisen das gähnende Ungeheuer, die Zeit, zu töten,'" in vol. 3, ed. M. Rainer Lepsius, of Werner Conze and Jürgen Kocka, eds., *Bildungsbürgertum im 19. Jahrhundert,* 4 vols. (Stuttgart: Klett-Cotta, 1985), 3:65–81, at p. 78. On Heinrich Brunn, professor at Munich and Director of the Glyptothek, Adolf Michaelis, professor at Strassburg, and Brunn's student Adolf Furtwängler as advocates of the independence of the visual image from the word in the study of classical art and culture, see Suzanne Marchand, *Down from Olympus: Archaeology and Philhellenism in Germany, 1750–1970* (Princeton: Princeton University Press, 1996), pp. 143–48.

22. *Handbuch der Architekturgeschichte* (1855), *Grundriss der Kunstgeschichte* (1860), *Geschichte der Renaissance in Frankreich* (1868), *Geschichte der deutschen Renaissance* (1873), *Geschichte der deutschen Kunst* (1889), *Handbuch der Kunstgeschichte* (1861), itself an updated edition of an earlier standard work by Franz Kugler, already revised at Kugler's request by Burckhardt.

23. Schlink, "'Kunst ist dazu da, um geselligen Kreisen das gähnende Ungeheuer, die Zeit, zu töten,'" pp. 68, 78.

24. Thomas Bernhard, *Old Masters,* trans. Ewald Osers (London: Quartet Books, 1989), pp. 14–15, 22–23. (orig. German: *Alte Meister* [Frankfurt am Main: Suhrkamp, 1985], pp. 34, 49).

25. G. P. Gooch, *History and Historians in the Nineteenth Century* (London: Longmans, Green, 1935 [1913]), p. 581.

26. Wilhelm Waetzoldt, "Von Passavant bis Justi," vol. 2 of *Deutsche Kunsthistoriker,* 2nd ed., 2 vols. (Berlin: Bruno Hessling, 1965), 2:180–82.

27. See Jörn Rüsen, *Ästhetik und Geschichte: Geschichtstheoretische Untersuchungen zum Begründungszusammenhang von Kunst, Gesellschaft und Wissenschaft* (Stuttgart: J. B. Metzler, 1976), p. 89.

28. Introduction to Carl Schnaase, *Geschichte der bildenden Künste,* 2nd ed., 8 vols. (Düsseldorf: Julius Buddeus, later Stuttgart: Ebner and Seubert, 1866–1874), 1:49–52.

29. Kaegi, *Jacob Burckhardt,* 2:166–68; Maurer, *Jacob Burckhardt und Rubens,* p. 136 note; Peter Paret, *Art as History: Episodes in the Culture and Politics of Nineteenth-Century Germany* (Princeton: Princeton University Press, 1988), p. 19. One scholar even faults Burckhardt for excessive emphasis on "eine optische, malerische Modalität" (Reinhard Liess, *Die Kunst des Rubens* (Braunschweig: Waisenhausbuchdruckerei und Verlag, 1977), pp. 266–67.

30. See Georg Leyh, ed., "Vier Briefe Jacob Burckhardts an Friedrich Theodor Vischer," *Corona* 7 (1937): 485–509. The examples quoted by Leyh date from the 1850s. Burckhardt's ironical professions of incompetence in matters philosophical turned to hostility to Hegelianism in the years after 1848.

31. See Douglas Crimp, "The End of Art and the Origins of the Museum," *Art Journal* 46 (1987): 261–66.

32. Support for this view is in Sir Ernst Gombrich, *In Search of Cultural History* (Oxford: Clarendon Press, 1967) (the Philip Maurice Daneke Lecture of 1967), p. 13.

33. Quoted by Gabriele Bickendorf, *Der Beginn der Kunstgeschichtsschreibung unter dem*

Paradigma "Geschichte": Gustav Friedrich Waagens Frühschrift "Über Hubert und Johann van Eyck" (Worms: Wernersche Verlagsgesellschaft, 1985), p. 104.

34. H. Dilly, *Kunstgeschichte als Institution. Studien zur Geschichte einer Disziplin* (Frankfurt am Main: Suhrkamp, 1979), p. 88, quoted in editor's introduction to Jacob Burckhardt, *Aesthetik der bildenden Kunst,* ed. Irmgard Siebert (Darmstadt: Wissenschaftliche Buchgesellschaft, 1992), p. 21; see also Kugler's review of vol. 1 of Schnaase's *Geschichte der bildenden Künste* (1843; dedicated to Kugler) in *Kunstblatt* (1844), reprinted in Franz Kugler, *Kleine Schriften zur Kunstgeschichte,* 3 vols. (Stuttgart: Ebner and Seubert, 1853–1854), 2:436–45.

35. *Gesamtausgabe,* 1:114.

36. Kugler insisted that the artist must fully grasp and represent the historical significance of the moment that is being represented. Criticism of the composition in Edouard de Bièfve's *Compromise of the Netherlands Nobility* was to some degree justified, he granted, but any other arrangement of the figures would have failed to do justice to the meaning of the historical action, and in such a case, he asked, "should history be shaped in obedience to some putative law of composition and clear historical characterization sacrificed to a dubiously successful artistic outcome?" Kugler advised idealizing German history painters to get closer to reality and to temper their symbolism and "aristocratic idealism" with the necessary counterweight of a "democratic element." Quoted by Leonore Koschuik, "Franz Kugler (1808–1858) als Kunstkritiker und Kunstpolitiker" (Ph.D. diss., Freie Universitat Berlin, 1985), p. 131. The "democratic element," Koschuik explains, was virtually identical, in Kugler's mind, with the notion of popular national consciousness. On Kugler's emphasis on the need for the painter to grasp the essence of the historical moment, see also Peter Paret, *Art as History; Episodes in the Culture and Politics of Nineteenth-Century Germany* (Princeton: Princeton University Press, 1988), pp. 23–24, 91.

37. *Kunstblatt,* no. 1, 12 January 1843, quoted by Kaegi, *Jacob Burckhardt,* 2:235. On the efforts of the Bavarian state authorities to create a Bavarian "national consciousness" and the use of the term *Bavarian nation* in the period between 1815 and 1848, see Theodor Schieder, "Partikularismus und Nationalbewusstsein," in Werner Conze, ed., *Staat und Gesellschaft im deutschen Vormärz* (Stuttgart: Ernst Klett, 1962), pp. 9–38, at p. 30. Count Armansberg, the Bavarian finance minister, referred to the frescoes that had been commissioned for the arcades of the Hofgarten as "a tribute to the justified national pride of the Bavarian people" and a "celebration of the honor of the nation."

38. "System der gesammten Philosophie und der Naturphilosophie insbesondere," 319, in *Sämmtliche Werke,* ed. K. W. F. Schelling (Stuttgart and Augsburg: Cotta, 1856–1861), 6:572. Cf. ibid., p. 573: "Where the freedom of public life declines into the slavery of private life, comedy is also inevitably enfeebled" (quoted in Manfred Frank, *Gott im Exil: Vorlesungen über die Neue Mythologie* [Frankfurt am Main: Suhrkamp, 1988], p. 11 and note).

39. See Willi Oelmüller, *Friedrich Theodor Vischer und das Problem der nachhegelschen Ästhetik* (Stuttgart: W. Kohlhammer, 1959), pp. 76–87. Characterized by Marx as "the Virgil of Wilhelm I" after he shifted his political and aesthetic views first in the wake of the Revolution of 1848, then again after the triumph of Prussia in 1866, and finally after the victory over France in 1870–1871, Vischer had been considered "on the left" in the early 1840s and Ruge proposed him to Marx in 1842 as a potential spokesman on aesthetics. Ibid., pp. 25–26. On the relations of Burckhardt and Vischer, see Leyh, "Vier Briefe Burckhardts an Friedrich Theodor Vischer," pp. 485–509.

40. On the friendship and intellectual affinities of Burckhardt and Vischer, see Oelmüller, *Friedrich Theodor Vischer,* pp. 102–3.

41. *Gesamtausgabe,* 1:179.

42. See Nikolaus Meier, *Stiften und Sammeln für die öffentliche Kunstsammlung Basel:*

Emilie Linder, Jacob Burckhardt und das Kunstleben der Stadt Basel (Basel: Schwabe, n.d. [1997]), p. 56.

43. *Niederländische Briefe* (Stuttgart and Tübingen: J. G. Cotta, 1834), pp. 80–89.

44. There are four sections: 1. "The relation of the arts to each other"; 2. "Inclinations, talents"; 3. "Historical aspects of art," subdivided into (i) "The architechtonic period until about 1400," (ii) "The plastic-painterly period from the 15th to the 17th century," and (iii) "The dramatic-harmonic period, 17th and 18th centuries"; and 4. "Consideration of the Historical."

45. Heinrich Wölfflin in his eulogy of Burckhardt, in *Jacob Burckhardt und Heinrich Wölfflin: Briefwechsel und Dokumente ihrer Begegnung, 1882–1897*, ed. Gantner, pp. 177–86, at p. 180. See also the comments of Leyh, "Vier Briefe Jacob Burckhardts and Friedrich Theodor Vischers," pp. 485–509, Introduction, pp. 498–500. Leyh compares the style of Burckhardt with that of both F. T. Vischer and his son, the art historian Robert Vischer.

46. Thus the harmonious religion and culture of the Greeks "spiegelt sich in ihrer Kunst" (quoted from the 1844–1845 lecture notes by Kaegi, *Jacob Burckhardt*, 2:466).

47. This view also appears to underlie the argument of the art historian Martina Sitt in her *Kriterien der Kunstkritik: Jacob Burckhardts unveröffentlichte Ästhetik als Schlüssel seines Rangsystems* (Vienna: Böhlau, 1992). In a shorter article in English, Sitt has argued that Burckhardt's surprising decision to hand over his work on the architecture of the Renaissance to his colleague Wilhelm Lübke and his renunciation of all rights to the book reflect his acute feeling that he had run up against "an insurmountable wall of methodological problems which he had no hope of ever scaling" ("Jacob Burckhardt as Architect of a New Art History," *Journal of the Warburg and Courtauld Institutes* 57 [1994]: 227–42, at p. 228).

48. See Kaegi, *Jacob Burckhardt*, 3:464. On the aesthetics of the visual arts in nineteenth-century Germany, see the invaluable introduction by Harry Francis Mallgrave and Eleftherios Ikonomou to their translation of essays by Robert Vischer, Conrad Fiedler, Heinrich Wölfflin, et al., *Empathy, Form, and Space: Problems in German Aesthetics, 1873–1893* (Santa Monica: The Getty Center for the History of Art and the Humanities, 1994), pp. 1–85.

49. "I will not write anything purely philosophical again. It's no good. I'm simply not cut out for it. My philosophy is nothing but a bird's stomach that needs sand, stuff, to grind down. The pure grind of metaphysics is not for me. I'm a hermaphrodite, made up of poetry and philosophy" (letter of 27 May 1838, in Adolf Rapp, ed., *Briefwechsel zwischen Strauss und Vischer*, 2 vols. [Stuttgart: Ernst Klett, 1952], 1:60). Later, on the publication of his *Aesthetics*, he wrote: "Now the crap—dirty, bad, and tasteless as it may be—is in print," and wondered "whether the whole first part, the metaphysics of the beautiful, has any right to exist. I have no strong conviction on that score, and had and still have no way to get help" (letter of 7 June 1846, ibid., 1:174). "Nothing keeps one from creating works of beauty as effectively as philosophizing about the beautiful," he had confessed to the poet Mörike in a letter of 7 June 1837. "If I really knew that I was born to be a thinker rather than a poet, I would have no good reason to torment myself. But I often find myself falling back into the notion that there is a poet in me somewhere" (quoted ibid., p. 288 note 22).

50. Letter to F. T. Vischer in Tübingen, from Basel, 19 December 1854, *Briefe*, 3:201–2.

51. Wölfflin, "Jacob Burckhardt und die Kunst," pp. 135, 137. See also Kaegi, *Jacob Burckhardt*, 6:635. The absence of method and systematic organization at first bothered the philosophically inclined Wölfflin, who had taken a degree in philosophy at Munich. He complained that the descriptions of artworks in Burckhardt's *Cicerone* were superficial and that Burckhardt had no organizing philosophy of history. See Joan Goldhammer Hart, "Heinrich Wölfflin: An Intellectual Biography" (Ph.D. diss., University of California, Berkeley, 1981), p. 34; Meinhold Lurz, *Heinrich Wölfflin: Biographie einer Kunsttheorie* (Worms: Werner'sche Verlagsgesellschaft, 1981), pp. 117–18.

52. Karl Swoboda, the editor of Riegl's book on the Dutch group portrait, defines the *Kunstwollen* as "an internal organizing principle of works of art that is to be discovered behind currently accepted notions of style and explained in terms of the *Weltanschauung* of a particular time" (*Das holländische Gruppenporträt* [Vienna: Oesterreichische Staatsdruckerei, 1931], p. vii). Riegl himself explained that he hoped to discover through his study of the peculiarly Dutch phenomenon of the group portrait the special *Kunstwollen* of early modern Holland. The aim, he wrote, is not to judge these works by *our* interests and desires, but to inquire what the Dutch artists and public wanted and were trying to achieve. Only in this way can we arrive at a proper aesthetic judgment of the art of other times (p. 5).

53. Not, however, to Max Frisch. See his Tagebuch, 1946–1949 in his *Gesammelte Werke* (Frankfurt am Main: Suhrkamp, 1976–1986), Taschenbuch ed., 1986, 2:508–10. With only *The Cicerone* and *The Civilization of the Renaissance* in mind no doubt, Frisch found Burckhardt exclusively sensitive to the art of the Renaissance, incapable of responding to the baroque: Burckhardt "suddenly becomes professorial; that's to say he suddenly loses his antennae and can hear nothing except himself, his own opinions." He then went on to ask: "But where is the criterion of right, which decrees that one style shall be superior to others? Jacob Burckhardt and the baroque. His indignation is understandable. He does not measure the baroque according to its own artistic objectives, but according to those of the Renaissance." See, in contrast, the comments of Felix Stähelin in the introduction to his edition of Burckhardt's lectures on ancient art, *Gesamtausgabe*, 13:14–18.

54. Alois Riegl, "Kunstgeschichte und Universalgeschichte," *Gesammelte Aufsätze* (Augsburg and Vienna: Benno Filser, 1929), pp. 3–9. On Burckhardt's use of the term *rococo* to designate the moment when an art transforms its ornamentation into substance—whether that moment occurs in late imperial Rome or in the late Middle Ages or in the eighteenth century—see Waetzoldt, *Deutsche Kunsthistoriker*, 2:191–92. Emil Maurer, however, has raised the plausible question whether Burckhardt was actually convinced that there is a single, internally unified baroque style; see *Jacob Burckhardt und Rubens*, p. 248.

55. See Oelmüller, *Friedrich Theodor Vischer*, p. 144.

56. Quoted in Udo Kultermann, *Geschichte der Kunstgeschichte* (Vienna and Düsseldorf: Econ-Verlag, 1966), p. 288.

57. "In den Kunstwerken nicht das dem modernen Geschmack Zusagende aufzusuchen, sondern aus ihnen das Kunstwollen herauszulesen, das sie hervorgebracht hat und so und nicht anders gestaltet hat" (*Das holländische Gruppenporträt*, p. 4).

58. *Aesthetik der Bildenden Kunst*, pp. 89–93.

59. On the relation of "Kunstwissenschaft" and "Kunstgenuss" in Burckhardt, see Wilhelm Schlink, "Jacob Burckhardt über den 'Genuss der Kunstwerke,'" *Trierer Beiträge* 11 (1982): 47–57, at pp. 52–53. On the importance of both imagination and education in art history for the appreciation of art works by nineteenth century viewers, see also Martina Sitt, "The Dilettante as Ideal Viewer? Goethe and Burckhardt: Two Approaches to a Problem," forthcoming in *Beiträge zu Jacob Burckhardt: Proceedings of the Basel and Princeton Colloquia* (Basel: Schwabe; Munich: Christian Beck).

60. The American art historian Michael Ann Holly has gone so far as to describe *The Cicerone*, arguably Burckhardt's most influential work of art history, as a model of connoisseurship. "Wölfflin and the Imagining of the Baroque," in *Europäische Barock-Rezeption*, ed. Klaus Garber (Wiesbaden, 1991), quoted in John Hinde, "Jacob Burckhardt: Politics, History, and Modernity," (Ph.D. diss., S.U.N.Y. Buffalo, 1995), p. 304.

61. *Aesthetik der bildenden Kunst*, pp. 56, 164, See also Martina Sitt, "Jacob Burckhardt as Architect of a New Art History," p. 231.

62. "Über erzählende Malerei" (1884), *Gesamtausgabe*, 14:303. This is the celebrated *"Zeitenthobenheit"* ("temporal transcendence") of art. See Dieter Jähnig, "Jacob Burckhardts

Bedeutung für die Ästhetik," *Deutsche Vierteljahrsschrift für Literaturwissenschaft und Kunst* 53 (1979): 173–90, at p. 182. In an important discussion of the successive levels of *"Genuss"* in Burckhardt, however, Wilhelm Schlink pointed out that the historian was less inclined than some contemporaries (F. T. Vischer, for instance) to make a radical distinction between *"Kunstwissenschaft"* and *"Kunstgenuss."* Schlink, "Jacob Burckhardt über den 'Genuss der Kunstwerke,'" p. 52.

63. Maurer, *Jacob Burckhardt und Rubens,* p. 175.

64. "Über erzählende Malerei," *Gesamtausgabe,* 14:306.

65. Kultermann, *Geschichte der Kunstgeschichte,* p. 288. On Burckhardt and Semper, see Martina Sitt, *Kriterien der Kunstkritik,* p. 138. Hegel also emphasized the importance for the appreciation of individual works of art of knowledge of the "technical development of art." *Vorlesungen über die Ästhetik,* ed. Eva Moldenhauer and Karl M. Michel, Einleitung, in *Werke* (Frankfurt: Suhrkamp, 1970), 13:55–56.

66. Quoted by Wölfflin, "Jacob Burckhardt und die systematische Kunstgeschichte," p. 149.

67. For a stimulating discussion of Burckhardt's dilemma as a writer of art *history* and a *cultural historian,* whose task is to integrate individual items into a general category, see Benjamin Richter, *Jacob Burckhardt als Schriftsteller* (Rome: Edizioni dell'Ateneo, 1968). Though Burckhardt's reputation rests on his work as a cultural historian, Richter argues, "another interest is far more important to him: his interest in the individual objects from the past that offer themselves to our immediate perception" (p. 37). For that reason he could not make artistic style the unifying category that would allow him to solve the theoretical problems he had encountered in trying to write his *Kunst der Renaissance.* What prevented him was "the subordination to which this would subject the individual work. For it was the individual art work that was of the highest importance to Burckhardt. Even though understanding of individual works promotes insight into their interconnectedness, the general fact represented by that interconnectedness should never become our express theme, in his view, or in any way overwhelm the true individual object" (p. 55).

68. On Burckhardt's method, see Maurer, *Jacob Burckhardt und Rubens,* pp. 115–16.

69. Schlink, "'Kunst is dazu da, um geselligen Kreisen das gähnende Ungeheuer, die Zeit, zu töten,'" p. 70. See also Sitt, "Jacob Burckhardt as Architect of a New Art History," p. 228. The view expressed by the American scholar Bernard Weinberg in relation to Burckhardt's approach to literature—that he was not concerned with literature itself but only with literature "as document and testimony" and that "this means really, that what interests Burckhardt in a work of literature is its subject matter or its content"—is probably inaccurate as concerns literature and certainly inaccurate in relation to the arts. See "Changing Conceptions of the Renaissance: Continental Literature," in *The Renaissance: A Reconsideration,* ed. Tinsley Helton (Madison: University of Wisconsin Press, 1961), pp. 105–23, at pp. 107–8.

70. Meier, *Stiften und Sammeln,* p. 116.

71. F. T. Vischer, *Das Schöne und die Kunst* (Stuttgart: Cotta, 1898), p. 77, quoted by Schlink, "Jacob Burckhardt über 'den Genuss der Kunstwerke,' " p. 53.

72. See Oelmüller, *Friedrich Theodor Vischer,* pp. 98–103.

73. See Kaegi, *Jacob Burckhardt,* 6:770. On the disconnection, in Burckhardt, of art and the historical circumstances of its production, see Sitt, "Jacob Burckhardt as Architect of a New Art History," p. 233.

74. On Spain, see Kaegi, *Jacob Burckhardt,* 6:668. Kaegi quotes here from Burckhardt's revision of Kugler's *Handbuch,* 2:438. The passage on Italy is quoted in Wilhelm Schlink, "Jacob Burckhardt und die Kunsterwartung im Vormärz," *Umgang mit Jacob Burckhardt: Zwölf Studien,* ed. Hans R. Guggisberg (Basel: Schwabe; Munich: C. H. Beck, 1994 [Beiträge zu Jacob Burckhardt, 1]), p. 243.

75. Kaegi, *Jacob Burckhardt*, 6:459. Cf. Ernst Gombrich's comparison of art and games in "Art History and the Social Sciences" (in his *Ideals and Idols* [Oxford: Phaidon, 1979], pp. 131–66, at p. 154): "Games, like art, need a social atmosphere and tradition to reach that high level of cultivation that goes with true mastery. In a champion, be it of tennis or chess, certain skills and expectations have to become automatic. For this to happen, it needs the kind of atmosphere to which I have alluded, the eager interest of whole groups, the debates about standards. . . ."

76. See Kaegi, *Jacob Burckhardt*, 6:686–87, quoting from the lecture course on the art of the seventeenth and eighteenth centuries (entitled "Modern Art since 1550" in Burckhardt's notes). In his important study of the modern movement in art, Julius Meier-Graefe argued that German artists had always been essentially graphic artists and had been untouched by the Italian Renaissance exploration of the possibilities of color, but he too refused to accept the common explanation that this was a consequence of the Thirty Years' War. See *Entwicklungsgeschichte der modernen Kunst*, 3 vols. (Stuttgart: Julius Hoffmann, 1904), 1:70.

77. *Essai sur les moeurs et l'esprit des nations*, ed. René Pomeau, 2 vols. (Paris: Garnier, 1963), ch. 82, 1:766–67.

78. Editor's introduction to *Aesthetik der bildenden Kunst*, ed. Siebert, pp. 20–22.

79. Maurer, *Jacob Burckhardt und Rubens*, p. 37.

80. Letter of 19 June 1841, *Briefe*, 1:206.

81. Quoted in editor's introduction to *Aesthetik der bildenden Kunst*, ed. Siebert, pp. 21–22.

82. *Gesamtausgabe*, 1:141.

83. Maurer, *Jacob Burckhardt und Rubens*, p. 187.

84. Quoted in ibid., p. 187.

85. In the historicist conception of history, Jörn Rüsen argues, "art is the guarantee that that conception itself is realistic; for art is the realization *within* history of the spiritual principle *of* history" (Jörn Rüsen, *Ästhetik und Geschichte*, p. 89).

86. Quoted in Maurer, *Jacob Burckhardt und Rubens*, pp. 185–87.

87. "Rubens ist ein grösserer Erklärer seines damaligen Belgiens als alle damaligen Gelehrten, Dichter und Künstler seines Landes zusammengenommen. Er ist das Form und Farbe gewordene Belgien seiner Zeit" (quoted by Wölfflin, "Jacob Burckhardt und die Kunst," p. 142; see also Maurer, *Jacob Burckhardt und Rubens*, p. 238).

88. Quoted in Maurer, *Jacob Burckhardt und Rubens*, p. 188. See also Emil Maurer, "Burckhardts Michelangelo: 'der Gefährliche,'" *Neue Zürcher Zeitung*, 20/21 June 1987, pp. 65–66.

89. Quoted by Joseph Gantner, "Jacob Burckhardt's Urteil über Rembrandt und seine Konzeption des Klassischen," in Joseph Gantner, ed., *Concinnitas: Beiträge zum Problem des klassischen* (Basel: Schwabe, n.d. [1944]), pp. 83–114, at p. 94 (Festschrift for Heinrich Wölfflin on his eightieth birthday).

90. *Über die Epochen der neueren Geschichte: Vorträge dem König Maximilian II von Bayern gehalten*, ed. Hans Herzfeld (Schloss Laupenheim: Ulrich Steiner Verlag, n.d.), p. 30.

91. Letter of 4 May 1847, *Briefe*, 3:70–71.

92. Letter of 13 August 1852, *Briefe*, 3:161.

93. Kaegi, *Jacob Burckhardt*, 3:504.

94. See Bickendorf, *Der Beginn der Kunstgeschichtsschreibung*, pp. 105–17.

95. Quoted from the introduction to the lecture course General History of Art (1851), in editor's introduction, *Aesthetik der bildenden Kunst*, ed. Siebert, p. 23.

96. Ibid., p. 93.

97. ". . . einzige Zeugen einer sonst ganz lautlos gewordenen Existenz" (ibid., p. 35).

98. See Wölfflin, "Jacob Burckhardt und die Kunst," pp. 142–43.

99. Quoted by Wölfflin, ibid., p. 143 ("In der Kunstgeschichte ist meine individuelle Aufgabe, wie mir vorkommt, diejenige, über die Phantasie vergangener Zeiten Rechenschaft zu geben; zu sagen, was diese und jene Meister und Schulen für eine Vision der Welt vor sich gehabt haben. Andere schildern mehr die Mittel der vergangenen Kunst, ich mehr den Willen [das heisst, so gut ich kann]").

100. *Aesthetik der bildenden Kunst*, p. 93.

101. *Griechische Kulturgeschichte*, ed. Felix Stähelin, in *Gesamtausgabe*, 8:2.

102. Quoted by Oelmüller, *Friedrich Theodor Vischer*, p. 32.

103. *Jacob Burckhardt und Heinrich Wölfflin*, ed. Gantner, p. 28.

104. Wölfflin, "Jacob Burckhardt" (eulogy), in ibid., p. 182; Maurizio Ghelardi, introduction to the English translation of Burckhardt, *Die Gattungen der Malerei* (forthcoming: Oxford University Press and Getty Center Publications).

105. See editor's introduction, *Aesthetik der bildenden Kunst*, ed. Siebert, p. 27: "The historical aspect of art lies for Burckhardt partly in completely profane factors like the mentality of the patron, the nature of the available materials or particular popular forms of art collecting and commissioning." See also Wölfflin, introduction to *Gesamtausgabe*, 12:x–xi.

106. *Aesthetik der bildenden Kunst*, p. 35.

107. *Über das Studium der Geschichte*, ed. Peter Ganz (Munich: C. H. Beck, 1982), p. 183 (re-edited text of the lectures originally published by Burckhardt's nephew Jacob Oeri under the title *Weltgeschichtliche Betrachtungen*).

108. "Bleibt dem Genuss sein Teil?" (quoted by Maurer, *Jacob Burckhardt und Rubens*, pp. 184–85).

109. Quoted by Kaegi, *Jacob Burckhardt*, 6:765–66.

110. Quoted in editor's introduction, *Aesthetik der bildenden Kunst*, ed. Siebert, pp. 28–29. Cf. Wölfflin's comment that "we have but to read Hans von Marées when he writes that he is learning to attach less and less value to schools and personalities in order to keep in view the solution of the artistic problem, which is the same for Michelangelo as for Bartholomeu van der Helst" (*Principles of Art History*, trans. Mary Hottinger [New York: Dover Publications, 1950; orig. German 1915; 1st English ed., London: G. Bell, 1932], p. 11).

111. Waetzoldt, *Deutsche Kunsthistoriker*, 2:180–81.

112. Letter to Willi Beyschlag, 14 June 1842, *Briefe*, 1:204. On history as *Bildung* in Burckhardt, see the comprehensive article by Joseph Mali, "Jacob Burckhardt: Myth, History and Mythistory," *History and Memory* 3 (1991): 86–118.

113. "Auf den Cicerone schaue ich mitleidig herab," he declared in 1875; quoted in Wölfflin, "Jacob Burckhardt und die Kunst," p. 143.

114. Wölfflin, "Jacob Burckhardt und die Kunst," pp. 142–43; Maurer, *Burckhardt und Rubens*, pp. 136, 250, 256.

115. See the essay on Murillo, originally in a "journal" that circulated in manuscript among Burckhardt, Kinkel, and their friends in the circle of the "Maikäfer" in Bonn, in Schiff, *German Essays on Art History*, pp. 111–24, at p. 112. This early essay was first published in *Die Kunst der Betrachtung. Aufsätze und Vorträge zur bildenden Kunst*, ed. Henning Ritter (Cologne: Dumont, 1984).

116. Quoted in Kaegi, *Jacob Burckhardt*, 6:702–3.

117. Jacob Burckhardt, *Recollections of Rubens*, trans. Mary Hottinger (London: Phaidon Press, 1950), pp. 90–91.

118. *The Cicerone: An Art Guide to Painting in Italy for the Use of Travellers and Students*, trans. A. H. Clough (New York: Charles Scribner's Sons, 1908), p. 191. Future references to *The Cicerone* will be to this outdated edition, still the only one available in English. The translator's sometimes obscure or inaccurate translations have been corrected, however, as

needed. In addition to *La Bella* and *Flora,* Burckhardt mentioned another *La Bella* in the Sciarro-Colonna collection in Rome, which he attributed to Titian. (Among early guidebooks to the collections in Rome, Friedrich von Rumohr, *Über Malerei und Bildhauerarbeit in Rome für Liebhaber des Schönen in der Kunst,* 3 vols. [Leipzig: Weidmanns Erben, 1787], listed seven paintings by Titian at the "Pallast Colonna" but none of those corresponds to the *La Bella* described by Burckhardt; Antonio Nibby, *Roma nell'anno MDCCCXXXVIII,* 4 vols. [Rome: Tipografia delle belle arte, 1841], listed two paintings in the Palazzo Sciarro-Colonna: a Titian family portrait, which he claimed was painted *"di mano dell'artefice stesso"* and the portrait of an unknown person. The latter, which is not described, may be Burckhardt's Palazzo Sciarro *La Bella.*) Burckhardt also believed that the same woman may be represented in the famous *Venere di Urbino* in the Uffizi, and possibly in the portrait of Eleonora Gonzaga, Duchess of Urbino, also in the Uffizi. Unlike some other art historians, however, he was not interested in identifying the sitter.

119. Editor's introduction, *Aesthetik der bildenden Kunst,* ed. Siebert, pp. 30–31; Wolfflin, "Jacob Burckhardt zum 100. Geburtstag," *Gedanken zur Kunstgeschichte,* p. 156.

120. "Jacob Burckhardt zum 100. Geburtstag," p. 157: "Die Belesenheit Burckhardts war ausserordentlich. . . . Er ist wohl einer der letzten gebildeten Europäer gewesen." See also Waetzoldt, *Deutsche Kunsthistoriker,* 2:198: according to Waetzold, the *Geschichte der Renaissance in Italien,* which appeared as the first half of volume 4 of Kugler's *Geschichte der Baukunst* in 1867, "ruht auf dem Fundament ungeheurer kunst- und kulturgeschichtlicher Erudition." Likewise Gottfried Boehm, "Genese und Geltung: Jacob Burckhardts Kritik des Historismus," in *Umgang mit Jacob Burckhardt: Zwölf Studien,* ed. Hans R. Guggisberg (Basel: Schwabe; Munich: C. H. Beck, 1994), p. 80: "Die *Kultur der Renaissance in Italien* ist völlig aus den Quellen erarbeitet, sie ist noch heute ein Exempel stupender Gelehrsamkeit. . . ." The French historian, Jules Michelet, whom Burckhardt much admired, expressed irritation with those who insisted on praising him for his style, "me louant pour me détruire et m'ôter toute autorité: 'C'est un écrivain, un poète, un homme d'imagination'" ("Préface de 1869," in *Histoire de France* [Paris: Calmann Lévy, 1898–1899], 1:xxiv).

121. "No living art historian could open [*The Architecture of the Italian Renaissance*] and read for a quarter of an hour," Peter Murray wrote in his Introduction to the recent English translation (London: Secker and Warburg, 1985), "without coming across at least one reference to an author—Leandro Alberti, Corio, Eccardus, even Milanesi and Müntz, with whom his familiarity is less than complete and who may . . . offer a new insight into what seemed known territory." In addition, "Burckhardt's approach through such things as diaries . . . and chronicles . . . , or even guide books . . ." pointed art history in new directions, according to Murray, and strongly influenced modern art historians like Rudolf Wittkower. A similar point about Burckhardt's command of available sources and imaginative exploitation of them, rather than discovery of new sources, was made by G. P. Gooch about Burckhardt the historian. Gooch, *History and Historians in the Nineteenth Century,* pp. 580–84.

122. See Kaegi, *Jacob Burckhardt,* 6:137.

123. *Über das Studium der Geschichte,* ed. Ganz, p. 182. Despite the significant differences dividing them, Ruskin and Burckhardt were in agreement at least on one point: that modern industrial society was radically unfavorable to art as it had been understood and practiced hitherto.

124. Letter to Max Alioth, 2 August 1879, *Briefe,* 7:43. On F. T. Vischer's reservations concerning the museum, which he saw as a sign of the autonomization of the aesthetic and its exile from everyday life, see Oelmüller, *Friedrich Theodore Vischer,* p. 177 and note 54.

125. Quoted by Wilhelm Schlink, "Jacob Burckhardt über das Amt des Kunsthistorikers" (unpublished paper), p. 22.

126. See Giovanni Morelli, *Italian Masters in German Galleries,* trans. L. Richter (London: George Bell, 1883), pp. 88–89 (shape of the ear and of the hand in Mantegna and Giovanni Bellini; pp. 110–11 (shape of the ear and the hand in Francesco Bianchi); p. 122 (shape of the ear and the hand in Correggio); pp. 172–73n (a painting of the Virgin and Child in Dresden, attributed by J. A. Crowe and G. B. Cavalcaselle to Andrea Schiavone, is reattributed to Titian on the basis of a "purely material sign, but one very characteristic of Titian. A peculiarity which I have observed in more than fifty authentic works of his is that the base of the thumb in his men's hands is abnormally developed, somewhat as I produce it here. The hand of the Baptist has it in this picture, in the "Assunta" the hand of the Apostle with the red garment, in the "Tribute-Penny" the hand of the Pharisee, etc.").

127. In a letter to Robert Grüninger, 22 August 1882, *Briefe,* 8:71–74. On Burckhardt and "der schreckliche Morelli," see ibid., Gesamtregister (index vol.), p. 228, and Wilhelm Schlink, "Die lange Übung des Auges: Giovanni Morelli und Jacob Burckhardt," *Neue Zürcher Zeitung,* 18/19 March 1995, section "Literatur und Kunst."

128. "Über die Echtheit alter Bilder" (February 1882), *Gesamtausgabe,* 14:270. Cf. letter to Heinrich von Geymüller, 8 May 1891: "I am still of the same opinion today as my old, long dead friend Gioacchino Curti, who used to say: Provided the stuff is good, why ask for the name of the author" (*Briefe,* 9:299). On Burckhardt and Morelli, see Schlink, "Die lange Übung des Auges: Giovanni Morelli und Jacob Burckhardt." As early as the introductory lecture to his course on ancient art of 1874 ("Über die Kunstgeschichte als Gegenstand eines akademischen Lehrstuhls"), Burckhardt had warned that people can acquire extensive connoisseurship and great learning in the arts without ever being able to respond to the essence of art ("das Innere der Kunst") (*Gesamtausgabe,* 13:27).

129. Waetzoldt, *Deutsche Kunsthistoriker,* 2:194–95.

130. Kaegi, *Jacob Burckhardt,* 6:539–41.

131. Maurer, *Jacob Burckhardt und Rubens,* p. 116.

132. Ibid., p. 133.

133. Ibid.

134. Letter to F. T. Vischer in Tübingen, from Basel, 19 December 1854, *Briefe,* 3:201–2. In his recent study of Wölfflin, Meinhold Lurz compared Burckhardt's account of Renaissance architecture with his student's *Renaissance und Barock* and found a far tighter logical and systematic organization in the latter: Burckhardt's text "lacks a rigorous logical and systematic structure" ["eine streng logische Systematik fehlt bei Burckhardt"]. Burckhardt did arrange the material he collected in connected categories; nevertheless, chapters on the Renaissance treatment of form stand on the same plane alongside chapters on individual thematic domains. Whereas Wölfflin's interest was primarily methodological, the Italian Renaissance serving as an illustrative test case, the interest of his teacher, Lurz concluded, remained essentially historical. Lurz, *Heinrich Wölfflin,* pp. 117–18. Even *Die Cultur der Renaissance,* generally viewed as the most comprehensive and tightly organized of all Burckhardt's works, is seen by Peter Ganz as marked by the coordination rather than the subordination of its component parts. "Jacob Burckhardt's 'Cultur der Renaissance in Italien' und die Kunstgeschichte," *Saeculum: Jahrbuch für Universalgeschichte* 40 (1989): 193–212, at p. 204. On the difference between Burckhardt and Wölfflin, see also Podro, *The Critical Historians of Art,* p. 99. According to Podro, "Burckhardt's study of the social life of the Italian Renaissance was only implicitly linked to the study of its art. His study of Italian Renaissance architecture, *Die Kunst der Renaissance in Italien* (1867) and his *Cicerone* (1855), as well as his schematically arranged surveys of the genres of altar painting and the portrait (*Beiträge zur Kunstgeschichte von Italian,* posthumously published in 1898) do not present any general argument in the light of which particular works are seen. His short comments

on particular works possess a remarkable capacity to give focus to a work, particularly in these late papers on Renaissance art and his posthumously published *Recollections of Rubens"* (p. xxiv).

135. Richter, *Jacob Burckhardt als Schriftsteller,* pp. 51–69.

136. "Über die Echtheit alter Bilder," *Gesamtausgabe,* 14:265–66. Kugler (*Handbook of the History of Painting,* 2:224–25) and Burckhardt himself (*Kunstwerke der belgischen Städte, Gesamtausgabe,* 1:140) had duly noted the large numbers of paintings that emerged from Rubens's studio and had pointed out that his students had had a large hand in the production of many of them. In the 1840s, however, this had been seen as highly regrettable. Color and expression suffered in those works, according to Burckhardt. In the 1882 lecture, Burckhardt was far more cautious in his judgment.

137. Burckhardt might have found that the authenticity of the *Madonna del passeggio*—long considered an original Raphael of high quality—had been questioned by Johann David Passavant in his *Raphael* (London: Macmillan, 1872; orig. German 1832, rev. 1852), p. 293. Passavant argued that the original of this work is lost, and that only "numerous copies of it have rendered it familiar to us. One of the best is in the Bridgewater Gallery." In their classic *Raphael: His Life and Works,* 2 vols. (London: John Murray, 1882–1885), J. A. Crowe and G. B. Cavalcaselle attributed "this pretty picture" to Penni, but conceded that it "may have its origin in some sketch by Raphael" (2:552). On the "Bridgewater Madonna," see ibid., 1:345–47; on both paintings, see C. Thompson and H. Brigstocke, *The National Gallery of Scotland: Shorter Catalogue* (Edinburgh: National Gallery of Scotland, 1978), pp. 85–86.

138. "Über die Echtheit alter Bilder," *Gesamtausgabe,* 14:267–68. See likewise a letter to Friedrich Keller (Basel, New Year's Day 1868): "Nothing is more difficult than deciding whether the *inventio* of a work not actually executed by the artist who conceived it is truly that of the artist, whether we are dealing, for instance, with a Holbein *inventio* or a non-Holbein *inventio.* The common artistic treasury of that time was vast and even in Holbein's immediate circle there were several masters who occasionally attained a degree of freedom and freshness of inspiration which can easily deceive the viewer as long as the execution itself does not betray the lesser artist. How many works by Urs Graf, for instance, have I not myself taken at first glance to be by Holbein" (*Briefe,* 5:17–18). The reference to Caspar Hauser is to a lost child of mysterious background discovered by the Nuremberg authorities in the early years of the nineteenth century. He died at a young age from wounds inflicted either by himself or by an unknown assailant. There was speculation that he was the true hereditary prince of Baden and that he had been the victim of a court intrigue to deprive him of his identity.

139. *The Architecture of the Italian Renaissance,* ed. Peter Murray, trans. James Palmes (London: Secker & Warburg, 1985), p. xviii.

140. See editor's introduction, *Aesthetik der bildenden Kunst,* ed. Siebert.

141. Quoted by Kaegi, *Jacob Burckhardt,* 6:545, from mss. "Notizen zur italienischen Kunst seit dem XV. Jahrhundert" (notes for his university lecture course). On rivalry among the cities, despots, princes, popes, and other *magnifici* as a stimulant of building projects, see *The Architecture of the Italian Renaissance,* pp. 3–10. See also Waetzoldt, *Deutsche Kunsthistoriker,* 2:197.

142. Lecture on "Rembrandt" (6 November 1877), *Gesamtausgabe,* 14:178–97, at p. 179.

143. "Über die niederländische Genremalerei," *Gesamtausgabe,* 14:110.

144. Quoted by Kaegi, *Jacob Burckhardt,* 6:765–66.

145. Quoted by Meier, *Stiften und Sammeln,* p. 56.

146. On the Venetians, notably Giorgione, Titian, and Veronese, see *Cicerone* (Engl.), pp. 183–85, 208–9. Cf. *Gesamtausgabe,* 4:330, 332. On Rubens as *"Existenz-Maler ohne*

Idee," see Maurer, *Jacob Burckhardt und Rubens,* pp. 195–96. Perhaps also the term *Existenzbild* was intended to emphasize the relation between the beautiful and the sensuously existent, in opposition to the view of many idealist philosophers that the latter is secondary or even insignificant—a "disturbance" banished to the "antechambers of the system," in the words of Burckhardt's contemporary, the art historian Anton Springer (*Die Hegel'sche Geschichtsanschauung* [1848], p. 9, quoted by Podro, *The Critical Art Historians,* p. 154). Springer (1825–1891), a friend of F. T. Vischer's, was professor of art history at Bonn (1860–1872) and Leipzig (1873–1891). See also Robert Zimmermann, *Geschichte der Aesthetik als philosophische Wissenschaft* (Vienna: Wilhelm Braunmüller, 1858), p. 695: "Since only the idea, the logical, has real being for Hegel and the sensuously existent does not therefore exist, the latter is the epitome of the negative, and the concept alone is positive. But in the beautiful, sensuous existence lays claim to be positive. However, as it can attain this only through the concept, which alone is positive, beauty is not truly realized, despite assurances to the contrary, and the difference lies only in that in one case the concept is grasped by the understanding, and in the other contemplated by the senses. There is never any question of reaching beyond the concept."

147. *Cicerone* (Engl.), p. 185. Cf. *Gesamtausgabe,* 4:333.

148. Otto Fischer, *Geschichte der deutschen Malerei* (Munich: F. Bruckmann, 1956; 1st ed. 1942), pp. 396–97.

149. The painters associated with the Nazarene movement included Philipp Veit, 1793–1877; Julian Schnorr von Carolsfeld, 1794–1872; Moritz von Schwind, 1804–1871; Julius Oldach, 1804–1830.

150. See Meier, *Stiften und Sammeln,* p. 56: "Burckhardt adopted a vehemently polemical tone because he spoke as an art historian, who wanted to exert an influence on the art of his own time. He wanted to bring art history and the practice of art together."

151. Franz Kugler, *Handbuch der Geschichte der Malerei* (Berlin: Duncker & Humblot, 1837), 1:306–7, quoted by Wilhelm Schlink, "Paolo: Existenzmalerei bis zu ihren höchsten Konsequenzen (Jacob Burckhardt)," in *Paolo Veronese: Fortuna Critica und künstlerisches Nachleben,* ed. Jurg Myer zur Capellen and Bernd Roeck (Sigmaringen: Jan Thorbecke Verlag, 1990), Studî del Centro Tedesco di Studî Veneziani, 8, pp. 7–15, at pp. 11, 13. Cf. Franz Kugler, *A Handbook of the History of Painting,* ed. Sir Charles Eastlake (London: John Murray, 1867), pt. 2, p. 441: "The beings he [Titian] creates seem to have the high consciousness and enjoyment of existence; the bliss of satisfaction, so like yet so different from the marble idealizations of Grecian antiquity—the air of an harmonious, unruffled existence seems to characterize them all. Hence they produce so grateful an impression on the mind of the spectator; hence they impart so refined and exalted a feeling, although generally but a transcript of familiar and well-known objects—representations of beautiful forms, without reference to spiritual or unearthly conceptions. It is life in its fullest power—the glorification of earthly existence, the liberation of art from the bonds of ecclesiastical dogmas." Similar comments on Veronese: "Paolo infused a magic into his pictures which surpasses almost all the other masters of the Venetian school. Never had the pomp of colour been so exalted, so glorified, as in his works; his paintings are like full concerts of enchanting music. He loved to paint festive subjects for the refectories of rich convents, suggested of course from particular passages in the Scriptures, but treated with the greatest freedom. . . . In these and similar examples, we have the most beautiful display of grand architcture . . . the most brilliant and gorgeous costume; above all, a powerful and noble race of human beings, elate with the consciousness of existence, and in full enjoyment of all that renders earth attractive" (p. 464). In general, Venetian painting combines the familiar and the grand, the sensuous and the ideal: "It is the enjoyment of life and of its splendour which speaks in all the nobler produc-

tions of this school. And although this general aim would appear to restrict imitation to familiar objects and circumstances, yet they knew how to penetrate life in all its aspects and in all its depths; and, on the other hand, to treat the grandest themes" (p. 431).

152. Quoted by Schlink, "Paolo," p. 13, from a note in Basel Staatsarchiv, 207, 36, fol. 10 recto.

153. Quoted in Waetzold, *Deutsche Kunsthistoriker,* 2:155. On Kugler, see Kaegi, *Jacob Burckhardt,* vols. 2, 3, and 6, *passim;* and Waetzold, *Deutsche Kunsthistoriker,* 2:143–72.

154. See, for instance, his response to a request that he suggest all-round candidates for the chair of art history at the Federal Polytechnic left vacant by the death of his one-time friend Gottfried Kinkel: "There are many learned and meritorious specialists in art historical research in the German lands at the present time," he replied, "but who can guarantee that any one of them would have the necessary dedication to the teaching of art history as a whole?" (letter to Carl Keppeler, 7 December 1882, *Briefe,* 9:347).

155. Kugler's wife Clara Hitzig, a daughter of one of Berlin's most prominent Jewish families, had grown up in a house regularly frequented by the romantic writers Chamisso and E. T. A. Hoffmann.

156. Of this work Burckhardt, reviewing his friend Kinkel's *Geschichte der bildenden Künste bei den christlichen Völkern* (Bonn, 1845) in the *Kölnische Zeitung,* declared that it was "die erste allgemeine, alle Völker und Zeiten umfassende Kunstgeschichte" (quoted in Kaegi, *Jacob Burckhardt,* 3:133).

157. Kaegi, *Jacob Burckhardt,* 3:504.

158. Quoted by Waetzold, *Deutsche Kunsthistoriker,* 2:149.

159. *On the Aesthetic Education of Man,* trans. Reginald Snell (New York: Frederick Ungar, 1965), letters 14 and 18, pp. 74, 88–89. Cf. the words of the "Philosopher" in letter 6 of Goethe's *The Collector and his Circle:* "The human mind is in an exalted state when it venerates, when it worships, when it elevates an object and is in turn elevated by it. However, the mind cannot stay long in this state. The generic representation left it cold, the ideal elevated it beyond itself. But now the mind longs to return to itself. It would like to savour again its earlier liking for the individual object, without, however, returning to the limitations of this position and without giving up that which is significant and elevating. What would happen to the mind in this dilemma if beauty did not step in and solve the problem! Only beauty can give life and warmth to what is presented with scientific exactitude. By muting what is significant and elevated and suffusing it with extraordinary charm, beauty brings the individual object back to us. A beautiful work of art has come full circle: It is again something individual that we can take to our hearts and make part of us" (*Essays on Art and Literature,* ed. John Geary, trans. E. and H. von Nardroff [New York: Suhrkamp, 1986], p. 145).

160. Quoted by Karl Gotthilf Kachler, *Schinkels Kunstauffassung* (Basel: Volksdruckerei, 1940), p. 26.

161. *Aesthetik der bildenden Kunst,* p. 164.

162. Ibid., p. 56.

163. Ibid., p. 58. Cf. *Über das Studium der Geschichte,* p. 182: "The highest thing of all is art, which gathers up what is imperishable in a chaotic world"; and p. 107: "The only restriction imposed by the eternal on earth: art."

164. "Über erzählende Malerei" (11 November 1884), *Gesamtausgabe,* 14:306. Cf. Goethe: "The poet will love his country as a man and a citizen, but the country of his *poetic* talents and of his activity as a poet is the Good, the Noble, and the Beautiful, which are bound to no particular province and to no particular place. He takes and forms these wherever he finds them. In this he resembles the eagle which freely surveys many lands and to which it is a matter of indifference whether the hare it swoops down upon is running in

Prussia or Saxony" (Johann Peter Eckermann, *Gespräche mit Goethe* [Basel: Birkhäuser, 1945], 2:479 [March 1832]).

165. See Schlink, "Jacob Burckhardt über den 'Genuss der Kunstwerke.'" Schlink's article explores the ramifications of Burckhardt's use of the term *Genuss* in the subtitle of *The Cicerone* and amply justifies the importance attributed to it here.

166. Friedrich Schiller, "Über den Gebrauch des Chors in der Tragödie," preceding *Die Braut von Messina, Werke,* ed. R. Borberger (Berlin: G. Grote'sche Verlagsbuchhandlung, 1901), 4:158. This passage was cited by Grimm in his *Wörterbuch,* under *"Genuss."* Grimm also cited a more religious usage in Adelung: "Die Seligkeit des Menschen besteht in dem Genusse Gottes." The reading "das heilige Abendmahl geniessen" is found in Trübner's *Deutsches Wörterbuch.* On Burckhardt and Schiller in the matter of aesthetic pleasure, see Martina Sitt, *Kriterien der Kunstkritik. Jacob Burckhardts unveröffentlichte Ästhetik als Schlüssel seines Rangsystems* (Vienna: Böhlau, 1992), p. 152.

167. While it is "a natural characteristic of all rational creatures to find *Genuss* in the contemplation of singular phenomena"—according to Schinkel, people "experience themselves at such moments as other than they are and, forgetting themselves, emerge out of themselves to freedom"—the experience of *Genuss* is "higher still" when a higher, ideal form is perceived in the individual phenomenon. Alfred Freiherr von Wolzogen, ed., *Aus Schinkels Nachlass* (Berlin: Verlag der Königlichen Geheimen Ober-Hofbuchdruckerei, 1862–1866), 3:347–48, 360.

168. Quoted by Emil Maurer, "Burckhardts Michelangelo: 'der Gefährliche," *Neue Zürcher Zeitung,* 20/21 June 1987, p. 65.

169. ". . . eine zweite Schöpfung, im Grunde das einzige Unvergängliche und Allgültige auf Erden" (*Aesthetik der bildenden Kunst,* p. 93). Thus he spoke of "die Kunst, die aus der wirren Welt, das Unvergängliche zusammenfasst" (*Über das Studium der Geschichte,* ed. Ganz, p. 182). On the aestheticizing of history as consolation for the horror and violence of lived history, see Egon Flaig, *Angeschaute Geschichte* (Rheinfelden: Schäuble, 1987), pp. 16–19, 27–34.

170. *On the Aesthetic Education of Man,* letter 21, p. 101.

171. Thus Schinkel argued that man should "make himself beautiful, so that every action he performs will become thoroughly beautiful in both its motive and its execution." Where beauty reigns, "the concept of duty in the crude sense of an oppressive, onerous obligation fades away; man then acts at all times in a condition of blissful joy [*Genuss*] . . . In other words, every action should be an opportunity for artistic creation. In this way, man will enjoy blessedness on earth and live in the presence of the divinity, and from that perspective, duty in the sense indicated above will appear half sinful, or rather we might put it this way: A man who acts solely out of duty still stands on an imperfect level of existence, in which sin must still be combatted, still exercises its oppressive power over him, and has not yet been driven back by the love of beauty" (*Aus Schinkels Nachlass,* 3:348).

172. *Reflections on History,* Trans. Mary Hottinger (London: George Allen & Unwin, 1943), p. 58 ("Nicht ganz abschliessend für die Stellung der Kunst in der Weltliteratur sind Schillers 'Künstler.' Es reicht nicht, dass das Schöne als Durchgangspunkt und Erziehung zum Wahren dargestellt wird; denn die Kunst ist in hohem Grade um ihrer selbst willen vorhanden" [*Gesamtausgabe,* 7:45]); cf. *Über das Studium der Geschichte,* ed. Ganz, p. 278: "Schillers Gedicht: Die Künstler, für die Stellung der Kunst in der Weltcultur abschliessend; das Schöne als Durchgangspunct und Erziehung zum Wahren. Es reicht nicht, denn die Kunst ist in hohem Grade um ihrer selbst willen vorhanden."

173. G. W. F. Hegel, *Vorlesungen über die Ästhetik,* ed. Moldenhauer and Michel, vol. 3 (vol. 15 of Hegel's *Werke*), pp. 23–25.

174. Schlink, "Paolo," pp. 14, 15.

175. Wölfflin, *Principles of Art History*, p. 10. Cf. Goethe: "The true art lover sees that he must raise himself up to the level of the artist himself in order to truly enjoy (*'geniessen'*) works of art, . . . that he must focus all the fragmented aspects of his life, live with the work of art, constantly view and re-view it, and thereby acquire for himself a higher existence (*'eine höhere Existenz'*)" (*Wahrheit und Wahrscheinlichkeit der Kunstwerke* [1798] in *Goethes sämtliche Werke*, Propyläen ed., 45 vols. [Munich: Georg Müller; Berlin: Propyläen Verlag, 1909], 12:59).

176. See Schlink, "'Kunst ist dazu da, um geselligen Kreisen das gähnende Ungeheuer, die Zeit, zu töten,'" pp. 65–81; "Jacob Burckhardts Künstlerrat," *Stadeljahrbuch*, n.s., 11 (1987): 269–90.

177. "The Great Men of History," in *Reflections on History*, p. 176. This lecture series was given in 1870, but the ideas expressed in it can already be found in the *Basler Zeitung* articles of the 1840s. In fact, Diderot had expressed similar concerns a century earlier; see "Salon de 1767" and "Salon de 1769," *Salons*, 3:52–56 and 4:111–12.

178. "Nous avons interrogé le passé au profit de l'avenir" ("Winckelmann," in *L'Artiste* 11 (1835): 221–23, quoted by Frances Suzman Jowell, *Thoré-Bürger and the Art of the Past* [New York: Garland Publishing, 1977]). The art historical writing of Eugène Fromentin, which Burckhardt studied closely, was also infused with contemporary concerns and also served as a vehicle for the judgment of contemporary art and artists. See the introduction by Pierre Moisy to his edition of *Les Maîtres d'autrefois* (Paris: Garnier, 1972), pp. xi–xii, xxix, xxxi. See also Schlink, "Jacob Burckhardt über den 'Genuss der Kunstwerke,'" pp. 48–51.

179. *Griechische Kulturgeschichte*, in *Gesamtausgabe*, 1:7. On Egyptian art, see also *Aesthetik der bildenden Kunst*, p. 38.

180. See on this topic the suggestive reflections of Joseph Gantner, "Jacob Burckhardts Urteil über Rembrandt und seine Konzeption des Klassischen," pp. 111–12.

181. *Kunstwerke der belgischen Städte*, in *Gesamtausgabe*, 1:142.

182. *Cicerone* (Engl.), p. 57.

183. Maurer, *Jacob Burckhardt und Rubens*, p. 188; lecture notes for course "Italian Art since the Fifteenth Century," quoted by Kaegi, *Jacob Burckhardt*, 6:570–71.

184. In spite of his keen sensitivity to what Wölfflin was to call the "autonomous life of color," line appears always to have been the *ultimate* guiding principle for Burckhardt. "Lack of feeling for line is equivalent in his art criticism to lack of feeling for art," according to Wölfflin ("Jacob Burckhardt und die Kunst," pp. 139–40).

185. *Gesamtausgabe*, 14:197.

186. Maurer, *Jacob Burckhardt und Rubens*, pp. 265–66.

187. Kaegi, *Jacob Burckhardt*, 6:782, quoting from the lecture notes for the course "History of Art Outside Italy since 1400."

188. *Recollections of Rubens*, p. 62.

189. *Cicerone* (Engl.), p. 111.

190. *Aesthetik der bildenden Kunst*, p. 65. Burckhardt's idea of Renaissance *"Raumstil"* thus seems to anticipate Riegl's view of Renaissance architecture as a free combination of disparate elements. See Margaret Olin, *Forms of Representation* (University Park: Pennsylvania State University Press, 1992), p. 33.

191. *Recollections of Rubens*, p. 29. The broad lines of this account of the history of art may well have been fairly common coin. A similar account, which appears to be Hegelian in inspiration, is found in Carel Vosmaer's pioneering study of Rembrandt (1868); see *Rembrandt: sa vie et ses oeuvres*, 2nd rev. ed. (The Hague: Martinus Nijhoff; Paris: Renouard, H. Loones, 1877), pp. 36–41, 418.

192. *Recollections of Rubens,* pp. 32–33.

193. Ibid., p. 9.

194. *Ästhetik der bildenden Kunst,* p. 158. Representing literary subjects, according to Burckhardt, is a "dubious task" for an artist, because he "makes himself dependent, like the painter of historical subjects, because poetic and painterly beauty are not the same, and most of all, because the artist's representation must compete with an image that the viewer has already formed of the scene."

195. Quoted from Burckhardt's lecture notes by Kaegi, *Jacob Burckhardt,* 6:456. Cf. a note on Hobbema: With him, as with other Dutch painters, according to Burckhardt, "it is not the subject matter that is the main thing but how the artist has viewed it and impelled us to find significance in it" (ibid., p. 764). See also Maurer, *Burckhardt und Rubens,* p. 234.

196. *Kunstwerke der Belgischen Städte,* in *Gesamtausgabe,* 1:115. *Die Kunst der Renaissance in Italien,* ed. Wölfflin, in *Gesamtausgabe,* 6:23: To see the Renaissance as simply a revival of antiquity is to see only half the picture: "Die freie Originalität, womit das widergewonnene Altertum aufgenommen und verarbeitet wird, die Fülle ganz eigentümlichen, modernen Geistes, welche bei der grossen Bewegung sich mit offenbart, kommen dabei nicht zu ihrem Rechte." Likewise, p. 47: The Renaissance "hat . . . keinen einzigen Tempel repetirt, und überhaupt das Antike nur im Sinn der freiesten Kombination verwertet" ["did not replicate a single temple and in general made use of antiquity only in a spirit of extremely free recombination"]. Cf. *The Architecture of the Italian Renaissance,* ed. Murray, p. 15. The poet Carl Spitteler, who had been Burckhardt's student, once noted that "Burckhardt's ideal is not so much antiquity itself as the study of antiquity"—that is, not slavish imitation, but willingness to learn and build on antiquity, often enough by transforming it. "Böcklin, Burckhardt, Basel," *Gesammelte Werke* (Zurich: Artemis, 1945–1958), 6:164.

197. *Kunstwerke der belgischen Städte,* in *Gesamtausgabe,* 1:141.

198. Quoted by Gérard Georges Lemaire, *Esquisses en vue d'une histoire du Salon* (Paris: Henri Veyrier, 1986), pp. 32, 38.

199. Quoted by Kaegi, *Jacob Burckhardt,* 6:456–57. For a vivid account of the place of art in the culture of the last four decades of the nineteenth century in Germany, see Schlink, "'Kunst ist dazu da, um geselligen Kreisen das gähnende Ungeheuer, die Zeit, zu töten.'"

200. From Burckhardt's lecture notes, quoted by Kaegi, *Jacob Burckhardt,* 6:727.

201. *Nachlass,* 1883/1888, in *Nietzsches Werke* (Taschenausgabe; Leipzig: Kröner, n.d.), 11:52, no. 94. See also the critique of romantic sensibility and of the modern need for sensations as "plebeian" in contrast with the great writers and the public of the French seventeenth century (ibid., pp. 59–60). Concern about the transformation of the conditions of artistic production goes back before the French Revolution. The pernicious effect on artistic taste and production of the substitution of the market for royal and ecclesiastical patronage was a recurrent topic in the debate over the rococo in France in the eighteenth century. It was a major theme of Diderot's art criticism in the 1760s. In the "Salons" of 1767 and 1769, for instance, Diderot defended public exhibitions and criticism on the grounds that they help to uphold standards, preserve the artist's pride in his reputation, and check the influence of the ephemeral tastes and demands of individual clients; for when artists become the servants of wealth and luxury, "great talents are degraded and made to produce works of no consequence and the subject matter of art is diminished to insignificant bambochades" (*Salons,* 3:56, 4:65–66). Diderot's critique of Boucher and Baudouin, in particular, focuses on the influence of the *"petit goût"* of well-to-do private patrons. Despite all its qualities, according to the author of the "Salon" of 1765, a sketch by Greuze for a work on "Le mauvais fils puni" may never be made over into a finished painting because of the "wretched taste of the times." Even if it is, "Boucher will have sold fifty of his indecent, stale marionettes before Greuze sells his two magnificent paintings. . . . I know what I am talking about. Isn't his 'Paralytique' or

'Récompense de la bonne éducation donnée,' still in his studio? Yet it is a masterpiece. They heard about it at Court. They had it brought there. It was admired. But it was not purchased. Thanks to the Empress of Russia this painting is no longer for sale. But it has been lost for France" (*Salons*, 2:159).

202. See *The Journal of Delacroix*, ed. H. Wellington, trans. Lucy Norton (London: Phaidon, 1951), pp. 85 (1848), 97–98 (23 April 1849). Cf. Baudelaire's description of Delacroix as "sceptique et aristocrate. . . . Haïsseur des multitudes, il ne les considérait guère que comme des briseurs d'images" (*La Vie et l'oeuvre d'Eugène Delacroix*, preface by J. Crépet [Paris: René Kieffer, 1928], p. 33).

203. Letter of 17 February 1884, *Briefe*, 8:183.

204. Burckhardt, *Aesthetik der bildenden Kunst*, p. 164. Cf. Goethe: "The English poet Thomson wrote a very good poem on the seasons but a very bad one on freedom, and not because the poet was unpoetic but because the subject matter was" (Eckermann, *Gespräche mit Goethe*, 2:479).

205. "Über die Echtheit alter Bilder," *Gesamtausgabe*, 14:270.

206. *Recollections of Rubens*, p. 115. See also the lecture "Über erzählende Malerei" (1884), *Gesamtausgabe*, 14:301–15; and the passages quoted from Burckhardt's university lectures on the baroque art of the Netherlands in the seventeenth century in Kaegi, *Jacob Burckhardt*, 6:706–7.

207. *Recollections of Rubens*, p. 115.

208. *Aesthetik der Bildenden Kunst*, pp. 161–62. This section of the lectures on aesthetics is devoted to the question of history paintings based on works of historical literature and scholarly studies of historical costume, as these developed in Europe after 1815. Burckhardt listed a number of disadvantages of this kind of history painting, among them, that historical accuracy, in details of costume and architecture, for instance, attracts attention to itself and distracts both the artist and the beholder from the painting as a work of art ("*vo. 'Jauptsache*"); that the choice of subject matter is dictated by nonartistic (historical or ideological) considerations of what counts as significant; that there is a temptation to make up for deficiencies in the commission by multiplying episodes and exaggerating the emotions of the figures represented; and that the pathetic moment to be represented is selected entirely on the basis of the contemporary public's ability to project its own feelings on to it. In this way "painting becomes the servant of contemporary politics and ideas [*"Zeittendenzdienerin"*] and the importance of the subject matter lies entirely outwith art, in the notoriety of the event and above all in the celebrity of the actors in it" (p. 161).

209. Ibid., p. 163.

210. *Recollections of Rubens*, p. 116.

211. Ibid., p. 114.

212. "Über die Richtung der Kunst in Bayern," in Kugler, *Kleine Schriften und Studien zur Kunstgeschichte*, 3:503–5. On the demand for patriotic paintings in Switzerland, see Franz Zelger, "Künstlerfreuden und Künstlerleiden: Streiflichter auf die Situation der Schweizer Künstler im neunzehnten Jahrhundert," in *Von Anker bis Zünd: Die Kunst im jungen Bundesstaat 1848–1900* (Zurich: Kunsthaus Zürich and Scheidegger & Spiess, 1998), pp. 321–31, at pp. 327–28.

213. In the lecture "Über erzählende Malerei" Burckhardt gave examples of such frescoes: that on the middle floor of the National Museum in Munich, which recounts the history of Bavaria and of the house of Wittelsbach, and Kaulbach's depiction of the history of humanity on the great staircase of the New Museum (destroyed) in Berlin. *Gesamtausgabe*, 14:301–2. See Kugler on the Bavarian monarchy's art projects in "Über die Richtung der Kunst in Bayern," *Kleine Schriften und Studien zur Kunstgeschichte*, 3:503–5.

214. Quoted in Kaegi, *Jacob Burckhardt*, 6:707. It is worth noting that as a member of

the city-state's *Kunstcommission*, Burckhardt did not recommend the purchase of a single history painting. On his increasingly reserved view of history painting, see Meier, *Stiften und Sammeln*, p. 88.

215. Quoted from Burckhardt's lecture notes on Dutch painting in the seventeenth century, Kaegi, *Jacob Burckhardt*, 6:722.

216. *Gesamtausgabe*, 14:189.

217. "In modern art, the artist's means of representation develop here and there an existence of their own, independent of any purpose. The purpose and the object of representation are only pretexts for exercising these means. Incredible artistic skill, which at times seems to disdain any task [*Aufgabe*], moves to the fore. . . . How does Rembrandt differ from all previous painters? In his subordination of the object, whatever it may be, to the two unconstrained great powers of air and light. These have become in his work the true rulers of the world" ("Rembrandt" [public lecture given in Basel, 6 November 1877], *Gesamtausgabe*, 14:178, 180–81). On Michelangelo, see Kaegi, *Jacob Burckhardt*, 6:590–97 (presentation of material in lecture notes for course "Italian Art since 1400," given in 1883–1884.) Burckhardt reproached Michelangelo with having treated "Aufgaben und Themen in völliger Wilkür" ("artistic tasks and themes in the most aribitrary manner possible"). "He is and remains *in rebellion* against every external content," he concluded (6:592; italics added). See also *Cicerone* (Engl.), pp. 122–23, 126; and Burckhardt's revised edition of Kugler's *Handbuch* (Stuttgart: Ebner & Seubert, 1848), pp. 671–72 (on Michelangelo as architect): "In contrast to earlier masters who were able to accommodate their needs with naive grace to the forms of the Ancients, in contrast to his own contemporaries, who at least observed these forms with a certain conscientious fidelity, he [Michelangelo] begins to transform them, according to his whim and mood, or under the pressure of that pursuit of material effects, which in his case shows little inner necessity. He thereby opens the gates to the degeneration of the following age."

218. Kaegi, *Jacob Burckhardt*, 6:595.

219. Ibid., 3:486.

220. *Recollections of Rubens*, pp. 23–24 (translation slightly modified in the interests of clarity).

221. "Rembrandt," in *Gesamtausgabe*, 14:179.

222. Kaegi, *Jacob Burckhardt*, 2:237, quoting an article in *Kunstblatt*, 9 March 1843.

223. Letter of 14 June 1881, *Briefe*, 7:246. Burckhardt would doubtless have been surprised by the degree to which Delacroix's judgments in political and aesthetic matters—on the importance of the "ideal" element in art, for instance, or of line and contour as well as color—coincided with his own. Delacroix's *Journal* was not published until 1893, four years before Burckhardt's death.

224. In a talk given in Brussels after Delacroix's death; *La Vie et l'oeuvre d'Eugène Delacroix*, p. 1. Burckhardt appears to have been closer to "la plupart des gens" for whom the name of Delacroix conjures up, according to Baudelaire, "je ne sais quelles idées vagues de fougue mal dirigée, de turbulence, d'inspiration aventurière, de désordre même" ("Salon de 1846," ibid., p. 67).

225. Aby Warburg, for instance, associated Burckhardt for a time with *Renaissancismus* and *Heroenverehrung* (the cult of heroes). See Berndt Roeck, "Aby Warburgs Seminarübungen über Jacob Burckhardt im Sommersemester 1927," *Idea* (Jahrbuch der Hamburger Kunsthalle) 10 (1991): 65–89, at p. 66.

226. Letter to Ludwig Pastor, 13 January 1896, *Briefe*, 10:263. Burckhardt's claim was strongly supported by the sociologist Alfred von Martin (1882–1979) in a courageous book, published under the Nazis, *Burckhardt und Nietzsche* (Munich: Ernst Reinhardt, 1941).

Throughout his book von Martin emphasized Burckhardt's moderation and his adherence to basic principles of morality in contrast to Nietzsche's unrestrainted commitment to "living dangerously." (Because of his opposition to National Socialism, von Martin gave up his teaching position in Germany in the 1930s and lived the life of a private scholar in Munich. After the war he returned to teaching at the University of Munich.)

227. *Cicerone* (Engl.), pp. 122, 126.

228. "Die Kunst der Renaissance in Italien," ed. Wölfflin, bk. 1, ch. 4, *Gesamtausgabe*, 6:35.

229. See Maurer, *Jacob Burckhardt und Rubens*, p. 255.

230. Kaegi, *Jacob Burckhardt*, 6:595 (quoted from lecture course "Art in Italy after 1400").

231. On Donatello as a "Naturalist," who "kannte in seiner Kunst keine Schranken" ("recognized no limits in his art") and "übte eine ungeheure und zum Teil gefährliche Wirkung auf die ganze italienische Skulptur aus" ("had a huge and in part dangerous effect on the whole of Italian sculpture"), see *Cicerone, Gesamtausgabe*, 4:13–16. (Parts 1 and 2, on architecture and sculpture, were not included in the English translation.) On Correggio, see *Cicerone* (Engl.), pp. 178–80, 182; see also Maurer, *Jacob Burckhardt und Rubens*, p. 248; Kaegi, *Jacob Burckhardt*, 6:619. On Michelangelo, see *Cicerone* (Engl.), 122–28. Burckhardt's reservations with respect to revolutionary, obsessive geniuses were anticipated, with a curious, ironical twist, in Diderot's *Rameau's Nephew*, where they are placed in the mouth of the talented but low-life nephew. To the narrator's question whether his uncle, the great composer, ever did anybody a kindness, Rameau replies that, if he did, it was unintentionally. "He thinks of no one but himself: the rest of the universe doesn't matter a tinker's damn to him. His wife, his daughter may die as soon as they please. Provided the parish bells that toll for them continue to sound the intervals of the twelfth and the seventeenth, all will be well. . . . That's what I especially envy in men of genius. They are good for one thing only— apart from that, zero. They don't know what it is to be citizens, fathers, mothers, cousins, friends. Between you and me, one should try to be like them in every way, but without multiplying the breed. The world needs men, but men of genius, no, I say, no! No need of them. They are the ones who change the face of the earth, and even in the smallest things stupidity is so common and powerful that it can't be reformed without creating mayhem. . . . If I knew any history, I could prove to you that evil has always come about on this earth through some man of genius . . ." (Denis Diderot, *Rameau's Nephew and Other Works*, trans. Jacques Barzun and Ralph H. Bowen [Indianapolis: Bobbs-Merrill, 1975], p. 12 [translation slightly emended]).

232. Quoted by Waetzold, *Deutsche Kunsthistoriker*, 2:173.

233. *Cicerone* (Engl.), p. 141.

234. Ibid., p. 111.

235. Thus Tintoretto, in contrast with Titian, is seen as having many mannerist traits, notably "a complete lack of control over his imagination, not because it was in itself too powerful, as one might think, but because his artistic will was not strong enough to contain and direct it" (quoted from notes on "History of Modern Art since the End of the Sixteenth Century" in Kaegi, *Jacob Burckhardt*, 6:643). Some reflections by Goethe on "Imitators" and "Imaginers" in *The Collector* strike a remarkably similar note: "Imitation can be considered the basis of the visual arts. . . . If the artist starts out as an imitator, he may yet rise to the highest level. If he stays with imitation, we may call him a Copyist. The Imitator only reproduces the subject, without adding anything to it or telling us anything beyond the obvious. . . . [His] work cannot really satisfy us because it lacks the beautiful radiance of artistic truth. If this radiance is present, even just a trace, the work has great charm." Imaginers, in contrast, "compete with poets by chasing after effects that are the domain of poetry, while

failing to understand and exploit the strengths of their own art. . . . I asked if genius did not manifest itself primarily through inventiveness? . . . If this quality . . . was not the basis of the highest art? . . . If there was anything more powerful to counteract the tedium of the prosaic than this capacity to create new worlds? If it was not a rare talent? Even if it had gone astray, if we should not talk about it with reverence?" The answer ran that it is only the "one-sided" Imaginer who is to be condemned: that the quality of imagination "because it could be so beneficial to the whole of art, was so much more damaging when it claimed to be self-contained, autonomous, and independent. The Imitator never harms art because with his efforts he brings it to a level where the true artist can and must assume responsiblity. The Imaginer, on the other hand, does infinite harm because he pushes art beyond its limits, where only the greatest genius can reclaim it from vagueness and boundlessness and lead it back toward its true essence and its own prescribed domain" (*Essays on Art and Literature*, ed. Geary, pp. 154–55). For Burckhardt, the Imitator of other works of art, the academic artist, performs a similar function to the imitator of nature for Goethe. He maintains the conditions that permit the truly gifted artist to do his work: the accumulated skills, practices, rules, and forms. The "Titan," in contrast, like the Imaginer, may destroy those conditions.

236. "Die Kunst der Renaissance in Italien," bk. 1, ch. 4, *Gesamtausgabe*, 6:35.

237. *Cicerone* (Engl.), p. 112.

238. Ibid., p. 140: "It is not the height of genius but the power of the will, which is grandest. The first would not have kept him from mannerism; it is the last which never suffered him to rest on his laurels, but always urged him to higher modes of expression." See also p. 164: "The highest personal quality of Raphael was . . . not aesthetic but moral in its nature, namely the great honesty and the strong will with which he at all times strove after the beauty which at the time he recognized as the highest."

239. Quoted by Kaegi, *Jacob Burckhardt*, 6:608. A remark by Oskar Fischel, who lectured on art history in Berlin in the early 1930s, goes to the heart of Burckhardt's well-known enthusiasm for Raphael. Raphael's portraits, according to Fischel, allow the viewer to experience "a humanistically—which at that time meant harmoniously—cultural society majestically interpreted in accordance with [its] own desires. So long as this culture was dominated by an ideal, until the triumph of the new bourgeoisie in the French Revolution, Raphael was accepted as the painter [of that ideal], without any question. It embodied itself in the symmetrically developed man, full of poise and spiritual energy, and in the fact that these figures gave outward effect to the inner moderation of their character. Herein lay Raphael's profound influence, peculiar and ennobling, on life" (Oskar Fischel, *Raphael*, trans. Bernard Rackham [London: Kegan Paul, 1948], p. 125).

240. Baudelaire in "Salon de 1845" and "Salon de 1846," in *La Vie et l'oeuvre d'Eugène Delacroix*, pp. 61, 63, 80. In the public mind, according to Baudelaire, Delacroix and Ingres had long been seen as two wrestling champions, representing two opposing views of art. "Exposition universelle de 1855," ibid., p. 82.

241. *Kunstwerke der belgischen Städte*, in *Gesamtausgabe*, 1:113–98, at p. 140.

242. Maurer, *Jacob Burckhardt und Rubens*, p. 177; *Kunstwerke der belgischen Städte*, in *Gesamtausgabe*, 1:153.

243. *Kunstwerke der belgischen Städte*, in *Gesamtausgabe*, 1:177.

244. Ibid., p. 153.

245. "Er hat die Natur oft weit übertrieben" (ibid.).

246. Ibid., pp. 154, 177.

247. Ibid., p. 140.

248. ". . . riesenhafteste Phantasie und Darstellungsgabe" (ibid., p. 154).

249. Ibid., pp. 153, 156.

250. Ibid., p. 140.

251. Maurer, *Jacob Burckhardt und Rubens*, pp. 193–95.

252. *Kunstwerke der belgischen Städte*, note 26, in *Gesamtausgabe*, 1:153.

253. "Rubens is in the highest degree *dramatic;* one should not forget that he was the contemporary of Shakespeare" (ibid., p. 153) Cf. Maurer, *Jacob Burckhardt und Rubens*, pp. 136, 177–81.

254. *Gesamtausgabe*, 1:140; Kugler, *Handbook of the History of Painting*, ed. Sir Edmund Head (London: John Murray, 1846), 2:230.

255. Maurer, *Jacob Burckhardt und Rubens*, pp. 100, 137.

256. *Recollections of Rubens*, p. 5.

257. Ibid., p. 157. Some judgments, it is true, repeat judgments made in the past, by Burckhardt himself or by Kugler. For instance, that Rubens's "figures, from the skeleton outward, lack ideality"; that "his selection of types was not always aimed at perfection, as we can see in the ugly and ungraceful stride of his male figures"; that the lack of "ideality" is "counteracted by the enchanting splendour of his treatment of flesh in itself, especially in paintings by his own hand, by the famous beauty of his nudes and their setting in light and chiaroscuro, by his general use of the nude in his work, harmonized by an unparalleled range of tones, of deeply luminous or softly shimmering colours in the drapery and setting"; or that the central female figure in *Andromeda Liberated by Perseus*" "in herself so fat and insignificant," must be appreciated "in all her luminous plenitude, from head to foot" (ibid., pp. 36, 40). Almost a half a century earlier, Kugler had written that Rubens's "figures are ennobled by the peculiar glow and vivid splendour of his colouring, and sometimes he seems to show even a . . . preference for common and vulgar forms. A sort of light from within shines through his figures . . . ; the glow, if one may so say, of a material inspiration, bursts through his compositions and reconciles us even to his less pleasing subjects" (*Handbook of the History of Painting*, 2:223–24).

258. *Recollections of Rubens*, pp. 40, 50–51. Burckhardt's view of Rubens' figures as ideal constructions by the Flemish artist rather than images of a given Flemish reality is quoted with approval by Robert Vischer in the essay on Rubens, which he published in 1904, six years after the appearance of Burckhardt's essay. See Robert Vischer, *Raffaele e Rubens: due saggi di critica d'arte*, trans. Elena Craveri Croce (Bari: Laterza, 1945), pp. 99, 152.

259. *Recollections of Rubens*, pp. 61–62.

260. Ibid., p. 66.

261. Ibid., pp. 66–68.

262. "Die Originalität der Themata das bekannte Hauptunglück der jetzigen Kunst, das Neuerfindenmüssen der Sachen" (quoted by Kaegi, *Jacob Burckhardt*, 6:650).

263. *Reflections on History*, p. 92.

264. In his 1877 lecture on Rembrandt, Burckhardt acknowledged Rembrandt's unique gifts as a painter of light and shadow, as Kugler had done several decades earlier in the unrevised edition of his *Handbuch*—though the acknowledgment is tinged with irony.

> Events, forms, natural objects are present for Rembrandt only insofar as air and light play magically on them. And the spectator is often carried away to the point that, along with the artist, he forgets what is being represented for the sake of the representation. . . . Rembrandt can discover unsuspected magic even in the coldest daylight. . . . But can we not see for ourselves, one might ask, the play of sunlight both in the open air and in enclosed spaces? Why need we follow this odd painter who often seems completely indifferent to objects? The answer to those questions runs that we could indeed see the light, but that

we discover how beautiful and infused with life it is only through the work of the painter. Only when the image of the world passes through an immortal human soul can the insignificant, even the unbeautiful—and there is never any shortage of either in Rembrandt—be mystically transfigured, as the Rembrandt enthusiasts say.

"Rembrandt," in *Gesamtausgabe,* 14:181.

265. Ibid., pp. 178–97.

266. Quoted by Joseph Gantner, "Jacob Burckhardts Urteil über Rembrandt," pp. 96–97.

267. Ibid., pp. 90–91.

268. *"Brutta e plebea"* ["ugly and vulgar"] was how Vasari's successor, Filippo Baldinucci, judged his work in 1686. See ibid., pp. 86–88; Vosmaer, *Rembrandt,* pp. 399–400.

269. In C. H. Balkema's *Biographie des peintres flamands et hollandais* (Ghent: H. Hoste, 1844), for instance, we still read that "son dessein est souvent incorrect, et ses ouvrages manquent du beau idéal de l'antique" (p. 274). On Rembrandt in Germany, see Johannes Stückelberger, *Rembrandt und die Moderne: Der Dialog mit Rembrandt in der deutschen Kunst um 1900* (Munich: Wilhelm Fink, 1996), pp. 30–53; on Rembrandt as "fantastic" and "bizarre," see ibid., pp. 31–32.

270. See Stückelberger, *Rembrandt und die Moderne:* "Many of the critics who were most enthusiastic about Rembrandt were also enthusiastic republicans" and "they saw a connection between Rembrandt's revolutionary art and the political and religious revolution in the Holland of his time" (p. 26; see also pp. 20, 30).

271. Théophile Gautier, *Critique artistique et littéraire,* ed. F. Gohim and R. Tisserand (Paris: Larousse, 1929), pp. 30, 69. Article in *Le Moniteur* (21 May 1859), in Marie-Hélène Girard, ed., *Théophile Gautier critique d'art: Extraits des Salons, !833–1872* (Paris: Séguier, 1994), pp. 176–77. "Un profond et mystérieux penseur," Gautier adds in a review of the *Histoire de la peinture flamande et hollandaise* by the popular writer Arsène Houssaye (1846) in the newspaper *La Presse* (11 January 1847).

272. *The Journal of Eugène Delacroix,* ed. Wellington, trans. Norton, pp. 109, 143, 356. G. F. Waagen described Rembrandt as "the Dutch Correggio" (*Handbuch der deutschen und niederländischen Malerei,* 2 vols. [Stuttgart: Ebner & Siebert, 1862], 2:96).

273. Théophile Thoré, *Musées de la Hollande,* 2 vols. (Paris: Jules Renouard, 1858, 1860), 1:ix–xi, 2:ix–xv. See also Jeroen Boomgard, *De verloren zoon. Rembrandt en de Nederlandse kunstgeschiedschrijving* (Amsterdam: Babylon-De Geus, 1995), pp. 101–2.

274. Vosmaer, *Rembrandt,* p. 413; other references: pp. 21–22, 112, 398–99. See also Vosmaer's earlier essay *Rembrandt Harmans van Rijn: les précurseurs et les années d'apprentissage* (The Hague, 1863).

275. Vosmaer, *Rembrandt,* p. 41.

276. In the sense that art had rendered itself incapable of expressing content and was thus no longer able to contribute to the coming into being of the absolute spirit. See *The Philosophy of Fine Art,* F. B. P. Osmaston's translation of the *Aesthetik* (London: G. Bell & Sons, 1920), 2:382–86 (pt. 2, subsection 3, ch. 3, sec. 3c).

277. The rooms in the Rijksmuseum were arranged so that the visitor would be led inevitably to that in which the *Night Watch* was hung, like the altarpiece in a house of worship. From the beginning, however, while the building was appreciated as a concept, a temple in honor of the nation and its national art, it was severely criticized as a place where paintings could be exhibited to advantage. Even the room devoted to the *Night Watch* was poorly lighted. See J. Becker, "'Ons Rijksmuseum wordt een tempel.' Zur Ikonographie des Amsterdamer Rijksmuseums," *Nederlands kunsthistorisch jaarboek* 35 (1985): 227–326; also An-

nemieke Hoogenboom, "Vaterlandse schilders verbeeld: Leven en werken van oude meesters als thema in de nederlandse beeldende kunst in de negentiende eeuw," in *Romantiek en Historische Cultuur,* ed. Jo Tollebeek, Frank Ankersmit, Wessel Krul [Groningen: Historische Uitgeverei, 1996], pp. 273–96).

278. Letter to Heinrich von Geymüller, 27 December 1874, *Briefe,* 5:260 ("Anstössige Gedanken" in German).

279. Maurer, *Jacob Burckhardt und Rubens,* p. 284, quoting from Burckhardt's lecture notes. Cf. the view of Thomas Thoré that Rembrandt offers a paradigm of a "democratic" way of painting, an "art for Man" (*Musées de la Hollande,* 1:ix–xi, 21–23; 2:ix–xv). See also Jeroen Boomgaard, *De verloren zoon.*

280. Cf. Stückelberger, *Rembrandt und die Moderne:* "In proportion as the veneration of Rembrandt increased, Burckhardt became more intensely critical of him. Burckhardt understood very clearly that the growing reputation of Rembrandt was intimately related to the coming of modernity. . . . His critique of Rembrandt was also a critique of modernity" (p. 232). Though a Rembrandt cult was slower to establish itself in Germany, Burckhardt was well acquainted with the art historian, Wilhelm von Bode, one of Rembrandt's major German champions. Burckhardt had given Bode carte blanche to revise *The Cicerone* for a new edition, and the two men had spent time together in Rome in 1875. It is conceivable that Rembrandt came up in their conversations and that this is what provoked Burckhardt to give his lecture on Rembrandt two years later. Ibid., p. 35.

281. Letter of 2 May 1855, *Briefe,* 3:213.

282. Bernd Roeck, "Aby Warburgs Seminarübungen über Jacob Burckhardt," pp. 67–69, 73. See also E. H. Gombrich, *Aby Warburg: An Intellectual Biography* (Oxford: Phaidon, 1986; 1st ed. 1970), pp. 254–59.

283. *Reflections on History,* p. 91.

284. Meier, *Stiften und Sammeln,* pp. 71–74. The comment was made by Albert Gessler.

285. It is only fair to note that French romantic critics like Théophile Gautier or Théophile Thoré found the stark, revolutionary realism of Courbet no easier to accept than Burckhardt. If Burckhardt was attached to the humanist tradition, they in turn clung to the romanticism of their youth; see Jean-Pierre Leduc-Adine, "Théophile Gautier et les réalistes," *Théophile Gautier: L'Art et l'Artiste,* Actes du Colloque International (Montpellier: Université Paul Valéry, 1982), 1:21–33.

286. On the falling out of Burckhardt and Böcklin, see *Böcklin Memoiren: Tagebuchblätter von Böcklins Gattin Angela,* ed. with commentary by Ferdinand Runkel (Berlin: Internationale Verlagsanstalt für Kunst und Literatur, 1910), pp. 127 ff. Runkel related that for a painting of Mary Magdalen grieving over the body of Christ in 1867–1868, Böcklin originally wanted to depict the dead Christ in profile, as Holbein had done in the striking *Leichnam Christi* in the Basel Kunstmuseum that so gripped Dostoievsky. Burckhardt dissuaded him from presenting such a stark and uncompromising image of death and in the finished painting the face of Christ is half turned toward the viewer and the whole figure is softened in relation to the Holbein Christ. Böcklin apparently always regretted that he had allowed Burckhardt to talk him around. "Burckhardt," Runkel commented, "hatte Muster im Kopfe" ("had models in mind") and he considered it a virtue in modern painters to imitate great masters from the past. "Das Neue an Böcklin befremdete ihn, es war ihm mehr Fehler als Vorzug" ("He was put off by what was new in Böcklin, judging it more a defect than a quality") (p. 132). See also the discussion of Böcklin's *Trauer der Magdalena an der Leiche Christi,* in the Basel Kunstmuseum, by Dorothea Christ in Dorothea Christ and Christian Geelhaar, eds., *Arnold Böcklin: Die Gemälde im Kunstmuseum Basel* (Basel: Kunstmuseum; Einsiedeln: Eidolon, 1990), p. 94. Likewise Böcklin's *Magna Mater* fresco for the museum

in the Augustinergasse in Basel, with its reminiscences of Rubens and classical allegory, stands in striking contrast to the later extremely simplified images of antique womanhood, as in the painting entitled *Das Drama*, executed after he had thrown off the protection and tutelage of his influential fellow citizen. On Burckhardt's ignorance of newer trends in German painting, see Schlink, "Jacob Burckhardts Künstlerrat," p. 286. For an extremely nuanced view of the Böcklin-Burckhardt falling out and a partial justification of Burckhardt as adviser, see Meier, *Stiften und Sammeln*, p. 96.

287. Adolph Bayersdorfer, article in the Vienna *Neue Freie Presse* (1874), reproduced in *Adolph Bayersdorfers Leben und Schaffen: Aus seinem Nachlass*, ed. Hans Mackowsky, August Pauly, Wilhelm Weigand (Munich, 1908), pp. 221, 223, and quoted in Anne-S. Domm, *Der "Klassische" Hans von Marées und die Existenzmalerei am Anfang des 20.* Jahrhunderts (Munich: Kommisverlag Uni-Druck, 1989; Miscellanea Bavarica Monacensia, 146), pp. 58–59. On the contrast between the "descriptive" emphasis of northern, particularly Dutch art and the "narrative" and rhetorical character of Italian art, see Svetlana Alpers' now classic study *The Art of Describing* (Chicago: University of Chicago Press, 1983), Introduction.

288. Letter to Conrad Fiedler, 21 September 1877, in Hans von Marées, *Briefe*, ed. Anne-S. Domm (Munich and Zurich: Piper, 1987), p. 169.

289. Letter to his brother Georg, 1 May 1879, in *Briefe*, ed. Domm, p. 189; letter to his patron, Dr. Conrad Fiedler, 15 July 1883, ibid., p. 264.

290. Letter to Conrad Fiedler, 12 June 1876, ibid., p. 146: "Freilich bin ich überzeugt, dass meine Bestrebungen mich immer weiter aus dem Getümmel des modernen Wirrwarrs entfernen werden." Letter to Fiedler, 15 August 1878, ibid., p. 181: ". . . nach Klarheit zu ringen und gegen den Strom der Zeit nach Kräften zu stemmen."

291. Letter to Conrad Fiedler, 21 September 1877, ibid., p. 169. Cf. another letter to Fiedler, 21 January 1878, ibid., p. 176: "Art without externally established constraints seems to me like a woman deprived of the guiding hand of the male. That is certainly the cause of our contemporary directionlessless. Where one does find common effort, it is directed toward a miserable goal and the realm of genuine representation is more and more abandoned. The majority [of artists] would rather outlive themselves as quickly as possible [i.e., by producing what the market wants] than strive to achieve what can be built upon and developed [as Marées himself believed he was doing in his search for the true 'grammar' of painting]."

292. Konrad Fiedler, *Schriften zur Kunst*, with an introduction by Gottfried Boehm (Munich: Wilhelm Fink, 1971; reprint of 1913–1914 Munich ed.), 1:165. The son of a wealthy Jewish industrialist from the Leipzig area, Fiedler was a considerable figure in the philosophy of aesthetics. His work provides a surprisingly early philosophical justification of "abstract" painting. An English translation of one of Fiedler's essays, "Über die Beurteilung von Werken der bildenen Kunst" (1876), was published in 1949, as abstract painting began to win general acceptance: *On Judging Works of Visual Art*, trans. Henry Schaeffer-Simmern and Fulmer Mood (Berkeley and Los Angeles: University of California Press).

293. "Über erzählende Malerei," *Gesamtausgabe*, 14:303, 315; see also the lecture "Die Malerei und das Neue Testament" (1885), *Gesamtausgabe*, 14:331–44, where Burckhardt contended that "the decisive factor in art is not an ever new 'This,' not the continual material discovery of hitherto non-existent topics, but the 'How' which is revealed in ever new ways of conceiving and modelling that which is permanent" ("in der Kunst nicht ein stets neues *Was*, nicht die beständige materielle Neuerfindung von noch nicht dagewesenen Aufgaben das Entscheidende ist, sondern das *Wie*, welches sich hier in der stets neuen Auffassung und Gestaltung des Feststehenden offenbart") (p. 332).

294. See the fine pages in Schlink, "Jacob Burckhardts Künstlerrat," pp. 283–86.

295. Meier, *Stiften und Sammeln*, p. 116.

296. See Joseph Mali, "Jacob Burckhardt: Myth, History and Mythistory," pp. 99, 103–5.

297. Letter of 21 May 1852, *Briefe*, 3:151.

298. *Cicerone* (Engl.), pp. 178, 190.

299. *Gesamtausgabe*, 13:23–28.

Chapter Fourteen

Author's note: The first epigraph that opens part 4 is from a letter by Gerhard Ritter to his teacher and friend, Hermann Oncken, 11 October 1934, in *Gerhard Ritter: Ein politischer Historiker in seinen Briefen*, ed. Klaus Schwabe and Rolf Reichardt (Boppard am Rhein: Boldt, 1984), p. 275. Ritter was teaching at the University of Freiburg and had been sounded out about his interest in the chair of history at the University of Basel. He was at the top of the list, he had been told, should there be no suitable Swiss candidate. In the end, the chair went to Werner Kaegi.

The second epigraph is from Friedrich Meinecke, "Ranke und Burckhardt," a lecture delivered to the German Academy of Sciences, May 22, 1947, published in the Academy's *Vorträge und Schriften*, no. 27 (1948), reprinted in *Aphorismen und Skizzen zur Geschichte* (1952) and in Friedrich Meinecke, *Werke*, ed. Hans Herzfeld et al. (Darmstadt: Toeche-Mittler; Munich: R. Oldenbourg; Stuttgart: K. F. Koehler, 1957–1979), 7:93–110. English translation (not used here) in Hans Kohn, ed., *German History: Some New Views* (Boston: Beacon Press, 1954), pp. 141–56.

1. In his letter to Vischer-Bilfinger, Ritschl noted that the young man was "not without some private means—which in my opinion is relevant to an appointment at Basel" (quoted by Carl Paul Janz, *Friedrich Nietzsche: Biographie* [Munich: Carl Hanser, 1978], 1:255). Nietzsche's salary was set at three thousand francs. This was raised to four thousand francs in 1872, after the young professor turned down an offer from Greifswald.

2. In vol. 1 (correspondence) of *Overbeckiana*, ed. E. Staehelin and M. Gabathuler (Basel: Helbing & Lichtenhahn, 1962), 1:178.

3. Franz Overbeck, *Über die Christlichkeit unserer heutigen Theologie* (Darmstadt: Wissenschaftliche Buchgesellschaft, 1981; orig. 1873), afterword to the second edition (Leipzig, 1903), pp. 168–69 (hereafter *CHT*).

4. Ibid., p. 169.

5. Janz, *Friedrich Nietzsche*, 1:324.

6. *Selected Letters of Friedrich Nietzsche*, ed. and trans. Christopher Middleton (Chicago and London: University of Chicago Press, 1969), p. 62.

7. David Marc Hoffmann, "Nietzsche und die Schweiz," in *Nietzsche und die Schweiz*, ed. David Marc Hoffmann (Zurich: OZV Offizin Zürich; Strauhof Zürich, 1994), pp. 7–16, at p. 10.

8. Quoted by Andreas Cesana, "Bachofen und Nietzsche," in *Nietzsche und die Schweiz*, ed. Hoffmann, pp. 55–63, at pp. 57–58. Cf. Lionel Gossman, *Orpheus Philologus: Bachofen versus Mommsen on the Study of Antiquity* (Philadelphia: American Philosophical Society, 1983; Transactions, 73, 5), p. 5, note 11.

9. Letter of 29 May 1869, in Friedrich Nietzsche, *Briefwechsel*, ed. G. Colli and M. Montinari (Berlin: De Gruyter, 1975–1984), in 3 sections and 16 vols., sec. 2, vol. 1, p. 11.

10. Letter of 29 May 1869, *Briefwechsel*, sec. 2, vol. 1, p. 13.

11. Letter to Erwin Rohde, 27 November 1870, *Briefwechsel*, sec. 2, vol. 1, p. 159.

12. Letter to Elisabeth Nietzsche, 29 May 1869, *Briefwechsel*, sec. 2, vol. 1, p. 11.

13. Letter of 7/8 November 1872, *Briefwechsel*, sec. 2, vol. 3, p. 89.

14. Letter of 29 March 1871, *Briefwechsel*, sec. 2, vol. 1, p. 190.

15. Letter of 26 August 1872, *Briefwechsel,* sec. 2, vol. 3, p. 48. For Schopenhauer on education and the universities, see "On Philosophy at the Universities," *Parerga et Paralipomena,* trans. E. F. J. Payne (Oxford: Clarendon Press, 1977), 1:137–97, and "On Learning and the Learned," ibid., 2:479–90.

16. Letter to Erwin Rohde, 15 December 1870, *Briefwechsel,* sec. 2, vol. 1, p. 165.

17. Nietzsche received only one invitation—from tiny Greifswald—and that was before *The Birth of Tragedy* had been reviewed.

18. See Gordon A. Craig, *The Triumph of Liberalism: Zurich in the Golden Age 1830–1869* (New York: Charles Scribner's Sons, 1989).

19. See above all Carl Albrecht Bernoulli, *Overbeck und Friedrich Nietzsche: eine Freundschaft,* 2 vols. (Jena: Diederichs, 1908); Janz, *Friedrich Nietzsche,* 1:358–63; Barbara von Reibnitz, "'Ich verdanke Dir soviel, lieber Freund . . .' Nietzsches Freundschaft mit Franz Overbeck," in *Nietzsche und die Schweiz,* ed. Hoffmann, vol. 5, pp. 47–54.

20. Von Reibnitz, "'Ich verdanke Dir soviel, lieber Freund . . .' Nietzsches Freundschaft mit Franz Overbeck," p. 48.

21. "Kirchenlexicon," ed. Barbara von Reibnitz, vol. 4 of *Werke und Nachlass,* ed. Ekkehard Stegemann et al. (Stuttgart and Weimar: J. B. Metzler, 1994–) (hereafter "Kirchenlexicon"), p. 63.

22. On "die industrielle Ausbeutung des Nietzsche'schen Nachlasses durch seine Schwester," see ibid., pp. 91–92.

23. There is a good account, in English, of the relations between Overbeck and Elisabeth Förster-Nietzsche in H. F. Peters, *Zarathustra's Sister: The Case of Elisabeth and Friedrich Nietzsche* (New York: Crown Publishers, 1977), pp. 30, 70, 98, 129–30, 135, 147–48, 180. See also Elizabeth Förster-Nietzsche, *Das Nietzsche Archiv, seine Freunde und Feinde* (Berlin: Marquardt & Co., 1907), which openly attacks the Overbecks, and Carl Albrecht Bernoulli, *Franz Overbeck und Friedrich Nietzsche,* 2 vols. (Jena: Eugen Diederichs, 1908), which presents Overbeck's side in the dispute with Förster-Nietzsche.

24. For a more detailed account in English of Overbeck's background and education, see Lionel Gossman, "Antimodernism in Nineteenth-Century Basle: Franz Overbeck's Antitheology and J. J. Bachofen's Antiphilology," *Interpretation* 16 (1989): 359–89. See also Janz, *Friedrich Nietzsche,* 1:358–63.

25. See Janz, *Friedrich Nietzsche,* 1:361.

26. See Gossman, "Antimodernism in Nineteenth-Century Basle," 16:364.

27. Walter Benjamin testified to Overbeck's integrity by selecting a letter from him to Nietzsche (25 March 1883) to close the collection of letters by upright Germans between the 1780s and the 1880s that he published under the pseudonym Detlef Holz in the mid-1930s in order to counter the image of German culture being propagated by the National Socialists: *Deutsche Menschen: eine Folge von Briefen* (Lucerne: Vita Nova Verlag, 1936; new ed. Frankfurt am Main: Suhrkamp, 1962).

28. Franz Overbeck, *Selbstbekenntnisse,* ed. Eberhardt Vischer (Basel: Schwabe, 1941) (hereafter *Selbstbekenntnisse*), pp. 116, 118.

29. Quoted by Hans Schindler, *Barth und Overbeck* (Gotha: Klotz, 1936; Darmstadt: Wissenschaftliche Buchgesellschaft, 1974), p. 141. On Overbeck's theology, see the fundamental study by Walter Nigg, *Franz Overbeck: Versuch einer Würdigung* (Munich: Beck, 1968). A sharp, succinct presentation of his thought is to be found in English in Karl Löwith, *From Hegel to Nietzsche,* trans. David E. Green (New York: Holt, Reinhart & Winston, 1964; orig. German, Zurich, 1941), pp. 377–78.

30. *Selbstbekenntnisse,* pp. 140, 159.

31. The question of Overbeck's faith remains disputed. Karl Barth took him most seri-

ously as a theologian (Barth, "Unsettled Questions for Theology Today" [1920], in his *Theology and Church: Shorter Writings 1920–1928*, trans. Louise P. Smith [London: S.C.M. Press, 1962], pp. 58–73); likewise John E. Wilson, "Die Zweideutigkeiten in Franz Overbecks Aussagen über sein Unglauben," *Theologische Zeitschrift* 40 (1984): 211–20. In the entry under his name in the *Evangelisches Kirchenlexikon* (Göttingen: Vandenhoek & Ruprecht, 1958), p. 1786, W. Philipp offers a clear and simple summary of his main ideas and characterizes him as *"der radikale Agnostiker."*

32. Quoted in Bernoulli, *Franz Overbeck und Friedrich Nietzsche*, 1:17–18. Surprisingly, remarkably similar reservations were expressed in 1871 by the Hegelian literary scholar Gervinus: "It would be a sorry perversion of developments if Germany were to give up her activity as a people of culture [*Kulturvolk*] in favor of that of a people of power [*Machtvolk*] and were to be caught up in one war after another" (*Hinterlassene Schriften* [1872], p. 29, quoted by Friedrich Meinecke, *Ausgewählter Briefwechsel*, ed. Ludwig Dehio and Peter Classen [Stuttgart: K. F. Koehler Verlag], 1962], letter to his former student, Siegfried Kaehler, 26 March 1948, in Meinecke, *Werke* [Darmstadt: Toeche-Miller; Munich: R Oldenbourg; Stuttgart: K. F. Koehler, 1958–1968], 7:521).

33. *Christentum und Kultur: Gedanken und Anmerkungen zur modernene Theologie von Franz Overbeck*, ed. from Overbeck's *Nachlass* by C. A. Bernoulli (Basel: Schwabe, 1919) (hereafter *CK*), p. 293. This text has been reprinted as vol. 6/1 (1996) of the ongoing scholarly edition of Overbeck's Complete Printed Works and *Nachlass* (Stuttgart: J. B. Metzler). The text prepared by Bernoulli from Overbeck's copious notes in his "Kirchenlexicon" (now accessible in their original form in vols. 4 and 5 of the new edition) strongly influenced the view of Overbeck handed down by way of Karl Barth, Martin Heidegger, Karl Löwith, and others. In important respects, however, it presents a distorted and particular account of Overbeck's ideas according to the editors of the new edition. For a discussion of Bernoulli's text and its relation to Overbeck's notes in the *Nachlass*, see Barbara von Reibnitz's introduction to vol. 4, *Werke und Nachlass*, pp. xiv–xviii.

34. Quoted by Franz Herre, *Nation ohne Staat* (Bergisch Gladbach: Gustav Lübbe, 1982 [orig. Cologne, 1967]), p. 266.

35. *CHT*, p. 169 (postscript to the 2nd edition of the pamphlet). The empire Germany had become since he left it in 1870, he explained, "has been in a state of war with me since 1873."

36. *Selbstbekenntnisse*, p. 122.

37. *CK*, pp. 13, 236, 273, 274, 253, 273 (in the order quoted).

38. Ibid., p. 242.

39. Ibid., p. 124.

40. *Overbeckiana*, 1:119 (letter of 1 November 1875). There is an echo of Overbeck's views in Thomas Mann's *Dr. Faustus* (XI): "In my view, liberal theology is a *contradictio in adjecto*. . . . A proponent of culture, ready to adapt itself to the ideas of bourgeois society, it degrades the religious to a function of the human . . . an ethical progressiveness."

41. *CHT*, p. 129. Cf. Nietzsche's comment in *The Birth of Tragedy* (sec. 10) that "[i]t is the sure sign of the death of a religion when its mythic presuppositions become systematized" (*The Birth of Tragedy; The Genealogy of Morals*, trans. Francis Golffing [Garden City: Doubleday, 1956], p. 68). The recently published correspondence of Overbeck and Lagarde, spanning the years 1864–1882 shows that Overbeck read Lagarde attentively and quite enthusiastically, especially in the years 1872–1878, and that he passed Lagarde's *Über das verhältnis des deutschen staates zu theologie, kirche und religion* (Göttingen: Dieterich, 1873) on to Nietzsche (who judged it 50 percent true and 50 percent false). The relationship between the two men in these years appears to have been quite friendly and it was only later in his

private notebooks that Overbeck became very critical of Lagarde. Even in these letters from the 1870s, however, Overbeck politely expressed reservations. After receiving from Lagarde a copy of his *Politische Aufsätze* (Göttingen: Dieterichs, 1874) he wrote (30 December 1874): "My reservations here, as in your previous work [*Über das verhältnis . . .*], concern your expectations with respect to a national religion. In fact, your own critique of the current situation makes even more problematic the issue of where the energies are to be found, on which such hopes could be grounded." In a later letter (14 January 1876) written in response to the receipt of another work by Lagarde—*Über die gegenwärtige lage des deutschen reichs* (Göttingen: Dieterichs, 1876)—he takes up this matter again: "May I hastily express my dissent on one matter: . . . Since I am deeply concerned, like you, with the threat of state omnipotence in Germany, it appears to me all the more inadvisable to ascribe tasks to the state, which it could carry out—if at all—only through the most extreme exercise of its particular powers and which would in any case drive us even deeper into the grip of the state." See Niklaus Peter and Andreas Urs Sommer, "Franz Overbecks Briefwechsel mit Paul de Lagarde," *Zeitschrift für neuere Theologiegeschichte* 3 (1996): 127–71.

42. "Kirchenlexicon," *Werke und Nachlass,* 4:107–8.

43. *CHT,* p. 77. For a brief account of Overbeck's distinction between modernity and modernism, see my article "Antimodernism in Nineteenth Century Basle: Franz Overbeck's Antitheology and J. J. Bachofen's Antiphilology," 16:370–73.

44. *Selbstbekenntnisse,* p. 166.

45. See my "Antimodernism in Nineteenth-Century Basle," 16:376.

46. *CK,* p. 286.

47. See Janz, *Friedrich Nietzsche,* 1:244–45, 258–59. Even when Nietzsche criticized Schopenhauer on philosophical grounds, he continued to venerate his basic approach to philosophy: "This is the Age of Schopenhauer," he declared. The qualities in Schopenhauer that were relevant to the times were "a healthy pessimism that arises from commitment to the Ideal, a manly seriousness, a distaste for everything hollow and airy, and an inclination toward what is sound and simple. In contrast to Kant, Schopenhauer is a poet, in contrast to Goethe, he is a philosopher. He has a style of his own, whereas most philosophers do not. . . . Schopenhauer is the philosopher of a revived classicism, of a Germanic Hellenism; Schopenhauer is the philosopher of a regenerated Germany." Even if it is not possible to accept all his philosophical arguments, "he is right in his being, and we want to stick to that. A philosopher can be something that no philosophy can ever be: the source of many different philosophies, the great man." Nietzsche and Rohde religiously noted Schopenhauer's birthday and felt impelled to write to each other with special seriousness at that time. "On this festive day (*'dies festa'*), permit me to praise you openly to your face," Rohde wrote. And on 22 February 1869 Nietzsche answered: "On this day, Schopenhauer's birthday, there is no one to whom I can speak as freely as to you. . . ." (*Gesammelte Briefe,* ed. E. Förster-Nietzsche and F. Schöll, 5 vols. [Berlin and Leipzig: Schuster & Loeffler, 1900–1909], 2:134.)

48. Letter of 29 May 1869, *Briefwechsel,* sec. 2, vol. 1, p. 11.

49. Letter of 28 January 1872, *Briefwechsel,* sec. 2, vol. 1, p. 279.

50. Letter of mid-November 1872, *Briefwechsel,* sec. 2, vol. 3, p. 89.

51. Letter from Ritschl to Nietzsche, 14 February 1872, *Briefwechsel,* sec. 2, vol. 2, pp. 541–43.

52. *Birth of Tragedy,* p. 9.

53. Ibid., pp. 59–60.

54. Ibid., p. 108.

55. Ibid., p. 60.

56. Ibid., p. 108.

57. Ibid., p. 72. On the face of it, it is hard to see why the slave should be complacent or

content with his condition. Nietzsche presumably has in mind the bourgeois—the *"satisfait"* in Overbeck's terms—who is enslaved by his material comforts, no longer capable of heroism or imagination, and unmoved by any self-transcending vision.

58. Ibid., p. 77. See also pp. 88–89.

59. Ibid., pp. 110, 88, 93, 83, 109 (in order of quotation).

60. Quoted ibid., p. 11.

61. Ibid., p. 82.

62. Letter of 13 December 1834, quoted in Max Hoffmann, *August Boeckh: Lebensbeschreibung und Auswahl aus seinem wissenschaftlichen Briefwechsel* (Leipzig: B. G. Teubner, 1901), p. 181.

63. *Birth of Tragedy*, p. 29.

64. Ibid., p. 39.

65. Ibid., p. 94.

66. Quoted by Janz, *Friedrich Nietzsche*, 1:245.

67. Letter of 7 November 1870, *Briefwechsel*, sec. 2, vol. 1, p. 156.

68. *Birth of Tragedy*, p. 124.

69. Ibid., p. 137.

70. Ibid., p. 138. It should be obvious that the Germany from which Nietzsche hoped for renewal was by no means the Germany of Kaiser Wilhelm I. Of that Germany, Nietzsche had the following to say in the *Nachlass:* "'Deutschland, Deutschland über alles' may be the most idiotic phrase ever uttered. Why Germany, I ask, as long as it aims at nothing, stands for nothing, proposes nothing that is worthier than anything any power up to now has represented! In itself Germany is just one more great state, one more stupidity in the world" (*Der Freie Geist: Ein Nietzsche-Brevier,* ed. J. Leithäuser [Wiesbaden: Limes-Verlag, 1947], p. 111. Likewise in *Human All Too Human:* "To be a good German means to de-Germanize oneself" (Part 2, trans. Paul V. Cohn, in *The Complete Works of Friedrich Nietzsche,* ed. Oscar Levy, [Edinburgh and London: T. N. Foulis, 1909–1911], 7:154).

71. *Birth of Tragedy*, p. 110.

72. *On the Future of our Educational Institutions; Homer and Classical Philology,* trans. J. M. Kennedy, in *The Complete Works of Friedrich Nietzsche,* 3:12–13.

73. Ibid., p. 140.

74. Ibid., p. 31.

75. Ibid., p. 38.

76. Ibid., p. 36.

77. Ibid., pp. 95–97.

78. Ibid., p. 39.

79. Ibid., pp. 80–81.

80. Ibid., p. 135.

81. Ibid., p. 41.

82. Ibid., p. 34. "Here lies the whole secret of culture—namely, that an innumerable host of men struggle to achieve it and work hard to that end, ostensibly in their own interests, whereas at bottom it is only in order that it may be possible for the few to attain it" (ibid.).

83. Ibid.

84. Ibid., pp. 67–68.

85. Ibid., p. 142.

86. Ibid., p. 38.

87. Janz, *Friedrich Nietzsche*, 1:448.

88. *On the Future of Our Educational* Systems, in *The Complete Works of Friedrich Nietzsche,* 3:8, repeated in first lecture, 3:16.

89. Letter to Richard Wagner, 7/8 November 1872, *Briefwechsel,* sec. 2, vol. 3, p. 89. Likewise to Erwin Rohde, November 1872: "That our little university should suffer because of me is very hard for me to bear" (*Briefwechsel,* sec. 2, vol. 3, p. 85).

90. Letter of 26 August 1872, *Briefwechsel,* sec. 2, vol. 3, p. 48.

91. *"Ein ewiges Pfeifen und Heulen"* (letter of 17 March 1872, *Briefe,* ed. Max Burckhardt, 10 vols. plus index vol. (Basel: Schwabe, 1949–1994), 5:154.

92. See letter to Friedrich von Preen, 23 December 1871, *Briefe,* 5:148–49.

93. Letter of 3 April 1879, *Briefwechsel,* sec. 2, vol. 5, p. 402. Nietzsche defined his "Basileophobia" as "a true anguish and fear of the bad water, the bad air, the whole oppressive nature of that accursed breeding ground of all my ills." A few days later in another letter to Overbeck he wrote that he was looking forward to their reunion but wished it did not have to take place "in that accursed Basel, which fills me with the dread people have of ghosts" (letter of 18 April 1879, *Briefwechsel,* sec. 2, vol. 5, p. 409). On Nietzsche's ambivalent relation to Basel, see the excellent pages in Alfred von Martin, *Nietzsche und Burckhardt,* 2nd ed. (Munich: Ernst Reinhard, 1942), pp. 18–24.

94. *Protestant Theology in the Nineteenth Century* (London: S.C.M. Press, 1972), p. 145 (translation slightly modified).

95. "My Life in Retrospect" (much abbreviated English version of *Selbstbiographie,* in *Myth, Religion, and Mother Right: Selected Writings of J. J. Bachofen,* trans. Ralph Mannheim, introduction by Joseph Campbell (Princeton: Princeton University Press, 1967; Bollingen Series, 84), p. 9.

96. Josef Oswald, "Basler Milieustudien," in his *Unbekannte Aufsätze Jakob Burckhardts aus Paris, Rom und Mailand* (Basel: Schwabe, 1922), pp. 11–22, at p. 11.

97. *Overbeckiana,* 1:192.

98. "Kirchenlexicon," 4:129.

99. Cesana, "Bachofen und Nietzsche," p. 59.

100. *Gesammelte Werke,* ed. Karl Meuli (Basel: Schwabe, 1943–1967; publication interrupted at vol. 10), 6:431 note 2.

101. Ibid., 1:364. For an excellent overview, see Cesana, "Bachofen und Nietzsche."

102. "Kirchenlexicon," *Werke und Nachlass,* 4:118–19. See also pp. 297–98.

103. Ibid., p. 212.

104. In a humorous passage of his essay "Jacob Burckhardt und der Student" the poet Carl Spitteler recalls that Burckhardt had high regard for learning, despite his denigrating remarks about the *viri eruditissimi.* "He vastly overrated the value of hard work in education," Spitteler—who seems not to have been a particularly good student—noted. "During my student days, when I used to visit him in his rooms, I regularly observed . . . such a deep veneration for learning, and especially for philological learning, both in his language and in his tone of voice that I constantly found myself wondering whether this remarkable fondness for cramming and dimwitted crammers might not be a weakness of some sort. How he would roll his eyes in veneration, for instance, as though at the sight of the holy monstrance, as he announced: 'The Saxons are excellent Latinists.' . . . And how proud he was of his own (not insignificant) philological learning. How he reveled in Latin and Greek expressions! On one occasion I wanted to talk to him about a work of Lucian's. No sooner had I mentioned the title than he cried out in a transport: 'Did you notice? Did you notice?' 'Notice what?' 'Did you really not notice?' 'Not notice what?' 'That it's an akephalon.' 'That it's what?' 'An akephalon.' 'What's an akephalon?' 'A book, the beginning or head of which has been lost,' he answered seriously and ponderously. . . . He was so carried away by the excitement of his philological delight that he had not a word left for the content" (*Gesammelte Werke* [Zurich: Artemis-Verlag], 6:407). Similar memories of Burckhardt's veneration for learning can be

found in the essay entitled "Böcklin, Burckhardt, Basel": "The 'sources' have a sacred quality for him, and if they are read in the original, even something 'magical,' as he himself liked to put it. He has an immense respect for philology. . . ." (ibid., pp. 163–65).

105. "Kirchenlexicon," *Werke und Nachlass,* 4:120.

106. Ibid., p. 381.

107. Ibid., p. 383.

108. Individual freedom is harder to achieve for an aristocrat than for a bourgeois, Overbeck suggested, but there is a greater danger that the freedom of the bourgeois will have something "Philistine" about it. As the aristocrat is used to exercising self-discipline, his individual freedom is more likely to have a noble quality. See ibid., p. 616.

109. "The world was not created for the individual and in no circumstances is it the world's job to concern itself with the individual. But it is the individual's job, in all circumstances, to find his place in the world. If it comes to a conflict, it goes without saying that it will be at the expense of the individual" (ibid.).

110. Ibid., p. 614.

111. Ibid., p. 618.

112. Ibid., p. 618.

113. Ibid., pp. 212–13. The lines are from the end of *Faust,* pt. 1.

114. Ibid., pp. 18–19.

Chapter Fifteen

1. Hugh Trevor-Roper, "Jacob Burckhardt," *Proceedings of the British Academy* 70 (1984): 359–78 (Master Mind Lecture, 11 December 1984). See also the equally pithy and even shorter introduction Trevor-Roper wrote for the English translation of *Historische Fragmente,* published as *Judgments on History and Historians,* trans. Harry Zohn (Boston: Beacon Press, 1958), pp. xi–xxi.

2. Trevor-Roper, "Jacob Burckhardt," p. 361.

3. Ibid.

4. Ibid., p. 364.

5. Ibid., p. 365.

6. Ibid., p. 370.

7. Ibid.

8. Ibid., p. 378. Meinecke's treatment of Burckhardt in his 1906 review of *Weltgeschichtliche Betrachtungen* is a good deal more even-handed than Trevor-Roper indicated. Meinecke himself objected to the view that he had held Burckhardt's nonparticipation in the national struggle for a German state against him—a view reiterated fairly recently in Sergio Pisone, *Federico Meinecke e la crisi dello stato nazionale tedesco* (Turin: Edizioni Giapachelli, 1969). "No," Meinecke wrote in 1943 to his colleague Walter Goetz, "I only pointed out that by not participating in this struggle he inevitably had to come to a different historical vision of things, and I still remember very vividly the reflective mood I was put in by my reading of the *Weltgeschichtliche Betrachtungen* and how unsatisfactory I considered Erich Marcks's oral comment that Burckhardt saw the world only from the narrow corner of the Basel patriciate. That mood first found full expression at the end of the First World War, but the seeds of it lie far further back in my past" (Friedrich Meinecke, *Ausgewählter Briefwechsel,* letter of 22 March 1943, in *Werke,* ed. H. Herzfeld et al. [Darmstadt: Toeche-Mittler; Munich: R. Oldenbourg; Stuttgart: K. F. Koehler, 1957–1979], 7:214–15). Meinecke's correspondence and his other writings lend support to his claim that he was preoccupied throughout almost his entire career with Burckhardt as the representative of a significant *historia altera.* On the Burckhardt–Ranke "parallel" as a persistent theme of

Meinecke's work, see J. L. Herkless, "Meinecke and the Ranke–Burckhardt Problem," *History and Theory* 9 (1970): 290–321, especially pp. 291, 319.

9. Trevor-Roper, "Jacob Burckhardt," p. 378. Even Max Weber—while conceding, as did Meinecke in his review of the *Welthistorische Betrachtungen* for the *Historische Zeitschrift* (1906, 97:557–62, at p. 559), that small states have their own part to play in history and in promoting German culture—was committed to the idea that Germany had a historical destiny that can only be played out on the stage of global politics and through the agency of the *Machtstaat;* see Max Weber, "Zwischen zwei Gesetzen" and "Deutschland unter den europäischen Weltmächten" (1916), in *Gesammelte Politische Schriften,* 2nd ed., ed. Johannes Winckelmann (Tübingen: J.C.B. Mohr, 1958), pp. 139–42, 170–72; Raymond Aron, "Max Weber and Power-politics" in *Max Weber and Sociology Today,* ed. Otto Stammer, trans. Kathleen Morris (Oxford: Basil Blackwell, 1971), pp. 83–100.

10. Trevor-Roper, "Jacob Burckhardt," p. 378. Erich Rothacker's essay on Burckhardt in the biographical dictionary *Die Grossen Deutschen* (ed. Willy Andreas and Wilhelm von Scholz [Berlin: Propyläen-Verlag, 1936], 3:620–35) attempts to "salvage" Burckhardt for the new National-Socialist Germany by interpreting his views of power as virtually identical with those of Treitschke (p. 633). Two books by the sociologist Alfred von Martin, who resigned his academic position in 1933—*Nietzsche und Burckhardt* (Munich: Ernst Reinhardt, 2nd ed. 1942] and *Die Religion Jacob Burckhardts: eine Studie zum Thema Humanismus und Christentum* (Munich: Ernst Reinhardt, 1942; 2nd ed. 1947)—were not incorrectly understood to be covertly critical of the Nazi regime and were not widely distributed. In 1943, all copies of *Die Religion Jacob Burckhardts* were confiscated by the Gestapo.

11. *Overbeckiana,* ed. E. Staehelin and M. Gabathuler (Basel: Helbing & Lichtenhahn, 1962), 1:105; cf. Heinrich von Treitschke, *Briefe,* ed. Max Cornicelius (Leipzig: Hirzel, 1914–1920), 3:375, letter of 28 October 1873.

12. *Christentum und Kultur: Gedanken und Anmerkungen zur modernene Theologie von Franz Overbeck,* ed. from Overbeck's *Nachlass* by C. A. Bernoulli (Basel: Schwabe, 1919), pp. 198, 209; cf. the re-edition of this text, Franz Overbeck, *Werke und Nachlass,* vol. 6/1, at pp. 235, 246.

13. Letter of 7 November 1870, *Briefwechsel,* ed. G. Colli and M. Montinari (Berlin: De Gruyter, 1975–1984), in 3 sections and 16 vols., sec. 2, vol. 1, p. 155.

14. Not surprisingly, Schmitt reviewed Steding's book enthusiastically. See Carl Schmitt, "Neutralität und Neutralisierungen: zu Christoph Steding, 'Das Reich und die Krankheit der europäischen Kultur'" [1939], *Positionen und Begriffe: in Kampf mit Weimar-Genf-Versailles 1923–1939* (Hamburg: Hanseatische Verlagsanstalt, 1940), pp. 271–95.

15. See, for instance, "Das Zeitalter der Neutralisierungen und Entpolitisierungen," presented at Barcelona in 1929 and published in *Positionen und Begriffe,* pp. 120–32. Even after the catastrophic collapse of the Third Reich, Schmitt explicitly rejected Burckhardt's characterization of power as evil. Evil, he argued on the basis of his own variety of Christian theology, lies not in the will to power, but in the will to powerlessness. Carl Schmitt, *Glossarium: Aufzeichnungen der Jahre 1947–1951,* ed. Eberhard Freiherr von Medem (Berlin: Duncker & Humblot, 1991), p. 139.

16. Christoph Steding, *Das Reich und die Krankheit der europäischen Kultur* (Hamburg: Hanseatische Verlagsanstalt, 1938), pp. 39–40, 60, 65–67, 94, 101–2, 145–46, *et passim.* The similarity between the obsession with *Baseliansierung* and the obsession with *Judaisierung* needs no comment. In similar vein, Gerhard Schröder, *Geschichtschreibung als politische Erziehungsmacht* (Hamburg: Hanseatische Verlagsanstalt, 1939). Both authors were associated with Walter Frank's notorious "Reichsinstitut für Geschichte des neuen Deutschlands."

17. See the excellent pages in Carlo Antoni, *From History to Sociology: The Transition in*

German Historical Thinking, trans. Hayden V. White (Detroit: Wayne State University Press, 1959; orig. Italian: Florence, 1940), pp. 86–92.

18. See Dietrich Schäfer, *Das eigentliche Arbeitsgebiet der Geschichte* (Jena: Gustav Fischer, 1888); Eberhard Gothein, *Die Aufgaben der Kulturgeschichte* (Leipzig: Duncker & Humblot, 1889).

19. Gerhard Oestreich, "Die Fachhistorie und die Anfänge der sozialgeschichtlichen Forschung in Deutschland," *Historische Zeitschrift* 108 (1969): 320–67. Oestreich reports (p. 360) that after World War II, Meinecke told Fritz Epstein and Hajo Holborn that he had not done justice to social and economic history as practiced in nineteenth-century Germany.

20. Friedrich Meinecke, review of Burckhardt's *Weltgeschichtliche Betrachtungen,* in *Historische Zeitschrift* 97 (1906): 557–62, at pp. 557–58.

21. Ibid., p. 559.

22. Ranke himself denied that there is progress in morality or art; see *Über die Epochen der neueren Geschichte: Vorträge dem König Maximilian II von Bayern gehalten,* ed. Hans Herzfeld (Schloss Laupenheim: Ulrich Steiner Verlag, n.d.), pp. 30–31. But he not only believed in material progress (ibid., p. 30), he exulted in it and saw the enormous expansion of European power over all the continents as an admirable achievement of the "Germanic-Romanic" spirit (ibid., p. 195). See above all a famous passage in the second edition of *Die serbische Revolution* (1844; 1st ed. 1829), retained in the revised and expanded 1879 edition, entitled *Serbien und die Türkei im neunzehnten Jahrhundert* and published in a single tome as vols. 43–44 of the 54-volume complete works: *Leopold von Ranke's Sämmtliche Werke* (Leipzig: Duncker & Humblot, 1868–1890), pp. 518–19:

> The past saw the flowering of other nations and other groups of peoples, animated by other principles. They created their own institutions and developed them to a remarkable extent: today, virtually nothing is left of them. How threatening and powerful Islam once stood in the face of Europe! Not so long ago the Tartars swept across Poland as far as the borders of Germany; the Turk occupied Hungary and besieged Vienna. Today, however, . . . the Ottoman Empire has been overwhelmed by Christianity, and penetrated from all sides. When we speak of "Christianity" we do not refer to religion alone; the term "culture" or "civilization" would be just as inadequate. It is the genius of the West. It is the spirit that transforms people into well organized armies, that builds roads, digs canals, takes possession of the seas by covering them with fleets, fills distant continents with colonies, probes the depths of nature by means of exact sciences, penetrates into all domains of knowledge renewing them through incessant labors, without however losing sight of the eternal truth, the spirit that maintains the rule of law and order among men despite the diversity of their passions. This spirit is making tremendous advances before our very eyes. It wrested America from the raw forces of nature and the indomitable tribes that inhabited it; by various roads it penetrates into the most distant regions of Asia where only China remains closed to it; it encompasses Africa along her entire coastline. Irresistible, multiform, unequaled, invincible thanks to its arms and science, it is conquering the world.

Quoted from the English translation by Mrs. Alexander Kerr, *History of Servia and the Servian Revolution* (London: Henry G. Boon, 1853), p. 365.

23. Friedrich Meinecke, review of Burckhardt's *Weltgeschichtliche Betrachtungen,* in *Historische Zeitschrift* 97 (1906): 561–62.

24. Friedrich Meinecke, "Johann Gustav Droysen: Sein Briefwechsel und seine Geschichtsschreibung," *Historische Zeitschrift* 141 (1929): 249–87, at p. 249. A year before, reviewing Carl Neumann's *Jacob Burckhardt* (1927) in the *Historische Zeitschrift* (1928, 138:79–83), Meinecke again evoked the "einsame Stellung Burckhardts innerhalb der historiographischen Richtungen des neunzehten Jahrhunderts."

25. Robert A. Pois, *Friedrich Meinecke and German Politics in the Twentieth Century* (Berkeley and London: University of California Press, 1972), pp. 127–29.

26. Letter of 16 April 1943, Friedrich Meinecke, *Ausgewählter Briefwechsel*, in *Werke*, 7:420.

27. Letter from Kaehler to Meinecke, 8 June 1943, *Ausgewählter Briefwechsel*, p. 423.

28. Letter of 15 April 1944, *Ausgewählter Briefwechsel*, p. 223.

29. Letter of 4 September 1944, *Ausgewählter Briefwechsel*, p. 458.

30. Letter of 22 March 1946, *Ausgewählter Briefwechsel*, pp. 247–48.

31. Letter of 14 March 1947, *Ausgewählter Briefwechsel*, p. 276.

32. Letter of 16 March 1947, *Ausgewählter Briefwechsel*, p. 514.

33. Letter to A. Friis, 18 April 1947, *Ausgewählter Briefwechsel*, p. 279.

34. Letters to Gustav Mayer, 24 March 1947, and to G. P. Gooch, 15 April 1947, *Ausgewählter Briefwechsel*, pp. 276, 277.

35. The lecture was published in 1948, but delivered the previous year; see letters to Ludwig Dehio of 15 May 1947 and 21 July 1947, *Ausgewählter Briefwechsel*, pp. 280, 282.

36. The Ranke–Burckhardt parallel is also developed in the fourth and final volume of Ernst Cassirer's *Das Erkenntnisproblem in der Philosophie und Wissenschaft der neueren Zeit*. This work first appeared in English translation with Yale University Press in 1950; see Ernst Cassirer, *Das Erkenntnisproblem* (Stuttgart: Kohlhammer, 1957), pp. 270–84. It is again the theme of the last work of Felix Gilbert, Meinecke's student in Berlin before his emigration from Germany in 1933: *History: Politics or Culture: Reflections on Ranke and Burckhardt* (Princeton: Princeton University Press, 1990). In his final chapter, however, Gilbert rightly emphasized how much Ranke and Burckhardt had in common. The American historian Burleigh Taylor Wilkins had already argued that the contrast of Ranke and Burckhardt is "exaggerated." "Some Notes on Burckhardt," *Journal of the History of Ideas* 20 (1959): 123–37. Like all parallels, that of Ranke and Burckhardt was developed in large measure as a rhetorical device.

37. Friedrich Meinecke, "Ranke and Burckhardt," in Hans Kohn, ed., *German History: Some New Views* (Boston: Beacon Press, 1954), pp. 141–56, at pp. 151, 153, 154, 156.

38. *Die Deutsche Katastrophe* (Wiesbaden: F. A. Brockhaus, 1965; orig. 1946), pp. 159–60.

39. Ibid.

40. *Reflections on History*, trans. Mary Hottinger (London: George Allen & Unwin, 1943), p. 41.

41. Thomas Paine, *Common Sense* (1776) (Harmondsworth: Penguin Books, 1976), p. 65.

42. *Ideen zu einem Versuch, die Grenzen der Wirksamkeit des Staates zu bestimmen* (1792), in Wilhelm von Humboldt, *Werke*, ed. Andreas Flitner and Klaus Giel (Stuttgart: J. G. Cotta, 1960–), 1:64, 69.

43. Humboldt, *Ideen zu einem Versuch, die Grenzen der Wirksamkeit des Staates zu bestimmen*, pp. 69, 71.

44. *Über den Gemeinspruch: das mag in der Theorie richtig sein, taugt aber nicht für die Praxis* (1793), in Immanuel Kant, *Kleinere Schriften zur Geschichtsphilosophie, Ethik und Politik*, ed. Karl Vorlander (Hamburg: Felix Meiner, 1964 [1913]), p. 88.

45. Humboldt, *Ideen zu einem Versuch, die Grenzen der Wirksamkeit des Staates zu bestimmen*, pp. 71–90.

46. Kant, *Idee zu einer allgemeinen Geschichte in weltbürgerlicher Absicht* (1784), in Immanuel Kant, *Kleinere Schriften zur Geschichtsphilosophie, Ethik und Politik,* pp. 9–10. Cf. Humboldt, *Ideen zu einem Versuch, die Grenzen der Wirksamkeit des Staates zu bestimmen,* p. 67.

47. *Selbstbiographie und Antrittsrede über das Naturrecht,* ed. Alfred Bäumler (Halle/Saale: Max Niemeyer, 1927), p. 37.

48. On the "conflict between liberalism and democracy," see the lucid short study of Norberto Bobbio, *Liberalism and Democracy,* trans. Martin Ryle and Kate Soper (London: Verso, 1990; orig. Italian 1988).

49. "Über erzählende Malerei" (November 11, 1884), *Gesamtausgabe,* ed. Emil Dürr et al., 14 vols. (Stuttgart, Berlin, and Leipzig: Deutsche Verlagsanstalt, 1930–1934), 14:306.

50. *Über das Studium der Geschichte,* ed. Peter Ganz (Munich: C. H. Beck), p. 276; cf. *Reflections on History,* p. 55.

51. *Griechische Reise,* ed. Georg Schmidt (Heidelberg: Richard Weissbach, 1927), p. 111.

52. Matthew Arnold, *Culture and Anarchy* (1869), ed. J. Dover Wilson (Cambridge: Cambridge University Press, 1963; orig. 1932), pp. 75–76. As regards England, Arnold's position was that culture was the only cement holding society together and that it might still protect English society from the corrosive effects of political liberalism run riot, but that, as a force "in the highest degree animating and nourishing to the creative power . . . permeated by fresh thought, intelligent, and alive," its decay had proceeded so far in England that it would have to be artificially resuscitated by means of a national program of education administered by the state. In the end, therefore, for Arnold, the power of the state—so weak in England that people were virtually unaware of it—needed to be strengthened precisely in order to bring about the return of culture, that "nationally diffused life and thought," which Arnold associated with the vanished days of Shakespeare in England or Pindar in ancient Greece. To the Basel critics, of course, such an extension of the power of the state would not revive a genuinely free culture, but would create only a pseudo-culture completely subordinate to the goals of the state. One of Arnold's arguments in favor of improving state-administered education was in fact that modern business and industry require a modern, well-educated managerial class and that it is the responsibility of the state to create such a class in order to meet growing competition from the continent. See my "Philhellenism and Antisemitism: Matthew Arnold and his German Models," *Comparative Literature,* 46:1–39, at pp. 20–25; also "The Figaros of Literature," in *Between History and Literature* (Cambridge: Harvard University Press, 1990), pp. 55–79, at pp. 68–71.

INDEX

Houston Bruce

Dr. O'Brien

Thanks for your
Encouragement
your Quiet Confidence
in Us

Dr. O'Brien,
   Thank you so much for a wonderful life experience all those years ago. Greetings from Guilford, CT.
                    George Peetjers

Dr O'Brien,
   We miss you! The year in Basel had such an impact on my life and provided many, many wonderful memories. Thank you for your part in that!
   All the best, Leslie Flowers

Dr. O'Brien,
   I hope you feel privileged to have been a great, and lasting, influence on many of us. You were a scholar and helped us grow in many ways.
                    Martha Jay Schultz

Dr. O'Brien
   Hope you are well & happy. Sorry you couldn't make the reunion. (Your ears must be burning).
                    David Goff